Bedouin Law from Sinai and the Negev

CLINTON BAILEY

Bedouin Law from Sinai & the Negev

JUSTICE WITHOUT GOVERNMENT

Yale University Press
New Haven &
London

Set in Sabon type by Keystone Typesetting, Inc.
Printed in the United States of America.

Library of Congress Cataloging-in-Publication Data
Bailey, Clinton.
Bedouin law from Sinai and the Negev : justice without government /
Clinton Bailey.
p. cm.
Includes bibliographical references and index.
ISBN: 978-0-300-15324-8 (cloth : alk. paper)
1. Law, Bedouin. 2. Bedouins—Legal status, laws, etc.—Egypt—Sinai.
3. Bedouins—Legal status, laws, etc—Israel—Negev. I. Title.
KM88.5.B44B35 2009
342.53′10873—dc22 2009025121

A catalogue record for this book is available from the British Library.

This paper meets the requirements of ANSI/NISO Z39.48-1992 (Permanence of Paper).

10 9 8 7 6 5 4 3 2 1

To my sons,
Michael, Daniel, Benjamin, and Ariel,
whose
humanity, honesty, and humor
are ever a source
of pleasure and pride

طويل السيف للحق راجع

Even he with the long sword must submit to the law.
—Bedouin proverb

Contents

Illustrations follow page 8

Acknowledgments

I hereby reiterate what I wrote in the preface to my book on Bedouin proverbs, *A Culture of Desert Survival*—namely, that my gratitude is forever extended to Bedouin culture itself for having endowed me with a lifetime of fascination and to the many Bedouin friends who illuminated the significance and nuances of the customs I witnessed and the words I heard. In the forty plus years that I have studied Bedouin culture in the Negev and Sinai Deserts of Israel and Egypt respectively, I have been repeatedly struck by the fact that almost every facet of Bedouin life that I observed was shaped by the need to survive under desert conditions. This was also the case with Bedouin law, which addressed the need to provide security to desert dwellers in the absence of any governmental or tribal authorities to do so. Among the many Bedouin who enlightened me over the years, those who taught me most on Bedouin law were Swaylim Sulaymān Abū Bilayya, Frayj Ḥimayd as-Saddān, and Judges Salmān Ḥusayn Ibn Ḥammād and Imsallam Abū Jaddūaʿ of the ʿAzāzma confederation; ʿAnayz Sālim al-ʿUrḍī, Jumʿa ʿĪd al-Farārja, and Judge Muḥammad Ḥusayn al-ʿAlowna of the Tarabīn; Mūsa Ḥasan al-ʿAṭowna and Muṣliḥ Sālim Ibn ʿĀmir of the Tiyāha; Rāḍī Swaylim ʿAtayyig of the Muzayna; and Judge Amīra Salāma Abū Amīra of the Masaʿīd Awāmra. Without the knowledge and understanding they imparted, I could not have written this book.

Most of my study of Bedouin culture was funded from the modest legacy of my parents, the late Benjamin and Edna Glaser of Buffalo, New York. Occasionally I also received funds from additional sources, such as the Harry S. Truman Institute for Peace of the Hebrew University, Jerusalem; the Division of Research Programs of the National Endowment for the Humanities, an independent federal agency; and a recent generous grant from the Kronhill Pletka Foundation. I am particularly indebted, however, to two foundations that have contributed generously to my ability to complete this book. One is the Dorot Foundation of Providence, Rhode Island, which has covered most of my research expenses since 1997. The other is the Alan B. Slifka Foundation of New York, whose writing grants in 1999 and 2000 and from 2006 until the present have allowed me to devote six years to the writing of this book, the one on Bedouin proverbs, and yet another that is currently in preparation. Like the Dorot Foundation, Alan Slifka, a leading exponent of Jewish-Arab coexistence in Israel, for which he established the Abraham Fund, understood the importance of preserving Bedouin culture and imparting it to the non-Bedouin, mainly Western, reader.

Certainly my abiding debt is to my wife, Maya, who has graciously shared my experience of studying Bedouin culture over the years, often at the expense of other, more normal things. My gratitude extends to others as well: to my sons and many Western friends who greatly encouraged me with their interest; to Jonathan Brent, who, appreciating the uniqueness and importance of conveying Bedouin law, initiated the acquisition of my manuscript for Yale University Press (YUP); to Margaret Otzel and Sarah Miller at YUP, who amiably saw this book through the publication process; to Bojana Ristich, who copyedited this difficult text for Yale with incredible skill and obvious dedication; and to both the Israel Exploration Society and Trinity College, Hartford (where I spent several happy years as a visiting professor) for facilitating the flow of my grant funds. Finally, I am grateful to the island of Skiathos, in Greece, where I wrote up much of this book amid beautiful and congenial surroundings, and to Jerusalem, also beautiful and my home.

Notes on the Arabic Text

This book is primarily a legal study, designed to portray Bedouin law as a means for providing security in the desert in the absence of governmental or tribal authority. It is not a study in linguistics. Nevertheless, as it presents proverbs and other materials in the Bedouin dialects of Sinai and the Negev, it should be of use to linguists and students of the Arabic language if the following comments are taken into account and reference is made to my book *A Culture of Desert Survival: Bedouin Proverbs from Sinai and the Negev*, its transliterations, and its glossary of Bedouin words and meanings.

The Phonemic Transliteration

Rather than list my own, nonprofessional, observations on the dialects of Sinai and the Negev, I would refer the reader to the excellent studies by Haim Blanc ("The Arabic Dialect of the Negev Bedouins") and Heikki Palva (*Artistic Colloquial Arabic*).

My transcription of the materials into vernacular Arabic was made according to how I heard them from Bedouin informants in Sinai and the Negev.

1. The greatest inconsistency in my transcription is found in the alternating sounds of "i" and "a" for the vowel that precedes a *tā marbūṭa*; a third-

person singular possessive pronoun; the initial vowel of the definite article; and in certain verb forms.

2. Occasionally I metathesize words, changing the order of a vowel and a consonant at the beginning of a word, especially in participles (*Imsallam/ Musallam*), words with a short vowel/long vowel sequence (*izlām/ zilām*), and the prefixes of second-person future tense verbs (*itgūm/tigūm*).
3. The signs used as equivalents for certain Arabic letters are as follows: th = ث; j = ج; ḥ = ح; kh = خ; dh = ذ; sh = ش; ṣ = ص; ḍ = ض; ṭ = ط; ẓ = ظ; ʿ = ع; gh = غ; g = ق; w, ū = و; y, ī = ي; ō, ow = او; ei, ay = اي.
4. Long vowels have a macron above them (ā, ī, ū). However, a long "i" accented by a *shadda* will be followed by a double "y" (for example, *shargiyya* instead of *shargīya*).
5. The diphthong اي appears in some words as *ay* (as in *day*) and in others as *ei* (as in *eye*); the diphthong او appears in some words as *ow* (as in *cow*) and in others as ō (as in *so*).
6. Long vowels that are not pronounced as such in Arabic words and proper nouns (for example, names of persons, tribes, and places) are transliterated throughout the book as short vowels (*Tarabīn* instead of *Tarābīn; Sarahīn* instead of *Sarāḥīn*). In the bibliography, all Arabic proper nouns appear in their Classical form.
7. A long "ī" and a long "ū" preceding an *ʿayn* glottal stop will be immediately followed by a short "a" to facilitate the pronunciation (for example, *rabīaʿ* instead of *rabīʿ; usbūaʿ* instead of *usbūʿ*).

As the Bedouin occasionally accent the article of a noun rather than a syllable within the noun (for example, *al'-bil*, "camels," rather than the more regular *al-bil'*), such places will be marked by an acute accent mark.

The *tā marbūṭa* is not marked by a final "h." By contrast, a final (ه), serving as an accusative or possessive pronominal suffix, is marked by an *"h,"* even though it is not aspirated in the vernacular.

Pronunciation

The pronunciation of the symbols used for the various forms of the Arabic letters is as follows: "th" as in *think*; "j" as in *jam*; "ḥ" as in *help*, deeply aspirated; "kh" like "x" in the Spanish pronunciation of *Mexico*; "dh," "ḍ," and "ẓ" like the English "th" in *these*; "ṣ" like in *bus*; "gh" like "r" in the French pronunciation of *Paris*; an "ʿ" like a glottal stop before or after a vowel.

The short vowel "a" is actually pronounced like "u" in the word *up* or like "e" in *tell*, especially before an "l"; a long "ā" (with a macron over it) has an *ahh* sound, as in *car*. A short "i" is pronounced as in *sit*: a long "ī" is pronounced like "ee" in *screen*. A short "u" sounds like "oo" in *book*; a long "ū" is pronounced like the "u" in *truth*.

In keeping with the pertinent Bedouin dialects, the Arabic letter ق is represented by a hard "g" except in derivatives of the root for "kill," قتل, where "k" is used to convey the peculiar pronunciation of these words (for example, *katal*, *maktūl*, *kitāl*).

Miscellaneous

All transliterated Arabic words are italicized, except Arabic proper nouns (names of persons, tribes, and places), the word Qurʾān, and words in certain subheadings, in order to differentiate them from italicized English words.

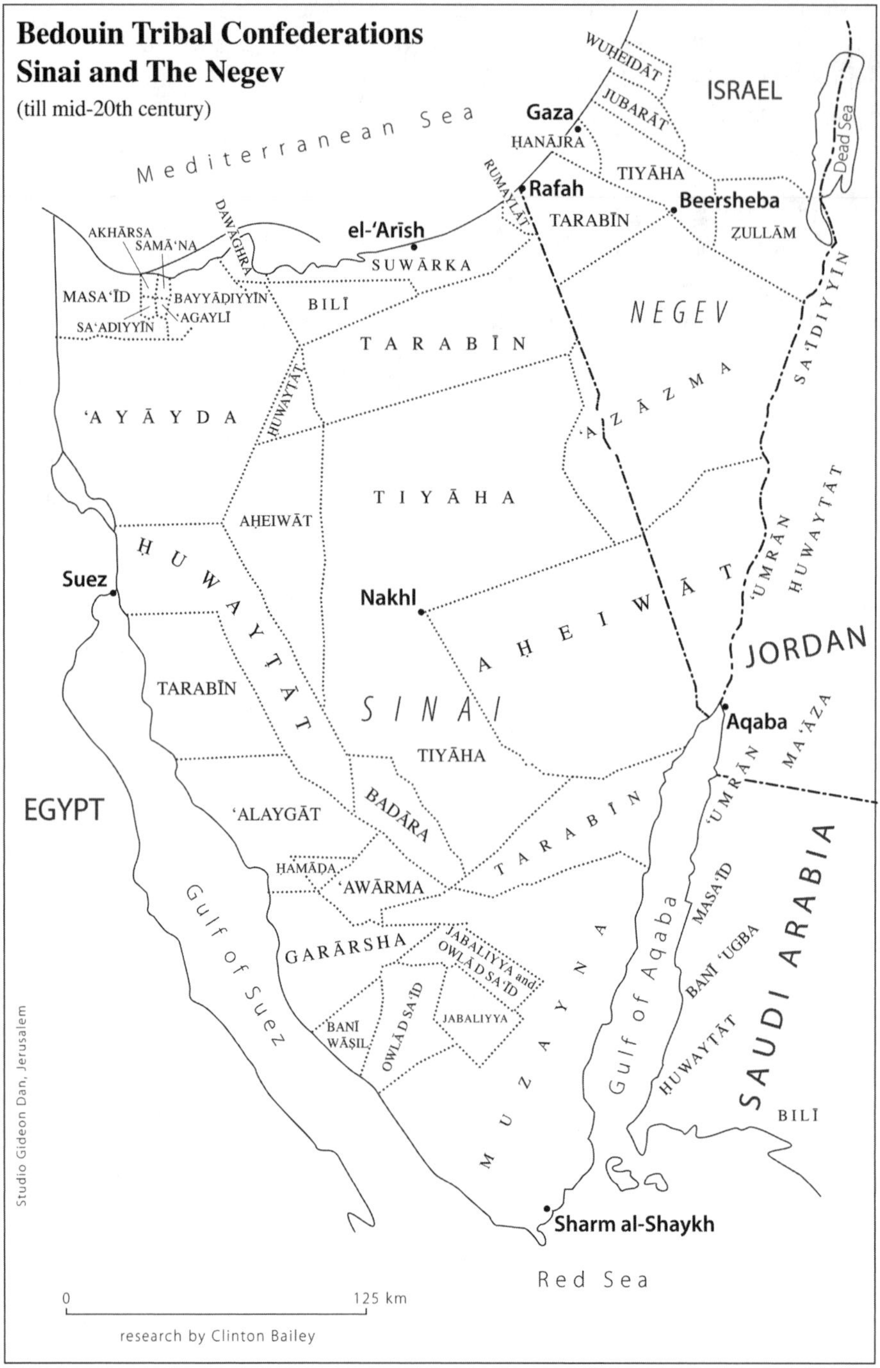
Bedouin Tribal Confederations
Sinai and The Negev
(till mid-20th century)
Mediterranean Sea
ISRAEL
Dead Sea
WUHEIDĀT
JUBARĀT
Gaza
ḤANĀJRA
TIYĀHA
RUMAYLĀT
Rafah
Beersheba
TARABĪN
ẒULLĀM
el-'Arīsh
AKHĀRSA
SAMĀ'NA
DAWĀGHRA
SUWĀRKA
MASA'ĪD
BAYYĀḌIYYĪN
'AGAYLĪ
SA'ADIYYĪN
BILĪ
TARABĪN
NEGEV
SA'ĪDIYYĪN
ḤUWAYTĀT
'AYĀYDA
'AZĀZMA
TIYĀHA
AḤEIWĀT
Suez
ḤUWAYTĀT
Nakhl
'UMRĀN
ḤUWAYTĀT
AḤEIWĀT
JORDAN
TARABĪN
SINAI
Aqaba
TIYĀHA
'UMRĀN
MA'ĀZA
EGYPT
'ALAYGĀT
BADĀRA
TARABĪN
'UMRĀN
SAUDI ARABIA
ḤAMĀDA
'AWĀRMA
MASA'ĪD
Gulf of Suez
GARĀRSHA
JABALIYYA and OWLĀD SA'ĪD
Gulf of Aqaba
BANI 'UGBA
BANĪ WĀṢIL
OWLĀD SA'ĪD
JABALIYYA
MUZAYNA
ḤUWAYṬĀT
BILĪ
Sharm al-Shaykh
Red Sea
0
125 km
research by Clinton Bailey
Studio Gideon Dan, Jerusalem

Introduction

What Is Bedouin Law?

Bedouin law (called *al-ʿurf wa-l-ʿāda*; lit. "that which is known and customary") is a system of rules that emerged in the deserts of the Middle East to provide protection to individuals and nomadic society alike. The need for this indigenous legal system stemmed from the absence in the desert of any other authority, governmental or tribal, that could offer such protection. Although noninstitutional and diffuse, this legal system furnishes the Bedouin, traditionally nomads, with all the means necessary for preserving law and order in accordance with their culture, and their law has enabled them and their society to survive for the thousands of years that they have dwelled in these arid, remote, and desolate lands. Even in modern times, Bedouin, in conflicts among themselves, mainly turn to their own laws, where permitted in the Middle Eastern countries they inhabit, rather than seek recourse in the civil law of the state or in Islamic law, the *sharīʿa*.[1]

A detailed examination of Bedouin law is important to an understanding of the origin of law in general. Many legal systems beyond the writ of civilized governments began as customary law, in conditions where people had to defend themselves and their rights in the absence of law-enforcement agencies. Bedouin law, suited so well to the circumstances of desert life, could not have changed much over the ages, given the limited options that always existed for desert survival. Thus, a presentation of this law, as imparted to me mainly by persons who grew to maturity in the premodern period, offers a unique opportunity to observe a customary law in its natural and original state.

Although a comparison is not developed in the present study, a detailed knowledge of Bedouin law might also enlighten us to aspects of Islamic law, which originated, as did Islam itself, in a primarily Bedouin culture area, the Arabian peninsula. It should be stressed, however, that Bedouin law emerged to address problems that the natural conditions of desert life pose to a society and does not derive from the religious law of the Muslims, despite the fact that almost all Bedouin adhere to Islam. Major differences exist notwithstanding the Bedouins' own proverbial assertion that their law is but "a branch of the religious law" (*faraʿ min ash-sharaʿ*), often reiterated in an effort to establish themselves as worthy followers of the faith.[2]

To make Bedouin law rational and clear to the reader, this book attempts to analyze its workings and logic by showing the close connection between the law and the culture from which it emerged. Owing to this approach, it is a chapter in ethnography. At the same time, it is also a book of law in that it presents the normative rules for maintaining law and order in the desert and describes the penalties for violating them. As a conceptual whole, the book portrays the manifold mechanisms that deter violations, as well as those that punish them. It shows how the law enlists the raw materials of the culture—such as honor, might, violence, religious faith, and clan solidarity—in the service of justice. It also depicts the effort of the law to afford individuals justice by sanctioning private violence, while keeping the fabric of Bedouin society unrent by it. One should note, though, that the strictures of Bedouin law pertain, first and foremost, to any given tribal confederation in order for that particular society to survive; beyond that, they are relevant between confederations in a state of friendship or confederations not in an actual state of war. However, as confederations are a Bedouin's nation, his "national" law and its safeguards may not always apply to belligerents in warfare, just as happens among states in both the East and the West.

I came upon Bedouin law in the context of my field research on Bedouin culture, which I began in 1967, when I was a teacher of English at a regional secondary school and teachers' training college called Midreshet Sde Boker, in the heart of the Negev Desert, surrounded by encampments of Bedouin of the ʿAzāzma Saraḥīn and ʿAṣiyāt tribes and the Ẓullām Janabīb. Although my main interest for the first twenty years was Bedouin poetry, close contact with Bedouin from almost all the tribal confederations in Sinai and the Negev exposed me to additional aspects of their culture, which kindled my curiosity about their law. Often this was a matter of a person's inadvertently relating to me recent or ongoing events that had legal elements, accounts that I was careful either to jot down in detail or to tape-record for additional insight into Bedouin life. Sometimes materials of a legal nature would appear in a poem that I recorded, even perhaps serving as the impetus for its composition. In order to understand the relevant point of law, I would clarify it with one of the elderly men who helped me transcribe the poems.

In this way, I also acquired a reserve of legal principles, frequently in the form of maxims or proverbs, which my tutors would use as an aid in helping me fathom legal matters. Such proverbs might have been the judgments and pronouncements of now anonymous, but once well-known and respected, judges in the desert over the centuries and the arguments of spokesmen for the contestants in important trials. Initially, persons present at a trial may have related such statements, in their context, to listeners in tents where they stopped off on the way home or subsequently. The listeners, impressed, would in turn relate them to gatherings of men in tents that they visited, perhaps when a case of the same type was discussed. Some of these countless statements apparently made so great an impression on the minds of listeners that they stuck and became proverbs, often serving thereafter as precedents in Bedouin law. These mainly rhymed, alliterative, and assonantal proverbs functioned as a mnemonic device that enabled the Bedouin to retain the principles of their oral law for many centuries. I was also able, by attending trials and hearings in the Sinai and Negev Deserts over the years, to record from the proceedings and conversations that accompanied them even more such principles and proverbs. One of my books, *A Culture of Desert Survival: Bedouin Proverbs from Sinai and the Negev*, contains numerous legal maxims, many of which are cited throughout the present work in order to highlight various points. Additional legal maxims not found in the above book are herein listed in the Index of Bedouin Legal Maxims.

Over the seventeen years from 1991 to the present, during which I focused on consolidating my knowledge and understanding of Bedouin law, mainly through the deliberate questioning of knowledgeable elderly Bedouin equipped with a long memory of conflicts and their resolutions, I was able to sharpen my discernment of legal principles with additional explanations, legal proverbs, and the stories of cases that happened in former generations. In annotating what I learned in the present book, I cite the oral sources for accounts of cases and conflicts but do not reference most points of the law, feeling that this would have been cumbersome and superfluous.

This is my practice too with information I gleaned from my other source of knowledge, the literature. Between the late eighteenth and early twentieth centuries, a number of travelers and officials in Sinai and the Negev, such as the Comte de Volney, John Lewis Burckhardt, E. H. Palmer, Alois Musil,

Na'ūm Shuqayr, Austin Kennet, George William Murray, and 'Ārif al-'Ārif, recorded aspects of Bedouin law that they had heard from informants they met. Because much of what they encountered is also what I learned from my many informants during the forty years that I was engaged in the subject, I utilized their material mainly for corroboration or, where we differed, for researching further into a specific matter.

In the mid-twentieth century, scholars began to take a deliberate interest in Bedouin law in the two regions under study, Sinai and the Negev, and their materials were of use to me mainly for the examples of cases and conflicts that complemented those that I had heard and enabled me to increase the number of legal principles that I could analyze and illustrate with real-life examples. The richest source of such examples was *Jurisdiction among the Negev Bedouins*, by Sasson Bar-Tsvi, who presided for nine years, in the late 1940s and 1950s, over Israel's erstwhile Bedouin Tribal Court (in Beersheba), which adjudicated disputes among the Negev Bedouin through their own judges. In addition to the numerous cases that Bar-Tsvi recorded in that capacity, his familiarity with the Bedouin and abiding interest in their law enabled him to record many more cases in subsequent years. Another valuable source of cases and conflicts was *Texts in Sinai Bedouin Law*, a two-volume series of conversations among members of the Aḥeiwāt confederation of central and eastern Sinai between 1978 and 1982 recorded, transcribed, translated, and annotated by Frank H. Stewart. These conversations reveal many nuanced aspects of the law, especially in regard to legal procedure and the background to conflict, notably between members of the same clan.

Bedouin law in the two areas of focus in this book is a standard example of Bedouin law, not differing significantly from the law of Bedouin in far-flung parts of the Middle East. This similarity emerges from a reading of books that describe Bedouin law in Jordan (by Muḥammad Abū Ḥassān and Aḥmad 'Uwaydī al-'Abādī), Iraq (by 'Abd al-Jabbār al-Rāwī), and elsewhere, examples from which are herein used to corroborate points of law from Sinai and the Negev. While a small percentage of the principles and practices in these other areas may differ from those in Sinai and the Negev, the similarities predominate, owing partly to the fact that most tribes in each of the areas originated in the Arabian peninsula and brought many of their laws with them when they emigrated and in part to there being few options for laws that protect individuals and their societies under desert conditions.

Bedouin law within Sinai and the Negev is even more uniform, owing to the factors mentioned above and to the fact that three of the four major tribal confederations in the Negev—the 'Azāzma, Tarabīn, and Tiyāha—came there from Sinai, where some tribes of each still live. Before dwelling in Sinai they, as most of the other confederations there, came from the Arabian peninsula, as did the ancestors of the fourth major confederation in the Negev, the Ẓullām. Hence, they had much common legal experience behind them. Accordingly, we find that the major differences between the two areas under study are really minor, manifesting themselves in terminology; for example, a person who denies another justice is called in the Negev an *ʿadmān* (lit. "one who destroys another's right"), whereas in Sinai he is termed an *ʿāṣī* (lit. "one who disregards another's right").

By contrast to the above, differences of opinion regarding various principles of the law—such as whether a victim has legal permission to attack his violator in his tent if the latter has denied him justice or whether an avenger has legal permission to pillage a murderer's livestock when seeking blood-revenge—belong to neither Sinai nor the Negev exclusively but may be encountered among different individuals, even of the same tribes in both areas. As Bedouin law is an oral law, with no codex to which to refer, there is ample room for such differences of opinion to emerge. Though every Bedouin knows something of the law, it being the set of rules that regulate his relations with others, his knowledge is only of what he has either inadvertently heard, observed in his immediate environment, or personally experienced. Hence, a litigant or anyone who has heard the ruling of a particular judge, whose knowledge of the law is normally broader than that of the average person, may deem it an affirmation of the specific law that was considered. Or if a problem is resolved out of court, observers may note this resolution too as an example of justice in keeping with the law. The practice of appeals in trials is aimed at settling many natural discrepancies.

It also happens that a type of problem may not occur within a given Bedouin society for a long while, perhaps even a few generations, leaving its members without any precise knowledge about it. If such a problem then suddenly arises for the elders to resolve or if these members are asked by an outsider about such a problem, they will have to improvise, extrapolating from aspects of the law that they do know, often with the help of an all-but-forgotten legal maxim that suddenly surfaces in their memory. By the same token, some rare events with legal ramifications that are not experienced within people's lifetimes may even be declared by them as impossibilities. Examples I heard from some persons in Sinai and the Negev included a woman killing her husband, a woman taking revenge for a clansman, an avenger taking blood-revenge from a sleeping man, and one brother killing another. The answer to queries about such occurrences might well be, "A thing like that never happened." Such are the founts of knowledge of a law that is totally oral, an understanding of which requires patience, repetitive questioning, careful observation, and attentive listening. Only after a time and much gathered detail can a non-Bedouin gain a comprehensive picture.

Chapter 1 of this book substantiates the historical lack of government in the Middle Eastern deserts and describes how the Bedouin had to conceptualize law and justice in a way that enabled a legal system to emerge. Chapter 2 explores how Bedouin society utilizes people of honor and might to prevent violence and violations and to hold people to their legal obligations, tasks that in other societies are discharged by the courts and police. Chapter 3 describes how collective responsibility serves as a deterrent to violations on all levels of social organization, beginning with the clan. Chapter 4 explains how the law allows for private violence to be used, either as a first or a last resort, to restore justice, as well as to deter violations, and how laws exist that prevent private violence from harming society. Chapter 5 describes the processes of litigation by which Bedouin attempt to attain justice by peaceful means. Chapter 6 is an in-depth look at the laws pertaining to three central, though not necessarily related, elements of Bedouin life: women, property, and the sanctuary of tents.

Some explanations of various of my usages in the book will render the reading more comprehensible. First, I often refer to a cited person's belonging to a confederation—namely, his tribal confederation, which is his ultimate identity and point of loyalty. In most cases, the reference is to his confederation followed by his tribe, such as ʿAzāzma Saraḥīn or Tarabīn Ḥasāblah. Two kindred confederations in Sinai, the Aḥeiwāt Shawafīn and Aḥeiwāt Ṣafeiḥa, have two parts to their name, requiring a third name to indicate the tribe—for example, Aḥeiwāt Shawafīn Guṣayyir. Also, because tribes, each with a chief, or *shaykh*, at its head, may be constituted and reconstituted by successive rulers in the desert, their names in the past, at the time of a particular legal event, may differ from their current names. In some such cases, I present them with their tribal name as concurrent with the event (and this past tribal name may be their current sub-confederation name—for example, Tiyāha Ḥukūk instead of Tiyāha Huzayyil, or Tiyāha Nutūsh instead of Tiyāha ʿAṭowna). The reader interested in these specific structural aspects may find instruction in the works of Alois Musil, Max von Oppenheim, and Clinton Bailey and Rafi Peled. In the footnotes, it is my practice to cite a Bedouin source together with his father's name and the name of his clan (ʿAnayz Sālim al-ʿUrḍī) or family (Swaylim Sulaymān Abū Bilayya), followed by his confederation and tribal identity. In the few cases where I had failed to record the name of a person's clan or tribe, I simply omit it in both the text and the footnotes.

Second, although members of the same clan are often termed "kinsmen" in the literature, it is my practice in this book to refer to them as clansmen or clanswomen. I prefer this term because it is less ambiguous than "kinsmen," as not all members of a clan are of the same kin descended from a common ancestor, some having been appended by agreement in the distant or relatively recent past. Third, I use the term "violator" to indicate someone who might elsewhere be called a criminal. As "criminal" denotes someone who has transgressed the law of the land, a discussion of Bedouin law, which deals with the violation of an individual's personal rights, is more clearly served through the designation "violator" or, as occasionally appears, "offender."

Fourth, the term "Bedouin" by itself refers in this book primarily to Bedouin males, as the realm of legal affairs belongs to them alone, the women playing a secondary role as passive, protected people represented by the men. Finally, I cite the values of fines and concessions in U.S. currency for the sake of clarity, even though the sums involved were originally designated in the British, Jordanian, Egyptian, and Israeli currencies in use among the Bedouin studied. As the values of these currencies periodically changed relative to the dollar, my considerable efforts to discern the precise equivalents in the various periods under study were nonetheless insufficient to achieve total accuracy. However, the equivalents used are sufficiently approximate to convey the scale of awards and punishments.

A word of explanation may also be in order regarding my practice of presenting some cases more than once in the book. Conflicts, cases, and procedures embody more than one aspect of the law. Thus, their retelling to highlight the different aspects they comprise is helpful to our understanding of each of them. For example, in an oft-mentioned conflict between two members of the Muzayna confederation in southeast Sinai, Sālim Abū Ṣabḥā and Munayfī Jabalī, the following subjects are all present and require several, at least partial, retellings, each with its own relevant emphasis: raiding a person in his tent, the fine-value of different wounds inflicted, the violation of a woman's honor, pillage in order to regain one's rights, truces, judges and trials of honor, and the right to use force as a last resort. An index of cases and the subjects they embrace may be found at the end of the book.

This book is set in the present tense, an option that may seem strange to a majority of Bedouin, who, at the outset of the twenty-first century have already adopted permanent settlement, Western education, and a modern lifestyle. Some may not find the material in the book reflective of their experience. I nevertheless rejected the option of writing about Bedouin law as a dead phenomenon. One reason is that the materials I encountered and learned among the Bedouin, from 1967 on, belonged to a traditional culture that I personally witnessed. Second, as indicated by several cases in the book, the law as described here is still practiced by many Bedouin as a way to resolve internal conflicts. Some adjustments have to be made: a tent may now be a solid structure, and camels have largely been replaced by cars. The principles and the atmosphere of the law, however, remain the same and continue to attract legal contestants owing to the sense of trust and intimacy that their customary law elicits. Finally, although Bedouin are increasingly changing their way of life, a fundamental knowledge of the rules that guided their society for centuries should help us understand these former nomads as they move into modernity.

The author with judges of the Badāra, ʿAlaygāt, and Ḥuwayṭāt tribes in central Sinai, 1971. Photographer: Joe Shadur.

Judge Salmān Ḥusayn Ibn Ḥammād, of the ʿAzāzma Masʿūdiyyīn, issuing a judgment. Photographer: Alan B. Slifka.

Swaylim Sulaymān Abū Bilayya, of the ʿAzāzma Saraḥīn, who taught the author much Bedouin Law. Photographer: Ricardo Iscar.

A judge of the Tarabīn Ḥasāblah, Muḥammad Ḥusayn al–ʿAlowna, listening to pleadings. Photographer: Benjamin Bailey.

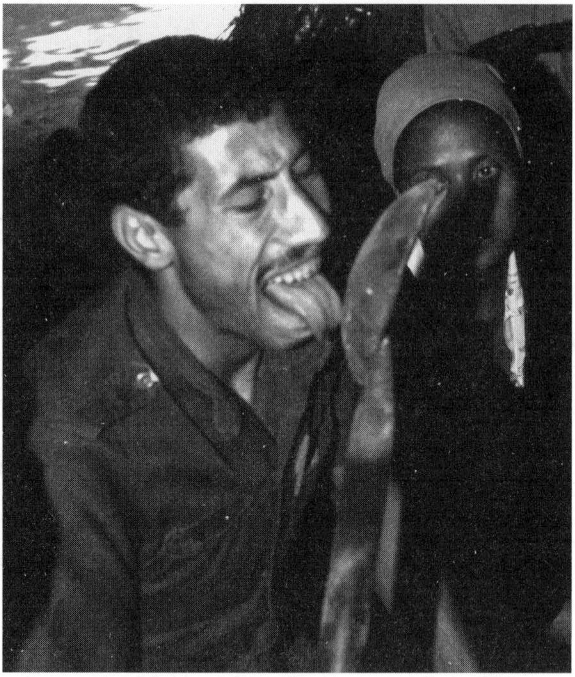

A defendant licking hot iron in the *bish'a* fire ordeal. Photographer: Danchu.

Judge Sulaymān Muḥammad al-ʿUgbī, the main honor judge in the Negev. Photographer: Nūrī Sulaymān al-ʿUgbī.

I

Justice without Government

The Absence of Law Enforcement in the Desert

NO CENTRAL AUTHORITY

The deserts of the Middle East, since time immemorial, have been a wilderness too daunting for the governments that claimed authority in them to penetrate sufficiently to make their rule effective. As a result, governmental authority was scarcely, if ever, available for the protection of desert dwellers.

As far back in recorded history as the Assyrian period in Mesopotamia, in the ninth to seventh centuries BC,[1] up to the end of the Ottoman Empire in 1918, governments confined their presence to imperial or provincial capitals located at the edges of the desert. Examples of such capitals include fifth-century AD Sassanid al-Ḥīra,[2] as well as Ottoman Damascus,[3] Gaza,[4] and Maʿān.[5] In the Arabian peninsula, although the nineteenth-century Saʿūd and Ibn Rashīd native dynasties ruled from oases in the heart of the desert, they mainly stayed confined to their respective seats of government at Dereiʿa[6] and Ḥā'il.[7] As a result, their sway over the daily lives of the widely scattered desert-dwelling Bedouin was slight.

Nor were the successive premodern rulers over desert lands ever interested in affecting the nomads' lives. Only three aspects of their contact with the desert people occupied their attention. One was to guarantee that caravans could pass to and from their capitals in safety. In this regard, their efforts mainly involved buying protection through the grant of direct payments;[8] profit sharing;[9] or patronage to the tribes through whose lands the caravans passed or, alternatively, to other tribes that possessed sufficient power to deter the latter from attack.[10] In southern Sinai at least since the fourteenth century, successive governments distant from Sinai made such arrangements with various tribes, with whom they guaranteed the profitable conveyance of provisions and Christian pilgrims to and from the remote St. Catherine's Monastery.[11]

Another aspect of governmental interest in neighboring nomads was to exact taxes from them.[12] Even here, however, the task was deemed possible only if delegated to friendly and powerful tribal leaders. In the Negev of the seventeenth and eighteenth centuries, for example, chiefs of the dominant Wuḥeidāt and Huzayyil tribes collected taxes on behalf of the Ottomans. Oral traditions tell of how a Wuḥeidāt chief took revenge on a man of the Ẓūllām Janabīb tribe for cheating on his taxes by substituting a skin full of whey for one filled with clarified butter[13] and how the Turks hanged Salmān ʿAzzām al-Huzayyil for withholding part of the taxes he had raised.[14] When the British took over the Negev in 1917, they delegated tax collection to chiefs from the Tarabīn and Ḥanājra confederations.[15]

The third governmental interest in the desert dwellers was that governments throughout history were often dependent on the goodwill and services of nearby nomads for ensuring security for their own administrative centers and outposts against the attacks of other nomads. Thus, the ancient Assyrians gave fiefs to chiefs of neighboring tribes in exchange for their keeping hostile tribes away.[16] The Byzantine and Sassanid Empires in the fifth and sixth centuries AD delegated control of their desert border areas to the Bedouin Ghassanids and Lakhmids respectively.[17]

Occasionally, when the three traditional interests of governments in the desert were jeopardized, they might conscript a large force to make pointed attacks against their nomadic adversaries. Assyrian sources mention such expeditions sent by Kings Sennacherib and Ashurrbanipal in the seventh century BC.[18] In AD 632 the first caliph of Islam, Abū Bakr, governing from Madīna, sent columns to force recalcitrant tribes throughout Arabia to pay the tribute on which they had been reneging since the death of the Prophet Muḥammad.[19] As with all the subsequent Muslim regimes throughout the ages, the Ottomans too occasionally sent expeditionary forces, including one from Jerusalem to the Negev in 1890 to halt a series of destabilizing tribal wars there[20] and another from Damascus to southern Jordan in 1894 to enforce the payment of taxes.[21]

The Bedouin, however, were mainly a formidable military match for government forces. In addition to their superior knowledge of the desert, affording them an advantage in maneuverability, the weaponry they possessed was equal in quality to that of government troops, at least until World War I.[22]

Hence, columns of soldiers sent to subdue them could be defeated, as were the six thousand government horsemen dispatched against the Rawala tribe by the Ottoman pasha of Baghdad in 1809[23] or those sent from Maʿān, in southern Jordan, to subdue the ʿUmrān tribe of northwest Arabia in 1814 and 1815.[24] Strategically, too, the nomads had an advantage in being able to disappear into the vast desert, with which they were more familiar than any pursuing troops.

As a result, Bedouin could always feel sovereign in most of their deserts and confident about dealing boldly with the peripheral governments. They not only demanded payments (called *ṣurra* or *maʿāsha* during the Ottoman period) for allowing caravans to cross their territories,[25] but they were also quick to pillage these caravans if the payments were withheld. We read, for example, of such raids on caravans bearing pilgrims to and from Mecca in the early nineteenth century.[26] Even after the building of the Ḥijāzī railroad, which replaced the camel pilgrimage caravans out of Damascus from 1910 on, the tribes along the way demanded what they deemed their due.[27] They were also not reluctant to attack actual seats of government. When denied their payments in the case of the Ḥijāzi railroad, for example, forty Bedouin of the Ḥuwayṭāt tribe laid siege to the sub-district fortress in Maʿān for three days, threatening to shoot anyone who came in or out. Finally, they received a down payment on the sum they were demanding and a promise of more.[28] The reporter of this event, the Czech scholar-explorer Alois Musil, also related a siege of the government post in the north Arabian oasis of Ṭubūq in 1902 by fifty warriors of the al-ʿEida tribe.[29] The Bedouin had already divested the soldiers of their camels, and Musil expressed his opinion that had they pressed their attack, "not a single soldier or gendarme would have escaped."

Owing to these disadvantages, governments shied from maintaining a presence in the deserts of the Middle East. In 1910 Musil noted that "the authority of the Turkish government did not extend more than a very short distance from the railway track."[30] A hundred or so years earlier, the Wahhābī government, which ruled much of the Arabian peninsula, did not have a garrison in the entire Ḥijāz (the size of California) except in the provincial capital, Madīna.[31] In 1886 the traveler Charles Doughty did not hear of more than twelve garrisons, built as pilgrim stations, all the way from northern Jordan to just north of Madīna, with an average of six men in each such *kella* (*sic*; *qalʿa*); these men survived only by "making the Bedouin allies [through gifts] and entertaining them [with meals]."[32] These soldiers were sufficiently neglected by the sub-district command and so underpaid that they often sold or traded their arms and ammunition to the Bedouin.[33] Musil, visiting the newly established Ottoman sub-district capital at ʿAqaba, in 1910, found the commander living in "a low, dirty hut," where he was "lying on a carpet, reading a Turkish newspaper." He was supposed to have had at his disposal 150 foot soldiers and 26 men mounted on camels, but 120 of the foot soldiers were "lying ill, suffering from fever and malaria," while the mounted men had only two camels, "which were deteriorating because of insufficient food."[34] The post had not been supplied with money, food, ammunition, medicine, or a doctor.

In Sinai and the Negev, the areas central to this book, the situation was no better. Until 1900 the only government presence in the Negev was the sub-district garrison at Gaza, far removed from most of the Bedouin tribes.[35] In Sinai in 1910 British intelligence officer W. E. Jennings-Bramley reported seeing only one manned government garrison, at Nakhl, which comprised the governor of the entire peninsula and ten soldiers.[36] By 1916 the number of garrisons had increased to nine, according to another such agent, Naʿūm Shuqayr, bringing the total of soldiers in all of Sinai to only 126.[37]

Certainly such traditionally weak and sparse governmental presence in the deserts of the Middle East could not have affected the daily lives of the nomadic Bedouin, who were by nature dispersed over vast expanses. Nor could it have provided them with law and order. Thus, the Bedouin maintained their own laws, which had kept them safe from time immemorial without the help of centralized government. Even Saudi Arabia, which ruled autocratically from the early twentieth century, enjoying the advantage of modern transportation, could not enforce the law of the land in the desert until 1953. Only then did it feel it could fulfill its decades-long intention to dispense with Bedouin law and impose the Islamic *sharīʿa* law on the Bedouin of its kingdom, in keeping with its national ideology.[38]

NO TRIBAL AUTHORITY

One might assume that in the absence of centralized government to enforce law and order in the deserts of the Middle East, the tribal system of the Bedouin themselves would constitute a law-enforcement authority. That, however, is not the case. Traditional Bedouin society is basically amorphous and acephalous. This society must be seen as essentially an amoeba-like swarm of independent families, each with its own desire to live and survive in the desert, finding there a livelihood, however meager it might be. Each family's membership in any definable communal group derives from the need for security. This extends from membership in the basic unit, the clan (*khamsa*), up to the tribal confederation (*gabīla*), a Bedouin's nation—the largest context with which he identifies.[39] For example, a Bedouin belongs to a clan because it assures him safety from physical assault and constitutes an association that deters theft and other sorts of violation.[40] Up the scale of size, he belongs to a sub-tribe (*rubaʿ*), which may come to his aid against members of other sub-tribes within his tribe. He belongs to a tribe (*ʿashīra*), which stakes out a certain area for its use within the land of the confederation. He belongs to a sub-confederation (*fakhdh*), which will side with him in conflicts with people from other sub-confederations within the same confederation. He belongs to a tribal confederation because it maintains a defined area of the desert, with its water sources and pasturelands, exclusively for its member tribes. Also, the members of a confederation may jointly assist a fellow member in various disputes that arise with members of other confederations.

Of all these associations to which any Bedouin belongs at one and the same time, only two have a permanent, institutionalized head: the clan, led by "an elder" (*kabīr*), and the tribe, with its "chief" or *shaykh*. All the other Bedouin communal units may delegate one of their members to be an ad hoc spokesman or leader, as in warfare, but only for the purpose at hand.

Whether permanent or provisional, however, all Bedouin leaders have three things in common. First, their role is mainly external. As the repositories of majority consensus in their respective groups, they represent them in matters pertaining to outside groups. Second, all agreements that leaders conclude with other groups must ultimately be acceptable to the members of their own group, who are largely autonomous, feeling but barely obligated to act upon another's directives. The importance of consensus among Bedouin is captured in some proverbial advice to a leader—namely, "It is better to destroy a people's interests with their consent than to enhance them on one's own initiative" (*takhrab bi-rei al-jamīʿa wala taʿmar bi-rei wāḥad*).[41]

By the same token, a leader who proves unable to further the interests of his group, as perceived by its members, will lose either support or actual members. When, in 1894, the chief of the Ḥuwayṭāt tribe of southern Jordan, ʿArʿār Ibn Jāzī, agreed under duress to pay taxes to the expanding Ottoman authority, the Taweiha section, under its leader, Ḥarb Abū Tāyah, broke away, persisting in its nonpayment.[42] A similar disaffection occurred in the Negev in the 1970s, when the chief of the ʿAzāzma tribe, ʿOwda Manṣūr Abū Muʿammar, lost the support of the ʿAṣiyāt and Saraḥīn sections, who opposed his cooperation with the Israeli authorities in trying to sedentarize his entire tribe.[43]

Chiefs may also be challenged on issues of only mundane importance. As personally witnessed by Musil in 1910, the son and successor of Ḥarb Abū Tāyah, ʿOwda, though a renowned warrior, proved unable to compel his tribesmen even to honor his traditional prerogative as a chief to determine their campgrounds and camp near a water source he had chosen; the tribesmen preferred to encamp sooner at a place lush with pasture for their herds.[44] Similarly, in the Negev in 1974, members of the ʿOwdāt clan of the ʿAzāzma Saraḥīn tribe sought to depose their elder, Ḥimayd as-Saddān, owing to his confrontational behavior toward other groups.[45]

The third condition common to all Bedouin leaders is that a leader's writ for coercing his people into any sort of action is limited. A Bedouin saying imparts that "A hand forced to grip the sword won't strike" (*al-īd illī maʿṣūba ʿa-s-seif lā tuḍrub*).[46] Thus, every chief understands that it is inviting trouble to try and force a tribesman to do what he feels is not in his interest. In 1974 Munayfī Sālim Jabalī, a powerful chief of the Muzayna Jarābʿa tribe in southern Sinai, got himself shot for insisting, on behalf of smugglers in Egypt, that his fellow Muzaynī, Sālim Jumʿa Abū Ṣabḥā, go to them to report how a consignment of contraband that he was supposed to deliver had disappeared.[47] (This is Case 1 in the Index of Cases and Conflicts below.) A chief who manages to exercise powerful sway over his independent tribesmen does so only under the fortuitous circumstances of either belonging to a strong and menacing clan or personally possessing a charismatic ability to persuade and lead.

As a rule, however, chiefs enjoy no special status. Indeed, they often depict their own office as a burden, owing to their obligation to take up the problems of their tribesmen, and they themselves are probably the authors of self-deprecatory proverbs, such as "A chief is a rag on which everyone wipes his dirty hands" (*ash-shaykh bursh—w-illī yijīh yimishsh fīh*) and "A chief's cloak must be wide" (*ash-shaykh—ʿabātah wasīʿa*)—that is, to have room for everyone's troubles.[48] These are allusions to the mediation of conflicts among his tribesmen that a chief is often asked to perform as the most prominent figure in the tribe.

Nevertheless, chiefs are only *primus inter pares*, with neither privileges nor authority. This is confirmed by the saying "No chief can force the divorce of a shepherd's wife" (*mā shaykh yiṭallig marat rāʿī*), it being understood that hired shepherds are among the lowliest members of Bedouin society.[49] Indeed, we have the testimony of Lady Anne Blunt that a shepherd even had a chief's wife divorced in his favor (Case 2). Searching for purebred Arabian horses to buy with her husband, the poet Wilfred Scawen Blunt, in 1878, Blunt stopped off with one of the most powerful chiefs in Syria, whom she called Jedaan (*sic*; Jadhʿān), on April 5, which was the third day of the chief's wedding celebration.[50] On April 7, she recorded that "an important suit" was being tried that day.[51] "It is nothing less than an action brought against Jedaan by his new wife's cousin, a young man of the Sirḥān tribe, for her recovery, on the plea of his not having consented to the marriage;" that is, as her closest cousin, the young man had been promised the girl at birth.[52] Later Blunt wrote, "The betrothed cousin brought forward his complaint for judgment by the judge; who decided that, the bride having taken no step to oblige her cousin to keep his promise and marry her, his right remained valid. This was signified to Jedaan, who at once put the bride on a camel and sent her to the chief of the Sirḥān."[53]

By the same token, no chief or other leader is above the law, and his meddling in the conflicts of others may render him a party to a conflict, with all its risks.

> In northern Sinai in 1976, for example, the chief of the Dawāghra Inghaymish tribe, Sālim Salāma Rajawīn, intervened in the marriage of a divorced woman, whom her uncle, as guardian, had married off to a man not of her liking (Case 3).[54] By law, a previously married woman (*ʿazaba*) may exercise a veto over her clansmen's choice of a subsequent husband.[55] The woman in question managed, with the help of a younger brother, to evade the first attempt to marry her to this man by seeking the protection of Shaykh Sālim, who thereupon undertook to defend her rights.
>
> The second time around, however, her uncle, concerned lest she shame the family in her unmarried state, contrived for the intended husband to abduct her and carry her off to his encampment in a remote sand dune area. Upon hearing of this abduction, the chief summoned Israeli troops, claiming that elements hostile to Israel were involved in the abduction. When they finally got to the prospective husband's encampment, the army entered his tent and arrested all the men present, while the chief took the woman's arm and escorted her out. Her uncle and the husband were quick to press charges against him, the former because the chief had touched his niece's arm, the latter because the chief had violated the sanctity of his tent and caused him and his friends to spend time in jail. The chief consequently faced fines amounting to the equivalent of $5,000, indicating that he was no more above the law than any of his tribesmen.[56]

Leaders, including chiefs, may not even receive respect. Musil reported several examples. One was the refusal by ʿOwda Abū Tāyah's slaves to break his tent prior to migration, exposing him to the indignity of pulling out the tent pegs himself.[57] While on the road migrating, Musil and Abū Tāyah were prevented from conversing by an impudent shepherd, who kept riding his camel between theirs.[58] While the Czech explorer conceded that the Ḥuwayṭāt were known to be unruly, "paying scanty attention to recognized chiefs,"[59] the same would not have been expected in regard to the paramount chief of the mighty Rawala tribe of the Syrian desert, Nūrī Ibn Shaʿlān. Yet when Musil was living with him in 1909 and Ibn Shaʿlān sent him the cooked foreleg of a camel he had slaughtered, giving clear and specific instructions to the bearers not to take any of the meat for themselves, it all disappeared along the thirty-four paces that separated the two tents.[60]

The foregoing indicates that the tribal political hierarchy does not constitute government in the sense of possessing inherent and structural authority to impose law and order. This, together with the traditional absence of state authority among the Bedouin, therefore meant that nobody historically existed to issue or enforce laws or to ensure the provision of justice.

Bedouin Law as a System

As the Bedouin nonetheless comprise a society, a system had to emerge to regulate relations among all its members and prevent people from violating each other. Time and experience eventually created such a system, which compensated through its own available means for the lack of what governments otherwise provide by way of institutionalized law enforcement, such as the authority to make laws and punish their infraction, the ability to issue subpoenas, a neutral police to arrest suspects and criminals, and jails in which to confine them.

DEFINING LAW AND JUSTICE

The Bedouin Concept of Law

Basic to the Bedouin legal system are its unique definitions of law and justice, which endow it with logic and direction. In non-Bedouin, sedentary societies, a law is understood to set limits to human behavior, the transgression of which is punishable. The existence of such laws, however, presupposes the presence of an authority that can punish their transgression. When, for example, in the seventh and eighth centuries AD, the new Islamic religion took form alongside Islamic government, a law was initially called a "border" (*ḥadd*, pl. *ḥudūd*; see Qurʾān 2:229, 45:2) and designated which behavior was beyond a border and thus liable to punishment. The emerging Islamic states could issue such "borders" as they gradually developed law enforcement agencies.

By contrast, Bedouin society, marked by the absence of an authority that can punish, needed a different definition for the concept of "law." The meaning of law that emerged in the desert was that of "a right" (*ḥagg*, pl. *ḥugūg*), in the sense of an entitlement. The term "right" connotes three related things. First, every person has a right, or is entitled, to what Bedouin view as the basic and inviolable elements of a human being: life, limb, honor, and property. The enjoyment of these entitlements unviolated by other persons is seen as the natural condition of life: a state of natural justice. Thus, the violation of any one of them constitutes an act of injustice. Indeed, when such a violation occurs, the violated Bedouin expresses it as, "My right is in a state of injustice" (*ḥaggī māyil*).[61]

Second, right denotes the permission granted by society to rectify a violation, including the ways by which a victim can effect a rectification. Taken together, these ways constitute "*the* law" as a system, with each specific way being a law in itself. Each such law, in turn, can be defined as a right that Bedouin society has provided a victim for restoring justice. When a violation has occurred, therefore, the victim possesses the right to enforce that law and to try and restore justice through one of the ways permitted. If murder occurs, for example, a clansman of the victim can choose the way of blood-revenge and proceed to kill the murderer or one of his clansmen with impunity. He does so under the claim, "This is my right" (*hādha ḥaggī*), in the dual sense of "This is what is permitted me" and "I am applying the law." By the same token, however, the law gives him the right to take revenge upon one man only. Should he kill two, the original murderer's clansmen would then have the right to take revenge on him or his group for the additional victim of his vengeance.*

Third, the right to act in order to rectify a violation is not an imperative. The law exists only to the extent that the violated party himself utilizes his right to activate it. "A right is got," proclaims a Bedouin proverb, "in keeping with the resolve of him who pursues it" (*al-ḥagg ʿala gadr sāyigah*). In cases of murder, for example, if a victim's clansmen choose to ignore the permission that exists for them to take revenge, no one else will or has the right to take action against the murderer. As no agency of society exists with the authority to effect punishments, Bedouin law does not recognize punishable offenses against society. There are merely offenses against persons or clans. These, however, get rectified only if the affected party decides to act. Adroitly, Bedouin society depicts a right that a violated person concedes (because he shrinks from pursuing it) with the scornful term "a right gained by a strong one at the expense of someone weak" (*ḥagg gawīy maʿ aḍ-ḍaʿīf*).[62]

The Bedouin Concept of Justice

In Bedouin eyes, rectifying the violation of a right is what restores justice. To understand the logic in the ways that Bedouin law provides for this rectification, we must first appreciate the Bedouin view of justice. Central to this view is the realization that in the absence of government to protect him from violations, each man, or the clan to which he belongs, must provide for his, or its, own protection.

Security is thus the focal, obsessive concern of every Bedouin man, and he has a strategy for maintaining it. It begins with the understanding that he must, first and foremost, deter others from violating him and that his first line of defense in deterring violations is to project an image of strength and sus-

*Also, when a judge issues a judgment, it is called "exposing the law" (*ṭulūaʿ al-ḥagg*)—that is, he is affirming the law as it pertains to the case at hand; see chapter 5 for more.

tain a reputation for being resolute in rectifying each and every infraction of his rights.

Given the contentious and predatory nature of Bedouin society—the result of life under conditions of bare subsistence—a man's abiding dread is that if he neglects to rectify any violation of his rights to life, limb, honor, or property, others will see him as weak or cowardly. In either case, his security will be forfeit, as others, on the lookout for some increment to help themselves survive, come to view him as easy prey and consistently attempt to violate his rights. The only way to avert this affliction is ever to be prepared to show one's mettle upon even the slightest infraction, a principle that every Bedouin instills in his children through the age-old saying, "Beat the dog, and the panther will stay away" (*uḍrub al-kalb—yistaydib al-fahd*).[63]

To illustrate this principle, Bedouin tell the following story:

> An aging man heard that eating turkey meat could restore his virility. The man thus bought a turkey chick in the market and eagerly watched it grow, feeding around his tent. Then, one day, the turkey disappeared, apparently stolen. Directly, the man convoked a meeting of his sons, all young men, and told them to drop everything and find his turkey. Outwardly they agreed but scoffed in their hearts, saying, "Why does he need that turkey, anyway? It is just vanity. Does he imagine himself marrying a younger woman and starting a new family? Vanity! Let's not waste our time looking for a turkey!" And they ignored his order.
>
> A short time later, returning from pasture, the shepherdesses reported that two goats were mysteriously missing. The sons said, "What shall we do?" The father said, "Find my turkey!" The sons scoffed, "Vanity! And two goats, too, are not worth our time." Some days later, a camel went missing, and in the evening conclave, the father again counseled, "Find my turkey!" but was again ignored. Finally, one day, the sons came back to the tent in alarm, reporting that their sister had been abducted while out at pasture and asked, "What can we do?" Their father glared at them bitterly and said, "It is too late. You thought that my turkey was a trifle, but others saw it as a sign. They understood that we lacked the will to defend our rights. It began with my turkey, but it led to your sister. Now, our reputation is in ruins."[64]

This story stresses the Bedouin conviction that a man who has been violated and has not reacted so as to rectify the violation cannot go on living in the desert, as he will be viewed as easy prey. Metaphorically he is likened to a camel that cannot go on walking in the desert because its load is unbalanced. Accordingly, Bedouin express "out of balance" and "violated" by the same adjective, *māyil*, while "restored balance" and "a rectified right" are expressed by the same noun, *ʿadl*. Thus, *ʿadl*, balance, as in the balancing of a camel's load, also became a Bedouin's term for justice because, in his eyes, justice is primarily the restoration of his reputation for strength and resolve, once this reputation has been challenged and thereby questioned through a violation of one of his rights. It is when a Bedouin has obtained justice in this sense that he can go on living in the desert, just as the balancing of a camel's tilting load enables it to go on walking. A Bedouin father who managed, after great difficulty, to avenge the murder of his son, captured this image of justice in lines of a poem that he composed the day following his revenge, as he watched the burial of his victim from a nearby mountain hideout:

> I retired encumbered, but arose feeling light
> My sideheavy saddlebags have now been put right.
>
> *Imsayt mahamūmin w-aṣbaḥt fāḍī*
> *sawwayt li-l-khurj ath-thagīl ʿadīl.*[65]

Violence, however, is not the only means for restoring justice. Bedouin law also provides peaceful ways for rectifying a violated right, such as mediation and litigation. Still, whether violent or peaceful, the means for restoring justice must all have one thing in common: making the violator hurt. That is how a violated party reaffirms his strength, giving out the message that whoever takes his strength and resolve lightly will suffer. A camel thief, for example, may have to return the stolen camel and pay a fine equivalent to four times its worth. An aggressor who has caused the loss of another man's arm may have to pay him twenty camels as compensation, half the "blood-price" (*diya*) of a murdered man. A Bedouin who has slandered a girl's reputation for moral probity may have to ignominiously proclaim that he is a liar before three tents filled with men. These punishments certainly hurt. Nevertheless, neither compensation nor material, physical, or moral punishment in themselves constitute an enactment of justice; they are but the means to it. It is the attainment of these punishments that constitutes justice, because it results from a show of strength and resolve in defending one's rights. Therefore, justice is seen by Bedouin as the restoration of a reputation for these attributes, once a violation has called such a reputation into question.

This equation of justice with the restoration of reputation is demonstrated by various voluntary practices that exist among the Bedouin. One practice is that of "concession" (*fawāt*), wherein most of the financial rewards accruing to a victim of violation through litigation or mediation are relinquished.[66] A Bedouin proverb urges, "Win your right and concede it" (*ḥagg lak ū-fūtah*).[67] Accordingly, once a judge or mediator has announced the size of a fine to be paid by a violator, people customarily intercede and ask the violated party to relinquish it. Although the law neither stipulates nor compels relinquishment (except for a percentage to honor a presiding judge or mediator), the general practice is to comply with the requests. Such concession confirms the Bedouin view that the receipt of compensation or a punitive fine in itself is less important as an enactment of justice than the fact, illustrated by a court's decision or a mediator's success, that a violated party has pursued his right and was able to make his violator suffer had he so wished. In forgoing an opportunity for gain, the violated party is merely adhering to the dictum, "Getting justice is for reputation, not for filling the belly" (*al-ḥagg sumʿa—mū hū dabb karsh*).[68]

Another practice concerns striking the perpetrator of a violation who has refused to make amends. The law allows for such an attack, but only after peaceful efforts have been made to persuade the violator to render justice.[69] If such efforts fail, leading the violated party to resort to force, Bedouin law may nonetheless hold him liable for any wounds he has inflicted on his adversary.[70] Yet, although the avenger is deemed responsible for any physical harm he causes his violator, thereby losing all, or at least part, of the fines and damages otherwise due him for the original violation, he can nonetheless proudly proclaim, "I have gained my right" (*jibt ḥaggī*), meaning that having made his violator suffer, he has restored justice by demonstrating his reputation for strength and resolve.

> In 1975 (Case 1), the aforementioned chief of the Muzayna Jarābʿa tribe in southern Sinai, Munayfī Sālim Jabalī, was owed the equivalent of $900 by a man of the Ghawānma clan, Sālim Jumʿa Abū Ṣabḥā, for the remainder of a fine that was guaranteed by Muḥammad Ḥamdān Abū at-Tiyār, the maternal uncle of Abū Ṣabḥā.[71] The sum was for fines and damages resulting from an attack upon the chief by Abū Ṣabḥā, an attack that included a gunshot wound and the chief's being conveyed to a more remote place in the desert, where he was abandoned. Though humiliated by the repeated postponement of the payment by either Abū Ṣabḥā or his "guarantor of the remainder" (*kafīl as-sāmil*),[72] Jabalī had two legal recourses for settling the problem peacefully; he could either have impounded the attacker's livestock or denounced the guarantor for being remiss in his guarantee.[73] Instead, he decided that his sons would attack Abū Ṣabḥā, especially after a noninvolved outsider insulted one of his sons, saying, "Your father is a crybaby" (*inti—abūk biyibkī*).[74] Jabalī thereby incurred several fines: for causing the amputation of Abū Ṣabḥā's finger in the resultant fray (a twofold fine, as the attack was in violation of the truce that was to be in effect until the time of payment); for violating the honor of the guarantor of the truce; for violating the sanctuary of Abū Ṣabḥā's tent; and for mauling his wife. These cost Jabalī nineteen legally pillaged camels and the equivalent of $57,000,[75] a much greater sum than that which had been due him. Nevertheless, he found this materially costly course prefer-

able so that he could establish that he was both strong and resolved and thus restore his reputation for these traits.

No less significant for confirming the centrality of reputation in the restoration of justice are stories, current among the Bedouin, relating occasions on which avengers conceded their right to blood-vengeance after receiving manifest proof that they were feared by the murderers. One such story from the central Negev concerns two clans of the ʿAzāzma Saraḥīn tribe, the Kallāb and the Ḥawaṣa (Case 4):

> After a man of the Kallāb killed one of the Ḥawaṣa, all the Kallāb fled eastward to the ʿAraba Valley, in present-day Jordan, and took refuge with people of the Saʿīdiyyīn confederation that dwelled there.
>
> After they had been there awhile, an argument broke out one day at a well where shepherds had brought their livestock for watering. A man of the Kallāb pushed in before a Saʿīdī, who, angered, said, "If you are so strong, why are you hiding among us from the Ḥawaṣa?" The man of the Kallāb replied, "Indeed, we are hiding among you from the Ḥawaṣa, because they are fearful. They are strong and determined and will not tolerate the shedding of their blood. Yet it would be better to risk their vengeance than, as ʿAzāzma, to suffer your contempt. We shall leave."
>
> So the Kallāb came back to the central Negev but kept their distance, camping in Wādī al-Figrī [present-day Nahal Tsin]. When others who were camping there saw them, they asked, "What are you doing here? Are you mad? Why did you leave Jordan? The Ḥawaṣa will slaughter you!" The Kallāb, in turn, told them their story: how they had acknowledged the strength of the Ḥawaṣa before the Saʿīdiyyīn and had decided, as ʿAzāzma, not to let the Saʿīdiyyīn insult them. So these people went to the Ḥawaṣa and told them how the Kallāb had spoken about them to others, and asked them to relent and forgo their vengeance in favor of blood-money. In light of how the Kallāb had behaved, the Ḥawaṣa agreed.[76]

Another such story enjoyed widespread currency among the Bedouin; it had been cited in a book by ʿĀrif al-ʿĀrif,[77] and I heard it orally related in both the Negev and southern Sinai.[78] It concerns two persons from the Tiyāha confederation in the Negev, ʿUṣaybī Abū Shunnār of the ʿAlamāt section and ʿAdaysān Abū ʿAbdūn of the Ḥukūk section (Case 5):

> ʿUṣaybī Abū Shunnār murdered ʿUwaymir Abū ʿAbdūn and fled with his wife, camping in a new spot every day, until he reached upper Egypt. The murdered man's brother, ʿAdaysān, was relentlessly on Abū Shunnār's trail until he located him one evening and crouched behind his tent waiting for the chance to spring upon him and kill him in revenge.
>
> It was Abū Shunnār's habit not to sleep at night out of fear of ʿAdaysān, but

that night, his wife, feeling that they were a safe distance from the avenger, chided him for staying awake and said, "Come to your sleeping place" (*taʿāl nām fī manāmak*). "I won't sleep in my sleeping place," he replied, "so long as ʿAdaysān is hunting me" (*mā anām fī manāmī wi-ʿadaysān ṭarrādī*).

Hearing this, the avenger leapt into the tent, calling, "Sleep with the Tiyāha woman! Don't be afraid" (*nām maʿ at-tihiyya; lā tikhāf*). "As you have shown me regard in my absence, the evil is over, and the blood-price is accepted. Return home and I guarantee that we'll be reconciled" (*yōminnak ḥāsib ḥisābī warāyy, maktūl as-seiya ū-magbūl ad-diya; rawwiḥ w-āna kafīl aṭ-ṭīb*).

A final example of the centrality of reputation in justice: on January 31, 1977, I attended a reconciliation conclave between members of the largest confederation in Sinai, the Suwārka, and members of one of the smallest, the Bilī, held in the sand dunes of Rās al-Aḥmar, in the north-central part of the peninsula (Case 6). Some days previously, a man of the Suwārka, during an argument with a man of the same confederation, killed the latter's guest, a man of the Bilī, who had tried to shield his host from being shot.[79] Under pressure from their powerful and numerous Suwārka neighbors, the Bilī agreed to consider the killing an accident. Although the Suwārka could have easily decimated the latter in battle, their leaders felt that they should ease the Bilī concession by praising their strength. One of their leaders, Salām Ghānmī al-Ḥowṣ, thus publicly proclaimed, "We know that the Bilī are a proud and resolute tribe and that, if they felt that the murder was intentional, they could have inflicted great losses upon us."[80] This public acknowledgment proved sufficient to restore the impaired reputation of the Bilī, making it easier for them to accept a blood-payment instead of taking revenge and indeed to accept an award of only twenty camels, half the blood-price for an intentional homicide.

2

Honor and Private Might in the Service of Justice

In addition to defining justice and the law as the point of departure for a legal system devoid of law-enforcement authorities, the Bedouin summon two innate elements in their own social environment to play a vital role in preventing violations and restoring justice that in sedentary societies is played by institutionalized force. These elements are the honor and the private might of parties not involved in a particular conflict, and they manifest themselves in four common Bedouin procedures: "delegation" (*wisāṭa*, *badwa*, and *jāha*); "guaranty" (*kafāla*; alternatively *wijih*); "throwing the face" (*ramī al-wijih*); and "protection" (*dakhāla*). Performing the roles played by the threat of arrest in sedentary societies, these procedures, separately and together, act to limit the spread of conflict, bring violators to justice through litigation, ensure compliance with judicial decisions and the terms of agreements, prevent violence when conflicts erupt, and redress the relative weakness of a party to a conflict and ensure him equality before the law. They also combine to eliminate the need that exists in other societies for penal installations in which suspects and lawbreakers can be confined—installations that Bedouin, traditionally nomadic for most of their history, could not maintain.

In Bedouin society, honor and might largely overlap. While honor, which endows individuals with social respect, often adheres to those who comport themselves with dignity and wisdom, abide by their commitments, receive guests hospitably, or speak eloquently, the honor that is most important to a man is determined by the number of other men—presumably fighting men—in his clan. If the number is great relative to other clans, people will fear him and treat him with caution and respect, lest they arouse the hostility of his clansmen, who are duty-bound to aid him under the obligations of collective responsibility.[1] Consequently, when a neutral party backed by considerable male power gets involved in a conflict not his so as to effect a just resolution, the adversaries in the conflict rarely allow themselves to ignore or challenge him and his honor. Ignoring it would signal that they are not afraid of this more powerful player, an impression that he will feel constrained to dispel, lest others too see him as weak. This may lead to hostility between him and the adversaries, causing the latter dire consequences, either physical or financial. A notable might avenge his wounded honor by attacking the party that scorns it. More commonly, Bedouin law stipulates the harshest of fines—"the fine of honor" (*manshad*)[2]—for disregarding the position of such a notable and the commitments that devolve from it.

Delegation

VOLUNTARY MEDIATION (*WISĀṬA*)

Owing to the tribalist relationships that prevail among Bedouin, commonly obliging them to show solidarity with others in their various groups, a conflict is rarely between individuals alone. As a result, the probability of a conflict spreading to include many people of different groups is ever present, and when it happens, the normal progress of society is disrupted to the disadvantage of all. In the nineteenth-century Negev, for example, a squabble between brothers led to the renowned "War of ʿOwda and ʿĀmir" (Case 7), which came to embrace at least twenty tribes over a period of twenty-two years (1842–64).[3] To avert such disruption, other persons in the broader society customarily make voluntary efforts to reconcile adversaries and contain a conflict, whatever its origin, before it spreads. Indeed, hardly a conflict erupts among Bedouin without an attempt at mediation by people not directly involved. For example, in southeast Sinai, Bedouin relate an early twentieth-century case of such mediation undertaken by a Nāṣir Ibn ʿUṣbān of the Arabian ʿUmrān confederation (Case 8).

> The mediation followed upon the murder of a young and yet uncircumcized shepherd of the Aḥeiwāt Ghuraygāniyyīn tribe of east-central Sinai by camel raiders from the Maʿāza tribal confederation of northwest Arabia. The raiders had killed the boy and buried him in Wādī al-Ithla. That evening, after he had not returned to his family's tent, his four brothers and three paternal

cousins set out to find him. They discovered the grave and followed the raiders' tracks over to the Ḥijāz, where, spotting them from a vantage point, they shot one dead as his companion fled.

For the next two years, the Ghuraygāniyyīn raided the Maʿāza, taking many of their camels. Finally, Nāṣir Ibn ʿUṣbān of the ʿUmrān—a confederation that was neighbor of both groups—told the Maʿāza, "This is revenge. There is no safety from it. The Ghuraygāniyyīn feel they must slaughter us [that is, you]" (*hādha ṭrād—mā minnah salāma—ghayr yidhbaḥūna khālis*). He said, "Let me go and ask for a 'camel-truce' (*jīra*)."[4] They said, "Fine." So Ibn ʿUṣbān went to the Ghuraygāniyyīn and paid them for a camel-truce. They told him, "The camel-truce payment is accepted, and the evil is killed" (*magbūla aj-jīra ū-maktūla as-seiya*)* and that they would meet with the Maʿāza in Ibn ʿUṣbān's tent—all this, however, on condition that Ibn ʿUṣbān guarantee them that resolution of the conflict would take account of their claim to three payments of blood-money, their remaining due for the murder of an uncircumcized boy.

The Maʿāza came, bringing two unmarried girls with them. When they met, the Ghuraygāniyyīn said to the Maʿāza, "Our man was an uncircumcized boy. We are entitled to take 'the lives of four men' (*arbaʿ rigāb*)." The Maʿāza said, "You've already killed one." They replied, "That leaves three." The Maʿāza said, "Here's payment for one life, and here is a 'marked girl' (*ghurra*) for one of your men to marry without bride-price."* The Ghuraygāniyyīn said, "That leaves two." Ibn ʿUṣbān said, "I, the master of this tent (*rāʿī al-bayt*), concede one to the Maʿāza." Thereupon, the Ghuraygāniyyīn conceded another, and the problem was resolved.[5]

A similar example of voluntary mediation to prevent a conflict from becoming violent occurred in western Sinai in 1993.[6] When Slaym Abū Ḥunayk of the Aḥeiwāt Ṣafeiḥa heard that a fellow tribesman, an Abū Maḥamūd, had stopped off and drunk tea with Abū Ḥunayk's shepherdess daughter under reportedly suspicious circumstances, he and his son grabbed their weapons—rifles with which to shoot Abū Maḥamūd and swords with which to hamstring his camels—and went off to find him (Case 9). On their way they ran into Ḥājj ʿOwda Abū ʿAgfa, another fellow tribesman who, noticing their agitation, questioned them as to the matter. He said, "Hey, Abū Ḥunayk, you have a bad

*This declaration usually stipulates accepting the blood-price (see Bailey, *Proverbs*, p. 342). Here the reference to a camel-truce, unless uttered by mistake, would have the same effect, as there is an obligation to accept blood-money instead of taking revenge once the truce is accepted (ibid., p. 278).

*A *ghurra* is given to a close relative of the murdered man in order to replace him with a son she will bear. Sometimes a *ghurra* is given instead of a blood-price, sometimes in addition to it. See chapter 6 for more on *ghurra* marriage.

look on your face. I don't like it. What's happened?" After Abū Ḥunayk told him what he had heard, Abū ʿAgfa immediately decided to mediate. He took some money from his pocket and said, "Here is Abū Maḥamūd's *jīra* fee for a camel-truce. This fee will open a discussion of the case at the tent of the *manshad* judge, Amīra Abū Amīra, next Tuesday. Abū Maḥamūd will state his case and you will state yours. If he has violated your right, he will pay you, and if he hasn't, he will be safe from you. I will be his guarantor for anything he might owe you." Because Abū Ḥunayk agreed, this mediation prevented violence, and perhaps bloodshed, among the Aḥeiwāt Ṣafeiḥa.

Conceivably the most common goal of mediation is to procure justice for a violated person. An example from the central Negev, among members of the ʿAzāzma Saraḥīn tribe, happened in 1978 (Case 10):

> Ever since ʿOwda Jumʿa al-Owradī absconded with his maternal cousin, the daughter of ʿOwda Sulaymān al-Hadōbe, in 1971, taking her from the central Negev to his home in east-central Sinai, Hadōbe refused to recognize the marriage, and a state of hostility existed between him and the abductor for seven years. This without Hadōbe regaining his violated right to engage his daughter in marriage according to his own choice. Finally, in 1978, he sought the protection of Sālim Sulaymān al-Kishkhar, chief of the Ẓullām Janabīb tribe, asking him to act on his behalf. Kishkhar went to Sālim Ibn Saʿad, the most prominent person in the ʿAyāl Silmī sub-section of the ʿAzāzma Saraḥīn tribe, to which both Hadōbe and his son-in-law belonged, presenting Hadōbe's demands. These were to return him his daughter, pay the "carrying off" and "unaccompaniment" fines (*jarra ū-rafīga*, consisting of a young camel and a full set of arms), and pay the sum of 20,000 Egyptian pounds for having ignored his rights for seven years.[7] Ibn Saʿad agreed to the terms, stressing, however, that they were harsh in light of the poverty of the abductor and his supporters.
>
> Still, Ibn Saʿad undertook to mediate and, with the help of men from the ʿAyāl Swaylim section of the Saraḥīn, tried to get Hadōbe to reduce his demands. They came to Hadōbe and, using meat-preparing metaphors for the solution of his problem, told him, "We have butchered, skinned, cut, and boiled it, and now we want to eat." "What do you want to eat?" he asked. "The twenty thousand pounds you want for your honor. They have been agreed to, but you must concede them." Hadōbe agreed to the concession, now satisfied that his right to honor had finally been recognized, as well as his ability to hurt his violator with a punitive fine had he so wished. He was quick, however, to assert that he would relinquish no more. It was only after the mediators persistently pressed him to relinquish part of the carrying off and unaccompaniment fines, ascribed to equal another 10,000 Egyptian pounds, that he also agreed to concede half the amount. Since they had helped

> him regain his honor, Hadōbe was not eager to confront them. Moreover, he had regained his daughter, whom he could now marry off in an exchange marriage that would yield a wife for his newly mature son without payment of a bride-price.[8] Mediation had brought Hadōbe justice, resolving a conflict without resort to either litigation or violence.[9]

Mediation by outsiders may occur even when people of the same clan clash, especially if their conflict threatens to spill over and affect a larger tribal group to which the clan belongs, as in the following example (Case 11).

> In 1979 among the Aḥeiwāt Shawafīn confederation in eastern Sinai, Sālim Ibn Naṣṣār felt abused by his cousin, ʿAlī Gāsim al-Guwāsma, and believed that no one in his own confederation would dare help him bring his stronger clansman to justice. Therefore, he sought and found protection from a man belonging to a totally different tribal confederation, the ʿAlaygāt of southwest Sinai, which was part of a group of tribes collectively called Ṭawara (lit. "people of Mt. [Ṭūr] Sinai"—that is, the southern part of the peninsula). Ibn Naṣṣār was also vocal about his intention to quit his native clan and tribe and join the ʿAlaygāt.
>
> Disturbed by this possible defection from a sister Aḥeiwāt confederation, a chief of the Aḥeiwāt Ṣafeiḥa, Salīm Salāma Ibn Rāḍī, took it upon himself to mediate this dispute and get ʿAlī Gāsim to give Ibn Naṣṣār justice in order to avert the latter's threatened departure. Accordingly, he went to ʿAlī Gāsim and is recorded as saying, "ʿAli, why won't you go to court? You're [denying justice], and you're causing Ibn Naṣṣār to go off with the Ṭawara; it's your misdeeds that are driving him away. Do you intend to kick out all the Aḥeiwāt and drive them over to Wādī aṭ-Ṭūr? That'd be the end of the tribe. Why won't you pay whatever you are legally obliged to pay and accept what is legitimately yours? Why don't you name a guarantor [that you will go through with litigation]?" Ibn Rāḍī's mediation between members of the Aḥeiwāt Shawafīn confederation led ʿAlī Gāsim to render Ibn Naṣṣār justice.[10]

BADWA

Unlike voluntary mediation, which has no legal status, a formal type of delegation exists called "appearance" (*badwa;* pl. *badwāt*), specifically devised to urge recalcitrant violators to render justice. A *badwa* is initiated by a self-perceived victim of violation, or plaintiff, who requests personages from Bedouin society to appear as a delegation, normally unannounced, at the tent of his suspected violator, state his claims and suspicions, and persuade the visited person either to admit his guilt and give the plaintiff his due or submit to litigation in order to establish the merits of the case.

In an attempt to prevent legal conflicts from leading to violence, Bedouin law stipulates that a plaintiff must send three such delegations before he may resort to force or "denunciation" (*taswīd* or *sawād*; lit. "blackening") to regain his rights.* The legal maxim states, "Outlaw him through three delegations" (*ʿāddmah bi-thilāth badwāt*).[11] Thus, among the Ẓullām confederation in the northern Negev in 1938, a *manshad* judge reduced the award accruing to Salāma Abū Graynāt after he had been attacked by his host, ʿĪd as-Sareiʿa, in the latter's tent, on the grounds that Abū Graynāt had blackened Sareiʿa before asking him for justice through *badwāt* (Case 12).[12] Had he gone through the *badwa* procedure without receiving satisfaction from his adversary, he could then have blackened him, after which the members of the three delegations would have come to a judge to testify to his failed efforts, thereby legally justifying his denunciation. The same type of testimony will also justify a plaintiff who has physically attacked his foe after having vainly resorted to *badwāt*. In other words, the law views the *badwa* procedure as a mandatory stage in a violated person's efforts to obtain justice.

Typically, *badwa* delegations are sent to open the door to justice only when there is proof or suspicion of theft, insult, damages, nonviolent or nonsexual violations of a woman's honor, violations of the tent, misuse of another's land, or commercial misconduct—problems that Bedouin term "concerns" (*humūm*; sing. *hamm*). They are not sent to ask for justice in the wake of what they term "blood" (*damm*)—that is, a violent physical attack by one man upon another or a sexual attack upon a woman—because the violators, being subject to automatic retaliation in such cases, are expected to placate their victims rather than be entreated. For a *badwa* to ask such a violator for any consideration would highlight his victim's weakness, thereby adding insult to injury. This attitude is also manifest in cases of murder, when it is customary for the perpetrators to flee their victim clan's expected revenge.

As honor and respect are important to Bedouin, they deem it difficult for a suspected violator to dismiss dignitaries who have appeared before him to plead a claim that they ostensibly endorse. In reality, however, it does occasionally happen. In the central Negev in 1987, a man of the ʿAzāzma Saraḥīn rejected a *badwa* sent to ask him to take responsibility for his wife's (and paternal cousin's) insulting the honor of another man by imputing that his daughter had borne children out of wedlock (Case 13).[13] Like many other reticent suspected violators, the accused tried to dissuade the delegation from supporting the sender. First, he argued the legal impossibility of the claim against him—that is, it wasn't he, a man, who had insulted the other woman's

*See below for more on blackening. Three *badwāt* must also be sent to an unregenerate member that a clan wishes to expel before taking this measure (see chapter 3 for more on expulsion).

honor, but only his wife, a woman. Accordingly, he could not be tried by a *manshad* judge, who rules in cases of sexual violation. He also argued that he was the party wronged and entitled to justice, because his wife had said what she had said in response to the other woman's threat to hit her. A defendant might try, as well, to impute dishonesty to a plaintiff or may pose conditions for agreeing to litigate, such as the plaintiff's requesting a truce from him for having supposedly initiated the conflict. This happened, for example, in 1974, when ʿOwda Sulaymān Zanūn of the ʿAzāzma Saraḥīn refused to ask a truce from fellow tribesman Ḥimayd Salmān as-Saddān after one of his clanswomen struck the latter's elderly sister; Zanūn protested that Saddān should have requested the truce, since his sister had started the brawl (Case 14).[14] If a *badwa* delegation sees no reason in the arguments of a defendant, it will leave him, considering that its mission has failed.

So long as the suspected violator remains intractable, another delegation is sent, up to three, adding new and more numerous dignitaries to the second and third in order to make the suspected violator's rejection more difficult. The size of *badwa* delegations often varies but must not exceed five persons so as not to seem like an attack party.* Still, among the Aḥeiwāt Shawafīn, an initial *badwa* in 1979 consisted of five persons.[15] By contrast, the ʿAzāzma Saraḥīn are quite consistent in composing the three successive delegations of two, three, and five persons respectively.[16] In the central Negev in spring 1973, for example, when ʿĪd ʿAtayyig al-Khiraynig felt violated because his cousin Ḥusayn Swaylim al-Khiraynig refused to wed his daughter to ʿĪd's son, despite the son's "closest-cousin's right" (*ḥagg ibn al-ʿamm*),[17] he managed to send two delegations, hoping to persuade Ḥusayn to relent; the first consisted of two men (himself and the elder of the Saraḥīn, ʿOwda Sulaymān Zanūn) and the second of three men (the previous two persons plus the paramount chief of the ʿAzāzma) (Case 15). A third delegation proved unnecessary as the problem was resolved through informal mediation.[18] The members of the successive delegations may be totally different or the same plus new members, as in the previous case, depending on the preference of the claimant. Naturally a claimant will seek to send a *badwa* composed of people he can trust, as manifest in the proverbial perception, "No one joins a *badwa* except a friend" (*mā yibdī ghayr ar-rafīg*).[19]

In Bedouin terminology, a plaintiff both "defines and sends" (*yifaṣṣil wi-yirassil*) his *badwa* delegations—that is, he defines exactly the message they are to convey. Those who stray from his definition are subject to an honor trial

*Hilw and Darwish, *Customary Law*, p. 20. For the same reason, a *badwa* is sent by day, except during Ramaḍān.

for having demonstrated disdain. In 1984 a judge of the Tarabīn, Ḥamdān aṣ-Ṣūfī, made Imsallam Abū Jaddūaʿ of the ʿAzāzma Masʿūdiyyīn swear an oath to clear himself of the charge that he had intentionally distorted the message entrusted to him as the head of a *badwa* delegation sent by Ḥimayd Salmān as-Saddān of the ʿAzāzma Saraḥīn (Case 16). Saddān, whose daughter had absconded with a fellow tribesman, had delegated Abū Jaddūaʿ to demand of ʿAbdallah Muʿattig al-Wajj of the Ẓullām Janabīb, the man in whose tent she had found refuge, that the girl be returned. Instead of arranging for her return, however, Abū Jaddūaʿ imparted that he would get Saddān to agree to the marriage and guarantee that his daughter would be safe from him. Refusing the judge's orders to take an oath, Abū Jaddūaʿ had to pay Saddān a fine of 1,000 Jordanian dinars ($1,500).[20]

JĀHA

By contrast to a *badwa* delegation, which is sent to a violator asking him for justice, another type of delegation, called "notables" (*jāha*; pl. *jahāt*; lit. "faces"), is sent to victims of violation asking for leniency that will serve to avert further violence. Five different roles are played by a *jāha* toward this end: it asks the victim to soften his claim, asks him for a truce, asks that he allow for an end to the conflict, asks him to concede some of the fines awarded him either by a judge or by his own determination, or requests that he relinquish the right to revenge. Unlike in a *badwa*, the number of members in a *jāha* delegation is not limited. I have participated in *jahāt* that varied in number from seven (1977) to forty persons (2004).

Asking a Victim to Soften His Claim

Often an offense may be viewed in different ways, which variously determine its gravity. For example, the law forbids a man to attack a woman for sexual objectives; such an attack is deemed one of the most serious of violations and requires an honor trial (*manshad*). The law also forbids a physical attack upon a woman for reasons other than sexual, though the penalties for such an attack are less than those for sexual assault. In a case that took place among the ʿAzāzma in the central Negev in the 1980s, two shepherdesses began to fight at a cistern over whose turn it was to water her animals (Case 17). When the husband of one of the women, Abū Lugayma, saw his wife being beaten, he picked up a stick and beat the other woman until she bled and her dress tore. On the basis of the rip, the latter girl's father, a Swaylim Sulaymān Zanūn, charged Abū Lugayma with sexual assault rather than beating. Consequently, Abū Lugayma sent Zanūn a *jāha*, which tried to move him to soften the charge to beating, through both confession and an offer to let him determine the award to which he was due.[21]

By the same token, while Bedouin law considers an affront to a woman's moral probity as warranting a *manshad* trial and punishment, it also takes into account background factors for the affront as attenuating circumstances that could lessen the penalty. Accordingly, when in the aforementioned case of a girl of the ʿAzāzma Saraḥīn asserting in public that another woman, whom she had met at pasture, had borne her children out of wedlock (Case 13), the latter's father challenged the former's paternal cousin and husband to a *manshad* trial. This would restore the father's honor for having raised his daughter properly. The challenged husband, however, unwilling to submit himself to *manshad* penalties, sent what was essentially a *jāha* delegation of one messenger to the father advising him to soften his case lest he, the husband, raise a counterclaim—namely, that whatever his wife had said was only in reaction to a threat by the former's daughter and that "words exchanged in argument do not shame" (*kalām fī kalām mā bitʿayyib*) and neither violate a right nor warrant a trial.[22]

Asking a Victim for a Truce

Truces are called for under Bedouin law only in cases of murder, physical violence against men or women, or sexual violence against women, these violations being subject to physical retaliation.[23] Thus, a violator in these categories is constrained to request a truce to ensure that he is safe from the danger of revenge. Among the Ẓullām confederation of the northern Negev in 1954, for example, Sulaymān Salāma Abū Rubayʿa was murdered by his clansman and cousin Ṣubayḥ Abū Rubayʿa, who subsequently fled. However, his sons found refuge with the chief of another Ẓullām tribe, ʿAli Abū Graynāt, who led a *jāha* delegation to the victim's brother requesting a truce (Case 18).[24] Within the neighboring Tiyāha Abū Rugayyig tribe, a truce was similarly sought by a *jāha* sent in 1961, immediately after a member of the Abū Ṣulb section had shot and wounded a member of the Hawāshla section (Case 19). Although the angry Hawāshla rejected the request, a second delegation was sent, proclaiming that the Abū Ṣulb now enjoyed the protection of three Bedouin dignitaries whose honor the Hawāshla could not ignore, and the Hawāshla felt obliged to accede.[25] In the early 1980s, when a lad of the Tarabīn confederation in central Sinai abducted a shepherdess of the Tiyāha, raids by members of the latter upon the livestock of the former impelled the Tarabīn to send a *jāha* delegation of their own notables to request a truce that would terminate the pillage (Case 20). The Tiyāha demanded to have the girl returned to her father as a condition for the truce, and the Tarabīn hastened to do so.[26]

As truces are extended for limited periods, during which the recipients are expected to take steps necessary for restoring justice to their victims, their lapse without justice being reestablished returns the adversaries to a state of potential belligerence unless a specific request for renewal of the truce is made. This too is the task of a *jāha*. For example, the ʿOwdāt, a clan of the ʿAzāzma Sarahīn of the central Negev, tell of a nineteenth-century happening in which a shepherd of the neighboring Saʿīdiyyīn confederation attacked, beat, and took the rifle of one of their camel herdsmen (Case 21).[27] When news of the assault spread, the Saʿīdiyyīn sent a *jāha* requesting a truce from the ʿOwdāt, only to be surprised at the unusually long period they were granted: an entire year. Neglecting to resolve the conflict during that time, however, they dispatched another *jāha* to ask for a renewal of the truce. Again the ʿOwdāt elder, ʿAwwād Ibn ʿOwda, granted them a full year, much to the consternation of his clansmen. After granting the Saʿīdiyyīn two long truces, thereby causing them sufficiently to believe that the ʿOwdāt were afraid to confront them so that they let the second truce lapse without a renewal, the ʿOwdāt were able to surprise them with a harsh reprisal attack. The ʿOwdāt relate this story to honor the memory of their ancestor and erstwhile elder, whose wisdom and patience led to their ability to retaliate.

Asking a Victim to Allow for an End to His Conflict

As stated above, Bedouin fear that conflicts permitted to fester too long may spark a larger conflagration throughout their society. They proverbially observe that "Evil [of conflict] is like a spark" (*ash-sharr sharāra*).[28] Thus, as we have seen, when a conflict erupts, Bedouin attempt to extinguish it by sending a *badwa* delegation to the violator, trying to persuade him to give his victim justice. Even if the *badwa* succeeds in opening the door to justice, however, the victim's pride, in particular, may prolong the conflict. In such cases, a *jāha* delegation may be sent to induce the victim in such a prolonged conflict to resolve it.

Take the aforementioned example from the central Negev in 1974 (Case 10):

> ʿOwda Sulaymān al-Hadōbe of the ʿAzāzma Sarahīn was still smarting from the abduction of his daughter by his maternal nephew, ʿOwda Jumʿa Salmān, who had carried her off to his tent in eastern Sinai three years earlier. Refusing to sanction the subsequent marriage, Hadōbe was seen as a source of dangerous tension within the tribe. Accordingly, the members living in Sinai asked the unofficial chief of the Sarahīn in the Negev, ʿOwda Sulaymān Zanūn, to lead a *jāha* delegation of the son-in-law's supporters to get Hadōbe to change his mind.
>
> When the *jāha* asked the aggrieved father to state what he demanded in order to reconcile, he gave them a choice: either he got the return of his daughter, plus the carrying off and unaccompaniment fines and an honor trial for the violation of his daughter's honor, or the marriage could continue with

> his recognition upon payment of a bride-price of 13,000 Egyptian pounds and a young camel (to symbolize the camel upon which Hadōbe's daughter had been abducted). The lad's relatives agreed to the latter option but said that they had neither the sum nor the camel with them. Hadōbe said, "When you bring what I am asking, I'll recognize the marriage." A time limit was set for delivery of all the requests, but when the in-laws failed to raise the full sum, Hadōbe refused to receive part of it as a deposit. Thus, Zanūn's *jāha* was doomed to failure.[29]

A more successful *jāha* took place at the oasis of Dhahab in southern Sinai in 1991, when notables of several confederations—the ʿAlaygāt, the Bilī, the Suwārka, the Tarabīn, and the Tiyāha—came to Sālim Jumʿa Abū Ṣabḥā of the Muzayna Ghawānma, requesting him to terminate his fifteen-year conflict with a rival, Munayfī Sālim Jabalī of the Muzayna Jarābʿa (Case 1). Of the three issues that constituted Abū Ṣabḥā's original claim—Jabalī's violation of Abū Ṣabḥā's tent and his wife and the amputation of his finger—the first two were settled before a *manshad* judge in 1976. However, Abū Ṣabhā kept the third one, a matter of bloodshed, open in order to keep Jabalī and his clansmen insecure and anxious, living under the threat of retaliation. In 1991, however, Jabalī, exploiting the occasion of Abū Ṣabḥā's imminent departure for the Muslim *ḥajj*, with its intimations of peace among the believers, sent him the high-powered *jāha* delegation, and Abū Ṣabhā felt he could not reject its pleas to bring the conflict to an end. He thus demanded immediate payment of the equivalent of $30,000, which the notables duly produced.[30]

Another successful *jāha* occurred in the northern Negev in 1976, after a black member of the Tiyāha al-Asad tribe, Sālim Abū Jidayaʿ, was beaten by a Caucasian fellow tribesman, Ḥusayn al-ʿOwdāt (Case 22).[31] The background, as claimed by Abū Jidayaʿ, was that the aggressor's flocks were entering his field and destroying the winter crops he had planted. After appealing to the ʿOwdāt elders for damages several times in vain, Abū Jidayaʿ impounded some of ʿOwdāt's animals, whereupon the latter and a few of his clansmen beat him severely, necessitating his hospitalization.[32] Adding insult to injury, they also took Abū Jidayaʿ's staff and dagger and refrained from either visiting him in the hospital or asking for a truce—all signs of contempt. Realizing the danger inherent in insult ("The wounds of weapons heal, but not the wound of words"—*jarḥ as-silāḥ yibra, walla jarḥ al-kalām mā yibra*),[33] a *jāha* composed of three important Bedouin notables visited Abū Jidayaʿ and asked him, as is customary, to specify what award was due him from his violators. First, he demanded a guarantee for the return of his staff and dagger ("even broken") because, as weapons with which he could ordinarily defend himself, these were symbols of his self-esteem. Second, he demanded the equivalent of

$7,500 as a fine and compensation for expenses incurred, most of which amount he later conceded.[34] As a final sign of respect, the members of the ʿOwdāt clan joined the session and kissed him on the head. Another case took place in 1977 in the central Negev (Case 23):

> Swaylim Abū Bilayya of the ʿOwdāt clan of the ʿAzāzma Saraḥīn was repeatedly violated by children of the family of Sālim al-Ameiṭil of the Muṭlān clan of the ʿAzāzma ʿAṣiyāt. The children killed one of his donkeys and put twenty-one of his goats and seven donkeys inside the fence of neighboring Kibbutz Sde Boker, where the animals were attacked by watchdogs and guards; told the kibbutz that Abū Bilayya's flock was pasturing on the kibbutz's sown fields (in order to effect Abū Bilayya's eviction from the area); and informed the police in the town of Dimona that an Abū Bilayya son had stolen objects from the cars of tourists in the desert. As Abū Bilayya had no hard evidence to establish the truth of his grievances, Ameiṭil rejected his repeated protests. When, however, Ameiṭil's sons beat up Abū Bilayya's son Sālim at the weekly market in Beersheba and the Ameiṭil found themselves subject to retaliation by the entire ʿOwdāt clan, they needed a truce from Abū Bilayya, which he would give them only if they confessed to all their offenses against him.[35]
>
> Ameiṭil, with no other option, agreed to these terms, thereby enabling the paramount chief of the ʿAzāzma confederation, ʿOwda Manṣūr Abū Muʿammar, to lead a *jāha* delegation to the Abū Bilayya encampment at a place called Khirbit ar-Rās, in the southern West Bank, where the group was then migrating.[36] The *jāha* included the main judge of the ʿAzāzma, Imsallam Abū Jaddūaʿ; the head of the Saraḥīn in the Negev, ʿOwda Sulaymān Zanūn; a dignitary of the Jordanian ʿUmrān tribe living in the Negev, Nazzāl Abū-l-Misk; a notable from the West Bank village of Ẓāhariyya; and Sālim al-Ameiṭil himself.
>
> Fearing that this conflict between the ʿOwdāt and Muṭlān clans might lead to warfare between their respective tribes, the Saraḥīn and ʿAsiyāt, the delegation sought to get Abū Bilayya to reconcile with Ameiṭil and end the conflict. This it did by allowing the ʿOwdāt spokesman, Ḥimayd Salmān as-Saddān, to enumerate the offenses perpetrated by the Ameiṭil family and designate the awards he wanted for each. Before doing so, however, Saddān posited new conditions—namely, that the *jāha* would leave until last the physical attack against Sālim, the most urgent problem for the Muṭlān to solve, as it threatened the safety of their whole clan; for the same reason, Saddān also threatened to terminate the truce that had been given them if a resolution of all the issues was not achieved in the present session. Ameiṭil was in no position to reject these terms, because the rules of *jāha* stipulate that the violator must be like "a dumb one that doesn't speak" (*balam mā yitikallam*). After all, "A reconciliation delegation, itself, spells recognition of the other's right" (*al-jāha—iʿtirāf fi-l-ḥagg*).[37] In Saddān's strategy, Ameiṭil would be less challeng-

ing about the penalties he planned to impose upon his clansmen for their relatively minor offenses so long as retaliation for the beating still hung over their heads.

Also, to relieve Abū Bilayya of the case that Ameiṭil had precipitated against him with the police, Saddān demanded a guarantee that Ameiṭil see to its closure or pay Abū Bilayya the equivalent (in Israeli pounds) of $25,000. In the end, the fines that Saddān laid on Ameiṭil amounted to $31,425. The *jāha* immediately reduced them, through the process of "concession" (*fawāt*),[38] to the equivalent of $3,625, which was paid out of hand by the designated guarantor, Nazzāl Abū-l-Misk. With that, reconciliation was achieved, and the mission of the *jāha* was accomplished.

In December 2004, I attended a *jāha* among the ʿAzāzma Saraḥīn in the central Negev at which forty persons came to ask Jumʿa Salāma ar-Rimāg to reconcile with the Dilīaʿ clan (Case 24). Approximately a month earlier, a few Dilīaʿ lads had tried to abduct his daughter but were prevented from doing so by one of Rimāg's sons. Soon, however, the Dilīaʿ came back with a larger group of clansmen and beat the son badly, even breaking his knee bones.[39] The *jāha* spokesman, ʿAṭiyya Abū Girshayn of the Jordanian ʿUmrān living in the Negev, began with a speech praising Rimāg as a reasonable and generous person and asked him how much he wanted for the blows and damages. Rimāg said he wanted the equivalent of $7,500 and asked to know who the guarantor of payment would be. At first, there was reticence within the *jāha* to name a guarantor before the members knew how much of the sum Rimāg would concede, but Rimāg held his ground until one participant, Swaylim Ḥimayd Zanūn, announced that he would guarantee the full sum if that was his wish. Thereupon, Rimāg announced that he would concede $2,500, stating explicitly that he was not doing so to honor the Dilīaʿ, "who attacked my womenfolk and then attacked my son," but rather to honor the *jāha*. At that, Zanūn sprang forward to hand him the remaining $5,000 in cash. A man called Abū ʿAtayyig al-Ghidayfī then undertook to be a "guarantor of warmth" (*kafīl dafā*) to ensure that none of the Rimāg attacked anyone of the Dilīaʿ in the aftermath of the reconciliation.[40]

Asking a Victim to Concede the Fines He Was Awarded

As seen in the above accounts of *jāha* delegations that come to induce the victim in a prolonged conflict to resolve it, the delegations most often play a second role as well—namely, asking the victim to concede the award he has determined for himself. Hence, after pressure exerted by the aforementioned *jāha* on Sālim Abū Jidayaʿ (Case 22), he conceded the equivalent of $6,500 of the $7,500 he had set for himself.[41] Similarly, Swaylim Abū Bilayya conceded

$22,500 out of his original award of $26,000, and Jumʿa ar-Rimāg conceded $2,500 out of $7,500.

When, however, an award has been made to the victim of a violation by a judge following litigation, part or all of the amount awarded is normally conceded on the spot, just after the announcement of the award. Occasionally further concessions are also made upon the winner's return to his tent, but only if he is visited by a *jāha* delegation specifically asking him to make them.

In 1976 such a further concession occurred in southern Sinai after Sālim Jumʿa Abū Ṣabhā of the Muzayna Ghawānma received an award for violations incurred at the hands of Munayfī Sālim Jabalī, chief of the Muzayna Jarābʿa tribe, whose three sons, in addition to violating the sanctuary of Abū Ṣabḥa's tent and cutting off one of his fingers, also mauled his wife (Case 1). For the first and third offenses, the noted *manshad* judge, Sulaymān Muḥammad al-ʿUgbī, in the Negev, awarded the victim a total of $60,500 (242,000 Israeli pounds) and immediately ordered the obligatory deduction from the award of one-third (approximately $20,000) in honor of himself,[42] in keeping with the legal maxim, "A third of the entitlement is at the judge's discretion" (*thilth al-ḥagg fī lisān al-gāḍī*).[43] This left Abū Ṣabḥā's award at $40,000. Pressed by some Negev Bedouin notables attending the trial to concede in their honor, Abū Ṣabhā relinquished another $4,000, thus returning to southern Sinai with a guaranteed sum of $36,000.[44] However, once Abū Ṣabhā had been home for a few days, a *jāha* of notables came to him to ask him to relinquish even more of his award. After much argument and negotiation, he surrendered another $9,000, leaving himself only $27,000 out of an original award of $60,500.[45]

Asking a Victim to Relinquish His Right to Blood-Revenge

As murder signals the possibility that the clansmen of the victim are weak insofar as their reputation for strength did not suffice to deter the bloodshed, they will be keen to dispel this image and show their strength through an act of blood-revenge. "Revenge dispels shame" (*ath-thār yijlī al-ʿār*) is the proverbial expression of this urge.[46] Nonetheless, there are cases when groups are relieved not to have to take revenge but rather to accept blood-payment. One occasion for desisting from vengeance is when the victim and murderer are in different families of the same clan, meaning that revenge upon someone from the immediate family of the murderer will weaken that clan, whose main function is to protect its members on a daily basis, mainly (as noted) through the number of its male members. Such, for example, was the problem in 1954 of ʿOwda Salāma Abū Rubayʿa of the Ẓullām confederation in the northern Negev when his brother Sulaymān was killed by a cousin, called Ṣubayh (Case

18). It was only relieved by a *jāha* delegation led by Sasson Bar-Tsvi, who headed the Israeli Bedouin Tribal Court in the Negev, and the chief, ʿAlī Salāma Abū Graynāt, who had given refuge to the murderer's two sons. The *jāha* came to ʿOwda Abū Rubayʿa and asked him to spare these sons, who were also ʿOwda's cousins, and the chief undertook to pay whatever blood-payment Abū Rubayʿa asked. In the end, he received the equivalent of $1,000.[47]

Another circumstance for desisting from even trying to take revenge is when the murderer's group is stronger and attempted vengeance might subject the victim's group to more danger and perhaps humiliation. In north-central Sinai in January 1977, a member of the Bilī confederation, one of the smallest in Sinai (679 persons at that time), was shot to death by a member of the Suwārka confederation, the largest in the peninsula (14,584 persons) (Case 6).[48] Although the Bilī could have found a way to take revenge for the murder, they did not, fearing that it might jeopardize good relations with their larger neighbors. Here again, a *jāha* delegation came to their aid, sent by the Suwārka on January 31, 1977. Led by Chief Sālim Salmān Abū ʿAnga of the Tarabīn Giṣār and including the Suwārka judge Ḥājj Murayshid Rashīd al-Murāshda and two Suwārka chiefs, Ṣabāḥ Rabāʿ Salāmiyyīn and Salām Ghānmī al-Ḥowṣ, it came to the renowned Bilī judge Ibrahīm Abū Dahathūm and stressed the need for peace in the area. Moreover, in addition to glorifying the courage and resolve of the Bilī, it agreed to give them twenty camels as the blood-payment they chose.[49]

The above special circumstances notwithstanding, *jāha* delegations whose mission is to ask victims of murder—that is, the clansmen of a murdered person—to forgo their right to revenge are mainly undertaken with thought of the murder's detrimental effect on the immediate society.

The Ẓullām confederation in the northern Negev—whose name means "offspring of the 'unjust one' (*ẓālim*)"—relate that when the son of their seventeenth-century ancestor aẓ-Ẓālim was killed, the father sought to take revenge on the killer (Case 25). Notables of his erstwhile area in the northern Ḥijāz, however, formed a *jāha* delegation that came to entreat him to relinquish his right to blood-revenge in exchange for a blood-payment.[50] The man demanded forty camels, as is normal under Bedouin law, and gave the killer and his clan a truce. The epithet, "the unjust one," then adhered to him because when the murderer's clan came to him with only thirty-nine camels—the most that they could gather, even with great difficulty—aẓ-Ẓālim took them but took revenge to boot. His subsequent flight is what brought the Ẓullām to the Negev.[51]

Another such story of *jāha* occurred in the early twentieth century among the ʿAzāzma Saraḥīn tribe in the central Negev when, as related above, a man of the Kallāb clan killed a man of the Ḥawaṣa clan (Case 4). The Kallāb thereupon fled from blood-revenge to the ʿAraba rift valley (which separates the Negev from Jordan), finding refuge among the Saʿīdiyyīn confederation; but they had, after some years, to return to the central Negev when a shepherd of the Saʾīdiyyīn insulted one of them for preceding him with his camels to a watering source. Before leaving, however, they praised the strength of both the Ḥawaṣa and the ʿAzāzma. Nevertheless, when they arrived in Wādī al-Figrī, the Bedouin there, knowing that the Kallāb were liable to blood-revenge, decided they must try and reconcile them with the Ḥawaṣa. So they formed a *jāha* delegation and went to the Ḥawaṣa, describing how the Kallāb had praised them before the Saʿīdiyyīn and asked that they welcome them back and reconcile with them on the basis of blood-payment, stressing that such mercy would be to the benefit of all the ʿAzāzma.[52]

Traditionally a *jāha* delegation that comes to ask a victim to relinquish his right to blood-revenge for murder follows certain procedures. First of all, the violator himself is not a part of the delegation so as not to put the victim in a dilemma between his perceived duty to avenge and his duty to ensure the sanctuary of his tent. In cases of murder, the *jāha* does not come without previous agreement on the part of the victim's clansman so as not to intimidate him into agreeing to its request without his having an opportunity to consult with the other members of his clan, who have as equal and legal an interest in the revenge as he has. Again, so as not to compromise him, as a host, into agreeing to their demands, the members of the *jāha* bring their own tent so as to demonstrate their independence. Similarly, they bring their own food (an animal to slaughter, flour for the bread, rice, tea, sugar, and coffee beans); utensils (cooking pots, bowls, teapots, coffee pots, cups, glasses, and trays); firewood; and the persons, male and female, who will prepare the festive meal that follows agreement and will be served in their own tent, where the victim group will be honored as guests.

As with any *jāha* for whatever purpose, and although the negotiations are held in the victim clan's sitting space, members of the delegation will neither eat nor drink anything offered to them so long as a resolution has not been reached—that is, not until after the concession procedure has ended and "the remainders of the entitlement" (*sawāmil al-ḥagg*) have been determined. At that point, the participants can drink and eat what is offered or what they themselves have brought, as in cases of murder, thereby indicating the end of conflict, as expressed in the saying, "He who is friendly toward you will eat your food" (*man rādak akal zādak*).[53] Further to symbolize the new accord, the violators will kiss the beard or forehead of the elder of the victim group or perhaps, in the case of wounds, the victim himself. As opposed to conflicts that have involved murder, however, a *jāha* in cases concerning wounds comes unannounced unless previous agreement to reconcile has occurred, as in the Rimāg-Dilīaʿ conflict mentioned above (Case 24). In May 1974, for example, I joined a delegation sent by Ḥimayd Salmān as-Saddān of the ʿAzāzma Saraḥīn to his fellow tribesman, ʿOwda Sulaymān Zanūn; the delegation was led by an elder of the ʿAzāzma ʿAṣiyāt, Sālim Ḥasan Abū Gardūd. The conflict between Saddān and Zanūn had begun the previous winter, when, in a brawl between women, Saddān's widowed sister was beaten by women belonging to the Zanūn clan (Case 14). As disagreement over responsibility for the origins of the beating persisted, the two elders refused to grant each other truces. In this atmosphere, Saddān stabbed Zanūn's son, Swaylim, exacerbating and prolonging the conflict, which proceeded in the absence of any truce.[54]

Such were the reasons for the *jāha* to Zanūn. At the meeting, Abū Gardūd said, "O Zanūn, I have come to you regarding the 'case of Ḥimayd' (*ṭalābit Ḥimayd*). First of all, you are clansmen; second, this is a simple case. It doesn't warrant a bigger problem. The *jāha* has come here in keeping with our necessary law: 'He who has angered a soul must placate him' (*man ghaḍḍab nafs yiraḍḍīh*).[55] We want to placate you and compensate you for your lost blood." At first, Zanūn showed impatience with the *jāha* delegates and did not requite their friendliness. But when he looked at the delegation's tent, filled with women and children and all the things necessary for a festive meal, he relented and asked Abū Gardūd if he would pay him for the wounds incurred. The latter answered that he wouldn't have come if he wasn't ready to compensate him; at that Zanūn said he wanted 10,000 Jordanian dinars (approximately $20,000). Following that, the concession process took place, leaving Zanūn with $2,000. Abū Gardūd appointed a guarantor of payment, and Zanūn named a guarantor of warmth. After that, as the meal was being prepared, someone fetched Saddān from the market in Beersheba, as he could now sit safely with the Zanūn in the wake of the reconciliation agreement. When he arrived, he paid Zanūn the outstanding $2,000 and kissed him on the head. The *jāha* had ended with success.[56]

Guaranty

MAKING PERSONS COMPLY WITH JUDGMENTS AND UNDERTAKINGS

Among the nomadic or semi-nomadic Bedouin (as in Sinai and the Negev), where, as noted, neither centralized government nor its law-enforcement agencies have historically existed and in which installations for detainment were practically impossible to maintain, other means for constraining people to honor their obligations had to be devised, enabling society to function. The main system that emerged was "guaranty" (*kafāla*; lit. "twofold"—that is, the involved party and his guarantor). Virtually every agreement between Bedouin, whether pertaining to litigation, judicial decisions, truces, the abstention from revenge, financial transactions, or clan membership, is normally backed up by a guarantor (*kafīl*). For example, guaranty is crucial to bringing adversaries to litigate their problems peacefully. If there has been some form of bloodshed between them, making revenge a possibility, other people in the society try to establish a truce that prohibits one side from attacking the other until they adjudicate or settle through mediation. Here a "guarantor of truce" (*kafīl ʿaṭwa*) is appointed to ensure that the truce is not violated. When the adversaries have agreed to meet for trial at the venue of a judge, their appearance at the "designated time and place" (*mādd ū-mīʿād*) is guaranteed by what Bedouin call "a guarantor against absence or fright" (*kafīl ʿan gheiba ū-heiba*), also called "a driving guarantor" (*kafīl sawwāg*), derived from the image of driving livestock forward. If one adversary's offense is expected to exact penalties, material as well as moral, he must engage a "guarantor of completeness" (*kafīl wafā*) who will ensure that he discharges them completely; often, in the event of a fine only, the designation is "guarantor of the remainder" (*kafīl as-sāmil*)[57]—that is, what is left of the fine after concessions are made. If the offender has physically violated his victim, it is incumbent upon the latter to engage a guarantor of warmth (*kafīl dafā*), who ensures that he will not strike back after receiving his fine.

In everyday life, too, guarantors are appointed to secure obligations undertaken in a wide variety of other realms. One is divorce. In 1961, for example, when the renowned poet ʿAnayz Sālim al-ʿUrḍī of the Tarabīn Ḥasāblah in southern Sinai divorced two of his wives after receiving a fifteen-year prison sentence in Egypt for smuggling, he sent a letter to a clansman, Ḥājj Ḥimaydān ʿUbaydallah al-ʿUrḍī, in which he appointed guarantors to disavow any marital claims against him or any claims by him against these women remarrying other men (Case 151).[58]

Guarantors may also play a role in upholding marital agreements, especially if there is to be a prolonged delay between the agreement and the actual marriage. Among the ʿAzāzma Sarahīn tribe in the central Negev, for example, when the daughter of Frayj Ḥimayd as-Saddān was abducted by her clansman, Sulaymān Swaylim Abū Bilayya, in 1995, one of Saddān's terms for his agreement to their marriage was that Abū Bilayya's brother, Salāma, pledge his oldest daughter in marriage to one of Saddān's sons when she came of age in fifteen years' time (Case 26). To ensure the implementation of this condition, they appointed a fellow tribesman, Sālim Salāma ar-Rimāg, to be its guarantor. The conditions of the guaranty were that Salāma Abū Bilayya would present his daughter for marriage when the time came, and Frayj as-Saddān would pay him 20,000 Jordanian dinars (the equivalent of $30,000) upon receipt of the girl; if Salāma defaulted, he was to pay that sum to Saddān.[59] Other agreements that involve delays also utilize guarantors. When, for example, thoroughbred female horses are sold, the seller is entitled to the first two female foals born to her. Bedouin call this arrangement "returned foals" (*mathānī*), and a guarantor is enlisted to ensure their delivery to the seller.*

Often the honor of a guarantor is a condition for the return of a woman to her husband after she has complained of mistreatment at his hands and he has been called to account by her father or an *ʿugbī* judge, who rules in problems between husband and wife.[60] Such a guarantor, appointed by the husband, must ensure that henceforth he, the husband, will treat his wife well; if she is mistreated, either she or her father (or guardian) will activate the guarantor. Similarly when Bedouin sell or give away land to others, this act too must be endorsed by a guarantor. Early in the twentieth century, when people of the Tiyāha Ṣugayrāt relinquished a cultivable area in eastern Sinai called Wadeiy al-Bayḍ to a group from the Aḥeiwāt Shawafīn, they provided four guarantors to confirm that they had no further claims to ownership of the site (Case 27). Subsequently, when the Aḥeiwāt group sold the land to fellow tribesmen, they appointed one guarantor to affirm that none of the seller clan would subsequently challenge the sale by claiming the right of preemption.[61] Yet another use of guaranty, highlighting its ubiquitous nature, occurred in the Negev in 1984, when Jumʿa Abū Huwayshil of the Tiyāha Gudayrāt denounced Ḥimayd as-Saddān of the ʿAzāzma Saraḥīn for denigrating the guarantee of a third party, ʿOwda Abū Rāghib of the Ẓullām Abū Graynāt, in the tent of Ṣāliḥ Abū Samra of the ʿAzāzma Ṣubayḥāt (Case 28). Saddān, in his defense, demanded that they jointly return to Abū Samra's tent and engage him as a paid witness (*marḍawī*)[62] to confirm or reject the allegation. Abū Samra, for his part, agreed to act as a witness only on condition that each party appoint a guarantor to ensure that the party against whom he testified would accept his testimony as the tent owner—that is, that the party would press no subsequent claim against him.[63]

Guarantors are also called upon to ensure that relations between members of a clan are upheld within the rules of clan association. In 1978, for example, when Frayj Muḥeisin of the Aḥeiwāt Karādma was affiliating with, or joining, the Guṣayyir clan of the Aḥeiwāt Shawafīn, both sides appointed guarantors to ensure that they would respectively abide by conditions pertaining to the period of affiliation, mutual obligations and rights, and the nature of relations between the veteran members and the joiners (Case 29).[64] In the same year,

*Al-ʿĀrif, *al-Qaḍā'*, pp. 144–46; however, al-ʿĀrif explains *mathānī* as deriving from two, as two colts are generally (though not always) returned to the seller.

guarantors of affiliation were also mutually appointed among the Tiyāha Ḥukūk of the northern Negev when the clan in which Ḥājj Khalīl al-Asad was the elder admitted to full membership blacks (*ʿabīd*; sing. *ʿabd*; lit. "slave") who lived among them (Case 30).[65] Similarly, in the event that a clan from which dissatisfied members threaten to disaffiliate attempts to block their leaving, they may be asked to appoint a guarantor to ensure that the other members of that clan henceforth treat them fairly if they refrain from leaving.[66] Further, if a member of a clan has proven to be a repetitive thief, his clansmen must post seven guarantors to the effect that he will not steal again.[67] Or when a clan expels a member for habitual troublemaking, it must provide three guarantors to ensure that it will have no future relations with or obligations toward him.[68]

PUNISHMENTS FOR VIOLATING GUARANTY

Bedouin law ensures the effectiveness of guaranty by specifying heavy punishments both for its violation by those who are guaranteed and for its neglect by guarantors. For example, a person who violates a guarantee or imputes neglect to a guarantor, thereby "cutting his face" (*gaṭʿ al-wijih* or *tagṭīaʿ al-wijih*, "face" being a metaphor for honor) will have to pay the guarantor an honor fine imposed at the discretion of a *manshad* judge. Bedouin fear these fines, which they hyperbolically depict as being "as extensive as the entire Beersheba district" (*ʿala gadd as-sabaʿ*)—that is, the entire Negev.[69] Among the Ẓullām confederation in 1932, for example, Muḥammad al-Gabbūaʿ violated the honor of Salmān Abū Rubayʿa, a truce guarantor, when he accused him of not helping the Gabbūaʿ get their rights after one of their lads was ostensibly beaten up by their adversary, Salāma Ibn ʿAyyāda, during a truce (Case 31). When it turned out that the lad had not been beaten, Gabbūaʿ was fined by a *manshad* judge for slandering Abū Rubayʿa. The overall punishment comprised forty full-grown and sound camel-mares, 40 gold pounds, and a man and woman slave for each peg in the tent of Abū Rubayʿa (to be evaluated in cash); in addition; Gabbūaʿ was ordered to cover the roof of the guarantor's tent with white cloth and proclaim the honor of his guarantee in the tents of three notables, a humiliating moral punishment.[70] Such are the enormous *manshad* penalties that deter people from violating any type of guarantee.

An alternative punishment, though less common, is a guarantor's resort to force against the violator of his honor, the threat of which is not easily ignored, owing to his presumably more numerous and powerful clan. Among the Tiyāha Gudayrāt of the northern Negev in 1958, when Ibrahīm al-Aṭrash was told that a man called Abū Khubayṭa had named him as an accomplice in a murder, he challenged him to a trial for slander (Case 32).[71] Abū Khubayṭa engaged a guarantor of completeness, who would ensure the payment of any fines imposed on him, but he himself failed to appear at the trial. He was therefore deemed guilty, and a fine was imposed upon him and guaranteed. After he also failed to pay that, his adversary, Aṭrash, went to the guarantor, who paid it in his stead but then proceeded to demand that Abū Khubayṭa compensate him—and twofold, as the laws of guaranty require. When Abū Khubayṭa again refused to comply, the guarantor's clan prepared to attack him as punishment for his repeated defaults, a prospect that was sufficiently fearful to make Abū Khubayṭa pick up and flee.

An additional way through which the law fortifies the importance of guaranty may also be observed from the above case. When Abū Khubayṭa saw that the guarantor and his people were about to attack him, he appealed for the protection of the chief, Ḥammād Abū Rubayʿa, as stated. This was refused him, as was later explained by the *manshad* judge, Sālim Muḥammad al-ʿUgbī, because guaranty must take precedence over protection (*dakhāla*)—that is, if a person has violated a guarantee that he himself initiated, he cannot ask for protection in order to avert the consequences. As one legal maxim asserts, "Protection doesn't take precedence over guaranty" (*ad-dakhal mā biyirkab ʿal al-kafal*).[72]

No less important for guaranty to be effective, however, is that guarantors too must be held to account. The indispensability of guaranty in the absence of law-enforcement agencies in the desert depends on guarantors not defaulting on their commitments. So strong is this awareness that a Bedouin sentiment considers a guarantor who is remiss (in Bedouin parlance "treacherous"—*bāyig*) the worst source of evil.[73]

Bedouin law employs three means for ensuring that guarantors remain constant. The first is a prohibition against renouncing their obligation. The relevant quadruple-rhymed legal maxim makes this injunction explicit: "Guaranty is like mountains that cannot be broken nor conveyed away" (*al-kafāl zay al-ijbāl—lā tinhāl wala tinshāl*).[74] The obligation can be annulled only by the party to whom it was made—in litigation, for example, by the claimant in the case of a *kafīl wafā* and the defendant in the case of a *kafīl dafā*. If not annulled by agreement with them, the law deems the guaranty valid and any dereliction of duty on the guarantor's part an offense.[75]

The second means for keeping a guarantor engaged is to make responsibility for the guaranty collective. Primary, and most operative on a daily basis, is the responsibility of the guarantor's clan, or *khamsa*. A traditional Bedouin saying holds, "Commitment to guaranty is not just yours; the commitment is for the whole clan" (*al-wijih mū hū lak min ḥālak—al-wijih la-l-khamsa kullha*),[76] instructing that if a guarantor himself is remiss in fulfilling the obligations of guaranty, others in his clan must fulfill them upon demand. In the same context, if a guarantor dies, the primary responsibility for the commitment passes to his heir: "The heir bears the guaranty" (*al-wārith—al-wijih maʿah*).[77] In cases where a guarantor extends guaranty to someone from another confederation, his obligation is binding on his entire confederation, some member of which must fulfill it in the event of his being remiss. For this intent, we have the maxim, "The confederation name includes everyone" (*al-ism biyishmil al-kull*).[78] In sum, any remissness on the part of a guarantor affects those with whom he is affiliated as well.

A third way of keeping a guarantor to his commitment is to allow the guaranteed party to denounce (lit. "blacken"—*yisawwid*) him for being derelict. Such dereliction may occur, for example, when a *kafīl wafā* reneges on paying a fine that the delinquent person he has guaranteed shrinks from paying. This guarantor of completeness has forty days, from the time of request, to present his payment, in accordance with the maxim, "The guarantor enjoys delays—forty nights of reprieve" (*al-kafīl lah mawajīl—arbaʿīn layla mafnūnīn*).[79] Dereliction may also occur when a *kafil dafā*, who is supposed to keep someone secure, desists from acting against one who has attacked or threatened to attack, once he, the guarantor, has been alerted. According to Bedouin law, he must "get up" and act immediately. If not, he will be blackened, a consequence that affects all his clan, as "the blackening blotches the whole *khamsa* group" (*as-sōda ʿal al-khamsa kullha*).[80]

Blackening (*sawād* or *taswīd*) is normally performed by the disappointed person erecting a cairn of blackened stones or placing black flags at frequented junctions or by tying a black dog to his tent, all announcing that these actions were taken to call attention to the remissness, indeed "treachery" (*bōg*), of the guarantor. Or he may do something more dramatic, such as taking hold of and shaking the edge of the roof of a remiss guarantor's tent (which is typically black in the winter, being woven from the hair of black goats), shouting at the owner, in the presence of many visitors, "This is your flag, O so-and-so!" (*haydhī reitak yā flān*). In the central Negev in 1983, Ḥimayd Salmān as-Saddān of the ʿAzāzma Saraḥīn used another formula at the guest tent of ʿAbdallah Muʿattig al-Wajj of the Ẓullām Janabīb, whom he wished to blacken for not resolving, in disregard of his guarantee, the problem of Saddān's daughter, who had absconded with her rejected suitor and found refuge in his tent (Case 16). Enraged by the delay of over forty days, Saddān, using the rhymed imagery of black objects, vociferously proclaimed the following to the many guests in Wajj's tent:

The flag of al-Wajj, my foe, is seven [times as black as] crows
(*Al-Wajj gharīmi—reitih saba' ghirbān*)
and seven [times as black as] pitched tents
(*ū-saba' buyūt imbanniyāt*)
and seven [times as black as] veiled girls
(*ū-saba' banāt imnaggabāt*)
and seven [times as black as] horses sent out for aid*
(*ū-saba' mahār imjabbabāt*)
and seven [times as black as] slaves from Cairo to Port Sa'īd
(*ū-sab'a 'abīd min maṣr ila būr sa' īd*)
and seven [times as black as] kilograms of iron.
(*ū-saba' kīlāt min al-ḥadīd*).[81]

Being blackened as a "remiss guarantor" (*kafīl bāyig*) and thus being exposed as untrustworthy in a public, undeniable, and indelible manner is the worst source of defamation among Bedouin, jeopardizing the guarantor's subsequent reputation and social status. A defamed guarantor is known as a "cracked guarantor" (*kafīl mathlūm*), "cracked" referring to his honor, which, like a tiny China cup, may prove irreparable.[82] Guaranty is thus a recurrent test of a guarantor's honor, and Bedouin law and sentiment give him little room for dodging. His condition is depicted in the proverb, "The guarantor must act rapidly like a thoroughbred horse, and his face [that is, honor] is but two fingers wide" (*al-kafīl aṣīl ū-wijhah garaṭayn*).[83] Blackening is thus greatly feared, impelling a guarantor who is threatened or actually afflicted with it to take quick action to annul it. Such a guarantor would demand trial before a *manshad* judge, within whose competence fall most cases pertaining to honor. Because the institution of guaranty is essential to the conduct of life in Bedouin society, the law is resolute to discourage unjustifiable blackening, thus mandating heavy *manshad* punishments for this offense.

Blackening may also be the punishment for negligent Bedouin guarantors who have appointed themselves to guarantee their own obligations, a common procedure. Such a guarantor, invoking his "word of honor" (*kilmit sharaf*), is called "a guarantor-executor" (*kafīl ū-'amīl*). For example, in the late nineteenth century 'Adaysān Abū 'Abdūn renounced revenge on 'Uṣaybī Abū Shunnār, the murderer of his brother (Case 5). 'Adaysān had pursued the man from

*The reference is to the past Bedouin custom of people threatened by aggression sending a messenger on a horse or camel with a strip of black tent cloth around its neck to request aid; oral communication from Mūsa Ḥasan al-'Aṭowna of the Tiyāha Nutūsh, October 1, 1973; cf. Bailey, "Arabah," p. 261.

the northern Negev deep into Egypt until, finally finding him in an isolated spot, ʿAdaysān, satisfied that Abū Shunnār feared him, proclaimed, "Return home and I guarantee that we'll be reconciled" (*rawwiḥ w-āna kafīl aṭ-ṭīb*).[84] Again, within the Aḥeiwāt confederation in eastern Sinai in 1978, when the fathers of lads who had attacked each other on a number of occasions mutually agreed to end this violence through litigation, each one gave his own guarantee that their respective people would honor the truce and halt hostilities until they met before a preliminary judge (Case 33).[85] Often in financial transactions, such as contracting a loan, the borrower will be his own guarantor of repayment, as was Sālim Salāma ar-Rimāg of the ʿAzāzma Saraḥīn in 1999, when he borrowed money from a fellow tribesman, ʿOwda Ibn Saʿad (Case 34).[86] Ultimately a remiss guarantor-executor who denies his guaranty can be required to swear an oath as to whether he made it or not, a procedure that Bedouin traditionally dread.[87] If he recoils, he may be blackened.

"Throwing the Face"

For deterring violence or imminent violations between Bedouin, the law sanctions the custom of "throwing the honor" (*ramī al-wijih*; lit. "throwing the face") of a notable man between two hostile persons. Once a bystander at impending violence says to the rivals, "I hereby throw the face of so-and-so between you" and (normally) reports his initiative to the notable (*wajīh*; lit. "a person of face") whose name he has summoned, the latter's honor should be sufficient to keep the peace between the contestants for a period of anywhere from three days to a month. The same procedure may be utilized by one of the parties to a dispute toward his rival. In Sinai and the Negev, a widely heard story and its attendant poem from northwest Arabia tell of a chief of the Ḥuwayṭāt Tihāma tribe, Muḥammad Abū Ṭugayga, who early in the twentieth century cast his honor between the Slaymiyyīn section of his own tribe and a section of the neighboring Masaʿīd confederation in order to prevent blood-revenge following the murder, by the Masaʿīd, of a Ḥuwayṭāt man (Case 35).[88] In the northern Negev in the mid-1960s, persons aware that blows were being exchanged between the Abū ʿAyyāsh section of the ʿAzāzma Masʿūdiyyīn and the Tiyāha Abū Rugayyig threw the honor of Chief Ḥammād Abū Rubayʿa between the adversaries lest hostilities increase between the two tribes (Case 36).[89] In 1978 in eastern Sinai, when Sālim Ibn Kureidim, visiting two brothers of the Kubayshāt section of the Aḥeiwāt Ḥamadāt tribe, saw lads of the Aḥeiwāt Ghuraygāniyyīn apparently on their way to beat the brothers up, he shouted at them to halt (Case 37). When they refused, he cried, "The face of Jumʿa Ibn

Ghayth is on you two, and the face of Shaykh Sulaymān al-Guṣayyir is on the Kubayshāt." At this, the comers, though protesting, turned back.[90]

Throwing the face of a notable may also be practiced by one party to a conflict to freeze a situation in order to prevent an anticipated violation from taking place. In the northern Negev in the mid-1940s, for example, when a Salmān Sālim saw his brother, ʿĪd Sālim, cultivating a field that Salmān considered his own by inheritance, he proclaimed, "This piece of land and the cistern upon it are under the honor of Shaykh ʿAlī Abū Graynāt; don't make any changes, lest you 'cut his face' (*tigṭaʿ wijhih*—that is, violate his honor) (Case 38)."[91] Likewise, in 1973 in the central Negev, when Sulaymān Ḥusayn al-Khiraynig of the ʿAzāzma Saraḥīn feared that his cousin, ʿĪd ʿAlī al-Khiraynig, was about to abduct his sister, pursuant to his "closest-cousin right" to marry her, he tried to stop the move by throwing the honor of three chiefs—ʿOwda Abū Muʿammar, Ḥammād Abū Rubayʿa, and ʿAlī Abū Graynāt—upon her not being abducted (Case 15).[92] In 1979, among the Aḥeiwāt Shawafīn in eastern Sinai, ʿAliyyān Ḥamdạn of the Najamāt section, fearing that claimants to ownership of a plot he had been cultivating for fifteen years would destroy his crops, threw the honor of three notables—one each from the Aḥeiwāt, Tiyāha, and Tarabīn confederations—against any harm being done to his field, the wire fencing surrounding it, and the crops growing in it (Case 27).[93]

If one of the adversaries should commence hostilities or otherwise violate the honor that has been thrown, it would constitute a statement of contempt for the notable's strength, which the latter would consider an intolerable situation and be loath to ignore. Although the law falls short of obliging him to take action against the offender, it does sanction his doing so. The system calls for him to demand an honor trial, where the offender will be heavily fined and severely shamed. For example, in the northern Negev in 1960, when a passerby, an Abū Ḥimayd, saw members of the Ṭurshān and Abū Kaff sections of the Tiyāha Abū Rugayyig tribe about to brawl, he threw the faces of two chiefs, Ḥasan Abū Rubayʿa and ʿAwwād Abū Rugayyig, to prevent them from fighting (Case 39).[94] When it subsequently turned out that the Abū Kaff attacked a man of the Ṭurshān after the throwing of the face, the two notables demanded a *manshad* trial, which was conducted by the judge and chief, Muḥammad Abū Juweiʿid, who ordered the Abū Kaff to pay to Abū Rubayʿa and Abū Rugayyig forty white camels, forty yellow camels, and forty brown camels (totaling the equivalent of $60,000); the equivalent of $3 for each step taken in pursuit of the Ṭurshān and $3 for each step in return (totaling $3,000); and payments to the Ṭurshān covering all expenses incurred as a result of the attack, $3,000 as ransom for the (otherwise amputated) Abū Kaff hand that struck the Ṭurshān man, and twofold the assessment of damages caused him. In addition, the assailants had to proclaim before three tents of notables filled with men that the honor of the two notables was clean and its protection effective, and the Abū Kaff also lost any claim relating to the original conflict with the Ṭurshān. Even if a violated notable willingly concedes much of such a fine, as did Abū Rubayʿa and Abū Rugayyig, these punishments largely serve to deter the violation of a "thrown face" throughout Bedouin society, thus helping to keep violence down.

In cases that require the throwing of face to freeze a certain status quo, Bedouin law stipulates two rules for making it valid. First, because the conflicts involved are subject to eventual legal resolution, mainly through litigation, it is mandatory for the person who throws the face (necessarily a party to the conflict) not merely to name the notable whose honor he is throwing, but also to name three judges who will decide the case.[95] This is deemed necessary for showing that he intends to bring the matter to litigation, thereby granting his adversary a chance to state his claims too. Neglect of this proviso may subject him who "threw the face" to a trial of honor. Such was the case in the conflict between the brothers Salmān Sālim and ʿĪd Sālim (Case 38) after the former neglected to name judges while throwing the face of chief ʿAlī Abū Graynāt to deter his brother ʿĪd from cultivating a plot he considered his own. When Salmān complained to Abū Graynāt that ʿĪd was continuing to prepare the disputed plot for cultivation and Abū Graynāt challenged ʿĪd to an honor trial, the judge deemed that Salmān had alerted the chief unjustifiably, as the throwing of his face had not been valid. Consequently he was ordered to compensate the notable for violating his honor.[96]

Second, one who throws a face to freeze a situation must inform the invoked notable of his action, thus giving him the latitude to take steps necessary for discharging his commitment as the maintenance of his honor requires. Accordingly, when ʿAliyyān Ḥamdān neglected this condition when throwing the face of Farrāj ʿĪd al-Musāʿida of the Tarabīn Ḥasāblah, his fence poles, fencing, and crops were destroyed by his adversaries without the notable's even knowing (Case 27).[97]

By contrast, when honor is thrown in order to prevent violence, it is not legally necessary to inform the notable. For example, the Czech traveler-scholar Alois Musil relates a story he heard in the Syrian desert early in the twentieth century wherein a woman of the Shammar confederation in central Arabia, being beaten by her husband, threw the face of a renowned (though distant) warrior, Fiheid Ibn Maʿabhil of the ʿAneza Rawala tribe, between them, albeit to no avail (Case 40). Her husband merely mocked her, asking, "How can my wife call on Fiheid when he camps a month's journey from us?" However, itinerant merchants who heard the woman's cries later recounted the event to people they met along their way until the story finally reached the ears of Ibn Maʿabhil himself. Directly assembling his men, the offended warrior set out to find the battering husband, traversing a distance that took twenty-five days to cover, until he found him. Thereupon, he stabbed him in the thigh, asking, "Did you really doubt that your wife was under my protection?" and threatened to kill him if he beat her again.[98]

Protection

OBSTACLES TO JUSTICE FOR THE WEAK

Numerical Disadvantage

The absence of any governmental or tribal authority to enforce equality before the law disadvantages a violated party in seeking the redress of his violation from someone stronger, strength being measured mainly by the number of men in the ranks. Bedouin awareness of this condition is reflected in the proverb, "The strong one rejects justice" (*al-gawīy ʿāyib*).[99] Under such circumstances, it is not surprising that Bedouin respect the role of might, as embodied in fighting men, in the pursuit of a conflict. Proverbial lines of a widespread poem counsel people to count the number of their men before getting themselves into battle.[100] In the confrontation between clans, it is often the size of their respective adult male membership that determines the result. "Numbers overcome bravery" (*al-kuthra ghallabat as-sibāʿa*) is ever on a Bedouin's mind.[101]

Numerical advantage manifests itself in conflicts on all levels of Bedouin society, including confederations and tribes. Commonly it breeds disdain for a smaller group, often leading the larger, stronger group to violate the former's dignity with reference to its legal rights. Such disdain was manifest between the Tiyāha and ʿAzāzma confederations of east-central Sinai, just west of the Israeli-Egyptian border, ever since the latter became refugees there from the 1948 Arab-Israeli War and were only a quarter the size of the native Tiyāha (Case 41).[102] Accordingly, in spring 1999, members of the Tiyāha Binayāt stopped, at gunpoint, the pickup truck of an ʿAzāzma man who was taking his ill wife to a doctor in the Guṣayma oasis, and while some of the attackers led the man aside, others violated the honor of the woman.[103] These attacks, though reportedly committed against the background of smuggling disagreements, revealed, by their abandon, the contempt for a smaller, presumably powerless, tribal group.

Although men of the ʿAzāzma took revenge within a few days, killing the original attacker and his brother, the traditional disdain resurfaced among the Tiyāha, as the total confederation declared its intention to seek revenge from anyone belonging to the ʿAzāzma confederation, regardless of his clan affiliation. In this, the Tiyāha were denying the ʿAzāzma, as a refugee group, the right, then current among all the native tribes of Sinai, to limit any blood feud between people of different confederations to their respective clans rather than to all members of both confederations, as tradition had always endorsed. Consequently all the ʿAzāzma of Sinai—some two thousand persons—were obliged to flee to Israel to save their lives. Only the subsequent guarantee of protection by the Egyptian Army enabled their return.

Another example of disdain for a weaker tribe occurred in northeast Sinai in about 1933, when Khalaf Khalafāt of the largest tribal confederation in the peninsula, the Suwārka, killed a man of the Abū Aʿraj, one of the smallest tribes in the vicinity and one of its least prestigious, owing to its reputed descent from Ottoman garrison soldiers (Case 42). Murder being the most extreme violation in Bedouin society and tangible testimony to the victim clan's weakness, Bedouin deem it imperative that the murderer's clan act with haste so as to restore their victims' reputation for strength, by either requesting reconciliation or fleeing from revenge.[104] In this case, disdain for the victims, the Khalafāt's neighbors in the vicinity of Shaykh Zuwayd, kept the Khalafāt from doing either. This forced the Abū Āʿraj, in order to salvage their self-esteem, to leave the area themselves, returning only after they had managed to take revenge against the Khalafāt nine years later.[105]

Numerical advantage is also evident in relations between clans belonging to the same tribe. Among the ʿAzāzma Saraḥīn in the central Negev, for example, a conflict broke out between two relatively small clans, the ʿOwdāt and the Rimāg, in 1974, when a squabble over the grazing of their respective flocks led the daughter of Ḥimayd as-Saddān to throw a stone that left a cut on the head of Sulaymān ar-Rimāg (Case 43). Disagreement over responsibility for the outbreak of the conflict and each party's consequent refusal to take a truce from the other threatened to ignite broader hostilities. The Rimāg clan enlisted the support of the Dilīaʿ clan, thus acquiring a numerical advantage over the ʿOwdāt. This advantage was upset, however, when the ʿOwdāt recruited support from the even larger Zanūn clan, resulting in a settlement that favored the ʿOwdāt.[106]

Indeed, although numerical advantage is mainly a factor in conflicts between different clans or between different larger social contexts (sub-tribes, tribes, sub-confederations, and confederations), it is also present in conflicts that erupt among members of the same clan. Among the Nuṣayrāt clan of the Aḥeiwāt Shawafīn in central Sinai, for example, Sālim Ibn Naṣṣār, who had only one small son, was greatly mistreated by his assertive paternal uncle, ʿAlī Gāsim, and his two grown sons (Case 11). Among other misdeeds, one of the sons in 1979 beat Ibn Naṣṣār's wife and refused to accept legal responsibility toward Ibn Naṣṣār (for violating his tent, in which she was beaten) or her brothers, members of a different clan (who were legally responsible for their sister's physical integrity). Ibn Naṣṣār, being numerically disadvantaged toward these clansmen (as well as dependent upon their support against potential adversaries from other clans), found himself unable to challenge them in order to obtain justice.[107]

Weakness in number may also induce Bedouin to jeopardize their own interests and rights in order to avoid a potential conflict with stronger parties. For example, in 1974 fellow tribesmen of ʿOwda Sulaymān al-Hadōbe of the ʿAzāzma Saraḥīn got him to end his three-year rejection of his daughter's marriage to a maternal cousin (who had absconded with her from the Negev to eastern Sinai), in exchange for 13,000 Egyptian pounds as a bride-price and the fine of a young camel for the carrying off of the girl by her husband (Case 10).

> When the absconder's clan, however, managed to gather only 7,000 pounds by an agreed date and asked Hadōbe to accept the sum as an advance, to be supplemented by the balance in two weeks' time, he refused. Then a prominent fellow tribesman, ʿOwda Sulaymān Zanūn, offered his personal guaranty that the balance would be paid within the fifteen days suggested. Hadōbe, however, suspecting that his son-in-law's family might ultimately default, proved wary about having to challenge Zanūn by demanding that he fulfill his guarantee, lest the latter's more numerous fellow clansmen fabricate excuses for possible remissness on the part of the guarantor, and he find himself both without his payment—after recognizing his daughter's marriage in principle—and in conflict with the Zanūns. He consequently declined ʿOwda Zanūn's offer of guaranty and the ostensible opportunity it presented for obtaining his payment. As a result, the unguaranteed balance was never paid and the conflict with his son-in-law continued.[108]

Timidity in Conflict

In addition to—or irrespective of—numerical advantage, the outcome of conflicts may also be determined by the personal assertiveness and recklessness of one of the parties, as opposed to the timidity and caution of the other. The role of assertiveness was caught in a conversation recorded among the Aḥeiwāt Shawafīn in eastern Sinai by Frank Stewart:

> IBN NAṢṢĀR: It's a fact, Salāma, it isn't the fear of God that stops people from wronging you.
>
> SALĀMA ḤUSAYN: Absolutely. The only thing that will stop them is if they're afraid of you.
>
> IBN NAṢṢĀR: Only if they're frightened of you—either because you know how to talk, or because you have men who will back you up.[109]

Assertiveness is especially effective in conflicts between members of the same clan. For example (Case 26):

> Among the ʿOwdāt clan of the ʿAzāzma Saraḥīn tribe, the reckless tenacity of Frayj Ḥimayd as-Saddān, whose daughter had absconded with her cousin, Sulaymān Swaylim Abū Bilayya, in May 1995, enabled him successfully to threaten and challenge Abū Bilayya's father and ruin him with ever-increasing financial demands in return for granting the elopers permission to marry. At first, he imposed the fines for unchaperoned abduction, the equivalent of $16,000 (that is, 11,000 Jordanian dinars), demanding that they also return the girl to her father's tent, an arrangement sanctioned by Bedouin law. Then, ten days after securing the fines, Saddān summoned the abductor's father, Swaylim Abū Bilayya, offering to give his son the girl's hand in exchange for an additional $20,000 bride-price. As that demand was about to be met, he raised another one—namely, that the three-year-old daughter of the absconder's brother be promised to his son in marriage in another fifteen years or that an additional $30,000 be paid him at that time. The Abū Bilayya family, deferring to Sulaymān's wish to marry his cousin, agreed to this additional condition too, which was guaranteed, according to Bedouin legal custom, in the tent of a neighbor, Sālim Salāma ar-Rimāg. Finally, Saddān raised the extraordinary demand that the agreement be registered and recorded in the Islamic *sharīʿa* court in Beersheba, a precaution that was an added insult to the Abū Bilayya family.[110]

Another incidence of timidity on the part of the weaker party to a conflict in 1974 was evident in the central Negev (Case 44). After Hilayyil al-Wajj of the Ẓullām Janabīb tribe paid a nocturnal visit to the wife of an absent Ḥimayd as-Saddān of the ʿAzāzma Saraḥīn, Wajj's small clan was sufficiently intimidated to agree, on demand by the woman's own and larger clan (the group responsible for a woman's sexual behavior and welfare), the Nashmiyya of the ʿAzāzma Saraḥīn, to attend an honor trial, where it was certain to be subject to heavy fines.[111] In reality, the clan's agreement was not at all inevitable, as the woman, rather than report Wajj's advances immediately, had waited until the next morning, a delay that made her suspect of collusion in the tryst, thus denying her clansmen the right to an *honor fine,* according to Bedouin law.[112] Similar timidity in 1987 cost a man of the ʿAzāzma ʿAṣiyāt tribe in the central Negev a deserved legal award when his daughter was publicly slandered for adultery by a woman of the ʿAzāzma Saraḥīn (Case 13). The slanderer's brother, assertive and confident owing to the strength of his larger clan, threatened that if the father pressed his suit, he would claim in court that his sister's remark had simply been uttered as a retort to a prior threat by his daughter, thus posing a legal challenge that the father felt himself too weak to pursue, even though his honor might remain impaired.[113]

ASSURING THE WEAK ACCESS TO JUSTICE

It is when people such as the aforementioned victims of violation feel too weak to obtain justice from a violator by themselves that they may seek the help of persons strong enough to challenge him. Among the Bedouin, faith in the efficacy of engaging a protector is depicted in the imagery of their dictum, "Against oppression there's protection, like there's a windbreak against the cold" (*al-jōr ʿannah al-jīra—wa-l-bard ʿannah aṣ-ṣīra*),[114] alluding to the windbreak of shrubs that they erect around a campfire sitting space or a tent as proven protection against the cold winds of the desert winter. Protection, as help against injustice, is mainly called "entrance" (*dakhāla*), indicating the tradition whereby a seeker of protection, entering a tent (passing the tent pegs), utters, "I am entering upon you" (*āna dākhil ʿalayk*), with the implication of "I am entering the realm of your protection."* Hence, both the provider of protection and the protégé will individually be called "partaker in protection," or *dakhīl*. By tradition too, each party may also be called a "person of the tent rope" (*ṭanīb*), the supplicant having reached, or actually taken hold of, a rope (anciently *ṭanab*) leading into the tent or having pitched his tent so that its ropes and that of his protector's are intertwined—the latter act often serving to depict the request for protection as, "He entwines his ropes with that of another" (*hū yuṭnub ʿalayh*). Accordingly, an alternative term for protection is *jīra*, which literally means "neighboring."

The Bedouin have developed guidelines to make this indispensable institution accessible and effective. First, it is extended free of charge, protectors often providing for destitute supplicants and defraying in their stead payments incurred in the settlement of a problem. When in 1967, for example, the paramount chief of the ʿAzāzma in the Negev, ʿOwda Abū Muʿammar, gave protection to ʿOwda Sulaymān al-Hadōbe of the ʿAzāzma Saraḥīn of eastern Sinai, he himself paid $1,500 to the family of a woman who had been killed by her husband, Hadōbe's clansman, thus relieving Hadōbe of having to give his daughter to them in free marriage (Case 10).[115]

Second, when approached by a supplicant, a prospective protector will assess his claim and take him on if he is "a protégé in the right" (*ṭanīb ḥagg*)—that is, one who is "clean of [legal] defects" (*sālim adh-dhawārib*) and not a fugitive from Bedouin justice. A relevant maxim holds, "There is no protection for one who is denying justice" (*al-ʿāyib mā lah dakhal*).[116] A murderer, however, may

*As further endorsed by the alternative, "I am entering the realm of God's [protection] and yours" (*āna dākhil ʿal allāh wi-ʿalayk*), occasionally chosen to show the ultimate supremacy of God. See chapter 6 for the sanctuary that a tent confers and for more on protection.

receive protection. In the 1960s a homicide took place within the Tiyāha Huzayyil tribe in the northern Negev (Case 45). The murderers took refuge with the paramount chief of the ʿAzāzma, ʿOwda Abū Muʿammar, for two years, until the latter, through mediation, succeeded in resolving their conflict without blood-revenge occurring.[117] Often, too, people who have taken revenge for an act of murder seek protection with a powerful person until a formal reconciliation has occurred. Sometime prior to World War I, for example, a man of the Tarabīn Abū ʿUwaylī, in the northwest Negev, killed a poet belonging to a quasi-Bedouin family, Abū Hānī, following some insulting lines he had composed at a wedding celebration (Case 46). After the victim's brother took revenge upon the murderer, he requested protection from the chief of the Tiyāha Huzayyil, who thereupon used his good offices to put an end to the conflict without further murder taking place.[118]

Third, the refusal of a person to extend protection when requested may sully his reputation, in accordance with the legal directive, "Protection is obligatory while guaranty is by agreement" (*ad-dakhal lizām wa-l-kafal iḥshām*),[119] referring to the indispensable institution of guaranty in Bedouin law, as described above. When a supplicant comes to a powerful person with a message of despair, protection will be extended with traditional phrases such as, "Welcome on the basis of your claim! The moonlight's before you, and the darkness behind" (*marḥabābak ʿala gadr ʿilmak—al-gamr guddāmak wa-ẓ-ẓulma warāk*).[120] If the supplicant is indeed a person denied justice or threatened with injustice, the only legitimate excuse a prospective protector might have for refusing protection would be his feeling insufficiently strong to protect him, in which case he would be obliged to "convey the protection" (*yungul ad-dakhal*) to someone more powerful or capable. Among the Ẓullām Janabīb in 1986, when Midʿān al-Wajj of the Wujūj clan killed an Ibn Imṭayr of the Kishkhar clan, one section of the Wujūj, the Abū Dāyaʿ lineage, came to the tent of Ḥimayd as-Saddān of the ʿAzāzma Saraḥīn, asking for his protection (Case 47). Saddān, feeling that he was living too close to the Kishkhar people to afford effective protection, personally removed the Abū Dāyaʿ some sixty kilometers away, to the tent of the paramount chief of the ʿAzāzma, ʿOwda Abū Muʿammar, after securing his agreement.[121]

Fourth, a protector must act so as to obtain justice for his protégé. In particular, he must represent him in meetings with his adversaries and try to force the latter to deal with him justly. One example of a protector acting on behalf of a protégé during the Ottoman period is heard among the Tiyāha confederation in the northern Negev, whose members tell of a poor lad of the Shalāliyyīn tribe who found work as a shepherd among people of the ʿAyāyda confederation in western Sinai (Case 48). One day, leaders of that group made a covenant with him, according to which the two parties would each see to the return of camels pillaged from each other by their respective tribesmen. The lad, however, was not an elder who could give his word of honor to such a covenant, something he learned when men of the Shalāliyyīn indeed raided the camels of the ʿAyāyda. When the ʿAyāyda came to collect their camels, he was unable to persuade the raiders to return them. In anguish, he went to the chief of the Tiyāha Ḥamāmda, a man called Abū Ḥammūda, and requested his protection for retrieving the pillaged camels. Abū Ḥammūda acceded and ordered his men to go and force the Shalāliyyīn to surrender them. Through Abū Ḥammūda's intervention, the lad was enabled to retain his honor, though the covenant he had made was henceforth invalid.[122]

Other examples of protectors who labor on behalf of their protégé's rights are rife in the desert, such as one heard among the ʿAzāzma confederation (Case 10):

> In 1959 Sulaymān al-Gurʿān of the Owraydāt clan of the ʿAzāzma Saraḥīn tribe in east-central Sinai struck and killed his wife, a member of the Izʿaylāt clan of the same tribe. In order to stay blood-revenge for the murder, the man's cousin and leader of the Owraydāt, ʿOwda Salmān al-Owraydī, pledged the daughter of another cousin, ʿOwda Sulaymān al-Hadōbe, in marriage to a brother of the murdered woman, in the absence of the girl's father and without his consent. As the girl was still a minor (eight years old), it was agreed that she would remain with her father until maturity (sixteen years old).
>
> Still, Hadōbe demanded the dissolution of his daughter's engagement, claiming that no one may engage a girl but her living father, that there were other eligible girls in the clan who could have served as such a *ghurra*, and that he had already raised a blood-price of 300 Jordanian dinars and five camels as a bride-price, with which the murdered woman's clan could acquire a woman to replace its loss. Too weak to gain regard for his demand or claims, however, Hadōbe moved away from his people to the area of the Guṣayma oasis, aggrieved.
>
> Eight years later, a day after the Israeli conquest of Guṣayma in the Six-Day War of 1967, Hadōbe crossed the newly opened border between Egypt and Israel, heading straight for the tent of the paramount chief of the ʿAzāzma in the Negev, ʿOwda Abū Muʿammar, to request his protection and help in the gaining of his rights. He pitched his tent in the chief's encampment, where he remained as a protégé for two months and eighteen days.
>
> During that time, the chief made two visits to Hadōbe's clansmen in Sinai. On his first visit, he offered them a blood-price for the murdered woman totaling the equivalent of approximately $1,500. This was on condition that they agreed to come before a "blood-pool judge" (*mangaʿ ad-damm*), one who judges in cases of clan matters, in order to examine the correctness of the

> girl's engagement. They rejected the offer, demanding four blood-prices and four camel payments for a truce, a fourfold fine being the legal award for a woman's murder.
>
> On his second visit, the chief dropped the demand for a trial before the blood-pool judge, and the murdered woman's clan dropped its demand for the fourfold payments. The chief thereupon paid the clan $1,500 out of his own pocket, and the clan annulled the engagement of Hadōbe's daughter. People of the ʿAzāzma presumed that the chief's prominence and closeness to the Israeli Army, at a time when Israel was in military occupation of Sinai, fostered the readiness of the murdered woman's clan to recognize Hadōbe's claims.[123]

Again, in 1977, six years after Hadōbe's daughter was abducted by a fellow tribesman, he sought protection with Sālim Sulaymān al-Kishkhar, chief of the Ẓullām Janabīb, to help have her returned. Within a few weeks, the chief betook himself to Sālim Ibn Saʿad, the elder of the ʿAyāl Silmī section of the ʿAzāzma Saraḥīn, to which both the father and the abductor belonged, persuading him to accept the father's claims. Following Kishkhar's intervention, Ibn Saʿad arranged that the marriage be annulled and the girl returned.[124] Another case of protection occurred in central Sinai in 1979, when Sālim Ibn Naṣṣār of the Aḥeiwāt Shawafīn, seeking help against fellow clansmen who had been persecuting him (ʿAlī Gāsim al-Guwāsma and his sons), became the protégé of ʿĪd Abū Hāshim of the ʿAlaygāt Zumayliyyīn (Case 11). Abū Hāshim threatened to enlist his entire Zumayliyyīn tribe and make war on the entire Aḥeiwāt Shawafīn, impounding their camels, unless they forced the Guwāsma to resolve all the disputes they had with Ibn Naṣṣār. His intervention proved fruitful.[125]

Owing to its roles in obtaining justice for the weak and providing sanctuary to persons pursued and persecuted, Bedouin view protection as a hallowed institution. Those who extend it augment their prestige in society, as in the sayings "Protection is a way to gain honor" (*ad-dakhāla dawwārit ʿizz*) and "He who comes to your tent increases your esteem" (*illī biyjīk fī wahadak biykabbir jahadak*). It affords one a reputation coveted and zealously guarded. It is thus imperative for a Bedouin protector to succeed in the mission he assumes, which is not always easy, as expressed in the saying "Protection is affliction" (*ad-dakhāla balwa*).[126] First, he must study the problem that has brought a supplicant to him, as remarked by the aforementioned Sālim Ibn Naṣṣār of the Aḥeiwāt Shawafīn when receiving protection from ʿĪd Abū Hāshim of the ʿAlaygāt Zumayliyyīn (Case 11)—namely, "A man who's got some sense, when you take refuge with him, he asks you what it's all about; he doesn't just welcome you without hearing the whole story."[127] Second, a protector may have to spend money for the protégé in order to gain him justice, as

Abū Hāshim, above, put out 5,000 Egyptian pounds ($1,000) to ensure the holding of the desired trial for Ibn Naṣṣār and even made a pledge (though not legally binding) to pay his possible fines, even if they came to 300,000 pounds ($60,000).[128] Similarly, as mentioned above, Chief ʿOwda Abū Muʿammar of the ʿAzāzma paid the equivalent of $1,500 in blood-money on behalf of ʿOwda Sulaymān al-Hadōbe in 1967 (Case 10). And in 1977 the chief of the Tiyāha al-Ḥukūk, Salmān ʿAlī al-Huzayyil, paid the bride-price incumbent on his protégé, the son of an Abū Girshayn of the Jordanian ʿUmrān Gurūsh living in the Negev, who had abducted a girl of the Ẓullām confederation and taken refuge with Huzayyil against expected revenge by her clansmen (Case 49).[129]

Finally, as a protector has willy-nilly become a party to the conflict of his protégé, he will find himself under pressure from the adversaries to tread lightly and from his ward to act quickly. In addition, his performance is always under scrutiny by the surrounding society. Accordingly, Bedouin have proverbially depicted a protector as "a bitch between two dogs and a light between two lights" (*ḍowa bayn ḍowayn ū-kalba bayn kalbayn).*[130] However, if he should fail in his mission, it will be enough that "his protégé holds him to account" (*ṭanībah ḥasībah*)[131] and resorts to blackening him, one of the most dreaded punishments in the desert—and one that may stain his reputation forever.

Thus a protector may go to great lengths—even of threatening war—to succeed in his mission and preserve his reputation as a provider of protection.* We have seen how ʿĪd Abū Hāshim threatened war against the Aḥeiwāt in central Sinai to help his ward, Sālim Ibn Naṣṣār (Case 11). Another such threat was issued by a protector in northern Sinai in 1933 in an effort to get protection for a supplicant and preserve his reputation (Case 42):

> Khalaf al-Khalafāt, a member of the Suwārka confederation, the largest in Sinai, shot and killed a man called Abū Aʿraj, who belonged to a small group of quasi-Bedouin living among the Suwārka. In contempt of the murder victim's clan, and by way of highlighting the size and power of the Suwārka, no one of the Khalafāt clan fled the common area to take refuge from revenge with a distant tribe. They remained where they were and made no effort to appease the victim's group. To escape this insult, the Abū Aʿraj themselves relocated to a place distant from the murderers. Seven or eight years later, however, one of the Abū Aʿraj took revenge by shooting a man of the Khalafāt in the market of Rafaḥ, on the Egyptian-Palestinian border. He then raced westward seeking refuge from the anger of the Suwārka.
>
> At a place called al-Baraṣa, near Shaykh Zuwayd, some twenty kilometers

*By way of comparison, the reader is reminded of Prosper Mérimée's story "Matteo Falcone," in which the hero murders his beloved only son for disclosing to the police a fugitive who had found refuge in their home.

> from Rafaḥ, both the man and his mount being tired, he stopped at a small summer tent occupied by a chief of the Bayyāḍiyyīn confederation of distant northwest Sinai, who had rented from the Suwārka, with whom the Bayyāḍiyyīn were in alliance, a little plot for growing watermelons, as fodder for his horse. The chief, ʿAlī al-Hirsh, was alone with his wife, removed from his tribe and even his sons, who were grazing his camels far away. When Abū Aʿraj exclaimed, "I seek your protection," Hirsh was perplexed, wishing to extend protection but unable to do so effectively, owing to his isolation in the heart of Suwārka territory.
>
> Immediately, therefore, he sped to the tent of a nearby Suwārka chief called Ḥasan, asking to let him transfer the protection of Abū Aʿraj to him. Seeing Shaykh Ḥasan balk, Hirsh threatened to abrogate the alliance between their two confederations and embark on war against them unless he relented. This sufficed to persuade Shaykh Ḥasan to agree that the Bayyāḍiyyīn chief bring him Abū Aʿraj as his protégé.[132]

Indeed, affording protection is so compelling a value in Bedouin life that the theme of killing a violator in defense of a protégé's rights has long fascinated the Bedouin mind. In pre-Islamic times, the famous War of Basūs is alleged to have begun when Jassās, the chief of Bakr bin Wāʾil, killed his brother-in-law, Klayb ibn Rabīʿa, chief of the powerful Banū Taghlib tribe, for spearing the she-camel of a woman protégé.[133] A similar theme exists among the Suwārka confederation in a legend of origins dealing with their purported ancestors in northern Sinai (Case 50):

> Among the forefathers of the Suwārka in Sinai was a man called Nuṣayr and his cousin, Manīaʿ. The latter had as a protégé an old and solitary woman without a family to look after her interests. She owned a small flock of sheep, and when she was out grazing one day, Nuṣayr exercised his right to raid her flock for a sheep to slaughter for guests. Bedouin law stipulates that for this practice, called "aggression" (*ʿadāya*),[134] such a raider has forty days to make reparation. Nuṣayr, however, let the period elapse and persisted in ignoring the old woman. She therefore petitioned her protector, Manīaʿ, to help her retrieve a sheep in place of the one she had lost. Manīaʿ, however, needed some prodding, so one day the woman composed and recited a short, hyperbolic, but caustic, poem about his laxity as a protector:
>
> By my life, a protégé's sheep warrants four,
> except to lowly men;
> My sheep's wool weighed a kantar,
> and her milk flowed like the best water-holes run.*

*Ar. *fī ragabatī shāt aṭ-ṭanīb murabbaʿa, ila ʿend rijālin dhilāyil/yā ṣūfha yījī gunṭār, ū-labanhī yishādī jiyyidāt ath-thamāyil.*

> Stung by these demeaning lines, Manīaʿ went to Nuṣayr, whom he found lying on the ground, his back turned to him, playing the *sīja* game with someone, and said, "Either replace my protégé's sheep or litigate with me!" The reply, uttered without Nuṣayr's changing position, was, "O backside, go litigate with Manīaʿ" (*yā jaʿabī, gāḍī Manīaʿ*). Deeply insulted by such contempt, Manīaʿ raised his spear and pierced him dead. Thereupon, he fled to northwest Arabia to escape revenge, finding refuge with the Bilī Magābla tribe, among whom he lived for many years before returning to Sinai.[135]

In the seventeenth century, a war actually broke out between sections of the Banī ʿUgba and Masaʿīd confederations, currently in the northern Negev and northwest Sinai respectively, over an attempt to violate a protégé (Case 51):

> A large party of the Banī ʿUgba and the Masaʿīd, from northwest Arabia, migrated up the ʿAraba rift, which separates the Negev from southern Transjordan, and encamped near the spring called ʿAyn Ḥuṣub. Hearing of this advance, the Negev tribes, led by the Wuḥeidāt, were concerned lest this formidable force invade the Negev and conquer their pasturelands. To thwart this possibility, al-Wuḥeidī, the paramount chief of the Negev tribes, resorted to a ruse.
>
> Wuḥeidī had been informed that the leaders of the Masaʿīd and Banī ʿUgba tribes—Saʿūd Ibn Masʿūd and Dāʿūd respectively—were totally different in character; Saʿūd was a vile libertine, while Dāʾūd was sober and trustworthy. With the aim of setting the two leaders against each other, Wuḥeidī sent a beautiful girl in the company of her brother, both strangers from the Arabian Muṭayr tribe, to take refuge with Dāʾūd, expecting Saʿūd, on seeing her beauty, to try to violate her honor.
>
> This expectation was realized when Dāʾūd's beautiful ward came to water her camel at the ʿAyn Ḥuṣub spring, where Saʿūd was reclining in the shade of an adjacent tree, playing the *sīja* game with Dāʾūd's slave. Letting her veil slip, she was observed by Saʿūd, who became determined to have her, expressing his intentions to the slave (in a poem that accompanies the tradition). The latter directly informed his master, Dāʾūd, who, concerned lest his reputation and honor be sullied, challenged Saʿūd, a step that led to a war of mutual destruction between the two tribes, just as Wuḥeidī had planned.[136]

3

The Role of Collective Responsibility in Achieving Justice

*The Workings of the Clan (*khamsa*)*

MUTUAL LIABILITY

In addition to the various ways by which Bedouin law utilizes honor and private might to perform the roles played by law-enforcement agencies in settled societies, it also seeks to maintain and restore justice by defining the legal personality as a collective. There are few acts that an individual can perform toward people of other clans without ultimate legal ramifications for his clansmen in the context of mutual liability. Among the few are choosing a wife and extending protection. Other than these, when a man's acts entail a legal commitment to others or impinge upon the rights of others, he is seen in the eyes of the law as acting on behalf of his basic group, the clan (*khamsa)*, which comprises his kinsmen (herein called clansmen). Thus, for example, when a member of one clan assaults the member of another clan, the law views the event as being perpetrated by the first clan in toto against the second clan in toto. Accordingly, any male member of the first group bears responsibility for the perpetrator's act no less than the perpetrator himself and can be punished for it. The perpetrator is but an agent of the group, an extension of it, much as, metaphorically, a limb is but an extension of the human body. When in 1996 the erstwhile Iraqi ruler Saddam Husayn sought to justify the murder of his sons-in-law by their families for having betrayed their country, he borrowed this metaphor to depict the act as "a hand ridding itself of infected fingers."[1] A member of the Āl Bū Nāṣir tribe, Husayn had grown up in a village, ʿOwja, strongly influenced by the culture of the surrounding deserts.

The many opportunities that the desert affords an individual Bedouin to flee from justice and from his obligations toward others justify the need for collective responsibility. If the actual perpetrator of a violation manages to abscond, his victims simply "hold his clan to account" (*yiḥāsibū al-khamsa*). In most cases, its members remain accessible and accountable, as affirmed by the proverb "What they've got on your cousin they've got on you; there's no way to evade it" (*ibn ʿammak illī fīh fīk—mā lak ʿannah imjannab*).[2] In 1959, for example, among the ʿAzāzma Saraḥīn tribe in eastern Sinai, when Sulaymān al-Gurʿān of the Owraydī clan struck and killed his wife and then fled to Jordan, the woman's clan, the Zuʿaylāt, held all his clansmen, still in place, liable to revenge, and the clan ultimately received from them a blood-payment for their woman (Case 10).[3] Thus too in southeast Sinai in 1976, after the sons of Munayfī Sālim Jabalī of the Muzayna Jarābʿa attacked their foe, Sālim Jumʿa Abū Ṣabḥā of the Muzayna Ghawānma, violating the honor of his wife and then fleeing, Abū Ṣabḥā's clansmen pillaged camels belonging to the entire Jabalī clan until the Jabalī finally confessed to their offense and agreed to submit to an honor trial (Case 1).[4] In the same area in 1997, when Salmān Zaydān of the Munāṣra clan of the Tarabīn Ḥasāblah tribe in southeast Sinai fled to remote mountains after killing ʿĀyid ʿAṭeiwī of the ʿAlōwna clan, who had made Zaydān's sister pregnant out of wedlock, the ʿAlōwna initially laid siege to all the Munāṣra, their neighbors, until the Munāṣra were able to obtain truces for themselves (Case 52).[5] As expressed by a noted judge of the Masaʿīd confederation in northwest Sinai, collective responsibility guarantees that in the prosecution of justice, "there is no vacuum ever" (*mā fīh fowḍa abadan*).[6]

A legal principle stipulates that "Compelling the unruly one is incumbent on his clansmen" (*ḥukm al-ʿāyib ʿa zlāmah*), meaning that they must bring him to justice or face it themselves. The logic is reflected in the saying, "Your cousin's misdeed is yours too, and the blame he incurs blames you" (*ibn ʿammak—ʿeibah zay ʿeibak ū-mizrātah tazrīk*). A debt, for example, is contracted individually, with the expectation that the individual that incurs it will repay it. At the same time, it is also considered a group debt that must, in the event of default, be repaid by the clan. "The balance is borne by his clan" (*al-mitibaggī ʿal khamsitah*) is the Bedouin dictum in this regard, perhaps the retained judgment of a long-past judge.[7] This principle—namely, that the group is ultimately responsible for repaying debts—was inversely confirmed in the central Negev in a case that took place in 1998. A member of the ʿAzāzma Saraḥīn tribe, Sālim Salāma ar-Rimāg, was asked to repay a debt to a fellow tribesman, ʿOwda ʿĪd Ibn Saʿad, whose clan lived mainly in Sinai (Case 34). Rimāg, however, posited that his debt should be voided against one owed to him by Salāma al-Braym, a man in Sinai who, he claimed, had joined Ibn Saʿad's clan, which had people living in both Sinai and the Negev. Ibn Saʿad did not challenge the principle of letting the two debts be settled between members of the same group. It was only when an investigation disclosed that Braym had never joined Ibn Saʿad's group that Rimāg himself had to pay his debt.[8]

Bedouin law also specifies the process of gaining redress. It says, "The closest clansman to you will deliver you" (*agrab mā lak hū owla bak*),[9] meaning that a creditor must first turn to the debtor's closest relatives, or agnates. Appeal may also be made to the clan leader, called the "elder" (*kabīr*; pl. *kibār*; lit. "big," as in "old" or "big of tooth" [*kabīr fi-s-sinn*]), who represents the group to all "outsiders" (*ajānib*) and is the member mainly responsible for its obligations toward them.

Fines and damages imposed as part of the resolution of a conflict are also, like debts, the ultimate responsibility of the clan to which the perpetrator of an offense belongs. Here, however, the Bedouin differentiate between fines that members of a group jointly pay as part of their standing obligation, without reimbursement from the perpetrator of an offense, and those for which the latter must reimburse them. The first category consists of indemnities that arise from physical assault and are mainly defined as "problems of blood" (*damm*). Payments in this category comprise blood-money for murder, compensation and fines for wounds, and fines for insults or other offenses committed during a violent conflict. Because violent conflict is concomitant to a life of scarcity in the arid desert and a show of force may serve the long-term security of a group by conferring it with deterrence, Bedouin law views the payment of fines stemming from such a demonstration as a justifiable contribution to the group's welfare.[10]

The second category consists of fines or compensations imposed on an individual for all other offenses, unless he committed them with the concurrence of a majority of his clan. Bedouin consider that an act perpetrated without such consensus does not fall within the context of a group's interests. The consequent punishment is thus ultimately to be borne by the individual himself, in keeping with the maxim, "He who takes on problems will bear the burden alone" (*illī biyḥammil yiḥammil ʿa nafsah*).[11] This is particularly so in regard to the violation of a woman's honor, seen as performed for the individual's own pleasure, or in regard to theft, for which the law stipulates that "The thief steals on his own" (*as-sārig yisrig ʿala nafsah*).[12] For such offenses, the offending individual must reimburse those of his clan who have paid all or a part of the indemnity. Nonetheless, in the eyes of the law the responsibility of the clan *per se* for indemnifying the victim of a violation caused by any of its members remains unalterable and must be discharged, regardless of whether the actual perpetrator reimburses the other members or not.

Bedouin law also holds an entire clan liable to physical punishment for any physical and certain sorts of sexual violation perpetrated by any one of its members against an outsider. Such violations are mainly murder, woundings, or rape. As with payments, Bedouin law is intent on ensuring that a perpetrator of such acts cannot obstruct justice by his own disappearance into the desert, as in the cases among the ʿAzāzma (Case 10), Tarabīn (Case 52), and Muzayna (Case 1) mentioned above. A no less important intent of the law in making all the adult male members of a clan liable to physical punishment for one individual member's violence is to deter violence in general. By allowing any member of a violated clan to physically assault any member of the violator's clan, Bedouin law anticipates that potential perpetrators of violent acts will feel obliged to restrain themselves as they consider the consequences of their actions for the other members of their group.

MAINTAINING COLLECTIVE RESPONSIBILITY: DISCOURAGING EARLY DISAFFILIATION

In recognition of the fact that the collective responsibility of a clan is indispensable for maintaining justice in the desert, Bedouin law is stringent in keeping the system from dissipating. Above all, it makes the early disaffiliation of members very difficult. Early disaffiliation means quitting one's clan prior to one's passing the fifth generation, as follows.

The word for clan, *khamsa*, means "fiver," denoting that membership in the group spans five generations, as comprising a male and all his living relatives descended from his great-great-grandfather, in the male line. Thus, as in the hypothetical diagram in Table 3.1, which shows a man called Sālim's direct line of descent (marked by Y) from his great-great-grandfather (marked by A), as well as all the other male issue (marked by x) of the first generation, we see the composition of a *khamsa* that would include twenty-two members (that is, males), assuming that only the members of Sālim's generation (Sālim, a brother and cousins) and those of his father's are still living.

Sālim's normal disaffiliation from this group will come when he, his brother, or one of his closer cousins of the same generation gives birth to a male child, who, counting back to the fifth generation (starting with himself), will only get to Sālim's great-grandfather, rather than the great-great-grandfather who served as the progenitor of Sālim's clan at his birth. Thus the newborn child's clan would be all the living descendants of his father's great-grandfather (Y/B in table 3.2)—that is, the child's great-great-grandfather.

As Sālim and his son must belong to the same clan in order to be responsible

Table 3.1. Sālim's Clan (Schematic)

<table>
<tr><th>Forefather</th><th>Generation</th><th colspan="13">Male Members</th></tr>
<tr><td>Great-great-grandfather of Sālim</td><td>1st</td><td colspan="13">A</td></tr>
<tr><td>Great-grandfather of Sālim</td><td>2nd</td><td colspan="6">Y</td><td colspan="4">x</td><td colspan="3">x</td></tr>
<tr><td>Grandfather of Sālim</td><td>3rd</td><td colspan="4">Y</td><td colspan="2">x</td><td colspan="2">x</td><td colspan="2">x</td><td colspan="2">x</td><td>x</td></tr>
<tr><td>Father of Sālim</td><td>4th</td><td colspan="2">Y</td><td colspan="2">x</td><td>x</td><td>x</td><td>x</td><td>x</td><td colspan="2">x</td><td colspan="2">x</td><td>x</td></tr>
<tr><td>Sālim</td><td>5th</td><td>Y</td><td>x</td><td>x</td><td>x</td><td>x</td><td>x</td><td>x</td><td>x</td><td>x</td><td>x</td><td>x</td><td>x</td><td>x</td></tr>
</table>

for each other's legal rights and misdeeds, the child's birth creates a new clan (B in table 3.2), which relates to Sālim's great-grandfather as its progenitor and disaffiliates all of the latter's descendants from those of his brothers (C in the table), who will now constitute a new clan by themselves. Henceforth, the two groups will not be responsible for each other's deeds or welfare. This type of disaffiliation, called "by count and the distance of a forefather" (*ʿadd ū-baʿad jidd*), is discretionary, requiring no agreement by the other members of the clan. Its validity begins with the naming of the first son born into the hitherto youngest generation. The wording of the law is, "The child can remove you as soon as he's named" (*al-walad mā dām tisamma yiṭillʿak*).[13] At the same time, people who have passed the five-generation mark but wish to remain affiliated are not obliged to quit. They can remain even for a number of successive generations. If they enjoy good relations with the other lineages in the clan, maintaining the numerical advantage of their continued membership will add to the security of all.

As opposed to this normal form of disaffiliation, however, Bedouin law, which is geared toward keeping the collective responsibility of clans alive and effective as a deterrent to violation, places obstacles on the path of early disaffiliation—that is, one's disaffiliation before he has passed the fifth generation. A Bedouin might seek such release for two reasons. One is general friction or non-cooperation within the group or the feeling that his kinsmen abuse him. In 1967, for example, ʿOwda Sulaymān al-Hadōbe of the ʿAzāzma Saraḥīn tribe distanced himself from his Owraydāt clan by relocating from Sinai to the Negev because his clan elder had pledged Hadōbe's daughter in

Table 3.2. Breakup of Sālim's Clan through Birth of Sālim's Son

<table>
<tr><th>Forefather</th><th>Generation</th><th colspan="6">Male Members</th></tr>
<tr><td>Great-great-grandfather of Sālim</td><td>6th</td><td colspan="6">A</td></tr>
<tr><td>Great-grandfather of Sālim</td><td>5th</td><td colspan="2">Y/B</td><td colspan="2">x/C</td><td colspan="2">x/C</td></tr>
<tr><td>Grandfather of Sālim</td><td>4th</td><td colspan="2">Y x</td><td>x</td><td>x</td><td>x</td><td>x</td></tr>
<tr><td>Father of Sālim</td><td>3rd</td><td colspan="2">Y x</td><td colspan="2">x x x x</td><td>x x</td><td>x</td></tr>
<tr><td>Sālim</td><td>2nd</td><td>Y</td><td>xx</td><td colspan="2">x x x x x</td><td>x x</td><td>x x</td></tr>
<tr><td>Sālim's son</td><td>1st</td><td>Y</td><td></td><td colspan="2"></td><td></td><td></td></tr>
</table>

marriage without prior consultation with him (Case 10).[14] At the time, he sought to disaffiliate but was ultimately prohibited by the fact that no other group would admit him.[15] In 1977 among the Aḥeiwāt Shawafīn Guṣayyrāt tribe of east-central Sinai, a man disaffiliated from the Nujūm clan, claiming that clansmen had not paid him various debts, had insulted him by not greeting him, and had fornicated with his daughter (Case 53).[16] Within the same tribe in 1978, Sālim Ibn Naṣṣār succeeded in disaffiliating from the Nuṣayrāt clan on the basis of a cousin's having violated his tent by entering it in his absence, beating up his wife, and then refusing to give him justice (Case 11).[17] While Ibn Naṣṣār was deliberating this move, which might expose him to the dangers of non-membership in a clan, one of his interlocutors advised him that it might be better to endure the occasional abuse of an outsider than the constant abuse of a fellow member of the clan.[18]

A second reason for a Bedouin wishing to quit his clan is his feeling endangered by the repeated and unjustifiable misdeeds of contentious clansmen toward people of other clans. Among the ʿAzāzma Saraḥīn tribe in 1971, the Abū Bilayya section of the ʿOwdāt clan took steps to disaffiliate, claiming that the elder of the group, Ḥimayd as-Saddān, was frequently contentious with outsiders, often to the point of violating them (Case 54).[19] When Sālim Ibn Naṣṣār, mentioned above, explained his reasons for disaffiliating from the Nuṣayrāt clan, one of them was the behavior of his clansman ʿAlī Gāsim al-Guwāsma toward others (Case 11). Ibn Naṣṣār was recorded as saying, "ʿAlī was going to make things worse and worse for me, and the next thing would have been him beating or killing someone, and then either I'd have been stripped of my property, or my son would have become the victim of someone seeking revenge, or my stock would have been seized."[20] For such cases, a Bedouin adage counseling an anticipatory disaffiliation from a troublesome clan holds that "He who exits today will be safe tomorrow, just as he who ablutes early is ready for prayer" (*illī yiṭlaʿ al-yōm yislim minnih bākir—w-illī yitiwaḍḍaʾ badrī biyṣallī ḥāḍir*).[21]

The above justifications for disaffiliation notwithstanding, Bedouin law, seeking to prevent the debilitation of the clan system through early disaffiliation by members, empowers other members of the clan to try and prevent it. If they wish, they can insist on a hearing with a judge sitting in the capacity of a "blood pool" (*mangaʿ ad-damm*), a judge to whom cases of murder and assault are referred, cases to which the composition of a clan is relevant.[22] It is then he who will have to decide whether the claim of those wishing to quit is justified. In addition to the reasons noted above, if a Bedouin contends that his clansmen failed to come to his aid in paying fines, seeking vengeance, or supporting him publicly, the judge will weigh the import of the circumstances. In the event of a serious dereliction—such as not extending aid following the rape of a fellow clansman's daughter—the judge will almost certainly authorize the disaffiliation. Another effective claim might be the violation of neutrality within the clan itself in cases of violence between related but separate member lineages (*arbāʿ*, sing. *rubaʿ*; or *gīmān*, sing. *gōm*). Such a violation is morally condemned as "deceit and treachery" (*ʿowg ū-bōg*). In the event of murder within the clan, for example, the law limits the right of revenge to the victim's lineage itself. Other member families have no right to aid the lineage. It is also forbidden for someone of a third lineage to intervene in a fray when blows are exchanged between people of two other lineages, other than to separate the fighters.[23] Hence, if someone from lineage "A" intervened in a fight between men of lineages "B" and "C," striking "C" in support of "B," lineage "C" would have grounds for disaffiliation.

By contrast, a judge may deem some claims insufficient. If, for example, one's fellow members refused to participate in the payment of a fine, the judge may deem it sufficient to exact the payment, as well as a guarantee against a repetition of such failure, upon the understanding that a future violation of this guarantee might justify disaffiliation. Or a judge may disallow a claimant's disaffiliation if the clan's failure to side with him was in a dispute that most of the others counseled him not to pursue or owing to frictions within the clan for which those wishing to disaffiliate are responsible. In 1996 Swaylim Abū Bilayya of the ʿAzāzma Saraḥīn tribe in the central Negev wanted to quit his ʿOwdāt clan when its most dominant figure, Frayj Ḥimayd as-Saddān, exacted from him exorbitant fines and an unusually high bride-price following the abduction of his daughter by one of Abū Bilayya's sons (Case 26). The majority of his clansmen, living in Jordan, barred him from quitting, citing the unlawful manner in which the abduction had taken place, which, in their eyes, justified Saddān's anger and consequent demands.*

Moreover, the law seeks to hamper early disaffiliation, even where the grounds for it may be justifiable. For instance, no judge will authorize a disaffiliation (even for those who have passed the fifth generation), if the quitter owes his clan any obligations stemming from prior conflicts with other clans, especially regarding his participation in the payment of fines. Although a judge may have validated all of a potential quitter's reasons for disaffiliation, he will still oblige him to settle his residual obligations beforehand, using traditional expressions such as, "Pay the group all that is due and quit" (*waffī al-khamsa w-iṭlaʿ*) or, metaphorically, "Wash your pail-rope and leave" (*ghassil irshāk w-iṭlaʿ*),[24] likening such residual obligations to the filthy residue in and around a well so that Bedouin shepherds must wash off their ropes before leaving with their watered flocks.

Yet further to impede disaffiliation, an early quitter is obliged to pay his clan a severance charge, called a "camel of exit" (*jamal aṭ-ṭulūaʿ*), an actual camel or its equivalent in cash. Although a seemingly minor encumbrance, many Bedouin would feel it a heavy burden to bear. When Sālim Ibn Naṣṣār, mentioned above, quit the Nuṣayrāt clan in 1978 (Case 11), he paid 6,000 Egyptian pounds ($500) for a camel that was so mediocre that his previous clansmen were loath to accept it.[25] An even more effective obstacle set by Bedouin law is the prohibition against disaffiliation, early or normal, so long as one's clan is engaged in an unresolved conflict and liable for payments to, or retaliation from, a clan it has violated. Were Bedouin law to permit disaffiliation "under fire," a mass exodus from a clan threatened with retaliation could be expected to take place, divesting the collective responsibility system of its ability to deter violence and other violations.

THE CLAN'S PROTECTION OF ITS MEMBERS

The liability before the law that each member of a clan bears for the misdeeds of any fellow member is only one facet of a clan's personality. The

*Oral communication from Swaylim Sulaymān Abū Bilayya of the ʿAzāzma Saraḥīn, December 18, 1996. The abductor (a) did not have a companion (*rafīg*) with him continually, from abduction to the depositing of the girl in a neutral tent, and (b) he neglected to deposit her in a nearby tent but rather deposited her in a distant one. See chapter 6 for more on abduction.

law also provides for a second, perhaps more important, facet, which in the eyes of its members is the main rationale for their belonging—namely, it protects them. Every male in the clan is expected to rally to any other member's defense when he is threatened and avenge him when he is violated and to be prepared to subordinate all other interests and activities to these goals. Accordingly, a Bedouin is traditionally advised that "If men violate you, rouse your clansmen" (*in māl ʿalayk ar-rijāl istaʿdī ʿala zlāmak*).* If a member of a clan has been murdered, "One fiver seeks vengeance from another" (*khamsa tuṭrud khamsa*), meaning that any member of the murder victim's clan may take revenge upon any member of the murderer's clan. The threat of such sweeping retaliation goes far toward guaranteeing a Bedouin's safety, whether in regard to murder or otherwise.

The same principle of mutual responsibility, as intimated, also pertains to lesser violations. A Bedouin belonging to a clan normally never feels abandoned in his dealings with the outside world, for whatever problem he may encounter with others, he can rely on the support of his clansmen and the intrinsic threat of their resorting to force on his behalf. Likewise, if he incurs a fine for practicing violence against an outsider, the fellow members of his clan, bound by the principle of collective responsibility, must participate in its payment, and every Bedouin is aware that "The burden, if divided, can be borne" (*al-ḥimil lō tifarrag inshāl*).* Not surprisingly, therefore, the prevailing sentiment is that "A man without a *khamsa* is like a garment without sleeves" (*al-wāḥad bila khamsa zay thōb bila irdān*),[26] inferring that a person without clansmen to protect him is insecure (often depicted as "cold," which in turn lends itself to the simile of a man's *jalabiyya* dress, if sleeveless, providing insufficient cover to the man wearing it). The same perspective makes Bedouin characteristically loath to dwell far from their fellow members. Another proverb affirms this: "Everyone absent returns but he who's absent in a grave" (*kull ghāyib yiʿūd ila ghāyib al-luḥūd*).[27] Accordingly, in 1876, when friendly Arabian Bedouin learned that the explorer Charles Doughty was from faraway England, they were shocked and cautioned him, "Thou art alone, and if thou wast made away, there is none would avenge thee. . . . *The stranger is for the*

*Bailey, *Proverbs*, p. 122. As in this dictum, the generic name for the members of a clan is *zilām*, which indicates the mutual responsibility that each bears for the others; it derives from the Bedouin term for pack camels, *zimāl* (sing. *zamal*), with the letters of the root inverted.

*Bailey, *Proverbs*, p. 132. As a rule, the person who inflicts a wound or perpetrates a murder pays one-fourth of the penalty, and the lineage of the person who suffers the violation receives one-fourth of the payment made by the other party (see ibid., p. 133).

wolf! . . . The stronger eat the weaker in this miserable soil, where men only live by devouring one another."[28]

Owing to the role of the *clan* as their main provider of security, moreover, Bedouin are ever conscious of how central and vital it is to their survival. The very word *khamsa*, meaning "fiver," as noted, they associate with other areas in which the number five plays a vital role in their lives. For example, five months is the gestation period of the goats and sheep they raise, as well as the growing period for the winter wheat and barley they sow. They also deem five generations of purebred breeding essential for producing a thoroughbred camel. Accordingly, they express the vitality of the clan in the proverb, "As wealth comes by five, so men come by five" (*khams bi-māl ū-khams bi-rijāl*).[29]

The Importance of Size

New male members add to the ultimate effectiveness of a clan in protecting its members, as the effectiveness is largely determined by its size. A widespread adage among the Bedouin says, "Count your clansmen before going to battle" (*ʿidd zlāmak w-ird ʿa-l'-mī*),* uttered to cite the importance of numbers in a clan. Regardless of how valiant the men of a group may be, they know that "The many overcome the brave" (*al-kuthra ghallabat as-sibāʿa*).[30]

One ramification of this reality in Bedouin culture is that Bedouin—and by extension all Middle Eastern peoples—prefer to father male children. Significantly, Bedouin congratulate the father of a newly born son by expressing the wish, "May he grow to be a horseman!" (*inshallah khayyāl*), and begetting sons is also the main justification for polygamy among Bedouin, as captured in their expression, "Marriage is for making men" (*al-jīza marājil*).[31] Accordingly, the birth of a male is met with celebration, that of a female, with silence; a man, asked how many children he has, will normally relate only the number of his sons, that of his daughters being irrelevant. It is the number of sons that determines one's status, both within one's clan and at large, as well as the status of the clan. Members of a small clan find they must be cautious in their contacts with members of larger ones, lest their actions arouse the latter's ire. This may prejudice the welfare of the former in several areas of life, particularly their honor and safety. Moreover, the opportunity for a small clan to play roles of leadership in the larger bodies to which Bedouin belong (subtribe, tribe, sub-confederation, confederation) is largely curtailed.

In terms of general vitality, therefore, the preference for sons is great, ex-

*Bailey, *Proverbs*, p. 125. "Battle" in the original is "before going down to the water," meaning a well. "Watering" is often a metaphor for battle, water always having been a resource for which Bedouin might fight.

pressed in the adage, "He who begets will not die, unless his offspring is daughters" (*illī ʿaggab mā māt—ghayr wi-ʿigbah banāt*). Indeed, the value of a male child is so great that all assume him to be endangered by the evil eye, which Bedouin appropriately call "the eye of the envious" (*ʿein al-ḥāsid*). To mislead the evil eye they will clothe an infant boy in girl's garments, especially a bonnet, and, as he grows, they may deliberately dress him in shabby clothes to avert undue regard.[32]

Another way to increase the size of a clan is to have people join it. However, while this possibility should be welcome and theoretically exists, there are rules for affiliation that often preclude it. First, as noted above, the clan from which the applicant wishes to disaffiliate must agree. Bedouin in southern Sinai recall that in the late nineteenth century a man of the Muzayna confederation wished to join a clan in the Tarabīn Ḥasāblah tribe, only to be thwarted by the refusal of his current clan to release him.[33] Similarly, all the members (married or formerly married males) of the desired clan must agree to admit the applicant. When in 1964 Ḥasan az-Zinayd of the ʿAzāzma Muḥammadiyyīn tribe, the only member of his original clan to remain in Israel after the Arab-Israeli War of 1948, sought to join that of his in-laws, the Muṭlān of the ʿAzāzma ʿAṣiyāt, he was prevented from doing so by the veto of a single member (Case 55).[34]

The desire to take on new members nonetheless exists, a manifestation of which is the custom called "purchase" (*sharwa*). One form of purchase is when a clan pardons a person or group that has killed one of its members on condition that he or they join the victim's clan. This happened early in the twentieth century among the Khawāṭra section of the ʿAzāzma Saraḥīn tribe when the Badrān clan appended the smaller Khiraynig clan, which had killed one of its members.[35]

Another form of purchase takes place when a clan appends someone by paying the blood-price he has incurred through the murder of someone from a third group. An example from the nineteenth century concerned Dakhalallah Ibn Sarīaʿ of the Tarabīn Nabaʿāt tribe in southeast Sinai, who had a shepherd from the neighboring Aḥeiwāt Ghuraygāniyyīn tribe called Farajallah Abū Rushaydī (Case 56).

> One day, Abū Rushaydī and a companion met and joined three people from the Tiyāha confederation transporting two camel-loads of wheat. As they saw that Abū Rushaydī had a rifle better than theirs, they secretly plotted to kill him along the way and take it. Sensing their intention, the shepherd took advantage of an occasion when they laid their guns down to reload the wheat onto their camels and shot at them. After killing one, the other two fell upon him with their swords, wounding him gravely. At this, Abū Rushaydī's companion ran

off to notify his employer, Dakhalallah Ibn Sarīaʿ, that he might have been killed. The latter came and found him lying bloody with his wounds next to the body of the man he had shot. The others had run away. Ibn Sarīaʿ ultimately arranged for a trial, in which Abū Rushaydī's wounds would be assessed against the blood-price of the murdered man, which usually was forty camels. Having gotten the fine reduced to twenty, which neither the shepherd nor his clan were yet able to pay, Ibn Sarīaʿ offered to pay it instead, on condition that Abū Rushaydī quit his clan and join that of Ibn Sarīaʿ in perpetuity. One hundred years later, following an internal dispute, the descendants of Abū Rushaydī, some ten men, sought to disaffiliate. The current Sareiʿa leader, with the size of his clan in mind, strove to stop them from quitting by insisting that each individual man pay back the twenty camels. He argued that Abū Rushaydī was only one person but that under the protection of the Ibn Sarīaʿ he was able to foster two generations of men, each of which now had to pay as if he was the forefather himself. Unable to make such a payment, Abū Rushaydī's descendants stayed on in the Ibn Sarīaʿ clan.[36]

If a clan decides to accept a person to membership, the successful applicant must go through a ceremony of affiliation to be witnessed in three separate tents, a way of ensuring that the mutual responsibility thus created will gain wide publicity. In each of these tents, he and the elder of his new clan will both bury, in the presence of the tent owner, some pebble-sized stones in the ground to symbolize the permanence of the new affiliation. This is called "burying the pebble" (*dafn al-ḥaṣā*).[37] The elder thereupon recites the traditional formula admitting a new member: "You are leaving a *khamsa* and returning to a *khamsa*: we are completely of one blood" (*inti ṭāliʿ min khamsa ū-tithannī fī khamsa—damm mā fīha kharam*). The joiner then dons a new garment and burns an old one to symbolize that he is exchanging the protection, or cover, of his former clan for that of the new one, and he enumerates his obligations to the latter by pronouncing the formulaic oath of allegiance:*

I hereby burn my dress and join with you
(*Āna madʿag thōbī ū-baṭlaʿ maʿak*)
In problems of blood and others.
(*fī damm ū-fī hamm*)
I'll pursue when you pursue and flee when you flee.
(*baṭrud miṭrādak ū-bashrud mishrādak*)
My son will suffice like your son;

*Oral communication from Muḥammad Ḥusayn al-ʿAlowna of the Tarabīn Ḥasāblah, October 20, 1999; cf. Stewart, Texts, vol. 1, pp. 56–57, 98; Stewart uses the term "blood money group" instead of clan but is obviously referring to the clan, which is evident from the obligations to seek and be subject to revenge that he quotes herein.

> (*ibnī yisidd fī ibnak*)
> My daughter will suffice like your daughter;
> (*bintī bitsidd fī bintak*)
> My camel-mare will suffice like your camel-mare.
> (*ū-nāgtī tisidd fī nāgtak*).

This oath signifies that the applicant and his male offspring (to the fifth generation) will seek vengeance for the murder of fellow members and will flee with the others from retaliation; he will allow his girls to be given in bondage-marriage to avert retaliation against the clan; and he will participate in the payment of fines, traditionally paid in camels.[38]

The Importance of Solidarity

While the size of a clan largely determines its effectiveness, the cohesion of the group is also essential. One element is the readiness of its members to act. "A spear with no one to raise it is worthless" (*ar-ramḥ illī mā lah sunūd dhalīl*) is a widespread maxim.[39] Another element is the solidarity among its members. An ancient adage cautions that "There is no gain in a clan whose right gets lost among themselves" (*lā khayr bi-gōm yiḍayya' al-ḥagg mā baynhum*).[40] In addition, Bedouin are urged to support a fellow clansman against any outsider, under any circumstances. One of their adages instructs, "When one turns to his cousin, even if he's wrong, he's not" (*illī biyījī l-ibn 'ammah — lō lih shī mā lih shī*).[41]

An example of unquestioned solidarity took place in the central Negev in 1974, during a conflict between two clans belonging to the 'Azāzma Saraḥīn tribe, the Rimāg and the 'Owdāt (Case 43). The conflict erupted over an argument between a shepherd of the 'Owdāt and a shepherdess of the Rimāg, during which the latter threw a stone at the former's head, wounding him. Prior to this fray, the two groups had enjoyed peaceful and friendly relations, and two elderly shepherds in their seventies, Hilayyil ar-Rimāg and 'Ayyāda Abū Bilayya, of the two groups respectively, were accustomed to camp together in remote parts of the desert, where they pastured their camels. They were the best of friends and jointly welcomed the occasional visitor in their itinerant encampments with good cheer. When the conflict between their clans erupted, however, the two elderly friends broke camp, each seeking pasture in a different direction. Moreover, Abū Bilayya related the following to me:

> "I was returning to my camp via the mountain pass called Nagb Ghawārib when suddenly I spotted Hilayyil ar-Rimāg coming up the pass with 'Īd al-Ḥawaṣa [of a neutral clan], apparently on their way to the latter's tent. They didn't see me, so I hid behind a boulder until they passed. Then I followed

> them, and from a hillock near Wādī ad-Damāth, I spied on the tent where they were sitting. I noticed that they were dressed up, as for a holiday; and then I saw that the pot was on the fire and smelled the aroma of boiling meat. Suddenly I realized that it was the ʿĪd al-Fiṭr holiday and that Ḥawaṣa had slaughtered a goat for his guest. I, living in isolation, was still observing the Ramaḍān fast, unaware it had ended the day before. When I smelled the cooking meat, my stomach ached with hunger. I was sorely tempted to climb down the hill, join them for lunch, and get something to drink. But I desisted," he said after a pause, "because Hilayyil was there."
>
> "So what?" I said. "You and Hilayyil are friends."
>
> "True," he replied, "but there is blood between his men and mine, and one's first loyalty is to his kin. If I had just entered the tent, Hilayyil would have hit me or else picked up his things and left. That is what he would have had to do. It would have shamed him to just sit there with me."[42]

Bedouin are also encouraged to support their clansmen against outsiders instinctively. As affirmed by a member of the ʿAzāzma Saraḥīn tribe, "No one should desert his cousin, even if he is angry with him. When your cousin is in conflict with an outsider, you must support him, no matter what. Only when you finish with your cousin's conflict can you go back to your own anger."* By the same token, Bedouin are noticeably indulgent of their clansmen's faults and usually prepared to overlook their misdeeds. In metaphor, they are cautioned to remember that "Your nose is yours, even if it's snotty" (*khashmak minnak lō jayyaf*).[43]

Dissensions within a Clan

Although clan solidarity toward outsiders is a conscious sentiment among Bedouin, internal conflicts do occur, sometimes leading to litigation even between brothers, let alone cousins. Especially dreaded is murder within the ranks, as expressed by the rhymed maxim "The greatest ill is killing a cousin" (*awwal hamm katl ibn al-ʿamm*).[44] In particular, internecine murder is a threat to a clan's position. The clan is seen to be divided, it has been weakened in manpower by the murder, and the possibility of internal revenge may weaken it further. To make the best of a bad situation, many clans agree to forgo internal revenge and settle for the payment of blood-money, which includes the grant of a *ghurra*, or "bondage-wife," whereby the murderer gives

*Interview with Swaylim Sulaymān Abū Bilayya of the ʿAzāzma Saraḥīn, May 12, 1998. The Arabic is *Wala wāḥad mā bikhallī ibn ʿammah, low zaʿlan ʿal ibn ʿammah. Fī wagt az-zaʿl ʿa-l-ajnabī ibtizrim maʿ ibn ʿammak. Ū-baʿd mā tikhalliṣ maʿ ibn ʿammak bitʿāwid ʿala zaʿlak.*

for free (without bride-price) his closest female kin, his sister or daughter, in marriage to the closest male relative of the victim so that she can bear his immediate family a male to compensate for the deceased.[45]

While the law itself permits internal revenge, in keeping with the addage "I and my brother will fight our cousin" (*āna w-akhūwī ʿal ibn ʿammī*), it is kept within specific bounds.[46] As many clans consist of various family lineages, each relating back to a son of the common forefather (or having joined at some point), the law permits revenge to be taken only by the lineage of the murder victim; members of other lineages in the clan must remain neutral and desist from taking vengeance. If they do not, it will be considered murder compounded by treachery, itself subject to revenge.[47] The law of neutrality between lineages also pertains to internal conflicts of lesser import.

Indeed, murder within a clan is rare, mostly heard of within particularly powerful chiefly families, when there is rivalry among siblings over leadership. One example took place in the Syrian desert early in the twentieth century among the chiefly Ibn Shaʿlān family of the huge Rawala tribe, which numbered thirty-five thousand souls.[48] Nūrī Ibn Shaʿlān killed his half-brother Mishʿal, who he believed had usurped the leadership of their tribe, in order to replace him with his full brother, Fahad, preferred by all the tribesmen. Then, when the tribe found Fahad ineffective and corrupt and would supplant him with Nūrī, Fahad plotted to assassinate Nūrī but was killed by Nūrī in advance.[49] In the Negev desert the most famous nineteenth-century war, as noted above, was the War of ʿOwda and ʿĀmir (1842–64), ʿOwda being chief of the powerful Tiyāha al-ʿAṭowna tribe and ʿĀmir his brother (Case 7). Although the oral tradition relates that the immediate cause of the conflict was an argument among women, there was also widespread discontent with ʿOwda's leadership; ʿĀmir saw fit to exploit this discontent in order to replace him as chief.[50] The above examples notwithstanding, internecine murder may also take place within rank-and-file clans. In 1954, for example, the Ẓullām confederation in the northern Negev experienced such a murder in its midst when a Ṣubayḥ Abū Rubayʿa killed his cousin and clansman, Sulaymān Salāma Abū Rubayʿa (Case 18).[51]

As in any other society, most internal disputes between closely related clansmen are over relatively mundane matters, even if some get to litigation. Frank Stewart cites an uncle taking his nephew to court for violating his tent by beating his (the nephew's) wife in it (Case 57) and a nephew trying to sue his uncle for stealing his camels (Case 11).[52] Brothers may dispute the division of their inherited property, as did Salmān Sālim and ʿĪd Sālim of the Ẓullām Abū Rubayʿa in the northern Negev in the mid-1940s, when the former accused the latter of cultivating his land (Case 38),[53] or as in 1961, when a man of the Tiyāha Afinish accused his sister of stealing their late mother's jewelry (Case

58).[54] As we saw above, in 1977 Silmī Ṣwayrī an-Nujūm of the Aḥeiwāt Shawafīn al-Guṣayyir in eastern Sinai claimed that his daughter was seduced by clansmen (Case 53),[55] and the wife of Sālim Ibn Naṣṣār of the same tribe was beaten up in her husband's tent by his clansman in 1979 (Case 11).[56] Among the Suwārka ʿAradāt of northern Sinai in 1998, a man beat his female paternal niece for gathering tall grass on his land for her flock (Case 59),[57] and in southern Sinai in 2005, ʿAnayz ʿAnayzān al-ʿUrḍī beat his clanswoman, ʿĀyisha, for grazing her flock on his sown crops, much to the dismay of the girl's brother, his paternal first cousin, ʿIshaysh ʿAnayz al-ʿUrḍī, who then brought him to trial for the act (Case 60).[58]

Expulsion from the Clan

Internecine disputes are as dangerous for clan solidarity as they are natural, and Bedouin law has made allowance for them, as we have seen, without undermining the clan system of mutual responsibility. Nevertheless, occasions arise (by most accounts rarely) when a member's behavior is deemed intolerable and may necessitate his expulsion from the clan. Such behavior may involve not rallying to the aid of kinsmen in trouble or not participating in the payment of fines imposed on the clan. The main cause of expulsion, however, is a propensity to stir up conflict with outsiders; such behavior may result in great harm or loss to the whole clan, owing to the mutual responsibility the members hold for each other's actions. For example, in the northern Negev in 1942, the Ghūl clan of the Ẓullām Abū Graynāt expelled Sulaymān al-Ghūl after having had to pay blood-money for a murder that he committed and heavy fines to the father and husband of a woman he abducted and after having suffered from much internal dissension that he provoked within the clan (Case 61).[59] Bedouin liken such a person to a monkey (*gird*), seen as never at rest and always up to mischief, and his danger to the clan is caught in the rhyming proverb, "Just as one scabby camel infects the whole herd, so one troublemaker (*gird*) gets his whole group into trouble" (*al'-bil yijrib-ha mafrūd—wa-l-ʿarab yugrud-ha magrūd*).[60]

The Bedouin call expulsion *tashmīs* (exposing one to the sun [*shams*]). With it they renounce any responsibility for the expellee's actions and divest him of their protection. The imagery indicates that the *mushammas* (lit. "one exposed to the sun") will no longer enjoy the shade, or protection, of his clansmen.* Indeed, the binding rhymed edict of expulsion, uttered before witnesses and guarantors, is as follows:

*In Bedouin eyes, the scorching sun, which desiccates their pasture and crops, is an enemy that would destroy them (see Musil, *Manners*, p. 1).

Carry your evil between your own wings!
(*Sharrak bayn jinḥānak*)
We'll neither pursue your vengeance nor flee for your misdeed;
(*mā nuṭrud miṭrādak wala nushrud mishrādak*)
Not for stolen livestock nor a murdered man.
(*lā fī māl mashlūl wala rājil maktūl*).

At the expulsion rite, the elder of the clan may also highlight its detachment from the expellee by proclaiming that if he be murdered,

Even his cloak will be due recompense,
(*Diytah ʿabātah*)
And his killer may have lunch in our tents:
(*w-illī yiktilah yitaghadda ʿendī*)
I'll pursue him neither by night nor by day.
(*lā asrāh wala abrāh*).[61]

To ensure maximum dissemination of the fact that the members of the clan will henceforth bear no responsibility for the actions of the expellee and are not, for example, to be pursued in revenge for a murder he may commit, Bedouin law requires that this rite be performed in three separate tents, just as it specifies when people affiliate with a clan. In addition, the law stipulates that nine guarantors enforce the expulsion to make certain that the expelling clan honors it and refrains from extending support or aid to the expellee in the future, such as taking revenge for his or his children's murder(s) or giving him refuge or intelligence when he is fleeing after having committed a murder. In the event that the clan violates this undertaking, it will have to pay each of the nine guarantors a heavy fine, as determined by the rigorous judges in cases of honor, the *manāshid*.

WOMEN IN THE CLAN

Inferior Status

Any presentation of Bedouin law must clarify that in almost all contexts the term "a Bedouin" refers to a man specifically and not to a woman. Bedouin society is a male society in the sense that men are the members active in intercourse with others. At best, women are represented by men. At worst, they have no rights, especially of appeal, as when they are married off without their agreement or clansmen kill them for moral impropriety. The fact that a woman may not sue or speak in court on her own behalf indicates that the law regards her as a different order of humanity than a man.[62] Indeed, even when the paths of a man and a woman cross, she is legally obliged to halt and allow him to proceed.[63]

This condition of inferiority before the law is manifest in the status of women in the clan. Every woman is born into the clan of her father, membership in which she retains all through her life. She is not an active member, however. She neither pays fines incurred by the clan nor receives fines accruing to it; nor is she expected to avenge the murder of a fellow clansman. As the adage holds, "Men don't figure women into their accounts" (*ar-rijāl mā bitiḥāsib an-niswān fī ḥagg-hum*).[64] A woman does not vote on matters affecting the clan, such as who a new leader should be, whether or not to establish a coexistence agreement with a clan of a different confederation, whether or not to admit an aspiring joiner, or whether or not her lineage should disaffiliate. Her children belong to her husband, and when her father dies, she has no right to inherit his land, in contrast to her brothers, or, if there be none, her paternal cousins.[65] On occasion, she may gain active participation in clan affairs by ad hoc permission but not by right.

Perhaps the origin of the secondary status of women in the clan derives from the traditional condition of Bedouin society, constantly on the move and exposed to attack. In order to afford security to man and beast under these conditions, marked by the absence of law-enforcement agencies in the desert, the men of the society had to be permanently on guard to provide protection. To assure this availability of the men, the women were assigned the burden of daily chores, which the men deemed secondary to their task. These chores included herding, raising the children, gathering the firewood, cooking, weaving the tent pieces, and even pitching the tent in new campgrounds (so that the men could remain on the lookout for foes). All these chores had to be done involuntarily, and the law provided the means for imposing them, including the right of a man to strike his wife or clanswoman and to divorce the former for neglect in their dispatch.[66] As security was the central concern of a nomadic society, its assumption by the men rewarded them with dominance. This condition was succinctly elucidated to the Czech explorer Alois Musil by the chief of the Syrian Rawala tribe, Nūrī Ibn Shaʿalān, in 1908 as follows: "Lookest thou, brother Mūsa; when the enemy appears and the sound of the battle cry arises, is it the women who rush to the defense? Is it the women who undertake aggressive raids? Is it the women who return with the booty? We keep women to bear us children and to care for our tents. We do not oppress them, but a woman must always be conscious of the fact that man is her master. Thus Allah has willed; our ancestors observed this order and we likewise observe it. It is our habit, our custom, our law."[67]

Another reason for the passive role assigned to women in the clan is the clan's patrilineal structure. Every member is descended from the group forefather through the male line—that is, through his (or her) father's father and the latter's father's father through to the fifth generation, as depicted above. Consequently the children of any woman belong to her husband's clan, as mirrored in the proverbial advice to grandfathers: "You can command the son of your son, but not the son of your daughter" (*iḥkim ʿala ibn ibnak—w-ibn bintak lā*). Although the practice of endogamous "closest-cousin" (*ibn al-ʿamm*) marriage is common among Bedouin, making many children members of the same clan as their mothers, the prevalent assumption is that a woman will marry out of the clan, and that her sons may eventually be its enemies. This attitude, and fear, is conveyed in the sayings "The sister's son is his maternal uncle's enemy" (*ibn al-ukht ʿadū la-khālah*) and "Woe to a maternal uncle from the spear of his sister's son" (*yā wayl al-khāl mi rumḥ ibn ukhtah*).[68]

The Protection of Clanswomen

One right that women nevertheless have in a clan is to be protected. The adage instructs that "Every woman has a shepherd behind her" (*kull mara warāha rāʿī*), meaning that there is a clansman to look after her.[69] From the time that a female is born until she dies, she is under the protection of her clansmen (in this capacity called *ʿizwa*), the responsibility starting with her immediate family and extending to her cousins. In 1973, as part of a squabble between women of the ʿAzāzma Saraḥīn tribe who were migrating in the northern Negev, girls of the Zanūn clan attacked girls of the Ghidayfī clan in the tent of the elderly sister of Ḥimayd as-Saddān (Case 14). Although the widow of a Ghidayfī man, she was a lifetime member of the ʿOwdāt clan. In the attack, Saddān's sister also suffered some wounds, but when men of the Zanūn and Ghidayfī subsequently sat down to reconcile and balance accounts for the blood that their respective girls had shed, they left Saddān's sister's wounds for him to settle, knowing that responsibility for problems bearing on her safety resided with him. Although Saddān and his sister had not been on speaking terms for several years, he, upon hearing of the circumstances, was quick to demand reparation and even went into conflict with the Zanūn clan over its version of the fight, which would leave it unaccountable.[70]

Another example of such responsibility took place in central Sinai in the early 1940s. A woman of the Ḥuwayṭāt Dubūr tribe in southern Jordan was married off to a man of the Aḥeiwāt Ṣafeiḥa (Case 62).[71] After a time, one of the men in the husband's clan made stubborn advances toward her, about which she kept silent. She divulged the information only about a month later, when visited by her brother, Salāma Ibn Aḥamad, who thereupon went to a prominent Aḥeiwāt leader, ʿOwda Ibn Huwayshil, demanding a trial of honor. Learning that the incident had taken place a month before, Ibn Huwayshil asserted the legal position that "after three and a third days, she no longer has a valid complaint" (*baʿd thilāthit iyyām ū-thilth mā ilha shakwa*). He changed his contention, however, upon hearing Ibn Aḥamad's rhymed defense, which depicted her as "a woman whose complaint and weeping were concealed in her bosom till her clansmen came" (*illī ṣārat shakwit-ha ū-bakwit-ha fī khubnit-ha limma jāwū ʿizwit-ha*). Ibn Huwayshil knew that because the woman was a stranger among the Aḥeiwāt, none of the Aḥeiwāt men, including her husband, would have taken up her cause. Only her clansmen could be expected to do that.

The vulnerability of women removed a great distance from their clansmen was also affirmed by the bards who sang the saga of Abū Zayd, the semi-legendary leader of the Banī Hilāl tribe, which emigrated from central Arabia to North Africa in the tenth century. The narrative poem relates that prior to the grand departure

> Abū Zayd convened his tribe and said: On Thursday and Friday we move!
> (*Nādī fī banī hilāl nādī—yōm al-jumʿa wa-l-khamīs raḥīl*)
> He whose wife is a girl of his clan will bring forth his camel and pack.
> (*illī ḥalīltah bint ʿammih—yidannī ʿowj al-ʿaragīb wi-yishīl*)*
> He who has two wives, one an outsider, should ask her choice between family and spouse.
> (*illī ʿendih thintayn, wāḥda ajnabiyya—yishāwirha mā bayn al-ahal wa-l-mīl*).[72]

In these lines, while it is taken for granted that a wife married to a clansman may safely go anywhere with him, under his assumed protection, it is inferred that a wife from a different clan cannot be arbitrarily removed from its proximity and protection without her consent. If she agrees to the separation, her clansmen must also concur. If she objects, however, they have a right and duty to prevent it as her legal protectors.

As implied in the foregoing, the responsibility for the physical safety of a woman pertains even after she is married. The legal instruction is that "The good of a woman is for her husband, the bad is for her clansmen" (*al-mara—khayrha li-jōzha ū-sharrha li-zlāmha*), thereby differentiating between the two legal entities.[73] On the face of it at least, this is a fairly clear-cut formula. From his wife the husband gains children, a home, and the care of his livestock. Her clansmen, by contrast, are there for her problems, which, in addition to physical protection, also include protection from sexual violation. Under specific conditions, clansmen are empowered by the law to kill the men who dishonor their clanswomen—such as rapists, abductors, and fornicators—even if the

*The Arabic expression "of crooked hocks" (*ʿowj al-ʿaragīb*) is one Bedouin term for a camel.

liaison in the latter two offenses is consensual. This aspect of clansmen's responsibility for "the bad" is no less exacting than their responsibility for her physical safety. It stems from the societal mission, which Bedouin society requires each family to pursue, of raising its daughters to refrain from sexual contacts. In this society, a woman's prime role is to bear males to her husband's clan or kinship group — males upon whom all the kin will one day depend for protection when endangered; males who will help them seek revenge when they have been violated; and, by contrast, males who may cause their clansmen to suffer through their own violation of people outside the clan. Such far-reaching obligations upon clansmen are weighty — too weighty, indeed, to be borne for people not of their blood. The possibility of an outsider implanting strange seed in their wives is something that Bedouin are zealous to avoid. Thus they seek to prevent women's fornication through the early discipline of girls. A Bedouin family is expected to keep a girl under close scrutiny all the years of her youth and to duly reprimand her for socializing with boys and for any other deviation from modest behavior. Social convention warns of the woes that result from a family's lenience in moral matters. One Bedouin adage instructs that "A loose girth brings the gall" (*al-ibṭān ar-rukhū yātī bi-d-dabr*).[74]

Accordingly, if a post-pubescent girl strays, society views it as a sign that her family has been shamefully negligent. This blaming of a girl's family was reflected even in lines of repartee poetry from the time of the British Mandate in Palestine (1919–48), composed after a woman from the area of the Gaṭya oasis in northwest Sinai, living under the protection of the powerful Tiyāha Huzayyil tribe in the northern Negev, was found fornicating with British soldiers. These lines followed an allegation by a man called al-ʿAṭashī of the Dawāghra tribe:[75]

> The Huzayyil didn't rescue a ward in their tent when the English screwed her in the ass.
> (*Āma al-huzayyil mā sallam dakhīlat baytah yōm khannathū-ha al-inglīz ū-saṭū fī-ṭīzha kibrītah*).

Hearing this, a man of the Huzayyil answered:

> The tent of Huzayyil is renowned for its protection;
> (*Āma bayt al-huzayyil al-kull biyismaʿ bi-ṣītah*)
> It's not our shame that the Gaṭawiyya girl strayed, but that of her family that let her go free.
> (*in ʿābit al-gaṭawiyya, ʿeibit-ha mī hī makhzitna — ʿeibit-ha ʿa jamāʿit-ha illī ṭalagūha falīta*).

To avert this type of shame, the family of Sulaymān Swaylim Abū Bilayya of the ʿAzāzma Saraḥīn tribe in the central Negev, for example, asked an Israeli court to transfer his two-year-old daughter to his family's custody in 1998 (Case 26).[76] When the child was still nursing, the father of Abū Bilayya's wife had her divorced from him and in turn married her off to a man of the ʿAbays clan of the same tribe; she took her daughter with her. Abū Bilayya's family, knowing that it would ultimately be responsible for the girl's moral probity, was intent on raising her. As, according to Bedouin law, a child belongs to its father's family, a divorced mother must return the child to that family once it is weaned. In this case, however, Abū Bilayya's ex-wife persisted in retaining custody of the child, knowing that an Israeli court would support her stance as the mother.

Honor Killings

To help remove a family's reputation for ostensible laxity in raising girls—gained through the wayward behavior of one of its women or girls—Bedouin law permits her closest clansmen to kill her with impunity.* Appropriately, it terms this category of killing "restoring station" (*radd ash-sharaf*). In May 1985, for example, the brothers of Ḥamda al-Ḥamāmda of the ʿAzāzma Masʿūdiyyīn tribe in the Negev burned her after her husband, returning home unexpectedly from the army, discovered her sleeping with another man (Case 63).[77] Similarly in March 2006, the brothers of Rīm Abū Ghānim of the Tarabīn Jarawīn strangled her and threw her corpse into a deep well for having trysted with a Palestinian man. At the time, the eldest brother, who organized the killing, was a pediatrician at a prominent hospital near Ramle, in central Israel (Case 64).[78]

Perhaps an even greater incentive of the law in sanctioning the dispatch of such a girl derives from the view that it is the surest "backup" method for edifying the youth. An oft-heard legal maxim confirms that "Punishing a girl educates the girls and teaches the boys to keep away" (*aydib al-ʿār yādib al-ʿār ū-yādib ʿannah*).* Bedouin men claim this educational measure as their right, referring to the metaphorical legal directive, "The blood of a mangy one will be let by her people" (*al-jarba yiṭlowha ahalha*),[79] which borrows the image of

*Closest clansmen are, first and normally, a girl's brothers. In the absence of brothers, the duty falls upon the sons of her father's older brother, and so forth throughout the clan, with men more remotely related acting in the absence of more closely related cousins. However, any man encountering a fellow clanswoman behaving contrary to Bedouin moral standards with an outsider man has the right to beat the woman as well as the man (cf. Stewart, Texts, vol. 1, pp. 60–61). See chapter 6 for more on the right to beat women.

*Bailey, *Proverbs*, p. 266. As in this maxim, Bedouin refer to a woman or women in a moral context in the masculine gender through the term *ʿār*, in its sense as womankind. By extension, it also means the violation of a woman's honor.

"mangy" from the mange skin disease common among their livestock and known to be highly contagious. Accordingly, a wayward girl, through her example, and a mangy animal, through proximity, are each seen as infecting their entire respective communities. The perceived merit in the dispatch of a wayward girl was conveyed in a story of such a case, which left us the phrase, "His daughter died, for his outlook was pure" (*mātat wiliyyitah min ṣafa niyitah*).[80] One option open to a father is to marry a girl off to her lover, an option that took root in the saying, "Cover the shame of a girl with marriage or death" (*al-bint sutrit-ha jīzit-ha ow maytit-ha*),[81] the shame being that which the girl is causing her family. As the proverb confirms, however, honor killing remains a prominent option, and its perceived justification is a difficult sentiment for Bedouin men to ignore.

Indeed, in the northern Negev in 2003, the maternal uncle (*khāl*) of a girl of the Tiyāha Abū ʿAbdūn who had absconded with a young man of the Tiyāha Abū-l-Gīʿān allowed himself to contribute to her murder—this, despite his having no responsibility for the girl's moral probity, she belonging to a different clan (Case 65). It was to this maternal uncle that the girl's boyfriend returned her, after they had had a week together, in the hope that he could mediate her safety with his in-laws, her clansmen. Ultimately, however, on the ostensible basis of the clansmen's promise not to harm her, the uncle took her to the local council offices in the Bedouin town of Lagiyya, where he was to turn her over to a paternal uncle. At one point, however, he told her to fetch something from his car, where her paternal cousins were lying in ambush to shoot her dead. While the maternal uncle, presumably, normally entertained feelings of affection for his sister's daughter, the social pressure for him to act in the public interest evidently overcame them.[82]

Responsibility for Wives of a Different Clan

As if to highlight the responsibility of clansmen, a husband whose wife is not a member of his clan (that is, is nonrelated) has little inherent right to strike at those who violate her honor.* The law entitles him to kill a man in the act of fornicating with his wife or sleeping beside her within his tent, considering it an act of aggression upon the dwelling; otherwise the right to kill a fornicator with impunity belongs only to her clansmen. The same pertains to gaining satisfaction from litigation. In 1971 in the central Negev, Hilayyil al-Wajj of the Ẓullām Janabīb tribe came to the wife of Ḥimayd as-Saddān of the

*Bedouin do not consider relatives through one's mother (*khwāl*) as legal relatives, in the sense of having any inherent legal commitment to them, as opposed to patrilineal relatives, who are one's clansmen (see Bailey, *Proverbs*, pp. 161–64).

ʿAzāzma Saraḥīn, who was not her clansman, and made advances toward her that, she later claimed, she rejected (Case 44). When she reported this to her father, ʿOwda an-Nashmī, he quickly demanded from the Wujūj clan a trial of honor, which he was granted. The husband, Saddān, on the other hand, received only his "right of the tent" (*ḥagg al-bayt*) in which his wife was approached, receiving, from Judge Ḥasan Abū Rubayʿa, a financial award (the equivalent of $5,000) and the restoration of his honor through the offender's covering his tent with white cloth and admitting his offense in three notable tents filled with men.[83] Hence, the non-clansman husband got his due for his violated tent but not for the violated honor of his wife. That was the preserve of her clansmen.

The legally divergent roles played by a husband and a clansman in a woman's defense were also witnessed among the Aḥeiwāt Shawafīn in 1979, when Sālim Ibn Naṣṣār took no action to redress the beating that his nonrelated wife received from a man, understanding that her sores were the legal concern only of her brothers, as clansmen (Case 11). As in the previous case, his concern in the beating was limited to the fact that it had taken place in his own tent, for the violation of which he sought compensation.[84] Again, in the mid-1980s in the central Negev, when a woman belonging to a clan of the ʿAzāzma ʿAṣiyāt was slandered to the effect that her children were born out of wedlock, she immediately went to her father to get him to try and redress the insult, knowing that her nonrelated husband was in no legal position to do so (Case 13).[85]

On the other hand, the law considers it the duty of a husband to try and protect his nonrelated (or related) wife from imminent violation, just as if she were a guest or ward in his tent.* By the same token, it grants a nonrelated husband the right to shed the blood of someone who has just then raped or struck his wife, either injuring or killing her. The chief honor judge (*manshad*) in Sinai, Amīra Salāma Abū Amīra, called this "the husband's permission" (*dustūr al-jōz*).[86] Bedouin in general strongly endorse such action by a husband, even if they cannot classify his right to it in the same way. Justifications stress that a woman is entitled to her husband's protection as part of his household, as the mother of his children, and by dint of their intimacy.[87] Certainly a woman encamped with her husband far from her clansmen might frequently be vulnerable to physical or sexual violation if she were bereft of his protection.

Perhaps indicating that social values may occasionally override legal considerations, many Bedouin also apply a husband's right of protection to the abduction of his nonrelated wife, deeming it incumbent upon the husband to

*See Smith, Kinship, p. 77, for corroborative evidence on considering a non-clan wife as a ward in pre-Islamic Arabia.

respond violently against the offender. In the central Negev in the 1940s, for example, the nonrelated wife of Sālim al-Owraydī of the ʿAzāzma Saraḥīn tribe was abducted by her cousin, who claimed that his "closest-cousin" right had been unlawfully bypassed when she was married off to Owraydī. The opinion of all the men in Owraydī's area was so strongly in favor of his taking blood-revenge against the abductor that they would not give him a carpet to sit on in their midst until he did so (Case 66).*

Again, among the Tiyāha in the northern Negev in 1958, when the wife of al-ʿAbd Abū-l-Gīʿān was sent to a traditional healer, Khalīl al-Fagīr, for an apparent nervous disorder, she fell in love with the healer's son and absconded with him (Case 67). Despite the absence of any kinship between Abū-l-Gīʿān and his wife, he went after the couple and slew the man. Although he possessed no legal right to murder his wife's abductor, the disgrace attached to the abduction of a married woman who had come to his father's tent for treatment was sufficient for the murderer's clan neither to flee revenge, in keeping with the customary practice, nor accept any of the conditions for reconciliation that the Fagīr put forward.[88] Nor did the Fagīr feel justified to take revenge.[89] After spending eighteen years in prison for murder, under Israeli law, al-ʿAbd Abū-l-Gīʿān, upon release, paid the Fagīr clan blood-money for the murder, partly as a gesture to others of the Tiyāha confederation, who were ill at ease with an ongoing feud in their midst.[90] Whatever the reason for the blood-payment, it served only to substantiate that according to Bedouin law, a husband cannot murder with impunity the abductor of a wife not of his clan.

Definition of a nonrelated husband's rights may come inversely from a case of abduction that took place among the Tarabīn Ḥasāblah of the Jabal Rāḥa area of western Sinai (Case 68):

> In the mid-1980s, a man of the Durūz clan married his daughter off to Sālim Abū ʿUbayd of the ʿUbaydāt clan, circumventing the clansman who had the "closest-cousin" right to marry the girl. The ʿUbaydāt set up a wedding tent and a *birza*, or tent for the bride to sit in, and had already slaughtered the wedding goat, the blood of which was sprinkled on the *birza*, signifying that the couple were married and their families bonded.[91] The next morning, a party of the Durūz raided the ongoing celebration, encircled the guests, fired into the air, toppled the tents, and went off with the bride, unhampered by the ʿUbaydāt. The latter, however, feeling violated, brought the Durūz to trial before the renowned Tarabīn judge Ḥājj Jāzī al-ʿArādī.
>
> ʿArādī questioned the assembled parties about the case, including whether

*The clansmen said, "Fold the carpet away from him" (*kiffū al-firāshʿannah*). Oral communication from Frayj Ḥimayd as-Saddān of the ʿAzāzma Saraḥīn, July 4, 2001.

> or not the ʿUbaydāt had been armed at the time of the raid. Learning that they were, he ruled, "He who has a weapon and does not keep men away from his wife cannot claim that he defends her honor" (*illī ʿendah silāḥ ū-mā yidāfiʿ dūn al-mara mā yilḥag al-bayḍā*).*

The same legalistic ambivalence exists in regard to the son of a mother who is not of his father's (and therefore not of his) clan. Does he have a specific right to use violence to defend her? The instinctive readiness to do so is reflected in a ditty sung while shepherds draw water for their herds: "The camels and Mommy, the camels and Mommy; you who hit them better not trust me" (*al'-bil w-ummī al'-bil w-ummī, yā ḍāribhum lā tāminnī*).[92] There is also a tradition in the central Negev that a shepherd called Ibn ʿĀyid, of the Saʿīdiyyīn confederation in the ʿAraba rift valley, struck a woman married to a man of the Abū Ruwaydī family, of the same confederation but not of the same clan (Case 69). Only one son was then in the area, herding the camels, the other men of the family being away at a distant market. This son, upon hearing of the assault, swore an oath: "The hand that struck my mother will be cut off" (*al-īd illī ḍarabat ummī ghayr tingaṭaʿ*). Thereupon, he took several clansmen with him to look for the culprit and, finding him, stripped off his clothes so that he could amputate his hand.[93] Contrary to the foregoing, however, bringing a nonrelated mother's claim to litigation is beyond the authority of her son, as demonstrated in the central Negev in 1973. When Ḥimayd as-Saddān's elderly sister, married to a man of the Ghidayfī clan, was injured in a fight with girls from the Zanūn clan, her son could not activate her case for reparations in litigation, as that right was the preserve of her own ʿOwdāt clan (Case 14).[94] The son professed, however, that had he been present at the time of the fight, he would have physically protected his mother, despite her being of a different clan.[95] This case helps put into focus the difference between a clansman's role, which is to obtain redress for the violated rights of a woman, and that of a nonrelated son or husband, which is to protect her against violation.

Collective Legal Personalities beyond the Clan

The individual Bedouin finds himself responsible before the law as part of collective groups other than his clan when his clan joins these groups in

*Oral communication from Zāyid ʿUbaydallah al-ʿUrḍī of the Tarabīn Ḥasāblah, December 2, 1997. The reference to "defending the honor" of a woman (lit. whitening [*bayḍā*]), stemming from the revenge that a husband takes for the violation of a non-clan wife, is a syllogistic way of stating that the ʿUbaydāt had forfeited their claim to the woman as a wife.

certain actions. His obligations to these groups are far less inclusive than those to his clan, but there are nevertheless laws that regulate their operations and that are binding upon him. Some groups are those with which his clan joins for paying and receiving fines in accord with a standing agreement; others are ad hoc groups that may help in conflict, on the basis of common origin, choice, or chance. In addition to the above-mentioned groups, there are certain individual connections that occur at times of conflict and that also are subject to the law.

THE BLOOD-FINE GROUP

The most common form of extra-clan cooperation among Bedouin is for two or more families that are not members of the same clan to join forces in paying fines that any of their number incur for assaulting or killing someone not belonging to this extended group, which they call a "blood-fine group" (*damawiyya*) in Sinai and "placing the coin" (*ḥaṭāṭ girsh*) in the Negev. (The terms will appear in this text interchangeably.)* Often these cooperating families will have belonged relatively recently to the same clan. Among the Tarabīn Ḥasāblah in southeast Sinai, for example, five clans that were a single clan seven to nine generations earlier (the Farārja, Muṭāwʿa, Musāʿida, Munāṣra, and ʿAlōwna) were still part of the same blood-fine group at the end of the twentieth century.[96] Likewise, barely related Bedouin living in the same area may form a blood-fine group, as did the Tarabīn Jawāzya clan, which claims descent from an early (perhaps sixteenth-century) forefather called Ḥasaballah,[97] and the Tarabīn Sareiʿa, professed descendants of Ḥasaballah's brother, Nabaʿ; the two clans are neighbors in Wādī Watīr, also in southeast Sinai.[98] One also meets blood-fine groups composed of families who have moved away from their parent clans or stayed behind after their parent clans moved away, such as those Bedouin in the pre-1948 Negev who moved to Jordan or Sinai following the Arab-Israeli War of that year. Hence, as of 1975 in the central Negev, Ḥasan as-Zinayd of the ʿAzāzma Muḥammadiyyīn, almost all of whose clan had moved to Jordan, "placed the coin" with his in-laws, the Ameiṭil of the ʿAzāzma ʿAṣiyāt (Case 55).[99]

The blood-fine group arrangement exists in order to relieve the individual member groups, especially the small families, of the danger of incurring fines for bloodshed or wounds that they may find difficult or impossible to defray.

*The individual member of this group is called a "placer of the coin" (*ḥaṭṭāṭ al-girsh*) or a "coin blood-member"(*damawī girsh*). When referring to such an individual, a Bedouin will simply say "my blood kin"(*damawiyyī*), as distinguished from a full member of his clan, whom he will call a "member of my clan" (*khamstī*) or, more directly, "my paternal cousin" (*walad ʿammī*).

Such relief fortifies each original party's confidence while pursuing its interests and rights, secure in the knowledge that it can endure any financial damages that might ensue. This advantage was captured in a line of light verse recited during a festive dance in Sinai: "Strike the shirker from justice with a sword, and the blood-fine group will pay for the reconciliation" (*uḍrub al-ʿāyib bi-s-seif—wa-ṭ-ṭība ʿa-d-damawiyya*).[100] Similarly, as in a clan, fines accruing to any member of the blood-fine group are shared by all the others, whatever their clan of origin.

Unlike full members in a clan, however, the people bound by this agreement of "placing the coin and gaining the coin" (*ḥaṭāṭ girsh ū-akāl girsh*) are not subject to any physical vengeance for the misdeeds of fellow members who are not of their specific clan; nor do they seek revenge for attacks against such unrelated persons. Accordingly, some Bedouin term these two categories differently, the larger being the "coin blood-fine group" (*damawiyyit girsh*) and the smaller, actual clan, the "stick blood-fine group" (*damawiyyit ʿaṣa*).*

To ensure the maintenance of this distinction, the law requires Bedouin entering a blood-fine-group arrangement to do so before witnesses, one of whom will serve as a paid witness (*marḍawī*; lit. "satisfied by payment") to whom the members will have recourse in the event of disputes over their rights and obligations. For example, if people have been fellow members in a blood-fine group for a long while, others may imagine them to be of one clan and hold them jointly liable to retaliation for physical violations perpetrated by a person of another clan. Hence, a *marḍawī* who was present at the formation of a specific blood-fine group will have to affirm that no physical punitive liabilities mistakenly pertain to those members, because they do not belong to the specific clan that perpetrated the assault in question. On the other hand, when the member of a blood-fine group defaults in "placing the coin" for fines incurred, it will be the duty of a *marḍawī* to reconfirm his membership so that his fellow members in the blood-fine group can take legal recourse; the law empowers them to impound the property of a recalcitrant payer, just as with similar default in an individual clan. By the same token, the disaffiliation from a blood-fine group must also be announced in the presence of witnesses to avoid claiming its obligations from someone that has quit. Unlike the clan, however, members of a blood-fine group are entitled to disaffiliate at will, providing they owe no outstanding debts to the others.

Similar to the workings of a clan, responsibility for the discharge of any

*Oral communication from Swaylim Sulaymān Abū Bilayya of the ʿAzāzma Saraḥīn, May 17, 1995. Although Stewart (*Texts*, vol. 1, chs. 3 and 4) uses "blood money group" instead of "clan" for *khamsa*, his intention is evident from the obligations he quotes for affiliation with a *khamsa*; these include seeking and being subject to revenge (pp. 56–57, 98).

penalties ensuing from one member's violation of a fellow member belonging to a different part of the blood-fine group will be singly borne by the violator's clan alone. In late 1997 in southeast Sinai, where, as noted above, five of the clans of the Tarabīn Ḥasāblah tribe form one large blood-fine group, one of them, the Munāṣra clan, was independently supposed to pay the blood-price when one of its members, Salmān Zaydān, killed ʿĀyid ʿAṭeiwī of the ʿAlōwna clan, also part of the same blood-fine group (Case 52). This obligation became hypothetical when the case was ultimately settled by an act of blood-revenge in 2001.[101] By contrast to the clan, members of a blood-fine group, while mutually responsible for paying fines for bloodshed or wounds, are not obligated to make good on any other losses caused by a culprit of their ranks not belonging to their specific clan.

CONTEXTS FOR SUPPORTING PEOPLE OUTSIDE ONE'S CLAN IN CONFLICT

Occasionally Bedouin will support others not of their clan in conflict, on the basis of either tribal solidarity (*ʿaṣabiyya*) or manly virtue (*murūwa*). The first grounds, *ʿaṣabiyya*, has always been renowned among Arab nomads, mainly impelling a Bedouin to side with people more closely related to him against people more remotely related, as expressed by the maxim, "I and my brother will oppose our paternal cousin, and I and my paternal cousin will oppose the rest" (*āna w-akhūwī ʿal ibn ʿammī—w-āna w-ibn ʿammī ʿal al-gharīb*).[102]

The outer limit of binding tribal solidarity is one's confederation (*gabīla* or *ṣaff*), which is the unit responsible for preserving the territory in which all its members have access to pasture and water.* In descending order of size, the subgroups within a confederation to which any member will concurrently belong are as follows: a sub-confederation and its sub-sections (formed by generational fission); a tribe; a sub-tribe and its sub-sections; and a clan. Schematically, a Bedouin of the Tarabīn Munāṣra clan in southeast Sinai in 1980, for example, would simultaneously belong to the following groups:

Confederation: Tarabīn
Sub-confederation: Nabaʿāt (one sub-confederation out of three)
Secondary sub-confederation: Ḥasāblah (one secondary sub-confederation out of three)
Tertiary sub-confederation: Muṭāwʿa (one tertiary sub-confederation out of two)

*For the structure of Bedouin society in the Negev, see Marx, *Bedouin of the Negev*, pp. 10–11 and passim. The terms for confederation, *gabīla* and *ṣaff*, denote a battle line or a row respectively, indicating the classical Bedouin form of battle, with which lands were conquered and defended by those who rallied to the confederation banner.

Tribe: Ḥasāblah (which embraces the Muṭāwʿa, who live in southeast Sinai)
Sub-tribe: Owlād ʿIshaysh (one sub-tribe out of two)
Secondary sub-tribe: ʿAreiḍa (one secondary sub-tribe out of two)
Clan : Munāṣra (one clan out of four).[103]

According to *ʿaṣabiyya*, the Munāṣra will support any of the other two clans in the ʿAreiḍa secondary sub-tribe against anyone in the other sub-tribe of the Owlād ʿIshaysh; any of the Owlād ʿIshaysh against anyone in the other sub-tribe of the Ḥasāblah tribe; any of the Ḥasāblah tribe against anyone in the other two tribes of the Muṭāwʿa tertiary sub-confederation not living in south-eastern Sinai; any of the Muṭāwʿa against anyone in the other sub-group of the Ḥasāblah secondary sub-confederation; any of the Ḥasāblah against anyone in the other two sub-groups of the Nabaʿāt; any of the Nabaʿāt against anyone in the other two main sub-confederations of the Tarabīn; and, finally, anyone in the Tarabīn against anyone of a different confederation.

Occasionally, if rarely, sentiments of *ʿaṣabiyya* may transcend the confederation and extend to the Bedouin as a people, over and against settled populations. In 1981, for example, Ḥammād Abū Rubayʿa, a Bedouin chief from the Negev in the south of Israel and a member of the Israeli Knesset, was shot dead by the sons of a Druze leader, Jabr al-Muʿādī, who was contesting the Bedouin's Knesset seat (Case 70). The next day, in the long mourning tent set up by the deceased man's clan, a large delegation of Bedouin from the Galilee, in the north of Israel, appeared, demonstratively shouting, "Your destiny is ours!" (*maṣīrna wāḥad*)—that is, "We are willing to fight alongside you." Although the Bedouin from the north of Israel are entirely unrelated to those in the south (their ancestors having emigrated from the Syrian desert, whereas those of the southerners came from the Arabian peninsula), their anger at so great a violation of a Bedouin leader by traditional enemies, such as the sedentary Druze of the Galilee, gave rise to this expression of support based on common Bedouin identity, even if it was only sentimental.*

Mazramiyya

One form of *ʿaṣabiyya* support is called *mazramiyya*, which literally means "rallying as if in a clan."* *Mazramiyya* may take place in support of a relatively closely related group against others who are inside or outside the

*Expressions of Bedouin enmity toward the Druze can also be heard in Syria (see Musil, *Arabia Deserta*, pp. 439–40).

**Mazramiyya* (also *zaram* or *zarma* as a noun) derives from the Bedouin verb *zaram* (*yizram*): to behave like a *zalama*, which in Bedouin parlance is a member of one's clan. Hence, one could say, "He supported me [as if he were in my clan]" (*hū zaram ʿendī*; *hū zaram lī*). We have here an example of the 'l' and 'r' interchanging in Arabic.

same tribal confederation. The operation of the ʿ*aṣabiyya* principle in *mazramiyya* may be seen through two intra-confederation conflicts that took place within the ʿAzāzma confederation of the central Negev in the 1970s. In 1973 ʿOwda Sulaymān as-Zanūn, the leader of the Zanūn clan of the ʿAzāzma Saraḥīn tribe, took a stand in support of a fellow Sirḥānī from a different clan, Sālim ʿAtayyig al-Khiraynig, after the latter's unmarried daughter was slandered as being pregnant by Sālim ʿOwda aṭ-Ṭimṭāwī of a different ʿAzāzma tribe, the ʿAṣiyāt (Case 71).[104] In 1974 we again find ʿOwda Zanūn taking sides in a conflict, this time, however, within his own Saraḥīn tribe. Here he was supporting Ḥimayd as-Saddān against Jumʿa ar-Rimāg when the former's daughter threw a rock and injured the latter's son for allegedly approaching her improperly (Case 43). The reason for Zanūn's support of Saddān was that he was more closely related to him than to Rimāg. Although all three parties belonged to the same tribe, Zanūn and Saddān also belonged to the tribal subsection, the ʿAyāl Swaylim, and Saddān belonged to the ʿOwdāt clan, from which the Zanūn had disaffiliated only three generations before. By contrast, the Rimāg were a clan in a completely different sub-section of the Saraḥīn tribe, the Khawāṭra.[105]

In the case of calculated (as opposed to spontaneous) *mazramiyya* support, the law determines that liability for wounds or homicide caused by the supporting parties rests upon them. Although there is a Bedouin sentiment that "a sense of decency" (*ḥasāsiyya*) obliges the supported party (called the "reason" [*sabab*]—that is, the reason for the support) to "wash the other" (*yighassil ʿalayh*) of responsibility and bear the indemnity, no Bedouin judge will hold the supported party legally liable. Hence, while the threat to use violence is a necessary component in the support of a party to a conflict, a supporting group must consider that using physical force may expose it to vengeance and fines. Its members might talk tough when representing the cause of their adopted ally, or, for example, they might demonstratively cease to greet their new adversaries in the market. But they will generally try to draw the line at that. We have an example from the Saddān-Rimāg clash of 1974, cited above (Case 43), when a clan called Dilīaʿ, supporting the Rimāg, joined in an armed pursuit of members of the Saddān family, deeming the latter and the rest of their ʿOwdāt clan too small and weak to retaliate. However, when the populous (thirty men) Zanūn clan declared its readiness "to similarly act as a clan" (that is, use physical violence) in support of the ʿOwdāt, the new scope of the possible danger awaiting the Dilīaʿ clansmen convinced them that henceforth it was best to refrain from violence on behalf of the Rimāg.

The above instance also instructs us about the dynamics of *mazramiyya*. First, the Dilīaʿ, angry over the contentious and imperious behavior of Ḥimayd as-Saddān in their common social environment, decided to support the Rimāg (a fellow clan in the Khawāṭra sub-section of the Saraḥīn tribe), and the Dilīaʿ clansmen were even willing to use violence against Saddān so as to teach him a lesson in humility. The lesser commitment of *mazramiyya* as compared to that of membership in a clan, however, became clear when the danger of armed conflict with the Zanūn emerged, causing the Dilīaʿ to reduce their obligation to the Rimāg to nonviolent measures. Second, the Zanūn, prior to the Saddān-Rimāg conflict, were also angry with Ḥimayd as-Saddān for the same reasons that aroused the anger of the Dilīaʿ with him and were in actual conflict with him over a women's brawl in which Saddān's sister had been struck (Case 14). Consequently they were initially not intending to support him in this quarrel. However, upon learning that the Dilīaʿ, who were not an original party to the Saddān-Rimāg conflict, had resorted to force against Saddān, they rallied to his defense on the basis of the same primordial instincts of tribal solidarity for the sake of security that motivate members of the same clan. In the context of *ʿaṣabiyya*, such instincts oblige one group to subordinate its anger toward another once the latter's safety is threatened by a third, more distantly related (or nonrelated) group. After the threat is raised, however, the first group can resume its conflict with the second, as the Zanūn subsequently did with Ḥimayd as-Saddān in the aforementioned case concerning blows between the latter's sister and women of the Zanūn clan.

Mazramiyya can also be spontaneous, as in the case of someone suddenly seeing a relatively closely related person being harassed by more distantly related (or nonrelated) people and coming to his aid. Even seeing property of more kindred people threatened by a less kindred person can evoke *mazramiyya*. In the 1940s ʿAyyāda Sulaymān Abū Bilayya of the ʿAyāl Swaylim section of the ʿAzāzma Saraḥīn tribe was watering his camels at the well named Bīr Ḥafīr, in the central Negev, when he saw a shepherd called Abū-l-Mannāʿ, belonging to the Janabīb tribe of the Ẓullām confederation, strike an unattended she-camel with a rope, so hard that the camel collapsed into the watering trough (Case 72). Noting that the camel bore the Saraḥīn camel brand (*wasm*), Abū Bilayya doubled his own rope and beat the shepherd badly, saying, "How dare you strike a camel bearing the Saraḥīn brand!" When a trial over the matter was ultimately held, the camel's owner, called Abū Ḥuwayḥī, of the ʿAyāl Silmī section of the Saraḥīn, came forward and "washed" Abū Bilayya of the need to pay the fines imposed for the wounds he had caused. He declared to the judge, "It is I who caused Abū-l-Mannāʿ his wounds. Leave Abū Bilayya out of it! He has protected my she-camel 'as if we were from the same clan' (*hū zirim ʿend nāgtī*)." Although they came from different sections of the ʿAzāzma Saraḥīn tribe, Abū Bilayya had risen to the defense of Abū Ḥuwayḥī against someone from a totally different confederation, the Ẓullām.[106]

War between Confederations (*Ṣaff Yigūm ʿa Ṣaff*)

Just as *mazramiyya* embodies the tribal sentiment of helping those more closely related against a group more distantly related, usually within the context of a single tribal confederation, there is a similar *ʿaṣabiyya* sentiment to support fellow confederates against antagonists from another confederation. This support is called "confederation rising against confederation" (*ṣaff yigūm ʿa ṣaff*) and is tantamount to war between two confederations in their entirety. Such wars purportedly stem from disputes concerning "land and women" (*arḍ ū-ʿarḍ*).

Land As a confederation is primarily a territorial unit that guarantees its members access to the water sources and pasturelands in the territory it controls, the preservation of the integrity of its common territory is what binds its component tribes together in membership. Accordingly, whenever a group belonging to confederation "A" threatens the territory inhabited by any tribe of confederation "B," it is the duty of all the other component tribes of confederation "B" to defend that land.

I experienced this confederal imperative in the spring of 1974, when I met a chief of the Ḥasāblah tribe of the Tarabīn confederation of Sinai in the small Mediterranean town of El-ʿArīsh (Case 73). The chief, Sulaymān Ibn Jāzī, invited me to join him at the festivities to be held that day for members of another Tarabīn tribe, the Nadayāt, who had just returned from performing the pilgrimage to Mecca. We traveled by jeep to the lands of the Nadayāt, some one hundred kilometers to the south, just beyond a large mountain in northeast Sinai called Jabal Ḥalāl. Indeed, the Nadayāt were the only Tarabīn Bedouin of northeast Sinai that lived south of this mountain, all the others of that region living to its north.* Hence, the neighbors of the Nadayāt were a number of tribes belonging to a different confederation, the Tiyāha, whose lands stretched from there southward to central Sinai.

The festivities consisted mainly of men sitting decorously along the length of the very long black guest tent and being served platters of mutton and rice. All the while we were there, I was anticipating the arrival of one particular guest, a venerable and respected elder of the Tiyāha, Muṣliḥ Sālim Ibn ʿĀmir, who camped just a few kilometers to the south and whom I had known to enjoy

*The powerful Tarabīn possessed four different regions in the Sinai peninsula: the northeast plain north of Jabal Ḥalāl, the Jabal Maghāra area in west-central Sinai, the northern half of the southeastern coastal area, and the northern part of the southwestern coastal area, near Jabal Rāḥa.

close neighborly relations with the Nadayāt. When I finally asked the hosts why he was not present, they diffidently replied that they did not know. When, therefore, the festivities ended without Ibn ʿĀmir's appearance, I suggested to my companion, Shaykh Ibn Jāzī, that we stop off at Ibn ʿĀmir's encampment and visit him before returning to El-ʿArīsh. The chief at first demurred, claiming it was late and the road back was long, but, in light of my urging, he finally acceded.

When, however, we arrived and were shown into Ibn ʿĀmir's tent, the welcome was not hearty, as previous visits had led me to expect, but coldly formal. Without the leaders' exchanging words other than the perfunctory greetings, we drank the coffee that Ibn ʿĀmir prepared for us and left.

On the road, I expressed my surprise over our chilly reception. How often I had heard Ibn ʿĀmir express his affection for Ibn Jāzī and praise his generosity. Only months before, he had related how the chief had found him stranded in El-ʿArīsh after nightfall and hired a car to take him back to his distant desert encampment. Ibn Jāzī too was always mindful to address Ibn ʿĀmir respectfully as "maternal uncle" (*khāl*), evoking the memory of the Jawāziya woman of a previous generation who had been married to one of Ibn ʿĀmir's paternal forbears.

Finally, the chief explained. "Our relations with the Tiyāha have been severed. They have been claiming possession of some of the lands that the Nadayāt cultivate, and I, as a Turbānī, a member of the Tarabīn, am forbidden to socialize with them. We are in a state of war. I have nothing personal against Muṣliḥ Ibn ʿĀmir. To the contrary, I respect and love him; he is my maternal uncle. And for that reason, I deigned to drink his coffee, although, in truth, that was a great deviation from our conventions, for which all the Tarabīn would rebuke me." "How extensive is the area under dispute?" I asked. "Less than a hundred acres," he said, and noticing my wonder, added, "But it is Tarabīn land, and when it comes to land, we must all stick together." I recalled that although the Jawāzī and the Nadayāt tribes were both Tarabīn, even belonging to the same sub-confederation of tribes called the Nabaʿāt, their lineages must have split at least ten generations, or three hundred years, before: the Jawāzī were the descendants of one of the sons of Nabaʿ, Ḥasaballah, and the Nadayāt were descended from another son, Shibayth. Three hundred years and three hundred miles separated the two tribes, but all of that was as nothing when it came to confederation land—even a spot of land that was less than a hundred acres, out of a total confederal acreage of many millions.

Almost ninety years before, in 1887, this phenomenon had occurred in reverse (Case 74). By that date, the Tarabīn in the Negev had been allies of the Tiyāha Ḥukūk tribes in a war against other of the Tiyāha tribes, whom they finally subdued after twelve years of fighting.[107] When, however, the Tarabīn prodded the Ḥukūk leader, Fiheid al-Huzayyil, to divide up the lands of the defeated Tiyāha tribes with them, Huzayyil, responding to the confederation instinct, balked, telling his erstwhile allies that their northern border was Wādī Shallāla and that all lands to the north of it must remain with the Tiyāha.[108]

Women The sexual inviolability of its women being so vital to the honor of a Bedouin group, it affects those at all levels of tribal organization, from the clan up to the confederation, each of which will deal with the violator in accordance with its own level. When the perpetrator of such a violation is a man from a different confederation, his violation is taken as an affront to the honor of the woman's entire confederation and hence becomes the common concern of all the confederation's component parts. Initially the problem must be addressed at the level of the clan to which the woman belongs. If, however, the clan can obtain no justice on its own, it becomes an all-confederation matter.

In west-central Sinai in 1981, for example, when a lad of the Tarabīn confederation absconded with a girl of the Tiyāha confederation and refused to return her, the entire Tiyāha, led in this case by their paramount chief, ʿĪd Muṣliḥ Ibn ʿĀmir, rallied to the cause and succeeded in convening a trial of honor (Case 20). However, when the judge gave them no satisfaction, deeming the girl's family partly responsible for her errancy, the danger of inter-confederation war arose. In their efforts to avert it, several chiefs of the Tarabīn called upon their fellow confederate, ʿAnayz Abū Sālim al-ʿUrḍī, a poet, and asked him to compose a poem that might mollify his friend, Ibn ʿĀmir, and foster a reconciliation with all the Tiyāha. Although belonging to a totally different section of the Tarabīn from the absconder, ʿUrḍī acceded to their request, impelled by feelings of confederal loyalty and responsibility.[109]

Again, in 1983 the daughter of Ḥimayd as-Saddān of the Saraḥīn tribe of the ʿAzāzma confederation was consensually abducted by Ḥasan al-Atayyim of his own ʿAzāzma Saraḥīn tribe, who entrusted her to the tent of ʿAbdallah Muʿattig al-Wajj of the Ẓullām Janabīb tribe, where her moral propriety would be maintained (Case 16). According to the rules of abduction that are valid among the Saraḥīn, the man in whose tent the girl has found shelter must either seek her father's permission for her marriage or bring the girl back to her father's tent within three days, pending further deliberation of the abduction and the penalties resulting from it. Unwilling to return the girl to her father, who had objected to the marriage, Wajj instead sent notables of three large tribes of the Ẓullām confederation—including ʿOwda Abū Rāghib and Chief Muḥammad Abū Graynāt—who devised ways of procrastinating and forestalling the girl's return. Thereupon, Saddān asked help (*ankha*) from leading figures in the ʿAzāzma confederation—the paramount chief, ʿOwda Abū Muʿammar; the main judge, Imsallam Abū Jaddūaʿ; and Sulaymān ad-Dinfīrī—claiming that "a confederation was rising against a confederation." These leaders accordingly warned the Ẓullām of imminent war unless they agreed to hold a trial of honor that would give Saddān justice. Reflecting the tribal attitude, Saddān's spokesman at the trial, Imsallam Abū Jaddūaʿ, although from a totally different tribe in his confederation, repeatedly referred to Saddān as "my paternal cousin" (*ibn ʿammī*), thus signaling that the lines of conflict had been drawn between the ʿAzāzma and the Ẓullām, as if each was that basic unit of conflict, a clan.[110]

Aid in Taking Revenge for Homicide (*Nashr ad-Damm*)

Just as an entire confederation might feel obliged to rally behind a fellow member whose woman had been violated or a fellow confederate whose possession of land had been threatened by someone from another confederation, both in the context of "a confederation rising against a confederation," the Bedouin also have a legal context for aiding a fellow confederate who is unable to take revenge for the murder of a person of his clan by someone of another confederation. This context is called "spreading the blood" (*nashr ad-damm*). Taking revenge on a murderer from a different confederation is viewed as more urgent than revenge for murder within the same confederation, owing to the pride associated with *ʿaṣabiyya*.

In many such cases, the homicide in question will have been perpetrated by a clan from a neighboring confederation, whose evasive behavior will be seen as insolent and insulting, not just to the victim's clan but to his confederation as a whole. For example, that clan may refuse to acknowledge its guilt in the murder or refuse to flee (*yijlū*) from the presence of its victim's kin, one of the greatest insults of all. Unlike *ṣaff yigūm ʿa ṣaff*, however, "spreading the blood" does not entail the enlistment of the entire confederation but only a section, such as a tribe, a tribal sub-section, or another clan. Solidarity, again, is the reason that such a group might be impelled to gather the "spread blood" of another—sharing common dread of the ignominy that derives from another confederation's deigning to violate the rights of one of the members of one's own with impunity. It is thus understood that the avengers are not primarily acting on behalf of the actual victims but on behalf of their common group, whether it is the confederation, tribe, or sub-section. Accordingly, if the blood of the ʿOwdāt clan "is spread" upon the entire ʿAzāzma Saraḥīn tribe (to whom it belongs) and the tribe manages to end the conflict by making the homicides pay blood-money, the payment, by law, will be distributed among all members of the Saraḥīn.

In the event of such inter-confederation murder, the clansmen of the victim, too weak to retaliate themselves, will come to a larger group from their confederation and request help in seeking revenge. Naturally, the murder victim's clansmen will be reluctant to take this step, as it is tantamount to a confession of weakness, which no clan is keen to make. Furthermore, owing to the gravity and danger involved in seeking revenge, people are not quick to ask others to undertake it for them. This is especially so if the circumstances surrounding the murder are not clearly honorable. For example, following the murder of Fiheid Slaym Ibn Jāzī of the Tarabīn Ḥasāblah tribe by someone of the Aḥeiwāt Karādma in southeast Sinai in 1979, his clan, although too small and weak to take revenge, refrained from "spreading the blood" to the rest of the Ḥasāblah tribe, to which it belonged, although thirty years would elapse without its taking revenge (at the time of this writing) (Case 75). Fiheid Slaym Ibn Jāzī was murdered while sleeping in the proximity of an Aḥeiwiyya girl. Although all the Tarabīn ostensibly subscribed to the view that the actual murder was unjustified, the possibility that Ibn Jāzī had violated her honor was sufficiently dishonorable to deter his clansmen from involving fellow tribesmen in his revenge by "spreading their blood."[111]

Whenever spilled blood is spread, however, it is necessary to ensure that the consequent act of revenge is legal. First, the "spreading" must be public, made in a council (*majlis*) of Bedouin, who witness that "the blood has been spread" (*ad-damm manshūr*) to such and such a group. This is to prevent the original killer(s) from deeming the revenge a fresh act of murder, itself warranting a separate act of revenge against the clan of the avengers, rather than a closing of accounts. A guarantor will also be present to guarantee any agreements that might be made between the murder victim's clansmen and the avengers, such as the former agreeing to join the latter's clan once retaliation has been taken or retribution gained.

The traditional method of eliciting a proxy avenger is for the leader of the victim's clan to convoke a council where he says either, "I spread my blood upon . . ." (*āna nāshir dammī ila*) or "My blood is spread upon . . ." (*dammī manshūr ila*) and then names the group. Compliance with the request, as indicated above, is not mandatory. If, however, the petitioned group accedes, it traditionally utters responses such as, "We welcome you as you are! We shall bring you revenge and expel your neighbor" (*marḥaba bi-ʿuyūnak — injīb ath-thār wi-nraḥḥil al-jār*). The leader of the declared avengers will then proceed to the killers or send them a message to announce his group's legal intervention in the blood-feud and serve them warning, as traditionally expressed in the following rhyming formula:

Beware, you are pursued and your heels are black.
(*Ithrāk inti maṭrūd ū-kuʿūbak sūd*)
Gather your livestock and people.
(*tilimm ṭurāfak ū-ḥurāfak*)
You have three days and a third for fleeing and making tracks.
(*maʿak thilātht iyyām ū-thilth; muharribāt musarribāt*)
I am your pursuer.
(*w-āna ṭarrādak*).[112]

As proclaimed, the new avengers must then wait three and a third days before attacking in order to give the murderers, who had expected no assault from this quarter, a chance to flee. A failure to observe this period of grace and the obligation to warn the threatened party would disqualify any resultant act of revenge, rendering it a simple act of murder. Alternatively, if the guilty clan is sufficiently intimidated by the prospect of a more powerful group now seeking revenge, it may be impelled to achieve reconciliation through the payment of blood-money, normally by way of mediation.

Defense of a Companion (*Rafīg al-Janb*)

The Bedouin value of manly virtue, or *murūwa*, manifests itself in the readiness to extend protection to an endangered person. Accordingly, it may lead one man to try to defend another who has been attacked, especially if they are companions. This specific context of defending someone not of one's clan, or even confederation, who is suddenly endangered is called "the companion alongside" (*rafīg al-janb*). Although there is no legal imperative to try and defend a beleaguered companion, Bedouin consider the failure to do so a manifestation of cowardice and bad character, the opposite of manly virtue. The moral directive, expressed in a maxim, is, "A companion delivers his companion" (*rafīg yiwaṣṣil rafīg*).[113]

As in *mazramiyya*, there is also a moral obligation for the person attacked (lit. "the reason" [*sabab*])—namely, to defray all fines and damages resulting from wounds or bloodshed that the "companion alongside," or defender, inflicts. The expression is, "He is washing [the defender] clean" (*hū biyghassil ʿalayh*). The law, however, distinguishes between two conditions. If the defender has entered the fray on his own initiative, the obligation to relieve him of the consequences may be moral but not legal. The person who benefited from the defense can claim that he did not require it, and the court must uphold him.

The law, however, does enforce this obligation in the event that the person assailed has actually called upon (*ankha*) the defender to act, even if a judge stops short at homicide. In the event that the defender kills the attacker, the responsibility remains with him, and he and his clan become subject to revenge or blood-payment. No legal obligation to absolve him devolves upon the defended party. Only social pressure may compel him to comply.

In late 1967, for example, such circumstances arose within the ʿAzāzma confederation in eastern Sinai (Case 76):

> It began when a member of the Ṣubḥiyyīn tribe, Muḥammad al-Angar, stole a rifle from a member of the Saraḥīn tribe, Shtaywī al-Braym. On a further occasion, when Braym was in the company of Salāma al-Ḥammādī, also of the Saraḥīn but a different clan, he ran into Angar bearing his rifle and tried to take it from him. Angar, a solidly built man, extricated himself from Braym, who cried out to his companion, saying, "He'll kill me, Salāma. Shoot him!" Thereupon, Ḥammādī shot and killed Angar and fled from vengeance all the way to Jordan. Eventually, when a reconciliation based on blood-payment was arranged through mediation, Braym refused to participate in the payment, asserting that he did not mean, nor ask, for Ḥammādī to kill Angar but merely to shoot and wound him. Only after heavy social intervention, based on the fact that Ḥammādī had willingly complied with Braym's specific request for help, did Braym agree to pay a part of the blood-price.[114]

Rafīg al-janb also pertains to persons sitting together in a tent, whether guest or host. Two widespread Bedouin stories bear this out. One tells of a judge who staged a fake raid on his camel herds in order to test the relative abilities of two wounded petitioners to defend themselves (Case 77). They were from different tribes that had been at war but had come to him for a judgment as to which was entitled to greater compensation, the one with a blinded eye or the other with a severed arm. When the call came that the camels had been raided, the two men rallied with the chief's people to pursue the raiders. The one-eyed man saddled his camel with ease and rode off, whereas the amputee could barely strap his saddle on, therefore receiving the larger award from the judge. (In no telling of the story did any reciter consider the rallying of the guests to the aid of their host as anything but natural.)[115]

The other story indicates that hosts too will seek to defend their guests. Members of the Tarabīn Wuḥeidāt tribe in the Negev tell of ancestral tribesmen who saw a fugitive from the Turkish police come to their encampment and dash for the chief's tent (Case 78). When the police arrived, the chief took his rifle and went out to meet them. They demanded to enter the tent and apprehend the culprit. The chief blocked their way, and when they began to push him aside, he shot. It was clear he was going to do battle for his guest.[116]

Benefaction (*Ḥisnī*)

Another form of manly virtue is for a Bedouin to requite a great benefaction conferred on him or on one of his ancestors in an hour of danger or need by aiding the benefactor when he is in dire need. Such a benefaction, or *ḥisnī* (*ḥasana* in Classical Arabic), performed by a person normally from a different tribal confederation, may consist of saving someone's life, extending him crucial financial aid, recovering his pillaged camels, or even burying someone's dead clansman found in the desert.[117] For example, an act of benefaction that "saved his life" was declared in the central Negev in the eighteenth century by a man called Sālim al-ʿĀgir (Sālim the Impotent) (Case 167). It was a gesture of gratitude to camel owners who took him captive when he was raiding their herd. By way of warning him and his people of the ʿUmrān confederation of Transjordan not to raid them again, ʿĀgir's captors, of the Ẓullām Janabīb tribe, cauterized him from head to toe on his front and back. When they finally released him to return to his tribe, he was able to impregnate both his wives, who bore him sons. Attributing this turn in fortune, which saved his line from extinction, to the cauterization he had endured, ʿĀgir undertook a *ḥisnī* obligation, characteristically on behalf of his clan and its descendants to the fifth generation, never again to raid the Abū Ṭrayfāt clan and its descendants to the fifth generation and to guarantee the return of its camels if pillaged by any other clan of the ʿUmrān.[118]

In the seventeenth century a man called Abū Khashshān of the Suwārka confederation of northeast Sinai owed a *ḥisnī* obligation to a fellow tribesman, a Manīaʿ, who had fled and taken refuge among the Bilī confederation in Arabia after killing his cousin in a squabble (Case 50). While Manīaʿ was with the Bilī, the latter carried out a raid upon the distant camels of Abū Khashshān. Recognizing the camels by their brand mark, Manīaʿ prevailed upon his protectors to take them back, asking them also to stress that the herd was released owing to his efforts. Abū Khashshān thereupon had the Bilī people bear witness that he considered Manīaʿ his *ḥisnā*, or benefactor. He then requited him by successfully securing him a pardon from the murder victim's brother, which enabled Manīaʿ to return home, where he and his wife of the Bilī became the forebears of several sections of today's Suwārka.[119]

In the nineteenth century a man of the Arabian Maʿāza confederation, whose impounded camel had once been ransomed from a merchant in Egypt by a man called Imsallam al-Ḥājj of the Tarabīn Ḥasāblah of southeast Sinai, repaid his debt of gratitude, a year later, by personally releasing al-Ḥājj's camels when his own tribesmen raided the herd (Case 162).[120] Similarly, in the early twentieth century, people of the Tarabin Ḥasāblah fulfilled a *ḥisnī* obligation owed to a clan of the ʿUmrān of northwestern Arabia by identifying the murderer of an ʿUmrān clansman (the murderer had come to Sinai to sell goats among the Bedouin of the Muzayna confederation), thereby enabling the ʿUmrān to take revenge (Case 110).[121]

The above examples are all of benefaction being requited out of voluntary manly virtue, as is often the case. Bedouin law applies to the practice of *ḥisnī* only when benefactors have specifically asked a former "recipient of their benefaction" (*muḥsin*) to help them and are met by refusal, deliberate delay, or inexcusable ineffectiveness. In such a case, they are entitled to "blacken" his reputation in the various ways cited in chapter 2. However, the law stipulates that before blackening him, they must produce witnesses that *ḥisnī* was declared in their favor at the time of the benefaction, as well as eye witnesses to testify that the benefactors indeed asked the recipients to extend them aid.

4

The Role of Private Violence in Achieving Justice

Private Violence to Protect the Individual

As already seen, Bedouin, in the absence of law-enforcement agencies to wield the threat of government-sanctioned force, were obliged throughout history to find their own ways of protecting the individuals who comprised their society and deterring potential violators of the rights of others. One of their solutions was to substitute the threat of their own violence for that of governments in settled societies. Thus Bedouin law empowered the victims of violation to use force to rectify their losses. For most offenses against the rights of an individual or group, however, the law sanctions the use of force as a last resort to be used only when justice has been denied through peaceful means.

ALLOWED VIOLENCE AS A FIRST RESORT

The law allows force to be wielded as a first resort for rectifying two sorts of violations: murder and certain sexual violations of what non-Bedouin would call "women's honor." The legal maxim "Revenge does not require judicial consent" (*ad-damm — mā bih gōm ū-gaʿada*; lit. "going to sit before a judge") empowers Bedouin to act directly when their clan has suffered from murder. In their view, the reason for this primacy of violence is that the sacredness of life, as well as the sexual inviolability of women, must be crystal clear.

Indeed, the law, in order to further deter potential murderers and sexual violators, augments vengeance for these violations with two fearsome components that militate toward this end: scope and ruthlessness.

Vengeance for Murder

Owing to the components of scope and ruthlessness, the dread of committing murder is deep among Bedouin. They say, "Murder is like a witch's cave" (*ad-damm juḥur ghūla*)—that is, easy to enter but impossible to exit. For a Bedouin who might nonetheless feel entitled to kill, a widespread proverb cautions to "Sleep with regret, but not with murder" (*nām ʿal an-nadam wala tinām ʿala damm*).[1]

Deterrence through Scope To ensure that the threat of revenge for murder is daunting, Bedouin law broadens the circle of those who can punish and be punished. "Vengeance for murder" (*thār*) is not confined to the offender alone, but extends to his entire clan, as noted in chapter 3. If "A" violates "B," it is not just "A" but "A" 's whole clan that is liable for punishment, as dispensed not just by "B" but by anyone in "B" 's clan. The Bedouin legal maxim states, "One clan seeks vengeance from another" (*khamsa tuṭrud khamsa*). When we consider that one's fellow clan members are all those living males descended from the great-great-grandfather of the youngest generation, we can begin to visualize the deterrence that is implicit (see table 4.1).

Let us assume that the number 22 in table 4.1 is a lad called Sulaymān, the youngest member of his clan, who is aged sixteen and "able to bear a sword" (*ḥammāl seif*). All the men of his grandfather's generation (generation 3) and all of their forebears are already dead. However, all those in his father's generation and in Sulaymān's generation (nos. 7–22) are still alive (that is, his father and his father's brother and cousins and Sulaymān and his own cousins of various degrees), so there are sixteen men in his clan. Accordingly, if someone murders Sulaymān, he is in fact violating Sulaymān's clan and opening a conflict with the fifteen remaining men, all of whom may strike him. Moreover, there is a double deterrent to scope. In keeping with the principle of collective responsibility, not only is the murderer of Sulaymān now vulnerable to attack by fifteen men, but so is each of the other men of his clan, however many or few they may be, thus subjecting them to a constant state of anxious alert.

In cases of murder, this anxiety is further compounded by what Bedouin call "exile" (*jalāya* or *majla*). To avoid retaliation, which is seldom averted through an early truce, all the clansmen of the murderer (unless special arrangements are made) pick up and flee, often for years, abandoning their possessions, grazing grounds, and perhaps fields sown with grain.[2] Moreover, these "people

Table 4.1. Sulaymān's Clansmen Avengers

<table>
<tr><td rowspan="2">Let us suppose that the "uniting forefather" (al-jidd al-jāmiʿ), who constitutes the first generation, had two sons (second generation).</td><td colspan="8">Uniting Forefather</td></tr>
<tr><td colspan="4">1</td><td colspan="4">2</td></tr>
<tr><td>For the sake of clarity, let us say that each of these sons, in turn, had two sons (nos. 3–6, comprising the third generation).</td><td colspan="2">3</td><td colspan="2">4</td><td colspan="2">5</td><td colspan="2">6</td></tr>
<tr><td>Each of these sons had one son (nos. 15–22, comprising the fifth generation.</td><td>7</td><td>8</td><td>9</td><td>10</td><td>11</td><td>12</td><td>13</td><td>14</td></tr>
<tr><td>Each of these sons had one son (nos. 15–22, comprising the fifth generation.</td><td>15</td><td>16</td><td>17</td><td>18</td><td>19</td><td>20</td><td>21</td><td>22</td></tr>
</table>

in exile" (*jalāwiya* or *majālī*) will be confronted with a life of almost constant humiliation, becoming dependent on the tribe among which they take refuge for the privileges of staying with it and using its lands for pasture and cultivation. Bedouin dread such dependence, as it curbs their ability to act emphatically on behalf of their own interests, particularly their physical and economic security. Although Bedouin law does not specifically require exile after murder and commands no penalty for its omission, the imperative nature of vengeance, in Bedouin eyes, impels all the liable persons to flee the wrath of the victim's group, as anticipated in the saying, "Murder compels migration" (*al-katl biy-waṣṣlak li-r-raḥīl*).[3] It is through these threats of blood-revenge and the discomforts to which a potential murderer thus exposes all his clansmen that Bedouin law seeks to deter potential murderers, thereby erecting a barrier to bloodshed.

Deterrence through Ruthlessness

The Primacy of Blood-Revenge over Other Values In order to augment the fearfulness of blood-revenge, Bedouin law holds that "Nothing obstructs vengeance for murder" (*ar-ragaba mā ʿanha*).[4] The law stringently maintains this principle though it clashes with otherwise cherished values in Bedouin society. It is formulated in the maxim "An avenger may be bold, by night or by day" (*ṣāḥib ad-damm jassār—layl ū-nahār*).[5] Accordingly, an avenger may even flout the hallowed values of sanctuary and protection that a Bedouin tent is supposed to afford anyone in danger. Although the law normally awards the owner of a tent heavy fines for an attack perpetrated against anyone within its bounds, it stops short of an act of blood-revenge against a guest or a ward. Under the law, the avenger would owe the tent owner nothing.*

Bedouin law also allows an avenger to choose any male of the murderer's clan that he himself deems fit to be the object of retaliation. The oral tradition recalls that when a now forgotten judge was asked, "Who suffices for vengeance?" he replied, "All males [born] of nine months" (*kull owlād tisʿa*).[6] Another anonymous judge stated the principle in metaphor as "Every bent-necked beast is a camel" (*kull āʿwaj ragaba jamal*).[7]

Accordingly, even considerations of defenselessness are set aside. By tradition, Bedouin are solicitous of persons they deem defenseless: children, cripples, helpless elders, and persons who are asleep. Seeking to protect such people, Bedouin law stipulates that any unprovoked wound inflicted upon them "is to be assessed and doubled" (*yingaṣṣ wi-yinthanī*). But for blood-revenge, the defenseless count as anyone else. The avenger's wish is the ultimate criterion. He may kill any male he wants. If he himself considers it revenge, the law is on his side. In reality, however, tradition and social values often serve to mitigate the harshness of legal stipulation so that Bedouin bent on revenge may choose not to exploit the law to its fullest. First, they may share the oft-expressed and natural ambition to wreak vengeance on an able-bodied man in order to do justice to the presumably able-bodied victim of homicide and derive commensurate satisfaction for themselves.

More important, if a main purpose of vengeance is to demonstrate the ability of any violated party to make its violators suffer, as noted above, the victims of homicide should be particularly keen to make the violators suffer through a show of manhood. It is thus incumbent upon them to prove their prowess by striking at someone that can resist. Taking revenge against defenseless persons might lead to a further weakening of their image, as society comes to doubt their strength. People might remind them that a "weak elder" (*gāṣir*) or handicapped cripple (*muʿawwag*; lit. "twisted") "cannot strike and must not be struck" (*lā yuḍrub wala yinḍarib*), as the rhyming maxim instructs.[8] They will certainly be mocked for killing "a tearful one" (*abū damʿa*), the term for a small child, or a boy still too weak to "bear a weapon" (*ḥammāl silāḥ*) or "wield a sword" (*ḍarrāb seif*). Yet, as stated above, the choice of victim is ultimately the avenger's right. The British explorer Wilfred Thesiger reported from southern Arabia how his traveling companions of the Rashīd

*That is the case unless a suspected avenger is warned off by the tent owner. If he then forces himself into the tent, he will owe the owner a heavy fine for violating the tent's sanctuary. In that sense, we have the maxim, "The tent saves lives [from vengeance]" (*al-bayt biysallim ar-rigāb*) (Bailey, *Proverbs*, p. 362). See chapter 6 for more on this legal issue.

confederation had, with no apparent misgivings, killed a fourteen-year-old boy of the Sār in revenge for one of their own lads, shot while raiding the Sār the previous day (Case 79).[9] It is also conceivable that, their victim being of a different and hostile tribal confederation, the restoration of respect for the Rashīds' own confederation was felt to be urgent, permitting them to surpass the limits of law and custom.

One particular source of scorn, however, is for what Bedouin consider the cowardly blood-revenge taken upon a man in his sleep, as such revenge is surely no sign of strength.* Tradition — as opposed to Bedouin law — exhorts an avenger to awaken the sleeping object of revenge and indicate his intention. At the turn of the century, the Czech explorer and scholar Alois Musil was told that the formula an avenger must utter, waking his victim, is "Do you remember that So-and-so is in your stomach?" (*inti dhākir innuh fulān fī baṭnak*) — that is, that you are responsible for his death.[10] Without witnesses, naturally, it is difficult to substantiate that a victim of revenge was indeed asleep when killed. His clansmen might try to establish a claim by indicating signs, such as the position of the body, a wound in the back, or the type of tracks found around the corpse.[11] Such "proof" might invite moral censure of the avengers, but under the law the act of revenge would be valid.

Another breach of values permitted in the case of blood-revenge pertains to the role of women. For reasons of demonstrating prowess, as discussed, Bedouin consider vengeance to be the business of men. Their sentiment is expressed in the sayings, "It is men who must pursue men" (*ṭard ar-rijāl li-rijāl*) and "A man does not charge a woman with his right" (*ar-rijāl mā bitḥāsib an-niswān fī ḥagghum*).[12] Accordingly, some consider it shameful for a woman to avenge a man, such as a brother, as this might arouse doubts about the martial ability of her male clansmen. Yet this sentiment notwithstanding, the law itself would view her act as closing the blood account. A past story of such an incident bequeathed to the Bedouin heritage the saying, "She has undertaken the duty of her menfolk" (*saddat masadd rijālha*) — that is, her vengeance has ended their need for revenge. While some Bedouin use this expression to ridicule the lack of manhood in a group, others might even hold a woman's act in high regard, seeing it as a reflection of her clansmen's mettle.[13] A member of the Tarabīn confederation in southern Sinai proudly related an act of revenge

*The Bedouin also believe that a sleeping person is unacceptable for vengeance because he is tantamount to dead. A Bedouin poet in the 1980s gave expression to this sentiment, bemoaning a case of vengeance perpetrated upon a fellow tribesman presumed to have been sleeping: "Those who die fighting, their dignity keep / Others lose life as though dead — in their sleep" (Bailey, *Poetry*, p. 78).

in which two women of his tribe participated by toppling a man who belonged to a group of raiders from Arabia, thus enabling a clansman to dispatch him in retaliation for one of their own men, whom the raiders had just slain.[14]

No Mitigating Circumstances Further to underline the ruthlessness of revenge, the law allows for no circumstances to mitigate the accountability and liability of a murderer unless his act was clearly an accident. Even self-defense does not acquit one. In 1816 in southern Sinai, for example, when Bedouin of the Owlād Saʿīd tribe, escorting the Swiss explorer J. L. Burckhardt, fought back night-time attackers of the ʿUmrān tribe and killed one of them, they knew, and greatly feared the fact, that they were liable to blood revenge (Case 80).[15] Similarly, even a highway robber or a thief making off with one's livestock cannot be killed with impunity.[16] In the 1940s in southern Arabia, the murdered lad for whom the guides of Wilfred Thesiger took revenge had just stolen eight camels from the killer's tribe (Case 79).[17]

By the same token, even a host defending an attacked guest and the honor of his tent, or a man seeking to protect an assaulted companion, had best be careful not to let his efforts get to homicide, lest he find himself and his clansmen subject to revenge. As we saw above, such was the case in late 1967, when Salāma al-Ḥammādī of the ʿAzāzma Saraḥīn in eastern Sinai responded to a call for help by his companion, Shitaywī al-Braym, and shot dead the man who was about to kill him (Case 76). Ḥammādī found himself subject to blood-revenge and had to flee to Jordan.[18] The same caution must be exercised in defending even the hallowed honor of an assaulted woman. Indeed, Bedouin law deems a nonrelated husband liable to retaliation for killing his wife's lover even though he has found them *in flagrante delicto*.[19]

No Statute of Limitations Finally, to leave as much latitude for blood-revenge as possible from the temporal aspect as well, Bedouin law imposes no statute of limitations. To the contrary, it specifically stipulates that "Blood is an item that neither frays nor decays; generation after generation will seek vengeance" (*ad-damm khalag mā yabla wala yisawwas—jīl yuṭrud wara jīl*).[20] Indeed, a common saying that survives from a now forgotten story makes a virtue of letting time pass. An avenging Bedouin is recalled to have said, "I took my revenge after forty years; I was hasty!" (*astathart baʿd arbaʿīn ʿām—astaʿjalt*).[21] If vengeance takes time, as in this case, the avengers console themselves with the knowledge that the murderer and his clansmen are all the while suffering from constant insecurity and hardship, in exile among strangers.

Examples of deferred blood-vengeance are rife. At the time of this writing (2009) in southeastern Sinai, for example, the murder of Fiheid Slaym Ibn Jāzī of the Tarabīn Ḥasāblah, who was found sleeping near a girl of the Aḥeiwāt Karādma in 1979, still had not been avenged (Case 75); nor in the northern

Negev had the murder in 1981 of the chief of the Ẓullām Abū Rubay'a tribe (the chief was murdered for not having relinquished his seat in Israel's parliament to a Druze notable, whose sons were the killers) (Case 70).[22] In both cases, the conflict remained active, the victim clans vowing ultimate revenge.[23] In the central Negev among the ʿAzāzma Ṣubḥiyyīn, the Lugaymāt clan, one of whose men was killed by someone of the Rahāyif clan in 1985, let the Rahāyif remain in exile among people of the Ẓullām confederation until 2000, when they surprised them in the market of a small town, Yeruham, and took revenge (Case 81).[24] In 2006 in the market town of Tell as-Sabaʿ, a man who was yet unborn in 1975, when his father was killed by Hilayyil Abū Silmī of the Suwārka (of the Negev), took his revenge upon the killer by stabbing him to death after thirty-one years (Case 82).[25]

One also finds killer clans whose flight from revenge has become all but permanent—for example, the now notable Majālī family of Karak, Jordan, whose ancestors fled there hundreds of years ago after perpetrating the murder of a man of the Tamīmī clan in Hebron. In the case of the Majālīs, the name they were given by local people—namely, "fleers from revenge" (*majālī*)—became their abiding clan name (Case 83).[26] In the Galilean village of ʿArāba resides a family called al-ʿAyāyda, named after its past tribal confederation in western Sinai, from which it fled from revenge for a murder its members committed in the late nineteenth century (Case 84).[27]

The above notwithstanding, all Bedouin avengers, in order to dispel the doubts of others concerning their determination and power, instinctively prefer to retaliate as quickly as possible. They thereby trust that others, recalling a surviving line from a now forgotten story, might say of them reverentially, "They took revenge while his blood was still hot" (*raddū ath-thār wa-d-damm sākhin*).[28] Accordingly, a traditional saying counsels, "[Kill] the first one you meet and evade disdain" (*al-mawālī bi-l-mawālī wi-tiʿaddī al-mazārī*).[29] This haste may explain why Wilfred Thesiger's companions in southern Arabia deigned to take revenge on a fourteen-year-old boy they encountered the day after his people had killed one of their lads (Case 79).

Vengeance for Violating "a Woman's Honor"

The Sanctity of Women's Honor In addition to vengeance for the murder of a man, the law entitles victims to use violence as a first resort in obtaining justice for the violation of a woman's honor. Whereas the preeminence of the right to life among Bedouin is as self-evident as in most other societies and warrants no special explanation, the sanctity of what the Bedouin call "woman's honor" is unique to their culture.

As mentioned in chapter 3, Bedouin attribute prime importance to the moral probity of their women to ensure that the children a woman bears belong biologically to her husband and his clan. Clansmen want to believe that the severe sacrifices they make for each other are warranted by blood affiliation. Therefore, Bedouin society charges each family to begin the moral education of girls at an early age, expecting that such education will make them chaste wives. Consequently if a girl or woman behaves in an immoral way—that is, not commensurate with morality as understood by Bedouin—great shame adheres to the clansmen of her father for having betrayed their societal trust.

The problem of ensuring women's chastity is compounded by the fact that Bedouin women are often in remote places and on their own, whether by day, when they are alone at pasture with the flock, or by night, when the man of the household may be away, engaged in social, economic, or security activities of importance. The temptation and occasion for another man to violate the honor of so isolated a woman or girl is thus great, and all that deters him from doing so is the fear of her menfolk. Hence, the inviolability of his women became the touchstone of every Bedouin's strength and deterrence. In particular, it indicated that people feared him even in his absence. Hence, the "violation of a woman's honor" really means the devastation of her menfolk's deterrence, expressed by the Bedouin themselves as "the destruction of the tent" (*kharāb al-bayt*)—the tent, that which physically shields a family, being a metaphor for a reputation that conceals weakness.* Accordingly, the term *ʿār*, which Bedouin law uses for problems of what is often known as "women's honor," is best understood as "a man's honor in regard to his women."*

Therefore, if Bedouin law deals harshly with homicide in order to prevent it, it is no less severe when a woman's honor has been violated. The gravity with which Bedouin view such offenses of "inexcusable shame" is reflected in the sayings, "Touch fire, but not a female!" (*an-nār wala-l-ʿār*) or "Grasp an asp, but not a girl!" (*ulguṭ al-ḥayya wala-tulguṭ al-banayya*).[30] It is also manifest in the practice, observed with legal impunity, of mutilating a murdered sexual violator's genitalia and stuffing them in his mouth, as happened in the northern Negev in the 1950s to a man who had absconded with a married woman

*This metaphor was also used in a poem by a man insulted publicly by his brother, indicating dissension, which weakens: "O woe the tent that's just been rent where it was tightly sewn / While some things may a secret stay, others will be known" (Bailey, *Poetry*, pp. 222–23).

*ʿĀr is the verbal noun of the root *ʿ-r-y* (naked) in its indefinite genitive form, meaning "of bare (inexcusable) shame—that is, a shame for which there is no justification. *ʿĀr* is also a designation for women in the context of "the problems that arise from women" (*mashākil ʿār*), and a man refers to a woman or women under his responsibility as *ʿāriy*—that is, they are "my honor [as it derives from them]." Classical Arabic uses *ʿarḍ* for what the Bedouin term *ʿār*.

of the Tiyāha Abū-l-Gīʿān (Case 67)[31] and to a man of the Tiyāha Banī ʿUgba who often trysted with a woman of the Tiyāha Ramaḍīn (Case 85).[32]

In principle, Bedouin law permits the clansmen of a violated woman to wield violence as a first resort against the perpetrators of three separate types of violation of "a woman's honor": rape, certain abductions, and consensual fornication. This is not, however, an unrestricted permission. For each category of violation, the law differentiates among the issues of what sort of force may be used, by whom it may be used, against whom it may be used, and when it may be used.

Rape Rape (*ghaṣab* or *dagga*) in Bedouin law is a violent assault upon a woman with intent to have sexual intercourse with her against her will.[33] Even attempted rape is considered rape. The law is aware that if rape were commonplace, women could not go alone to pasture and men would have to stay close to home. Such restrictions would obstruct the Bedouins' economy, as well as the maintenance of their security interests, which often necessitate the presence of the men elsewhere. To deter potential rapists, therefore, the law allows for the victims' clansmen to carry out both murder and pillage, against not only the rapist himself, but also his whole clan. Bedouin cite the authority for this harshness in a thrice-rhymed threat issued to a rapist's group by an anonymous avenger in the distant past:

> Within three and a third days
> (*Thilāthit iyyām ū-thilth*)
> We shall kill your men and take your wealth
> (*nadhbaḥ rijālak ū-nākhidh mālak*)
> And whatever falls in that time's lost.
> (*w-illī ṭāḥ fīhin rāḥ*).[34]

In some ways, then, the punishment for rape is more severe than revenge for murder. First, although killing is limited to three and a third days, the law ignores parity and allows for killing as many men of the rapist's clan as circumstances permit, all with impunity. Second, the law allows what in some tribes is forbidden in vengeance for murder—namely, the pillage of livestock and movable property.[35] Unlike the killing of men, moreover, pillaging may continue beyond the three and a third days so long as the rapist's clansmen have not requested a truce and agreed to sit for trial. In addition, these spoils "are lost" (*biyrūḥ*)—that is, they are not deducted from the final indemnity, as are items pillaged during blood-vengeance, if pillage is practiced.*

*Property does not include the tent and its elements of sustenance, such as food or grain. Oral communication from ʿAnayz Sālim al-ʿUrḍī of the Tarabīn Ḥasāblah, June 17, 1998.

Harsh as this punishment is, however, Bedouin differ over whether the law permits such a use of force as a first resort or only after attempts to clarify the case have been taken. To be sure, many believe that acts of rape may legally be met by immediate and automatic retaliation. The oft-quoted line of a now forgotten story seems to confirm this position: "Her brothers set out upon her complaint; May God have mercy upon him" (*ʿizwit-ha ʿagabū shakwit-ha—allah yarḥamah*).[36] The argument underlying this position is that a woman's family and clansmen would know how to discern whether or not her account of rape is true. If the attack takes place in the morning or during the shepherdess's return from pasture in the evening, a woman will traditionally be depicted as "a mid-morning complainer" (*shākyit aḍ'-ḍaḥa*) or "one who precedes the flock home" (*sābigt as-saraḥ*), indicating that she has indeed been assaulted. Her people would also expect her to be "screaming" (*ṣāyiḥa*) or "crying her distress" (*shākī bākī*; lit. "complaining and crying")* and perhaps "waving the edge of her head-cloth" (*bi-ṭarf gunʿit-ha lāyiḥa*) to signal alarm. Similarly, if an attack takes place after nightfall and the girl or woman is alone, she should directly "light a campfire and wake her neighbor" (*tōgad nārha ū-tihibb jārha*).[37] Another traditional depiction of such a girl is fixed in a formula recited by the fathers of raped girls (in the event that the case gets to litigation); it describes her with clothing torn and jewelry in disarray.[38] In such a condition, her clansmen would recognize that she is abnormally agitated and feel justified in slaying her rapist straightaway.**

Bedouin recognize however, that immediate retaliation entails a risk, insofar as the accused rapist's clan might challenge the accusation of rape and hold the girl's group subject to blood-revenge for killing him unjustifiably. Those accused of rape could maintain, for example, that the encounter between the couple was in fact consensual but that the girl, subsequently fearing she might be found out, chose to claim she had been raped. Faced with such an allegation, the only recourse of the girl's family is to deny it through swearing an oath or submitting her to the ordeal by fire.[39] However, commonly believing that rendering a false oath based on the fabrication of their girl might expose them, their offspring, and their livestock to the anger of God, many families can be expected to check the veracity of her account before swearing in her favor. If satisfied that their woman is innocent, they then have the option of summoning the accused to a trial of honor, a *manshad*; only if the accused perpetrator balks would they then resort to the use of force, as described.

*This expression appears in the masculine gender, perhaps originally relating to such a raped female as "womankind" (*ʿār*), which similarly appears as a masculine noun.

**By contrast, the account of a girl who tells of an attack only as "she follows the flock home" (*ʿāgibt as-saraḥ*) is met with doubt.

The argument for caution was stressed by Bedouin judges from Jordan in an academic discussion with their counterparts from the Negev held at the Museum for Bedouin Culture, near Beersheba, in June 2002. The local judges submitted a hypothetical case. It posited a woman who was unhappily married to a husband from another tribe, with whom she lived in isolation in a remote part of the desert. One day a man of her tribe passed by; after hearing her complaints, he secretly agreed to return her to her family, three days' journey away, when he left. As they approached her encampment, however, she waved her head-cloth and shouted out, alleging that her purported rescuer had tried to rape her along the way, whereupon her clansmen immediately rallied and killed him. Whereas the Negev judges in the discussion endorsed this reaction, those from Jordan asked how the man could have been slain straightaway on the claim of a woman whose morality was clearly dubious for having forsaken her husband and for having spent three nights on the road alone with a man not of her clan.[40]

This ambivalence regarding the legal right to use force as a first resort in cases of rape is characteristic of various aspects of an unwritten law. One may assume that the ambivalence is often resolved according to the circumstances of a specific case, such as the unmistakably harmed condition of the allegedly raped girl, the presence of witnesses, the prior reputation of the girl for moral probity, the relative strength of the two opposing groups, and the nature of the groups' overall relationship.

Abduction More intricate than rape in Bedouin law is the carrying off of a girl or woman (*nihibi* or *shrād*). Under some circumstances Bedouin law views abduction as rape and accordingly sanctions the use of force, including murder and pillage, as a first resort. Thus, upon hearing that a girl has been abducted, her clansmen may immediately—or "after only a step and a half" (*baʿd khaṭwa ū-nuṣṣ*), as commonly expressed—set out to kill the abductor and pillage his clan, regardless of whether the abduction was consensual or by force. As in cases of rape, murder is not legally limited to the abductor himself but extends to any male in his clan. Moreover, the murder and pillage is not limited to three and a third days but may continue until the girl is returned to her family. The law's authorization of such extreme action is a major way by which it seeks to prevent the abduction of women. It pertains, however, only to abductors from different tribal confederations or distant tribes in the same confederation with which the girl's group (either clan, sub-tribe, or tribe) has made no special agreement, which they call a "coexistence" agreement (see below).

Under this agreement, which moderates the reactions of the parties to acts of abduction, the father or guardian of an abducted girl will refrain from pursuing the abductor for three and a third days, giving him this reprieve in which to ask for the girl's hand in marriage and, in the event that his suit is denied, to return her to her father's tent. The same terms apply to a man who abducts a fellow clansman's sister or daughter. Here, however, the right to murder is relinquished so as not to weaken the clan by lessening the number of men that comprise it.

Only if a rejected suitor belonging to a group with whom there is a coexistence agreement refuses to return the girl does Bedouin law entitle the father and the other members of his clan to use force, either slaying the abductor himself or pillaging movable property of his clansmen until they see to the girl's return. In 1981 in central Sinai, a coexistence agreement between neighboring tribes of the Tarabīn and Tiyāha confederations served to prevent immediate killing between the two when a lad of the former abducted a girl of the latter. It was only when he fled with her to Israel that the Tiyāha utilized their legal right to pillage camels from the Tarabīn, until leaders of the latter finally made a successful effort to bring the girl back and agreed to have the abduction judged at a trial of honor (Case 20).[41]

Fornication In an effort to prevent fornication (*zinā*), in the interests of families of women potentially affected, Bedouin law permits the murder of the man as punishment for it. However, as fornication is a consensual act on the part of the woman, it signifies that the woman's family has been remiss in raising her to moral probity. This failure limits the latitude her family possesses for punishing the man involved, despite the law's recognition that his tryst with the girl is a punishable violation of her family's rights. Accordingly, although the law allows the use of force as a first resort against a fornicator, it limits it in ways that are not applicable to rapists and abductors. These limitations concern who can be killed, who can kill, and under what circumstances the killing can take place.

First, the fornicating man, but not others in his clan, can be killed, and the most respected honor judges in Sinai—those of the Masaʿīd confederation—state two conditions under which the law permits such killing. They say that he can be killed if found "lying on the bedding of a woman" (*nāyim ʿala frāsh-ha*) or "between her legs" (*bayn arbāʿha*; lit. "between her four," meaning her two calves and two thighs).[42] When asked if these conditions pertain to any place in which the man is found, many Bedouin give ambivalent answers. The most certain one limits the allowable killing to the tent, especially that of a woman's husband. If killed there and under the above circumstances, the fornicator will be considered "a dog that's died" (*kalb ū-māt*), and his death will be like "killing a wolf" (*katlit dhīb*)—that is, warranting neither blood-revenge nor blood-payment. Often Bedouin explain that the violation of the sanctity of a tent and the fornicator's entering it with evil intent justify his being killed there with impunity—an argument that is contradicted, however, by the fact that one cannot kill a thief in one's tent with impunity. A more likely consideration is that if a fornicator is killed in a tent, his clansmen will find it difficult to disprove the reason for his death and will be deterred from seeking revenge.

Further to avert the possibility of revenge, Bedouin would caution a husband against pursuing a fleeing fornicator and killing him, even within the boundaries of the tent area, let alone beyond them. His legal recourse against a fornicator who has fled is to bring him to trial and have him pay both a fine for the violation of his tent and the bride-price for a new wife of his choice to replace the adulteress, whom he will divorce. This payment is called "rebuilding the tent" (*iʿmārat al-bayt*), as the banishing of the original wife is tantamount to "the destruction of the tent" (*kharāb al-bayt*), in keeping with the view that "The life of the tent comes from the wife" (*al-mara ʿammār al-bayt*).[43]

The above notwithstanding, Bedouin law also allows for the killing of a fornicating man discovered "lying on the bedding" or "between the legs" of a woman or girl somewhere away from her tent.* Still, murder for an act of fornication "out in the open" (expressed as "on the firm, flat ground": *fi-l-ḥamād*) is more difficult to defend. First, if some enmity already existed between the killer and the killed or their respective clans, the former might be suspected of killing for ulterior motives, merely using the allegation of fornication as a false pretext. Second, as opposed to a man's being in a tent, it is impossible to prejudge his intent when he is with a woman out in the open. He could merely, for example, have been passing by a shepherdess's resting spot and stopped to get a drink of water, sitting beside her—in itself an act forbidden to a nonrelated man but not an offense that warrants murder. Of course, emotions have been known to prevail over legal considerations. In west-central Sinai in 1993, when a shepherdess of the Aḥeiwāt Ṣafeiḥa was seen by a passerby pouring tea for a fellow tribesman not of her clan who was out searching for his grazing camels, her father, Slaym Abū Ḥunayk, upon hearing the report, directly set off to kill him (Case 9).[44]

Two cases of "murder for a woman" (*katl ʿend al-ʿār*) from southeast Sinai illustrate how an allegation of fornication committed out in the open desert may be insufficient to avert blood-revenge. In southern Sinai in 1979, Ḥimayd Ibn Kureidim of the Aḥeiwāt Karādma tribe killed Fiheid Slaym Ibn Jāzī of the

*Bedouin label a woman who fornicates away from her tent "one who pastures freely at night" (*nāfsha*).

Tarabīn Ḥasāblah, claiming that he had found him lying with a girl of his clan, both of them on her bedding (that is, a cloth on the ground) (Case 75). By contrast, Ibn Jāzī's clansmen, after going to the spot and retrieving his body, argued that he was sleeping by himself and, in the absence of any evidence of a struggle, was killed in his sleep.[45] They thereupon declared revenge, at which the killer and his people had to flee for their lives to a distant place in central Sinai, where they still were hiding as of 2005.[46] Again, in 1997, among the Tarabīn Ḥasāblah themselves, Salmān Zaydān of the Munāṣra clan killed ʿĀyid ʿAṭeiwī of the ʿAlowna clan, claiming that he had found him sleeping with his sister (Case 52). For their part, the ʿAlowna claimed that Zaydān had previously married off his sister to ʿĀyid, who therefore had a right to be sleeping with her. Although no one in the area had attended such a wedding, the ʿAlowna declared revenge, the Munāṣra fled, and Salmān Zaydān was killed in an act of vengeance in 2001.[47]

To establish that an act of fornication has taken place and precipitated his killing of a man out in the open desert (rather than in the tent), the killer needs the testimony of the woman involved, alive or dead. "Alive" would be if he bound her to the spot so that she could enlighten persons brought there as witnesses about the truth of what transpired. In that capacity, she is called "a light" (*nūra*). "Dead" would be if the killer slew her together with the man. If the woman was her killer's clanswoman (sister, cousin, niece), whether wife or not, such a killing would signify a sacrifice that a Bedouin might make in order to save the honor of his clan, rather than merely to cover up the murder of the man for other reasons. It would therefore be convincing evidence. On the other hand, the same Bedouin would be cautious about resorting to killing a non-clanswoman wife whom he found fornicating out in the open, lest her clan, in addition to that of the slain man, challenge the allegation of fornication and exact from him the blood-price for a murdered woman, which is four times that of a man. Her clansmen could claim that her husband had no right to punish her for immorality, as that right belongs to them alone.[48] Only if a wife's clan and her husband enjoy very good relations might her clansmen accede to his allegation and absolve him of culpability, asserting that in killing their wayward clanswoman, he has restored their honor (lit. "brought them whiteness": *jāb bayḍāha*).

ALLOWED VIOLENCE AS A LAST RESORT

Physical Assault

As seen, justice can be achieved directly where Bedouin law allows a violated party to use force as a first resort in redressing a wrong, as after murder and serious offenses against women. By contrast, for types of cases in which the use of force as a first resort is not sanctioned by the law, Bedouin find that owing to the traditional absence of law-enforcement agencies in their deserts, they might ultimately be able to redress a violated right only by wielding, or at least threatening to wield, force as a last resort. Hence, they bear in mind the old wisdom that "A right not accompanied by the sword is a lost right" (*ḥaggin mā yibrāh as-seif ḥaggin ḍāyʿa*).[49] Consequently when all other procedures fail to bring a violator to justice peaceably, they find no escape from applying force. Metaphorically the Bedouin know this truth as "Burning is the ultimate cure" (*ākhir aṭ-ṭibb al-keiy*), a proverb taken from their medical practice of cauterization.[50]

Thus, in the central Negev in 1955, a man of the Atayyim clan of the ʿAzāzma Saraḥīn tribe struck a shepherdess belonging to the Kishkhar clan of the Ẓullām Janabīb (Case 86). After rejecting several requests by men of the Kishkhar that he give them justice for the violation, the Kishkhar attacked Atayyim in his cousin's tent, scarring his head with sword wounds.[51] They were using force as a last resort to gain justice. Another story, from southern Sinai, also illustrates the use of force as a last resort (Case 87):

> People of the Tarabīn Ḥasāblah relate that in the mid-1930s a man of the Muzayna Sakhāna tribe called al-Aṭrash came to the oasis of ʿAyn Umm Aḥmad, in Tarabīn territory, and harvested the dates from a particular tree that he claimed had belonged to an ancestor. After checking out the claim with elders of their tribe, the Tarabīn were convinced that it was one of their own forebears who nurtured the palm tree in question and told the man to stop. Finally, after three years of such repeated harvesting and unheeded warnings, four of them raided the oasis of ʿAyn Ḥaḍra, in Muzayna territory to the south, where Aṭrash had his own palms.
>
> Finding some ten men sitting around the campfire, one of the raiders kept them seated with the threat of gunshots from the rifle he pointed in their direction while his companions cut enough date clusters from Aṭrash's trees to fill the saddlebags of four camels. In the midst of this action, however, Aṭrash's wife tried to prevent them from pilfering her husband's dates, whereupon one of the party hit her on the backside with the flat of his sword and sent her running. The upshot of the event was that the Muzayna, demanding a trial that would compensate them for the blow delivered to their clanswoman, finally agreed to the Tarabīn call to resolve simultaneously the question of ownership of the disputed palm through litigation. By applying force, the Tarabīn thus succeeded in obtaining justice from their foes.[52]

Owing to the nature of such orally conveyed and related accounts, certain details may be overlooked. Here, in particular, we are not told just how the Kishkhar and the Tarabīn made representation to the Atayyim and Muzayna respectively prior to their attacks upon them. This is significant in light of the legal process that Bedouin law stipulates, before a victim of violation may use violence as a last resort to redress an injustice. As seen in chapter 2, he is enjoined to send delegations, called "appearances" (*badwāt*; sing. *badwa*), to the alleged violators to persuade them to either litigate or mediate the problem at hand. A minimum of three such delegations must be sent unless, of course, success is achieved before that limit. The legal prescription is, "Make him an outlaw with three delegations" (*ʿādmah bi-thilāth badwāt*).[53] Once the victim has complied with this injunction, he is entitled to wield violence against his violators. The same equally applies to a temporary reprieve that Bedouin law also provides before ultimately allowing for a resort to force. Such a reprieve might, for example, be the three and a third days in which the abductor of a girl must return her to her father's tent. Only if he fails to do so within that allotted time will violence against him be legally justified.

Violence as a last resort, like as a first resort, consists mainly of physical assault and pillage. In contrast to first-resort violence, however, last-resort violence does not include homicide, as any person who commits an act of homicide will be subject to revenge, unless his act follows upon murder, rape, or certain conditions of abduction or fornication, as indicated above. When in 1958 among the Tiyāha Ḥukūk, al-ʿAbd Abū-l-Gīʿān murdered Ibrahīm al-Fagīr, who had absconded with his wife, the Fagīr clan declared blood-revenge against him on the grounds that the abscondment was not his legal affair, the woman not being of his clan (Case 67). If Abū-l-Gīʿān had been the woman's clansman and if the abduction had been forced, his award might be a harsh honor fine. These conditions being absent in this case, however, the most that the husband could claim was the fine called "rebuilding the tent"—that is, a payment sufficient for acquiring a new wife.[54]

Moreover, an act of last-resort violence cannot be performed with impunity, regardless of the amount of harm inflicted. In fact, the law actually deems last-resort violence unlawful, often designating it "violence bereft of justice" (*ʿadam, taʿdīm*). Thus, although Bedouin law allows the originally violated person to physically attack his violator after he has sent him delegations to determine whether or not he remains "one who flouts lawful procedure" (*ʿadmān* in the Negev) or "noncompliant" (*ʿāṣī* in Sinai), he must nonetheless compensate him for any wounds he inflicts, in keeping with the legal directive, "Every aggressor must lose" (*kull mitʿaddī khasrān*).[55] Even the Tarabīn, whose attack on the Muzayna (Case 87, cited above) brought them reparation for their pilfered dates, had nonetheless to pay a fine for the blow that the Muzayna woman received from the flat side of one of their swords.

Another example of responsibility for damages inflicted through force as a last resort was provided between 1974 and 1976 by a conflict between two members of the Muzayna confederation, Munayfī Sālim Jabalī and Sālim Jumʿa Abū Ṣabḥā, in southeastern Sinai (Case 1). In the initial phase of their conflict, Abū Ṣabḥā had left Jabalī to die in the desert with a bullet wound that he and his people had inflicted. A Bedouin court awarded Jabalī a considerable fine and designated a date for payment. When the date passed, Jabalī sent delegations to Abū Ṣabḥā, requesting compliance with the court order. Each delegation received assurances that payment would be made, only to be disappointed; and with every such disappointment comprising an insult to Jabalī in the form of disdain for his—and of course his clan's—power to challenge the default.

Finally, men of the Jabalī clan attacked Abū Ṣabḥā's tent with swords, at night, assaulted him, cut off one of his fingers in the fray, and pinned his wife down on the ground, a violation of her honor. The Jabalī attackers had to pay fines for Abū Ṣabḥā's lost finger, the violation of the sanctity of his tent, and the violation of his wife, as well as compensation for his vehicle (which they damaged to prevent his conveyance to a hospital in the Israeli town of Eilat), but their attack reinstated the reputation of the Jabalī people for resolution and power.[56] All together, their payments to Abū Ṣabḥā approximated $25,000, a sum far exceeding the fine that was due Munayfī Jabalī from the first stage of their conflict ($2,000), thus causing them great financial loss. However, from the Jabalī point of view, as this act restored their honor, the turn to violence as a last resort against Abū Ṣabḥā served to rectify their violated right.[57]

Pillage

When Bedouin law permits pillage with impunity as a first resort in redressing violations, it is specifically as a way either to punish a rapist or to force other types of violators of a woman's honor to send a truce-camel, asking for a truce, and submit to an honor trial that will impose a heavy fine. What may be pillaged is salable wealth (*māl*), such as livestock and sown or harvested grain (as opposed to land, tents, and food products). Bedouin explain this permission as deriving from the view that women too are saleable property—that is, at marriage, when a bride-price is both paid and received. A known Bedouin saying holds that "Livestock is property and women are property, and this property can dishonor its owner" (*al-māl māl wa-l-ʿār māl—wa-l-māl biylowwim ṣāḥbah*), meaning that just as men are responsible for the damages their livestock cause, they are also responsible where the honor of their women is concerned.[58]

By contrast, the law is more ambivalent about pillaging as part of revenge after murder. While some unreservedly assert that it is allowed during the first three and a third days of anger following the murder (called the "boiling of the blood" [*fowrit ad-damm*] or "the spreading of the news of bloodshed" [*ishāʿat ad-damm*]),[59]* others emphatically reject this possibility, arguing that bloodshed and the honor earned by taking revenge are central and essential subjects and must not be tainted with the quest for material gain, as is associated with pillage.[60] This ambivalence indicates that pillage is an unresolved issue in a society on the edge of subsistence.

Impoundment

The Impoundment of Livestock Less extreme than outright pillage as a method of using force to bring a violator to justice is the Bedouin right to impoundment (*wisāga*; lit. "driving [camels] along"), sanctioned by the law. The element of temperance in impoundment, as opposed to outright pillage, is that it is temporary. Property is seized only for as long as it takes the violator to agree to justice. The law allows an ignored plaintiff, after having sent three *badwa* delegations to his suspected violator, to seize and impound his livestock, traditionally one or more camels, in keeping with the seriousness of the case. It also sanctions creditors to use impoundment to induce a defaulter to pay a debt. Bedouin faith in this measure is reflected in their observations: "Camels are the tongs that catch men" (*al'-bil kalalīb ar-rijāl*) and "A man's rein is his camel-mare" (*ḥizām ar-rājil nāgtah*).[61] As raisers of livestock, Bedouin are not expected to endure the loss of their sustenance with indifference.

In 1952 in the central Negev, two men of the Ibn ʿAtayyig clan of the ʿAzāzma Saraḥīn were the guests of ʿOwda al-Kishkhar of the Ẓullām Janabīb, who slaughtered a goat in their honor (Case 88). The next morning, after leaving Kishkhar's tent, they stole some goats from his flock and sold them in the market at Guṣayma, in eastern Sinai. The angry Kishkhar people sent several *badwa* delegations to persuade the Ibn ʿAtayyig to come to trial over the theft, but they repeatedly refused. The Kishkhar even built a cairn of blackened stones to blacken their honor, but all to no avail. Finally, many of the Kishkhar themselves raided the Ibn ʿAtayyig camp, firing their weapons and sending the men fleeing, and impounded the latter's livestock. It was only this act that secured the agreement of the Ibn ʿAtayyig to litigate the offense.[62]

A plaintiff wishing to exercise the right to legal impoundment and not be accused of theft by the owner of the livestock must be accompanied at the act by a number of men who, if he is subsequently challenged, will testify under oath that he was not stealing but rather only impounding the camels he has

*This is an example of the word for blood (*damm*) used also for bloodshed or murder.

taken. "Bring sufficient witnesses and avert the livestock fines" (*waffī ash-shuhūd ū-baṭṭil az-zuyūd*) is the legal directive.[63]

After a plaintiff has impounded the camels, he must deposit them with a third, neutral party, putting them under his protection for safekeeping.[64] Traditionally he may utter things like, "I seek your protection for my right, which has been violated by so-and-so. This is his camel. Behold, it is couched with you, and only my right can release it" (*āna dākhil ʿalayk fī ḥaggī illī ʿend fulān, ū hādha jamalah; irʿah birk ʿendak; ma yiṭlig-ha ghayr al-ḥagg*).[65] "Only my right can release it" means that the protector himself will be liable to defamation ("blackening") and a legal claim by the impounder if he surrenders the camel or camels before their owner agrees to litigation or to paying an outstanding debt (according to the case) and also brings along a guarantor who will ensure that he is fulfilling his obligation. The guarantor is one of the necessities referred to in the rhymed directive, "Bring what is necessary and regain the camels" (*tilzim al-malazīm ū-tirudd al-marazīm*).[66] Moreover, an impounder must inform the livestock owner of the impoundment "within a day" (*mablagh yōm*). Once this is done, the law deters the owner from trying to retake his camel (or camels) by force with the double threat of a stiff honor fine for violating the sanctuary extended by the protector and "a multiple fine" (*ziyādī*) for the theft of what would not, under these circumstances, be deemed his camel, should he succeed in taking it.

Bedouin law imposes obligations on both the original owner and the impounder. The owner is responsible for the cost of fodder and any other expenses incurred during the impoundment, to be paid at the final reckoning of accounts. He is constrained to agree to litigate or pay his debt, according to the case, within forty days, after which the impounder may use—even sell—the camel as if it were his own. The impounder, for his part, must tend to the camel vigilantly, in terms of feeding it and attending to its ailments, within the forty-day impoundment period. Otherwise, he will be subject to a claim by the owner for either the death or decline of the camel stemming from misuse or neglect. Once the owner agrees to settle the problem and provides a guarantor of his obligation, his camel must be released immediately. Delay in restoring the camel to its owner is tantamount to theft, for which the law punishes the impounder or the protector accordingly.

Although reference is mainly made to camels as the objects of impoundment, other livestock, such as goats and sheep, may also be impounded. This is established in the legal maxim, "He who hasn't paid up in full, his smallstock will be couched" (*illī mā waffa al-ḥagg tubruk mawashīh*).[67] In modern times, motor vehicles are impounded too. However, the law imposes fines for the impoundment of specific objects—in particular, clothes, food, tents, weapons, water-bearing animals, and thoroughbred horses—each of which the law punishes as theft in its own category. For the impoundment of a camel belonging to a guest in the camp of the person denying justice, the latter has the right to demand from the impounder the normally large fine awarded for the violation of the sanctuary of a tent.[68]

The law also prohibits the impoundment of a swift camel (by inference thoroughbred); prior to the mid-twentieth century, such an animal, known as "warner of the camp" (*mundhirat al-ʿarab*), was necessary for bearing the shepherd who warned of a camel raid. Impounding such an animal jeopardized its owner's entire herd. Bedouin in southeast Sinai tell of a barely averted tribal war stemming from the impoundment of a thoroughbred in the early twentieth century (Case 89):

> A thoroughbred camel belonging to one of the "southern Sinai tribes" (Ṭawara) was impounded by people of the Aḥeiwāt Shawafīn tribal confederation of east-central Sinai, in order to force the distant Ṭawara to compensate them for one of their camels that the latter had stolen and butchered in Wādī Fīrān, in the south. The Ṭawara agreed to a trial at the tent of Judge Ḥusayn al-ʿAlowna of the Tarabin Ḥasāblah tribe, who dwelled midway between the two foes. On the day of the trial, the Ṭawara appeared with forty mounted warriors, ready to do battle unless their thoroughbred was returned. Only after the Aḥeiwāt swore under oath that they were unaware that the camel was thoroughbred and agreed to return it did the Ṭawara relent, also agreeing to pay the "multiple fine" for the original theft imposed by the judge—four camels for the one stolen.[69]

The Impoundment of Persons Although custom prohibits the impoundment of persons, stories from Sinai and the Negev testify to this practice, but under circumstances that indicate its legal permission in conflicts between persons of different and unfriendly tribal confederations, even if the practice is forbidden within the same confederation or presumably between those in relations of friendship. One such occasion (reminiscent of the infamous pre-Islamic kidnapping of the son of the Arabian-Jewish poet Samawʾāl Ibn ʿAdiya to force the father to surrender the tribal armor that a fellow, and most renowned, poet, ʿImrʾu ʾl-Qays, had left with him for safekeeping)[70] involves a lad: In the early twentieth century, a man of the Bayāḍiyyīn confederation stole a mare belonging to Muḥammad Abū Kaff, a chief of the Tiyāha Gudayrāt tribe in the northern Negev and fled with it to his home in northwest Sinai (Case 90). Abū Kaff went after him. After reaching the area, he learned that a boy in his presence was a son of the thief. He thereupon snatched the boy and brought him back to his tent in the Negev, where he stayed a captive for ten days, until his father came and returned the horse.[71]

Another incident of taking a person hostage for purposes of restoring justice took place in 1991.

> Men from the ʿAlaygāt confederation, living near ʿUyūn Mūsa, in southwest Sinai, kidnapped a shepherd from the Tarabīn Saḥābīn tribe living in the Jabal Maghāra hills of central Sinai and took him, bound, some forty kilometers to their camp at Rowiyayna, where they shamed him by letting their women observe and mock him (Case 91). The abductors had suspected him of reporting them to the Egyptian police for some offense. Although they released him the following day, they made no representations to the Tarabīn elders to request a truce. Traditionally the ʿAlaygāt and Tarabīn maintained relations of enmity. Hence, the Tarabīn, in order to force the ʿAlaygāt to give them justice, felt free to go to the camp where their fellow tribesman had been held and to kidnap one of its men, bind him, and take him to their own camp, one hundred and twenty miles distant. This brought the ʿAlaygāt to trial under a judge of the Aḥeiwāt Shawafīn Guṣayyir tribe, Salāma Ḥusayn az-Zimaylī, who did not reprimand the Tarabīn for impounding the ʿAlaygāt man.[72]

A third instance of impounding a person concerns a woman. It took place in the early 1950s and was widely known.

> A man of the Suwārka confederation and his wife were living among the ʿAzāzma near Bīr ʿAṣlūj in the central Negev (Case 92). One day a man of the ʿAzāzma, called al-Bagaʿ, abducted the wife, taking her to Jordan. Thereupon, her husband, with his children, returned to his home in northeast Sinai, telling his tribesmen of the abduction. These took counsel and decided, upon the advice of an old man of the southern Sinai Ḥamāḍa tribe living among them, that "Nothing will bring back a woman but a woman" (*mā yijīb al-ʿār ghayr al-ʿār*).[73]
>
> Accordingly, thirty to forty camel riders crossed the desert border into Israel and fell upon a camp, reportedly of the ʿAzāzma chief, where they checked all the girls in the light of a flashlight, finally choosing a beautiful one, whom they duly kidnapped on camelback and took with them to Sinai. There they deposited her in the tent of the mother of the Suwārka girl whose abduction was the cause of this impoundment, tying one leg of each of the females together to ensure that the impounded girl's honor would not be violated by a man.
>
> Finally, the ʿAzāzma forced the absconder to return the Suwārka woman, and an honor trial was held at the Guṣayma oasis, under Judge Salāma Abū Amīra of the Masaʿīd confederation. Abū Amīra fined the ʿAzāzma a great sum for every night of the abduction. The only fine incurred by the Suwārka was for turning a flashlight on the ʿAzāzma girls. No reprimand, however, was directed at them for the impoundment; to the contrary, the ʿAzāzma were

ordered to fly a white flag to honor the Suwārka for ensuring the honor of their girl.[74]

In the above three cases, the impoundment of people was allowed between confederations with a history of traditional enmity—that is, the Tiyāha and the Bayyāḍiyyīn, owing to the latter's friendship with the Tiyāha's traditional enemies, the Tarabīn; the Tarabīn and the ʿAlaygāt, owing to the latter's friendship with the Tarabīn's traditional enemies, the Muzayna; and the Suwārka and the ʿAzāzma, owing to the latter's friendship with the Suwārka's traditional enemies, the Tarabīn.[75] By contrast, however, the law, as stated above, forbids the impoundment of people within the same confederation (or presumably between friendly confederations). For example, in 1999 a Masaʿīd judge of honor, Amīra Salāma Abū Amīra, the son of the very judge who had absolved the Suwārka of human impoundment in the 1950s, imposed a heavy fine on a family of the Bayyāḍiyyīn confederation of northwest Sinai for trying to kidnap the female cousin of a man of the same confederation in order to force the latter to return their daughter, whom he had abducted (Case 93). Though not referring overtly to the tribal context, Abū Amīra simply ruled that "One woman cannot be impounded for another" (*al-ʿār mā biyitwassag ʿala bʿaḍah*).[76]

Protecting Society from Private Violence

In the foregoing, it has been seen that one way Bedouin law chooses to ensure that an individual's rights are not violated by others is that it allows him and his clan to wield private violence, which may come in the form of physical attack on persons and the pillage of property. Although clearly an instrument of punishment against the immediate violators, this violence is primarily viewed as the most effective deterrent to other potential violators, either of the victims in question or in general.

At the same time, the law also recognizes that private violence, however effective as a deterrent, could destroy Bedouin society if left unrestrained. Therefore, it furnishes the means to curb it. We have already seen, for example, the differentiation between the use of violence as a first resort as compared to a last resort. The intention to limit private violence is also evident regarding offenses committed against a woman's honor and the diverse punitive measures allowed. For example, while allowing the murder of both a rapist and members of his clan, it exempts from murder the clan of a man caught in an act of consensual fornication. Further, it forbids the murder of a man who forcefully violates a woman's honor without direct sexual intent, confining the punishment to pillage. Even where pillage is allowed, moreover, it is limited in time—that is, only until the violators agree to redress their action through nonviolent means. Clearly, then, the law consciously sets limits to the type of physical violence it will condone regarding each type of violation.

As we have also seen, where the law permits the use of violence as a last resort in rectifying a violation, it stipulates nonviolent measures that must first be tried. Ignoring them through a precipitate act of retaliation will cause the original victim to lose his violated right. Moreover, even damages inflicted after an abortive attempt at nonviolent resolution may be punished, the law calling for all wounds to be assessed and fined. By the same token, pillage is mainly limited to temporary impoundment, which in itself is hedged in by rules. Other pillage is heavily fined.

RESTRICTIONS ON BLOOD-REVENGE

Although the laws of blood-vengeance grant broad latitude in the use of violence, with the goal of deterring homicide, they too entail certain safeguards lest the use of force destroy Bedouin society through widespread belligerence.

Limiting Victims of Revenge to the Murderer's Clan

The first restriction posed by the law on revenge limits the liable persons to members of the offending clan, although the specific definition of which generations in the clan are liable to revenge may differ according to the time at which revenge is taken. For most of the period of revenge, the outer limit is set at five generations of common affiliation, comprising that of the youngest male member and that of his great-great-grandfather, as demonstrated in table 4.1 above. This is the prevailing rule, even though the scope is broader during the first three and a third days following news of a murder, when the victim's kin group is presumably so compelled that it has no time or mind to be precise in counting generations. In this period, therefore, the law allows an avenger to retaliate beyond the five-generation mark, striking equally at the descendants of earlier generations that have not yet formally disaffiliated, "even up to the tenth generation."[77]

In no case, however, may revenge be sought from people that have previously disaffiliated from the clan of the murderer, regardless of the reason or the generation to which they belong. The only exception pertains to revenge against groups with which the avengers have little familiarity, such as other confederations or distant tribes in an avenger's own confederation. A legal maxim affirms this exception, proclaiming that "During the boiling of the blood, vengeance is valid up to the seventh forefather; whoever falls suffices" (*fī fowrit ad-damm li-ḥadd sābiʿ jidd—illī yiṭīḥ yisidd*).[78] To avert counter-revenge for a miscalculation, however, an erring avenger must swear under oath that he acted out of ignorance.

After the blood cools down, the law makes specific provisions for further reducing the scope of revenge. Members of the murderer's clan who are descended from generations beyond the fifth (that is, the sixth, seventh, etc.) but who had not previously disaffiliated are now legally entitled to do so. One condition for such exemption is that each lineage among the petitioners pay the victim's clan a camel, called the "camel of sleep" (*baʿīr an-nōm*), denoting that the petitioners' sleep will no longer be hampered by the cares of a person who is being hunted down with the intent of being killed. The "sleepers," for their part, must agree to pay their allotted share of the blood-price, if such is the resolution of the murder, and must neither help those still being pursued to evade revenge nor hinder the avengers in their pursuit. This abstention from the conflict is a cardinal commitment and is assured by a guarantor, to whom the "sleepers" will pay a large fine if they break it. Such a contravention will also re-expose them to revenge. On the other hand, the same (or another) guarantor must ensure that the avengers too honor the new exemption from revenge. Although allowing sleep is the avenger's choice, once he grants such immunity, it is legally binding; by transgressing his commitment, he will be liable for the payment both of honor fines for the violated guarantor and fourfold blood-payment for the treacherous murder.[79]

Such exemption is assured for people belonging to the same confederation as the murder victim or to a different confederation with which their confederation has agreements regulating revenge (see below). Such an agreement exists, for example, between tribes of the Aḥeiwāt and Tarabīn confederations of southeast Sinai. Thus, when people of the Aḥeiwāt Karādma tribe killed Fiheid Ibn Jāzī of the Tarabīn Ḥasāblah in 1980 (Case 75), the Tarabīn exempted nearly all the Karādma from revenge except for the killer's immediate family. By contrast, no such agreement exists between the Tiyāha and ʿAzāzma confederations of east-central Sinai. Therefore, when people of the ʿAzāzma Saraḥīn tribe killed Ḥasan al-Aṣfar of the neighboring Tiyāha Braykāt tribe in 1998, none of the entire Saraḥīn tribe were exempted (Case 41).[80]

Through the same "camel of sleep" process, people descended from the fifth generation of the murderer's clan are customarily exempted from revenge and allowed to disaffiliate. The legal directive says, "He of the fourth forefather will bring the camel of sleep and sleep" (*illī fī-l-jidd al-khāmis yisūg baʿīr an-nōm ū-yinām*).[81] Here, however, more than with higher generations, it is incumbent upon the neutral envoy who delivers the camel of sleep to prove the claim that his senders are descended from the same fifth generation of common ancestry as the murderer—that is, that they are not from a lower generation (fourth, third, etc.). Customarily the envoy makes the case by holding a dagger between two fingers of one hand, and performing a ritual called "count and exit" (*ʿidd w-iṭlaʿ*). He begins by reciting the name of the murderer and each of his male-line ancestors in ascending order up to the fourth ancestor (that is, the fifth generation), who should be common to him and to a member of the generation that wishes to withdraw. With each ancestor named, he wraps a finger of the other hand around the dagger until all five fingers grip it. He then recites the name of the member representing the generation that wishes to withdraw, simultaneously extending the lower finger from the dagger; then the name of that person's father, extending the penultimate finger; then his grandfather, extending the middle finger; then the grandfather's father, extending the index finger; and finally the grandfather's grandfather, extending the thumb. No longer gripped, the dagger thereupon falls to the ground, symbolizing that the petitioning generation, being at least four times removed from the murderer, no longer bears responsibility for either his dagger or deeds. Accordingly, it should be exempt from retaliation and the consequent need to flee. If, however, the common ancestor's name comes up with the dagger still gripped, the suitors will be deemed liable to retaliation no less than the other members of their clan.[82]

Through this process in 1997, the Abū Huwaymil lineage (*ruba*ʿ) of the Munāṣra clan was allowed to sleep after Salmān Zaydān al-Munāṣra murdered ʿAyid ʿAṭeiwī al-ʿAlowna, both of the Tarabīn Ḥasāblah tribe (Case 52). The envoy for the Abū Huwaymil demonstrated to the ʿAlowna clan that it and Salmān's lineage had a common ancestor, Manṣūr, in the fifth generation, as shown in table 4.2. As a result, the Abū Huwaymil asked to be able "to sleep," and the ʿAlowna granted their request.[83]

Fifth-generation exemption, however, is not an entitlement, as with higher generations, but must take place by permission of the murder victim's clansmen, who also retain the right of refusal. A legal maxim holds, "Sleep [relief from vengeance] is by leave" (*an-nōm bi-l-khāṭir*).[84] Among the Tiyāha Gudayrāt in the northern Negev in 2005, for example, the Nabārī clan, one of whose members was shot by a man of the Ṣāniʿ clan, refused to exempt from revenge the lineage to which Ṭalab ʿUmr aṣ-Ṣāniʿ, a member of the Israeli Knesset, belonged, despite his sending the Nabārī (the monetary equivalent of) a "camel of sleep" (Case 94).[85] Although the law supports the "camel of sleep" custom for the fifth generation and sets punishments for the violation of its terms, it is nonetheless reluctant to dissipate the scope of retaliation as a main deterrent to homicide by making mandatory the exemption of people within the five generations of collective responsibility.

However, alongside the societal benefit in reducing the circle of those subject to revenge, the law, in supporting the "camel of sleep" custom in the fifth generation, also acknowledges additional interests that the avengers themselves might have in such reduction. In the case discussed above (Case 52), for

Table 4.2. Part of Munāṣra Clan Showing Distance between Huwaymil Lineage and the Murderer, Salmān

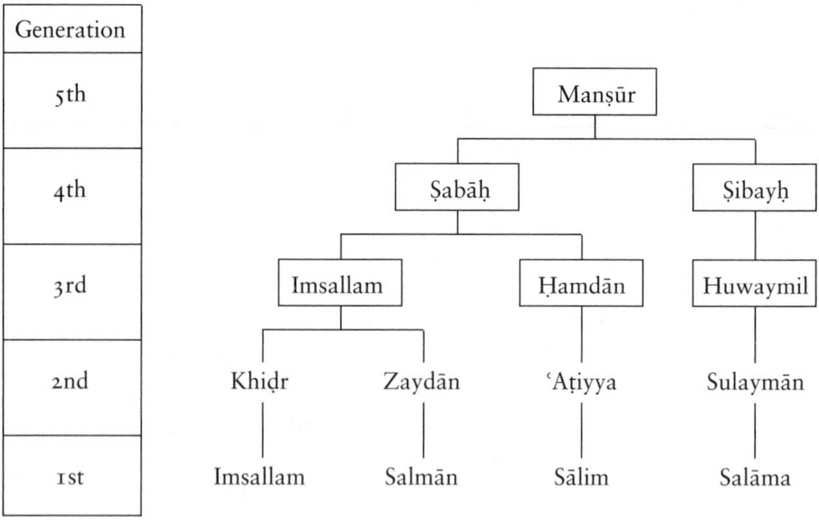

example, because the ʿAlowna and the Munāṣra clans were members of the same tribe and the same supra-clan blood-fine group (*damawiyya*),[86] the former felt a natural tendency to relieve as many of the latter as possible of the ordeals of flight and fear. Of a more practical nature, moreover, they figured that by limiting the quest for revenge to Salmān Zaydān and his brothers, they could prevent a whole lineage, such as the Abū Huwaymil, from extending aid to the murderer and make the task of revenge simpler. Indeed, this thought led them, after a year, to exempt from retaliation, first, the Abū Ḥamdān lineage (fourth-generation tie with the murderer) and finally even Salmān's first cousins of the Abū Imsallam lineage (third generation).[87] This was an activation of the legal maxim, "An avenger can let you sleep, even if you're in the clan" (*ṣāḥib ad-damm yinowwmak w-inti khamsa*).[88] Yet while all these "sleepers" are bound by the same obligations as those of the fifth and higher generations, their exemption, unlike the former, is temporary, not requiring them to disaffiliate from their clan.

Parity in Revenge

A second limitation on the scope of revenge pertains to parity in number, a principle deriving from the legal maxim, "A man for the blood of a man" (*damm ar-rājil bi-rājil*). For any individual murdered, revenge can be taken from one individual only; for two murders, vengeance is taken from two, etc. The law deems any retaliation in excess of parity as a further case of homicide, opening a new blood-feud. Parity in number, however, is not the same as parity in stature. Even in the event that a clan has lost a prominent member, such as a chief, and wishes to wreak revenge upon a man of like prominence so as to make the murderer's group suffer a loss of similar magnitude, it has only one act of revenge in which to succeed. To avoid the spread of a blood-feud, the law is careful to impose blindness in the choice of a victim; any man of the killer's group will do. Such blindness as to the status of the victims of both the original murder and the revenge is expressed in the maxims, "An unknown for an unknown" (*karīm fī karīm*) and "You have no choice among the [murderer's] men" (*mā lak fī-r-rijāl khiyār*).[89] If the victim of revenge turns out not to be commensurate in stature, the avengers must nonetheless rest content. The relevant maxim, "A shepherd can beget a chief" (*rāʿī biyʿaggib shaykh*),[90] instructs that the loss of a lowly person to revenge may ultimately deprive his group of someone substantial—that is, one of his unborn offspring—rendering the revenge worthwhile. As with parity in number, any additional retaliation made with the purported intention of achieving qualitative compatibility is a new case of murder, itself liable to revenge.

The only option to taking revenge upon a person of lesser quality than the murder victim is to make a deliberate choice. In northeast Sinai in 1982, for example, a tribal chief in the Suwārka confederation, Shaykh Sulaymān Ibn ʿAwwād, was offered a consignment of hashish by a smuggler from the Tiyāha confederation (Case 95). When he came to examine the goods in the hills of Jabal Ḥalāl, however, one of the smuggler band shot him dead. Fearing warfare with all the Suwārka (the largest confederation in Sinai), leaders of the Tiyāha brought the killer to them. The Suwārka, however, considering him far inferior to their slain, renowned chief, rejected him as an object of revenge. As of late 1999, their revenge had still not been taken.[91]

Excluding Women from Revenge

A third restriction on the scope of vengeance for the murder of a male is that the object of retaliation must be a male. This is one reading of the maxim, "A man for the blood of a man." Accordingly, women are totally exempted from revenge, as stipulated in the rhymed legal injunction, "Revenge is not taken from women" (*al-ʿār mā ʿalayh thār*).[92] This injunction is a part of the broader Bedouin effort to ensure the safety of their often isolated and thus vulnerable women, so the law plays its role by dealing harshly with a man who kills one. It stipulates that "The blood of a woman is fourfold" (*al-ʿār dammah murabbaʿ*),[93] allowing for retaliation against four men or the payment of four blood-compensations (or a combination of the two options).

Accordingly, in the almost hypothetical event that a Bedouin man were to claim that his striking down a woman was but an act of blood-vengeance, it would not close accounts. Even if the parties were to agree that the woman had fallen as revenge in place of a male clansman, the avengers themselves would now become liable to a triple revenge, or, alternatively, they would have to pay the blood-price for a man threefold; in other words, as the murder of a woman is assessed as equal to the murder of four men, the man for whom she supposedly fell the victim of revenge is deemed but one of the four now liable for her murder, with three retaliations still left to settle. The exemption of women from retaliation pertains even to a woman who is the actual murderer of a man. Rather than herself, the law designates the men of her father's clan as the proper objects of revenge.

The only occasion for which a woman may be killed in revenge, according to Bedouin law, is when she or one of her clanswomen has murdered another woman. In this case, a man is forbidden to carry out the revenge, leaving the task only to a woman of the original victim's clan. The same principle pertains to wounds, as demonstrated among the ʿAzāzma Saraḥīn in summer 1973, when two shepherdesses, one of the Ghidayfī clan and the other of the Zanūn clan, began to fight over watering procedure at a well called Bīr Ḥawwāsh, in the northern Negev (Case 14). As the Ghidayfī girl had gotten the best of the Zanūn girl, causing her a number of minor abrasions and wounds, the Zanūn men sent seven of their women to the Ghidayfī tents that night to beat the Ghidayfī girl up.[94]

Excluding Accidental Killing from Revenge

Bedouin law makes further provisions for limiting the violence that it allows in blood-revenge by curbing revenge against persons that have caused accidental death. The cultural latitude for setting this limit derives from that aspect of deliberate murder that Bedouin consider most pernicious—namely, the disdain it demonstrates for the power of the victim's clan to hurt the clan of the murderer in retaliation. In accidental murder, however, this element is missing, especially when it is clear that there was no intent to kill. For example, among the Tiyāha Ḥukūk in the northern Negev in the 1950s, Feiṣal Dirdāḥ Salmān al-Huzayyil was drinking tea with his lifelong friend, Sulaymān ʿAliyyān Abū Hānī, in the police station in Beersheba, where both young men were serving as policemen (Case 96). When Abū Hānī did not succeed in locking his revolver, Huzayyil took it, in order to see if he could lock it instead. Doing so, one of the bullets accidentally went off, hitting Abū Hānī in the heart with a fatal wound.[95] It was apparent, however, that the victim clan had no need to seek revenge because the accidental nature of the killing was clear, and it posed no challenge to the Abū Hānī reputation for strength. By the same token, among the ʿAzāzma Saraḥīn of eastern Sinai in 1998, a man called al-Braygī was cleaning his pistol during a midday break while traveling, when the weapon went off, killing his companion, Shitaywī ʿĪd Abū Rutayma (Case 97). Owing to their lifelong friendship, the Abū Rutayma clan pardoned Braygī with no penalty or compensation for their lost son.[96]

By contrast, there are cases of accidental murder in which the element of accident has to be established. In north-central Sinai in 1977, when an Abū Bilhān of the Suwārka came to another member of his confederation to collect an overdue debt and was about to shoot him with a rifle in a fit of anger, a chance visitor in the tent, a man of the neighboring Bilī confederation, jumped up to stop him, only to be hit and killed with the discharged bullet (Case 6). All the action was very quick, and an investigation was required to clarify that there was no intention to murder the Bilī man. As a result, revenge was waived in favor of the payment of twenty camels, the accepted payment for accidental murder, equaling one-half the traditional blood-price for an intentionally murdered man.[97]

Often the condition for a killer's exoneration from intentional murder is that he take an oath, usually performed at a holy tomb, disavowing any ill intent. Thus, in the Negev in the 1960s, when Chief Kāyid al-ʿAṭowna of the Tiyāha Nutūsh was firing shots of joy at a wedding celebration, one of the bullets accidentally hit a guest, Sālim al-ʿUbra, killing him (Case 98). In order to absolve himself, the chief was constrained to swear an oath at the holy tomb of al-Muʿafāt (in Wādī as-Sayyāl) that his killing ʿUbra was completely unintentional.[98] Finally, Bedouin law also exempts a person who causes death during play from both revenge and blood-payment. The legal precept is that "He who is killed at sport has no lawful claim" (*katīl al-malʿab hāfī*).[99]

TRUCES

Bedouin law also seeks to limit the violence allowed for revenge in cases of murder, physical wounds, and the violation of a woman's honor by supporting institutionalized truces that create the possibility for a nonviolent resolution of the conflict. These truces are of two types: a blood-truce, or *ʿaṭwa* (lit. "grant"), which comes to prevent further bloodshed following the infliction of wounds, and a camel-truce, or *jīra* (lit. "protection"), which seeks to halt further violence following upon murder or after the violation of a woman's honor.

The Blood-Truce

Aware that an act of physical violence against a person contains an element of disdain for his power and will almost certainly be followed by a retaliatory act of violence intended to prove that he has power, Bedouin law, aiming to check the resultant instability that might beset society in general, provides for a blood-truce. The violence that the blood-truce seeks to confine is that of blows and injuries. It does not apply to murder.* It does not even apply to a critically wounded person, lest his wound turn out to be fatal, warranting blood-revenge. Legal maxims determine that "There's no blood-truce for one who's critically wounded" (*al-mukhṭir—mā ʿalayh ʿaṭwa*), or more graphically, "For one whose skin is slashed and blood is in pools, there won't be a blood-truce for a year" (*illī ʿaṣabah gaṭīaʿ ū-dammah nagīaʿ—lā tisrī ʿalayh al-ʿaṭwa ila baʿd ḥowl*).[100] Unlike murder, however, for which the threat of violence can go on for years before revenge is had, the law is intent on bringing conflicts involving wounds to as quick a resolution as possible.

Every blood-truce entails a period of cease-fire. A legal maxim prescribes, in assonance, that "He who grants a blood-truce throws away his stick" (*illī biyiʿṭī al-ʿaṭwa biyirmī al-ʿaṣa*).[101] This period is expected to afford the conflicted parties time to compose their differences; most often, it is the person considered the violator who must either make amends during this period or at least agree to submit himself to mediation or litigation. During the *ʿaṭwa* period, the parties are mutually safe from violence; in particular, the original violator is safe from the wrath of the violated party. The law traditionally states that he is "safe from an erring word or the blow of a stick" (*maḥfūẓ ʿan kilmit khaṭa ū-ḍarbit ʿaṣa*) and free "to go watering and to pack his camel for migration" (*tōrd al-bīr w-itshidd ʿa-l-baʿīr*), as in normal times.[102]

Nevertheless, the blood-truce also entails provisions that keep the parties apart, as a safeguard against friction that might rekindle the violence. These include moving the encampment site of one of them, keeping a distance from each other at the market or other public places, not walking or riding in proximity of each other, and not socializing. In 1974 an elderly shepherd, ʿAyyāda Abū Bilayya, related that on the first day of feast after the month-long fast of Ramaḍān, he went to have lunch at the tent of people of the Ḥawaṣa clan, only to notice, on approaching, that another shepherd and friend, Hilayyil ar-Rimāg, was among the company inside (Case 43). Because the respective clans of the two men, both of the ʿAzāzma Saraḥīn tribe, were then in conflict and subject to an *ʿaṭwa*, however, ʿAyyāda agreed to the host's request and turned away from the tent, despite his hunger and the personal friendship

*While Bedouin in Sinai and among some tribes in the central Negev (for example, the ʿAzāzma) do not use the term *ʿaṭwa* for a truce pertaining to murder, choosing the term *jīra* instead, those in the northern Negev may use it for the period following a victim clan's agreement to resolve the conflict through a blood-payment (see al-ʿĀrif, *al-Qaḍāʾ*, pp. 81–84, and Bar-Tsvi, *Jurisdiction*, pp. 34, 97–98).

that prevailed between himself and Hilayyil. Had he entered the tent and sat down in such proximity to Hilayyil, whose people considered his clan their violators, his action would have constituted yet another demonstration of disdain for their power and an insult to Hilayyil himself, perhaps compelling his erstwhile friend to rise and strike him.[103]

An ʿ*aṭwa* is granted for a specific period of time, usually a week, fifteen days, or a month, during which the prohibition against striking one's enemy is valid. Should the blood truce elapse without renewal, the party that granted it is free to assault his adversaries, barring a prior agreement on a few days of grace. In the late nineteenth century, as related in chapter 2, the ʿOwdāt clan of the ʿAzāzma Saraḥīn tribe utilized the elapsing of an ʿ*aṭwa* to mount a calculated attack upon its neighbors of the Saʿīdiyyīn confederation (Case 21). After a shepherd of the ʿOwdāt had one day been beaten up by shepherds of the Saʿīdiyyīn, of Jordan, the violators' leader asked the ʿOwdāt for an ʿ*aṭwa*. The latter granted them a year and then a renewal of another year. He counseled his impatient clansmen patience, confident that the Saʿīdiyyīn would neglect to renew the ʿ*aṭwa* next time it elapsed. His scenario proved true, whereupon he activated his long-term strategy and, utilizing the permission granted by the law to attack an adversary that has neglected an ʿ*aṭwa*, led his people on a devastating attack against the Saʿīdiyyīn.[104]

In the interest of peace, however, the law expedites the request for the renewal of an elapsed ʿ*aṭwa* by imposing a fine for each day that passes without its having been made. Officially this is called the "fine for the blood-truce" (*iḥtūm al-ʿaṭwa*), specifically imposed for "leaving the blood-truce" (*tark al-ʿaṭwa*) or "ignoring the blood-truce" (*ihmāl al-ʿaṭwa*). As stipulated in the legal maxim, "Neglecting a blood truce will be fined: They'll count out the fine, before setting a new time" (*tark al-ʿaṭwa yitikayyal—yiʿiddū ʿidd-ha wi-yimiddū midd-ha*).[105] After the reprieve of a few days, the fines begin and are particularly heavy for the ensuing week. When a renewal is finally requested, payment of these fines will be a condition for its grant, as happened in the central Negev in 1977, when Sālim al-Ameiṭil of the ʿAzāzma ʿAṣiyāt was fined the equivalent of $25 for each night he neglected to renew the expired blood-truce given to him by Swaylim Abū Bilayya of the ʿAzāzma Saraḥīn after Ameiṭil lads had beaten up the latter's son (Case 23).[106]

The law also supports an ʿ*aṭwa* in other ways. First, it stipulates that a guarantor (often a guarantor for each side) be appointed to ensure the fulfillment of its conditions. Any violation of the truce thus becomes a violation of the guarantor's honor, entitling him to a typically large fine from the party that violates it, as imposed by a court of honor. Second, it imposes a double fine for any injuries inflicted while the blood-truce is valid. In the wording of the law,

He who is hit during a blood-truce will have his wound assessed and doubly fined" (*illī yinḍarib fī-l-ʿaṭwa yingaṣṣ wi-yinthanī*).[107] Finally, an attack during an *ʿaṭwa* may, in addition to the above fines incurred, automatically cost the attacker his initial right. This is the practice in the Negev.[108] In Sinai, it is not part of the law; there, however, the view is that the attackers who violate the truce lose what was their due because it gets submerged in the fines they incur from their attacking during the truce.[109]

If the law is so stringent about a violator's not letting a blood-truce elapse, it follows that it will be even more stern when a violator neglects to request an *ʿaṭwa* from the start. Although no financial indemnity is stipulated, the law deems this neglect as justification for a physical retaliation against the instigator of the original violence. In the central Negev in 1955, after a man of the Atayyim clan of the ʿAzāzma Saraḥīn beat a girl of the Kishkhar clan of the Ẓullām Janabīb and desisted from requesting an *ʿaṭwa*, a judge upheld the resultant physical attack perpetrated by the Kishkhar against him, in which he suffered serious head wounds, on the grounds of his neglect (Case 86).[110] In central Sinai in 1991, as well, a judge of the Aḥeiwāt Shawafīn, Salāma Ḥusayn az-Zimaylī, rejected the claim raised by people of the ʿAlaygāt confederation that the Tarabīn had unjustifiably bound and kidnapped one of their men on the grounds that they, having perpetrated a similar attack against the Tarabīn, had neglected to request a blood-truce (Case 91).[111] The law's clear dismay at a violator's failure to request a blood-truce is that it is tantamount to adding insult to injury—that is, after demonstrating disdain for the victim's strength through the very act of aggression against him (and his clan), neglecting to ease his shame by asking for a truce is a further insult and seen to ensure that the conflict will grow.

All Bedouin caught up in a violent conflict are obviously more keen to grant an *ʿaṭwa* than to receive it from their opponent. If they feel violated, the plea for a truce by the party that violated them, as indicated, restores their reputation for strength, which the violation has eroded. The act of granting the *ʿaṭwa* gives them an advantage in setting the agenda for the litigation that follows, as it establishes them as the party to fear and thus to be heeded. Several different criteria for determining who grants the *ʿaṭwa* exist. One is that the violent attack was unprovoked, in which case the party attacked and injured will grant it. A second is that there was a fight from which one party emerged more injured than the other. For such a case, a judge in the Bedouin past once ruled that "The one who is slightly wounded takes a blood-truce from the one with heavier wounds" (*ad-damm al-galīl yākhidh ʿaṭwa min ad-damm al-kathīr*).[112] A third criterion is that two parties to a fight have been injured to the same degree, in which case they will grant each other a truce, according to the process called "truce against truce" (*ʿaṭwa gibāl ʿaṭwa*).[113]

A fourth criterion is that the victim of the violation that led to the violence will grant the truce even though the initial violation was not a physical attack. Among the ʿAzāzma Saraḥīn tribe in 1973, for example, when the daughter of ʿOwda Zanūn, leader of the Zanūn clan, was injured by the sister of Ḥimayd as-Saddān, leader of the ʿOwdāt clan, in a scuffle between women, he warned Saddān that he had better take a blood-truce from him lest he retaliate (Case 14). Saddān refused, arguing that it was Zanūn who should request the *ʿaṭwa*, as it was his women who invaded, and thus violated, his sister's tent.[114] A year later, in 1974, Saddān again resorted to this tactic to evade taking an *ʿaṭwa* from the Rimāg clan for a wound that his daughter inflicted on one of their boys with a rock, asserting that the cause of the fight had been the boy's negligence in not keeping his camels away from the goats his daughter was herding (Case 43).[115]

When neither side proves ready to concede his position, one option is to agree upon a temporary truce in order to clarify the details and virtues of the case. Alternatively, this is called "an investigative truce" (*ʿaṭwa iftāsh*) and "a truce for preventing evil" (*ʿaṭwa manaʿ ash-sharr*). It does not usually last for more than a few days or a week, but it provides security to the parties in accordance with the conditions cited above. If successful, this temporary truce will lead to a "direct truce" (*ʿaṭwa rās*), which will have longer duration. If it does not succeed, however, a Bedouin notable may activate another option, which is to impose a truce upon the parties using his own honor as the guarantee for its conditions being observed. This may initially be a temporary truce, as described, or a longer one, lasting for months. The procedure is called "throwing one's face (that is, honor) between the two sides" (*ramī al-wijih bayn aṭ-ṭarfayn*), and it can be used, too, to stop people from fighting on the spot.[116] The law gives it muscle by empowering the notable, usually a dominant personality from a large clan, to demand an honor fine that the violators of the imposed truce will find difficult to pay.

The Camel-Truce

Whereas a blood-truce comes to prevent violence following the infliction of injuries by one party upon another, the role of a camel-truce (*jīra*) is to prevent violence during negotiations for reconciliation after murder or after the violation of a woman's honor. Bedouin law states this truce in two forms: "The camel-truce is for a murdered man and cracked [that is, irreparable] honor" (*al-jīra fī rājil madhbūḥ ū-fī ʿarḍ maflūḥ*), and "The camel-truce is for a fallen man and a shouting woman" (*al-jīra fi-r-rājil aṭ-ṭāyiḥ wa-l-ʿār aṣ-ṣāyiḥ*).[117] The camel of the image "camel-truce" is a camel traditionally sent as a deposit in requesting a truce. In common parlance among the Bedouin, *jīra*, which literally means protection, is often taken to mean the camel itself. Hence, the verbs used to request such a truce are "to couch the camel" (*yibarrik al-jīra*) and "to drive the truce-camel forward" (*yisūg al-jīra*), as a short form for "to couch (or drive forward) that with which one is requesting protection." Another mixed metaphor in common use is "to hang up the camel" (*yiʿallig al-jīra*), which may derive from the expression, "to hang up what's required" (*yiʿallig al-ʿānī*), as used in Jordan,[118] perhaps reflecting an ancient form of request for a truce.

The Camel-Truce after Murder Bedouin are wont to assert that there is no truce after murder, insisting that the victim's clan should be solely focused on seeking blood-revenge. When giving this opinion, however, they are conjuring the blood-truce, or *ʿaṭwa*, which, as described above, the law provides for stopping, rather than permitting, further bloodshed after injuries have occurred—and the sooner the better. Indeed, if a blood-truce is granted after murder takes place, it is mostly within the same clan, where little intention to take blood revenge exists in any case. Such was the case in the Ẓullām confederation of the northern Negev in 1954, for example, when ʿOwda Salāma Abū Rubayʿa, whose brother Sulaymān was murdered by his cousin and clansman, Ṣubayḥ Abū Rubayʿa, gave the latter an *ʿaṭwa* in preparation for a reconciliation (Case 18).[119] However, when someone is murdered by an outsider (that is, someone not of his clan), taking blood-revenge for the murdered clansman is vital to restoring the reputation of the clan for being strong and determined—the reputation that is the clan's first line of defense. Hence, the very idea of granting a blood-truce that checks bloodshed shortly after a murder is repugnant, indicating weakness.

Nevertheless, Bedouin law, in its desire to prevent violence for the sake of stability in the society at large, does provide for a truce after murder, in the form of the camel-truce. The practical difference between the camel-truce and the blood-truce lies in the date before which Bedouin victims are unwilling to accept the *jīra* and grant the truce. Those with manly pride (*shahāma*) will never accede to its request, preferring to utilize the revenge option only, though it takes years—perhaps generations. This is confirmed by the aforementioned proverb, "I took my revenge after forty years; I was hasty!"[120]

One reason for this abhorrence toward a camel-truce is that it marks the beginning of reconciliation (*ṣulḥ*) on the basis of a blood-payment, implying that one who accepts the *jīra* camel and grants the truce may be decadent, interested more in material gain than in the honor earned by taking revenge or, alternatively, the honor of the murdered clansman whose shed blood deserves vengeance. A legal maxim affirms that "He who accepts the camel-truce will accept blood-payment" (*illī biyigbal al-jīra biyigbal aṭ-ṭīb*).[121] A tradition in southeast Sinai tells of people who murdered their own clansman and fled to the Arabian peninsula but respectfully desisted from requesting a camel-truce until "ten years, ten months, and ten days" had elapsed, even though the murder victim was of the same clan.*

On the other hand, the law, while placing no obligation on blood avengers to assent to the request for a camel-truce, does not itself impose any time obstacle on granting it, even if directly after the murder, if such be the victim clan's wish. Moreover, it endorses such a truce in two significant ways. First, it puts the blood-revenge taken from someone who has been granted a camel-truce into the category of "treachery" (*bōg*), allowing for a fourfold revenge to be visited upon the avengers in return. In the Negev, as noted in chapter 2, an entire confederation (the Ẓullām) is named after a forefather, Ẓālim, who had to flee from this fourfold revenge after perpetrating the treacherous violation of a *jīra* back in the seventeenth century (Case 25). Ẓālim granted a "camel-truce" and agreed to accept a blood-payment of forty camels for the murder of his son but thereafter took revenge from the destitute homicides, who could bring him only thirty-nine.[122] His revenge would only have been valid if he had first returned the incomplete blood-payment.

In cases of such fourfold revenge taken for the violation of a camel-truce, the man whom the original victims have killed will be considered revenge for their murdered clansman, but this violation renders them liable to three fresh acts of revenge against them or the payment of three blood-payments or a combination of the two. Even if the resolution involves blood-payments only, three traditional payments would come to one hundred and twenty camels, a sum that would break the offenders. Traditionally it was rare for an individual family to possess more than ten camels, the average being even less.[123] In addition, the truce breakers must pay a large fine for the violated honor of the guarantor, whom the law requires be appointed to ensure the nonviolation of those granted a truce by the avengers.

The same penalties also pertain under a second type of camel-truce given in the wake of a murder, one that is requested, in this case, by the avengers after they have already carried out their vengeance for the murder. While blood-revenge taken within the bounds of parity may settle accounts between the parties legally, it may not necessarily dispel their mutual hostility, which might erupt again in an act of murder. For example, in a case of homicide in the central Negev between two clans from the ʿAzāzma Ṣubḥiyyīn tribe in 1986,

*Oral communication from ʿAnayz Sālim al-ʿUrḍī of the Tarabīn Ḥasāblah, June 17, 1998. The ten months and ten days were hyperbolically added to the alleged judgment of an ancestral judge in problems of blood, according to which a request for truce after murder should not be made until ten years have elapsed.

the Rahāyif killed a man of the Lugaymāt and fled into exile among the Ẓullām confederation in the northeast Negev. Fourteen years later, the Lugaymāt took their revenge. In the absence of a subsequent post-vengeance camel-truce and reconciliation, however, more violence was expected, compelling the Rahāyif to remain in exile as of 2001 (Case 81).[124] To prevent the possible destabilization of Bedouin societies from such continued feuding, Bedouin law counsels, "One who has taken revenge should ask for a camel-truce" (*astathār astajār*). The usual process would be to send a delegation of notables, a *jāha*, to the original killers to suggest that the two sides negotiate "to resolve [lit. "terminate"]the problem" (*yitammim ʿala-l-mushkila*). If, as a result, the parties reconcile, the settlement is called "washing the clothes" (*ghusūl ath-thiyāb*)—that is, of blood. In Sinai the original murderers possess a right to have reconciliation requested of them following the act of revenge. It is called a "camel-truce right" (*ḥagg al-jīra*), the neglect of which may cost the avengers a fine. If, however, the original murderers grant the avengers a camel-truce but violate it by killing one of them, the law will hold them liable to a fourfold penalty by killing or by fines, just as in the case of a camel-truce granted to resolve a homicide through blood-payment, as seen above.

The Camel-Truce after the Violation of a Woman's Honor More common among Bedouin than a camel-truce resulting from murder is the camel-truce that follows upon the violation of a woman's honor, this being a more frequent offense than murder. Here, however, the role of the truce is to halt types of violence otherwise allowed. Following an act of rape, for example, murder and pillage are allowed for three and a third days without the violated woman's clan being legally obliged to grant a camel-truce; after that reprieve, however, the violence must stop as soon as a truce-camel is delivered. Following abduction by an outsider (as variously defined), violence is permitted against the abductor until he returns the girl and conveys the truce-camel. Again, even after physical assault that violates the canons of women's honor but without sexual intent, her clansmen, though denied the right of murder, may pillage the offender until he couches the truce-camel.[125] Indeed, pillage can be used against anyone suspected of violating or attempting to violate a woman's honor until his people bring the truce-camel, signaling their readiness to render justice. Their belongings will be pillaged until they request a truce.[126]

The purpose of the *jīra* is to make certain that the offender stands trial at the harsh court of the honor judge. The law affirms that "A woman for whom a camel is couched will get her honor trial" (*illī tubruk jīrit-ha biyiṭlaʿ manshad-ha*).[127] Such a trial is crucial to the woman's clansmen. First, it may clear their reputation for neglect in the raising of their girls; second, it demonstrates that they can make anyone who denigrates their strength by violating their women suffer losses. Owing to the corollary disadvantages that standing trial before such a court entails for the offenders, they are naturally reluctant to pay the *jīra* and may try to avoid it. In 1975 among the Muzayna of southeast Sinai, after men of the Jabalī clan attacked Sālim Abū Ṣabḥā in his tent and held down his wife, they refrained from bringing the truce-camels demanded for more than a month, until constant pillaging by the Abū Ṣabḥā finally compelled them to comply (Case 1).[128] For the most part, Bedouin consider that "The request for a camel-truce is like a verdict of guilt" (*al-jīra garār*).[129] Thus, they call it "a decisive truce, canceling rights and the talk of men" (*al-jīra garḍ ū-farḍ—gaṭ' ḥuggān ū-sawālif 'urbān*),[130] meaning that unless specifically asked, the defendant cannot express his position but only listen to the claims against him and the verdict of the judge.

In Sinai, however, there is a provisional *jīra*, called "a camel-truce for searching" (*jīrit inshāda*), used to investigate the details of a case before demanding the couching of a "true truce-camel" (*jīrit ḥagg*). In west central Sinai in 1993, Ḥājj 'Owda Abū Akthar paid for such a truce to Slaym Abū Ḥunayk, both of the Aḥeiwāt Ṣafeiḥa confederation (Case 9). Abū Akthar met the latter as he was on his way to shoot another man of the Ṣafeiḥa, Salām Abū Maḥamūd, who was reportedly seen sitting next to Abū Ḥunayk's daughter in a field where her goats were grazing. It was to prevent the shooting that Abū Akthar proposed "a camel-truce for searching." It proved a helpful measure, for upon investigation, Abū Maḥamūd turned out to be free of evil intent.[131]

Thus, Abū Akthar had utilized the *jīra* as a measure that Bedouin law provides for checking the spread of violence. The law stands behind a *jī*ra by stipulating penalties for its violation. Requiring the involvement of guarantors (in this case, Abū Akthar himself), the law ensures that any such violation will result in a heavy fine awarded to the guarantor. As mentioned above, it also specifies that anyone assaulted and injured while supposedly protected by a camel-truce will receive a double-fine award for his wounds.

AGREEMENTS BETWEEN TRIBES TO LIMIT VIOLENCE

A further attempt by Bedouin law to curb violence in favor of the broader Bedouin society is its endorsement of two sorts of agreement between groups from different confederations. A tribal confederation, being the nationality of a Bedouin and the outer limit of his loyalties, is an independent territorial unit in the traditional desert. Moreover, since the confederation is the context that provides its members with water and pasture, so vital to their survival, one confederation is always on guard against the others, who, in the arid and sparse desert, might be coveting its resources for their own people. Thus, the natural state of relations between confederations is that of cold war, entailing constant suspicion, tension, and hostility.

Accordingly, any violation by a member of one confederation against a member of another is seen as an act of war committed by the former's entire confederation against that of the latter. Under normal conditions, the clan of a violator plays no individual role in cross-confederation violations. Every member of the respective confederations is involved. Thus, for example, an act of murder committed by a member of the ʿAzāzma confederation against someone of the Tiyāha confederation may be retaliated by any member of the Tiyāha against any member of the ʿAzāzma, as was the case in eastern Sinai in 1999 (Case 41).[132] Similarly, the abduction of a woman of the Suwārka confederation by any man of the ʿAzāzma confederation is, first and foremost, an act of war that is directly punishable by death, as inflicted by any member of the Suwārka (Case 92).[133] Animals pillaged by tribesmen of the Aḥeiwāt Shawafīn confederation from people of the Ṭawara supra-confederation are considered war booty and are not returned except by ad hoc agreement (Case 89).[134]

The "Coexistence" Agreement

All relations (such as the foregoing) change once an agreement is concluded between any two confederations. These agreements regulate offenses between them by applying the same rules and laws that prevail between groups belonging to the same confederation. One such agreement is called "coexistence" (*ʿimāra*; lit. "living together"). This agreement may pertain either to whole confederations or to separate tribes of one confederation and their immediate neighbors of another. In Sinai, for example, there is an *ʿimāra* agreement active among five of the largest confederations: Suwārka, Tarabīn, Tiyāha, ʿAyāyda, and Ṭawara. On the other hand, *ʿimāra* agreements on a small scale can be found among specific tribes of the Tarabīn and the Aḥeiwāt in southeast Sinai, or the ʿAyāl Swaylim sub-tribe of the ʿAzāzma Saraḥīn tribe and the Kishkhar sub-tribe of the Ẓullām Janabīb, neighbors in the hill country of the central Negev.[135] The latter agreements bear no legal validity toward other groups in the respective confederations.

The law stipulates that these agreements, to be legal, must be formed in the presence of witnesses sitting together in what is called "a tent of coexistence" (*bayt al-ʿimāra*) and through the simple but solemn ceremony of "burying the

*Oral communication from ʿAnayz Sālim al-ʿUrḍī of the Tarabīn Ḥasāblah, October 20, 1999. Actually, the term "Ṭawara" is a geographical designation for most Bedouin of southern Sinai, rather than a confederation.

pebble" (*dafn al-ḥaṣā*), during which the leaders of the two sides in turn recite the specific conditions of the agreement, each interring a stone in the sand in front of him to signify permanence.[136] Each confederation has a person or persons responsible for the redress of violations of such agreements and who accordingly must know the state of relations that his confederation has with all others. These people are called "those who enable coexistence between confederations" (*muʿammirit aṣ-ṣufūf*) or "elders of the confederation" (*kibār aṣ-ṣaff*).

The *ʿimāra* agreement deals specifically with physical attacks against men and sexual attacks against women. It makes such attacks the responsibility of the clan rather than the confederation, in keeping with the principle, "Each clan against its [specific] clan" (*kull khamsa bi-khamsit-ha*). Thus, for example, following the murder of Fihayd Slaym Ibn Jāzī of the Tarabīn Ḥasāblah by a man of the Aḥeiwāt Karādma tribe in 1980, revenge remained the prerogative of the Ibn Jāzī clan rather than of all the Tarabīn in the area, while the object of revenge was the Kubaysh clan alone, rather than the entire Karādma tribe (Case 75).[137] By contrast, the absence of an *ʿimāra* agreement between the Tiyāha and ʿAzāzma confederations in east-central Sinai led all the Tiyāha to hold the entire ʿAzāzma confederation subject to revenge when men of the latter killed two of their people in winter 1999 (Case 41). There is also no such agreement between the Tarabīn and their southern neighbors, the Muzayna confederation, in southeast Sinai (Case 100). Hence, in September 1973, when one of the two chiefs of the Tarabīn in that area, Sulaymān Salīm Ibn Sarīaʿ, died a natural death in his sleep, all the Muzayna who were encamped at the nearby oasis of Nuwaybaʿ made preparations to flee from revenge, on the instinctive assumption that if someone had murdered the chief, he might well be of their confederation.[138]

Violations of women's honor are also covered by an *ʿimāra* agreement. In Bedouin eyes, abduction, for example, is something natural, almost always deriving from a man's wish to marry that is frustrated by the father of the desired bride, who is the decisive factor. At the same time, Bedouin also acknowledge that without limitations on the reactions to abduction, neighbors, whose children get to know each other and may fall in love, might find themselves in frequent conflict with each other. Therefore, they set what they call "ground rules" (*magrūaʿ*) for the abduction of women that pertain to men of the girl's own clan or to a kindred group of the same sub-tribe and that are regarded as law. First, the abduction, from beginning to end, must take place in the company of a witness or "companion" (*rafīg* in the Negev; *imbarrī*, in Sinai) so that the abductor is never alone with the abducted girl and so that there is someone present who can, if necessary, attest under oath that the abductor has literally not touched her. Second, the abductor must deposit the girl in the tent of a notable (some say the nearest tent, even of a widow), where her virtue will be under close watch until the problem of the abduction is resolved. Third, he must return the girl to her father within three days, whether the latter agrees to the marriage or not. Fourth, whether or not his marriage proposal is rejected, he must pay the father or guardian of the girl "a camel of abduction" (*jamal ash-sharāda* in Sinai; *jarra* in the Negev), representing the camel on which the couple absconded. So long as an abductor in this category observes these rules, there will be no further legal claims or actions against him.

For the sake of peace in a wider context, Bedouin law extends these rules to other, neighboring tribes of the same or another confederation in the form of *ʿimāra* agreements. In the central Negev, for example, the Saraḥīn tribe of the ʿAzāzma confederation has an *ʿimāra* agreement with the neighboring Kashākhra (al-Kishkhar) section of the Ẓullām Janabīb. Accordingly, in the 1950s, when a lad of the Ḥammādī clan of the ʿAzāzma Saraḥīn abducted the daughter of Sālim Muḥammad of the Kashākhra, the problem was solved by a delegation of ʿAzāzma notables visiting the father (Case 99). The father used his prerogative to reject the marriage proposed, and the man brought the girl home and paid the abduction camel.[139] The resort to force, however, was averted, just as if the abduction had occurred between people of the same clan.

SWORN COVENANT

Another form of agreement that is meant to prevent violence in Bedouin society is the "sworn covenant," or *ḥilf*,[140] which is a peace agreement between entire confederations. Like the *ʿimāra* agreement, a *ḥilf*, to be legally binding, must be formed in a meeting between the two parties to it in the presence of witnesses, "made permanent" by the burying of a pebble, and defined by a declaration of goals and rules. The declaration goes as follows:

Allah, Allah and Muhammad, the messenger of Allah
(*Allāh Allāh ū-Muḥammad rasūl Allāh*)
A divine covenant exists between us.
(*baynna ū-baynkū ʿahd allāh*)
There will be no war nor raid between us.
(*lā yiṣīr baynna lā ghazū wala ḥarb*)
Whoever harms you harms us;
(*illī yiḍurrkū yiḍurrna*)
Whoever gladdens you gladdens us.
(*illī yisurrkū yisurrna*)
Our enemies are those who act against you
(*āʿdā man āʿdākū*)

Our friends are those who befriend you
(*aṣdigā man ṣādagkū*)
So long as the sea remains wet and the desert bare
(*mā zāl al-baḥar baḥar wa-l-barr barr*)
And the palm of the hand does not sprout hair.
(*wa-l-kaff mā yinbit minnah shaʿr*).[141]

The chief ingredient in a *ḥilf* agreement is a prohibition on pillage. One of the main manifestations of belligerence between confederations is the mutual pillaging of camels and other livestock, an act that the law forbids within the context of a single confederation, where it is considered plain theft, with its attendant penalties. Between confederations, however, camel raiding (*ghazū*) has always been considered a means of Bedouin survival, as expressed in the proverb, "Camels are only got by herding or raiding" (*al'-bil—jaybha ghayr ghizāya ow riʿāya*).[142] With rainfall spotty in the desert, drought that decimates herds of camels and flocks of goats in one area may be absent in another area, leaving the livestock there to thrive and reproduce. Hence, Bedouin that are deprived of rainfall and pasture have always been wont to raid those that have fared well.

The *ḥilf* agreement, therefore, aims to eliminate raiding as a source of friction between confederations. It provides for the mandatory return of the pillaged animals (or other property) and the payment of "fines for theft" (*zuyūd*), as pertains within an individual confederation. The people responsible for maintaining the agreements are called "bearers [of the responsibility]" (*galada*; sing. *galīd*; lit. "one who wears it around his neck," like a necklace, or *gilāda*).[143] If a member of one of the covenanted confederations is raided by someone of the second one, he will go to that confederation's *galīd*. The latter is accountable for returning the animals to their owners and securing the fine that has been stipulated in the agreement.[144] In Sinai early in the twentieth century, for example, the fine was set at two Egyptian pounds per camel, which was twice the cost of that animal in the market.[145]

The law specifies that renewed pillaging and the failure of a *galīd* to fulfill his commitment may restore the prior state of war. This was demonstrated in the 1950s in an incident that took place between the Tarabīn and ʿAzāzma confederations of east-central Sinai and the central Negev, who had a *ḥilf* agreement between them going back to the nineteenth century (Case 101). As in other agreements of this type, theirs too stipulated that livestock raiding could take place only after a formal declaration of war, which Bedouin call "removing the purity" (*radd an-nagaʾ*); otherwise the pillaged camels must be returned with a set fine.

> Between 1953 and 1955, however, Bedouin led by Ḥāmid ad-Duʿayjī, of the Tarabīn Dulūḥ tribe, began crossing the 1948 Egyptian-Israeli border from Sinai into the Negev and pillaging ʿAzāzma camels. The leader of the ʿAyāl Swaylim sub-tribe of the ʿAzāzma Sarahīn, Shitaywī Sālim al-Atayyim, thereupon went to the Tarabīn *galīd*, Sulaymān al-Aḥamar, citing their long-standing accord and asking for either a formal declaration of war or a return of the camels. Aḥamar prevaricated, protesting that the raids were the work of youth, who were hard to control, and not an intentional abrogation of the *ḥilf* agreement.
>
> Shortly thereafter, however, Duʿayjī stole goats from the Abū Bilayya family, whereupon its elder, ʿAyyāda Abū Bilayya, betook himself to the tent of Aḥamar, staying there for a month, until his host relented and asked him to summon Atayyim again. While reasserting his inability to halt the youthful thieves, Aḥamar pledged to Atayyim that henceforth whenever an ʿAzzāmī complained that his livestock had been stolen, he would see to its return or personally compensate the owner from his own pocket. Atayyim, for his part, undertook to act in like fashion, and the two sides renewed their covenant. As an opening gesture, all but five of the plundered goats were returned to the Abū Bilayya.[146]

Another element in a sworn covenant is the provision of procedures for litigating offenses, such as murder, theft, or the sexual violation of women, perpetrated by members of one confederation against those of another. In the absence of a *ḥilf* agreement, such violations are dealt with in two different ways. One is that they are considered acts of war, in which case retribution is meted out by any of the violated confederation attacking any of the offending confederation. Such was the case in the 1950s, when the Suwārka, of northern Sinai, resorted to the otherwise illegal action of kidnapping a girl of the ʿAzāzma, in the western Negev, in an effort to gain the return of a Suwārka woman who had been abducted earlier by an ʿAzāzma man (Case 92).[147]

The other, more peaceful, way is for leaders of one confederation (either the violating or the violated one) to establish contact with their counterparts in the other confederation and arrange for mediation. This happened in northern Sinai in 1977, when a man of the Bilī confederation was accidentally shot dead by a man of the Suwārka (Case 6). In the absence of a sworn covenant between them, and thus no contractual instrument for the Suwārka man to establish the accidental nature of the killing, danger loomed of revenge being taken against anyone in that confederation by anyone from the Bilī. Consequently it was leaders of the Suwārka that approached Bilī leaders, in order to work out provisions for the killer to absolve himself of deliberate homicide and for subsequent mediation and reconciliation.[148]

This more peaceful way of settling problems between confederations that have no *ḥilf* agreement between them is nevertheless idiosyncratic, depending on the current nature of their relations, as well as the balance of power between them, at the time. In the case of the Bilī and the Suwārka, relations were sufficiently cordial to enable a peaceful resolution of the killing, despite the dominant strength of the latter. On the other hand, an example of dominant power flouting justice between non-covenanted confederations took place in 1925, when a man of the Suwārka Khalafāt tribe killed a man of the Abū Aʿraj clan, which was tiny and of non-Bedouin origin but living as Bedouin near the village of Shaykh Zuwayd in northeast Sinai (Case 42). The Khalafāt, not considering the Abū Aʿraj a threat, neither fled into exile nor felt sufficiently compelled to try to mollify their victims by seeking reconciliation. The episode ended when the Abū Aʿraj shot a member of the Khalafāt in revenge at the Rafaḥ market eight years later, but it nonetheless demonstrates how an imbalance of power among confederations leads to a flouting of Bedouin justice when no sworn covenant exists.[149]

By contrast, once a *ḥilf* agreement is formed, the relations between confederations shed their dependence upon such variables as size, and the confederations turn to solving their mutual problems according to Bedouin legal principles. For this purpose, judges from each confederation are selected to rule on cross-confederation violations. During the first half of the twentieth century, before an international border between Israel and Egypt separated their respective Bedouin tribes, the ʿAzāzma and Tarabīn confederations had a judge each for mundane problems, problems of bloodshed, and problems of honor. The three ʿAzāzma judges were Ibn Ḥammād, Abū-l-Khayl, and Abū Samra; two of the Tarabīn judges were Abū Jilaydān and Abū ʿArādī. When conflicts emerged between members of the two confederations, the "brother judges" in these three jurisdictions (jointly called "the three disputants"—*thilāthit al-mikhtalfīn*) from each confederation sat as a court to resolve them.[150] In the absence of a sworn covenant, however, the sides turn to a judge from a neutral confederation in the event that their conflict leads to litigation. Thus, in the abduction case between the ʿAzāzma and the Suwārka in the 1950s (Case 92), the judge was Salāma Abū Amīra of the Masaʿīd confederation.[151] Likewise, when the Aḥeiwāt took a camel from the Ṭawara early in the 1930s, the judge was Ḥusayn al-ʿAlowna of the Tarabīn (Case 89).[152]

Further to mitigate tension between confederations, a *ḥilf* agreement confers permission on their members to enter each other's territory and utilize the pasture there. As mentioned above, a confederation is that organization whose member tribes jointly preserve its territory in order to assure access to pasture and water for their livestock. People of other confederations will thus be trespassing if they bring their herds into any particular confederation's lands unless they do so with specific permission. In the late sixteenth century the renowned Ṣawālḥa-ʿAlaygāt war in southern Sinai began when the latter invaded the former's territory for grazing (Case 102).[153] In the Negev in 1830, similar trespassing by a large Arabian tribe, Banī ʿAṭiyya, led to a war in which a combined force of local tribes succeeded in expelling it (Case 103).[154]

Permission to enter another confederation's lands for pasture may be either formal or casual. A *ḥilf* agreement stipulates formal permission, and the formula, "We are the same at the trough and the grassy valley" (*iḥna wāḥad fi-l-ḥowḍ ū-fi-r-rowḍ*), is uttered by each side at the meeting at which the covenant is formed.[155] In southeast Sinai, this *ḥowḍ ū-rowḍ* ("trough and grassy valley") arrangement exists between the Tarabīn and Aḥeiwāt, enabling each to utilize the other's pasturelands whenever its own are blighted by drought. If either party were arbitrarily to deny the other this right, the denied party could petition the other's *galīd*. If he is unable to produce a reason—such as heavy drought and an absence of sufficient pasture in his confederation's territory—the entire *ḥilf* agreement would be endangered. Where no agreement exists, by contrast, the casual permission that confederations extend to others when their relations are cordial may be revoked arbitrarily when hostilities occur, leaving no recourse to appeal. Such was the case in southeast Sinai between the Tarabīn and Muzayna confederations in 1972, when the former simply expelled the latter's shepherds from a *wādī* called Zaranīg, south of the ʿIjma plateau (Case 100). It was in response to the claims of ownership then being pressed by the Muzayna to date palms that the Tarabīn considered theirs at a spot called Wāsiṭ, which marked the border between the two confederations on the Gulf of ʿAqaba coast.[156]

LAWS TO PREVENT VIOLENCE AND CONFLICT

In the foregoing, we have seen how Bedouin law, in its concern for the welfare of Bedouin society at large, attempts to limit and contain violence through restrictions on blood-revenge, truces, and agreements between confederations. Out of the same concern, it also provides laws and provisions that seek to prevent conflict and the resultant violence.

Laws to Prevent Provocation

"Strike a man, but don't insult him" (*uḍrub ar-rājil wala tiʿayyirah*) is a widespread Bedouin sentiment. Insulting a man is a statement of disdain for his strength, implying that he can be disgraced or otherwise violated with impunity. Therefore, insult often precipitates instant physical retaliation, undertaken to quickly disprove the insinuation of weakness. This reaction is reflected in the popular saying, "A stick is the medicine for erring talk (*kalām al-khaṭa dawāh al-ʿaṣa*).[157] In the central Negev, people of the ʿAzāzma ʿAṣiyāt are proud to relate that a past fellow tribesman, called Ṭimṭāwī, struck and killed a guest whom he had just fed, because the guest said that he was a miser compared to other hosts (Case 104).[158]

To avoid the violence that may thus erupt from a slight to people's dignity, the law allows suit for several forms of insult. One is insulting behavior. For example, one person's refraining from greeting another person whom he knows and whom he encounters individually or at a gathering is in itself deemed a serious offense. This is reflected in the term for it—*aḥrab*—which literally means "He acts belligerently," as well as in the widespread expression, "He who ignores you, hates you" (*illī biyijhalak biyikrahak*).[159] Accordingly, among the Guṣayyir tribe of the Aḥeiwāt Shawafīn confederation in eastern Sinai in 1977, people of the Nujūm clan sued a fellow clansman for belligerence after he allegedly warned them not to approach him (Case 53). The claim was rejected, but only after witnesses established before the judge that hostility prevailed between the two parties at the time, thus justifying the warning—that is, if hostility had not existed, the claimants would have received a legal award. In the course of these proceedings, another element of violence prevention was revealed when it turned out that the defendant had not warned all the group from approaching him but rather differentiated, allowing one to come forward and represent the others. This measure too was upheld by the judge, who deemed that the law, further to its efforts to deter violence, also forbids the approach of more than one adversary into the presence of a foe. As if to highlight the sensitivity surrounding an act of greeting, the erstwhile defendant himself was quick to sue his accusers once they stopped greeting him out of pique—that is, upon losing their suit against him for not having greeted them.[160]

Similarly, other behavior that slights a Bedouin (however negligible it may seem to non-Bedouin) is also litigable. If a host neglects to offer a passing guest something to drink, in contradistinction to social convention (that is, "You have arrived together with your rights [as a guest]"—*jīt ū-ḥaggak maʿak*),[161] or if a host offers the guest food or drink and the latter avoids touching it, the slighted party may initiate legal procedures by sending a *badwa* delegation to clarify the reason for this flagrant neglect.[162] If it appears that there is no legal justification for it, the violator may have to pay his victim a fine. By the same token, in the northern Negev in early 1976, the fact that a black man, Sālim Abū Jidayaʿ, had his dagger and staff stolen from him when the sons of Ḥusayn al-ʿOwdāt of the Tiyāha al-Asad beat him up as he tried to stop their flocks from grazing on his sown crops constituted an insult, inferring his inability to defend himself (Case 22). Therefore, Abū Jidayaʿ insisted, when visited by a *jāha* delegation, that this theft, though less weighty than the reparational consequences of the pasturing and the beating he had endured, be redressed as the prime condition for his agreeing to litigation.[163] The relevance of this demand to the trampled honor of the black man was acknowledged, and a guarantee was given that either the dagger or the equivalent of $150 would be given him by a fixed date.[164]

In 1979 in east-central Sinai, Farrāj ʿĪd al-Musāʿida of the Tarabīn Ḥasāblah sued ʿAliyyān Ḥamdān Ibn Nijm of the Aḥeiwāt Shawafīn Najamāt for having insulted him by accusing him, as his supposed protector, of not protecting his property when it was damaged by people of another Aḥeiwāt clan (Case 27). An investigation revealed not only that Ibn Nijm had neglected to inform Musāʿida that he had designated him as protector—an insult as well as a procedural omission—but also that he had compounded his shame by making the accusation in the tent of another person. Accordingly, a judge of the Aḥeiwāt Shawafīn confederation awarded him an honor payment, his expenses in pursuing his right, and three white flags to be raised for him at different places in order symbolically to restore his injured honor.[165]

Another type of litigable insult is the demeaning of a person by treating him like an animal. For example, transporting a violated person from one place to another is viewed as reducing him to the status of a goat, thus constituting a violation in itself and entitling him to an "award for conveyance" (*ḥagg ash-shayla*). In southern Sinai in 1974, for example, Sālim Jumʿa Abū Ṣabḥā and his clansmen of the Muzayna Ghawānma shot and beat up Munayfī Sālim Jabalī of the Muzayna Jarābʿa and then took him some kilometers to a remote place, where they abandoned him (Case 1). The "blood-pool" judge, Rafīaʿ Abū Imṣayfir, of the Ḥuwayṭāt Dubūr, accordingly fined them a total of 25,000 Egyptian pounds (approximately $8,000) on the basis of every step taken during the conveyance, whereas the gunshot, not having damaged any bones, was assessed at only 105 Egyptian pounds. Had Jabalī died following his conveyance, his clansmen would have been entitled to a fourfold payment of blood-money or four acts of revenge.[166] In 1991, when people of the ʿAlaygāt confederation in western Sinai kidnapped, bound, and conveyed a lad of the Tarabīn ninety kilometers, subsequently to have one of their men treated in the same manner but transported one hundred and forty kilometers, they demanded the award for conveyance for the fifty-kilometer difference (Case 91). The judge, Salāma Ḥusayn az-Zumaylī, of the Aḥeiwāt Shawafīn, rejected their request only owing to their original binding of the Tarabīn lad, by which they demeaned him as if he were a donkey.[167] Likewise, in the northern Negev late in the nineteenth century, a man of the Tiyāha al-Asad tribe was fined 19 Egyptian gold pounds and sixteen camels for punishing his wife by "branding" her with a red-hot iron as if she were an animal (Case 105).[168]

Verbal insult is also litigable, in keeping with the stipulation, "He whose tongue torments will pay a fine" (*al-lisān al-ʿādhib biygharrim ṣāḥbah*).[169] If an insult leads to a violent clash in which the insulter gets injured, it will be considered the initial aggression and calculated into the fine as against the assessment of the wound it occasioned, in keeping with the injunction, "Every aggressor is a loser" (*kull mitʿaddī khasrān*).[170]

Some such insults, inferring misbehavior and uttered in public, may damage a person's reputation, such as calling him a dog (*dhīkh*)—that is, behaving without self-respect, as mongrel dogs are seen to do; a habitual thief (*khāyin*), one who steals from friends and neighbors; a betrayer of trust (*bāyig*); or a person devoid of religion (*galīl dīn*)—all of which may cost the maligner a fine of "two mature camels, male and female" (*rabāʿ ū-rabaʿiyya*) unless he can substantiate his charge.[171]

In 1977, among the Aḥeiwāt Shawafīn Guṣayyir, ʿAlī Salīm an-Nahārī was fined four mature camels and had to fly a white flag for saying to a fellow tribesman, Sālim ʿAlī al-Guṣayyir, that his business ventures "stunk," expressing it literally as, "[The ventures are] from your wife's ass" (*min ṭīz maratak*)[172] and thereby insulting his wife in public (Case 106).[173] A particularly serious insult is to imply that a man is behaving like a woman, thereby divesting him of manhood. In the northern Negev in June 2006, the chief of the Tiyāha Abū-l-Gīʿān, Khalīl Abū-l-Gīʿān, acting as judge, fined one fellow tribesman 450,000 Jordanian dinars (approximately $800,000) for threatening another in public that he would "come to him like a man comes to a woman" (*ajīk jei rājil ʿala mara*) and that he would "dress him in a woman's clothes" (*albisak labs al-mara*) (Case 107).[174]

Bedouin maintain that the worst insult is one that imputes base origins, in particular those of the outcast tribes generically called Hitaym, which are spread widely throughout the Middle Eastern deserts. Oral traditions relate that either the forefathers of the Hitaym demurred from helping construct the Kaʿba shrine in Mecca or that their ancestress, called Jarāda, betrayed the Prophet Muḥammad by smuggling his battle plans, concealed in her forebraid, to his infidel enemies. In either case, they are viewed as lowest (*magirr*) in the human scale, and "pure" Bedouin refuse to intermarry with them.[175] The insult of being called a Hitaymī in public is considered so vicious that a non-Hitaymī Bedouin can strike at his vilifier straightaway, even shooting him dead.[176] A judge in Sinai asserted that if the victim struck the vilifier and knocked his eye out, the fine for the insult would consume (*yākil*; lit. "eat") that for the missing eye. Moreover, if the victim chose to sue in court, his claim could be judged by an honor court, where he would be awarded a typically heavy fine, consisting of forty camels at the least. If this number was then balanced against the fine for an ejected eye, which is usually ten camels, thirty camels would be the insulted person's award.[177]

Another litigable form of insult is slander, particularly allegations concerning the moral impropriety of a woman. In 1973 Sālim ʿOwda aṭ-Ṭimṭāwī of the ʿAzāzma ʿAṣiyāt claimed to a company of fellow army trackers that the unmarried daughter of Sālim ʿAtayyig al-Khiraynig of the ʿAzāzma Saraḥīn was pregnant (Case 71). After hospital tests proved the accusation wrong, the judge and paramount chief of the ʿAzāzma confederation in the Negev, ʿOwda Manṣūr Abū Muʿammar, ordered Ṭimṭāwī to declare that he had lied before three notable tents filled with men.[178]

Finally, the law views as a serious form of insult the degrading of someone by "blackening" his reputation unjustifiably. Blackening, as we have seen, is a way to shame a foe into giving justice or a guarantor into fulfilling his commitment, especially by placing a cairn of blackened stones at a frequented venue.[179] In order to blacken, however, one must first have sent *badwa* delegations requesting a violator to relent. When in 1952, for example, ʿOwda al-Kishkhar of the Ẓullām Janabīb in the central Negev blackened a man called Ibn ʿAtayyig, who had stolen some of his goats after being his guest, his act was justified, as it followed several prior attempts to bring his foe to justice (Case 88).[180] By contrast, an example of an unjustified blackening took place in 1938 among the Ẓullām in the northern Negev, when Salāma Abū Graynāt built a black cairn to denigrate his host, ʿĪd as-Sareiʿa, after he had been attacked in the latter's tent (Case 12). *An honor* judge reduced the award accruing to him for the attack on the grounds that Abū Graynāt had blackened Sareiʿa before asking him for justice through a *badwa* delegation.[181] Unjustified blackening may also cost the violator from eight mature camels to the forty usually awarded by an honor judge.[182] In 1979, when ʿAlī Gāsim al-Guwāsma of the Aḥeiwāt Shawafīn confederation in eastern Sinai blackened a fellow clansman, Sālim Ibn Naṣṣār, ostensibly for not having agreed to litigate a dispute with him, the judge awarded the latter two honor payments, amounting to 8,000 Egyptian pounds ($2,000), because Guwāsma had neglected to take the required steps to secure this agreement before resorting to blackening Ibn Naṣṣār with a cairn of blackened stones (Case 11).[183]

In addition to punishing insult in order to prevent violence, Bedouin law also prohibits pointing a loaded firearm at someone. The relevant maxim says, "He who points a weapon has killed" (*man madd katal'*),[184] allowing for the imposition of a fine against him amounting to half the blood-payment for a man, or twenty camels. This fine, imposed in the event that he does not even fire the gun, is based on the presumption that there is intent to kill. Many Bedouin thus claim that it is preferable if the gun goes off and injures someone, as the punishment will exact a lower indemnity, in keeping with the usual provisions of the law for wounds.[185]

Even if no one is hit when an extended gun goes off, however, the law imposes a heavy fine, comprising one-quarter the blood-payment for a man. It is based on the claim that "You have killed him, but God saved his life" (*inti kataltah w-allah ḥayyāh*), as a judge from the distant past is recalled to have ruled. The same judge went on to deliver the sentence: "There was a shot and an impact. Therefore, I rule ten camels, five for the shot and five for the impact; and the rifle goes to him at whom it was pointed" (*ilha maṭlaʿ ū-maṭabb—ʿashr biʿrān—khamsa maṭlaʿ ū-khamsa maṭabb—wa-l-barūda tījīh ʿal illī madd-ha*).[186] These heavy fines are designed to highlight the gravity of provocation in the eyes of the law. The only reprieve from punishment for pointing a gun is if it was empty, in keeping with the maxim, "While a loaded gun kills, an empty one saves [the one who holds it]" (*al-milyāna katalat w-al-fāḍya aslamat*).[187]

Laws to Prevent Collusion

In its effort to prevent violence in Bedouin society, the law widens the circle of responsibility for it, as for any other violation, to include those who aid or even accompany the perpetrator. It thereby seeks to deflect potential accomplices from getting involved in acts of violence, even revenge, in matters that do not legally concern them. If, for example, a man accompanies his friend during an act of rape or an illicit tryst, he will be liable for fines together with the main offender. The law spells this out as, "Whoever smelled her campfire will share in the loss" (*illī yishimm nārha yiḥuṭṭ fī mikhsār-ha*),[188] depicting "her" in question as a shepherdess alone with her flock at night. While the law holds the perpetrator himself as the culpable party subject to all the permitted penalties, it also allots part of any fine imposed by a court of honor to his accomplice. The law stipulates the same liability in regard to an accomplice in theft. Using the imagery of a stolen camel-mare, the relevant legal maxim asserts that "Whoever's heard her groan will pay for part of her discomfort" (*man simiʿ irghāha yiḥuṭṭ fī balwāha*).[189]

Bedouin law also prohibits another sort of collusion in the violation of an individual's rights—namely, guiding the perpetrators to their destination. This injunction pertains whether one is leading people on a criminal operation or avengers on a mission of blood-revenge. Although avengers have a legal right to their vengeance, the guide (*dalīl*, *ibṭaynī*) has no right to endanger the security of the original murderers. Thus, he is a culpable person, and his crime is expressed in the legal directive, "He who guides kills" (*man dall katal'*).[190] All Bedouin agree that such a guide is subject to punishment. While some judges think that in cases where his guidance leads to murder he is subject to revenge in his own right, most hold that his penalty is half the blood-payment for a man, traditionally twenty camels.[191]

Thus, whatever the purpose of the persons he leads, Bedouin law holds the guide subject to a penalty. This is so even if he is leading governmental authorities to perform an arrest. In Sinai early in the twentieth century, the fine was a camel and an Egyptian pound for every day that the arrested people spent in jail.[192] Furthermore, if one should die in jail "even from a common cold" (*inshallah min ad-dishba*), he who guided the authorities will be subject to revenge. In northern Sinai in 1977, when a chief of the Dawāghra confederation, Sālim Salāma Rajawīn, led Israeli soldiers to arrest a contentious tribesman on the fictitious claim that he was a terrorist, a Bedouin judge fined him the equivalent of $50 per day as a "detainment fine" (*ḥabasiyya*) for each of the forty days that the tribesman and his clansmen sat in jail (Case 3).[193] In 1987 in the central Negev, when Frayj, a government tracker, the son of Sālim al-Ameiṭil of the ʿAzāzma ʿAṣiyāt tribe, led the police to the tent of Swaylim Abū Bilāyya of the ʿAzāzma Saraḥīn to search for stolen goods, he was eventually fined the equivalent of $500 (Case 23).[194]

The fact that Ameiṭil was then working as a police tracker and that his guiding was but a part of his job did not acquit him of responsibility by Bedouin law. By the same token, the Tarabīn of southeast Sinai relate that in the early twentieth century, a member of the Aḥeiwāt confederation, called Brīs, was working as a soldier in the Egyptian camel corps, which patrolled the coast of the Gulf of Aqaba (Case 108). One day the corps stopped and searched some Tarabīn youths; during the procedure Brīs slapped ʿĪd Imfarrij al-Musāʿida, who reported it to his elders when he returned home. So long as Brīs served in the camel corps, however, they found it impolitic to demand their right from him. But when, six years later, he quit his job, they were quick to send him a delegation offering him the option of taking an *ʿaṭwa* truce and litigating the blow or becoming subject to violent reprisal. Understanding the rules, Brīs asked for the truce.[195]

Laws to Prevent Treachery

Breaches of Trust The Bedouin in Sinai and the Negev view treachery (*bōg*) as the violation of trust, especially where safety is concerned. Violating trust is in itself sufficiently heinous to Bedouin, as they are particularly dependent on it in the absence of centralized authority and law-enforcement agencies in their deserts. However, when certain conditions of safety that they normally take for granted are jeopardized by deceit, they fear that the underpinnings of their society and culture are coming undone. Consequently the relevant legal maxim proclaims that "The punishment for treachery is compounded" (*al-bōg bizyid*).[196] We have already seen how Bedouin law uses compound punishments for violations of the "camel of sleep," the "blood-truce," and the "camel-truce"—all measures designed to contain and resolve conflicts under assured conditions of safety and based on trust. Thus, if someone exempts clansmen of a murderer from revenge through the "camel of sleep" and then kills one of them, he is subject to four acts of revenge and the payment of a fine for dishonoring the person who guaranteed the exemption. The same holds for someone who agrees to reconcile with the murderers of his clansman, extends them a "camel-truce," and then strikes one of them down. Likewise, if a person grants a "blood-truce" in order to resolve his claims peacefully but assaults his opponent in the midst of it, he too is deemed treacherous and charged a double fine for the wounds he has caused him.

In its effort to prevent violent conflict rather than merely contain it, Bedouin law also compounds the punishments for other breaches of specific trust. One such act of treachery is a premeditated violent attack against someone deliberately misled to think he would be safe. Among the Bayyāḍiyyīn of northwest Sinai in 1999, for example, men planning to kidnap a girl lured her and her father into accompanying them in their car, as if to look into a job opportunity that they were supposedly offering her (Case 93). It was a ploy to force a clansman of hers to return one of their own women, whom he had abducted. After the girl discovered the plot and managed to bolt from their car and escape, an honor trial was held in which the stringent Masaʿīd judge, Amīra Salāma Abū Amīra, not only issued a heavy fine for the deception, but also compounded it fourfold.[197]

In 1997 blood-revenge was permitted fourfold by a judge of the Aḥeiwāt Shawafīn tribe, Imsallam Abū Rās, for the "treacherous" murder of ʿĀyid ʿAṭeiwī al-ʿAlowna by Salmān Zaydān al-Munāṣra, both of the Tarabīn Ḥasāblah tribe in southeast Sinai (Case 52). According to the claim of the ʿAlowna clan, Munāṣra had agreed to marry his sister to her lover after the latter had held secret trysts with her and made her pregnant, but instead he killed him at the meeting that was supposed to be a private wedding attended only by the two men and the girl. Although the law would have allowed a fourfold punishment for Munāṣra's act of betrayal, the ʿAlowna proved content with a single act of revenge (which they subsequently carried out in spring 2000), preferring not to swear an oath as to the veracity of their claim, which was the judge's condition for allowing the fourfold punishment.[198]

Bedouin law also permits fourfold blood-revenge for treacherously murdering a person whose safety is otherwise assured by hallowed Bedouin traditions. Such would be a guest, a traveling companion, and a person asleep. All Bedouin understand that automatic hospitality to all guests is a requisite for survival in the desert, as is the attendant need of people to travel for one reason or another. This value is so ingrained in the Bedouin mentality that even an enemy must be received as a guest. Accordingly, we have the late-nineteenth-century story from the Negev of Muḥammad Ḥamdān aṣ-Ṣūfī, whose brother's murderer, Dahshān Ṣagr Abū Sitta, appeared unwittingly at his tent one night (Case 109).[199] Upon seeing him in the light of the fire he had kindled to prepare coffee, Ṣūfi, honoring the inviolability of a guest, immediately rose and darted for the women's section of the tent, claiming that he had become a woman, unable to execute his revenge like a man. Abū Sitta thus had a chance to flee the tent. This extreme solicitude toward guests is also reflected in the proverb, "A guest is inviolable, though he's a foe" (*aḍ-ḍeif min al-muḥṣināt—lō gōmānī*).[200]

Hospitality is so hallowed a value that it is binding even between confederations that do not share a mutual peace agreement. Moreover, its laws hold a whole confederation responsible for the welfare of visitors from another confederation, in addition to merchants—for example, Case 110:

> Early in the twentieth century, a man of the ʿUmrān confederation in western Arabia came to southeast Sinai to sell some of the prized Ḥijāzī goats of his homeland. He peddled them among the Muzayna, staying with them at night, until one day, a man called Ibn Bakhīt and another man of the Muzayna killed him, threw his body off a cliff, and took the remainder of his livestock. When clansmen from the ʿUmrān came to Sinai looking for him, they were told by a man of the Tarabīn living among the Muzayna that his shepherdess daughter had noticed that the daughter of Ibn Bakhīt had many more goats than usual. The ʿUmrān, knowing that the Muzayna were liable to a fourfold punishment, having murdered a guest in their midst, were quick to wreak blood-vengeance on two of them. The Muzayna thereupon sued for peace, agreeing to a trial in the neutral tent of a judge from the Aḥeiwāt Ghuraygāniyyīn tribe. The judge awarded the ʿUmrān two blood-payments in addition to their two acts of revenge, making the penalty for their murdered clansman fourfold.[201]

Like hospitality, trust in one's traveling companion is a sacrosanct value in the desert, without which the Bedouin would lose their mobility and thus their ability to survive as individuals or as a society. There are many proverbs that reflect the importance of good traveling companions, such as, "Inquire of your companion before choosing the route" (*isʿal ʿan ar-rafīg gabl aṭ-ṭarīg*), or "For a companion it pays to wait two days" (*ar-rafīg—tigūm lah yōmayn*).[202] The most important one, a legal maxim, stipulates that "Companions make sure each other arrives" (*rafīg yiwaṣṣil rafīg*),[203] expressing the rule that a Bedouin must make every effort and take every risk to ensure that his companion arrives safely at his destination. In addition to the great shame suffered by a Bedouin who falls under suspicion of betraying a companion, the law allows for his disqualification in the future from taking oaths that might normally exonerate him from accusations. If one companion murders another, moreover, his punishment will be fourfold, either through revenge or blood-payments.

Killing a sleeping person is also deemed treacherous, whether as an act of murder or an act of revenge. Recall that in revenge, tradition holds that one must awaken the intended victim and remind him that "So-and-so is in your stomach." As noted above, one explanation for the need to wake him up before killing him derives from the belief that when a person sleeps, he is tantamount to dead, and one does not take revenge on the dead.[204] This explanation, however, lacks the usual legal logic of Bedouin law. It also is not proffered to explain the prohibition on murdering a sleeping man when it is not in revenge.

Violations of the Helpless It is more likely that the answers to the enigma lie in two other directions. One is that sleep should be ensured under conditions of security so that people can sleep soundly. The second stems from the Bedouin repugnance toward violence wielded against the helpless.

An interesting corroboration of this possibility may be found in an old tradition among the ʿAzāzma Saraḥīn in the central Negev, where men of the Ḥawaṣa clan were seeking blood-revenge from the Kallāb (Case 111). The Kallāb had fled south and taken refuge among the Aḥeiwāt confederation, but one day their leader came to their usual camping grounds to fetch a supply of wheat he had stored in a narrow cave. Hearing of his whereabouts, the Ḥawaṣa crept up on him and shot him dead as he was penned in tight between the walls of the cave, unable even to turn around. Consequently the Kallāb demanded a trial, in which they claimed to be the victims of treachery, owing to the helpless state of their leader when shot. The judge awarded them four blood-payments, from which one was automatically deducted in the form of their leader, who had been killed as revenge for the Ḥawaṣa man that they had formerly murdered, thus relieving them of the threat of revenge. The second was the customary blood-payment of forty camels, and the third was a girl to be married in bondage-marriage with a close relative of the man killed in the cave until she bore and raised a son to replace the deceased. The Kallāb conceded the fourth award, in keeping with common practice.[205]

As Bedouin law does not explicitly prohibit or punish revenge taken against someone "helpless," as it does regarding the killing of a sleeping man, for example, many Bedouin I questioned cast doubt over the veracity or preciseness of the Kallāb tradition. Some pointed out that the law does not prohibit blood-revenge against other categories of helpless persons, such as cripples, the aged, or the infirm, even though injuries caused such people in assault are fined twofold. On the other hand, the Kallāb tradition is endorsed by all members of the ʿAzāzma Saraḥīn tribe, who volunteer the view that the condition of the man in the cave is identical with that of a person asleep, thus supporting the supposition that the origin of the prohibition on killing a sleeping person developed from his being helpless.[206]

Other cases that may be seen as a prohibition on killing helpless people pertain to women and children, who are not to be killed under any condition, even in revenge. The grounds for this prohibition might be explained in economic terms, as both women and children, in their capacity as shepherds, are essential to Bedouin livelihood. In addition, owing to the geographical spottiness of pasture, they and the livestock are often at too great a distance from other people to be aided if they are attacked. However, this explanation ignores the fact that grown men also serve as shepherds under the same conditions and, if killed, are also avenged, but not fourfold. Accordingly, we are led back to the difference between women and children, on the one hand, and men, on the other, the former being deemed physically weak and thus helpless. Definitions of the two often highlight the weakness. Of a woman it is said, "Her eye is sharp, but her arm is short" (*ʿeinha baṣīra ū-īd-ha gaṣīra*), signifying that she cannot defend herself. Children are generally termed "weak ones" (*ḍuʿūf*), and a child (as noted) is referred to as "a tearful one," about whom it is said, "A piece of plain bread will make him content, and a slap will make him cry" (*al-himsh yiraḍḍīh wa-l-kaff yibakkīh*).[207] As to revenge, the law stipulates, "Any circumcised boy is fit" (*kull imṭahhar biysidd*),[208] considering a boy eligible only after he has been circumcised, which traditionally happens in his early teens. Before that he is too weak to "wield a sword" and thus, "cannot take revenge nor help an assaulted girl" (*lā yākhidh ath-thār wala yinkhī li-l-ʿār*).[209]

The ʿAzāzma Saraḥīn of the central Negev highlight the caution they exercise so as not to take revenge on a minor child by relating an account of murder that transpired in the early twentieth century (Case 112).

> After a man of the Rugaydāt clan murdered someone of the Ibn Ṣughayyira clan, he fled from revenge to Transjordan, where he found refuge among people of the ʿUmrān confederation. A brother of the murder victim, who took up the task of revenge, pursued him to Jordan, asking Bedouin he met along his way if they had seen or heard about a stranger fitting the description of Rugaydī. One man, after asking what he would gain in return for guiding

> Ibn Ṣughayyira to his destination and learning that he would receive the rifle used for the vengeance, led him to Rugaydī's encampment. Ibn Ṣughayyira hid nearby, taking note of his intended victim's movements. He noticed that whenever he exited the tent where he had found refuge, he carried his infant son on his shoulder to deter any avenger from shooting him lest he kill the child and become liable to four acts of revenge in his own right. One day, however, going to a well to water his livestock, he put the child down in order to return for something he had apparently left behind. Ibn Ṣughayyira, exploiting the moment, lit the wick of his rifle and shot Rugaydī dead. The avenger's patience had paid off. All that was left was to present his guide the rifle he had promised him and return home.[210]

The prohibition against killing a child pertains not only to revenge, but also to outright murder.

> Among the Aḥeiwāt Shawafīn of east-central Sinai, they recall that early in the twentieth century two men from the Maʿāza tribe of western Arabia killed the uncircumcised son of Sulaymān ʿAlī Abū Ghuraygāna while the boy was out herding his father's camels (Case 8). They cut his throat, buried him, and went on. The boy's four brothers and three cousins went after the killers, managing to kill one as part of the revenge. For three years thereafter Aḥeiwāt raiders crossed into Arabia and pillaged livestock from the Maʿāza until the latter finally asked the leader of the neutral ʿUmrān confederation to request a camel-truce. At the subsequent reconciliation meeting, in the tent of the ʿUmrānī leader, Nāṣir Abū ʿUṣbān, the Maʿāza agreed that the boy's murder warranted four acts of revenge. One of the four was the killer, whom the boy's brothers had already shot. In place of the second revenge, the Maʿāza made a blood-payment of forty camels and added a *ghurra*-bride for a brother of the boy to have in bondage-marriage. Out of gratitude, the Aḥeiwāt conceded the third revenge specifically in honor of Abū ʿUṣbān, and they waived the fourth as a gesture of mercy.[211]

Finally, Bedouin concern for the vulnerability of children or mentally incompetent persons and the awareness of it as a source of conflict to be avoided are also manifest in the legal procedure of "dissolution" (*tafwīl*), which allows elders to dissolve (*yifowwil*) agreements that others have made with children or the incompetent through deceit. The law asserts that "Trickery and deceit toward the helpless won't work" (*al-ghaff wa-z-zaff mā yimshin ʿala ṣahghāya*), and it empowers the elders to redress the deceit with the provision, "The mature are responsible for a child's right" (*ḥagg al-jāhil ʿal al-ʿāgil*).[212] Deceitful agreements may jeopardize the interests of the child's family, clan, or tribe and may entail the cession or sale of land, implements, or livestock. An example of jeopardizing one's group was in the nineteenth century, when a lad from the northern Negev, working as a shepherd among the ʿAyāyda confederation in western Sinai, undertook, ostensibly on behalf of his tribe, the Tiyāha Shalāliyyīn, to return any camels his tribe might take in raids upon his employers (Case 48). When such an occasion actually arose, however, it became clear that his agreement was not binding, as he was incompetent to make it, owing to his age. His chief used his influence to persuade the raiders to surrender the stolen camels on a one-time basis, but only on condition that the ʿAyāyda consent to abrogate the agreement, which they had clearly obtained through treachery.[213]

Another case from the Negev past stresses helplessness, as well as immaturity, as grounds for dissolution (Case 113).

> A family of three brothers had its camel herd stolen. The two older brothers owned fleet horses upon which they could pursue the raiders. The youngest, who had no horse but was determined to join in the pursuit, asked a man to loan him his horse, for which he offered to give him a camel-mare once they retrieved their herd. Taking advantage of the boy's zeal, the man demanded three camels, to which the boy agreed, and the deal was ensured by a guarantor.
>
> When the brothers indeed released their camels and returned home, the owner of the horse came to them demanding his payment. The older brothers straightaway protested, on the basis of their right to dissolution, and challenged their creditor to a trial. There, the judge, after hearing the arguments of the respective sides, ruled, "The boy made a commitment, but it was after he had learned that his whole herd had been taken. So obviously he was crazy, as anyone in his place would be. He might equally have offered ten camels." The judge thereupon abrogated the agreement but awarded the owner of the horse one camel as recompense for its use.[214]

The law stipulates, however, that once the elder of a clan learns of a deception, he must request an appeal with no further delay. As the legal maxim states, "A dissolver is like a roaring flood: by night he gets moving, by day he runs" (*al-imfowwil sayl dāwī—laylah tisrī ū-nahārah tijrī*).[215] If this rule is observed, the person who has, for example, received an item through deceit must return it to the incompetent one's elders or be subject to a legal claim. Such dissolution is yet another attempt by the law to try and settle a problem quickly, before it spreads and involves more persons. By the same token, the law insists on haste out of consideration for those accused of deception, who may have paid money for what they received. Haste may save them from suffering financial loss.

The above notwithstanding, there is one important case in which no dissolution exists for the action of an incompetent person. If someone liable to blood-revenge elicits from the mouth of such a person a word of pardon for the murder committed against one of his clansmen, the victim clan automatically loses its right to revenge. Bedouin say of such a measure, "The blood is like broken glass" (*ad-damm imkassar gazāz*) — that is, the right to revenge is worthless.[216] Though seemingly incongruous, in light of the importance that Bedouin place on taking revenge, this practice comes to underscore the centrality of the clan in matters of bloodshed. Just as any member of the clan — however incompetent — can take revenge for a murdered clansman, so any member — however incompetent — can concede that revenge. All the Bedouin I consulted on this principle confirmed it, but none had ever heard of it happening.

5

The Role of Litigation in Achieving Justice

Most disputes in Bedouin society do not warrant the use of private violence, certainly not as a first resort, for achieving justice. Even when private violence is wielded as a last resort, it is usually to force a recalcitrant violator to give justice through litigation. Litigation is a victim's preferred way to resolve his problem, especially because victims are most often weaker than violators ("It is the strong one that starts the problem" [*al-gawīy bādī*]),[1] and might not be able to muster sufficient force for using violence as a first resort to regain justice. A victim's relative weakness may also be a drawback in trying to oblige his violator to litigate; even if he succeeds in bringing a stronger violator to litigation with the help of mediators or a protector, as seen in chapter 2, his problems have not yet ended. He still has to find a fair judge, produce persuasive evidence, and obtain a guarantor who will ensure the execution of the judgment. Hence, the Bedouin perceive that "He who accuses dives into fire" (*al-mit-him biykhūḍ fi-n-nār*).[2] Nonetheless, violated Bedouin mainly seek litigation, armed with the faith that "One's right will not disgrace him" (*al-ḥagg mā biylūm rāʿīh*).[3]

The Bedouin Judge

THE ROLES OF JUDGES

In Bedouin society, a judge (*gāḍī*, pl. *guḍā*; lit. "decider") is any person to whom Bedouin might turn when they have conflicts concerning legal rights. Judges stand at the disposal of Bedouin society for a variety of purposes. First, in cases that involve accusations of wrongdoing, a sentencing judge may determine if the defendant is indeed guilty. In 1993, for example, a judge of honor in northwest Sinai, upon personal investigation, absolved from guilt a man accused of trysting with a shepherdess (Case 9). Judges may also weigh the relative wrongs committed by parties against each other. In 1938 a judge heavily fined a man in the northern Negev for assaulting a guest in his tent but deliberately reduced the size of the fine, owing to the guest's precipitous public denunciation of his host before attempting to bring him to trial (Case 12).[4]

Second, in cases pertaining to honor (especially the honor of women) in which guilt has already been established, judges sit in court solely to hear the plaintiff's claim and determine the fine. Such was the case in the northern Negev in 1976, when a judge of honor issued a stiff sentence against persons from southern Sinai who invaded their opponent's tent at night and took hold of his wife (Case 1). Third, judges are also called upon to make procedural decisions on whether a prospective measure will be legal. For example, among the Aḥeiwāt Shawafīn of eastern Sinai in 1979, disputants over the use of land referred to a judge for a decision as to whether their conflict must be litigated by judges from their own confederation, in accordance with a standing arrangement, or whether a specialized judge from a different confederation could rule on it (Case 27).[5] Similarly, members of a clan attempting to stop one of their number from disaffiliating will request the ruling of a judge as to whether the latter has the right to quit.[6]

In addition to these functions, Bedouin have auxiliary judges that aid the litigation process. For determining innocence or guilt in cases lacking evidence, the ruling judge may send a defendant to a judge called a *mubashsha*ʿ, who administers an ordeal in which the accused licks a red-hot iron implement.[7] For deciding the size of fines imposed for bodily wounds, a judge will receive the services of an assessor, or *gaṣṣāṣ* (pl. *gaṣṣaṣīn*), someone skilled at measuring wounds. Indirectly too sentencing judges are aided by the services of a preliminary judge (*malamm* or *ḍraybī*), who hears the disputants' cases and suggests the proper judges for deciding the conflict.

PERSONS ACTING AS JUDGES

When parties to a conflict agree to resolve their differences through a trial and the accused has appointed a guarantor to ensure his attendance, they must decide on a judge to hear their case. Although some judges are themselves the sons and grandsons of judges — largely owing to the expertise gained through their lifelong, constant exposure to conflicts and to trials within their society — no professional corps of judges exists before whom the opponents in a conflict are constrained to litigate. Indeed, judging is rarely a judge's main livelihood — as opposed to livestock raising, agriculture, or (say) smuggling; many Bedouin feel that if it were otherwise, judges might be inclined to partiality, with intent to serve their own economic needs.

Thus, parties to a conflict can pick whomever they wish to judge between them. Any man they choose will have to enjoy their confidence for impartiality, intelligence, a sense of responsibility (as manifest in the conduct of his own life), and a sufficient knowledge of the law. The last quality comprises a familiarity with judicial procedure, the rules for establishing innocence or guilt, the formulas ("words of adroitness": *kalām shaṭāra*) in which contestants usually argue their cases and judges normally deliver their judgments, and the scope of punishments that a judge can impose on a violator for any specific category of crime. In many cases, anyone possessed of these attributes and having the advantage of dwelling near to the contestants may be selected by them as a judge. In southeast Sinai in September 1973, for example, I attended a trial in Wādī Watīr between lads of the Munāṣra and ʿAreiḍa clans of the Tarabīn Ḥasāblah that was adjudicated by Salīm ʿĪd Ibn Jāzī, who rarely acted as a judge but was conveniently encamped nearby (Case 114). As the contestants had injured each other in a fight, their respective clansmen thought it wise to quickly litigate the dispute with someone that was readily available, lest it spread and lead to more bloodshed. Opponents can even turn to a neighbor of a differing tribal confederation to be their judge, as did people of the Aḥeiwāt Shawafīn confederation when, in 1980, they chose Farrāj ʿĪd al-Musāʿida of the Tarabīn to try a case of public insult (Case 106).[8]

In most cases, the persons who serve as judges are men that are considered the elders of a group, such as the clan, sub-tribe, tribe, or confederation. In their capacity as leaders within their groups, elders often find themselves mediating conflicts between co-members, attempting to restore or preserve peace and quiet within the group. It is also they who frequently succeed in prevailing upon opponents to litigate their problem. An elder, by dint of his experience and the many litigations he has most likely witnessed throughout his life, is acquainted with the different branches of Bedouin law. Thus, for example, he can be called upon to try a case of camel theft. If he agrees, the elder will declare that he is sitting in the capacity of a *ziyādī* (pl. *zuyūd*), the designation for a specialized judge who rules by the laws pertaining to theft. This would be the practice of persons judging in any area of litigation, such as honor (a *manshad* judge; pl. *manāshid*); bloodshed and physical assault (a *manga*ʿ *ad-damm* judge; pl. *manāgi*ʿ *ad-dumūm*; lit. "a blood pool"—that is, the place into which all questions of blood drain); or property (an *ahl ad-diyār* judge). Bedouin see it as essential that a ruling judge designate himself accurately so that the punishments he imposes are properly understood. In 1980, for example, in a trial among the Aḥeiwāt Shawafīn in east-central Sinai over a humiliating insult uttered in public, the judge, in awarding the insulted man sixteen grown (five-year-old) camels from his violator, was careful to state that he was ruling as a plain elder rather than an honor judge (*manshad*) in order to avoid any mistaken assumption that his relatively light punishment represented an attenuation, as it might, if he had issued it acting in the capacity of a *manshad*, whose judgments are mainly more severe (Case 27).[9] Owing to this Bedouin obsession with a judge's ruling according to the correct category of the law, an approached elder who does not feel competent in a specific branch of the law will normally decline to rule in it.

Despite the competence of elders to act in the capacity of a judge specializing in a particular branch of the law—a competence that enables litigation to exist as a peaceful way to resolve conflicts in the desert—each tribal confederation contains a number of specifically specialist judges, normally three, who are deemed particularly adroit in their specific branch. In 1933, ʿĀrif al-ʿĀrif, the British Mandatory District Officer for the Negev (1929–39), published a list of these judges for five of the confederations under his jurisdiction.[10] As opposed to the elders, who normally dwell near to the problem at hand, Bedouin respectfully refer to these judges as "the distant judges" (*al-guḍā al-ba*ʿ*īdīn*), as they may live anywhere throughout the confederation's territory, in places often far from the conflict. Formally they are called "those who sustain the confederation" (*mu*ʿ*ammirit aṣ-ṣaff*), an allusion to their additional role in keeping the confederation together by resolving conflicts between members of its various constituent tribes.

Viewed as the most expert people in the different branches of Bedouin law in each confederation, the "distant judges" often also sustain relations between the various confederations of the desert, especially those maintaining a mutual "sworn covenant" (*ḥilf*).[11] In conflicts between individuals belonging to different confederations, these judges from each of the confederations in question will sit together in judgment. A judge of the ʿAzāzma, Salmān Ibn Ḥammād, related that during the British Mandate, his father, Ḥusayn Ibn

Ḥammād, one of three of their confederation's "blood-pool judges," had as "his brother" among the Tarabīn confederation Ṣubuḥ Abū Jilaydān, with whom he would jointly rule in conflicts of physical assault between members of their respective confederations. The other two distant "blood-pool judges" of the ʿAzāzma, Nāṣir Abū-l-Khayl and Sālim Abū Samra, also had their respective "brothers" among the Tarabīn.[12] By tradition, such pairs, each belonging to what the Bedouin designate as "the three disputants" (*thilāthit al-mikhtalfīn*), will sometimes act as judges of first resort, at other times as judges of appeal.

SPECIALIZATIONS AMONG JUDGES

The scope of punishments that judges may impose determines the relative degree of their importance, not as individuals, but deriving from the type of case they are judging at any one time. Cases concerning honor are the most important that come before a Bedouin judge, and the law entitles him to impose a punishment, normally severe, according to his own discretion. Typically, honor cases concern the following:

1. The sexual violation of a woman, allegations of sexual impropriety on the part of a woman, or forbidden entry into the women's quarters;
2. The violation of a guarantee or a false accusation that a guarantor has reneged on his guarantee;
3. Insult to a person by allusion to his having base origins or characteristics;
4. The use of violence in another person's tent.

In the Negev, a judge for all four of the above categories of offense, as well as the branch of the law he will be following, is called a *manshad* (lit. "place of entreaty," to stress the urgency of the problem). In Sinai, the same term is used for the first three categories, but in the fourth category, the term used for both the judge and the law according to which he will rule is *aḥmadī* (pl. *aḥāmda*), the origin of which is indistinct.* Whatever the appellation, the severity and size of the punishments that are at the discretion of judges of honor cause Bedouin to hold them in awe.

Another judge enjoying discretion in the imposition of fines is known, especially in Sinai, as the *ḍraybī* (pl. *ḍraybiyya;* lit. "one who blends claims"), even though the scope of his harsh punishments is less severe than that of either the *manshad* or the *aḥmadī*. Initially the *ḍraybī* is sought as a preliminary magis-

*Hilw and Darwish, *Customary Law*, p. 13, were told in northern Sinai that *aḥmadī* derived from the Prophet's name, Muḥammad, although no supportive material was presented to substantiate this assumption.

trate to decide whether a plaintiff's claim to adjudication before a *manshad* or an *aḥmadī* over a violation of honor is sufficiently sound and serious to be warranted. This is determined by the *ḍraybī*'s hearing the claims of both accuser and accused (hence "blending"). If he finds the case insufficient for a *manshad* or an *aḥmadī* trial, he may judge it himself or send it to a relevant judge; if he finds it deserving of such a trial, he will send the parties to a judge who will rule in these capacities. In 1960, for example, the chief of the ʿAzāzma Masʿūdiyyīn in the Negev, ʿOwda Abū Muʿammar, served as a *ḍraybī* to check if there had occurred a violation of the honor of two men, ʿAwwād Abū Rugayyig and Ḥasan Abū Rubayʿa, who had been called upon to guarantee nonviolence between two sections of the Tiyāha Gudayrāt—Ṭurshān and Abū Kaff (Case 39). As it turned out, the Abū Kaff assaulted a man of the Ṭurshān, who duly aroused the two guarantors of safety, apprising them of the slight to their honor and demanding that they obtain justice for him. While the Abū Kaff initially asserted that their assault had preceded the engagement of the guarantors, they ultimately confessed that it had occurred subsequently. The *ḍraybī*, Abū Muʿammar, thus felt justified to send the case to a judge acting as a *manshad*, Muḥammad Abū Juweiʿid, who had but to issue his harsh sentence.[13]

Similarly, in spring 1993 in northern Sinai, one of the noted *manshad* judges of the Masaʿīd confederation, Amīra Salāma Abū Amīra, acting in the capacity of a *ḍraybī* for a case concerning a shepherdess's moral probity,* sent it to be judged by a *manshad* judge, not in regard to the morality of the girl, however, but rather the immorality of the person who had slandered her (Case 9). The case revolved around a man of the Aḥeiwāt Shawafīn confederation who had informed the father of the shepherdess, of the Aḥeiwāt Ṣafeiḥa confederation, that he had seen her sitting in the company of a man from her confederation and that she had tried to conceal him with her head shawl upon hearing the horn of the informer's car. Abū Amīra, convinced that the implicated man had merely been getting information from the girl about his lost camels, absolved him, while ordering the deceitful informer to ask for a camel-truce from the girl's father, preparatory to a *manshad* trial over his offense against the girl's and the accused man's honor. He also suggested that the judge be a man from the informer's own confederation, Salāma Ḥusayn az-Zimaylī, who would rule in the capacity of a *manshad*, Abū Amīra being confident that "Zimaylī knows the rulings of the Masaʿīd well" (*hū biyʿarrif ḥagg al-masaʿīd zay kidhī*).[14] For rulings such as the two preceding ones, the *ḍraybī* is dubbed "the carpet of the *manshad*" (*frāsh al-manshad*)—that is, the *manshad* rests on his ruling.

* That is, a case affecting the honor of a woman but the details of which are open to debate, or *nagāsh*.

Next in importance are the judges that rule in cases of physical assault and in matters pertaining to the clan, which exists to prevent such assault. Although physical assault — in particular murder — is only slightly less serious to Bedouin than a violation of honor, the primary punishment is delivered through blood-retaliation rather than through the ruling of a judge; hence, the taking of a life may exceed the punishments for the violation of one's honor. However, if the monetary punishment for murder is decreed by a judge, although it might be material and heavy — say, forty camels — its scope will be set by the law and not result from the judge's discretion. As stated, a judge ruling in matters of physical assault is called a "blood-pool judge." One often meets the "measurer" (*gaṣṣāṣ*) as well. Whereas the original specific function of a *gaṣṣās*, as indicated by the name, is to assess the gravity of a wound as an auxiliary judge, someone ruling in the capacity of a *mangaʿ ad-damm* may also on occasion be entrusted to perform the originally auxiliary function of a *gaṣṣāṣ*.

Of the specialized areas of adjudication that impose lesser punishments than honor or physical assault judges, theft is the most important. The judge ruling in such cases will be called an "increase judge" (*ziyādī*; pl. *zuyūd*), as the law allows him to increase the victim's wealth by fining an accused thief normally three or four times the object stolen — a camel, for example — or more in extreme cases. Smaller fines are given for cheating on the boundaries of land, judged by a person or council called the "people of the properties" (*ahl ad-diyār*) or "people of the palm trees" (*ahl al-ʿarāyish*) if the land in question comprises date palms, which are characteristic to many places in Sinai in particular. Relatively small fines are also imposed by judges called "people of the reins" (*ahl ar-rasān*), who deal with problems arising from the sale or use of horses. The judge in cases of marital problems unconnected to honor, the *ʿugbī* (named after the Banī ʿUgba, or ʿUgbī, tribe), also issues judgments containing relatively light punishments. As stated, every confederation contains judges who specialize in almost each of these areas.

Throughout the desert, however, a broad consensus exists that supreme expertise in some branches of the law inheres in the judges of certain confederations, with whose judgments other judges ruling in these branches are expected to be consistent. One such confederation is the Bilī, which dwells in central northern Sinai and also (before 1948) dwelt just north of Beersheba, in the Negev. In ʿĀrif al-ʿĀrif's list of "distant judges" for five confederations in the Negev, four of the five he cites had no *manāgiʿ ad-dumūm* or *gaṣṣaṣīn* of their own. Instead, they referred to judges of the Bilī for major problems of physical assault, even in faraway Sinai.[15] This belief in supreme expertise may extend even to specific families within a confederation. Some of the Bilī family names of the judges that al-ʿĀrif listed in 1933, such as Abū Dahathūm and

Abū-l-Gīʿān, were still borne by *manāgiʿ ad-dumūm* in the early twenty-first century, persisting for at least seventy years.[16]

In Sinai judges from the Bilī are also considered the highest authority as *aḥāmda*, the judges who specialize in violations of a tent's sanctuary. Although Bedouin in the Negev have not traditionally regarded problems of "the rights of the tent" (*ḥagg al-bayt*) to be the specialty of an *aḥmadī* judge, referring such problems instead to *manshad* judges, we find in al-ʿĀrif's list that the Ḥanājra confederation of the Gaza area referred to a Bilī judge from Sinai as one of their *manāshid*, probably in regard to the problems that in Sinai are considered the ultimate domain of an *aḥmadī*.

According to the Bedouin of Sinai, the ultimate domain of a *manshad* resides within a particular confederation, the Masaʿīd, who dwell in the extreme northwest of the peninsula (and also west of the Suez Canal, in the northeast corner of Sharqiyya Province). They are looked upon by all the Bedouin of Sinai as severe guardians of honor, whether pertaining to that of women or men. The awe accorded them for setting the standard in *manshad* judgments is reflected in the alliterative proverb, "The ruling of Masaʿīd judges is harsh" (*ḥagg al-masaʿīd ṣaʿīb*).[17] Indeed, owing to the fact that Bedouin view questions of honor as the most important, the Masaʿīd term themselves "the ultimate terminal" (*magarr*) of judgment, while rhymingly labeling all other *manshad* judges as merely "the passage" (*mamarr*)—that is, to them.[18] For their part, accordingly, all other judges that rule as *manshad* are expected to issue harsh judgments and punishments, purportedly in keeping with those passed down by the Masaʿīd, for what the Bedouin imagine as untold generations. One Masʿūdī judge, Amīra Salāma Abū Amīra, claimed that they had been judges "for ten generations or more—ever since we came from the land of Ḥijāz." This may have been but an approximate estimate, for there is evidence that they came from Ḥijāz to Sinai in the sixteenth century;[19] the precise information, however, would have been lost in an unlettered society. Still, Judge Abū Amīra could name at least four generations of direct ancestors that had preceded him as *manāshid* from his own family—from his great-great-grandfather Ḥusayn, his great-grandfather Ḥasan, his grandfather Amīra, and his father Salāma down to himself.[20] In addition to the Abū Amīra family, the Masaʿīd name four others with a legacy of producing *manshad* judges: the Abū ʿAyyād, the Abū Ḥammādī, the Abū Ḥasan, and the Abū Rashīd.[21]

In the eyes of Negev Bedouin, by contrast to their fellows in Sinai, the ultimate expertise for *manshad* has traditionally resided not with the Masaʿīd but with the Banī ʿUgba, a tribe within the Tiyāha confederation, as represented in recent times in the person of the chief, Sulaymān Muḥammad al-ʿUgbī, until he died in the 1990s. In a *manshad* trial held before ʿUgbī in June 1976 between two families of the Muzayna confederation from southern Sinai, an argument broke out between the guarantors of the defendants and ʿUgbī, the former claiming that their mandate was to guarantee execution of the punishments imposed by a judge ruling in the capacity of a Masʿūdī (a member of the Masaʿīd), while the latter insisted that he, ʿUgbī, being the ultimate authority for *manshad*, could not rule according to a lesser version of the law (Case 1). This squabble reflected the seriousness with which Bedouin hold their convictions about the origins and validity of their laws, and it did not erupt from a theoretical point of view alone. The guarantors had been delegated to pay the fines imposed by a Masʿūdī judge, subsequently to be repaid by the defendants. If the judge was not acting in the capacity of a Masʿūdī, but rather an *ʿugbī* (an alternative appellation for *manshad* judges in the Negev), the defendants might have grounds for withholding their repayment.[22]

Whereas in Sinai the ʿUgbī family is in fact regarded as the ultimate authority in marital problems (called "problems of the night" [*mashākil al-layl*]), an *ʿugbī* judge is not recognized there as the authority for *manshad* law. Indeed, in regard to women, the proverb current among Sinai Bedouin says, "The ʿUgbī judge is the father of women and the Masʿūdi is their paternal uncle" (*al-ʿugbī abū an-niswān—wa-l-masʿūdī ʿammhin*), referring to the concern of a woman's paternal kin for her honor and the purported concern of a father for his daughter's marital welfare.[23] In the Negev, on the other hand, while the authority of an *ʿugbī* judge in domestic problems is acknowledged, he is called "women's paternal uncle" (*ʿammhin*), concerned, as a *manshad*, primarily with their honor. One wonders if the rivalry of these two tribes over preeminence in the *manshad* branch of Bedouin law doesn't somehow emanate from a sixteenth-century war that broke out between the Masaʿīd and Banī ʿUgba, when the two erstwhile neighboring tribes from western Arabia were jointly about to invade the Negev (Case 51). After that war, the remnants of the Banī ʿUgba stayed in the Negev, while the Masaʿīd went on to dwell in Sinai.[24]

Another example of the Bedouin belief that ultimate authority concerning the law resides in a particular confederation are the ʿAyāyda, who live in the deserts that straddle the central section of the Suez Canal.[25] Their specialization is not in ruling on the law, but rather in administering an ordeal by fire called *bishʿa*, which assists judges in establishing guilt or innocence, especially in cases of murder, rape, fornication, and theft, when doubt exists over the identity of the perpetrator or the circumstances of the act. In the ʿAyāyda *bishʿa* ritual, a defendant licks a red-hot iron implement, usually a long-handled pan for roasting coffee beans that is called in Egypt a *ṭāsa* and is known, on this occasion, as "the ʿAyāyda-man's roasting pan" (*ṭāst al-ʿayyādī*). This reference to the ʿAyāyda man is to the *mubashshaʿ*, who administers this ritual and who is normally the single person in any period qualified for the task.

For many decades, this office resided in the Salāṭna section of the ʿAyāyda, within a particular clan called the ʿAwāmra. The ʿAwāmra claim that the first *mubashshaʿ* of the ʿAyāyda was a Ḥamdān, who was followed by his son Ḥimayd. They tell that the *bishʿa* ability came to Ḥamdān, who was skilled at tracking, when his tent was burglarized. Although he knew the identity of the burglar, whom he had tracked, there were no witnesses. So Ḥamdān, in order to overcome the latter's denial, took a pair of red-hot iron tongs from the campfire and challenged the latter to an ordeal of proof: Ḥamdān would lick the tongs three times, to be followed by the thief doing the same. The liar would be burned, while he who told the truth would stay unscathed.[26]

Since then, the *bishʿa* irregularly alternated between the Salāṭna and the Jarābʿa sections of the ʿAyāyda. The practice was that when a *mubashshaʿ* died, "the *bishʿa* would halt for a year out of grief" (*al-bishʿa tugʿud sana, yaʿnī ḥazīna*). Then, one morning, an elder member of the ʿAyāyda would say to those assembled for morning coffee, "By God, I dreamt last night that the *bishʿa* came to me [that is, God revealed it to him in a dream], and I must undertake this duty." The people would then ask to see his tongue, which, if bearing a white mark, would substantiate the truth of his dream.[27] In the 1930s the British surveyor G. W. Murray reported that the current *mubashshaʿ*, called ʿĀmir, was of the Jarābʿa section and that he had followed his father, ʿAyyād, and paternal uncle, ʿUwaymir, in this position.[28] In the early 1970s the incumbent *mubashshaʿ* was an elderly ʿĪd Abū ʿĀmir, of the Salāṭna section, who practiced at his farm in Basatīn Barakāt, near Bilbays, just east of the Delta. At some point after the death of ʿĪd, no one apparently appeared among the Salāṭna to assume the office of *mubashshaʿ*, for by 1980 it had again passed to the Jarābʿa section of the ʿAyāyda, among whom ʿAwwād ʿUwaymir al-Jarabīaʿ performed the *bishʿa* at ʿIzbit al-ʿArab, his farm near Abū Sulṭān, south of Ismailia in the Suez Canal Zone, until 1987, when he was followed by his son, ʿAyyād.[29] Unlike the *mangaʿ ad-damm* and *manshad* branches of the law, in which any judge may rule in the capacity of a Bilī, Masʿūdī, or ʿUgbī ultimate specialist, an administering *mubashshaʿ* must by tradition be the single member of the ʿAyāyda confederation thus sanctioned;[30] nonetheless, since the 1990s there have indeed been two rival practicing administrators: Sulaymān ʿAwwād ʿĀmir of the ʿAyāyda Salāṭna, at Basatīn Barakāt, and ʿAyyād ʿAwwād ʿUwaymir of the ʿAyāyda Jarābʿa, at ʿIzbit al-ʿArab.[31]

TRUST IN JUDGES

Whichever judge they choose to adjudicate their conflict, Bedouin hope that he will be impartial in his judgment. Based on the fact that the Bedouin legal system has survived for millennia, one might safely say that impartiality prevails among judges. On the other hand, several indications exist that partiality in judicial decisions is not unknown. First, appealing a judge's decision before an additional judge, a process called "going up" (*istinād* in the Negev; *irtifāʿ* in Sinai), is built into Bedouin litigation as a right. Indeed, when a Bedouin requests an appeal, his disdain for the perceived partiality of the judge who has condemned him may be expressed in angry terms such as, "Your judgment is shit in a donkey's ass" (*ḥaggak mankūt fī ṭīz al-ʿeir*)—that is, it stinks. Second, Bedouin sayings belie a suspicion of biased judges, admonishing that, similar to witnesses, their future welfare, or "luck" (*ḥaẓẓ*, *bakht*), depends on honesty. One proverbial warning, often uttered to judges, holds, "A man should come to one's aid with money and men, but not with his luck" (*ar-rājil yifzaʿ bi-mālah wi-rijālah—lā bi-ḥaẓẓah*).[32] Another simply admonishes, "A judge should not sell his luck" (*al-gāḍī mā yibīaʿ bakhtah*).[33]Third, specific instances of partiality may be found in various accounts. In 1979 Frank Stewart tape-recorded the evidence of a party to litigation from the Aḥeiwāt Shawafīn confederation in eastern Sinai; it relates how a judge, ʿOwda Ṣabāḥ Abū Nada of the Tarabīn Shibaythāt, called him aside to coach him on what to do so that he, the judge, could rule in his favor (Case 27).[34]

Another instance, from central Sinai, occurred in 1991, when people of the ʿAlaygāt and Tarabīn confederations were in dispute over the former having kidnapped a lad of the latter, to be followed by the Tarabīn kidnapping a man of the ʿAlaygāt and the latter's demand for differential awards owing to the greater distance the second kidnapping covered (Case 91). The parties ultimately decided upon Salāma Ḥusayn az-Zimaylī, of the Guṣayyir section of the Aḥeiwāt Shawafīn, to try them, and they set a date.

> Before the arrival of the parties, a member of the Tarabīn Ḥasāblah residing in the south, ʿAnayz Sālim al-ʿUrḍī, betook himself to the tent of the judge on the basis of their being friends. ʿUrḍī's goal was to relate to the judge a story about Zimaylī's grandfather, ʿAliyyān al-Guṣayyir, a noted chief and judge in his own right, in order to sway him to favor the Tarabīn. According to the story, Guṣayyir once had a guest, Swaylim al-Galbāwī, an elder of the Aḥeiwāt, and the two men talked into the night, discussing matters of law. At one point, the host asked Galbāwī what, in his opinion, Bedouin law (*ʿilm al-ʿarab*) was really about. Galbāwī answered: "When you give me a riyal, I give you a riyal" (*yōm taʿṭīnī riyāl aʿṭīk riyāl*)—that is, one bad turn deserves another.[35] The next morning Zimaylī delivered his judgment—namely, that the first kidnapping (and the failure to ask for a truce) occasioned the second kidnapping and that the ʿAlaygāt deserved no award.[36]

Other accounts indicate that Bedouin judges have sometimes been unfair to the Egyptian peasants and merchants who live among them, cultivating their fields in the Negev or trading with them in Sinai. Apparently it stems from a reluctance to let non-Bedouin use Bedouin courts to overcome Bedouin. During the period of the British Mandate, this was at least one reason for the Tarabīn in the Negev to include a peasant judge, an Abū ʿArādī, as one of their three "blood-pool judges".[37] An early-twentieth-century story from there tells of a trial between the Tarabīn Jaladīn and the Tarabīn ʿAmarāt, the latter reported to be of peasant origin (Case 115). It was certain that the ʿAmarāt had the better claim and were bound to win the trial. Before it took place, however, a man of the Jaladīn agreed with the Bedouin judge, also of the Tarabīn, that the latter would help them. The plan was that this man, Abū Jilaydān, would come to the trial late but would be allowed to speak. Thereupon, he would tell a story that would insult the ʿAmarāt, who would indignantly get up and leave the trial, "making themselves the losers" (*yinfilijū*). Abū Jilaydān's story, which angered the ʿAmarāt, causing them to leave the trial, went as follows:

> I was on my way here this morning and stopped to rest near al-Khalaṣa. When I looked around, I saw "the Generous One" (*al-karīm*—that is, God) sitting on the ground and kneading the mud. I lit my *ghalyūn* pipe and watched him. He was creating little human figures, and when he had made them smooth, he laid each pair aside and said, with satisfaction, "These are the Tarabīn," "These are the ʿAzāzma," "These are the Ẓullām," and so forth, naming all the pure Bedouin tribes. Then he took to hand some mud that would not stick together but kept falling apart. So he got fed up and threw it away, saying, "These are the ʿAmarāt; nothing but cows!"[38]

Another account from the early twentieth century tells of a judge, the blind ʿAliyyān Farrāj al-Ghuraygāni of the Aḥeiwāt Shawafīn, who adjudicated a dispute between his sons and a merchant from El-ʿArīsh called Ismaʿīn (Case 116). The latter claimed that the sons owed him payment for merchandise they had received from him in the course of time. It was clear that the merchant was in his rights. When, however, the judge delivered his judgment, it went against Ismaʿīn. A judge of the Tarabīn Ḥasāblah, Ḥusayn al-ʿAlowna, sitting next to Ghuraygānī and surprised by the verdict, tapped his foot with his own and uttered, "May God help us!" (*yā sātir*). The Aḥeiwī judge asked, "Whose foot is next to mine?" And learning whose it was, he said to ʿAlowna, "Take your foot away from mine and don't open a door for the peasant (*fallāḥ*) to get the better of my sons" (*ibʿad rijlak ʿan rijlī ū-lā tibawwib la-l-fallāḥ yākil ūlādī*)! For the sake of justice, however, the sons of Ghuraygānī subsequently paid the merchant his due.[39]

The Litigation Process

DEFINING CLAIMS AND CHOOSING A JUDGE

Elders, in addition to mediating and adjudicating disputes, may also play dominant roles in the initial stages of the litigation process, particularly as preliminary magistrates, providing the site and forum for choosing the judge of first instance and for defining the claims that will be submitted to litigation. In performing these roles, an elder is specifically termed "site of gathering" (*malamm*)—that is, the place where opponents gather to settle their differences. A Bedouin legal maxim, using the same image, defines the *malamm* as "someone who gathers one opponent to another" (*yilimm as-sagīm la-sagīmah*).[40] Other than men designated as elders, however, anyone trusted by the parties, even a younger man, can act as *malamm*. In east-central Sinai in 1978, for example, two contestants belonging to the Aḥeiwāt Shawafīn confederation used as their *malamm* ʿAṭeiwī Rāshid al-Munāṣra, who was still in his thirties and also of a different tribal confederation, the neighboring Tarabīn (Case 106).[41]

Actually, the defining of claims must precede the choice of judge, as the claims will determine which branch of the law is applicable to the case and which judge will be appropriate for its adjudication. At the tent of the *malamm*, each party to the conflict states his claims by digging a hole in the sand in front of where he is sitting and "burying a pebble" (*dafn al-ḥaṣā*) for each claim he enumerates. This is the claimant's single opportunity to state his claims, for the law deems any claim not enumerated at this session, but subsequently pressed, to be invalid for judgment by trial. If, as often happens, a victim of violation has multiple claims, not all of which fall within the same category of law, he can insist on one or more of the claims being heard by different, perhaps specialist, judges. He does this by taking a separate pebble and casting it aside, declaring that each such pebble represents a further claim that will be dealt with at a later date. In 1975, for example, when, among the Muzayna of southeast Sinai, Sālim Jumʿa Abū Ṣabḥā was attacked in his tent by assailants who cut off his finger and violated his wife, he insisted on having the violations against his wife and the sanctuary of his tent tried by a judge of honor in one trial and his wound assessed by a "blood-pool judge" in another (Case 1). Therefore, while choosing the honor judge at a session with a *malamm*, he buried two pebbles stating his claims to justice for his woman and his tent, and he symbolically threw a different pebble aside, saying, "The pebble of my wound [lit. 'blood'] is cast aside" (*magrūṭa ḥaṣāt ad-damm*), to indicate that he was leaving this claim for a separate trial. This "throwing of the pebble" (*garṭ al-ḥaṣā*), as the procedure is called, later enabled Abū Ṣabḥā to plead his case before the renowned "blood-pool judge" as-Sulaylmī of the Bilī confederation. Had he neglected the *garṭ al-ḥaṣā* procedure, which preserved for him his deferred claim, the law would not have allowed him the subsequent trial over the spilling of his blood.[42]

A Bedouin may also activate this procedure to preserve the violated rights of someone of a different clan who is not present at the *malamm*. Among the ʿAzāzma Saraḥīn of the central Negev in 1973, for example, after women of the Zanūn clan beat the aged sister of Ḥimayd Salmān as-Saddān of the ʿOwdāt clan, along with her daughter-in-law of the Ghidayfī clan, the Ghidayfī men, demanding reparations for the wounds received by their own woman from the Zanūn, threw aside the pebble of Saddān's sister, knowing that the restoration of her rights was his responsibility (Case 14).[43] Similarly in 1979, when, among the Aḥeiwāt Shawafīn of eastern Sinai the nonrelated wife of Sālim Ibn Naṣṣār was beaten in his tent by his clansman, he threatened to convoke a trial over this violation of the tent, declaring, however, that he was throwing his wife's pebble aside—that is, for her own clansmen to deal with at another time (Case 11).[44]

To Bedouin the buried pebble also symbolizes permanence, signifying that what is stated through the procedure cannot be altered in any later stages of the litigation. Accordingly, they preclude the possibility that one of the parties will change his claims in order to gain some advantage as the trial proceeds. Burying a pebble, by focusing the attention of the *malamm* and others present on the claims stated, also augments their ability to remember them in the event of subsequent discrepancy. The *malamm* (or another designated witness from among those present), as the repository of the respective claims, will be the authority for what the litigants said when initially stating them. In this regard, therefore, the act of burying a pebble with the statement of each claim also offsets the absence of writing in the premodern desert.

If, as suggested, one of the contestants should deviate from his original statement while pleading before a subsequent judge (perhaps one of those originally selected in the presence of the *malamm*), this judge will send him back to the *malamm* (also termed "master of the dwelling" [*rāʿī al-bayt*] to stress the importance of his venue) so that his authoritative recall will resolve the discrepancy and allow for the proceedings to continue. This step is called "counting out [the witness's fee] and returning [to him]" (*ʿadd ū-radd*); in keeping with tradition, the judge will say, "I hereby cause you to count and return you to the burying place of your claims" (*āna ʿāddkū ū-rāddkū ʿala madfan ḥaṣākū*). Owing to the "satisfaction fee" (*raḍwa*) that the contestant who is shown to have deviated from his original claims will pay the *malamm*

—in keeping with the legal maxim, "The deceptive petitioner takes the loss" (*al-mughirr owla bi-l-khasāra*)[45]—the *malamm*, in this capacity as a paid witness, will also be called "the one to be satisfied" (*marḍawī*).*

After hearing the claims, a *malamm*, rather than name the judges who will try the case, may offer to judge it directly himself, suggesting in rhymed, traditional language "to solve the case upon the burial of your pebbles" (*al-fakāk ʿala dafn ḥaṣāk*).[46] Only if his offer is refused by the contestants will he begin the process of selecting prospective judges by making three lines (*khuṭūṭ*) in the sand and asking the defendant (as a gesture of appreciation for his agreement to litigate the conflict) to name three judges whom he agrees may adjudicate it. The plaintiff may reject one or all of those chosen by the defendant, in which case other names must be proffered. When agreement has been reached over these "people who have been indicated by a line" (*makhaṭīṭ*; sing. *makhṭūṭ*), the contestants decide which of them will be the judge of first instance and which the judges of appeal, since the right of appeal is part and parcel of the Bedouin legal system. This process of selection is called "preference" (*ʿadf*). The *malamm* now asks the plaintiff which of the three *makhaṭīṭ* he prefers as his appeals judge in the event that he should disagree with the judgment of the judge of first instance. The judge he chooses is then formally known as his "preferred one" (*maʿdūf*). Next, the defendant chooses his *maʿdūf*, leaving the yet unchosen one as the judge of first instance.

If the offer of the *malamm* to adjudicate the case is accepted, he becomes the judge of first instance. In the event that, after his decision, one of the parties feels the need to appeal, the *malamm* will name the appeals judges rather than resort to the *ʿadf* process. This procedure is called *ikhwānah fī lisānah* ("he names his brothers with his own tongue"). It is practiced too by the *ḍraybī* if he is in the capacity of a preliminary magistrate that adjudicates the problem before him rather than sending it to a specialist judge. It is also applied by both *manshad* and *aḥmadī* judges when they decide cases rather than merely determine awards and punishments.

In Sinai, however, the *ḍraybī*, for the most part, is the main forum for selecting *manshad* and *aḥmadī* judges, and, like an elder or other *malamm* (by which name the *ḍraybī* is known to most Bedouin in the Negev), he can either

*Another function of a *marḍawī* as a court's witness is to provide evidence on which a judge's conditional judgment rests. See Stewart, Texts, vol. 1, p.47, for an example of a judge asking a *marḍawī* (who happened to have been present when a group of foes approached a litigant) whether the latter vocally allowed one of them to come forward, which would have removed any claim against him for having insulted the entire group (Case 11).

aid in this selection or adjudicate the case himself. Two things differentiate the *ḍraybī* from the aforementioned judges. First, contestants refer to him for his decision on whether the plaintiff's claim is sufficiently serious to warrant being heard by judges specializing in questions of honor or, alternatively, whether they should be tried by him or someone else on the level of a nonspecialist. A frequent claim of this sort concerns the violation of a woman's honor. In 1973, for example, Īd ʿAtayyig al-Khiraynig charged Sālim aṭ-Ṭimṭāwī, both of the ʿAzāzma confederation in the central Negev, with slandering his unmarried daughter by alleging, before a number of fellow Bedouin soldiers with whom he was stationed, that she was pregnant (Case 71). After considerable mediation, Khiraynig got Ṭimṭāwī to go along with him to a *ḍraybī*, Sulaymān Ibn Rafīaʿ, of whom he requested that his case be tried according to the *manshad* laws of honor. In light of the fact that Khiraynig was able to bring witnesses who had heard Ṭimṭāwī's allegations, Ibn Rafīaʿ ordered the contestants to be tried by the head ʿAzāzma chief, ʿOwda Abū Muʿammar, in the capacity of a *manshad*.

A case in which a *ḍraybī* did not pass the case on to a *manshad* judge occurred among the Aḥeiwāt of eastern Sinai in 1978 (Case 57). The *ḍraybī*, Slaym ar-Rimāg, was petitioned by a fellow tribesman, Salāma Ḥusayn az-Zimaylī, who claimed that his tent had been violated when a husband beat his wife in it. "Beating a wife is forbidden in another's tent" (*al-bayt mā fīh marājil*).[47] Zimaylī thus demanded of the *ḍraybī* an honor trial before a judge acting as an *aḥmadī*, who adjudicates the violation of tents in Sinai. The *ḍraybī* ruled, however, that the case did not warrant the extreme penalties that an *aḥmadī* judge (or even a *ḍraybī*) is authorized to impose, sending him instead to be tried by an Aḥeiwāt elder, Ḥimayd Jumʿa Kureidim.[48]

Occasionally, when cases are particularly intricate and potentially volatile, three (or more) judges will sit together in council (*majlis*) and take a majority decision, after which there is no appeal. Such was the case in 1975, when a council consisting of nine judges from the Suwārka, Tarabīn, and ʿAyāyda confederations of northern and central Sinai tried to adjudicate a conflict between two members of the Muzayna confederation of southern Sinai, Sālim Jumʿa Abū Ṣabḥā and Munayfī Sālim Jabalī, over an attack that comprised wounds, the violation of a tent, and the violation of women's honor (Case 1). They sat as *ḍraybiyya*, trying to decide if the claim of the plaintiff, Abū Ṣabḥā, deserved a *manshad*. Ultimately they decided that it did.[49] Similarly in 1999 in eastern Sinai, a council of judges of the Tarabīn confederation, which included Judge Ḥājj Swaylim Zāyid al-Gunbayzī, ruled in a conflict between the Tiyāha and ʿAzāzma confederations in which a tribesman of the latter murdered a man of the former, accusing him of having violated the honor of his wife (Case 41).[50]

PROVIDING GUARANTORS

No less important to the litigation process than choosing the judge or judges that will adjudicate a conflict is the provision of guarantors (*kafala*; sing. *kafīl*; lit. "a doubler," "an endorser"). In the absence of other law-enforcement measures, the fact that a trial takes place "under guarantors and the honor of men" (*bi-kafāl wi-ʿurūḍ ar-rijāl*) makes its success certain. Guaranty ensures that violators will attend the hearings and abide by the judgments issued by the judge.[51] Accordingly, a guarantor is expected to be a man of relative means and power who can "put up the money and force the men" (*yiḥuṭṭ al-māl ū-yiḥkim ar-rijāl*).[52] It is the social weight of the persons who act as guarantors and the legal penalties that result from ignoring their honor that serve to deter the parties to a conflict from stopping litigation or dodging its outcome.

Toward ensuring that a person accused of committing a violation attends the trial to which he has assented and does not recoil from paying the judge's fee, he must appoint "a guarantor against absence or fright" (*kafīl ʿan gheiba ū-heiba*).[53] In 1952 such a guarantor was Chief Sālim Ibn Saʿad of the ʿAzāzma Saraḥīn, who undertook to have a fellow tribesman, an Abū ʿAtayyig, come to a trial at which his stealing some goats from a host, ʿOwda al-Kishkhar of the Ẓullām Janabīb, would be judged (Case 88).[54] Once this type of guarantee is obtained, the date, time of day (mid-morning or mid-afternoon), and place of the trial or claims session are set in the presence of elders, and as the Bedouin proverbially affirm, "Attendance at the trial is as binding as a debt that must be met" (*al-mowʿid dayn—lā budd ʿan sidādah*).[55] If one of the parties is delinquent, he will be deemed the "guilty one" (*maflūj*) in the case at hand unless he provides an acceptable explanation for his absence. Such an explanation might be an impassable flash flood, government detainment, an enervating illness, or someone's death and burial. When such excuses and sufficient notice are provided, the trial is postponed for a week. If, however, the absence is inexcusable, it constitutes an affront to the honor of the guarantor, subjecting the delinquent to an honor trial with a *manshad* judge, where he will incur the particularly severe punishments that this type of judge has the discretion to impose.

Another way of fostering the participation of a defendant at his trial, especially in a case entailing an accusation of physical assault or violation of the claimant's honor (via his womenfolk, his tent, or his reputation)—cases in which physical retaliation is possible—is to guarantee his safety so long as the litigation continues and the resolution of the conflict is in progress. In cases of violation by physical attack or sexual assault, the defendant will have been granted either a blood-truce (*ʿaṭwa*) or a camel-truce (*jīra*), during which he must act to give his victim justice; correspondingly, the latter must desist from assaulting him. These truces are extended even before the details of the impending trial are discussed. For every such truce, a "truce guarantor" (*kafīl ʿaṭwa*) is engaged who will ensure the fulfillment of the truce rules, in particular the immunity of the defendant from attack. Any breach of the rules will subject the violator to a *manshad* trial and its harsh punishments, in addition to his having to pay double fines for any wounds or damages he causes.

Minor differences pertaining to the period of a truce guarantee exist between Sinai and the Negev. In the Negev a truce guarantee applies only until the litigation begins, whereupon a new guarantor is appointed as "a guarantor of warmth [that is, safety]" (*kafīl dafā*). This guarantee is valid even beyond the apparent resolution of the conflict in order to protect the original defendant from attack from his perhaps still vengeful opponents. In Sinai the role of the *kafīl dafā* begins only after the defendant has discharged all the punishments imposed by the judge "completely" (*wāfī*), in keeping with the rhymed maxim, "Warmth comes with completeness" (*ad-dafā yōm al-wafā*).[56] In the event that a condemned defendant is accosted in connection with the original case, his recourse is "to arouse" (*yigowwim*) the *kafīl dafā*, whose responsibility is not only to bring the offender to a *manshad* trial in order to restore his own slighted honor, but also to ensure that the assaulted party is compensated for any harm with compounded fines. As under a *kafīl ʿaṭwa*, it is not any sort of violent action on his part that serves to keep a defendant safe, but rather the threat of *manshad* and damage fines, which serve to deter assault under a *kafīl dafā*.

To ensure that a guilty party submits to the punishments contained in the judge's sentence completely and does not abscond, a defendant must, after choosing the judges together with his opponent, appoint a "guarantor of completeness" (*kafīl wafā*), who has the wherewithal and power to "put up what's due and return the fugitive" (*yiḥuṭṭ al-bārid ū-yirudd ash-shārid*).[57] "What's due" is the fine imposed, meaning that the guarantor must pay it in the event of the accused's default, in keeping with the injunction, "If your adversary flees, collect your due from your guarantor's honor" (*in sharad gabīlak kayyil al-ḥagg fī ʿarḍ kafīlak*).[58] To "return the fugitive" means the action that the *kafīl wafā* must undertake to obtain his due after having paid the fine in the fugitive's stead. His due is double the sum. The relevant legal maxim stipulates, "The guarantor's due is double: two coins for one and two animals for one" (*ḥagg al-kafīl mathnī—girsh bi-girshayn ū-sōg bi-sōgayn*).[59] Ultimately a guarantor's obtaining this compound sum is his task alone, presuming that his power is sufficient to pose a threat to the remiss person whose payment he has guaranteed. Still, Bedouin law entitles a *kafil wafā*, when agreeing to guarantee completeness, also to demand a backup, or indemnifactory, guarantor, who will help him obtain his twofold due from the delinquent fugitive. This backup is called a "guarantor of doubleness" (*kafīl ṣaff ū-mathnī*; lit. "once and again"). A legal maxim counsels, "The guarantor of complete payment must know who's his guarantor of doubleness, even if the payment is certain" (*kafīl al-wafā ghayr biyʿarrif al-kafīl ṣaff ū-mathnī—lō al-ḥagg wākid*).[60]

The existence of this recourse indicates how a threat by the more powerful members of Bedouin society enables guaranty to be effective as the chief means to enforce the judicial judgments of litigation. In 1932, for example, among the Ẓullām confederation in the Negev, Muḥammad al-Gabbūaʿ, whose son was supposedly beaten up by Salāma Abū ʿAyyāda, blackened the chief, Salmān Abū Rubayʿa, for not taking action against the aggressor, despite his having guaranteed, as a *kafīl dafā*, his desistance from violence (Case 31). When Abū Rubayʿa and his accuser aired their respective cases before a *ḍraybī* judge, it turned out that Salāma Abū ʿAyyāda had not hit anyone. Thereupon, the chief, as a guarantor of warmth, pressed his right to an award from a *manshad* judge, who imposed the following punishment on Gabbūaʿ:

1. Forty unblemished four-year-old camels;
2. One hundred Palestinian *grūsh* (pennies) with every camel;
3. A tent covered with white cloth down to the ropes;
4. A male and female slave for each of the tent pegs;
5. The recitation of three words (*bayyaḍ allah wijhih*—May Allah whiten the honor [of Abū Rubayʿa]) in three prominent tents covered with white cloth and filled with men (each missing word of the three to be offset with a four-year-old camel).[61]

The fact that Abū Rubayʿa eventually conceded all the material awards that the *manshad* judge decreed in his favor but would not concede the proclamation of his honorable behavior in three tents filled with men attests to the supreme importance of an honorable reputation to a guarantor's status and welfare.

Similarly in 1957 an Abū Khubayṭa was fined in trial for having given false evidence alleging murder to Ibrahīm al-Aṭrash of the Tiyāha Gudayrāt (Case 32). When Abū Khubayṭa avoided paying the fine, Aṭrash turned to the *kafīl wafā*, who paid in his stead, lest he be blackened. The guarantor then pursued Abū Khubayṭa, demanding the customary double reimbursement and threatening him with physical assault if he desisted. So Abū Khubayṭa announced that he was under the protection of the new chief, Ḥammād Salmān Abū Rubayʿa, who would prevent any such assault. When the guarantor's threats nonetheless continued, Abū Khubayṭa aroused Abū Rubayʿa, but to no avail.

Threats to blacken the latter led the two to a trial with the *manshad* judge, Sālim Muḥammad al-ʿUgbī, who claimed that a party that has violated the honor of someone that guaranteed him is guilty of injustice and cannot summon notables to protect him. His alerting of Abū Rubayʿa was unfounded, and his threats to blacken him were unjust. ʿUgbī thus announced the following punishments for Abū Khubayṭa:

1. He must pay Abū Rubayʿa forty camels;
2. He must give him a male and female slave, each on a camel;
3. He must cover the tent of Abū Rubayʿa with white cloth;
4. He must announce at the tents of three notables (the chiefs of the Huzayyil, ʿAṭōwna, and Ṣāniʿ tribes) that Abū Rubayʿa was not remiss but that he (Abū Khubayṭa) was in the wrong.

Again, Ḥammād Abū Rubayʿa conceded all the material awards but insisted on the act of confession in order that his name be cleansed.[62]

PAYING THE JUDGE'S FEE

The appointment of guarantors is but one, albeit vital, part of the litigation process, ensuring first and foremost that in the absence of law-enforcement agencies, the verdicts of the judges will be implemented. The institution of guaranty, depending as it does on the honor of the guarantors, also lends a degree of prestige to the litigation process, and it facilitates compliance with its decisions through respect. This comes in addition to the prestige of judges, who, in general, are called the "masters of justice" (*siyād al-ḥagg*), as in the saying, "Justice will appear when its masters appear" (*al-ḥagg yiẓhar yōm tiẓhar siyādah*).[63] Judges who hail from prestigious families, even from dynasties of judges in certain fields—such as the *manāshid* Abū Amīra and ʿUgbī families, the *manāgiʿ ad-dumūm* Abū Dahathūm and Abū al-Gīʿān families, and the *mubashshaʿ* Jarabīaʿ and Salāṭna tribes of the ʿAyāyda confederation—enjoy additional esteem.

There is also a Bedouin sentiment that the setting of a trial is hallowed and its precinct sacrosanct. Hence, "Trial sessions are an obligation" (*al-magāʿid malāzim*),[64] and a party on trial must not absent himself for "The trial is like a debt that must be paid" (*al-mowʿid dayn—lā budd ʿan sidādah*).[65] Bedouin also have high regard for the seriousness of a trial. In particular, it is "an open men's tent with well-founded [that is, precise] talk" (*shigg imsharraʿ ū-harj imgarraʿ*),[66] not the well-known and frequented "mountain plains and pastures of camel herds" (*furūsh ū-marātiʿ ṭurūsh*), where talk is nonaccountable. Accordingly, Bedouin (especially claimants) feel that a main attribute of litigation is the airing of a conflict in public in "a gathering that hears" (*samaʿ ū-jamaʿ*), "a semicircle of men sitting cross-legged" (*ḥiniyya ū-rukba mathniyya*), or "a meeting-place with a full coffee-pot" (*dīwān ū-bakraj milyān*).[67] Such reverence for the setting of the trial facilitates compliance with the judgments that issue from it in a way more benign than guaranty.

However, respect for the trial is also augmented by the obligation of both parties to put up a judge's fee (*ruzga*; pl. *ruzag*; lit. "sustenance"). Indeed, a trial is often defined as the venue of "rights gained through the fees being paid [lit. 'thrown down']" (*ḥagg ū-garṭ irzag'*). Payment of the *ruzga* thus underscores a commitment to submit one's case to judgment and to accept the results. At trial's end, the full fee (for example, 2,000 Jordanian dinars), of which each contestant has paid half, remains with the judge, the winner retrieving his half from the sentenced party, who thereby bears the full sum himself. This repayment is also operative when parties go to a judge to obtain a conditional judgment regarding a point of law, a procedure that does not entail a judgment of innocence or guilt but only of right or wrong.[68] In a *manshad rās* trial, in which innocence and guilt are determined beforehand, only the defendant puts up a *ruzga*.[69]

The amount of the *ruzga* is determined at the discretion of the judge; if it is apparent that the sentence will comprise a fine, it may constitute some one percent of that sum. In the past, swords or other precious possessions were occasionally known to be deposited as a *ruzga*, to be replaced by a more modest sum when the trial was over. Sometimes too a man would put up his camel or horse to demonstrate confidence that his case would prevail.

PLEADING BEFORE THE JUDGE

Once the judge's fee has been put up by the parties, they state their cases to the judge, the claimant first, followed by the defendant. Although contestants may plead by themselves, most are represented by spokesmen who are usually more experienced in presenting a case before a judge, just as they are in discussions, negotiations, and arguments in general. These representatives are mainly the elders of a contestant's group, whether clan, sub-tribe, tribe, or confederation, often depending on his opponent's corresponding level of affiliation. If one's spokesman is of the same clan, he is known as an "elder for a day and forever" (*kabīr yōm ū-dōm*).[70] In this case, his overall participation in the trial is that of any other fellow clansman in that he pays part of the judge's fee (*ruzga*) as well as fines, if they result from the proceedings. This is expressed as "wearing his [the contestant's] gown and contributing to his share" (*lābis thōbah ū-gāyim bi-nōbah*); by contrast, if his contestant wins the case, the spokesman will regain his share of the judge's fee and take a portion of the fines accruing to his clan. As a fellow clansman, he may also endorse his contestant's oath with one of his own.[71] He also may swear an oath on his contestant's behalf. If the spokesman is not of the clan, he is called a "tongue for the occasion" (*lisān ḥāl*), a title that is thought to have come from the pronouncement of a long-past spokesman defining (perhaps defending) his role—namely, "I am a tongue for the occasion but a good man. I pour, but don't get drenched. I neither lay down a judge's fee nor swear an oath" (*āna lisān ḥāl w-ibn ḥalāl—sāgya wala babtalī—la baḥuṭṭ ruzga wala baḥlif aymān*).[72] Unlike an "elder for a day and forever," who is generally not paid for his representation, the "tongue for the occasion" is normally paid.

Respect for spokesmen is also a part of the overall respect for the litigation process. As Bedouin law has never been codified or written down, and given that certain aspects of the law in any one area do not come up often or even in every generation, what the spokesmen say in their pleadings, however mistaken, may easily be taken as the truth of a legal point. Accordingly, it is said that "The spokesmen of people write the law" (*ilsin an-nās galām al-ḥagg*).[73] Incidentally, this gives rise to a phenomenon peculiar to Bedouin litigation, whereby bystanders at a trial, though they have no stake in it, may speak out and contradict what they are hearing, even from a spokesman, lest the law (as they conceive it) be distorted. Still, all agree that "The spokesman destroys a defense and builds it" (*al-kabīr biyhidd aṣ-ṣīra wi-yibnīha*)[74]—that is, he has the responsibility for building his client's case. Accordingly, in order for Bedouin law to be able to continue to utilize his and others' experience in the service of sound litigation, the prestige of spokesmen must be secure. Thus, the litigant that a spokesman represents is forbidden to criticize or dismiss him. From a trial in the past, a criticized spokesman is recalled to have reprimanded his client proverbially as follows: "Appointing a spokesman and then limiting him can't happen: you're like a rooster in a cage that can't caw. Neither fidget nor gesture! You are dumb and can't speak" (*kabbarah ū-ṣaghgharah mā biyṣīr—inti dīk fī-l-gafaṣ mā tigōgī—lā tihiff wala b-īdak tiriff—inti balam mā titkallam*).[75] Though a litigant may be unhappy with his spokesman, he can replace him only when the case is appealed before a new judge. Such possible tension between litigant and spokesman, however, mainly pertains when the latter is a "tongue for the occasion." In the case of a spokesman of the same clan, the results of the trial affect both litigant and spokesman equally, owing to the clan principle of mutual responsibility. Hence, more trust prevails, even to the extent of the spokesman's waiving the litigant's original claim.

One reason for the widespread use of spokesmen for pleading before a judge is that the plea (*ḥijja*) is, in part, regularly delivered in formulas and rhymes not easily managed by a rank-and-file Bedouin. Between the formulas and rhymes, or after them, the spokesman (or a litigant speaking for himself) may supply details specific to his case or may be questioned on details by the judge. The traditional content of these pleas may be seen (through bold letters in the Arabic text), in the following examples, presented according to categories of the law. In the first plea, regarding a rape, the spokesman for the raped girl's father, or the father himself, uses mainly traditional formulas and rhymes, some in metaphor, to describe the violation. Then he absolves the girl of any suspicion of compliance, indicates the plaintiff's wish for a harsh sentence, and expresses deference toward the judge. This is the content of many pleas.

1. The plea of the father of a raped girl to a *manshad* judge:

By God, what is your judgment, o Judge,
(***W-allah w-aysh* ʿ*endak yā gāḍī***)
About one who came to her in her pasture,
(*fi-llī jāha fī **maflāha***)
Who came to her out of blindness and misguidance,
(*ū-jāha min* ʿ***amāh*** *ū-gillit* ***hadāh***)
She being innocent, having not anticipated him on the hilltops
(*ū-hī **sāhya lāhya,** lā wagafat lah* ʿ*ala* ***gīzān***)
Nor having sent him a message with people.
(*wala arsalat lah ma*ʿ *al-*ʿ***urbān***)
He did with her what he wanted and left off what he didn't,
(*ū-sawwa **mā rād** ū-khalla **mā kād***)
Leaving her dress tattered and her beads scattered
(*ū-khalla thōbha **gadāyid** ū-kharazha **badāyid***)
So that the very mountains split and the ground was pierced.
(*ū-sawwa fi-l-jibāl **thulūm** ū-fi-l-bilād **suhūm***)
But she directly lit her campfire and woke up her neighbor
(*ū-walla*ʿ*at **nārha** ū-habbat **jārha***)
And came to me shouting, her mouth open to the wind
(*ū-jatnī **tiṣīḥ** ū-fammha fātḥa la-r-**rīḥ***)
Wailing and weeping, still nighttime, not waiting for day.
(***shākya bākya*** *— layl **mū hū** nahār*)
God willing, I'll have him fined and condemned
(***inshallah agharrimah*** *w-ajarrimah*)
As though I'd put him in fire that burns or a sea that drowns.
(*w-aḥuṭṭah fī **nār itḥarrig** ū-**baḥr yigharrig***)
I seek protection from Allah and from you
(***w-adkhal*** ʿ***al allah*** *w-*ʿ***alayk***)
Concerning a judgment that is clear to you though hidden from me.
(ʿ***an*** *ḥagg* ***imbayyin lak ū-mitigī*** ʿ***annī***)
This is the plea of a dumb man to one who understands.
(*ū-haydhī* ***ḥijjat balīm*** ʿ***end ar-rājil al-fahīm***).[76]

The second plea is that of a man whose camels have been stolen. Although it is shorter than the first, merely describing the violation and expressing the wish for a harsh sentence, it employs the standard formulas and rhymes.

> 2. The owner of stolen camels pleading before a *ziyādī* judge:
>
> By God, what is your judgment, o Judge,
> (***W-allah w-aysh* ʿ*endak yā gāḍī***)
> About one who attacked my camels and took them,
> (*fi-llī hajam* ʿ*a-l-bi*ʿ*rān w-akhadh-hin*)
> Moving them from their pasture to where they were hid,
> (***ū-waddāhin** min **maflāhin** ila **makhfāhin***)
> Camels that never carried a heavy load nor plied a long road.
> (*ijmāl mā ḥāmla ḥiml **thagīl** wala lāgṭa khaṭṭ **ṭawīl***)
> God willing, I'll have him fined and condemned
> (***inshallah agharrimah w-ajarrimah***)
> As though I'd put him in fire or a stormy sea.
> (*w-aḥuṭṭah fī-n-**nār** wa-l-baḥr at-**tiyyār***).[77]

The third plea, of someone whose ownership to land has been disputed, is also replete with the standard formulas and rhymes, defining the case (by asserting the plaintiff's rights) and indicating his desire for a severe punishment for his opponent.

> 3. The plea of someone on whose land another has squatted, to the *ahl ad-diyār*:
>
> Take strength, o Judge, to give a right that isn't light
> (***Khudh lak*** ʿ***awāfī** yā gāḍī fī-l-ḥagg illī mū hū **ḥāfī***)
> For my land which is guaranteed by the honor of men.
> (*fī arḍī illī* ʿ*alayha **ikfāl** wi-*ʿ*urūḍ ar-**rijāl***)
> In its borders to the west and to the east
> (*min ḥudūd-ha min **gharb** ū-min **sharg***)
> Which I leveled with my feet, as with my hands I put a sky above
> (***illī baṣṣaṭṭ-ha bi-rijleiy ū-rafa*ʿ*t samāha bi-īdeiy***)
> And have been plowing it from the day a crow cawed in it
> (*ū-bi-yōm naghaṭ **gharābha** w-āna **karrābha***)
> As I was the first there to plant, to sow, and to cut the bushes.
> (*āna sābgah bi-**khaḍār** ū-**badhār** ū-gaṭa*ʿ ***ishjār***)
> And since I brought him near and had him join the semicircle on your carpet
> (*ū-yōm **dannaytah** ū-*ʿ*a-frāshak **ḥinnaytah***)
> God willing, I'll have him fined and condemned
> (***inshallah agharrimah w-ajarrimah***)
> As though I'd put him in fire that burns or a sea that drowns.
> (*w-aḥuṭṭah fī **nār itḥarrig** ū-**baḥr yigharrig***).[78]

The fourth plea, arguing for awards for the violation of the sanctuary of a man's tent, differs from the preceding pleas in that it was made by the plaintiff himself, a rank-and-file Bedouin, and is mainly stated in everyday prose, with only a few formulaic expressions.

4. The plea of the owner of a violated tent to an *aḥmadī* judge (Case 57):

I wish you good health, o Abū Sālim
(***Khudh lak ʿawāfi,*** *yā-bū sālim*)
I come to you rightly guided and will leave you rightly guided,
(***ajīk bi-hidī w-amshī bi-gidī***)
But nothing should be done without a blessing on the Prophet.
(***wa-lā tingiḍī al-ḥajjāt ila bi-ṣalātin ʿa-n-nabī***)
It happened that I, my neighbor, and my wife were away,
(*illī fīh: āna ghāyib ū-ṭanībī ghāyib ū-raʿiyyt al-bayt gheiba*)
And in our absence there was trouble, and she took refuge in my tent before the blows
(*w-ʿugibna ṣārat ṭowsha ū-tiwazzat li-l-bayt gabl aḍ-ḍarb*)
And he came to her in my tent and beat her and dragged her
(*ū-jāha fī baytī ū-ḍarabha ū-jarrha*)
And then forced her from my tent and pushed her into his tent
(*wi-ʿugib mā aṭlaʿha min duwārik al-bayt sāg-ha ila baytih*)
But after I returned she came back to me and told me what took place
(*ū-ʿugib mā jīt thannat ʿaleiy tathnāh ū-ballaghatnī*)
And since she told me, we were happily able to agree to bring the matter to court
(*ū-yōmin ballaghatnī ḥaṣal al-khayr ū-rabaṭna al-ḥagg*)
And to go to court averts evil.
(*wa-l-ḥagg nihāya ʿan ash-sharr*)
By God, I can say that now that I've found Allah and found you
(*wallah innī agūl* ***yōminnī liḥigt allāh wa-liḥigtak***)
I will get an award for her being dragged from my tent and an award for her for being beaten
(*l-āʿṭī jarrha bi-ganūn wi-ḍarbha bi-ganūn*)
And an award for his violating the precincts of my tent to come get her.
(*ū-tigaṭṭaʿ al-ḥaramāt ʿalayha bi-ganūn*)
If the law gives her a divorce, God willing you will award it
(*w-in-kān lihiyya frāg, in sha allah min ʿendak ghayr alḥagah*)
And if the law doesn't give her a divorce, I would not dare to break up the marriage.
(*w-in-kān mā liha frāg, ḥazzī mā yigṭaʿ ʿaysh aḥad*)
This is the plea of a dumb man to one who understands.
(***wa-ḥijjit balīm ʿend rājil fahīm***)
I seek protection with God and with you

(***ū-dākhil* ʿ*al allāh w*-ʿ*alayk***)
Concerning a judgment that is hidden from me but clear to you.
(ʿ***an ḥagg ghibī* ʿ*aleiy ū-bayyin* ʿ*alayk***).[79]

By contrast to the above plea and the everyday language of the plaintiff speaking for himself, the following plea, though also made by a plaintiff unaided by a spokesman, is replete with formulas and rhymes, the plaintiff having served as a spokesman for others in many trials. Not only is his rhetoric more traditional, but he is also careful to praise the judge at the outset, imbue his plea with religiosity, describe the violation, and express his wish for a harsh sentence for his violator. Then he describes another aspect of his problem, expresses his anticipation of a severe punishment, and shows deference to the judge. Some of the formulas were heard in more than one of the cited pleas.

Sālim Jumʿa Abū Ṣabḥā pleads before Sulaymān Muḥammad al-ʿUgbī, the *manshad* judge (Case 1):

I come before you with a blessing that pleases Muḥammad, o ʿUgbī.
(***Ajīk fī ṣalā illī tirḍī Muḥammad,*** *ya* ʿ*Ugbī*)
What is your opinion, o our Judge, who brings relief to our woes?
(*b-allah* ***w-aysh* ʿ*endak yā gaḍīna, yā imfarrij balawīna***)
What is your opinion of a woman sleeping at night curled up
(*w-aysh* ʿ*endak fī nāyimt* ***al-layl*** *ṭāwiyyt* ***adh-dhayl***)
And her close neighbor comes and attacks her through deceit and treachery,
(*illī ṭanība ū-jāra, wa-yindabb* ʿ*alayha* ʿ***owg ū-bōg***)
Comes and devastates her sacrosanct space, the barrier not to be passed without permission
(*ū-yījī ū-yihaddim maḥarimha, illī* ***ṣūr*** *mā yinkhashsh ghayr bi-****dustūr***)
But he destroys it upon her, she who's lying, not standing, o ʿUgbī
(*w-allah wi-yikassirūh* ʿ*alayha, wi-hī* ***nāyima*** *mī hī* ***gāyima,*** *yā* ʿ*Ugbī*)
And demolished my honor and disgraced my face, going up to my woman, violating my woman,
(*ū-haddamū wijhī wa-yisawwdū wijhī, wi-yifūtū* ʿ*al-*ʿ*ārī, ū-yifaḍḍiḥū fī* ʿ*ārī*)
Who, by God, is lying in only the garb her creator gave her.
(*illī, w-allah, hī nāyima fī ghayr thōb il-khālig*)
From ten o'clock till sunrise, they pushed her around
(*min as-sāʿa* ʿ*ashara limma ṭiliʿ aṣ-ṣabāḥ, wi-yidaffiʿū fīha*)
Marrying her to each other, one marrying, one divorcing;
(*wi-yijowwzūha bʿaḍ-hum, wa-dhī yijowwiz wi-dhī yiṭallig*)
Not marriage by the tradition of God and his messenger.
(*jīza ghayr bi-sinnt allāh wa-r-rasūl*)
By God, I hope, now that I've found God and found you
(*w-allah, innī* ***min yōm liḥigt allāh wi-liḥigtak***)
And brought him near you and kneeled him on your carpet

(*ū-thannaytah* ʿ*a frāshak ū-dannaytah*)
I'll have him as if he were in a burning fire and drowning sea.
(*l-āʿṭīh fī* ***nār itḥarrag*** *ū-fī-****baḥr yigharrig***)
Then, o ʿUgbī, he rejected taking the camel-truce
(*w-allah, yā* ʿ*Ugbī, illī baʿd kidhī yitʿaṣṣa ib-jīrtī*)
Which we demanded of him and pressed him to do
(*ū-nuṭulbah aj-jīra wi-ndizz* ʿ*alayh*)
But he got the government to attack me, using its orders
(*ū-yihajjim* ʿ*aleiy al-ḥukūma ū-yitrawwaḥ marasīm al-ḥukūma*)
To obliterate my case
(*wi-yirūḥ ib-gaḍiyyitī*)
And they put me on trial with tribal judges, the state trying me,
(*wi-yisawwī* ʿ*aleiy manadīb wi-tijībnī al-ḥukūma ū-tiḥākimnī ad-dowla*)
All from the oppression and at the behest of the violator, who should have been the one pursued.
(*min jōrtah ū-min sababah wa-hū maṭrūd*)
By God, they fined me all my money, everything left by my father and grandfather
(*w-allah ū-agharram kull māltī, kull ma* ʿ*aggab abūwī ū-jiddī*)
But I came to him and pursued him like a man
(*w-allah w-ajī* ʿ*alayh w-aṭrudah ṭrād rijāl*)
By way of our "taking livestock and killing men"
(***w-ākhidh minnah māl w-ashill minnah rijāl***)
Until the right overcame the wrong and I brought him with my bare hands
(*limma al-ḥagg ghalab al-bāṭil, w-ājībah* ʿ*ala ṭabaʿ īdī*)
And made them each take a camel-truce and throw the pebble over what they had denied;
(*ū-limma daffaʿt kull minhum ib-jīra wa-l-mankūr maṭshūsh al-ḥaṣā*)
And I brought him to your carpet, o ʿUgbī, making him kneel in a semicircle,
(*w-ajībah* ʿ*a frāshak, yā* ʿ*Ugbī,* ***w-aḥannīh w-athannīh***)
The criminal that blackened my face.
(*al-mijrim illī sawwad wijhī*)
God willing I should have him take a camel-truce for each day he balked
(*in sha allah l-āʿṭī* ʿ*alayh kull yōm ib-jīra*)
And each truce bought with four camels, and every *manshad* fourfold
(*ū-kull jīra ib-arbaʿa ū-kull manshad imrabbaʿ*)
He who used deceit and treachery on his woman neighbor, our flocks pastured with his flocks, our shepherdesses went to the well with his shepherdesses, the women visited each other, there was no warning nor pillage.
(*illī* ʿ***amal*** ʿ***owg ū-bōg,*** *illī ṭanībtah, al-ghanam fī-l-ghanam, wi-l-mīrād fī-l-mīrād wi-l-* ʿ*ār fī-l-*ʿ*ār, illī lā nadhr wala wākhidh*)
And this is the plea of a dumb man before one who understands.
(***ū-ḥijjit balīm*** ʿ***end ar-rājil al-fahīm***).[80]

After the pleading is finished, it is customary for the judge to repeat the pleas in a procedure called "revealing the pleas" (*tashrīaʿ al-ḥajaj*). It is performed, often in the actual original phrasing of the pleas, in order for each of the contestants to be sure that his points were properly heard and understood and for them and the other people present at the trial to feel that the upcoming judgment, called "exposing the law" (*ṭulūaʿ al-ḥagg*), will be well founded.[81] It is also important for sustaining the litigants' confidence in the judge.[82]

PROVIDING EVIDENCE

Confession

In trying to determine innocence and guilt in a case before him, a judge's task is facilitated if one of the parties confesses that he was in the wrong. "Confession is the lord of all laws" (*al-iʿtirāf sayyid al-aḥkām*) is a sentiment often heard among Bedouin, attributing to confession supreme merit in effecting justice.[83] We have seen how confession is ipso facto forthcoming when one requests a camel-truce, or *jīra*, especially after those violations of a woman's honor for which the law allows private violence to be wielded as a first resort. In 1975 among the Muzayna in southeast Sinai, the Jabalī clan sent four camels to request a truce from Sālim Jumʿa Abū Ṣabḥā after having violated the honor of his wife in a raid on his tent (Case 1).[84] They knew that the *jīra* camels were tantamount to a confession that would lead to a trial and a reprieve from revenge, in keeping with the legal maxim, "The request for a camel-truce is like a verdict of guilt" (*al-jīra garār*).[85]

In court, for cases less serious than murder or rape, however, violators are naturally not eager to confess their wrongdoing, except when confronted with irrefutable material evidence that leaves them no choice but to throw themselves at the mercy of the judge. This is so, for example, with thieves caught in the act or those asked to swear an oath or undergo the *bishʿa* ordeal. We have an example from 1946, when the tent of the future paramount chief of the ʿAzāzma, ʿOwda Manṣūr Abū Muʿammar, was swamped and its belongings scattered after a major flood in the central Negev (Case 117). Abū Muʿammar could not find his coffee utensils, which he eventually accused some neighbors of stealing. They denied the charge vehemently, claiming that they had bought the utensils in the market; they even stated their willingness to go to the *mubashshaʿ* in Egypt to prove their innocence. Abū Muʿammar took up their offer, having those present at the time bear witness to it. When the time came to leave, however, fear of the *bishʿa* led the thieves to confess, whereupon a judge of theft, or *ziyādī*, ordered them to return the utensils, pay their owner fourfold their worth, and compensate him for the expenses he had incurred in searching for them.[86]

Fear of a witness's testimony can also lead a violator to confess. In the northern Negev in 1960, it impelled the leader of the Abū Kaff section of the Tiyāha Abū Rugayyig tribe to admit that his people had violated a truce by beating up a man of the Ṭurshān section, with whom they were in conflict (Case 39). After Abū Kaff had denied that his clansmen had perpetrated the assault after the truce went into effect, the judge ordered the person who had arranged it, an Abū Ḥimayd, to testify as to when the truce had been called. Abū Kaff, expecting that the witness would tell the truth, thought it best to anticipate him and confess, even though he became obliged thereby to sit for a *manshad* trial that would affirm the reliability of the man who had guaranteed the truce, Ḥasan Abū Rubayʿa.[87]

Witnesses

Institutionalized Witness In the absence of a confession, a judge may have to base his judgment on the evidence he can garner, witnesses and oaths being the two main sources in Bedouin law. Witnesses are commonly used in legal conflicts between Bedouin. Some witness is even institutionalized. When, for example, a violated Bedouin encounters a refusal by his violator to litigate the problem, he sends him a delegation of people (*badwa*) to try and persuade him to relent. If he remains unyielding, the members of this, or further, delegations will be witnesses to the fact before a judge, should the violated party ultimately resort to violent action to regain his rights. Institutionalized evidence is also expected from witnesses in cases of abduction (*shrād*—that is, of women) and the impoundment (*wisāga*) of property, customarily camels. In cases of abduction, it is the "companion" (*rafīg*, *imbarrī*) of the eloping couple who must testify under oath that the man did not physically touch the woman, thereby averting a *manshad* trial. When a person resorts to impoundment, one or more witnesses testify that the camels were not taken for theft but for the purpose of forcing a violator to litigate a conflict, abiding by the dictum, "Provide sufficient witnesses and eliminate the fines for theft" (*waffī ash-shuhūd ū-baṭṭil az-zuyūd*).[88]

When, however, any chance violation has occurred, the victim will attempt to engage eyewitnesses to give evidence in court. Traditionally he would tie a knot into a witness's head-cloth, saying, "Your head-cloth is knotted. Bear it with you to pasture in the morning and back to the tent at dusk; wear it as a necklace by day and use it as a pillow by night (*inti maʿgūd al-ʿamāma—tisraḥ maʿāk al-misrāḥ ū-tiḍwī maʿāk al-marāh—fī nahārak gilāda ū-fī laylak wisāda*)[89]—that is, pay attention to this knot (a common method of recalling obligations), which you must keep with you during all hours and activities of the day.

Nonetheless, bearing witness is not a legal obligation; the designated eye-witness of a violation retains the option of testifying or not. Bedouin sentiments approving free choice impel a violated person to respect the prospective witness's prerogative (for example, "A hand that must be bound to the sword won't strike" [*al-īd illī maʿṣūba ʿa-s-seif lā tuḍrub*]).[90] In certain cases, a person may find that his testimony runs counter to social conventions. In a conflict between a fellow clansman and a non-clansman (*ajnabī*; lit. "outsider"), for example, there clearly is no question of a witness giving testimony that would harm the former. Clan solidarity is ingrained.[91] Loyalty to a traveling companion is another convention. Thus, if such companions were suddenly waylaid by a robber in the desert and both fired their weapons to defend themselves, killing their accoster, the one whose rifle may have jammed, or who simply missed the mark, would be roundly condemned in society for testifying that not he but his companion did the killing. Before a *mangaʿ ad-damm* judge trying to clarify who committed the murder, the non-killer might testify that he did not do the killing if he were suspected, but he could otherwise say nothing to directly implicate his companion.

In other circumstances, considerations such as one's safety or one's social relationship with the violator may also serve to deter one from getting involved in a conflict not pertaining to oneself. Accounts are rife of accused Bedouin trying to intimidate a willing prospective witness into not giving testimony. Often they may hint at possible revenge, rhetorically asking, "Why do you want to harm us?" Or they may suggest a way out for him. For example, in one infamous, albeit anonymous, case in the Negev, they even directed a prospective witness to go to a visible slope near to the judge's tent, crouch in the Bedouin manner, and urinate facing upward. As no sane Bedouin would urinate in a way in which he would soil himself with urine running downhill, the witness, if attention were called to him, would disqualify himself as mentally incompetent.[92]

The Acceptability of Witnesses In addition to mental competence, a person against whom a named witness is to give testimony can reject him for other reasons. First, since the witness will have to swear to the truth of his evidence, he must be deemed a God-fearing man. As conceived by Bedouin, this would be indicated by his having dear things to protect from the wrath of God, such as wealth and sons, which he would not endanger by bearing false witness—in other words, someone "whose tent is wide and who says his morning prayers; one who possesses livestock and children" (*wasīaʿ al-marāḥ w-imṣallī aṣ-ṣabāḥ—rāʿī māl wa-ʿayāl*).[93]

Second, a witness must be without public moral stain: "God-fearing and clean; he who seeks in him a blemish will not find it" (*tagī nagī—illī biydow-*

wir fīh al-ʿeib mā yilāgī).[94] A public stain might pertain to "a remiss guarantor" (*kafīl bāyig*), who has proven remiss in fulfilling the terms of his obligation, or a man who "knows [that one of his womenfolk has morally strayed] but ignores [punishing her or her consort]" (*dārī ū-mārī*).[95] To escape such devastating public shame, a guarantor accused of being remiss will demand a *manshad* trial to clear his reputation, as did Ḥasan Abū Rubayʿa, for example, when accused of not restoring the right of a man of the Ṭurshān who was assaulted while under his guarantee (Case 39).[96] Another example, this one of a cuckolded husband who sought to restore his reputation, occurred in the central Negev in the early twentieth century (Case 66). After his fellow tribesmen refused to let him sit with them (*kaffū al-frāsh ʿannah*; lit. "rolled up the carpets away from him"), reviling him for his counter-conventional submissiveness, a man of the Owraydī clan of the ʿAzāzma Saraḥīn went so far as to pursue and murder his wife and the man who had absconded with her, subsequently being killed himself by the abductor's clansmen.[97] Other causes of public shame, which could deny one the ability to bear witness at a trial, are what the Bedouin consider their three inexcusable transgressions: "stealing what has been stored" (*sirgit al-miṭmāra*), "fornicating with a neighbor's wife" (*dabbat al-jāra*), and "betraying a traveling companion" (*bōg ar-rafīg*).[98]

An accused aggressor may also reject as a witness someone who bears him enmity, a person whom he "may have offended" (*ḍarab fīh*) in the past. In a traditional story heard among the Muzayna in southern Sinai, a camel thief rejects as a witness someone whom he had promised an Egyptian pound to keep the secret of the theft, only to renege on his promise thereafter (Case 118). In this case, however, he could not reveal the offense he had committed against the man without also admitting to the theft.[99]

Finally, women are automatically disqualified from testifying in court. If a woman has witnessed an event with legal implications that might incriminate a man, she may offer it only as "a declarative oath" (*dīn bāligha*), normally via a clansman. If her evidence is denied by the accused, after an initial clarification with him through her clansmen, she must swear an oath to the rightness of her report, which is then deemed sufficient by a clansman for giving sworn testimony at the trial as if it were his own. In a highly unusual, and seemingly improbable, case that reportedly took place in the northern Negev in the 1930s, a woman gave such evidence through a brother, swearing that her son, whom she had inadvertently killed, did not belong to her husband and his clan, as generally believed, but was rather the issue of a romance between her and one of her paternal cousins (Case 119). The blood-pool judge, trying the husband's claim to blood-money compensation for his presumed child, deemed the woman's testimony as to the paternity of her child central to the case, even though it cast dishonor upon her clansmen for their immoral behavior and their failure to raise her to moral probity.[100]

Again, in central Sinai in the early 1940s, a man from the Ḥuwayṭāt Dubūr tribe in southern Jordan testified on the basis of a "declarative oath" thus delivered by his sister (Case 62). The woman, who had been married off to a man of the distant Aḥeiwāt Ṣafeiḥa confederation, claimed that one of their men had made stubborn advances toward her about which she, as a stranger, had been keeping quiet until her brother's visit.[101] Similarly in 1999, when Judge Amīra Salāma Abū Amīra of the Masaʿīd confederation of northwest Sinai was hearing a claim based on an unconfirmed report that a girl of the Aḥeiwāt Ṣafeiḥa was trysting with a man of her tribe, he traveled to her distant encampment to hear her version of the story, which subsequently disposed his judgment in her favor (Case 9).[102]

The only court that accepts a woman's claims directly is headed by a "judge of argumentation" or "hospitality judge" (*gāḍī al-ghalāṭ*), who decides which tent of an encampment is entitled to receive and feed newly arrived guests.[103] So important is hospitality as a social value that a solitary woman may argue a turn for her tent so as to preserve its (and her) honor.

Preventing False Witness Aware that evidence gained from declared witnesses may be false, Bedouin law has viewed witnesses with some reserve. For example, the law deems the evidence of witnesses in the most serious of legal problems among Bedouin—those dealing with murder or the violation of a woman's honor—as unacceptable in court. Hence, judges follow the legal maxim, "No informers for fornication nor witnesses for murder" (*al-ʿeib mā ʿalayh shuhūd wa-d-damm mā ʿalayh wurūd*).[104] Even more resolute is the judgment of a past judge when a girl's honor was maligned: "The eye that saw should be put out; how much more if it didn't see" (*ʿein in shāfat giliʿit—w-aysh ḥāl illī mā shāfat*).[105]

In cases in which evidence gained from witnesses is admitted, it must be firsthand, not the conveyance of hearsay or rumor. Accordingly the law says, "There is no evidence based on other evidence" (*lā ʿilm min warā ʿilm*).[106] Also, when witnesses are allowed, such as in cases of camel theft, the law is fastidious about details. In one early-twentieth-century case in the Negev, for example, a Bedouin of the Tarabīn who had spotted a fellow confederate in the desert with a camel bearing the ʿAzāzma brand offered himself as a witness to the camel's owner after hearing of its theft (Case 120). However, as he had personally never seen the camel prior to encountering it in the desert and had thus never seen it in herd at the owner's encampment before it was stolen, the judge invalidated his evidence.[107] Similarly in Sinai, also early in the twentieth century, the evidence of a witness who claimed to have encountered a camel thief presumably selling his loot in a market was also nullified because he had not actually seen the thief untie the fetters from the camels' legs, thus giving the thief the opportunity to claim that the witness had seen him merely looking the camels over as a prospective buyer (Case 118).[108]

Finally, Bedouin law curbs false witness by stipulating that it constitutes a violation of the reputation of the person slandered and is grounds for the offended party to demand an honor trial against the slanderer in order to restore it. In 1993, for example, the Masʿūdī honor judge Amīra Salāma Abū Amīra dismissed a claim made by Slaym Abū Ḥunayk against a man named Abū Maḥamūd, both of the Aḥeiwāt Ṣafeiḥa confederation, to the effect that the latter had stopped off to flirt with the former's daughter (Case 9). The claim was based on the purported evidence of a third party, called Bilān, who had reported to Abū Ḥunayk that he had seen the two together as he drove by. After checking the story out personally, the judge not only dismissed the claim, but also ruled that Bilān had to face honor trials for defaming both the girl and Abū Maḥamūd and exposing them to great danger, perhaps death.[109] In the central Negev in December 2004, ʿAliyyān aṭ-Ṭimṭāwī of the ʿAzāzma ʿAṣiyāt tribe accused Ḥusayn al-Kishkhar of the Ẓullām Janabīb for telling the sons of his late neighbor, Huwaymish al-Wajj, that he had been moving their father's land borders back in order to expand his own holding in Wādī Umm Iḥṣei. Ṭimṭāwī, after proving to his neighbors that the border markings had remained unchanged, challenged Kishkhar to an honor trial (Case 121).[110]

Despite these cautions concerning witnesses, many cases are decided according to the evidence they provide. In 1973, for example, three fellow Bedouin soldiers and tent mates in the Israeli Army testified before a *ḍraybī* judge that they had heard Sālim ʿOwda aṭ-Ṭimṭāwi of the ʿAzāzma ʿAṣiyāt tribe claim that the daughter of Sālim ʿAtayyig al-Khiraynig of the ʿAzāzma Saraḥīn was pregnant out of wedlock (Case 71). Apparently Ṭimṭāwī's assertion came when he learned that the girl was engaged to marry his retarded former brother-in-law, implying that she had to be married off to just anyone owing to the pregnancy. On the basis of the witnesses' evidence, the judge ordered the girl to be checked at a hospital in Beersheba, where she was found not to be with child. As a result, Ṭimṭāwī was obliged to sit before a *manshad* judge, who fined him heavily for slandering the girl's honor.[111]

Oaths

The Role of Oaths When neither a confession nor unequivocal evidence provided by witnesses is forthcoming, an oath (*yamīn*; *dīn*) is the main instrument in Bedouin litigation for facilitating a decision regarding innocence or guilt. In a court case (except in disputes over the ownership of land), it is the defendant who takes an oath while the claimant uses witnesses to bolster his suit.[112] The legal maxim establishes that "An oath is for him who denies, and witnesses are for him who accuses" (*al-yamīn ʿala man ankar—wa-sh-shuhūd ʿala man āddaʿa*).[113] Indeed, if the accuser can produce witnesses whose evidence satisfies the judge, as did the Khiraynig family in the aforementioned case of slander against their daughter, there will be no need to have the defendant swear an oath. For there to be an oath, at any rate, its request must come from either the claimant or the judge.

Without witnesses, the material evidence may not be sufficiently solid for a judge to forgo an oath by the defendant. Accordingly, Bedouin law holds that "What's clear requires only a statement, but what's concealed requires oaths" (*al-beiyina ilha bayān wa-l-gheiba ilha diyān*).[114] In 1976, while Sālim Abū Jidayaʿ of the Tiyāha al-Asad was being beaten up by men of the ʿOwdāt section of the same tribe out of anger at his accusation that their flocks were eating his crops, his traditional long *ghalyūn* pipe disappeared (Case 22). At the session for resolving the conflict, he was able only to recover the pipe or be compensated for it by demanding that his attackers swear to the veracity of their assertion that they had no knowledge of what had happened to it or of its whereabouts.[115] In 1983 Ḥimayd Salmān as-Saddān of the ʿAzāzma Saraḥīn, whose daughter had been abducted, delegated Muḥammad Abū Jaddūaʿ, a tribal elder of the ʿAzāzma, to arrange the return of the girl (Case 16). Learning, however, that Abū Jaddūaʿ had agreed, in Saddān's name, to let the couple marry, Saddān charged him with exceeding his delegation out of deceit. He could substantiate his claim, however, only by getting Abū Jaddūaʿ to swear an oath that he had been given authority to betroth the girl.[116]

Other defendants that must take an oath in order to prove their innocence are those who have been accused of deliberate murder but who claim that the killing was accidental. If, after mediation and in agreement with the murdered person's clansmen, they swear under oath that the murder was an accident (*zalla*; or, as in Islam, *qaḍāʾ ū-qadir*), they evade the danger of blood-revenge. Among the Ẓullām Abū Graynāt tribe in the Negev, for example, a story exists whereby in the late nineteenth century one of their people, walking in the desert with three others, dropped his rifle, which went off, killing each of the three (Case 122). The rifle owner went directly to the elder of their clan and confessed what had happened. After swearing an oath that their killing was an accident, the men's clan waived their right to revenge, asked only the blood-price of one victim, and conceded him the blood-price of the two others—all in light of the killer's admission and the oath that he swore.[117] Similar oaths were taken with like effect when, for example, an Abū Jābir accidentally killed Sālim Ḥasan Abū Rubayʿa in the 1940s, playing with the rifle of the victim's father, Ḥasan (Case 123); when Fayṣal Dirdāḥ Salmān al-Huzayyil, trying to lock his revolver, killed his friend and fellow policeman, Salīm Sulaymān Abū Hānī, in the 1950s (Case 96); and when Chief Kāyid al-ʿAṭowna, celebrating a wedding by shooting into the air, killed Sālim al-ʿUbra in the 1960s (Case 98).[118]

Although oaths are normally demanded of defendants, a judge, perceiving that an accusation might be invented, can alternatively order the claimant to swear an oath to substantiate it. In the 1960s in the Negev, an Abū Ruwaydī accused a man called al-Ghannāmī, both of the Ẓullām confederation, of throwing a block of earth at his daughter, purportedly on the grounds that she had let her flock graze in his sown field, a claim that Abū Ruwaydī's daughter denied (Case 124). The judge ordered Abū Ruwaydī to swear that his daughter's account was correct.[119]

Again, Bedouin in southern Sinai tell that among the ʿUmrān tribe of northwest Arabia in the mid-twentieth century, a *ḍraybī* judge, ʿAbdallah ash-Shamsān, ordered Ḥusayn Ibn ʿUṣbān to swear to the correctness of his claim that ʿĪd Ibn Magbūl had raped his daughter at knifepoint (Case 125). Ibn ʿUṣbān, known for his avaricious nature, was generally suspected of trying to gain financial awards through litigation by fabricating violations purportedly perpetrated against him. The story enjoys great currency owing to the exaggerated and graphic depiction of the event as uttered in the claimant's plea, which was as follows:

> What is your opinion, o Shamsān, of this man who met the girl
> (*W-aysh ʿendak yā shamsān fī-rājil illī lagāha*)
> And on the firm ground of a remote place mounted her from behind
> (*ū-fī ṣamm al'-khala tash-halbāha*)
> Putting his dick into the place of her droppings
> (*ū-ḥaṭṭ heifah fī mabʿarha*)
> While holding a knife to her throat
> (*ū-khōstah fī manḥarha*)
> And then climbed a hill and looked about
> (*ū-yishrif ū-yiṭill*)
> And came back and did it again.
> (*wi-yithannī wi-yiʿill*).
> God willing, he'll meet here a burning fire and a drowning sea.
> (*inshallah yilḥag nārin yiḥarrig ū-baḥrin yigharrig*).

The accused, Ibn Magbūl, simply replied that Ibn ʿUṣbān had no witnesses:

> By God, o Shamsān, lead me* to him who dragged me off her;
> (*W-allah ū-hādha shalīlī l-illī shaddnī min fōg-ha*)

*The expression "Lead me [to a witness]" is traditionally expressed as "Here is the hem of my cloak" (*hādha shalīlī*) (as in the present plea) or "Bring me your reins" (*hāt rasanak* —that is, items with which to lead.

If you find him, let me pay a fine; if not, fine Ibn ʿUṣbān for deceit.
(*yā aṭayyibha, yā yugʿud ila bōg-ha*).[120]

The judge, suspecting Ibn ʿUṣbān of lying, said he could win an award only if he swore by oath that his claim was true.

In Bedouin law, oaths can exonerate defendants from accusations and guilt. Thus, Bedouin maxims state that "He who swears is safe; he who fears to swear is fined" (*in ḥalaf silim w-in hābha ghirim*) and "To him who swears belongs the right" (*man ḥalaf al-ḥagg ḥaggah*).[121] After one swears, moreover, the case is closed. "After God's verdict there is no further discussion" (*mā baʿd ḥagg allah bayʿ ū-shrī*).[122] Thus in the northern Negev in the 1950s, when a man of the Ṭalālga section of the Tiyāha al-ʿAṭowna tribe accused his neighbor, Ḥusayn, of helping marauders from the West Bank steal his livestock, he insisted that Ḥusayn take an oath denying the accusation (Case 126). Ḥusayn thus swore: "In the name of our great God, the merciful and compassionate, I declare that all through life, from my first days until today—o Ṭalālga—I never guided nor aided thieves or treacherous people, neither against you nor against anyone else in the world. Your words to this effect are lies and a plot, invented only by yourself and the devil." Following the oath, pronounced in a crowded tent, Ṭalālga dropped the case against Ḥusayn for good.[123]

Preventing False Oaths A non-Bedouin might suspect that the Bedouin reliance on oaths for evidence constitutes a major loophole in the law. If the utterance of an oath is all it takes for a defendant to exonerate himself, one could imagine violators and criminals availing themselves of it on every occasion that they wish to perpetrate their violations with impunity. In fact, the Bedouin themselves are aware of this criminal escape hatch, as reflected in their ironic sayings, "A thief also swears" (*as-sārig ḥālif*) and "As a thief is perfidious, he'll surely also swear" (*al-khāyin khāyin—ghayr yiḥlif*).[124]

However, the law combines with Bedouin culture to curb such infractions. First, oaths may be deemed inadmissible or be rejected if the person swearing (*al-ḥālif*) is not considered morally suitable. As with the unsuitability of a witness, mentioned above, a person whose oath is unacceptable may be suspected of godlessness, owing to his lack of dear things he would not want to endanger through a false oath—in particular livestock and male children. Bedouin consider a godless person to be someone with nothing to lose. Hence, he is depicted in rhyme as "gray-skinned and devoid of offspring" (*ash-hab al-jild ū-gatīaʿ al-wild*), "gray-skinned" denoting an absence of generosity owing to indigence.[125] As in the case of witnesses too, other persons disqualifiable for taking an oath are remiss guarantors and men who do not punish their womenfolk for immoral behavior. In regard to the latter, a Bedouin legal maxim explicitly states that "One who knows but is patient can give no oath" (*khābir ū-ṣābir — mā lih yamīn*).[126] Finally, the oath of someone who has committed the three inexcusable transgressions — stealing what has been stored, fornicating with a neighbor's wife, and betraying a traveling companion — may also be disallowed. Indeed, the fear of losing the privilege to take oaths that can exonerate them from accusations of wrongdoing is one of the great incentives for people to live a life that observes Bedouin moral values and societal conventions.

Another way of guarding against false oath from a person suspected of a readiness to lie in order to avert a legal judgment against himself is to insist on others taking an oath that affirms what the suspected person has said. This is called "an oath and five more in train" (*dīn ū-khamsa mitgaṭṭrīn*),[127] and it can vary in that it includes the accused plus four or five other men or five men without the accused. In a case from the 1950s mentioned above (Case 126), in which a man called aṭ-Ṭalālga accused his neighbor Ḥusayn of abetting the theft of his livestock, the latter was obliged to swear and was followed by four members of his clan, each in turn saying, "I swear by our great God that whatever he said was the truth" (*aḥlif b-illah al-ʿaẓīm, innah fī kull mā gāl ṣādig*). The additional four men were from Ḥusayn's clan, on the basis of Ṭalālga's demand: "five from the clan" (*khamsa min al-khamsa*), as is often the case.[128]

It is the will of him who calls for an oath to determine whether or not those swearing and affirming that oath should be members of the clan of the accused. In Sinai in 1980, an elder of the Tarabīn Ḥasāblah, ʿAnayz Sālim al-ʿUrḍī, one of whose tribesmen had been killed by men of the Aḥeiwāt Karādma, demanded an oath that the killers had found the victim with one of their women *in flagrante delicto* and had not just murdered him in his sleep (Case 75). Refusing to accept the oath from the murderers themselves or their clansmen as morally unacceptable people — "I will not take an oath from a clan that kills a sleeper" (*al-khamsa illī tuktul an-nāyim mā bākhidh ʿalayha dīn*) — he rather called upon the chief of the Karādma, Jumʿa Ibn Kureidim, to swear in their stead (as the fellow tribesman bearing responsibility for a violation against someone from a different tribe) that the murdered lad, Fiheid, had been killed between the girl's legs, and Kureidim's oath was to be followed by four other fellow tribesmen swearing affirmation of his oath.[129]

Another method for preventing lying in the taking of an oath is found in the requirement that the opposing party be present, either in person or through a representative on his behalf, at the swearing ritual. This is to guarantee that the form of the oath, agreed upon by the parties in advance, will be maintained. If the contestants do not appear, any oath taken will be unacceptable. In 1997 the ʿAlowna clan of the Tarabīn Ḥasāblah tribe in southeast Sinai was ordered by a judge from the Aḥeiwāt Ṣafeiḥa confederation, ʿOwda Abū Agfā, to swear an oath at the tent of a Tarabīn man encamped in southwest Sinai, near Rās aṣ-Ṣadr (Case 52).[130] The oath was to state that one of their lads, murdered during a meeting with a girl of the Munāṣra clan, had come to marry her, as previously agreed to by her brother, bringing with him a goat with which to perform a ritual slaughter and whose blood he was to sprinkle on the girl, in keeping with tradition.[131] This claim was contrary to that of the girl's brother, Salmān Zaydān, who asserted that the man he murdered had not been betrothed and had only come to tryst with the girl, already pregnant with his child. The ʿAlowna duly appeared, ready to take the oath, but the Munāṣra stayed away, invalidating it thereby, as the law requires both parties to be present at a swearing.

The ultimate safeguard against lying under oath comes from traditional Bedouin religiosity and the belief that both God and the saints at whose graves swearing often takes place are involved in oaths as the forces that confirm them; it thus follows that they will be indignant over a false oath (which compromises their holiness) and punish anyone who gives it. This dread is reflected in sayings such as, "An oath won't leave a home to him who swears it" (*al-yamīn mā biykhallī li-ḥālfah dār*), and "An oath is a hot cauterization nail and can destroy a home" (*al-yamīn miḥwār ū-kharāb dār*).[132] "Home" is a reference to children and clansmen. Hence, after composing the oath that a Bedouin is asking his opponent to swear, he will warn of the consequences of a false oath with words such as, "One after another, may your clansmen and offspring be cut down!" (*leiya wara leiya—yigṭaʿin adh-dhara wa-dh-dhareiya*).[133] Danger to the offspring is specifically captured in the saying, "An oath entails danger to the offspring" (*al-yamīn ilha ḍarār li-l-maṭalīaʿ*). This is further spelled out by the proverbial warning that God's wrath from a false oath "will be visited on seven men ['head-cloths'], one in each of seven generations" (*al-yamīn muʿallag fī sabaʿ manadīl—ū-yuṭrud jīl wara jīl*).[134]

To underpin the connection between the deity and an oath, most oaths begin with a reference to God. Sometimes this reference is direct, with the utterance of His name (Allah) three times (for example, "By the great God, by the great God, by the great God: I killed him only between her legs" [*w-allah al-ʿaẓīm, w-allah al-ʿaẓīm, w-allah al-ʿaẓīm—innī mā kataltah ghayr bayn arbāʿha]*, as was demanded of members of the Aḥeiwāt Karādma in southeast Sinai, whose tribesmen were accused of killing a purported fornicator of the Tarabīn Ḥasāblah in his sleep, near one of their women [Case 75]).[135] This triple mention of God is sometimes termed "six precious words" (*sitt kalimāt ghawālya*)—that is, "great God" uttered three times.

Alternatively, the reference to God may be indirect, by allusion to his greatness. One example, heard in 1984, began, "By the life of Him who made the sun shine and separated man's fingers" (*wi-ḥayat illī aẓhar ash-shams ū-farrag al-khams*); it then continued with, "I didn't take authority for anything but what my tribesman detailed for me" (*mā malayt ḥālī ghayr b-illī faṣṣalnī fīh ibn ʿammī*) (Case 16). The oath was demanded by a Tarabīn judge, Ḥamdān aṣ-Ṣūfī, of an ʿAzāzma notable, Imsallam Abū Jaddūaʿ, to avow that he had not exceeded his mandate by undertaking to authorize the marriage of Ḥimayd as-Saddān's daughter to a suitor of a different sub-tribe. Saddān, having delegated Abū Jaddūaʿ merely to persuade leaders of the Ẓullām to have his abducted daughter returned to him, viewed the unauthorized marriage as a betrayal.[136] Another example of an oath sworn to disavow the intentional killing of three men of the Ẓullām Abū Graynāt tribe in the nineteenth century Negev, went as follows: "By the life of the annual plant and our worshipped Lord, the deaths of your clansmen are not my fault. It's like: I took aim, but God did the killing" (*wa-ḥayāt al-ʿūd wa-r-rabb al-maʿabūd, innah zlāmak mū hum ʿendī—āna maddayt w-allah katal*) (Case 122).[137] Further allusions to the actions of God, as well as references to a Bedouin's precious possessions (children, livestock, clansmen, annual pasture, grain) that may be endangered by a false oath, take several forms and can be integrated into oaths pertaining to any type of legal conflict.

The venue and performance of oaths also involve a sacred presence that reaffirms their holy character. Many oaths are sworn at the graves and tombs of revered saints (such as Abū Jurayr in El-ʿArīsh, northern Sinai, belonging to the Suwārka; or Abū Sākhna and al-Āʿsam, belonging to the ʿAzāzma and Tiyāha respectively in the central Negev).[138] In December 2004, for example, a young man of the Kallāb clan of the ʿAzāzma Saraḥīn tribe swore upon the grave of al-Āʿsam that he had not stolen money from a fellow tribesman, ʿAlī ʿOwḍtallah (Case 127).[139] On other occasions, Bedouin swear oaths at the tents of persons acknowledged to be reverential. In 1997 in Sinai, men of the ʿAlowna clan of the Tarabīn Ḥasāblah tribe went, by demand of a *mangaʿ ad-damm* judge, to the tent of a respected member of their tribe, Imsallam Abū Shnayf, living in Wādī ar-Rāḥa in western Sinai, to swear that one of their men had been killed deceitfully by someone of the Munāṣra clan (Case 52).[140] In the early 1960s, for another example, a man accused of aiding in the theft of a neighbor's livestock swore his innocence at the tent of a respected judge, Ḥasan al-Ḥujūj (Case 126).[141]

When performing an oath at a tomb, the person swearing will place his right hand on the structure in order to establish direct contact with the holiness. If the oath is taken at a revered person's tent, the holiness of the act is expressed in performing what is called "an oath with a line and a knife" (*dīn bi-khaṭṭ ū-sikkīn*). Usually in such a ceremony the oath-taking person faces Mecca ("I put Polaris [the North Star] over my shoulder and Canopus [a star on the southern horizon] between my eyes" [*aḥuṭṭ al-jidī bayn imṭūnī wa-s-suhayl bayn ʿuyūnī*]) and swears while standing in a circle drawn with a dagger in the sand and containing seven vertical and seven horizontal lines that form little squares or rectangles. The circle constitutes an area of sanctity, such as Bedouin delineate with lines in the sand or by placing a cloak (or, more rarely, a carpet) before them when praying. Believing that the Prophet Muḥammad swore an oath in such a circle renders a false oath an offense against his memory, and it will incur his wrath and revenge. Sometimes a camel udder-bag and an ant (*shamla ū-namla*) are placed in the circle as additional warnings against swearing a false oath, to the effect that it will wreak disaster upon the camel herd of the person swearing, symbolized by his being deprived of camel milk (udder-bags are used to wean calves from suckling) and will reduce his food supply to quantities that an ant stores up. Bedouin also heed the potential danger of a "circle and knife" oath by performing it behind rather than before the tent, the face of which is open and hence believed to be exposed to bad influences from that direction.[142]

Owing to the anticipated dangers of a false oath, people, whether defendants or claimants, are loath to risk swearing them. In the central Negev in 1945, for example, Salmān al-Kallāb was accused by his neighbor, Sālim Salīm al-Ghidayfī, both of the ʿAzāzma Saraḥīn tribe, of having moved the boundary markings between their agricultural plots so as to expand his own holding (Case 128). Although the judge, Salīm Ibn Saʿad, offered him the chance to absolve himself of the accusation by swearing an oath, Kallāb refused. Instead, he opted to undergo the more immediately harsh ordeal by fire, the *bishʿa*, preferring even to burn his tongue and pay all the fines and expenses deriving from his guilt rather than swear a false oath and expose seven generations to the deadly wrath of God.[143]

A further example of a claimant's being wary of swearing an oath took place in the northern Negev in the1960s. As we saw, a father, Abū Ruwaydī, accused a neighbor, called al-Ghannāmi, of assaulting his daughter, ostensibly for having let her flock graze in his sown field (Case 124). When the judge ordered him to swear that his daughter's denial of Ghannāmi's account was correct, Abū Ruwaydī withdrew his complaint.[144]

The reticence to swear a false oath prevails even when a party has much to lose by refraining from taking it. In 1980, as noted above (Case 75), the Tarabīn of southeast Sinai claimed that members of the neighboring Aḥeiwāt Karādma confederation had killed one of their young men in his sleep, a violation that warrants four acts of revenge or the payment of blood-money fourfold, totaling 160 camels, evaluated at the time as the local equivalent of approximately $80,000. The Aḥeiwāt countered that they had killed the man *in flagrante delicto* with one of their girls, which relieved them of any threat of revenge. To avert the danger of four acts of revenge or the enormous cost of blood-money resulting from the alleged circumstances of the case, all that the Aḥeiwāt had to do was swear, in the name of the main killer, "By the great God, by the great God, by the great God: I killed him only between her legs." They preferred, however, to bear the losses rather than to risk arousing the wrath of God.[145]

Another example of the fear of swearing a false oath took place among the ʿAzāzma in the central Negev in 1983, after a young friend of ʿAtayyig Ibn Saʿad drove him and the daughter of Ḥimayd as-Saddān, with whom he was eloping, from a spot where he had conspired to meet them to the tent of a local notable for safekeeping, as stipulated by the rules of abduction (Case 16).[146] According to these rules, the driver was in the legal capacity of a "companion" (*rafīg*), whose function was to testify that the eloper had not touched the girl from the very moment he had fled with her, but the fact that he had met the couple only half way made him wary to take an oath affirming that he had indeed been present during the entire abduction. Thus, when the girl's father demanded of him to swear an oath to that effect, he demurred. His reluctance to risk the consequences of a false oath thereby cost his friend, Ibn Saʿad, the fine of a camel for breaking the rules.[147]

So great is the Bedouins' fear of punishment for distorting the truth through an oath that they are reluctant to swear even when they are in the right. This is a sentiment they stress by enlisting a saying of the Prophet Muḥammad: "An oath is odious, though its content be true" (*al-yamīn makrūha wi-lō ṣādig*);[148] it may find explanation in what J. L. Burckhardt heard—namely, that any oath might anger God, who "would resent having his name made subservient to earthly purposes."[149] The power of an oath is so strong that Bedouin are even cautioned to refrain from making an opponent swear. Hence, they say, "Woe to him who must swear, if he swears; and woe to him who makes him swear, if he does not recant" (*yā wayl al-ḥālif in ḥalaf—ū-yā wayl al-muḥallif in mā ʿāf*).[150]

There is a way out, however, particularly for a defendant who is not in the right and if the matter is financial or pertains to matters of honor rather than to murder, rape, or land. It is called "buying the oath" (*sharwat al-yamīn*). Someone close to the defendant—a relative or a friend—offers (*yaʿrad*) a sum of money to the person imposing the oath, saying "I want to buy his oath" (*widdī ashrī dīnah*). Concurrence with the purchase (*sharwa*), including the sum, lies with the accuser, who, generally accedes, aware of the possible dangers of compelling an oath. In this way, he will have retrieved his expenses and losses and perhaps will have gained some additional money. In the Negev in

1984, for example, Imsallam Abū Jaddūaʿ of the ʿAzāzma was accused by a fellow tribesman, Ḥimayd as-Saddān, of misrepresenting him when delegated to negotiate the return of Saddān's abducted daughter (Case 16). Abū Jaddūaʿ balked at absolving himself through an oath, despite his claim that he had completely adhered to Saddān's directives. At that point, the chief of the Tiyāha Gudayrāt, Muḥammad Sālim al-Āʿsam, came to his rescue by putting up the equivalent of $2,000 (in Jordanian dinars) to buy his oath, with the consent of Saddān, to whom the sum reverted.[151]

"Buying the oath" saves face for a defendant, as innocence or guilt will not have been specifically determined. To endorse this face-saving device, a Bedouin maxim says, "An oath that cannot exact an offer is false" (*al-yamīn illī mā lih maʿrad bāṭla*), insinuating that the purchased oath is true.[152] If, however, the oath taker is subsequently revealed to have indeed committed the violation of which he was accused, he will be considered to have denied his crime deceitfully and have to pay the relevant fine fourfold when the case is retried before a judge.

Totally innocent persons too may occasionally resort to the practice from fear of the divine wrath they expect to afflict them, perhaps for neglect in the exact phrasing of the oath or because they may be attesting to events of which they do not have complete knowledge. In addition, selling their oath may be a face-saving device for them, particularly as a way to maintain their social status. They perceive that if they simply refuse to swear an oath demanded of them, people might suspect that they are trying to evade punishment for the violation of which they are accused. On the other hand, if they do swear, people might suspect them of taking a false oath.

The Fire Ordeal (*Bishʿa*)

The most drastic form of oath to determine innocence or guilt, as mentioned above, is called *bishʿa*, a word used by Bedouin to mean the ordeal itself, its personalized spirit, the mystical authorization for performing it, and the red-hot implement that is a part of the ordeal. The man who is exclusively sanctioned to administer the *bishʿa* is variously called the *mubashshaʿ* (lit. "the person in whom the sanction to administer the *bishʿa* inheres") or the *mubashshiʿ* (lit. "the person who administers the *bishʿa*"). However enunciated, the *mubashshaʿ* is (normally) the sole specific member of the ʿAyāyda tribal confederation who is exclusively qualified to administer (*yibshaʿ*) the *bishʿa* ordeal.* The ordeal is generally resorted to when witnesses are lacking or, as in

*In 2005 two rivals were administering the ordeal. (Oral communication from Joseph Ginat of Haifa University, January 2, 2005; see the bibliography for Ginat's book on *bishʿa*.)

the use of the above-mentioned "oath and five more in train," an accuser does not believe that his adversary will swear an ordinary oath honestly.

To Bedouin, if asked, it seems that the resort to the ordeal is mainly in cases involving murder, rape, fornication, and land ownership—that is, the most serious of problems. To a large extent, this is true. Records abound of suspected murderers being dispatched to the *mubashsha*ʿ to establish their innocence or guilt. For example, when Mūsa Farhūd Abu-l-Gīʿān, a man of the Ḥukūk section of the Tiyāha confederation in the Negev, was murdered in 1981, the three persons suspected of participating or aiding in the killing, Sulaymān Muḥammad al-Afinish, Saʿīd Abū Ruḥayyil, and Ismaʿīl al-Gaṣṣāṣī, were constrained, under the threat of revenge or the payment of blood-money, to "lick the fire" (*yilḥas an-nār*) (Case 129).[153] Similarly, Bedouin in the Negev tell of a chief of the Tarabīn, called Shaykh al-ʿĪd, who was obliged sometime during the first half of the twentieth century to visit the *mubashsha*ʿ to clear himself when a fellow tribesman accused him of attacking his daughter with intent to rape (Case 130).[154] In the mid-1960s among the Guṣayyir tribe of the Aḥeiwāt Shawafīn confederation of east-central Sinai, two sections, the Ḥusaynāt and the Nuṣayrāt, agreed to have their conflicting claims to ownership of a plot of land in Wadeiy al-Bayḍ resolved through the *bishʿa* ordeal (Case 27).[155]

Problems of lesser import too can be resolved through the ordeal. In 1946, when ʿOwda Abū Muʿammar, future chief of the ʿAzāzma in the Negev, found his coffee utensils, which had been carried off with his tent by a flash flood, in the possession of a family who refused to surrender them, alleging that they had bought them in the market, he demanded that they go to the *mubashsha*ʿ to ascertain the truth (Case 117).[156] Slander too is grounds for utilizing the *bishʿa*, as happened in the Negev in the interwar period, when a conflict erupted among the Tiyāha that led Salmān Swaylim as-Sawālma to oblige a man called Hāshim of the Tiyāha Braykāt from eastern Sinai to undergo the *bishʿa* (Case 131). Hāshim, who had borrowed 6 Palestinian pounds from the chief of the Tiyāha al-Asad tribe to pay the British Mandatory customs duty on his flock crossing the border from Sinai, later insisted that he had returned the loan through Sawālma, charging him with having stolen the money. Zealous to restore his reputation, Sawālma dispatched Hāshim to test his story at the *mubashsha*ʿ.[157]

There is a process for sending an accused person to the *mubashsha*ʿ. The one who demands the ordeal, whether it is a judge or the accuser himself, will define the oath to be sworn by the accused or suspected opponent before the latter "licks the fire." When, for example, Sulaymān Muḥammad al-Afinish underwent the ordeal in November 1980, on suspicion of aiding the murderers of Mūsa Farhūd Abū-l-Gīʿān, the latter's clansmen insisted that he swear,

"We neither guided nor aided. Neither male nor female. The night he was killed, even if he was our own son, we were ignorant of who killed him. No one of our clan saw the killers on their way to the murder or on their return from it" (Case 129). Then, when Saʿīd Abū Ruḥayyil and Ismaʿīl al-Gaṣṣāṣī underwent the ordeal in March 1981, accused of being the actual murderers of Abū-l-Gīʿān, the latter's clansmen ordered them to swear that they neither killed him "by hand or by iron" (*lā bi-īdī wala bi-ḥadīdī*), the iron referring to knives and guns.

In order to prevent any subsequent dispute over the verdict of the *mubashshaʿ* in conflicts between persons of different clans, their respective members must be accompanied to the *mubashshaʿ* by an agreed-upon witness (called the "listener": *sāmiʿa*), who observes the ordeal and reports its results to the judge who will later issue a sentence. When, for example, Sulaymān al-Afinish, on the one hand, and Saʿīd Abū Ruḥayyil and Ismaʿīl al-Gaṣṣāṣī, on the other, underwent the ordeal as noted above (Case 129), a chief of the Tarabīn, Yūsuf Salmān Abū Bilāl, acting as a *sāmiʿa*, accompanied the groups on both occasions.

If, however, a family resorts to the *bishʿa* in order to verify whether one of its members is indeed innocent of an accusation made against him or her, they can dispense with a listener. Such was the case when, early in the twentieth century, the brothers of a woman defamed for being licentious took her to the *mubashshaʿ* to establish that the assertion was groundless before demanding justice (Case 132). Having satisfied themselves as to their sister's innocence according to the results of the ordeal, they felt confident to assail their defamers.[158]

Upon arrival at the residence of the *mubashshaʿ*, the parties relate to him their cases and the oaths they will swear prior to licking the red-hot pan. An assistant of the ordeal administrator records this information in a ledger. Once apprised of the case, the *mubashshaʿ* may try to prevail upon the defendant to confess rather than submit himself to the ordeal or, alternatively, to make his oath more precise in order to lessen the chances of his being burned. The *bishʿa*, the Bedouin believe, is very sensitive to the exact truth. When, for example, Sulaymān al-Afinish went to the *mubashshaʿ* to swear that neither he nor anyone in his clan saw or knew the murderers of Mūsa Farhūd Abū-l-Gīʿān, mentioned above (Case 129), the *mubashshaʿ* warned him that he might be overestimating his knowledge—that some woman or child of his camp may have seen someone go by on the night of the murder without knowing his intentions. He suggested that Afinish simply swear that he did not know who killed Abū-l-Gīʿān (a suggestion that both the defendant and the accuser rejected).[159] Indeed, even after the aforementioned Tarabīn chief, called ʿĪd, was accused of attempted rape and had his tongue burned during the ordeal, the *mubashshaʿ* suggested that he change his oath and lick again

(Case 130). Instead of swearing "I never touched her," which may have been imprecise, perhaps ignoring his having once shook her hand in greeting or accidentally trod on the folds of her long dress, and thus incriminated himself before the *bishʿa*, he should simply say, metaphorically, "The twig never entered the kohol pot" (*al-ʿūd mā khashsh al-makḥala*).[160] Complying, Shaykh ʿĪd licked the hot pan a second time, only to be found innocent.[161]

It is generally determined, before setting off for the *mubashshaʿ*, that the parties name guarantors to ensure their subsequent compliance with the results of the *bishʿa*. The accused party will comply, if found guilty, by accepting the punishments subsequently meted out by a judge. The accuser will comply, if his opponent is found innocent, by terminating his accusations, as well as reimbursing him for all the expenses he will have incurred in the context of the ordeal. In cases of murder, moreover, the accuser must also appoint a guarantor to ensure that he will not attack the accused if the *bishʿa* finds him innocent.

Often defendants, laboring under the threat of retaliation or a heavy fine, agree to defray the expenses of the entire party on its journey and return, as well as the fees of the *mubashshaʿ* and his assistant, which are notably token, so that the ordeal is accessible to all as a means for resolving conflicts. If the *bishʿa* absolves the defendant of guilt, his accuser repays all his expenses, unless the matter submitted to the ordeal is murder. In a case of murder, the relief at being exonerated is deemed sufficient recompense.

Once the fee has been paid and the ledger inscribed, the *mubashshaʿ* instructs the accused how to lick so as to protect his lips and nose from burning and how to prevent his teeth from scraping his sensitive tongue in the moments before it is inspected.[162] The ʿAyāyda *mubashshaʿ* then bids his assistant place the coffee-roasting utensil (consisting of an approximately one-meter-long arm with a pan at one end) into a fire, lit for the occasion, until it is red-hot. At this stage, it is removed from the fire and handed to the *mubashshaʿ*, who quickly passes it over his forearm to indicate that the innocent do not get burned. Then, in successive steps, the person undergoing the ordeal shows the *mubashshaʿ* and others present the pre-ordeal condition of his tongue (for later comparison); rinses his mouth three times; licks the extended red-hot pan on its convex side three times; again rinses his mouth three times; and, after a pause of anywhere from one to fifteen minutes, shows his tongue for the *mubashshaʿ* to examine. If the latter finds no burns on the tongue, he declares the person innocent (*barī*). In the event that blisters or burns appear, he declares him guilty (alternatively *waghīf*, *meighūf*, *mowghūf*). In either case, he also calls upon the *sāmiʿa* to regard the condition of the tongue as part of his role in reporting the verdict. Other guests of the *mubashshaʿ* may also be asked to bear witness, thus affirming his decision. Next, the parties to the ordeal sign the ledger of the *mubashsha*ʿ (the unlettered persons with a thumbprint), thereby terminating the ritual. If a verdict of innocent has been given, the parties greet each other as an act of reconciliation.

The possible impression, perhaps gained from transmitted accounts, that *bish*ʿ*a* is an ordeal only for defendants or accused individuals is not accurate. First, judges who are doubtful of the veracity of claims made by claimants before them are wont to send them to the *mubashsha*ʿ for validation, just as they might send them to swear an oath. In 1982 in central Sinai, for example, when the paramount chief of the Tiyāha confederation, ʿĪd Muṣliḥ Ibn ʿĀmir, attempted to achieve a *manshad* ruling from an honor judge of the Masaʿīd, Amīra Salāma Abū Amīra, to the effect that a lad from the Tarabīn had forcibly abducted a Tiyāha girl and stolen her father's money, Abū Amīra, in his decision, told Ibn ʿĀmir: "Go to the pan of Abū Jarabīaʿ al-ʿAyyādī and lick the fire concerning what happened and what you claimed before me—the truth with no entry for a lie. When you emerge clean and noble, your tongue intact, come back and receive the right you had received previously [that is, from a prior judge] plus what will come after it" (*ʿaggid ʿa ṭāst Abū Jarabīaʿ al-ʿAyyādī ū-talḥas an-nār ʿal illī ṣār w-aḥtajjayt fīh ʿendī, ṣaḥīḥ wa-l-kidhib ma dakhal ʿalayh—ū-limma taṭlaʿ naẓīf ū-sharīf, lisānak tamām, itʿāwid tākhidh al-ḥagg illī ingāl ū-yinigil warāh*). Fearing to undergo the ordeal and be found untruthful, Ibn ʿĀmir refused and had to make do with the slight award that Abū Amīra saw fit to grant him (Case 20).[163]

Second, it often happens that persons accused of a violation will take the initiative in offering to expose themselves to the ordeal in order to refute the claim against them, even before litigation or retribution has taken place. For example, in 1980 Frank Stewart recorded that the chief of the Karādma tribe, Jumʿa Sālim Ibn Kureidim, volunteered to undergo the *bish*ʿ*a* in order to prove that his son, though suspected, had not aided the murderers of Fiheid Slaym Ibn Jāzī of the neighboring Tarabīn Ḥasāblah tribe (Case 75).[164] Stewart also recorded this phenomenon in a conflict between lineages of the Aḥeiwāt Ghinaymāt tribe in which a man of one clan was accused of inciting strife within another clan (Case 133). Although witnesses were lacking to support the accusation, the accused offered to "lick the fire" to show that he was in the right.[165] Bedouin regard this manifest willingness to expose oneself to pain and danger as an extreme demonstration of conviction that goes far toward validating a position of denial.

The sacredness of the *bish*ʿ*a* is also deduced from the belief that the ability to administer the ordeal is bestowed on a new *mubashsha*ʿ in an inspired dream[166] and that he himself subsequently receives, in a dream, advance information about cases that are brought before him. Such was the information the *mubash-*

*sha*ʿ claimed to have received concerning the three suspects in the murder of Mūsa Farhūd Abū-l-Gīʿān, cited above (Case 129), and the attempted rape of which Shaykh ʿĪd of the Tarabīn was accused (Case 130).[167]

Although non-Bedouin attribute the ability of people deemed innocent to endure the ordeal without their tongues being burned to an absence of fear, which allows their saliva flow to remain intact—as opposed to the knowingly guilty ones, whose dry tongues stick to the hot pan when they are licking it—the Bedouin believe in the inherent faculty of the hot pan, or the *bishʿa* spirit that it embodies, to be able to detect guilt. Thus, the ʿAyāyda relate that the first *mubashshaʿ* whom they collectively recall came to the vocation when he challenged a thief that had stolen from him, and whom he had tracked down, to take turns with him in licking red-hot tongs, he himself emerging from the ordeal unscathed. Perhaps as a replay of this event, every *mubashshaʿ* since then has run the red-hot pan, fresh from the fire, over his forearm. According to this belief in the prescience of the *bishʿa*, those who have endured it relate a lack of fear or a sense of ease before licking the pan. "I licked it as if I were licking this pack of cigarettes here," one of them asserted.[168] To endorse their belief in the efficacy of the *bishʿa* to discern innocence from guilt, a popular tradition relates how Bedouin convinced the quasi-legendary British governor of Sinai, Col. A. C. Parker (1907–23; he is reverently recalled as Bārkil Bey), of its worth.

> When Bārkil Bey was new to Sinai, a Bedouin whom he knew stole something and was brought to the *bishʿa*, which burned his tongue, finding him guilty. Hearing of this, Bārkil asked him why he had stolen, to which he claimed that he was innocent but that the "fire leaves no one unburned" (*an-nār mā bitkhallī ḥad*). So Bārkil convened the chiefs and asked why they had burned his friend's tongue. They said, "O Bey, this fire discerns the teller of truth from the liar" (*haydhī an-nār bitbayyin aṣ-ṣāḥḥ min al-kadhdhāb*). Bārkil said he had to check this himself. So he had some money secretly stowed with a man called ʿĪd and sent another to accuse him of having stolen it. ʿĪd, knowing that he was innocent, said that he would lick the *bishʿa* to prove it. So they brought him to Ḥamdān, the *mubashshaʿ*, where he licked the fire and emerged unscathed. Then he found someone who was known to have stolen a camel but whom Bārkil's men counseled to deny the theft. So they had him "lick the fire," and he was burned and deemed guilty. Satisfied with his investigation, Bārkil said, "All right! This *bishʿa* is just fine. It clears things up straightaway" (*mazbūṭ: hadhihī al-bishʿa tamām—bitbayyin ʿala ṭūl*).[169]

Indeed, one of the greatest advantages that Bedouin see in the *bishʿa* is its ability to bring incontrovertible results immediately. Unlike an oath, which may take time—maybe generations—before a calamity may reveal that it is false, the calamity upon the licking of the fire is the burning of the tongue itself.

To stress the incontestability of the ordeal ritual, the Bedouin coined the maxims, "He who emerges from the fire will not return" (*illī biyiṭlaʿ min an-nār mā biythannī*), and "After the fire, there is no slander" (*mā ʿugb an-nār miʿyār*).[170] After the *bishʿa*, the innocent one is "absolved and bare" (*barī wa-ʿarī*), "bare" meaning that he is not covered by guilt. One obvious effect of the finality of the *bishʿa* practice is that it puts an end to many conflicts that otherwise might fester, causing much instability in Bedouin society.

Judgments and Punishments

JUDGMENTS

Deciding innocence and guilt or right from wrong is no problem for a Bedouin judge when a confession is forthcoming or when evidence is available. As mentioned above, confessions are often forthcoming when an accused party is confronted with the need to swear an oath or endure the *bishʿa* ordeal. However, in the absence of clear evidence or a confession to help a judge issue a verdict, he must resort to a number of other resources—namely, his familiarity with characteristic Bedouin behavior, his common sense, his investigations into the problem at hand, and his superior knowledge of the law.

Verdicts Based on Familiarity with the Social Environment

A judge's first resource, based on personal familiarity with Bedouin behavior and character types, is his intuition, which endows him with insight into motives, often enabling him to detect false or exaggerated claims. Bedouin in Sinai, for example, tell that when in the mid-twentieth century ʿAbdallah ash-Shamsān, a judge of the ʿUmrān confederation of northwest Arabia, was confronted with the claim by Ḥusayn Ibn ʿUṣbān that ʿĪd Ibn Magbūl had raped his daughter at knifepoint, his knowledge of the claimant's contentious and avaricious nature led him to suspect its veracity and order the claimant to swear an oath that would substantiate it (Case 125). When Ibn ʿUṣbān refused, Shamsān felt justified to throw the case out.[171]

A case from the Negev in the 1960s also illustrates the role of a judge's knowledge of his litigants (Case 124). As seen above, it concerned two members of the Ẓullām confederation, an Abū Ruwaydī and a man called al-Ghannāmī. Abū Ruwaydī, the claimant, asserted that the latter had thrown a clod of earth at his shepherdess daughter and threatened her with further violence if he again caught her flock among the crops he had planted. Ghannāmī pleaded in his defense that the girl had made a habit of pasturing her father's livestock in his sown fields, and when he reprimanded her for it, she insulted him with the epithet, "camel-lipped" (*abū shallūfa*), implying that he was of Negroid, rather than Bedouin, origin. His resultant anger led him to pick up a clod of earth and fling it at her. Abū Ruwaydī, while not denying the insult, demanded a judicial award for Ghannāmī's accosting his daughter instead of asking him to examine if damage had indeed been caused to his field. Not only does Bedouin law outlaw any attack against a defenseless female, but it also discourages the use of physical violence as a first resort in seeking justice.

The judge in this case, ʿAlī Salāma Abū Graynāt, chief of the Ẓullām Abū Graynāt tribe, understood that Abū Ruwaydī held Ghannāmī in contempt and that he wanted to penalize him as a further humiliation to that already inflicted upon him by his daughter. The only way the judge could prove his suspicion, however, was to order Abū Ruwaydī to swear that his flocks had not grazed on his opponent's crops. When the claimant refused, Abū Graynāt realized that his story was insincere and that his flocks were indeed causing Ghannāmī damage. He made him an award to reaffirm the inviolability of women principle, but it was a token award amounting to little more than the equivalent of $1. To protect Ghannāmī from further incursions into his fields, he had Abū Ruwaydī designate a guarantor to ensure that if witnesses testified that his flocks were again seen among Ghannāmī's crops, Ghannāmī would receive, as a judicial award, all present damages plus any claim he would make for past damages.[172]

A further example, from central Sinai in 1983, was the suspicion held by the Masʿūdī honor judge Amīra Salāma Abū Amīra concerning a claim made for the father of a girl of the Tiyāha confederation by their paramount chief, ʿĪd Muṣliḥ Ibn ʿĀmir (Case 20). Ibn ʿĀmir argued that the girl had been forcibly abducted by a Tarabīn lad. Aware that the girl had willingly absconded with the same boy on a previous occasion, only to be forcibly returned to her father after major pressure exerted on the Tarabīn by the Tiyāha, the judge doubted whether the girl had to be coerced into fleeing with her lover this second time. Consequently he ordered Ibn ʿĀmir, if he wanted a proper award for the violation of the girl's honor, to undergo the *bishʿa* ordeal to substantiate his claim. When Ibn ʿĀmir refused, the judge was convinced that his claim was false. Accordingly, like Judge ʿAlī Abū Graynāt in the above case (Case 124), he granted the Tiyāha a token award merely to reaffirm the inviolability of a woman's honor, even though the violation was consensual.[173]

Verdicts Based on Common Sense

A second resource for arriving at a judicial decision is the common sense that judges use in deducing the truth from improbable aspects of a case. For example, in the case previously mentioned concerning the alleged abduction of a woman from the Tiyāha confederation by a young man of the Tarabīn (Case 20), the Tiyāha spokesman, ʿĪd Ibn ʿĀmir, also charged the Tarabīn lad of stealing six gold bars and 23,000 Egyptian pounds (approximately $7,000), which the girl's father had hidden away in his tent.

> The judge, Amīra Abū Amīra, believing that the girl had been eager to abscond with her lover, deduced that she must have shown him where the money was. Accordingly, he said to Ibn ʿĀmir during the trial, "O Ibn ʿĀmir, I don't want to leave the sitting area; so would you go to my tent and bring me 100 pounds? You just have to get up from the sitting place and put your hand on the money. Or, by God, would you prefer to have one of my people lead you to the stashed money?" Ibn ʿĀmir answered, "Of course I need someone to tell me where it is, to point it out to me." The judge then declared, "I beg your pardon, Ibn ʿĀmir, but it was your Tiyāha girl who showed the Tarabīn lad where the money was. Otherwise, how could he have known?"
>
> Then the judge, again using common sense and his knowledge of Bedouin behavior, pressed Ibn ʿĀmir: "Before coming to trial, why didn't you demand the money as a condition for giving the Tarabīn the camel-truce they were eager for in order to save their lives and livestock? If you wouldn't have given them the truce without receiving the stolen money, they wouldn't have dared withhold it from you, having violated the honor of your woman. Now that they have the truce, they can ignore the money. You can't kill them for the money." The Tiyāha spokesman feebly replied, "We forgot about it." Then Abū Amīra, apparently exasperated, reprimanded him: "That's the law; and you forgot about it? Now you can forget about the award!"[174]

Another example of common sense on the part of a judge was in connection to a dispute over land ownership in northern Sinai. In the mid-twentieth century, a clan of the Suwārka, the Abū Daʿās, claimed that people from the Mediterranean town of El-ʿArīsh had been cultivating their land in the Jūra area (Case 134). A panel of three land judges (*ahl ad-diyār*) was gathered to rule on the claim. To support their action, the ʿAreishiyya (people of El-ʿArīsh) defendants brought forward a bill of sale that their ancestors supposedly had received 170 years before from the previous owner, a Ziyyād Abū Mazyid. Studying the bill of sale, one of the judges, ʿAnayz Sālim al-ʿUrḍī of the Tarabīn Ḥasāblah tribe, noticed that it had been written with a ballpoint pen, "such as didn't exist 170 years ago," in handwriting that was still fresh. This discovery quashed their case.[175]

Verdicts Based on Investigation

Judges may also employ investigation and interrogation to aid them in coming to a judgment. Following are three examples.

1. In late 1993, as depicted above (Case 9), Slaym Abū Ḥunayk of the Aḥeiwāt Ṣafeiḥa charged a fellow tribesman, an Abū Maḥamūd, of having had a tryst with his daughter. The claimant asserted, on the evidence of a man called Bilān, a passerby in an automobile who saw them from a distance, that he was sitting next to her and that she shielded him from sight with her black head scarf when she heard the horn of the passing car. For his part, the defendant claimed that he was out looking for his freely grazing camels, stopped off to ask the shepherdess if she had seen them, and received from her a glass of tea.

Unable to decide on the basis of the respective pleas, the judge, Amīra Abū Amīra decided to question the girl herself. He asked her brother to drive with him to the family camp, some 130 kilometers distant, an arduous trip that included a drive from his home at Jalbāna on the northern Sinai road down to Jabal Boḍiyya, near the southern end of the Suez Canal, and a trek over rocky terrain at night. When the judge finally arrived at the encampment, the accused girl related to him that she had been sitting with shepherdesses of the ʿAyāyda confederation, making tea, when Abū Maḥamūd approached in his pickup truck and asked if she had seen his camels. She answered that she had not but offered him a glass of tea. The ʿAyāyda girls thereupon got up to leave so as not to be seen sitting in the company of a stranger, but as she knew him as a fellow tribesman and the tea was almost ready, the girl invited him to sit down as one should and drink. He drank the tea and directly left. "He neither said anything deviant (*miḥtirif*) nor made any immoral demands (*maṭālib ʿowjī*)."

Satisfied with the girl's version of the events and her blamelessness, Abū Amīra returned to the trial and the next morning announced his verdict. He declared the girl and Abū Maḥamūd innocent, giving them the right to honor trials against the informer, she for the slandering of her reputation and Abū Maḥamūd for being exposed to murder.[176]

2. Similarly, in the aforementioned land case in northern Sinai (Case 134), once the suspicion of the judge, ʿAnayz Sālim al-ʿUrḍī, was aroused by the obviously forged deed of sale, he noticed that it did not designate the exact plot supposedly sold. He told the "buyer" party, "All the deed says is that the land is 100 kilometers from El-ʿArīsh. Maybe you're the ones that chose this plot in the Jūra because it is close to you." They answered, "What are you, an interrogator or a judge?" Al-ʿUrḍī said, "I can act as both. And didn't you plant any trees, like fig or plum trees, to establish your ownership in all the 170 years that you've had this land?" They said, "We planted them, but they were all removed. Nevertheless, the land was bought from Ziyyād al-Mazyid." Al-ʿUrḍī asked, "Where are the descendants of the Mazyid clan, who can tell us if he had land in the Jūra and take us to it?" They said, "The family has died out." At this, the judges went out to see the plot of land themselves and spoke to the neighbors from all directions. Each of them reported that Abū Daʿās was

indeed their neighbor. When the judges returned to the trial and found the ʿAreishiyya demanding that Abū Daʿās swear an oath of ownership of the plot, they recited them the law—namely, that "Only a plot without neighbors [to testify to its ownership] requires an oath or the *bishʿa* ordeal" (*ad-dār illī mā liha jār—yā yamīn yā nār*). As a result of their investigation, the judges invalidated the ʿAreishiyya claim.[177]

3. Another example of investigation is from western Sinai in 1991, when a case was brought before a judge of the Aḥeiwāt Shawafīn, Salāma Ḥusayn az-Zimaylī, by members of the ʿAlaygāt and Tarabīn confederations (Case 91). The conflict began when people of the ʿAlaygāt abducted a lad of the Tarabīn on suspicion that he had informed the Egyptian police about their smuggling activities. They bound him, put him in their car, and took him as a captive to their camp, where they exposed him, bound, to their womenfolk to mock. They had chosen this violent method of avenging his alleged disclosures rather than turning to his elders and demanding justice. Binding someone, however, is considered a severe insult, likening him to a donkey. A Bedouin proverb says, "Kill a man, but don't bind him" (*uktul ar-rājil wala turbuṭah*),[178] meaning death is preferable to so great a humiliation.

After the ʿAlaygāt released the lad, following the interventions of neutral tribes, the Tarabīn retaliated in kind. They went to a camp of the ʿAlaygāt in Wādī ar-Rawiyayna, near the spring of ʿAyn Mūsa, forcefully entered tents to look for a young man, found and bound him, and took him 120 kilometers to their own camps in the Jabal Maghāra hills, where they exposed him to the ridicule of their womenfolk before releasing him.

When people of the respective confederations met in trial at the tent of Salāma Ḥusayn az-Zimaylī, the ʿAlaygāt demanded a judicial award for the Tarabīn violation of their women by their having entered the sacrosanct haven of their tents when seeking a lad to kidnap. Zimaylī, believing that this was not a case of violating women's honor, decided that he had to speak with the women involved in order to clarify his belief. So he drove the 250 kilometers to the ʿAlaygāt encampment that had been invaded. There, he asked the women, "Were there women in the tent when the Tarabīn came?" They said, "There were." He asked, "Did they say anything to you?" They said, "No." "Did they assault you when they took your man?" They said, "No." He asked, "Were they looking for women or looking for men?" They answered, "They were looking for men." As a result of this questioning, Zimaylī rejected the ʿAlaygāt request for a trial of honor.[179]

Verdicts Based on Superior Knowledge of the Law

A further resource that judges often possess over their litigants is their broader and more precise knowledge of the law, gained through more intensive exposure to legal conflicts as judges themselves or through apprenticeship with their fathers as judges, if such they were. This superior knowledge often serves them well in coming to a judgment, even if not always in determining innocence and guilt. Sometimes this involves expertise in procedural matters. The use of their knowledge of the law can be seen in the following three examples.

1. In the case noted above involving the kidnapping, binding, and shaming of a Tarabīn man and the retaliation in kind by the Tarabīn (Case 91), the other party, the ʿAlaygāt, demanded a judicial award for the attack on their tents when the Tarabīn were looking for a man to kidnap. During the discussion of the case in the tent of the judge, Salāma Ḥusayn az-Zimaylī, the judge asked the claimants if they had requested a blood-truce after their aggression against the Tarabīn man. The answer was "No." Hence, Zimaylī ruled that the ʿAlaygāt, after kidnapping, binding, and exposing the Tarabīn lad to shame and not asking for a blood-truce from his tribe, had laid themselves open to lawful retaliation, including the attack on their tent and the kidnapping of their tribesman. Moreover, their failure to ask for a truce deprived them of any entitlement to a judicial award or compensation.

2. An error in procedural matters also led to the condemnation of ʿĪd as-Sareiʿa for attacking a guest in his own tent (Case 12). The story, from 1938, began after Sareiʿa lent Salāma Abū Graynāt a gold pound, which he did not return though the due date had long passed. When, however, the borrower made a chance visit to the tent of the lender, the latter reminded him that he had not yet repaid his debt. In his defense, Abū Graynāt asserted that he had paid the debt to the lender's son, to which transaction there was also a witness, Sulaymān al-Gabbūaʿ of the Ẓullām confederation. Sareiʿa exclaimed that he would not accept that witness's testimony. As the argument proceeded, Sareiʿa flung the pestle of the coffee mortar at Abū Graynāt's head, missing the mark only because others present grabbed at his arm in time. Abū Graynāt thereupon set out to blacken the honor of Sareiʿa as a delinquent host by building black cairns at two wells in the northeast Negev, ʿArʿara and Bīr al-Māliḥ, and carved the camel brand (*wasm*) of the lender's tribe, the Ẓullām Abū Juweiʿid, on rocks beside each cairn so that people who came watering at the wells would know for whom the cairns were built.

The Abū Juweiʿid, burned by this defamation, were quick to resort to the recourse for obtaining justice for this affront, and they called for a *manshad* trial to restore their honor. After hearing the pleas of both sides, the now anonymous judge issued the following ruling: "As the borrower had said that he had repaid the debt, adding that he had repaid it in the presence of a witness, and as the lender failed to check, investigate, or make any demand but rather resorted directly to violence, he deserved the blackening for attacking his guest." In other words, Sareiʿa, who may have been correct in suspecting that Abū Graynāt had lied to him, lost the case owing to a procedural error: not checking his debtor's claim before assaulting him.[180]

3. Another case of a judgment based on procedural errors occurred in 1947, when two brothers of the Ẓullām confederation in the northeast Negev, an ʿĪd Sālim and a Salmān Sālim, inherited land from their father (Case 38). One day Salmān saw ʿĪd plowing his plot, which Īd also claimed to be his. So he resorted to the protection device of calling upon the honor of a powerful man, in this case the chief, ʿAlī Abū Graynāt, to protect his rights—meaning that any further use of his land by ʿĪd would be an affront to the notable. When, nevertheless, it turned out that ʿĪd kept up his cultivation of Salmān's plot, the latter aroused Abū Graynāt, demanding that he act in defense of his violated honor. At the resultant *manshad* trial, however, the judge, an ʿOwda Ṣubayḥ, ruled that no violation had taken place because Salmān Sālim had committed a procedural error when initially calling upon the honor of Abū Graynāt to protect his rights. He had neglected to mention, at the same time, the names of three judges before whom his claims could be adjudicated. This omission left his rival no opening for establishing his own claims.[181]

A judge's superior knowledge of the law may also help him clarify it through the judgment he makes. For example:

1. In the 1940s a man from the Tarabīn Jarawīn tribe in the Negev stole a camel from someone of the ʿAzāzma and took it to Egypt (Case 120). On his way, he met a fellow Tarabīn who, when he heard of the theft and the description of the camel, informed the owner of the identity of the thief and offered to serve as witness in a trial. Three years later, when the thief returned to the Negev, the owner charged him with theft and got him to submit to a trial of theft (*ziyādī*). After the thief denied the accusation, the owner produced the witness, who told how he had seen the thief with the camel. The judge, however, would not accept his testimony, ruling that a witness of camel theft must actually "see the camel in both couching-grounds" (*ḥāyif al-maraḥayn*)—that is, in the owner's possession before the theft and in the possession of the thief thereafter. In this case, the law, as defined by the judge, worked to the thief's advantage.[182]

2. Another example of a judge's defining the law for the disputants occurred in the central Negev in 1951, when a man of the Atayyim clan of the ʿAzāzma Saraḥīn tribe hit a shepherdess belonging to the Kishkhar clan of the Ẓullām Janabīb tribe (Case 86). Striking a female is considered a heinous violation, and wounds deriving from the blow are assessed twice those accruing for a man. When the Kishkhar demanded a trial to regain their rights, the Atayyim refused. Some time later, however, they met the actual violator in the tent of his clansman and beat him badly, causing him a head wound with the blow of a sword.

At the trial, which the tent owner subsequently demanded in order to reestablish the inviolability of his tent and to attain compensation for his guest's wounds, the judge dismissed his claims, ruling that the culprit himself was legally subject to attack for not having requested a blood-truce after striking the shepherdess—a procedural error. Hence, having refused to grant the Kishkhar clan justice, Atayyim left them no option but to resort to revenge. As to the tent and its rights, the judge defined the law as he understood it—that is, as the tent belonged to a clansman of the culprit, the latter could not find in it sanctuary from his injustices, as these were equally attributable to anyone in his clan. Accordingly, the law stating that "The tent of one who denies justice will not protect him" (*bayt al-ʿāyib mā yisallmah*) applies to all his kinsmen as well.[183]

3. Bedouin in the Negev also relate a case in which a man struck his brother's wife for refusing to perform a household chore (Case 135). According to the law, the only men who may strike a girl or woman are her guardians—in particular, her father or brothers or a clansman guardian in their absence—or her husband, but not her husband's brother. In this case, the man in question and his brother were married to sisters, but the accused supported his brother and sister-in-law. After the man hit his sister-in-law, she complained to her father, as the person ultimately responsible for her welfare, and at a subsequent trial, the father demanded justice from his son-in-law, who was married to his other daughter. On the one hand, the father naturally argued that the man had no legal right to strike his daughter for any reason, not being her father, brother, or husband. On the other hand, the accused son-in-law pleaded that he fed, clothed, and provided shelter for her as well as her husband, his brother. The judge, confronted with an unusual situation, defined the law as granting the man the prerogative he had taken. Finding a precedent in a rhymed phrase believed to have been part of the judgment of an anonymous judge from the past, he declared that whoever clothes and feeds a woman (lit. "covers her backside and apportions flour for her sack": *yiksī jaʿabit-ha ū-yithaṣṣaṣ fardit-ha*) has the right to discipline her with a blow.[184]

PUNISHMENTS

Prohibited Penalties

After delivering his judgment regarding innocence and guilt or right and wrong in the case before him, a judge must determine a sentence. Two forms of penalty are beyond his jurisdiction: physical punishment and detention.

Physical Punishment Although Bedouin law allows a victim of injustice to inflict physical punishment for certain categories of violation, it is as a private initiative, not the consequence of a legal judgment. The law allows the clansmen of a murdered person to avenge their group by murdering the original killer or someone of his group, as it also allows them to murder a rapist or someone of his group for violating one of their women. However, if the clansmen of the victims of such violations agree to litigate their grievance, the judge is authorized to decide, retroactively, that the original violation was indeed a violation and that subsequent retaliation, in life or limb, would have been justified if chosen. But he cannot prescribe any form of physical punishment. To do so would implicate him in the act of correction unjustifiably, his having no personal quarrel with the accused violator; accordingly, he would in practice be considered an accomplice to any physical damages inflicted, in keeping with the Bedouin legal maxim, "Directing is tantamount to killing" (*man dall katal'*),[185] and he would thereby make himself subject to a claim for them. This is a jeopardy that no judge would welcome.

While judges often allude to physical punishment in their sentences, it is only for the purpose of designating fines for certain violations. In particular, amputation of the offending part of the body—such as the tip of the tongue for slander or the hand for rape—is specified for ransom through the payment of a fine. This practice is mainly hyperbole; the allusion to amputation (perhaps borrowed from Islamic law, where amputation is actually practiced) serves to highlight the view of the ruling judge that the violation in question is grave. Such is the case of "the mangy camel" (*al-jamal al-ajrab*) in cases of rape. Hypothetically, it is legally permissible to seat a rapist, unclad, on the back of a camel smeared with oil (as if it were being treated for the mange) and then amputate all parts of his body on which the oil stuck. In fact, a fine, which is part of the rapist's penalty, is extrapolated from the assumedly amputated parts.[186]

Detainment Imprisonment, or detainment, the other form of punishment beyond the jurisdiction of a judge, is obviously not a practicable option within a society that traditionally has no permanent structures or law-enforcement agencies or personnel and which spends much of the year in movement and lacks the means to feed and otherwise maintain prisoners. However, even if these logistic obstacles could be overcome, Bedouin would reject detainment for running counter to their principles of honor and freedom, as expressed in the saying, "Kill a man, but don't bind him" and the sentiment that death is preferable to the humiliation of a life in which one is bound because "only an ass may be bound" (*lā yurabaṭ ghayr al-ḥimār*).[187] The sole circumstance under which Bedouin law permits detention (which practicably requires binding the detained person) is when an offender—such as a thief or sexual violator—has been caught in the act and the victims keep him as hostage until his clansmen agree to give them justice. In this sense, it plays the same role as the legal impoundment (*wisāga*) of property. For the purpose of punishment, as opposed to ransom, however, detainment is unlawful. Thus, as seen in the early 1990s, when people of the ʿAlaygāt confederation in western Sinai abducted and bound a man of the Tarabīn and displayed him, shamefully bound, to their womenfolk in order to punish him for allegedly informing against them to the Egyptian police, Salāma Ḥusayn az-Zimaylī, a judge of the Aḥeiwāt Shawafīn, deemed that they had laid themselves open to retributive counter-attack (Case 91).[188]

Permitted Penalties

A Bedouin judge may impose only two types of penalties on a violator: material and moral. Material penalties are mainly payments to the victim in livestock or cash, while moral punishments usually take the form of public confessions of wrongdoing. All penalties, however, whether moral or material, are imposed for three reasons: *to deter* others from committing the violation in question, *to compensate* the victim for losses and expenses, or *to set standards of behavior*. Some penalties serve more than one of these goals, even all three. They can deter, compensate, and set standards at one and the same time.

Penalties Imposed to Deter Deterrence, aimed at discouraging people from committing the offense being litigated, is most clearly observed in the penalties imposed for murder and rape, considered the worst crimes a Bedouin can commit. As we have seen, the law permits the clansmen of victims of these offenses to take revenge by killing the perpetrator or his clansmen with impunity. This is violence as a first resort, with no need of prior permission from a judge. The threat implicit in such categorical justice is in itself conceived to be daunting. To the same end, in cases of murder or rape that are not avenged directly but in which justice is rather eventually sought through litigation or mediation, the goal of deterrence is achieved by the imposition of heavy fines.

For murder, as noted above, the blood-money fine (*diya*) has traditionally been put at forty camels. In terms of late-twentieth-century values, this penalty was tantamount to $20,000, a fortune by Bedouin standards* — certainly suf-

*Toward the end of the twentieth century, when Islamism was pervading Bedouin life and culture, many Bedouin began even to speak of 100 camels (the blood-money in Sharīʿa law), which they designated "the Muhammadan *diya*" (*ad-diya al-muḥammadiyya*), based on the following Bedouin rendition of a story appearing in the Ḥadīth, as heard from Sulaymān Rizig al-Musāʿida of the Tarabīn Ḥasāblah, June 5, 2000:

> The Prophet's grandfather, ʿAbd al-Imṭallib, said, "O Lord, If you provide me with ten sons, I will sacrifice one of them." He got ten sons and said, "I've got to sacrifice one for the honor of God." They chose the youngest son, ʿAbdallah, but as he was the youngest, everyone loved him most, as did ʿAbd al-Imṭallib. The Jews in particular loved him. So all the chiefs and others got together and said, "You mustn't slaughter this child." He said, "I must." Finally, they said, "Okay, but ransom him." He said, "Fine, I'll ransom him with camels." He brought 10 camels and said, "Here is ʿAbdallah and here are 10 camels." But they said, "They are not his equal." He brought 20; still ʿAbdallah was

ficient to make Bedouin think twice before taking someone's life.* In addition, the murderer's clan is often constrained to provide a free bride (*ghurra*) to a close clansman of the murdered person.[189] The justification for the *ghurra*, as noted in chapter 3, is that she must bear the victim's clan a son to replace the male that has been killed.* She must remain with her husband until this son is mature—sufficiently so, according to tradition, that he can bring a handful of coffee beans to the sitting area (*mag'ad*) of his father's clansmen to symbolize his participation in their councils and affairs. On that occasion, the *ghurra* declares that she has fulfilled her clan's obligation to replace the dead man and is free to request divorce and return home. If her husband then wishes to keep her as his wife and she agrees, he must pay her family a bride-price.[190]

The surrender of a *ghurra* resulting from litigation or mediation is a harsh punishment for the murderer's clan to bear. First, the clan will be giving up a girl already promised in marriage (at birth) to a boy from the clan. Not only might this "closest male cousin" (*ibn al-'amm*) then have to pay a relatively high bride-price for an "outsider" girl, but also the father of the *ghurra* is deprived of the bride-price otherwise accruing for his daughter. Second, had the *ghurra* married her closest cousin, she might have borne sons for the strengthening of the clan. Finally, ceding one of its girls as a *ghurra* is a moral blow to the clan because it is thereby abandoning its responsibility for her welfare. Bedouin law denies the clan the right to interfere in marital matters on the *ghurra*'s behalf. Hence, she is equivalent to her husband's slave and, in being offered to him, is accordingly and metaphorically referred to as "a cold Kuḥeila mare without a blanket" (*kuḥeila bārda—lā ilha jalālha*) or "picked grapes without a watchman" (*gaṭf fī 'inab—mā warāh maṭlab*)";[191] in other

---

worth more. He brought 80; still 'Abdallah was worth more. Finally, he brought 100, and the people said, "All right; 100 camels have saved 'Abdallah" (*miyyt ba'īr sallam 'Abdallah*). Since that time, everyone's *diya* has been one hundred camels, like "the ransom of 'Abdallah's life" (*fidiyit rūḥ 'Abdallah*). As 'Abdallah begat Muḥammad, we call it "the Muhammadan *diya*."

*Some Bedouin believe that their blood-money of 40 camels is less than the Muhammadan *diya* because 100 camels would be impossible for Bedouin, relatively poor, to pay (oral communication from Jum'a 'Īd al-Farārja of the Tarabīn Ḥasāblah, January 30, 2001). The figure of 40 may have derived from the Muslim period of mourning or from the overall holiness of this number (see Bailey, "Religious Practices," p. 83).

*On occasion a *ghurra* is offered to replace a woman that has been abducted for marriage. In 1974 fellow tribesmen of 'Owda al-Hadōbe of the 'Azāzma Saraḥīn tried to placate him, following the abduction and marriage of his daughter by one of them, by offering him a *ghurra* to marry his son. (Oral communication from Swaylim Sulaymān Abū Bilayya of the 'Azāzma Saraḥīn, December 1, 1974).

words, she has no one to "cover" or "guard" her. As one Bedouin remarked, "Even if her husband kills her, her kinsmen have no claim."[192] For these reasons, the *ghurra* penalty, like a heavy indemnity, is imposed to serve as a deterrent to murder.

By the same token, sentences for rape, through their severity, also seek to deter men from perpetrating this much dreaded crime. In rape, as in other violations of the honor of persons or the violation of the sanctuary of tents, the material penalties are particularly fearful, especially as they depend on the total discretion of the judge, acting in the capacity of a or judge of honor. The sentences of these judges in a case of rape have been known to include the vehicle or camel that brought the violator to the place of offense; forty camels as ransom for the life of the rapist, who would otherwise be liable to revenge by murder; forty more camels of especially high quality; several other rarely hued and expensive camels; and varying numbers of camels as ransom for "the hand that grabbed her," "the tongue that commanded her," "the eye that saw her," and "the penis that penetrated her." Such a punishment may also comprise forty sheep and forty gold coins.[193] Moreover, in imposing the fines in kind, a *manshad* judge may also specify their financial value in local currency —again at his own discretion rather than in keeping with often lower market prices. Thus, the above list of separate fines might come to an aggregate sum reaching the equivalent of several hundred thousand dollars, which few Bedouin could ever defray.

Deterrence in questions of honor is also sought in the moral punishments imposed by a judge. If, for example, a man slanders a woman's reputation for propriety—as was the case in the central Negev in 1973, when Sālim aṭ-Ṭimṭāwī of the ʿAzāzma ʿAṣiyāt insinuated that the unmarried daughter of Sālim ʿAtayyig al-Khiraynig of the ʿAzāzma Saraḥīn was pregnant (Case 71)— one part of the judge's sentence will be for the man in question to confess that he has lied while standing before (normally) three tents filled with men. In the case cited, Ṭimṭāwī's father, moreover, had to vocally reaffirm before the same forums that his son had lied.[194] Such shame to a violator and his clan is clearly a punishment that Bedouin would be careful to avoid.

In yet another effort to deter violations through the imposition of fines, a judge may detail the various components of a violation so as to highlight them for the public imagination. To discourage the planning of violations, a thief or rapist, for example, is regularly fined for each step, or the general distance, between his tent and the scene of the crime, as well as the camel—more recently the vehicle—that conveyed him. In 1976, for example, when the *manshad* judge, Sulaymān Muḥammad al-ʿUgbī, in a trial between two members of the Muzayna confederation of southern Sinai delivered his sentence against the sons of Munayfī Sālim Jabalī for violating the sanctuary of Sālim Jumʿa Abū Ṣabḥā's tent and the bodily integrity of his wife while they were attacking his tent at night, he designated, as part of the penalty, specific fines for each step taken from one encampment to the other, for entering the tent of Abū Ṣabḥā, and for exiting the tent (Case 1).[195]

Camels stolen while grazing will characteristically be fined for each step "from their pasture to the place they were hidden" (*min maflāhin ila makhfāhin*). Thieves and rapists will also be given one fine for entering the tent of their crime and another for leaving it; often too the fine of a grown male and female camel (*rabāʿ ū-rabaʿiyya*) will be imposed for every turn, or *lafta*, within the tent. If implements such as coffee pots or cups are knocked over during his searchings, an intruder will be fined for those as well. As detailed above, a rapist may be sentenced to the amputation of the limbs or organs involved in his offense, as well as to the "mangy camel" ordeal. To deter people from shooting each other with firearms, those that do, even if they miss the mark, must surrender the weapon to the person at whom they have shot.

Penalties Imposed to Compensate Compensation to the victims of violation through litigation accrues to them through the fines that violators pay and the moral punishments they endure. The compensatory aspect of Bedouin law is often praised as one of its main merits. In cases of murder, as indicated above, the victim's clansmen are not only compensated by monetary or animal awards, but also actually regain, through the acquisition of a *ghurra*, at least one male for the male that was killed (let alone the bonus of all the children she will have borne her husband while his wife).

In a case of rape, further to the huge material fines awarded to the victim's clansmen, as in cases of murder, the clansmen also receive moral compensation intended to rehabilitate the woman's and their defamed reputation. Bedouin law awards moral compensation to all victims of dishonoring—whether compromised women or defamed men—and it generally takes the form of a public confession of wrongdoing, as explained. Often too the violator is ordered to fly white flags at spots that people frequent or to cover the complete exterior of the tent of the victim of dishonoring with white fabric to symbolize that the victim's honor is intact.[196] Such was the case in the central Negev in 1971, when the Wujūj clan of the Ẓullām Janabīb was ordered by the judge, Ḥasan Abū Rubayʿa, also of the Ẓullām, to cover the tent of Ḥimayd as-Saddān of the ʿAzāzma Saraḥīn with white fabric after one of its men, Hilayyil al-Wajj, visited Saddān's wife one night in the husband's absence (Case 44).[197]

In east-central Sinai, such fabric is called "the white cloth of Ibn Ghibn," as related in a case by a judge of the Aḥeiwāt Shawafīn confederation, Salāma Ḥusayn az-Zimaylī (Case 136):[198]

> The men of the tribe of Aḥeiwāt once went out on a raid. While they were away, Shaykh Ṭōg, an old man, ordered his family to grind a large quantity of wheat so that he could receive the men of the tribe hospitably when they returned. Upon their return, Shaykh Ṭōg told the men to slaughter one of his goats for every ten of them. But the men said they did not wish to eat meat. So Shaykh Ṭōg ordered flour and clarified butter (*samn*) to be brought instead. They made *fatt* (broken bread soaked in the *samn*) and ate until they were satisfied. When they got up to go, Shaykh Ṭōg asked which of them was the oldest, and they answered, "Ibn Ghibn." The shaykh turned to him and said, "I seek your protection from any poets of your party who may satirize me for not having slaughtered animals for you to eat" (*āna dākhil ʿalayk min mughannī ar-rikāb*). Ibn Ghibn answered, "You have come under my protection and are safe" (*dakhalt wi-silimt*).
>
> On the road, Ibn Ghibn heard a poet ridiculing his host: "Ṭōg is an old fart who has not oiled the beards of his guests" (*Ṭōg, yā faṣwa ʿajūz, mā dassam al-liḥāḥ*)—that is, with fat from meat. Ibn Ghibn retorted in rhyme,
>
> > O slaves of Abū Tamāma, Ṭōg does not deserve censure.
> > (*Yā ʿabīd Abū Tamāma—Ṭōg mā jā la-l-malāma*)
> > The wheat with butter was piled high and sheep were aplenty.
> > (*al-gamḥ wa-s-samn imtallal—wa-l-ghanim ʿala-l-matamma*).
>
> Ibn Ghibn then struck the offensive poet with his sword and cut off his hand. When the case was sent to a Bedouin judge, he considered that the cutting off of the poet's hand discharged Shaykh Ṭōg's claim for slander and warranted no further award. A white flag was raised for Shaykh Ṭōg's protector, Ibn Ghibn, to prove that he had performed what was required of him when he promised that Shaykh Ṭōg would not be ridiculed by the poets. From that moment, *shāsh Ibn Ghibn* became a proverbial expression, describing the whiteness of the flag decreed as a penalty by a judge.

Bedouin law also seeks to compensate victims of physical violence for damages lesser than murder. Hence, judges assess the loss or disability of limbs, organs, or other parts of the body in an effort to find commensurate recompense. Although Bedouin believe that compensatory awards are standard, a review of the literature and my conversations with judges reveal many inconsistencies in the size of the fines imposed for purposes of compensation. One reason for this discrepancy is that very localized figures are genuinely felt by all those who reported—to me personally or to those who have written on the subject before me—to reflect general Bedouin usage.

Another reason for discrepancy in fines results from a certain personal discretion that judges may exercise in their sentences. The greatest discretion is enjoyed by *manshad* (honor) judges or those ruling in cases of the violation of tents, the *aḥmadī* judges. However, a *ziyādī* judge, in cases of theft, may also exercise a certain discretion, such as imposing heavier sentences on repeat thieves than on first-time offenders. By the same token, a *manga*ʿ *ad-damm* judge ruling on the loss of a limb will often take into account the circumstances, such as provocation, that may have preceded the blow that caused a wound, as seen in the above story of Ibn Ghibn, where the loss of a hand received no compensatory award owing to the victim's slanderous line of poetry that occasioned it.

The above notwithstanding, Bedouin confidence in the uniformity of such compensations is strong, as manifest in a widespread story that was heard among the Ḥuwayṭāt in southern Jordan, the ʿAzāzma in the central Negev, and the Bilī in northern Sinai. The story explained how the levels of compensation for a lost eye and a lost hand were originally determined. As told by the ʿAzāzma raconteur, Swaylim Sulaymān Abū Bilayya, whose account localizes the story by "identifying" the central figures, the story goes as follows (Case 77):

> Two men of the Aḥeiwāt had a fight, one losing an eye and the other a hand. When they went to the "blood-pool judge" to see which of the two should receive more compensation, the one with the lost eye claimed that his award should be half that of a murdered man, and he with the severed hand said the same. They went from judge to judge, but none could decide who was entitled to a bigger fine. Finally they got to the seventh judge, ʿAtayyig ʿOwda as-Saddān of the ʿAzāzma Saraḥīn, who also struggled with the problem. There were many men in his tent that day, and as the weather was hot, he told the guests to unsaddle their camels. Then he called one of his shepherds and whispered something to him, whereupon the lad left the gathering. When lunch was served and the guests were eating bowls of mutton, they all heard shouts in the distance. The shepherd, standing on a hillside and waving his cloak in the air, was shouting, "O worthy men! Raiders have taken our camels and are racing off with them." All the men present straightaway couched and saddled their camels and rode off to pursue the enemy. The one-eyed man did likewise and was in the forefront of the pursuers. The man with the severed hand, however, struggled to saddle his mount, pulling on the saddle strap by putting it on the ground under his foot and tightening it with his good hand and his teeth.
>
> Seeing this, the judge called out to the riders, "Come back! God bless your effort! Come back! It was a mistake. An old woman mistook our people for raiders." When the gathering had reassembled, the judge announced his decision: "As the man with the gouged eye had his face disfigured and suffers

inconvenience, his compensation must be one-fourth the blood-price of a man. But he with the severed hand, though still alive, can barely defend himself like a man. He is therefore but half a man, and his compensation is one-half the blood price of a man—twenty camels."[199]

Although judges may award different numbers of camels or different equivalents in monetary fines for an eye or a hand, depending on circumstances, we can nonetheless discern certain bases for the size of the awards. The first, as seen in the story of the hand and the eye, is whether the wound limits one's ability to defend oneself or even take part in warlike pursuits, such as camel raids and acts of vengeance. Hence, an amputated hand or leg is seen to deserve twenty camels, or half the blood-price of a murdered man, whereas the same limbs, if merely broken or otherwise impaired but not totally unusable, command only half that figure, or ten camels.[200] An amputated finger is worth one camel, but the index finger, which must pull the trigger in conflict, is valued at five.[201] The loss of both eyes, through either blinding or extraction, may be assessed as high as thirty camels, as it makes a man totally defenseless. He is nevertheless awarded only three-fourths of a dead man's blood-price because being alive, though blind, he is still seen to carry certain advantages, such as the ability to father male children for his clan.

Another criterion, applied with the dual purpose of instilling caution against violent conflict as well as to compensate the victim, is the breaking or damaging of any limb or organ, even if nonessential. Thus, a tooth, a rib, an ear, or a finger, broken or lost, are generally assessed at one camel each, and a single eye at ten. As indicated, a lost eye, while entailing hardship, such as the difficulty in locating one's freely grazing camels, is also evaluated for its aesthetic disability. In this, it is similar to the face, where a scar is metaphorically depicted as a "valley," as in the maxim, "A valley on the face is a constant companion" (*al-wādī fī-l-wijih ṣāḥbah*), owing to its permanent visible disfigurement.[202] Accordingly, a scar on the face is assessed at double the value of a wound or scar elsewhere on the body—that is, two full-grown camels (*raba'ayn*; sing. *rabā'*) for each "finger-width of wound" (*ritba*, by which wounds are measured) instead of one.[203] Whereas a wound anywhere on the body is subject to compensation for the loss of one's blood, those that cause no impairment of bodily functions or disfigurement, permanent or temporary, are fined lightly. In 1974 in southern Sinai, a gunshot wound between the index finger and thumb of the right hand of Munayfī Sālim Jabalī of the Muzayna Jarāb'a that did not comprise damage to either bone or cartilage cost the shooter, Sālim Jum'a Abū Ṣabhḥā of the Muzayna Ghawānma, a fine of only 105 Egyptian pounds ($34) (Case 1).[204]

Tradition and symbolism constitute a third criterion for a judge's decision on the level of compensation to be awarded a victim of violation, especially in rape. As Bedouin law permits the murder of a rapist by his victim's clansmen, a case that comes before a *manshad* judge will result in part of the sentence being "forty standing camels or a bound lad" (*arbaʿīn wugūf ow ghulām maktūf*)[205] — that is, the blood-price of the otherwise-murdered rapist for having been spared (thus the forty camels) or, metaphorically, his being delivered up for murder (the bound lad). This formulaic sentence, devised sometime in the distant past, has become standard. Similarly, and together with this material fine, come "a black male and a black female slave" (*ʿabd ū-khādim*) dressed in white, the female to lead the camels and the male to drive them. Such slaves originated in the more practical *manshad* award to a raped woman who conceived a child, "the female to bear him in her arms and the male to fetch water" (*al-khādim tishīl al-walad wa-l-ʿabd yiwarrid yijīb miy*).[206] However, it became part of the award for rape itself, partly owing to the symbolism of black as representing the dishonor that was committed and the white as indicating that honor has been restored. White is frequently also included in other parts of a sentence for rape, such as the paying of forty white sheep or the payment of forty specifically white camels. The designation of penalties for rape by forties, such as forty sheep or forty gold coins, is also symbolic, evoking the alternative to death for a rapist and his ransom by forty camels.

Penalties Imposed to Set Standards In addition to the goals of deterring violation and compensating victims, judges also determine some fines in order to set certain standards of behavior that are not to be exceeded in committing violent offenses. This is mostly done by compounding the fines.

The first standard pertains to persons who are not to be physically assaulted owing to physical inferiority, women in particular. The unprovoked striking of a woman who is neither clanswoman nor wife commands a fine for damages twice as large as that for wounds inflicted on a man. In other words, a woman's wound is "assessed [like that of a man] and doubled" (*yingaṣṣ wi-yinthanī*).[207] For the murder of a woman by a man, Bedouin law allows for four acts of revenge or the payment of four blood-prices of a man or a combination of acts of revenge and payments up to a total of four. This compounding, in addition to setting limits to violent behavior, seeks to uphold the hallowed inviolability of women, thus enabling them to be left alone and often isolated, whether at pasture or at home.

Similar to attacks upon women, fines for wounds and injuries inflicted on cripples and children are also doubled in order to deter assaults upon them too. In the event of murder, the clansmen of a child, like those of a woman, are also entitled to four acts of vengeance or four blood-prices. When, early in the twentieth century, camel raiders of the Maʿāza confederation from western

Arabia killed a yet uncircumcised shepherd of the Ghuraygāniyyīn tribe of the Aḥeiwāt Shawafīn in eastern Sinai, the latter were entitled to four acts of revenge, of which they perpetrated one, received one blood-price payment, and voluntarily waived the receipt of the other two (Case 8).[208] As children serve as shepherds—a vital role in the economy of their families—this compounding, by signaling that they are inviolable, augments their security when alone at pasture.

Another standard that the law seeks to maintain through compound fines has to do with treachery or deceit (*bōg*). A Bedouin legal maxim holds that "Deception will compound its doer's fines" (*al-bōg bizyid ʿa rāʿīh*).[209] Generally treachery refers to an unanticipated physical assault. One such act is the killing of a man asleep. To Bedouin, sleep is a hallowed condition, during which one is entitled to security and peace of mind. Some believe that while sleeping, one's soul departs and moves about, leaving one lifeless.[210] For either reason, sleep is not to be disturbed, even by waking—let alone murder. Thus, a judge, to give expression to this sentiment in the law, will rule that the killers of a sleeper must pay the blood-price of a man fourfold; if, instead, the clansmen of the sleeper choose their right to revenge, it too is fourfold. In 1980 the Tarabīn Ḥasāblah of southeast Sinai claimed this right when Fiheid Slaym Ibn Jāzī, who was sleeping, was killed by men of the Aḥeiwāt Karādma (Case 75).[211] Even if a sleeping man is murdered in revenge for another killing, his death itself, while counting as revenge in its own right, may in turn be avenged threefold by his clansmen (the initial murderers); alternatively, three times the blood-price for a man must be paid. The laws of blood-revenge require an avenger to waken a sleeping man before killing him.

Treachery is also an attack or other violation against someone who believes he is enjoying friendly or peaceable relations with his assailant, owing to a prevailing absence of hostility or agreement between them. Among the Tarabīn of southeast Sinai in 1997, when ʿĀyid ʿAṭeiwī al-ʿAlowna was shot and killed by Salmān Zaydān al-Munāṣra, the brother of a girl with whom ʿAlowna had been trysting, his clansmen claimed their right to four acts of revenge, asserting that the murder took place at a meeting in which Munāṣra, by prior accord, was to give ʿAlowna his sister in marriage (Case 52). Hence, they argued, although ʿAlowna had every reason to feel secure, he had been led into a premeditated ambush. Munāṣra's seeming agreement to the marriage was thus deemed deceit.[212] A similar form of deceit is to feign friendship in order to disarm a companion and facilitate killing him for ulterior motives, such as robbery. These acts of murder, which intentionally abuse the victim's sense of trust and security, are termed "the killing of a traveling companion" (*bōg ar-rafīg*), the imagery deriving from the condition of companions joining for a journey through uninhabited desert in a state of mutual trust.[213] It is a type of trust normally enjoyed by neighbors in an encampment. Thus, "taking hold of a neighbor's wife" (*lāgtak ʿala jārtak*) in his absence is also a betrayal of trust. Indeed, as noted, betraying a companion, assaulting a female neighbor, and stealing anything stored by migrating Bedouin are the three offenses most despised in Bedouin society.[214]

A further category of treachery or deceit pertains to relations between hosts and guests. Hospitality being essential to survival in the desert, it is extended automatically. As a result, both hosts and guests are obligated to protect and respect each other so that the institution of hospitality can exist. Accordingly, any violation of one against the other, such as a host attacking his guest or a guest stealing from his host, is deemed faithlessness and is subject to the compounding of fines for wounds and thefts and the inflicting of severe punishments for related offenses. In 1938, for example, Ḥājj ʿĪd as-Sareiʿa of the Ẓullām Abū Juweiʿid was fined 100 gold pounds for attempting to strike his guest, Salāma Abū Graynāt, also of the Ẓullām (Case 12). The sum of the fine was sufficient to purchase twenty camels, according to values at that time.[215] When in the late nineteenth century men of the Muzayna Ghawānma in southeast Sinai murdered an Arabian ʿUmrānī Bedouin selling goats in their area (and was thus their guest), the latter's clansmen, entitled to four acts of revenge, killed two men of the killers' clan and were awarded, as their due, the cash equivalent of eighty camels as the blood-price for another two (Case 110).[216] In cases of a guest violating a host, the fines are also great. In the Negev in 1952 (Case 88), when a man of the ʿAzāzma Saraḥīn stole goats from his host of the Ẓullām Janabīb, he was fined the equivalent of $1 for each step he took from their pasture to the market; two grown camels, male and female; the equivalent of $400 together with each camel; and four goats for each one he had stolen.[217] Had it been a case of simple theft, rather than the betrayal of a host, the guest would not have been fined the two camels and the $800.

Yet a further category of treachery is the violation of agreements deliberately intended to ensure the safety of their recipients. One is the blood-truce, or *ʿaṭwa*, given by a victim of physical violence as safekeeping that the perpetrator will be free of any act of revenge until the problem is litigated.[218] Another is "the camel of sleep," which exempts certain, usually distant, clansmen of a murderer from revenge.[219] A third is the period following litigation over physical assault, during which the initial assailant, having completed his penalties, is guaranteed safety from attack by his former victim through a "guarantor of warmth."[220] For the violation of this category of treachery, a judge will fine the offender double for each wound inflicted, in addition to his honor fine for violating the guarantor of such an agreement.

Finally, there is a specific sort of treachery called *dalīkha*, a Bedouin term for the denial of a crime, murder in particular. To help dispel any resultant doubts that may unsettle Bedouin society after a murder has taken place, the law quadruples the blood-price to be paid by a murderer who initially denies his deed or, alternatively, the number of acts of vengeance that are allowed against his clansmen.[221]

The Relinquishment of Fines

Reasons for Concession At first sight, an ostensibly odd aspect of Bedouin legal custom is the voluntary concession (*fawāt*) of fines awarded to, and expenses incurred by, the victims of violation after they had been so eager to attain them. Such concession takes place after almost every trial or mediation in which punishments and awards are decreed. The only exception, occasionally practiced, is the nonconcession of blood-payments for acts of murder. Often, however, nearly all material awards are conceded, the victim of violation retaining only the expenses incurred in his efforts to obtain justice and the awards specifically designated to restore his honor.

Hence, in 1976, in the conflict between Sālim Jumʿa Abū Ṣabḥā and Munayfī Sālim Jabalī of the Muzayna confederation of southern Sinai (Case 1), the sons of the latter were fined a total of $60,500—for attacking Abū Ṣabḥā in his tent at night, hitting and holding his clanswoman wife, and puncturing the tires of his car, thus prohibiting him from obtaining medical aid; after concession this sum came down to $27,000.[222] In 1946, when the coffee utensils of ʿOwda Abū Muʿammar of the ʿAzāzma Masʿūdiyyīn were lost and pilfered after a flood and he was awarded the return of the utensils, their worth fourfold, the expenses he incurred in trying to obtain justice, and a public confession that he was right when he accused the thieves, he conceded everything except the utensils and the confession (Case 117).[223] In the late nineteenth century, when camel raiders from the Maʿāza confederation in northwest Arabia killed an as yet uncircumcised shepherd boy belonging to the Aḥeiwāt Ghuraygāniyyīn tribe of east-central Sinai, his family, though entitled (owing to the victim's age) to four acts of revenge or blood-payments, conceded two of them (Case 8).[224] In 1977, when members of the Ameiṭil family of the ʿAzāzma ʿAṣiyāt tribe perpetrated a series of violations against the Abū Bilayya family of the ʿAzāzma Saraḥīn (Case 23) and were fined a total of $31,425, the family conceded $27,800, keeping only $3,625, mainly representing their expenses.[225] In 2006, after a man of the Tiyāha Abū-l-Gīʿān tribe was awarded the equivalent of $800,000 for an insult to his manhood, he conceded the entire sum (Case 107).[226]

If, indeed, the reason for setting high fines for violations is to indicate that a violator will seriously suffer at the hands of his victim (called "the possessor of the right" [*ṣāḥib al-ḥagg*]), their punitive or deterrent effect seems ironic, in light of everyone's prior knowledge that the victim will concede much of the sum. Nevertheless, the Bedouin support this system and offer two main justifications for it. First, in keeping with the Bedouin proverb already mentioned in chapter 1, "Getting justice is for reputation, not for filling the belly," [227] every man's need to appear in society as totally devoted to the protection of his rights obliges him not to let financial gain play a role in this domain. If others suspect him of being motivated by thoughts of gain ("He measures his rights in his pocket" [*ḥaggah fī kīsah*]),[228] it will weaken the desired impression. Accordingly, a number of Bedouin proverbs denigrate the acceptance of blood-money in cases of murder or wounds: "Money is no compensation for men" (*al-maṣārī mā biyjāzin ar-rijāl*); "It is shameful to earn money from your blood" (*ʿeib tākil flūs fī dammak*); "Only a dog licks its own blood" (*al-kalb biyilḥas dammah*); "Either be generous [in concession] or strike [in revenge]" (*yā tikram—yā tuḍrub*).[229]

Second, in order to justify the security aspect of conceding fines, the Bedouin portray it as a sign of strength, the image that a violated person seeks to restore through justice. Hence: "Where there's concession, there's strength" (*al-ʿafū ʿend al-migdara*).[230] They also depict it as generosity, elevating it to a social virtue, as indicated by the proverbs, "True generosity is the concession of blood-money" (*al-karam karam ad-damm*), and "Get your right to the last gram, but be large by the *kantar*" (*al-ḥagg bi-l-aghrām wa-l-karam bi-l-gunṭār*).[231] In addition, Bedouin describe persons who concede the fines awarded them as people possessed of self-respect (*shahāma*), manliness (*murūwa*), generosity (*karam*), and humaneness (*insaniyya*).

Further to the theoretical explanation above, the Bedouin themselves explain the utility of setting high fines as a means of deterrence, even though they may be conceded. First, it sets a degree of punishment for the violation in question, and, as shown in the case of Abū Bilayya and Ameiṭil, it forces the violator "to scream as though he'd been bitten [by a snake]" (*yiṣayyiḥ umm gurṣ*).[232] Second, if the accused violates his victim again, he will have to pay the fines determined without any concession being asked. Third, Bedouin stress that concession "is not mandatory" (*mish ijbārī*). A Bedouin proverb says, "The one who's won justice is spoiled; if he wishes he's large, if he wishes he's tight" (*ṣāḥib al-ḥagg imdallal—yirīd yikram, yirīd yubkhul*).[233]

An Example of Concession One example of concession concerns a case that took place in the central Negev in spring 1977 (Case 23).[234] As related in chapter 2, the Abū Bilayya family of the ʿAzāzma Saraḥīn tribe had migrated to Wādī Abū Ḥiṣāya, just north of Kibbutz Sde Boker, a Jewish agricultural community, in order to avail themselves of the ample pasture of annual plants that had grown there. This move displeased the Ameiṭil family of the ʿAzāzma ʿAṣiyāt tribe, who had already been grazing their flocks in that area and enjoyed cordial relations with the kibbutz—relations they did not wish to share with the newcomers. Consequently they perpetrated a series of acts designed to prejudice the newcomers' relations with the kibbutz and discourage them from remaining in the area. These included putting twenty-one of Abū Bilayya's grazing goats into the fenced-off area of the kibbutz, where watchdogs bit five of them, killing one; placing seven donkeys into the kibbutz fields, where a watchman shot them dead; stabbing another donkey dead; reporting to the police in a nearby town, Dimona, that a son of the Abū Bilayya family, Sālim, was pillaging army depots and stealing from the cars of tourists in the area—accusations that led to two police searches of the Abū Bilayya tents and interrogations of Sālim. Finally, Ameiṭil lads beat Sālim up at the weekly Beersheba market in plain sight of many bystanders, after which they felt impelled to request a blood-truce, lest the entire ʿOwdāt clan turn upon them. They quickly violated the truce, however, in that one of their sons, working as a tracker, provoked the Abū Bilayya by flouting his presence when he led the police on one of its inspections of the Abū Bilayya tents. Even worse, the Ameiṭil allowed the blood-truce to expire—a further act of contempt. Under these volatile circumstances, which threatened to unsettle the ʿAzāzma confederation, tribal dignitaries, including the chief, ʿOwda Abū Muʿammar, formed a delegation (*jāha*) to persuade the Abū Bilayya to reconcile with their violators.

When the delegation came to the new camping grounds of the Abū Bilayya at Khirbit ar-Rās in the West Bank, they bid, as is customary, the head of the ʿOwdāt clan and its spokesman, Ḥimayd Salmān as-Saddān, to determine the awards they considered due their people for their suffering.

Saddān first stipulated that Sālim Abū Bilayya's beating be dealt with last and separate from all the material damages that the Abū Bilayya family had suffered. He also demanded that Ameiṭil pay them, up front, the equivalent of $375—that is, $25 for each night that they insulted the Abū Bilayya by not renewing their truce after it expired. After the delegation agreed to his conditions, Saddān began to specify the awards that his clansmen deserved for the Ameiṭils' initial harassments as follows:

Driving seven donkeys into the kibbutz—equivalent of $900
The stabbing of a donkey—$150
The first police search of the Abū Bilayya tent—$2,500 ($1,250 for making the inhabitants exit; $1,250 for their re-entrance)

The second police search of the Abū Bilayya tent — $2,000
The Ameiṭil son's leading the police to their tent on the second search — $500
Four goats bitten by kibbutz dogs — $1,000
One goat killed — $250.

These damages amounted to the equivalent of $7,300.

When he was finished, the *jāha* lost no time in demanding that Saddān make concessions. In the negotiations that followed, the position of the *jāha* was that, though the Abū Bilayya had suffered and thus deserved awards, it behooved them to be generous. Saddān's position, by contrast, was one of indignation over the *jāha*'s demands, repeatedly reviewing in detail the tribulations that his clansmen had endured. The argument over concessions lasted half an hour, during which Saddān, while adamantly rejecting the demands, would suddenly make a concession. The first, of $1,500, was made "to God and his Prophet," as is customary. The chief, Abū Muʿammar, thereupon protested, asserting, "God and the Prophet's share is very little. You should add to it. God is greater than all people together. You should give him more." Saddān shot back: "God isn't greedy, o Chief; fifteen hundred is enough for him."

The second concession was $2,500, for the "honor (lit. 'beard' [*liḥā*]) of the delegation," to which the chief protested that its members should not be lumped together but should rather receive concessions individually. So Saddān conceded another $1,250 for the delegation, insisting that he would concede no more. Still, the *jāha* pressed him to concede everything remaining so that they could drink and eat, whereupon Saddān asserted that he did not need the sheep they had brought to slaughter upon reconciliation, and if the delegation did not agree to the sum in balance, it had the option of resorting to a trial, which he had claimed from the outset as his preference so as to establish the guilt of the Ameiṭil. Nevertheless, he conceded $500, again for "God and his Prophet." Following a bit more bickering, Saddān acceded to the request of the guarantor of payment, Naṣṣār Abū-l-Misk of the ʿUmrān confederation, for a concession in his honor, which amounted to $750. The delegation now agreed to the balance remaining for the damages: the equivalent of $800.

Then Ḥimayd as-Saddān began to enumerate the awards accruing to the Abū Bilayya family for slights to their strength:

The insult uttered by one of the Ameiṭil about the Abū Bilayya in Chief Abū Muʿammar's tent ("We'll carve them up with an adze" [*widdna ninjar annās bi-l- gadūm*]) — $12,500
The grabbing of Sālim Abū Bilayya before the Ameiṭil beat him in the market — $2,500
The beating of Sālim — $5,000
The release of Sālim after the beating — $2,500
Two blows to Sālim — $1,250

The total thus came to $23,750, and the *fawāt* process began. As Saddān had assessed the pride and blood damages as a blood-pool judge would assess them (despite the session being defined a *jāha* rather than a trial), he "magnanimously" conceded one-third (the equivalent of approximately $7,200) to himself as if he were an acting judge. Then, in the course of a forty-five-minute heated dispute over whether the Abū Bilayya should make further concessions, the *jāha* pressed them to be generous, using precedents and proverbs (for example, "A lion eats his share and leaves some" [*as-sabiʾ biyākil min ḥaggah wi-yibaggī*]), and the Abū Bilayya countered with reiterations of their suffering from insult and with oaths ostensibly committing themselves to truculence (for example, "As God is my witness . . ." [*asūg ʿalayk allah*]; "Though I be expelled from the Islamic religion . . ." [*lō akūn barra min dīn al-islām*]; "Upon my very skull . . ." [*w-allāhī min dagshūm rāsī*]; and "Though my father, dead these past twenty years, were to come back . . ." [*lō yījī abūwī illī mayyit lah ʿishrīn sana*]—"I won't concede another penny of the sum" [*mā afūt minnah kamān girsh*]). Still, Saddān made eight more sporadic concessions—two to "God and the Prophet," one to the guarantor, five to the delegation, and two to its guests—the award coming down to $2,000. This, together with the $800 for the damages and the $375 for the Muṭlān's having abandoned the blood-truce for fifteen days, left a total balance (called "remainders of the entitlement" [*sawāmil al-ḥagg*]) of $3,625 out of the original $31,425 that the Ameiṭil owed the Abū Bilayya.

*Reconciliation (*Ṣulḥ*)*

Bedouin, realizing that violations are to be expected in a society such as theirs, which lives on the edge of survival, are not wont to bear grudges against their violators so long as they have received justice from them. This attitude is reflected in sayings such as, "A man is angry when he's in conflict, but when he's appeased, he's genial" (*ar-rājil yizʿal wagt az-zaʿal—ū-wagt ar-riḍā yarḍa*), and "The law applies against me as against you" (*al-ḥagg sārī ʿaleiy wi-ʿalayk*).[235] Consequently when justice has been meted out by a judge, a mediator, or a delegation and its terms are fulfilled, erstwhile enemies often reconcile and become friends. Bedouin, however, consider that justice is not complete by merely restoring rights to a victim of violation. It should also restore peace to society, a goal that is accomplished when both sides are content. Hence, they say, "A verdict satisfies one, but reconciliation satisfies two" (*al-ḥagg biyirḍī wāḥad wa-ṣ-ṣulḥ biyirḍī thinīn*).[236] Indeed, the expression "Reconciliation is the master of all laws" (*aṣ-ṣulḥ sayyid al-aḥkām*) holds reconciliation up as a main aspiration of the Bedouin legal system.[237]

Even blood avengers, who have taken justice into their own hands, are urged to reconcile with the original murderers, after revenge is had, in the emphatic (but nonbinding) dictum "He who has taken revenge should ask for a camel-truce" (*man astathār astajār*)[238]—that is, a truce during which the sides can discuss resolution of the reasons for the violence. Bedouin hope that such reconciliation will avert an ongoing feud and an attendant series of murders.

Before blood-revenge has taken place, however, as we saw in chapter 2, a *jāha* delegation often acts so as to effect reconciliation between a murderer and the clan of his victim; in successful negotiations the victim party or group concedes its right to take revenge and settles for a resolution of the conflict through peaceful means—that is, the receipt of blood-money. In such cases, the reconciliation takes place after the monetary or moral awards to the victim party are either paid or carried out or are guaranteed.

Then, the law stipulates symbolic measures that must be performed to restore the honor of the victim, the omission of which prevents the reconciliation. In cases of murder, the clan of the killer, as described in chapter 2, prepares a meal for the victim's clan, including the slaughter of an animal that it brings to the latter's camp, as a sign of gratitude for the pardon from vengeance and flight. The injured party's partaking in the meal is indeed seen as a gesture of pardon, in keeping with the expression, "He who likes you will eat your food" (*man rādak akal zādak*).* Even in cases lesser than murder, the violators prepare a meal for their victims. Hence, among the ʿAzāzma Saraḥīn of the central Negev in 1974, the ʿOwdāt clan, which had wounded a man of the Zanūn clan, served the Zanūn meat and coffee when the parties reconciled (Case 14), and in 1977 the Ameiṭil clan of the ʿAzāzma ʿAṣiyāt, who had caused the aforementioned ʿOwdāt many losses, prepared a meal for the latter following a reconciliation between the two groups (Case 23).

Another act of reconciliation in all conflicts is a violator's kissing the head of his victim, as a sign of deference toward someone he had allowed himself to violate. I have seen this custom on several occasions, among them when Ḥimayd Salmān as-Saddān, who had wounded a member of the Zanūn clan, kissed the head of its elder, ʿOwda Sulaymān az-Zanūn, in May 1974 (Case 14), and when Salmān ad-Dilīaʿ, whose sons had broken the kneecaps of the son of Jumʿa Salāma ar-Rimāg, kissed the head of the latter (*ḥabb ʿala rāsah*) at a conclave of reconciliation in December 2004 (Case 24).[239] Following this act, the sides customarily shake hands (*yitṣaffagū*) and utter expressions that affirm the termination of hostility between them, such as "What's past is dead"

*Bailey, *Proverbs*, p. 42. This is the adverse of refusing to partake of food or drink with someone, an act that signals conflict.

(*illī fāt māt*); "The cliff has collapsed on its shadow" (*al-jurf inhadam ʿala ẓillah*); "What was dug up is buried—all that was concealed or revealed" (*ḥafār ū-dafān—ʿala kull mā khifī ū-bān*); and "Reconciliation forever—until judgment day" (*aṣ-ṣulḥ deidāma—limma tigūm al-giyāma*).[240]

The maintenance of a reconciliation is guaranteed by a "guarantor of warmth," or *kafīl dafā*, who seeks to prevent a subsequent assault by one party upon the other through the threat of a heavy fine for violation of his honor and twofold payments for any damages caused. As in all violations of a right, it is the responsibility of the party accosted to arouse his guarantor, traditionally saying, "I arouse you and appeal to your pride over what has befallen me" (*āna bagāwimak ū-bashāwimak ʿal illī jarā lī*). The law specifies, however, that "There is no revenge after the arousal" (*ma baʿd al-gawām ṭard*)[241]—that is, the guaranteed person must not act to restore his right on his own, lest he release the guarantor of any further responsibility toward him. If the guarantor himself proves remiss in gaining the victim his violated right, the attacked party has the legal right to defame him by blackening his name, a measure meant to motivate the guarantor to honor his commitment.[242]

6

Laws Pertaining to Women, Property, and Sanctuary

Women

THE SEXUAL VIOLATION OF A WOMAN

Bedouin law understands what others may consider "the sexual violation of a woman" as "the violation of the honor of a woman's menfolk through a sexual act involving her," her menfolk being primarily her clansmen but in some cases her husband as well.* Such honor is violated by a sexual act in two ways. First, if the act is consensual, it implies that her clansmen have been remiss in raising her to moral probity, which is a social obligation expected of every Bedouin family.[1] To fail at this brings dishonor.

Second, regardless of whether the woman is coerced or acted consensually, the violator's willingness to perform such an act indicates that he holds the strength (and thus the honor) of her clansmen in contempt.[2] As Bedouin men are often away attending to the family's and clan's various needs and concerns and must frequently leave their womenfolk alone at pasture by day or in a remote tent by night, they can ensure the inviolability of their women only through a reputation for punishing any violation against them. Indeed, they consider their womenfolk the touchstone of their honor because anyone who

*The term "woman" in this section comprises both married and unmarried females.

dares assault a woman in the absence of her menfolk is signaling that the menfolk are not to be feared, even when they are present. This is poignantly expressed in the Bedouin saying, "If a man's back won't protect him, neither will his face" (*in mā ḥamāh gafāh, mā ḥamāh wijhah*)[3]—that is, the perception in a clan's immediate society that its women can be violated with impunity signals that the clan has lost its main deterrence against violation of any sort. To regain it, the clan must prove that it does possess both strength and resolve, and, as with any other violation, it does so by making its violators suffer.

Thus, when a clanswoman has been violated sexually, Bedouin law, as we have seen in previous chapters, allows the clan to resort even to murder to redress this violation in three categories of sexual offense: fornication, rape, and abduction. In the event that rape and abduction get to litigation, however, the law also allows for the most severe punishments a judge may impose, putting the violators under the jurisdiction of a judge of honor (*manshad*).[4] A *manshad* judge rules, too, in five other categories of sexual offense, which may also warrant heavy punishments, both financial and moral: touching a woman, violating a woman's modesty, violating a woman's seclusion, slandering a woman's sexual propriety, and being alone in the company of a nonrelated woman. These offenses are termed by many in the Negev as "a right akin to that of a *manshad*" (*ḥagg akhū manshad*)[5] and in Sinai simply as *manshad*, but in both cases they are adjudicated by an honor judge.

The *Manshad* at Work

The role of a *manshad* trial concerning the sexual violation of a woman is twofold. In addition to deterring such violations through its harsh punishments, it restores the honor of a woman's family for having raised her to moral probity. Accordingly, consensual acts, such as fornication and abscondment, which indicate that a family has been remiss in raising its daughter, are not the subjects of a *manshad* trial. They appear as *manshad* subjects only when attempts are made to claim that the acts were forced rather than consensual. In central Sinai in 1981, when the father of a girl from the Tiyāha confederation who absconded with a lad of the Tarabīn tried to incriminate the latter before a *manshad* judge, he claimed that the young man had forcibly abducted his daughter—which comes under the rubric of rape when the parties are of different confederations (Case 20). The judge, Amīra Salāma Abū Amīra of the Masa'īd Awāmra, however, citing that the girl had already absconded with the lad once before, rejected the claim of coercion. Although he imposed on the defendant a token fine of five camels, it was specifically to indicate that Bedouin law condemns any sexual liaison with a woman.[6] A Bedouin saying goes, "Whoever gets close to a woman will lose his camels and get his head smashed too" (*illī biygarrib la-l-ʿār—iblah tinwakhidh wiykassar rāsah fōgah*).[7]

Manshad trials are initiated either when the clansmen of a woman are informed by a chance observer that her honor has been violated or when a woman herself complains of a violation. Her clansmen cannot neglect any report or complaint of sexual violation, as it will signify, if true, that their honor and strength have been disdained. The proverb says, "As soon as a woman's dishonoring gets known, there must follow a camel-truce and a *manshad*, though the offense be light" (*al-ʿār yōm tisammaʿ lah sumaʿ—lāzim min jīritah ū-lāzim min manshadah—ḥatta iy-lō al-ḥagg mistagill*).[8]

The first step toward rectifying the violation through a *manshad* trial is for the accused, upon demand by the woman's clansmen or on his own initiative, to send a truce-camel (*jīra*), which represents his declaration of intent to give the woman's clan justice. A traditional maxim observes, "He whose camel is couched is ready for the honor trial" (*illī tubruk jīrit-ha biyiṭlaʿ manshad-ha*).[9] In the event that the accused balks at sending the camel, the law allows the plaintiff clan to pillage his livestock until he relents. Among the Muzayna in southern Sinai in 1975, the clansmen of Sālim Abū Ṣabḥā pillaged the camels of the clan of Munayfī Sālim Jabalī for an entire month before the latter agreed to dispatch the four truce-camels that were demanded and sit before a *manshad* judge for having attacked Abū Ṣabḥa in his tent and taken hold of his wife (Case 1).[10] In 1982 members of the Tarabīn confederation in central Sinai had their livestock pillaged for months before agreeing to return an abducted girl of the Tiyāha and undergo a *manshad* trial (Case 20).[11] If there is doubt concerning the offense, the accused will send a camel asking for an "investigative truce" (*jīrit iftāsh* or *jīrit ingāsh*), during which the parties will discuss the merits of the case before a preliminary judge (*malamm* in the Negev; *ḍraybī* in Sinai) until the judge decides whether it warrants a *manshad* trial or not. If it is clear-cut, such as when the accused has been caught or witnessed in the act, he must agree to "a decisive camel-truce" (*jīrit garḍ ū-farḍ*), which leads straight to a "direct honor trial" (*manshad rās*).

As the role of a *manshad* court is to condemn men for violating the honor of women, it does not try women. A woman who "has not restrained herself" (*mā ḥafaẓat ḥālha*) will be answerable to her family and clan and can be killed by them with impunity. However, when trying a man for a sexual violation against a woman's honor, both preliminary and honor judges must first be certain of a woman's honesty if it is she who has initiated the claim. First, a "complaining and crying woman" (*shākya bākya*) must act directly—that is, she must immediately inform of what she has experienced in order to be credible and deserve a judicial award. The relevant legal maxim says, "Each cry sounded at the time is a [relevant] reminder" (*kull ṣowt fī awānah dhakar*).[12] If a shepherdess, for example, is subject to violation while at pasture, she is expected to abandon her flock and come running to tell. Delay is perceived by the Bedouin as concealing a bad conscience for having willingly participated in the act—even an otherwise innocent tryst—and a fear of detection and perhaps murder by the woman's family.

The same pertains to a violation perpetrated at night. The law demands of women that they "complain and cry at night, not wait for morning" (*shākī bāki—layl mū hū nahār*).* As noted in chapter 4, whether alone in her tent or away from it at remote pastures, a violated woman must immediately either light a fire and wake her neighbor so that the fire at an unsuitable hour arouses the attention of neighbors camped within eyesight, or she must go to a more distant neighbor and waken him in order to have witnesses to her distress. If she waits until morning, she is suspected of collusion in the violation. In 1971, when Ḥimayd as-Saddān of the ʿAzāzma Saraḥīn in the central Negev was told by his wife that she had been visited the previous night by Hilayyil al-Wajj of the Ẓullām Janabīb, he straightaway divorced her (Case 44). Moreover, he subsequently criticized the Wajj clan for agreeing to a *manshad* trial at the request of his wife's kinsmen, asserting that her delay in informing of the visit affirmed that it was consensual and that her family did not warrant an honor trial.[13]

Rape If a case of rape is not settled through the murder of the rapist but gets to a *manshad* court, the law posits criteria for the woman who claims that she has been raped. These criteria are manifest in the plea (*ḥijja*) that the father or guardian of such a girl makes before a *manshad* judge or in a preliminary court hearing.[14] First, as with any woman who has suffered a sort of sexual violation, she should have come to inform her family or a neighbor of the attack immediately after it took place. Second, to indicate that she was agitated and had put up resistance, she normally would have come shouting, and her clothes would have been in disarray, her veil detached (see below). Hence fathers, in court, normally use the formulized claim that "She came to me shouting, her mouth open to the wind; her dress was ripped and her necklace scattered" (*jatnī bitṣīḥ ū-famha fātḥa la-r-rīḥ—thōbha gadāyid ū-kharazha badāyid*); or she came "shouting and waving the edge of her headcloth" (*ṣāḥat ū-bi-ṭarf gunʿit-ha lāḥat*); or "shouting and waving her extended sleeve" (*ṣāḥat ū-bi-ridinha lāḥat*); or "gesturing and shouting" (*showshaḥat bi-ṣ-ṣowt al-ʿalī*).[15] Indeed, to stress the importance of a woman's resistance, Bedouin law terms the victim of rape, whether attempted or consummated, "a screamer" (*ṣāyiḥa*).

Third, the woman must be convincingly "innocent" (*sāhya lāhya*; lit. "un-

*Language notes: (1) *shākī* and *bākī* appear here in the masculine, referring to one term for "a woman" (*ʿār*), which is also masculine; (2) *mū hū* is the Bedouin vernacular pronunciation for *mā hū*.

mindful") of collusion in the act. Hence, fathers often assert that "She neither "anticipated him on hilltops" (*lā wagafat lah ʿala gīzān*) nor sent him a message with people" (*wala arsalat lah maʿ al-ʿurbān*). In 1999 a girl of the Bayāḍiyyīn confederation in northern Sinai was abducted by a man of the same confederation (Case 137). When she was returned to her family by members of her lover's clan, her father demanded a *manshad* trial, alleging that she had been forcibly abducted. The judge, Amīra Salāma Abū Amīra, however, canceled the scheduled trial when he discovered that she had answered a letter sent her by the lad, agreeing to abscond with him again.[16]

If a woman should falsely accuse a man of rape (or any other sexual violation) or the man denies the accusation, he may send "an investigatory truce-camel" (*jīrit iftāsh*) to signal his consent to discuss the accusation and request a preliminary *manshad* hearing, where his denial will be heard and considered. This is called an "absolution *manshad*" (*manshad brāt*).* At it, the defendant, following the claimant, will state his case after uttering the formulaic statement, "What is your opinion, o Judge, of this remote garden talk* that neither took place nor was, except between the tongue of my accuser and the devil. I am innocent [of the claim]" (*w-aysh ʿendak yā gāḍī fī kalām al-bustān — mā jara wala kān — min lisānah li-sh-shayṭān — āna sāhī lāhī*). Then, the judge will try to assess the truth through carefully listening to the claims and through questioning the parties. In the northern Negev in the 1960s, the judge, Frayj al-Hawāshla, while judging a case of alleged rape among members of the Aʿsam tribe, heard the father of the girl claim that she was assailed while alone in a place where there was no one to hear her cries, but then he stated, by way of hyperbole, that the act was witnessed by both God and people (Case 138). The judge seized upon this inconsistency and asked the father if he could name the people who he said had seen it. When he could not, Hawāshla suspected his sincerity and gave the accused a chance to take an oath containing the euphemism "I did not hold her hand or kiss her brow" (*mā masakt-ha yamīn wala ḥabbayt-ha jabīn*). Taking the oath, the lad acquitted himself.[17]

On the other hand, if a "direct honor trial" takes place over rape, it is primarily an occasion for the judge to impose his punishments on the violator and his clan. The claimants do not pay the judge's fee, which is totally paid by the defendant. By contrast, only the claimants can "state their claims"

*Language note: the final "t" being silent, the word is pronounced "brā."

*Mountain gardens (as in southern Sinai), like remote pastures, are viewed as venues where Bedouin talk carelessly, often distant from where Bedouin migrate, live, and (especially) hold trials in which well-founded claims can be established and guaranteed. See Bailey, *Proverbs*, pp. 306–7.

(*yiḥtajjū*), while the defendant "is dumb, without words" (*mitiballam mā yitikallam*). The defendant himself need not be present at the *manshad*. However, the guarantors of fulfillment of the judgment must be there so that the punishments they are bound to guarantee will become clear to them in all their detail. These punishments, or awards, are both material and moral.

The material awards are often of a symbolic nature—for example, forty camels (forty symbolizing the number of camels constituting the blood-price of a murdered man and thus indicating that the rapist warranted execution). By the same symbolism (as noted in chapter 5), other punishments, such as forty gold pieces or forty sheep, are included in addition to the camels.[18] Additional camels may be added for each step taken in seeking the victim out or for the rapist's entering and exiting the victim's tent, if such was the venue of the violation. Camels (or their worth in money) are also imposed as symbolic ransoms for the parts of the man's body involved: "the penis that penetrated her or its ransom with ten camels" (*al-bashr illī khashsh fīha walla fadwāh ʿashar biʿrān*), "the hand that reached for her" (*al-īd illī maddat ʿalayha*), or "the tongue that talked to her" (*al-lisān illī naṭag-ha*). Another such symbolic punishment is the financial ransom of all parts of the rapist's body that become stained after he undergoes "the mangy camel" (*al-jamal al-ajrab*) procedure (see chapter 5).

The moral punishment imposed is the "whitening" (*bayāḍ*) of the face, or honor, of the woman and her father. Often this consists of "covering the tent" (*kiswit al-bayt*) of the victim or the tents of notable persons with white cloth, but it always comprises a declaration, in the presence of an assembly of men gathered in these tents, that the girl and her father are honorable, she for being moral and her father for having raised her to moral probity. All these punishments are guaranteed by guarantors, including the "whitening" procedures, for the neglect of which fines are also set.

If a woman becomes pregnant as a result of rape perpetrated by a known man, the child belongs to the biological father's clan but is nursed by the mother. At the man's *manshad* trial, the judge may award the woman's father a male and a female slave—symbolically, "the female to bear the child and the male to bring it water," but actually their arbitrarily determined worth in money needed for raising the child. The child's mother must do "nothing but offer her breast" (ʿalayha al-bizz ū-bass).[19] This award may stem from a proverbial claim by the father of a raped girl that "If I kill the child, I will have sinned before my Lord, but if I let him live, I won't tolerate his being borne on the hands of my daughter" (*in kataltah akhṭayt ʿend rabbī—w-in khallaytah mānī ḥāmlah ʿala īdayn bintī*).[20] If the rapist is unknown, the child stays with his mother's family, in accordance with the legal maxim, "The family gathers to itself" (*ad-dār hawwāsh li-ahalha*),[21] but the illegitimate child will be viewed as "a stray camel" (*jamal ash-shatt*),[22] not belonging to his mother's clan. If a raped woman is married, her husband must refrain from sexual intercourse with her for three months so as not to be considered the father of the child, in the event that she becomes pregnant. Once, arguing his freedom from responsibility for the child of his raped wife, a Bedouin stated, "I didn't come to her bed; I was only responsible for her upkeep. I sustained her but did not come to her" (*mā ṭabbayt ilha frāsh ū-mā ʿaleiy ghayr al-maʿāsh — aʿīsh-ha wala ajīha*).[23]

Touching a Woman Another subject taken up at a *manshad* trial is touching a woman (*madd al-yad*; lit. "extending the hand"). A Bedouin legal maxim asserts, "Laying one's hand on a female is fined" (*madd al-yad ʿal al-ʿār gharāma*).[24] Another says, "If touching a woman's dress is like sparks, touching her flesh is like fire" (*thōbha shirār ū-jild-ha nār*).[25] Accordingly, in March 1977 in northern Sinai, after Sālim Salāma Rajawīn, the chief of the Dawāghra Nighāmsha, rescued a woman ward from the tent of a man who had abducted her in collusion with her uncle (who wanted her wed), leading her out by the arm, the uncle charged him with violating "his niece" (that is, his honor) by touching her arm and received a *manshad* trial (Case 3). To symbolize the gravity of this act of touching, the *manshad* judge fined the chief fifty camels, which, however, he arbitrarily valued at a total of only 1,000 Egyptian pounds (the equivalent of $350), owing to the relative triviality of the incident.[26]

Less trivial was the deliberate holding of a woman by the sons of Munayfī Sālim Jabalī, the chief of the Muzayna Jarābʿa, when they attacked Sālim Abū Ṣabḥā of the Muzayna Ghawānma in his tent in March 1975 (Case 1).

> According to the sons, they attacked Abū Ṣabḥā in retaliation for his prolonged failure to pay their father the balance of a fine awarded him for wounds inflicted by the former in 1974 — that is, the attack was not intended to violate his wife. As Abū Ṣabḥā's wife was with him in the tent at the time of the attack, however, each of Jabalī's three sons held her down in turn while the other two struggled with Abū Ṣabḥā; cut off the little finger of one hand; searched the tent; and punctured the tires of his pickup truck so that no one could summon help or take him to the hospital. The attack, including the holding of the woman, lasted from ten o'clock in the evening until dawn the next day.[27]

Abū Ṣabḥā, considering that his wife, who was also his clanswoman, had been sexually violated, wanted an honor trial. He thus sent messengers to Munayfī Jabalī, demanding that he send him four camels to request a camel-truce: one, symbolically, for each of the offending sons and the fourth for the overall violation of the sanctuary of his tent.[28] As noted, such a camel-truce is a prelude to an honor trial.[29] Jabalī rejected Abū Ṣabḥā's demand, arguing that the attack was mounted by right, owing to Abū Ṣabḥā's default in paying him his fine, and did not warrant a *manshad*.[30] This unwillingness to give Abū Ṣabḥā justice for his violated woman provided him and his clansmen legal justification to go out and pillage nineteen camels belonging to the clan of their adversaries, in keeping with their professed right in such cases to "take livestock and kill men during three and a third days" (*thilātht iyyām ū-thilth—nākhidh mālak ū-nidhbaḥ rijālak*).[31]

This pillage was upheld by the law when a *manshad* trial was finally heard by the noted judge of matters pertaining to women, Sulaymān Muḥammad al-ʿUgbi of the Tiyāha Banī ʿUgba tribe, in the northern Negev, on June 26, 1976.[32] ʿUgbī rejected the claim of Abū Ṣabḥā's assailants that the laws of *manshad* did not apply to them, although they argued that their taking hold of the woman was devoid of sexual threat and was merely intended to keep her away from the physical violence surrounding her husband lest she be harmed. According to ʿUgbī, they should have sent the truce-camel when requested. Their failure to do so justified the pillage of their camels, which were also unredeemable, or, as Bedouin say, "folded under the carpet" (*tinṭiwī taḥt al-frāsh*; from the image of not discussing things that are under the carpet). This loss was in addition to fines imposed by the *manshad* judge himself. Together with those for the violation of Abū Ṣabḥā's tent, the fines came to the equivalent of $60,500. Thirty years later, Abū Ṣabḥā's remaining brother, Sulaymān, asserted that "Even had we killed ten men before the payment of the truce-camel, they would have been forfeit."[33]

Other than Sulaymān's claim, however, no mention of killing men as an option for the crime of touching a woman's body was mentioned either at the judicial hearing, consisting of nine judges, in August 1975,[34] or the trial itself in June the following year,[35] or in my conversations with Sālim Abū Ṣabḥā himself and the Muzayna judge, ʿOwda Ṣāliḥ Imbārak, on November 22, 1994, indicating that the law does not consider that "touching", unlike rape, fornication, or abduction, warrants the threat of murder as a deterrent.

Violating a Woman's Modesty The bodies of pubertal and post-pubescent women must be kept unexposed, in conformity with Bedouin rules of modesty. Modesty in dress is so important to Bedouin society that they consider the worst theft possible to be that of a needle or pin, always borne by a Bedouin woman so she can repair or hide a sudden rip in an outer garment that might otherwise expose her body to sight.[36] In Sinai and the Negev, moreover, the rules of modesty require a woman to keep her mouth veiled (*mulaththima*) and her head covered (*mughaṭṭiya*) in the company of non-clansmen and when out of doors. Women who fail to deport themselves in this way may humorously be depicted as demented (as in the stories of women—such as Galōla, the ancestral mother of the Ẓullām confederation, and the Bilī ancestral mother of the ʿAzāzma Abū Bilayya family, both in the Negev—whose clansmen deigned to marry them off to nonrelated shepherds that worked for them because they walked about bareheaded.

Men who violate a woman by forcefully "removing her veil" (*tafrīaʿ al-bint;* lit. "exposing her oral orifice") or "baring her head" (*jird al-bint*) are deemed violators of her honor and are subject to a harsh *manshad* trial. In the 1950s, when men of the Suwārka confederation of northern Sinai used a flashlight on unveiled ʿAzāzma girls, whose tent they had attacked in the Negev, to choose one that could serve as a hostage against the return of an abducted Suwārka girl, taken to Jordan by an ʿAzāzma man, their act was condemned and fined by the noted Masʿūdī *manshad* judge, Salāma Amīra Abū Amīra (Case 92).[37] Among the ʿAzāzma Saraḥīn in the central Negev in 1974, when Sulaymān Salāma ar-Rimāg chased the daughter of Ḥimayd as-Saddān and her flock away from the camels he was herding, causing her headdress (*gunʿa*) to fly off, the compensation for the head wound he suffered from the rock she subsequently threw at him was, as a result, forfeit (Case 43).[38] If unveiling and uncovering the head of a woman is a grave violation of a woman's modesty, how much more so, argued Sālim Abū Ṣabḥā in his effort to gain a *manshad* trial against the sons of Munayfī Jabalī (Case 1), was the sons' taking hold of his wife, who was totally bare, or as he put it, "in the garb in which the Creator had made her" (*thōb al-khālig*) and "her birth garb" (*thōb al-makhlūg*).[39]

Violating a Woman's Seclusion Protecting women's modesty is also the reason for secluding them from men not of their clan, whether they are out in the desert or in a tent. Accordingly, Sālim Abū Ṣabḥā, in arguing his case against Munayfī Sālim Jabalī at a judicial hearing, to decide whether he deserved a *manshad* trial (Case 1 above), said, "We all know that though a wolf be eating her flock, a man is forbidden to approach and awaken a shepherdess napping while at pasture, lest he see her "unveiled and bare headed" (*fārʿa w-imjarrida*).[40] Abū Ṣabḥā, aware that "the violation of a woman's seclusion" (*ʿār ʿala dār*) is a grave offense, also stressed it later, in stating his claims before the *manshad* judge. Using Bedouin legal terminology, he accused his assailants of "attacking on a starless night, when women are in the midst of the tent, asleep and with their heads uncovered" (*hujūm fī ghuyūb an-nujūm—wa-l-ʿār fī baṭn ad-dār—nāyimāt imjarridāt*).[41]

Bedouin law is fastidious in this regard in determining whether an attack warrants a *manshad* or not. It stipulates that if men intend to attack a man in a tent, they must either call upon him to remove the women from it or call to the women themselves to exit, rather than barge in on them unexpectedly, perhaps to find them immodestly clad. Only after a few minutes, whether women have meanwhile exited or not, may the attackers enter so as to carry out their plan, on the assumption that any women still inside will have had ample time to properly dress. Out of similar concern for the modesty of women, even a friendly non-clansman approaching a tent is legally directed to enter from the side of the men's section (*shigg* in the Negev; *magʿad* in Sinai), where male guests gather, rather than from that of the women's quarters (*maḥrama*), and to call out a greeting, such as "Peace be upon you" (*as-salām ʿalaykum*), to warn any women inside to prepare lest they be immodestly clad. The failure to respect the seclusion of women in a tent will result in more than a *manshad* trial; a past judge, using hyperbole to deter such violation, is recalled as having ruled, "Women in the tent have seven curtains, and passing each one calls for a camel-truce and an honor trial" (*al-ʿār fī-d-dār ʿalayh sabaʿ starāt—ū-kull stār illī tiʿadda bi-jīra ū-manshad*).[42] Indeed, this aspect of violating the sanctuary of a tent is deemed so serious that in the Negev, a trial for any violation of a tent's sanctuary is deemed a *manshad* so that the judge may impose a severe punishment based on his own discretion.

The above examples notwithstanding, there are Bedouin judges and others who feel that the presence of women in the tent of a wrongdoing man should not override an attacker's right to seek justice from him in it. This position—namely that "a wrongdoer's tent will not protect him" (*bayt al-ʿāyib mā biy-sallmah*)[43]—was expressed by ʿAnayz Sālim al-ʿUrḍī, the chief poet in Sinai and an occasional judge, in criticizing the ruling against the sons of Munayfī Sālim Jabalī for attacking Sālim Abū Ṣabḥā in his tent (Case 1). ʿUrḍī maintained that the sons acted by right, as Abū Ṣabḥā had consistently avoided paying Munayfī Jabalī the balance of the fine he owed him for wounds he had inflicted.[44] By the same token, when some thirty-five men of the Suwārka confederation of northern Sinai attacked a tent of the ʿAzāzma in the central Negev in order to kidnap a woman and thereby force the ʿAzāzma to return one of their own abducted women, the respected *manshad* judge Salāma Amīra Abū Amīra did not fine them for the attack, which he deemed to be their right, but only for exposing the faces of the young women present with a flashlight (Case 92).[45] Another such judgment was issued in 1991 (Case 91). After men of the ʿAlaygāt confederation of southwest Sinai abducted and held a lad of the Tarabīn confederation, whom they suspected of informing on them to the Egyptian police, and humiliated him by showing him bound to their womenfolk, the Tarabīn retaliated in kind. When they, however, invaded a tent to find a man to abduct, it was a tent filled with women. When the ʿAlaygāt subsequently charged the Tarabīn in court with violating "women in a tent" (*ʿār ʿala dār*), the judge, Salāma Ḥusayn az-Zimaylī of the Guṣayyir tribe of the Aḥeiwāt Shawafīn confederation of eastern Sinai, ruled that the attack had been made by right because the ʿAlaygāt had abducted and bound the Tarabīn lad and neglected to ask his people for a blood-truce.[46] His judgment was as follows:

> Regarding those who bind men and don't ask them for a blood-truce
> (*In illī biyurbṭ rijāl wa-lā biyākhidh minhum ʿamār*)
> I hereby rule
> (*āna min ʿendī*)
> that tents that are violated by [the bound] men will draw neither fine nor condemnation.
> (*in al-buyūt al-imḥaddira li-r-rijāl lā yighramin wala yijramin*).[47]

Being Alone in the Company of a Nonrelated Woman A man's spending time in the company of a woman not of his clan (*ṣuḥbat al-ʿār*), even if she is modestly dressed and he has not touched her, is considered the prelude to a sexual liaison and deemed a serious violation. A past judgment determined that "Talking with a girl is like sparks and walking with her brings affliction" (*kull khurāfak fi-l-ʿār sharār—ū-mashyak maʿha ʿawār*).[48] The Bedouin ethos even specifies that a man seeking directions from a shepherdess call to her from a distance and that she answer him while facing in the opposite direction. Similarly, if a man asks a shepherdess for water and receives it, he must drink it. Otherwise his approach to her is suspect and subject to a *manshad* trial.

Thus, a nonrelated man in the company of a Bedouin's women—wife, sister, cousin, or daughter—arouses concern and anger. In 1973, when Sālim ʿOwda aṭ-Ṭimṭāwī of the ʿAzāzma ʿAṣiyāt in the central Negev found a fellow tribesman, seventeen-year-old Muḥammad Sālim Abū Jilaydān, sitting with his wife in his tent, he beat him up (Case 139).[49] A year earlier, in 1972, the wife of Ḥimayd as-Saddān revealed that Hilayyil al-Wajj of the Ẓullām Janabīb had visited her when she was alone the previous evening (Case 44). Without checking the details of the account, Saddān, as indicated above, immediately divorced her, lest he be suspected of overlooking a possible moral lapse in his wife's behavior.[50] From the judge, Ḥasan Abū Rubayʿa, he also received, for his violated tent, a whitening confession in three prominent tents, his own tent covered with white cloth, and four camels, two for Wajj's entering the tent and two for his exiting it. For the same offense, a stiff *manshad* fine was awarded to Saddān's father-in-law, ʿOwda an-Nashmī, also of the ʿAzāzma Saraḥīn.

In 1993, among the Aḥeiwāt Ṣafeiḥa confederation in northern Sinai, a Sālim Abū Maḥamūd was only narrowly spared from murder and the loss of his camels after a report that he was seen sitting with a shepherdess out at pasture aroused her father, Slaym Abū Ḥunayk, and her brother to grab a rifle and two swords and go after him and his herd (Case 9). The man who saved Abū Maḥamūd was Ḥājj ʿOwda Abū Akthar, who, meeting the father and brother on their way, convinced them that they had no right to kill the suspect on the basis of what they knew. Instead, the father decided to bring the case before the noted *manshad* judge Amīra Salāma Abū Amīra to clarify the details before resorting to murder. Abū Amira ultimately believed Abū Maḥamūd's version — that is, that he was out looking for his freely grazing camels and had only approached the girl to ask if she had seen them, proceeding merely to drink a glass of tea she offered him and go on his way. By contrast, Abū Amīra directed the litigators to a judge of the Aḥeiwāt Shawafīn, Salāma Ḥusayn az-Zimaylī, who, as a *manshad* judge, tried the man that invented the account.[51]

Slandering a Woman As staining the reputation of a woman may precipitate her death in an honor-killing, potential slanderers are cautioned, "Guard your tongue when talking about a woman! The words, once out, will wound" (*iḥfaẓ lisānak ʿend dhikr al-wiliyya — al-kalām lō ṭiliʿ yijraḥ*). The disdain Bedouin feel toward slandering a woman (*masabba*) is highlighted by the proverbial judgment of a past judge that "The eye that saw should be put out; how much more the one that didn't see" (*ʿein in shāfat giliʿit — w-aysh ḥāl illī mā shāfat*).[52] Moreover, as Bedouin families are entrusted with the societal responsibility of raising their daughters to moral probity, the failure at which brings them dishonor, they are sensitive to any aspersion cast upon their womenfolk.[53] In a well-known Bedouin poem enumerating the ten best things in life, one of them is, "Cover for daughters to shield them from shame / Lest talk at a gathering of slanderers stain" (*sitr al-ʿadhāra min al-ʿār / min magʿad as-sifāh harjin yiṣīb*).[54] In the central Negev in 1998, the casual statement by a rejected suitor, Salmān Labbād az-Zinayd, suggesting that the girl he had wanted was trysting with her clansman and designated future husband, Salmān al-Ameiṭil, led the family of the latter to ambush and shoot to death the alleged slanderer's father (Case 140).[55] The Ameiṭil, of the Muṭlān clan of the ʿAzāzma ʿAṣiyāt tribe, had demanded a *manshad* trial for Zinayd's statement, "I want to marry my maternal cousin, even if her paternal cousins have been with her on the flat desert" (*widdī bint khālī wi-lō owlād ʿammha jāwūha ʿa-l-ḥamād*). The Zinayd's delay in accepting to sit before a *manshad* judge provided the Muṭlān with self-justification for committing the murder.

In the same area twenty five years earlier (April 1973), Sālim ʿOwda aṭ-

Ṭimṭāwī of the ʿAzāzma ʿAṣiyāt tribe declared before a tent full of fellow Bedouin trackers in the Israeli Army that the betrothed daughter of Sālim ʿAtayyig al- Khiraynig of the ʿAzāzma Sarahīn was already pregnant with child (Case 71).

His statement was made out of pique because the Khiraynig girl's betrothal, about which he had just heard, was part of an exchange marriage including Ṭimṭāwī's former wife, Ḥusn, who was to marry Khiraynig's son. After the statement was relayed to Khiraynig by two of those present, ʿĪd al-Ḥawaṣa and ʿAlī al-ʿAbays, the scandalized father ordered blood tests to be made on his daughter at the Beersheba hospital. The tests, however, showed no signs of pregnancy, whereupon Khiraynig demanded that Ṭimṭāwī agree to a *manshad* trial. The threat of the entire ʿAzāzma Saraḥīn tribe rallying with Khiraynig ultimately brought Ṭimṭāwī to heel, and the trial was held at the tent of the ʿAzāzma paramount chief, ʿOwda Abū Muʿammar.

Two punishments were decreed for Ṭimṭāwī, financial and moral. The financial was a fine the sum of which was designated to equal an amputated part of the tongue that slandered. It was stated as "a piece of his tongue the size of a coffee-bean, or its ransom in cash" (*yā bunāna min lisānah—yā yishtarīha bi-māl*). The moral punishment decreed by the judge is called "whitening," a Bedouin image for reaffirming honor. Accordingly, Ṭimṭāwī was ordered to "cover the tent" of Khiraynig with white cloth and make three declarations before those assembled in the tents of three prominent men, proclaiming

In what I said about the daughter of Khiraynig I was a liar.
(*Fī mā ḥakayt fī bint ikhraynig kadhdhāb*)
I swear that she [her honor] is as white as white cloth
(*ash-had inha abyaḍ min ash-shāsh*)
May God bring whiteness [honor] to the face of her father.
(*bayyaḍ allah wijh abūha*).

After Ṭimṭāwī made his declaration, his father was obliged to stand before the tents and announce the following:

My son's claim was a lie.
(*Waladī fī mā gāl kidhib*).[56]

By means of the *manshad*, therefore, Khiraynig was able to restore the honor and reputation of his family. As the Bedouin say, "The girl's father closed the crack" (*abūha sakkar ath-thilm*), "crack" being an image for dishonoring. A widespread Bedouin proverb using the same imagery holds, "The reputation of a woman is like glass; once cracked, it can't be closed" (*al-ʿār gazāz—w-in anthalam mā biyjabbar*).[57]

THE PHYSICAL VIOLATION OF A WOMAN

Women as Protected People

As discussed in chapter 3, women are born into the clan of their fathers and belong to it throughout their lives. Though their status is not overtly defined as inferior to that of men, the facts that their children belong to their husbands, that they do not inherit, or that they are not independent personalities before the law suffice to indicate that they are considered inferior. One explanation for this condition is that, like children, women are seen as weak and cannot carry out the celebrated main functions of men "to strike with a sword and feed meat to a guest" (*yuḍrub bi-s-seif ū-yigrī aḍ-ḍeif*)[58] — that is, they cannot protect the property of the group through warfare or the honor of the group through hospitality by slaughtering goats, sheep, or camels.

The inferior status is embodied in the term by which a woman is called — *wiliyya* — which literally means a "guarded person," one represented in all things by a guardian (*wilī*) — that is, her father first, if alive; her brothers after him, or her paternal uncle if her brothers are minors; and after them, her paternal cousins, beginning with the most closely related to her. Among their other functions as her guardians, these men are responsible for protecting her; they view any physical violation against her as a challenge to their power to protect her, and it must be addressed lest they be considered weak. Thus, in the central Negev in summer 1973, when the sister of Ḥimayd Salmān as-Saddān of the ʿAzāzma Saraḥīn, though estranged from him for years, was injured in a fight among women in her son's tent, Saddān, upon hearing of the injury, immediately took up the responsibility for reestablishing her right to physical integrity (Case 14).[59] In the same tribe in May 1974, when Ḥusayn Swaylim al-Khiraynig summarily divorced his wife, implying immoral behavior on her part,[60] her case was directly taken up by her uncle, Swaylim Sulaymān Abū Bilayya, as her father was dead and her brother was living in Jordan, which was inaccessible to Bedouin in Israel at the time (Case 141).[61]

In addition to clansmen's need to maintain their reputation for strength, a main reason for the protection of the womenfolk, as noted in chapter 4, is to enable them to be alone, as they often are, in isolated encampments and remote pastures, or while the men are attending to matters vital to the welfare of their family and clan. Women are therefore considered inviolate by men, in keeping with the principle, "No manliness is practiced on a woman" (*al-mara mā ʿalayha marājil*),[62] and the law endorses their physical safety. Not only is a woman exempt from blood-revenge (except by other women after she has killed a woman of their clan), but also a man's killing a woman can be punished fourfold — that is, revenge may be taken against four of the killer's clansmen, or a blood-payment (usually forty camels) can be demanded for any of the four not killed.[63] As noted in chapter 4, this principle is embodied in the proverb,

"The blood of a woman is fourfold."[64] By the same principle, an injury caused a woman by a man warrants a twofold fine, once it has been assessed.[65] There is no excuse for a man who is neither a woman's husband nor her kinsman to strike her. In 1973, when two shepherdesses of the ʿAzāzma Saraḥīn tribe got into a physical fracas at a well called Bīr Ḥawwāsh, in the Umm Khashram area (currently Kiryat Gat) of the northern Negev, over which of their flocks would drink first, ʿAbdallah Sālim al-Ghidayfī, the brother of one of the girls, resorted to slapping them both in order to separate them (Case 14). His slapping the one who was his sister was fine, but not his striking the non-clan girl, the daughter of ʿOwda Sulaymān Zanūn, who was quick to challenge Ghidayfī to a trial before a blood-pool judge.[66]

This inviolability of a woman pertains so long as she is in the role of the weak one in conflicts with or between men — particularly that she refrain from attacking a man. No injury suffered by a woman who raises a hand against a man warrants a twofold punishment. The man who struck her may be fined, one for one, as if his victim were a man; after all, she had behaved like a man. In the mid-1930s, for example, such was the case at the southeast Sinai oasis, ʿAyn Ḥaḍra, when the wife of a man called al-Aṭrash, of the Muzayna Sakhāna, pushed men of the Tarabīn Ḥasāblah away from her husband's palm trees, where they were cutting clusters of dates as part of a conflict (Case 87). When an injury she received on her backside from the flat of the sword of one of the pillagers, ʿAṭeiwī Imsallam al-ʿAlowna, was eventually litigated, Judge Jumʿa Abū Ṣabḥā assessed it as a single violation, rather than twofold, because the woman had assailed the invaders.[67]

According to the same principle of a woman attacking a man (and, by inference, forfeiting the status of weakness that grants her physical inviolability), the clansmen of a woman who kills a man, of whatever age, are subject to blood-revenge. Hence, in the 1930s among the Tiyāha confederation in the northern Negev, when a woman struck her small son, who fell down and died, her husband, the presumed father of the boy (who, *ipso facto*, belonged to his father's clan), asserted that he was entitled either to take revenge on one of his wife's clansmen or to receive from them a blood-payment, in keeping with his own choice (Case 119).[68] To further ensure that women retain their subservient status, the murder of a mature man by a woman who raises her hand against him entitles his clansmen to not one but two acts of revenge against men of her clan or two blood-payments from her clansmen.[69] Only the death of a man by a woman acting in self-defense is deemed to warrant no punishment upon her clansmen.

Violence by Husbands and Clansmen

The above description of the physical inviolability of a woman does not pertain to violence against her by her husband or clansmen. These are legally entitled to strike her for having committed "a wrong" (*dhanb*) of various sorts; they may not strike her, however, if she has not committed a wrong. A clansman may strike an unmarried girl for dubious moral behavior that he has spotted, such as her holding a conversation with a non-clansman; for the same type of behavior, a non-clan husband holds the right to strike his wife. In 2002, for example, when a tourist woman photographed the wife of a man of the Tarabīn Ḥasāblah in southeast Sinai and showed him the picture, he beat his wife, who was unrelated to him, for having exposed her unveiled mouth to a stranger—that is, to any man who might subsequently see the photo (Case 142).[70] Although a non-clan husband is not legally responsible for his wife's moral behavior, his failure to exercise the prerogative for striking his wife in matters of morality may present her family with a grievance against him for enabling her to stray and thereby to bring shame upon them.[71] If, for example, it can be shown that such remissness led to an act of fornication on her part, the husband would be deprived of any compensation from his wife's family in the event that he divorced her.

A husband may also strike his wife for being recalcitrant (*razīla*; lit. "unwilling"), such as her refusing to prepare food and drink for him or for guests in their tent. For example, among the Aḥeiwāt Shawafīn of east central Sinai in 1978, a man called Faraj beat his wife for refusing to make tea for him when he fell ill and for running off to a neighbor's tent for refuge (Case 57). When he was fined by a judge, it was for violating his neighbor's tent by hitting her *there*, but not for striking her as such, as the judge deemed that the husband's behavior was justified owing to his wife's reclacitrance.[72]

A wife may also be struck by her husband for being remiss in her various economic duties. Such remissness may include negligent supervision of the family's livestock, whose well-being is the responsibility of the women, or for desisting from getting up at night, when the dogs bark, to chase a prowling wolf away from the flock. This right of a husband to strike his wife stems from two sources. First are the responsibilities she takes on as a bride, such as pasturing the flock, baking bread, and fetching water and firewood.[73] Second is the fact that he maintains her. Indeed, a judge in the northern Negev in the mid-twentieth century, even acquitted a man of wrongdoing for slapping his brother's wife on the grounds that it was he who dressed and fed both her and her husband and thus had a right to discipline the woman for remissness (Case 135).[74]

Finally, as a way of ensuring the submissiveness of women, a man may strike his wife for using insulting epithets toward him—such as "Filthy one!" (*yā wisikh*), "Dog!" (*yā dhīkh*), "Pimp!" (*yā muʿarraṣ*), "Bastard!" (*yā ibn seiya*)—whether in public or privately. A perception exists among men that without exercising this prerogative, women would be quick to criticize their husbands, thereby undermining the social order. Their proverb goes, "If you want to shame a man, let his wife loose on him" (*widdak timsakh zalama—iṭlag ʿalayh mara*).[75]

The above notwithstanding, Bedouin law limits the use of force by a husband toward his wife, or a man toward a clanswoman, regardless of whether she has committed a legal wrong or not. First, striking a woman must manifestly be of disciplinary or educational value, not out of mere anger or spite. If, for example, a man plans to divorce his wife for an act deemed immoral or for any other (wrong) she may have committed, he cannot beat her first. In other words, if he is to divorce her, there is no need for him to discipline or educate her. That is the responsibility of her family or future husband, but not his. To strike a wife before divorcing her would thus be considered an injustice, and the husband would be liable to sit before an *ʿugbī* judge and be fined.[76]

Second, a husband, in beating his wife, cannot demean (*yahīn*) her. When he becomes betrothed, he undertakes to protect her in regard to "hunger, thirst, clothing, and demeaning treatment" (*al-jūaʿ aẓ-ẓamā al-kiswa wa-l-ihāna*).[77] One facet of such humiliation would be to beat her as if she were an animal. While the two permitted means of such assault are the bare hand and a stick (*maṭrag*), the latter must not be longer than twenty-two inches, or a common cubit, a measure known to the Bedouin as a "Hashimite forearm" (*dhrāʿ hāshimī*).[78] Anything longer would resemble a whip, and the law forbids whipping a woman, as that would reduce her to the level of an animal. A graphic example of preserving a wife's dignity above that of an animal comes from the northern Negev in the late nineteenth century (Case 143). The woman in question, whose husband was of the Tiyāha al-Asad tribe, purchased a goat with her own money and branded it with the brand (*wasm*) of her father's tribe. Her husband, considering this a slight to his own tribal identity, branded his wife with the *wasm* of his tribe. Subsequently her clansmen challenged him to a trial, in which the judge punished him with the amputation of the hand that took hold of his wife and branded her as if she were an animal. Although the hand was ransomed, the payment for it of 90 Egyptian pounds and sixteen camels illustrates how serious the offense was viewed.[79]

Another effort of Bedouin law to spare a beaten woman humiliation is its ruling that the beating must not take place before the eyes of others. Accordingly, a wife may not be struck in public or public view, but only in the privacy of her own tent, with the curtain flaps lowered. To stress the imperative in this injunction, a legal maxim holds, "A woman can't be hit but in her tent, though you pitch your cloak over her" (*al-mara mā tinḍarib ila fī bayt-ha—lō tibnī ʿalayha ʿabātak*).[80] By the same token, a man may curse his wife in private but not in public. A further ruling intended to spare a woman's dignity is that her husband cannot strip her for a beating, but rather must deliver the blows upon her outer garment. Moreover, in order to protect her appearance and vital organs, she may be hit only on the back side of her body.

As seen in the aforementioned case of the man who branded his wife, the law provides punishments for a husband who transgresses the limits on the physical force he can exert against her. The persons who activate the claim against him are the woman's clansmen, who are responsible for her physical integrity and her dignity. Any physical injury or humiliation she suffers, as a member of her father's clan, is a humiliation to her entire clan, which cannot afford to ignore it lest it acquire a reputation for weakness. If a woman complains to her clansmen of any illegal behavior by her husband against her—such as hitting her without justifiable reason, beating her with a long stick or on the front of her body, or striking her within eyesight of others—they will normally first clarify her claim with her husband. If he admits to the wrongdoing, he will have to pay the woman or her family a fine. If he denies it, her family may resort to having the woman swear an oath that her claim is true, or they may send her back to him on condition that a further complaint will justify her leaving him. As in any other Bedouin legal agreement or commitment, these arrangements will all be ensured by a guarantor.

In the event of disagreements over whether the force applied is justified or constitutes a wrongdoing, the parties will refer to an *ʿugbī* judge, as in the case of the brother-in-law who struck his brother's wife for remissness, mentioned above. If the woman is injured by her husband, regardless of whether she has committed a wrong or not, the man is liable to pay, after reference to "a measuring judge" (*gaṣṣāṣ*), the fine the latter determines twofold. If the woman is killed by her husband's assault, her clansmen have the right to four acts of revenge against the men of his clan or a blood-payment for each revenge not taken. Thus, in 1967 among the ʿAzāzma Saraḥīn in eastern Sinai, when Sulaymān al-Gurʿān of the Owraydāt clan killed his wife by striking her, the woman's clansmen of the Izʿaylāt clan demanded vengeance or compensation fourfold from the Owraydāt (Case 10). It was their legal due, which was reduced to only one blood-payment following the mediation of the paramount chief of the ʿAzāzma in both Sinai and the Negev, ʿOwda Manṣūr Abū Muʿammar.[81]

MARRIAGE AND DIVORCE

Marriage

Husbands Are Chosen for Women A woman has no choice concerning her future husband, whether she is a yet unmarried girl, defined as a "virgin" (*bint*), or one who is either a widow or divorcee, defined as a "solitary woman" (*ʿazaba*). Indeed, virgin brides are rarely informed of the identity of their groom until shortly before the marriage ceremony is to take place, either by days or by hours—or not until the groom actually comes to fetch her.[82] Symbolizing the dismay that virgin girls may feel over the choice of a groom for them is a mountain just north of Wādī Fīrān in southern Sinai, called "Mountain of the Virgins" (*jabal al-banāt*). Local tradition holds that from one of its peaks, two disappointed girls tied their braids together and leapt into the void to manifest their dissent.[83]

A previously married woman enjoys a slight advantage over a *bint* in that she can legally exercise a veto on the choice her clansmen make for her. The legal maxim holds, "A virgin is betrothed by her parents' discussion, but one who's been married before is consulted" (*al-bint bi-l-khaṭūba wa-l-ʿazaba bi-l-mashūra*); hence, Bedouin, perhaps exaggeratedly, attribute to an *ʿazaba* the right of choice, as in the saying, "She will sit in a camel litter [once used for migration] and her eye will choose" (*hiya rākba bi-l-ḥiṣār ū-ʿeinha tikhtār*).[84] Accordingly, in the 1970s among families of the Aḥeiwāt Shawafīn in central Sinai (the Abū Raḍwān and the Ibn ʿAtayyig), the brothers of two women, one an *ʿazaba*, agreed to undertake an exchange marriage (*badl*), in which they would each marry the other's sister (Case 144). Before the exchange took place, however, Salāma Ibn ʿAtayyig lost interest in marrying the woman to whom he was engaged and persuaded his brother, ʿId, to replace him. When the *ʿazaba* learned of the switch, she objected, and the marriage was annulled by the Aḥeiwāt judge, Ḥasan Abū Khalīl.[85]

Indeed, the right of a previously married woman to reject her designated groom may prevail in the face of heavy social pressure against it. For example, among the Dawāghra Nighāmsha of northern Sinai in March 1977, the uncle and guardian of an *ʿazaba* was displeased that she remained unmarried and conspired with a man to abduct her and remove her to a spot among remote sand dunes to the south, from where she would be powerless to protest his choice of a husband (Case 3). When, however, the plot was uncovered and challenged in court by her protector, the Dawāghra chief Sālim Salāma Rajawīn, the Bedouin judge, in accordance with the legal right of an *ʿazaba* to reject a proposed husband, annulled the betrothal.[86] This type of protest would be practically and legally impossible for a virgin.

According to the law, Bedouin marriages are arranged by the immediate families or (if these do not exist) guardians of the bride and groom, even if such a marriage conflicts with the interest that one partner's clan may or may not have in a connection with the other partner's family and clan. Any attempt to join a couple in marriage without the consent of the woman's family leaves the latter with a legal claim against the validity of the marriage and against the groom and his clan. One relevant legal maxim states, "A father has no partner in his daughter's betrothal, not even his brother" (*bint ar-rājil—mā lih fīha sharīk wi-lō akhūh*), the allusion being to the unique closeness that exists among brothers in Bedouin society. Another maxim, referring to the cut blade of grass or other plant (*gaṣala*) that a girl's father hands to the father of the proposed groom after he has agreed to the marriage, affirms, "No one presents the girl's plant but her father" (*mā yugṣul al-bint ghayr abūha*).[87] Accordingly, in 1967 among the ʿAzāzma Saraḥīn in eastern Sinai, when ʿOwda Salmān al-Owraydī, an ʿAzāzma chief and head of the Owraydāt clan, assumed to marry off, in her father's absence, the daughter of his clansman, ʿOwda Sulaymān al-Hadōbe, to a member of the Izʿaylāt clan as partial compensation for the murder of one of the Izʿaylāt women, Hadōbe protested that no one had the right to usurp his paternal right (Case 10). With the dissolution of the border between Israel and Egypt following the Six-Day War in June1967, he thus betook himself to the Negev, where he received the protection of ʿOwda Abū Muʿammar, the paramount chief of the ʿAzāzma, who succeeded in extricating Hadōbe's daughter from this attempt to circumvent the law.[88]

Another indication of the father's exclusive right to determine his daughter's spouse also occurred when the daughter of Ḥimayd as-Saddān of the ʿAzāzma Saraḥīn absconded with her desired husband in 1983 and was given refuge in the tent of ʿAbdallah al-Wajj of the Ẓullām Janabīb (Case 16). In light of Saddān's rejection of the prospective marriage, Wajj, in compliance with the laws of abduction, was obliged either to return the girl to her father within three days or take her to another tent for refuge. When he discharged his undertaking by bringing the girl to her father, however, Saddān was absent from the tent, and the only present man was his clansman, Salāma ʿĪd Abū Bilayya, who refused to be responsible for receiving the returned girl, asserting, "Give her to her father. This has nothing to do with me" (*āna mānī marbūṭ fīha*).[89] Abū Bilayya understood that his authority regarding his clanswoman fell short of anything pertaining to her matrimony.[90]

By way of confirming the father's exclusive right to choose his daughter's husband, the law denies a prospective bride any right to utilize the hallowed institution of protection (*dakhāla*) in order to protest her father's choice.[91] In October 1974, when Freija, the daughter of Sālim al-Ameiṭil of the ʿAzāzma ʿAṣiyāt in the central Negev, refused her father's choice of a husband for her, she sought refuge in the tent of Swaylim Abū Bilayya of the ʿAzāzma Saraḥīn, whom she asked to persuade her father to let her marry a fellow tribesman, Sālim ʿOwda aṭ-Ṭimṭāwī (Case 145). The next day, looking for their sister and finding her with Abū Bilayya, the girl's brothers insisted that he surrender her, citing the legal maxim, "No one precedes a girl's father in her defense" (*al-bint—mā ʿan abūha difāʿ*).[92] By way of saving face, Abū Bilayya, before duly yielding her to her brothers' custody, tried to extract an assurance from them that they would not harm the girl.[93]

"Closest-Cousin" Marriage The greatest obstacle to a father's right to choose his daughter's husband resides in "the right of the paternal uncle's son" (*ḥagg ibn al-ʿamm*). Whenever a girl is born, she is pledged in "marriage to a paternal cousin" (*jīzit ibn al-ʿamm*), if such already exists and is not already designated for another girl in the clan. This endogamous, or internal, form of marriage is apparently a clan interest, believed to be favorable to its solidarity and security; it is feared that an "outside girl" (*ajnabiyya*) will maintain strong loyalties to her paternal clan that will manifest themselves when it and her husband's clan are in conflict. According to the right of the paternal uncle's son, a man has legal priority to marry the cousin committed to him over any other man. In April 1878, for example, the English writer Anne Blunt was present at a Bedouin wedding in Mesopotamia when a lowly, but protesting, shepherd had the impending marriage of his designated cousin to one of the most powerful chiefs in the area canceled (Case 2).[94] In the central Negev in 1997, among the Ẓullām Janabīb tribe, ʿAbdallah al-Wajj took a paternal cousin's daughter (who had been designated for his son) from the house of her father in order to block her marriage to the son of a non-clansman, ʿĪd Ibn Darrāj, which the father had furtively arranged (Case 146). The removal of the girl was subsequently upheld by a judge, Salmān Ḥusayn Ibn Ḥammād, before whom Ibn Darrāj protested. The only award granted to the latter was a sum (to be paid by the girl's father) that covered expenses incurred for the bride-price (*siyāg*) and preparations for the anticipated wedding.[95]

Fathers have a variety of reasons for preferring to marry a daughter to an outsider rather than to her designated cousin. One is that they may want to receive a bride-price that is larger than the standard one paid by a closest cousin (traditionally fixed at only five camels). Another reason is that the father may be fond of an outside man, whose friendship he wishes to bind through marriage. When, for example, the daughter of Frayj Ḥimayd as-Saddān of the ʿAzāzma Sarahīn in the central Negev came of eligible age in 1995, he wanted to marry her off to fellow tribesman Labbād Ṭassān al-Khawāṭra, whose friendship he enjoyed, rather than to her cousin, Sulaymān Swaylim Abū Bilayya (Case 26). As his older daughters had already been married to cousins in the Abū Bilayya family, he argued that the interests of the ʿOwdāt clan, to which both families belonged, were jeopardized by too many inside marriages, which were isolating the ʿOwdāt from useful contacts with other clans.[96]

Family and clan interests are, indeed, often a prevalent reason for contracting marriages with outside men. Sometimes a family will seek marital relations with another that possesses a cistern on its yearly migration cycle so that it might gain access to nearby water toward summer.[97] Similarly in 1972, when I was traveling across southern Sinai from east to west in the company of a man of the Tarabīn Ḥasāblah tribe from the eastern coast who was responsible for his orphaned sisters, we stopped off on successive nights with two he had married off to men of the Aḥeiwāt Shawafīn and ʿAlaygāt confederations, inhabiting remote places in central and western Sinai respectively. It turned out that the brothers-in-law were his partners in moving contraband from Jordan toward Cairo.

A further reason for wanting to betroth a daughter to an outsider is to gain a bride for her brother through an exchange, or *badl*, marriage. Such marriages are often contracted by the fathers of two girls with the aim of betrothing each to the brother of the other or to some other man of the clan that is suitable. Among the ʿAzāzma ʿAṣiyāt of the central Negev, for example, ʿAliyyān aṭ-Ṭimṭāwī used his fine-looking sister, Ḥusn, as bait to attract a bride for their mentally retarded brother, Salāma, whom ʿAliyyān wished to see married in order to sire sons for their family and clan (Case 147). In 1971, he contracted an exchange marriage whereby Ḥusn would marry Sālim ʿOwda aṭ-Ṭimṭāwī (not a clansman) in exchange for Sālim's sister to marry Salāma. This marriage broke up, however, owing to the flight of the sister from Salāma and the subsequent beating she sustained at the hands of ʿAliyyān and his clansmen. In exchange marriages, when one couple divorces, the other must do so as well, so Ḥusn was divorced by Sālim aṭ-Ṭimṭāwī.[98] Still, in 1973, ʿAliyyān tried again to use his sister Ḥusn to attract a bride for their retarded brother through an exchange marriage with the son and daughter of Sālim al-Khiraynig of the ʿAzāzma Saraḥīn.[99]

Similarly, if the cousin who has a claim on the daughter has no sister that is suitable for her brother to marry—particularly owing to an age disparity—her father may want to arrange an exchange marriage whereby his son will obtain a bride without having to pay a bride-price.[100] This is in keeping with the perception that "My daughter is my wealth" (*wiliyytī hī mālī*).[101] To endorse this exigency, a Bedouin proverb emerged with the assertion, "The first daughter is for her brother, and the second is for her cousin" (*al-awwala l-akhūha wa-th-thānya l-ibn al-ʿamm*).[102] But the saying has no legal validity. For example (Case 15):

> In 1973 among the ʿAzāzma Saraḥīn of the central Negev, the son of ʿĪd ʿAtayyig al-Khiraynig had a closest-cousin claim on the daughter of Ḥusayn Swaylim al-Khiraynig. Ḥusayn, on the other hand, had a son, Sulaymān, who had reached marriageable age, and he wanted to get him married so that he could begin to sire sons for their family. ʿĪd al-Khiraynig's daughter, however, was sufficiently prepubescent (ten years old) so that Sulaymān would have to wait seven years before an exchange marriage between the two families could be consummated. As a result, Ḥusayn made an exchange-marriage agreement

with ʿAlī al-ʿAbays, who had both a daughter and a son suitable in age for his children. However, threats by ʿĪd al-Khiraynig and his sons to sabotage the upcoming wedding celebration, on the one hand—and the demand of Sālim Shitaywī al-ʿAbays to marry the betrothed daughter of ʿAlī al-ʿAbays, to whom he had a closest-cousin claim, on the other—combined to terminate the Khiraynig-ʿAbays exchange agreement.[103]

Finally, men may also exchange daughters to gain wives for themselves, such as did Farrāj an-Nakhlāwī and another man of the Nakhlawiyya tribe of central Sinai in the late 1960s (Case 148).[104] Similarly, a man may contract a marriage to gain a wife for himself by betrothing his daughter to the prospective wife's brother, as did Chief Khalīl Farhūd Abū-l-Gīʿān of the Tiyāha Abū-l-Gīʿān in the northern Negev in 2006 (Case 149).[105]

A father can try to overcome the closest-cousin marriage obstacle in one of three ways. The first is to prod the closest cousin to marry his daughter quickly, claiming that he has a prospective outsider groom who wants her hand. In the event that the cousin refuses, he is free to marry off his daughter to whomever he wants. The failure of the father to pursue this path in the nineteenth century case in Mesopotamia about which Anne Blunt reported (Case 2) annulled the marriage of the designated cousin of a lowly shepherd to a prominent chief. Blunt wrote, "The judge decided that, the bride [that is, her father] having taken no step to oblige her cousin to keep his promise and marry her, his right remained valid."[106] The second way for a father to betroth his daughter to a specific outsider is for him to try to persuade the closest cousin to concur. This may entail finding him an alternative bride and paying her bride-price.

Often the failure of a father to pursue these first two paths in favor of a third one—namely, to circumvent the cousin and carry out a "concealed marriage" (*jawāz dass*)—may have dire consequences for him, as it did in the 1960s in the Jabal Rāḥa area of southwest Sinai (Case 68).[107] There, among the Tarabīn Ḥasāblah, a man of the Durūz clan secretly married his daughter to an outsider from the ʿUbaydāt clan, Sālim Abū ʿUbayd. During the wedding ceremony at an ʿUbaydāt encampment, where the bride was brought and placed in the bridal tent (*birza*) for the duration of the celebration, a large party of the Durūz attacked and, at gunpoint, kept all the company seated while they snatched the girl and made off with her. Subsequently her closest cousin married her. The ʿUbaydāt took the case to a renowned judge of the Tarabīn in western Sinai, Ḥājj Jāzī al-ʿArādī, who, however, upheld what many believe to be the ruling of a past *ʿugbī* judge—namely, that "The closest cousin can take his designated cousin out of the bridal tent" (*ibn al-ʿamm yākhidh bint ʿammah min al-birza*).[108] When the ʿUbaydāt protested that the girl could not be abducted as she was already married to their man—inferring that her *gaṣala* plant had been presented and that Abū ʿUbayd had performed the marriage sacrifice (*ḥilliyya*), sprinkling the blood of an animal on the bridal tent to signify his bond with the bride—ʿArādī ruled that the right of a closest cousin terminates only once the husband has performed the "entry" (*dukhla*) into his wife—that is, consummated sexual relations with her, something that normally takes place only after the end of the wedding celebration and the departure of the guests.[109]

The possibility of a closest cousin actually raiding a wedding celebration and thwarting such a "concealed marriage" always exists as a last resort for him to preserve his right. Among the ʿAzāzma Saraḥīn of the central Negev in 1973, ʿĪd al-Khiraynig, upon learning that his kinsman, Ḥusayn al-Khiraynig, was to marry his daughter, the designated cousin of ʿĪd's son, ʿAlī, to an outsider, he threatened the prospective host of the impending celebration, Swaylim Abū Bilayya, with an attack that would bring the wedding tent down on the heads of his guests (Case 15).[110]

The Abduction of Brides Abduction (*shrād* or *nihibi*) is another resort often practiced by a closest cousin to realize his right in the face of the resolve of the father of his designated cousin to circumvent it. Such an abduction is generally a consensual act, tantamount to a mutual abscondment, and is treated by the girl's family less harshly than an abduction by a non-clansman.[111] The law, however, specifies rules whose omission exposes the abducting cousin to legal punishment. First, he must make at least one, if not more, requests of the girl's father to marry her. In spring 1973, when the aforementioned ʿĪd ʿAtayyig al-Khiraynig heard that the cousin designated for his son was promised to an outsider (Case 15), he made three representations to her father, Ḥusayn Swaylim al-Khiraynig: the first, only with his son; the second, with the head of the ʿAyāl Swaylim section of the ʿAzāzma Saraḥīn, ʿOwda Zanūn; the third, with Zanūn and the paramount chief of the ʿAzāzma, ʿOwda Abū Muʿammar.[112] Without giving the father a chance to refuse, there is no justification for the abduction of his daughter.

The second rule stipulates that the abductor must be accompanied by an adult man, called "companion" (*rafīg* in the Negev; *imbarrī* in Sinai), who must be in his company from the moment he meets the girl until the moment he places her in the tent of someone who will protect her honor (that is, from the abductor himself). The role of the companion is to testify, under oath if necessary, that the abductor neither touched the girl nor said anything improper to her. In 1995, when Sulaymān Swaylim Abū Bilayya abducted his designated cousin, the daughter of Frayj Ḥimayd as-Saddān, his companion, a neighbor of the Rimāg clan, testified that he joined the couple only on the road over which he was to drive them to a protective tent (Case 26). Although Abū Bilayya's marriage was ultimately allowed by the father, the partial absence of a companion enabled the father to demand a *manshad* trial,[113] for the concession of which he was able to exact an exorbitant bride-price (10,000 Jordanian dinars, or $15,000) and fines (8,000 Jordanian dinars, or $12,000).[114]

The third rule regarding abduction pertains to the tent to which the girl must be brought for safekeeping. The criteria for an acceptable tent range from that of a notable person to that of a widow (someone with a non-notable status) but insist that it be not far from the designated wife's home tent so that access to her father is easy. Accordingly, when Sulaymān Abū Bilayya took the daughter of Frayj as-Saddān a distance of sixty kilometers to the tent of his maternal relative, Ṣubḥī al-ʿUwaywī, he added a pretext to Saddān's demanding from him four times the usual fine for abducting without a companion (Case 26).

Fourth, the abductor must immediately (within three days) come to the father of the girl with the legal bride-price for a closest cousin: five camels with a year's age difference between each of them. The traditional rhyming declaration on such an occasion is as follows:

> Her bride-price is piled high and her protection is endless;
> (*Maharha kōm ū-dakhalha dōm*)
> I've put her under shelter by myself [with my own arms].
> (*w-āna jāyirha bi-bāʿī ū-dhrāʿī*)
> Behold! Led and driven, five camels of ascending age,
> (*irʿāhin gōd ū-sōg—khamsa min al-bil sinn yuṭrud sinn*)
> With my staff thrown behind them.
> (*ū-maṭrag-hin warāhin*).[115]

The above payment must be made by the abductor himself or his representative as part of a goodwill delegation (*jāha*) that will afterwards bear witness that the bride-price has been paid. Although the father must consequently permit the marriage, he can utilize his bargaining position at this session to raise the bride-price in the event that any of the rules of closest-cousin abduction have been transgressed. In the case of Sulaymān Abū Bilayya in 1995 (Case 26), the delegation sent by his father and led by a notable of the ʿAzāzma ʿAṣiyāt tribe, Dakhlallah Abū Gardūd, was able to gain the approval of the designated cousin's father, Frayj as-Saddān, but not before he demanded 18,000 Jordanian dinars (approximately $27,000) for the bride-price and the fines. One such fine, traditionally representing the camel used for the abduction, is called the "dragging-off fine" (*jarra*) in the Negev and the "camel of abduction fine" (*jamal ash-sharāda*) in Sinai; it is paid by the abducting closest cousin, whether he ultimately marries the girl in question or not. Traditionally it was a three-year-old camel (*marbūṭ*), whose price is arbitrarily evaluated at 1,000 Jordanian dinars. Owing to the fact that Abū Bilayya abducted the girl without the constant escort of a companion, which entitled the girl's father to a *manshad* trial, Saddān, by yielding the trial, was able to set the price of the dragging-off fine at 4,000 dinars. Such was the case too with a second fine, called the "companion fine" (*rafīga*—that is, the fine for not having an escort), which is traditionally a three-to-four-year-old camel (*ḥigg*), also evaluated at 1,000 Jordanian dinars, but which Saddān also increased fourfold the usual evaluation.* Finally, Saddān's concession of the *manshad* trial also enabled him to demand and receive a bride-price of 10,000 Jordanian dinars, which was at least double the price of the five camels traditionally paid by a closest cousin.[116]

Naturally, the right of a father to decide on the husband of his daughter may also be blocked if she is abducted by, or consensually absconds with, a man not of their clan, an "outsider" (*ajnabī*). If such an absconder is of the same tribe, or a neighboring but friendly tribe of the same or another confederation, he must abide by the rules that pertain to a closest cousin, such as the presence of an escort, the placement of the girl in a protective tent, and the dispatch of a delegation to request the father's accord within a short time (commonly three days; alternatively three and a third days). Among two different clans of the ʿAzāzma Saraḥīn tribe of the central Negev in 1983, Ḥasan al-Atayyim abducted Saʿīda, the daughter of Ḥimayd as-Saddān, and put her into the protective tent of ʿAbdallah al-Wajj of the Ẓullām Janabīb, in accordance with the rules (Case 16). His companion, Hilayyil al-Wajj, however, was not with the couple at the outset of their abscondment, and this cost Atayyim a camel as a *rafīga* fine when he married the girl.[117]

Unlike the case of Atayyim, however, the father of a girl abducted by an outsider does not always allow the abductor to marry his daughter. In the 1950s in the central Negev, for example, when ʿAlī al-Kishkhar of the Ẓullām Janabīb abducted the daughter of Sulaymān al-Ḥamāda of the ʿAzāzma Saraḥīn, he duly paid the *jarra* fine but had to return the girl to her father (Case 150).[118] An abductor's refusal to comply with a father's request to return his daughter to him, marrying her without the latter's agreement, is grounds for a legal claim against him. Such a marriage is called "a marriage that destroys rights" (*jīzat ʿadam*), the right of the father to determine his daughter's hus-

*A traditional alternative to the *ḥigg* camel is "a complete set of weapons" (*as-silāḥ al-kāmil*), consisting of either (1) a rifle, a bandolier, and an ammunition belt, or (2) a sword, a dagger, and a rifle (oral communication from Swaylim Sulaymān Abū Bilayya of the ʿAzāzma Saraḥīn, December 15, 1996.

band being thus destroyed. Among the ʿAzāzma Saraḥīn in eastern Sinai, a marriage of this sort between ʿOwda Jumʿa al-Owraydī and the daughter of ʿOwda Sulaymān al-Hadōbe remained unrecognized by the latter from 1971, when it was perpetrated, until 1978, when Hadōbe received the protection and intervention of the chief, Sālim al-Kishkhar of the Ẓullām Janabīb, who succeeded in facilitating a divorce (Case 10).[119] In the interim, several goodwill delegations of notables failed to persuade Hadōbe to relent.[120]

Moreover, if absconders are outsiders who ignore the wishes of a girl's father and neglect his honor by not returning his daughter within the three-day respite or not sending a delegation to negotiate with him, hostilities may exceed social ostracism and take the form of pillage and murder. In the event that the abductor is from a different or hostile confederation or tribe, as indicated in chapter 4, the girl's father and his people have a legal right to murder and pillage immediately, unlimited by the three and a third days' respite for negotiations stipulated for abductors from the same tribe or neighboring and friendly ones. Abduction by men of distant or unfriendly tribes, even of the same confederation, is viewed as tantamount to rape, warranting the same punishments. In 1977, when the son of a man called Abū Girshayn, belonging to the Jordanian ʿUmrān confederation but living in the central Negev, abducted a girl of the Ẓullām confederation of the northern Negev, men of the Ẓullām gathered and went off to kill as many of the lad's clansmen as possible, a prospect averted only by the offenders' finding protection with the powerful Tiyāha Huzayyil tribe (Case 49).[121] In 1981, when a lad called Ibn Fayyāḍ of the Tarabīn confederation in central Sinai absconded with a girl of the Tiyāha, people of her confederation pillaged the Tarabīn until they agreed to have the girl returned to her father and to sit before a *manshad* trial (Case 20).[122] If such a case ends in murder, it is over. If it gets to litigation before murder occurs, the father is entitled to seven camel-truces and seven *manshad* judgments, one for each of seven sunrises that the abducted girl was not yet returned.

Polygamy A final aspect of Bedouin marriage, polygamy, is allowed by Bedouin law and also permitted by the Muslim religion. The reasons mainly proffered for Bedouin men marrying more than one woman at the same time are to increase the chances of fathering male sons (for example, "Marriage is for making men"—*al-jīza marājil*) and to discipline an uncooperative current wife ("As breaking a camel is done with a stick, so breaking women is done with women"—*yadb al-hijn bi-l-ʿaṣa ū-yadb an'-nisī ba-n'-nisī*).[123] The main prescription for polygamy in Bedouin law is that the husband treat the fellow wives equally, a condition that each wife is keen to see upheld. Hence, the Bedouin proverb holds that "A fellow wife's eye is a scale, and her cheek is a steelyard" (*aḍ-ḍarra—ʿeinha mīzān ū-khadd-ha gabbān*);[124] the "scale," figuratively, is to examine the various goods and gifts her husband brings her fellow wife, and the "steelyard" (that is, more weighty) is for keeping account of the nights he shares her pillow. Complaints of mistreatment in any of these categories are dealt with by an *ʿugbī* judge, who specializes in marital problems.

Divorce

Divorcing an Honorable Woman A Bedouin man may divorce his wife at will. The reasons may be incompatibility, her failure to bear sons, perceived negligence in her duties pertaining to the livestock and household, or her assertive opposition to his taking an additional wife—all these being considered grounds for an honorable divorce. So long as the husband gives her such a divorce, her family has no right to interfere. Traditionally, an honorable divorce was signaled by sending the woman back to her family on what was called "the camel of the worthy one" (*jamal al-mufaḍḍala*). Such a woman could take with her her clothing and jewelry and the livestock she had received as presents from her father or guardian (for an independent source of spending money). In terms of ceremony, the husband has only to declare to the woman, "You are as something unbound" (*intī ṭālig*) or "you are divorced" (*intī muṭallaga*) and to engage a man, whether present at the declaration or not, as a witness to the divorce. When, in 1961, ʿAnayz Sālim al-ʿUrḍī of the Tarabīn Ḥasāblah in southeast Sinai divorced two of his wives from his place of imprisonment at Zagazīg, Egypt, he did it via a letter, written for him by a cellmate, that he sent to his cousin, Ḥājj Ḥimaydān ʿUbaydallah, thus announcing the divorces and delegating him to be the guarantor and witness (Case 151).[125] As in Islam, if a husband utters *intī ṭālig* or *intī muṭallaga* only once, he may thereafter remarry his ex-wife.[126] If, however, he wishes to signal that the divorce is irrevocable, he will utter it three times or say, "You are as if unbound threefold" (*intī ṭālig bi-thilātha*). One Bedouin interviewed understood this to mean that a man is forbidden to remarry the wife he has thus divorced, as if she were one of the "three forbidden women [for marriage]" (*thilāth al-muḥarrimāt*): one's mother, one's sister, and one's stepmother (*ʿammtah*), the wife of one's father.[127]

Divorcing a Dishonorable Woman A dishonorable divorce occurs when a man says to his wife, "Go to your clansmen!" (*rūḥī li-zlāmkī*). This implies that a woman has acted immorally, and it brands her as a "woman of misconduct" (*ʿāyiba*)—that is, she has trysted with a man or has even just exposed herself indecently. Cases indicate that the category of indecent exposure includes reciting poetry or playing music before men, as these may reveal emotions or desires. In particular, Bedouin men conventionally assume that women's poems are sexually suggestive. An eighteenth-century narrative from the Iraqi desert tells of a prominent chief, Jidayaʿ Ibn Hadhdhāl, who married a merchant woman from the city on the condition that she never again recite poetry, though she was widely acknowledged to be talented (Case 152). Indeed, when the chief learned that his wife, Irgeiya, had subsequently recited a poem to a camel raider in an attempt to regain her pillaged herd, Ibn Hadhdhāl summarily divorced her.[128] Similarly in central Sinai in the 1950s, ʿOwda Ibn Huwayshil, a leading figure among the Aḥeiwāt Ṣafeiḥa, divorced his wife, a woman of the Masaʿīd confederation, because she, though veiled, had played her shepherd's flute (*shabbāba*) in the presence of people, among them men, at the well where she watered her flock (Case 153). When informed of her divorce, her own father, a *manshad* judge of the Masaʿīd, justified it, ruling that playing the flute before men is a contravention of "moral self-respect" (*ṣāyinit nafs*).[129]

Sending a woman to her kinsmen, euphemistically called "describing [the whereabouts of] her family" (*towṣīf ahalha*), is a great shame to her.* Indeed, she is henceforth not commonly referred to as divorced (*muṭallaga*) but rather as "banished" (*maṭrūda*). Moreover, she is constrained to leave with nothing but the dress on her back, if that is her husband's wish. Owing to his moral leverage, he can make her leave all her jewelry and personal livestock behind. The legal maxim that affirms this condition goes, "Only a woman of misconduct is banished from her wealth" (*mā tinṭirid min mālha ghayr al-ʿāyiba*).[130] Her family, though normally the defender of her marital welfare, is often too compromised by her immoral behavior to fulfill this responsibility; it is as if it has failed in its societal task to raise her to moral probity.[131] If anything, it is keen to keep her behavior from public knowledge. This, in turn, accounts for her husband's rare opportunity to extort from the family the return of her bride-price.

A tradition exists among the Tarabīn Ḥasāblah in southeast Sinai that a husband returned one night early from a journey to hear a man's voice, together with that of his wife, coming from his tent (Case 154).

*This term is also used for divorcing an unloving wife (*ṭāmiḥ*; lit. "unsubmissive"). Indeed, in central Sinai in the 1970s, the *ṭāmiḥ* wife of ʿOwda Ibn Huwayshil of the Aḥeiwāt Ṣafeiḥa confederation was prompted by her father to ask her husband, on his return from journeys, if he had news of her family and where they were encamped. Ibn Huwayshil, sensing the ploy, always denied knowing where her family was. On one occasion, however, he slipped and told her where it was, whereupon she happily declared that she was divorced. Although Ibn Huwayshil rejected this claim, her family appealed to the *ʿugbī* judge in the Negev. The *ʿugbī* ruled, "As he described the whereabouts of her father's tent, she is henceforth divorced." (Oral communication from ʿAnayz Sālim al-ʿUrḍī of the Tarabīn Ḥasāblah, June 17, 1998.)

> He distanced himself to within eyesight of the tent, waiting for the man to leave before daybreak. Once the man had left, he entered the tent to his wife's fulsome greetings and her professions of desire to prepare him some coffee and breakfast. He ordered the woman, "Go to your clansmen!" and she left, banished. Her father and brothers thereupon came to the husband, inquiring about the reason for her banishment, whereupon the husband told them his story, demanding simultaneously that they return to him the bride-price he had paid. It was blackmail for keeping the story secret, an offer the girl's family could not reject.[132]

Otherwise the law itself provides little possibility for a man's retrieving the bride-price for a wife he has divorced, considering that he has used her for the goal of reproduction, successful or not. The main exception is in the case of a *ṭāmiḥ* wife who cannot bring herself to have sexual relations with her husband owing to her love for someone else. Such a woman, however, is not considered shameful so long as she has not trysted with her beloved. Thus, if her father or other guardian or protector is willing to take up her case, a judge will authorize her divorce, conditioning his judgment on her family's returning her bride-price to her current husband.

A banished woman's family will normally interrogate her as to the veracity of her husband's allegation before it accepts her alleged misconduct (*ʿeib*) and the consequent shame. In the aforementioned account of ʿOwda Ibn Huwayshil of the Aḥeiwāt Ṣafeiḥa in central Sinai (Case 154), his divorced wife's father, himself a *manshad* judge from the Masaʿīd, questioned her about her husband's accusation. He asked, "What is his grievance?" She answered, "He said that I was playing my flute at the well." "Is that true?" he asked. "Yes, but I was veiled all the time," she replied. "Were there men in the crowd?" he went on. "Yes" she admitted. He then ruled that it was improper to play music to men and consented to Ibn Huwayshil's divorce.

By contrast, however, there are families that interrogate their women but do not concur in a dishonorable divorce. In 1974 among the ʿAzāzma Saraḥīn in the central Negev, Ḥusayn Swaylim al-Khiraynig divorced his wife with the order, "Go to your clansmen!," implying that she had behaved immorally (Case 141).[133] Her closest relative in Israel (the rest having moved to Jordan) was Swaylim Sulaymān Abū Bilayya, a distant clansman and her mother's brother. In the absence of any closer kin, Abū Bilayya was delegated by the girl's relatives to be her guardian.* Knowing his niece to have been a faithful

*Bailey, *Proverbs*, p. 164. Stewart (*Texts*, vol. 1, pp. 71–72, 204–7) cites two cases of women's clansmen delegating non-clan persons to act as guardians of such women among the Aḥeiwāt Shawafīn confederation in eastern Sinai.

and efficient wife who had increased Khiraynig's livestock greatly through her diligence and who was generous in providing from their considerable bounty for the guests who visited their tent, Abū Bilayya was skeptical of her husband's slur. He was aware, however, of Khiraynig's displeasure over his wife's hospitality. Thus, after interrogating her, Abū Bilayya, feeling that the accusation was but slander against her reputation, summoned Khiraynig to a *manshad* trial before Sulaymān al-ʿUgbī, the leading *manshad* judge in the Negev. Hearing the pleas of both Khiraynig and his wife—her plea as presented by Abū Bilayya—ʿUgbī ruled that the woman was "pure and noble" (*naẓīfa sharīfa*). He therefore ordered Khiraynig to take her back (on condition that she was willing to go back to him); to give her a "conciliation gift" (*irḍāwa*), consisting of one herd of ten camels and two flocks of twenty goats each; and to cover the tent of Abū Bilayya with white cloth so that people would know that the woman's honor was "white" and that Abū Bilayya had gained her her rights.

Aiding Unhappy Wives A wife unhappy with her marriage might seek a divorce through the good offices of either her father, a guardian, or someone willing to extend her his protection. However, no Bedouin law obligates men to undertake to help an unhappy wife, whether for gaining her better treatment or a divorce. The law leaves such compliance to the complete discretion of the man to whom the woman appeals for help, even her father. Fathers, as directly responsible for their daughters' marital welfare, are notably solicitous of it. If, for example, a woman comes to her father complaining that her husband beats or vilifies her unjustly, denies her necessities, or treats her unequally in respect to a fellow wife, the father possesses the right to question her husband as to the veracity of her complaints and, if they are correct, demand that the husband improve his behavior and give her a conciliation gift as conditions for her continued marriage to him. If the complaints persist, however, and the husband refuses to reform or conciliate, the father has the right to obtain her divorce, as ordered by an *ʿugbī* judge in his capacity of what Bedouin call the "father of women" (*abū an-niswān*), ruling in marital problems referred to as "nighttime problems" but entailing all the mutual obligations of a man and his wife. Having once heard a case and its history, the *ʿugbī* is empowered by the law to order a divorce. It should be remembered, however, that fathers, in taking up their daughters' complaints, are nonetheless careful not to support those of an amorous nature so as not to undermine the Bedouin marital system, by which marriages are contracted to serve family and clan interests rather than the emotions and preferences of a bride.

Cases in which no man exists to help a woman in her marital difficulties are not unknown. In 1978, for example, two young men in the Tarabīn Ḥasāblah tribe of southeast Sinai decided to exchange their sisters in a *badl* marriage (Case 155). The son in one of the two families found his prospective bride very desirable, but his sister found her designated husband, the brother of her own brother's bride, disgusting. No sooner was she married than her behavior reflected this negative attitude, angering her new spouse. He thus attempted to break her will with beatings and deprivations and finally by encamping her in a remote place far distant from her shepherdess girlfriends, among whom she might otherwise have found some solace and pleasure. Her only company was her domineering, irritable, and suspicious mother-in-law. Her father being dead, the woman entreated her brother (and guardian) to extricate her from her marriage, but the latter, keen on preserving his own happy marriage and knowing that the rules of *badl* required the divorce of one woman to be followed by the divorce of the other, refused to help her. Finally, she took refuge in the tent of her stepfather, who was also the elder of their sub-tribe. He, however, having an interest in maintaining the friendship and support of the two *badl* husbands, limited his efforts on her behalf to trying (and failing) to persuade her husband to treat her better. Hence, the unhappy wife remained with her husband, her plight becoming hopeless once she bore him a son, whom she would have to relinquish to him if she were to obtain a divorce.[134]

One category of married woman exists in which a father is legally forbidden to intervene in his daughter's marital problems. It is that of a "bondage-wife" (*ghurra*; lit. "marked woman"), who is given as part of the blood-price to compensate a family for one of its males killed by someone of the girl's family.[135] Such a woman must remain with the husband to whom she has thus been married until she bears him a son to replace the murdered man and he lives to early puberty. In that interim, the man may treat his wife however he wants, without any interference.

By contrast to any right of men to intervene in their clanswomen's marital problems, Bedouin law grants no one other than a husband the legal right to dissolve a marriage, including the wife's father, who holds the exclusive authority to betroth her. A legal maxim stressing this point with hyperbole holds that "Even a chief cannot cause the divorce of a lowly shepherd's wife" (*mā shaykh yiṭallig marat rāʿī*).[136] The only legal exception pertains to a marriage in which the husband continuously mistreats his wife, as depicted above. Thus, the success of a father in dissolving the marriage of his daughter, despite the absence of mistreatment on the part of her husband, cannot follow from legal prescription but rather from the father's superior might.

One instance occurred within the ʿOwdāt clan of the ʿAzāzma Saraḥīn in the central Negev in 1997, when Frayj Ḥimayd as-Saddān succeeded in breaking up the marriage of his daughter, Farḥāna, to Sulaymān Swaylim Abū Bilayya, who had abducted her under his right as closest paternal cousin two years earlier (Case 26). The divorce was not achieved in pursuit of the law, however, but stemmed from the reality of the Saddān family's being stronger and more relentless than that of the Abū Bilayya. The Abū Bilayya family, committed to enabling its man to marry his designated cousin and owing to his blunder of not taking an escort along on his abscondment, found itself having to bear excessive payments for the bride-price and the fines he incurred. It also submitted to humiliations, such as the demands that it undertake to marry a then three-year-old Abū Bilayya girl to a Saddān boy when she came of marriageable age and that it even appoint a guarantor for the obligation, as if its word was not to be trusted. Moreover, the Saddān family demanded to have the obligation recorded at the Islamic *sharīʿa* court in Beersheba, to whose services the Bedouin rarely resorted. Thus, when Saddān subsequently refused to allow his daughter to return to her husband's encampment after a visit home and demanded a divorce, the Abū Bilayya were too spiritually exhausted to refuse. This all transpired despite the compatibility and happiness of the married couple and in the absence of complaint over mistreatment on the part of the wife.[137]

Finally, another limitation on the choice of a man not to divorce his wife occurs in *badl* marriages. If one of the husbands decides to divorce his wife, the coordinate husband is legally obligated to divorce his wife too. In 1972 among the ʿAzāzma ʿAṣiyāt in the central Negev, Sālim ʿOwda aṭ-Ṭimṭāwī was admittedly quite happy with his wife, Ḥusn, while his sister, Sālma, was quite miserable being married to Ḥusn's brother, Salāma, who was mentally retarded (Case 147). One day, Sālma came to her parental tent for a visit and refused to return to her husband. After a few weeks of entreating her family to send her back, the husband, in the company of some clansmen, found her at the watering spot, slapped her, took their infant son away from her, and divorced her. When news reached her brother Sālim, he divorced Ḥusn immediately. Indeed, he even slapped her in retaliation for her brother's slapping his sister. That too was within the context of equal treatment for the respective wives, which is one of the reasons for the rhyming proverbial sentiment "Exchange marriage is unjust" (*al-badl gillit ʿadl*).[138]

Property

LAND

Ownership Claims

For Bedouin, as raisers of livestock, the importance of land has traditionally been as a source of water and pasture. A tribal confederation — such as the Tarabīn, the Tiyāha, the ʿAzāzma, the Suwārka, and the Muzayna — is the group designated to provide its members access to these two resources — rhymingly called "trough and valley" (*ḥowḍ ū-rowḍ*) — within the confines of its borders, which had in most cases been cut out by warfare. Each member is supposed to have equal access to these resources according to his needs and the arrangements made between his and other tribal chiefs belonging to the same confederation. Only with the custodial confederation's permission are members of other confederations allowed to graze their herds on its pasture, compelled by drought in their own territories.[139] Indeed, the oral tradition of the Muzayna relates that when the first of the Tarabīn came to pasture their livestock in Wādī Watīr, an area of southern Sinai that the former had appropriated from their allies, the ʿAlaygāt confederation, Muzayna permission was hedged with the condition that the newcomers only "graze on dry annuals and sleep in shrub booths" (*yirtaʿū fī-l-gashsh ū-yināmū fī-l-khashsh*) — that is, they were prohibited from staying until the next winter rains sprouted fresh succulent pasture, and they had to leave their rain-proof goat-hair tents behind in their own territory to ensure that their presence was temporary (Case 100).[140]

In the case of semi-nomads like the Bedouin of Sinai and the Negev, characterized by their engagement in agriculture as well as animal husbandry, land also means areas for cultivation, marked by boundaries between one man's plot and another's, all within the borders of their tribal confederation. Initially a Bedouin belonging to the confederation would be attracted by the potential of such a plot and would legally appropriate it by a process called "stoning," which entails clearing it of stones and bushes that might impede cultivation, as well as marking its boundaries, commonly with rocks set in place or cactus or squills planted for the purpose. The privilege of cultivation was reserved for members of the confederation in whose territory the plot was found, members of other confederations being allowed to sow crops there only by specific permission. An attempt to grow crops without such permission could lead to war. In 1830, for example, when the Banī ʿAṭiyya tribe of northwestern Arabia entered the Negev in search of pasture and proceeded to sow lands east of Beersheba, the indigenous tribes, led by the Tiyāha Huzayyil, formed a fighting coalition that drove them out (Case 103). To make the prohibition on unallowed planting clear to the invaders, a poem of warning sent to them by the local tribes stressed the following:

> Before tobacco and melon, you'll meet spears of *zān*
> (*At-titin wa-l-baṭīkh dūnha khashab zān*)
> And mounts champing at the bit, tugging bridles aside!
> (*ū-khayl tigargaṭ ʿā-l-ḥasak wa-l-aʿinna*)[141]

The same prohibitions pertain to planting fruit trees and date palms. In the mid-1930s in southeast Sinai, a man called al-Aṭrash, of the Muzayna Sakhāna tribe, cut clusters of dates from a palm tree over which he claimed possession, a forefather having found it beginning to sprout in the flood course of a *wādī* near the oasis ʿAyn Umm Aḥmad and shored it up so that it could grow (Case 87). His claim to the tree, however, was rejected by the Tarabīn Ḥasāblah, in whose territory the tree stood and the early care of which they attributed to their own eighteenth-century forefather, Mughannam Slaym al-ʿUrḍī. When the case was finally adjudicated before a Muzayna judge, Jumʿa Abū Ṣabḥā, the tree was awarded to the Tarabīn claimants by dint of its location in their territory.[142]

Most problems concerning agricultural land, however, arise from conflicting claims to ownership of the same plot within the same tribal confederation. The background of such conflicts has to do with the traditional attitudes of Bedouin to agriculture. On the one hand, most of their cultivation is of winter grains — barley and wheat — the basis of 80 percent of their traditional diet.[143] The ability to supply these needs in grain by growing them themselves is felt to be a great relief, freeing them from dependence on markets and itinerant merchants whom they otherwise had to pay for their breadstuffs by bartering or selling their livestock. Accordingly, it often happened that a man migrating in search of pasture with his flocks and herds would encounter, slightly before the planting season in November or December, a stretch of land that could be utilized for cultivation; he would proceed to clear it of stones and bushes and then plant his crop. Having "stoned" the plot, he would henceforth claim it as his property.

A man might follow this procedure in various places over the years, leaving him with a number of plots scattered throughout his confederation's territory, some nearer to his summer camp, some farther. As the deserts of Sinai and the Negev, like those elsewhere in the Middle East, are subject to sporadic rainfall in time and place, the owner of a plot in an area where the rain that has fallen over a number of years is insufficient to sprout pasture for his animals will cease traveling there to cultivate, preferring to expend his labor on plots nearer to his pastures.[144]

Eventually, even after the "stoner's" lifetime, someone else may come along and find the long-unused plot, consider it (or not) to be ownerless, and sow his seeds, perhaps making improvements to facilitate his cultivation. If he stays in that vicinity, he may try to cultivate the field each year. It apparently is not rare, however, that others with some clanship contact to previous owners, seeing that the relative newcomers have improved a plot and are reaping harvests, challenge their presence in it. At that point, Bedouin law prescribes that the problem be solved by either elders of the confederation or "the people of the lands" (*ahl ad-diyār*) — that is, specialized judges in problems of landownership who are normally chosen from other confederations. The elders or judges will decide the case on the basis of either evidence, oaths, or the fire ordeal.

The testimony of neighbors—normally three, if such number are to be found—is valid if taken (in ascending order) from the closest neighbors up to the ones removed from the disputed plot by seven plots, on the assumption that such neighbors are well acquainted with the mutual borders that exist near to them. Indeed, testimony by witnesses is the preferred way of establishing a claim, as stated in the saying, "The neighbor has the right to bear witness" (*al-ḥadīd lah shihāda*).[145] In 1990 a dispute over lands in the Jūra area of northeast Sinai between a man called Abū Daʿās of the Suwārka confederation and residents of the town of El-ʿArīsh was settled by bringing in three neighbors who testified that the land belonged to the former (Case 134).[146]

In the absence of neighbors to bear witness or in the event that neighbors give contradictory evidence, the person who opens a case through his claim to ownership is asked to swear an oath or undergo the fire ordeal to establish its rightness. The relevant (and rhyming) legal maxim prescribes that "Proving ownership of land without a neighbor is by oath or by ordeal" (*ad-dār illī mā liha jār—yā yamīn, yā nār*).[147] Early in the twentieth century, for example, an oath taken by ʿAlī Ibn Khalaf of the Suwārka Manṣūriyyīn tribe established his ownership of a field in the Grāʿī area of northeast Sinai, against Ḥammād al-Gudayrī of the Suwārka Zuyūd, who had been cultivating it (Case 186). As described, Ibn Khalaf took hold of Gudayrī's belt in the presence of witnesses and swore the following:

> By God, by God, by God and by my prolific son and my pasturing livestock,
> (*W-allāhī w-allāhī w-allāhī ū-fī waladī al-fāliḥ ū-mālī as-sāriḥ*)
> This is the border of the land that I inherited from my father and grandfather.
> (*hādha hū ḥadd al-arḍ illī waratht-ha min abūwī ū-min jiddī*).[148]

As shown in the above example, it is the claimant who swears an oath in questions of land ownership, unlike in other domains of Bedouin law, where suspected wrongdoers are asked to take an oath.[149] False claimants, as persons accused of other types of wrongdoing, have been known to be sufficiently deterred by the imagined dangers of swearing a false oath as to retract their claim. One example of such recoil happened in east-central Sinai in the 1960s, when a Sālim Ṣāliḥ of the Ḥamadāt clan of the Aḥeiwāt Shawafīn, upon being told by a judge to take an oath, withdrew his claim to a field then being worked by a member of the Nijmāt clan (Case 27).[150]

Witnesses, oaths, and the ordeal by fire are also utilized in conflicts over the exact boundaries of neighboring agricultural plots. In the central Negev in

November 2004, the sons of Huwaymish al-Wajj of the Ẓullām Janabīb tribe accused ʿAliyyān aṭ-Ṭimṭāwī of the ʿAzāzma ʿAṣiyāt of changing, to the latter's advantage, the boundaries of the adjoining plots that they were plowing and that were marked by the placement of medium-sized boulders (Case 121). The accusation was based on the professed evidence of a fellow tribesman of Wajj, Ḥusayn al-Kishkhar, who claimed to have seen this violation. Ṭimṭāwī was asked, as the party accused of wrongdoing, to bring other neighbors to bear witness to the original borders. He brought Sālim Muḥammad Abū Jilaydān, also of the ʿAzāzma ʿAṣiyāt, who swore that he remembered that Ṭimṭāwī's grandfather had "stoned" and cultivated the disputed area and that he, Abū Jilaydān, was present when the original owner gave Huwaymish al-Wajj's father part of his land, as payment of a fine for wounds caused to one of the latter's clansmen, and marked the borders between him and his new neighbor at the same spot where the boulders presently stood. Through this testimony, Ṭimṭāwī succeeded in repelling the claims against him and was subsequently able to charge Kishkhar in court for defaming him.[151]

When witnesses are lacking or give conflicting evidence, the judge will ask the relevant party (the claimant regarding ownership and the accused in regard to moving boundary markers) either to swear his innocence or undergo the *bishʿa* ordeal. In 1945 in the central Negev, for example, two parties of the ʿAzāzma Saraḥīn tribe had a dispute over the position of the borders marking their respective plots (which they had appropriated from previous owners) in a *wādī* just north of the Ramon Crater (Case 128). Both plots having been long abandoned, Sālim Salīm al-Ghidayfī (the claimant) had taken that of a one-time clansman called Gāsim, while Salmān al-Kallāb (the defendant) had simply taken over the plot of a nineteenth-century figure called Abū ʿArgūb of the ʿAzāzma Faraḥīn, who had moved north in the Negev.[152] After three witnesses from each side gave contradictory evidence, the judge, Salīm Ibn Saʿad, an elder of the ʿAzāzma Saraḥīn, asked Kallāb to swear an oath, which he refused to do, demanding instead to undergo the fire ordeal at the ʿAyyādī *mubashshaʿ* in Egypt (despite the greater expenses involved). The *mubashshaʿ*, learning of Kallāb's refusal to swear an oath, designated him a wrongdoer (*midhnib*) even before he licked the red-hot iron. Accordingly, Kallāb had to pay the fees of the *mubashshaʿ* and the judge; reimburse Ghidayfī for all his expenses, including the trip to Egypt; pay him a fee for having utilized his land; restore the original border to its rightful place; and recognize Ghidayfī's right to all the territory he claimed as his.[153]

Bedouin law recognizes an individual's ownership of a plot of land regardless of whether he prepared it for cultivation himself, inherited it, purchased it, or received it as a gift. Although his rights to his plot are curbed concerning to whom he may sell it (see below), he is master of the plot in all other matters, insofar as they do not violate other aspects of Bedouin law. This individual proprietorship pertains even in disputes between members of the same clan. When, in 1948, for example, two brothers, Salmān Sālim and ʿĪd Sālim, of the Ẓullām Abū Rubayʿa tribe in the northeast Negev, disagreed over the location of the border that separated their respective inherited plots, they were acting as individual owners (Case 38).[154] Similarly in the mid-1960s in central Sinai, when a clansman of the owner of a plot at Wadeiy al-Bayḍ claimed ownership to it in light of the latter's having relocated to Jordan, his claim and the oath upon which it was to be substantiated were rejected by the judge in question (Case 27).[155]

One indication of individual ownership before the law is the right of a Bedouin owner of a plot to give part of it to whomever he wishes as a gift, called "an honoring with land" (*karam al-arḍ*). He need only mark the new boundaries and pronounce, in the presence of witnesses and guarantors, that the land henceforth belongs to the beneficiary. In the northern Negev in the nineteenth century, for example, Ḥasan ʿĪd al-Aʿsam of the Tiyāha Gudayrāt tribe made such a gift to a Bedouin called ash-Shaʿr, from the Jordanian Ḥuwayṭāt Ibn Jād tribe, out of admiration for his piety as shown by the frequent pilgrimages he made to Jerusalem through the Negev (Case 156).[156] In the same area in the early twentieth century, Sālim ʿĪd Abū Rubayʿa, chief of the Ẓullām Abū Rubayʿa tribe, gave land to the Abū ʿAyyāda family as a gift, in gratitude for its support in fighting peasants from the southern Hebron Hills in what was known as the Ẓullām-Yaṭṭa War (Case 157).[157] In east-central Sinai in the mid-1960s, ʿĪd Sālim of the Nuṣayrāt clan of the Aḥeiwāt Shawwafīn gave part of his land as a gift to his brother-in-law, ʿAliyyān Ḥamdān of the Nijmāt clan, for improving his entire plot at Wadeiy al-Bayḍ (Case 27).[158] The gift was acknowledged by the clansmen of ʿĪd Sālim who owned adjacent plots and who, when they considered selling the joint Nuṣayrāt holdings to people of the Ḥusaynāt clan, recognized a legal obligation to provide ʿAliyyān Ḥamdān with an alternative, even superior, holding.[159]

Land may also be given by its owner at will in order to discharge legal obligations. Thus, in the 1930s, in the central Negev, the aforementioned grandfather of ʿAliyyān aṭ-Ṭimṭāwī of the ʿAzāzma ʿAṣiyāt gave part of his land in Wādī Umm Iḥṣeiy to the Wajj clan of the Ẓullām Janabīb as defrayment of the fine it was owed for wounds inflicted by the former (Case 121). In the 1940s in the same region, ʿAyyāda Sulaymān Abū Bilayya of the ʿAzāzma Saraḥīn gave all his land at Rās Wādī al-ʿIjram, north of the Ramon Crater, to his clansman Ḥimayd Salmān as-Saddān as a bride-price for the latter's sister, with whom he had absconded (Case 158).[160]

The Sale of Land

Although Bedouin law recognizes individual ownership, when a Bedouin wishes to sell his own plot of land, his clansmen do have a right to interfere. They enjoy the right of preemption in such a sale in order to ensure the preservation of that property within the clan and, if neighboring on their own plots, to afford them trust and geniality with their neighbors, on the assumption that that is what can be expected from clansmen (even though experience indicates that trust does not always prevail).[161] In the 1940s among the ʿAzāzma Sarahịn in the central Negev, for example, ʿAyyāda Abū Bilayya demanded his right of preemption from his clansman Ḥimayd as-Saddān, who wished to sell the land (that he had acquired from the former as bride-price for his sister) to a nonrelated neighbor, Ḥājj Salīm Ibn Saʿad, who belonged to the Suʿūd clan of a different section of the Saraḥīn, the ʿAyāl Silmī (Case 158). Abū Bilayya owned no adjacent plot, but his right to preemption was accepted as valid so long as he fulfilled Saddān's conditions—that is, to pay him, within three days, the proceeds of three sackfuls of homegrown tobacco (*hīshī*) that he would have sold by then at the Guṣayma oasis in eastern Sinai.[162]

Another example of preemption took place in the 1930s in the northern Negev, when Jaddūaʿ al-Aʿsam of the Tiyāha Gudayrāt went into debt and, in order to extricate himself, secretly sold his father's land to a merchant from Gaza (Case 159). When the father died, the trickery was revealed, whereupon Aʿsam's brothers, each of whom was to inherit of their father's land equally, in keeping with the law, activated their right of preemption. Through litigation against their brother, the seller, they forced him to compensate them for the harvests they had forfeited until they won their case and had him effect the return of the land to them.[163] As in this case, all clansmen whose rights to preemption have been disregarded are bound by no statute of limitations from activating their claim to the sold land. Based on fresh evidence, such as newly found documents or new testimony, they can activate it at any future time. Once such a claim, initial or renewed, is accepted in litigation, moreover, the erring seller must reimburse the original buyer for the purchase price he paid, just as the judge in the above case ordered Jaddūaʿ al-Aʿsam to do.

Regarding a plot that the owner's clansmen have declined their prior right to buy, the right of preemption passes to its immediate neighbors, though not related—up to the seventh neighbor in each direction. The law stipulates that when wishing to sell such a plot, the owner must offer it to these immediate neighbors for purchase. His failure to do so entitles them to make a legal claim against him, just as in the case of clansmen. A recorded example of such a claim took place in the 1930s among the Owlād ʿAlī in the Western Desert of

Egypt (Case 160). There, a Gāsim Guwaydir claimed that a Ghāzī ʿAlī was cultivating a patch of land that was his by right, as he was the direct neighbor of a Kurayyim who had given it to a man called ʿAbd al-ʿAzīz, who sold it, in turn, to Ghāzī ʿAlī.[164]

Preemption, however, has its rules. First, the clansman or neighbor of the seller must be willing to pay the price that the seller can obtain from a different buyer; second, the buyer must make his payment by an agreed date.[165] Both these conditions, it will be remembered, were fulfilled by ʿAyyāda Abū Bilayya, who demanded preemption in purchasing the land that his kinsman Ḥimayd as-Saddān had put up for sale (Case 158). By contrast, when ʿAbd al-ʿAzīz (the seller) wanted 7 British pounds for his plot, his neighbor, Gāsim Guwaydir, agreed to buy it for that sum but failed to pay all but 2 pounds by the agreed date (Case 160). Subsequently ʿAbd al-ʿAzīz felt legally entitled to sell the plot to Ghāzī ʿAlī for 5 pounds. When the case came to litigation, the judges affirmed the ownership of Ghāzī ʿAlī, but in the interest of good neighborliness, they ordered ʿAbd al-ʿAzīz to compensate Gāsim Guwaydir the 2 pounds he had initially paid him.

The compensation in this case was made conditional on Guwaydir's guarantee that he would henceforth not reopen his claim. Similarly when Aṭrash of the Muzayna confederation, who had claimed ownership of a date palm in the territory of the Tarabīn in southeast Sinai, was paid by the latter, by court order, a quarter of an Egyptian pound as token payment for his cancellation of the claim, he guaranteed that neither he nor his offspring would activate it again (Case 87). Indeed, in order to avoid future contentions concerning the ownership of a plot of land or a tree, the legal transfer of ownership must be guaranteed. Accordingly, when people of the Tiyāha Ṣugayrāt tribe in central Sinai, during the first half of the twentieth century, sold the plots at Wadeiy al-Bayḍ (mentioned above) to the Aḥeiwāt Tiḥeitiyya, the sale was confirmed by four guarantors (Case 27).[166]

Mortgaging land is also covered in Bedouin law. In particular, when a plot is mortgaged as collateral for a debt, the creditor has the right to utilize it until the debt is paid, in keeping with the maxim, "The mortgaged land lives" (*dār ar-rahan ʿammār*).[167] Unless otherwise stipulated, there is no statute of limitations on repayment of a loan, the owner of the plot or his heirs being able to redeem their land whenever they get the sum together. On occasion, however, specific repayment dates are agreed upon, in accordance with the circumstances of the case. One particularly fertile area in east-central Sinai, the Wādī Gudayrāt, inhabited by people of the Gudayrāt section of the Tiyāha confederation, was mortgaged in the early twentieth century to merchants of the Shurafa family from the nearby oasis of Guṣayma as collateral for debts (Case 161). After the

Bedouin owners of plots there repeatedly defaulted on loans extended them by the merchants — local legend attributes their need for money to the great quantities of sugar with which they sweetened their tea, a new social drink introduced by the British rulers of Egypt — the Shurafa, by agreement, gained ownership of most of the *wādī*.[168]

LIVESTOCK

The animals that Bedouin raise come under the law in three categories: their sale, damages caused to and by them, and their theft.

The Sale of Livestock

Bedouin law aims to protect buyers of livestock from deceit and its sellers from default. If, for example, a Bedouin purchases a thoroughbred camel (measured by its having been sired by four generations of thoroughbreds of both genders) that turns out not to be purebred, he is legally entitled to return the camel and be reimbursed. This entitlement also pertains to the buyer of any camel, small stock, or dry goods whose seller neglects to apprise the buyer of its defects. The law, however, stipulates that there be witnesses to such sales who can testify in regard to the claims made by a plaintiff buyer.[169] Although commercial transactions in Bedouin areas were traditionally oral, an unfamiliar seller — of a camel in particular — could be obliged to detail his sale in writing.[170]

The law protects sellers by stipulating guarantors for buyers with insufficient funds to defray the payment of a purchase. If the buyer ultimately defaults, the guarantor must pay in his stead, and if the latter lacks the necessary cash, Bedouin law allows him to pay in small stock, after which he has the right to demand a twofold reimbursement, in cash or kind, from the delinquent. In commercial transactions between Bedouin themselves, a remiss guarantor can be held to account by the threat of "blackening" him, which constitutes a permanent blight on his reputation in Bedouin society. On occasion, a non-Bedouin merchant, who himself lacks the moral standing among Bedouin that makes blackening effective, can nonetheless resort to impoundment against the guarantor or the buyer if the opportunity presents itself. The Tarabīn Ḥasāblah of southeast Sinai relate that one of their nineteenth-century ancestors, called Imsallam al-Ḥājj, encountered in the market of Cairo a man of the Arabian Maʿāza tribe, sitting and weeping outside the shop of a merchant (Case 162). He was about to miss the returning caravan because the merchant had impounded his camel owing to a one-pound debt from the previous year. His relief came only when Imsallam al-Ḥājj offered to pay the debt himself.[171]

Through "dissolution" (*tafwīl*)—that is, the dissolving of a transaction—Bedouin law protects livestock sellers, too, from being cheated.[172] For the most part, dissolution is activated in cases of incompetent persons, especially adults of weak judgment and children, who have sold livestock for prices deemed too low or livestock that was not for sale. The principle is that "Trickery and deceit toward the helpless won't work" (*al-ghaff wa-z-zaff mā yimshin ʿala ṣaghāya*), and the role of the dissolver (*al-mufawwil*) is embedded in the legal maxim, "Deliverance and lawfulness are the elders' affair" (*al-fāyiz wa-l-jāyiz ʿend al-kibār*).[173] The law, however, insists that the elder, whether of the family or the clan, must immediately appeal the transaction before the buyer, and if the latter refuses, before a judge. The proverbial imagery for his expected haste is of "a roaring flood: by night he travels, by day he runs."[174] The time limit for seeking a dissolution is accordingly tight—sometimes three days, sometimes a week—unless it can be substantiated, through witnesses and perhaps oaths, that the dissolver only heard of the transaction after such a time but directly addressed the appeal as prescribed by the law.[175] Such mandatory haste is not only out of consideration for the buyer, who has disbursed money, but also from concern lest the sale precipitate a conflict between the respective clans. Dissolution is also exercised in order to restore a Bedouin's right of preemption, particularly in purchasing a thoroughbred camel or horse, if sold surreptitiously by a clansman to someone of another clan. In this case, as in the case of an inept sale, the buyer must be reimbursed for his abrogated purchase and compensated for any damages resulting from the dissolution.[176]

The most intricate laws pertaining to the sale of livestock are those concerning thoroughbred horses, in particular fillies. A swift filly (*faras*), viewed as a "handful of wind" (*gabḍa min ar-rīḥ*),[177] enabling a Bedouin before the twentieth century to mount surprise raids on distant camel herds, has remained a prized possession, bestowing its owner with honor and an image of daring. As pedigree is measured through the female line, the law seeks to ensure someone who would sell his thoroughbred filly the retention of its pedigree. It upholds, through the process of guaranty, a seller's right to receive, without payment, the first two female foals born to her. Bedouin call this arrangement "returned foals" (*mathānī*) and the animals returned as "the co-partner's share" (*fāyiḍa*; pl. *fawāyiḍ*).

The law also stipulates that a buyer who wishes to keep the first female foal must return the mother to the seller without recompense and provide him with his foal's first female foal. The law, moreover, prohibits the buyer from reselling the mother until the initial seller has received his first foal, and it grants the initial seller the right of preemption to repurchase the mother he once sold.

Even if he declines this right, he is nonetheless still entitled to receive from the second buyer the first female foal to be born to the mother under his possession. An initial seller of a thoroughbred filly is also protected from the neglect of his buyer during the period in which the foal he is to receive is nursing. The law stipulates that on the tenth day after the foal's birth, the buyer must bring the mother and foal to the seller for inspection by him and his witnesses. The condition of the foal at this time will provide the basis for judging its soundness after one hundred days of nursing. If, at the end of this period, the foal is found to be inferior, the seller has the right to reject it and to demand, instead, the mother's subsequent female foals (or foal, if the seller has already received one). If, however, the foal is unharmed, the seller must compensate the buyer for the efforts and expenses incurred during the nursing period. Finally, to ensure that terms of a *mathānī* sale are fulfilled in all their detail, Bedouin law forbids a buyer from selling a filly to a new buyer who lives a great distance from the initial seller before the latter receives all the *fawāyiḍ* to which he is entitled. Naturally *mathānī* sales are guaranteed under the usual rules of guaranty. Violations are tried by judges known as "people of the reins" (*ahl ar-rasān*).[178]

Damages by and to Livestock

The appetites of camels and goats are proverbial to the Bedouin. Encouraging a man to act like a leader, they tell him, "Eat voraciously like a camel and get up before the others" (*kul akl al-ijmāl ū-gūm gabl ar-rijāl*).[179] Their experience has also led them to conclude that "A migrating horde eats less than a permanent goat" (*as-salaf al-miẓʿin wala al-jidī al-magīm*).[180] The law has ignored neither this facet of desert reality nor its effect on the crops that semi-nomadic Bedouin, such as those in Sinai and the Negev, grow—wheat and barley in winter and tobacco and melons in summer—when these animals invade their sown fields. Accordingly, it rules on the damages caused, holding the owner of the herd or flock responsible. Their relevant legal maxim states, "Property [that is, livestock] does not damage property [in this case, crops]" (*māl mā biykharrib māl*);[181] thus, "The livestock's neglect is that of its owner" (*himālit al-māl min himālit ṣāḥbah*).[182] In the Negev during the 1960s, a judge, ʿAlī Salāma Abū Graynāt of the Ẓullām confederation, decreed that an Abū Ruwaydī, the owner of a flock of goats that had grazed on the crops of a fellow tribesman called al-Ghannāmī, must compensate him for all the damages that were caused (Case 124).[183] In July 2005 a similar sentence was issued by Judge Sulaymān ʿAṭeiwī al-ʿAlowna, of the Tarabīn Ḥasāblah tribe of southeast Sinai, against the brother of a shepherdess who was accused of letting her flock graze on the grown crops in her cousin's field (Case 60). In both cases, it was necessary for the claimants to provide witnesses who had actually seen the goats grazing on the crops.[184]

Bedouin call their method for gauging animal damage to crops "assessments" (*guṭʿaniyya*). If the grain is already high and can be nibbled off the top of the stalk, the owner of the field or someone acting on his behalf will tear a pod of seeds off one of the stalks, remove the husk, and count and weigh the granules inside. Then he will multiply that figure by the estimated number of stalks in the area covered by the invading animal or animals, the total being the basis for the fine. If the stalks are still short and dry, causing a scavenging animal to search for the pods, thereby crushing the stalks too, the cultivator will gather in one hand all that is left on the ground, weigh it, multiply it by five (symbolizing the mouth that ate and the four legs that trampled), and then multiply it by the estimated steps the animal or animals took inside the invaded field. This figure will be deemed tantamount to the amount of grain the area would have produced in a good year and will serve as the basis for the fine. To be legal and the grounds for litigation, the assessments procedure must be performed in the presence of witnesses and the invading animals.[185]

Bedouin law also covers damages caused to animals by other animals, under the rubric of "protecting livestock" (*ṣiyānit al-māl*). Based on the same principle of "Property does not damage property," the owner of the animal that does the damage is held responsible. Hence, in the southern Negev in the second decade of the twentieth century, a major clash between the ʿAzāzma and Saʿīdiyyīn confederations nearly erupted over the accusation that shepherds of the former had let their camel-mares pasture next to a stud camel belonging to the latter, and that this negligence led to his exhaustion (Case 21).[186] In 1974 among the Saraḥīn tribe of the ʿAzāzma themselves, a conflict between the ʿOwdāt and Rimāg clans began when a shepherd of the latter, Sulaymān Salāma ar-Rimāg, let his camels graze among the goats tended by the daughter of Ḥimayd Salmān as-Saddān (Case 43).[187] As letting camels and small stock pasture together or approach each other is considered dangerous, the employer of the negligent shepherd whose animal harms or is harmed by another animal is deemed responsible for the damages.

One major manifestation of this law is humorously related by the Farārja section of the Tarabīn Ḥasāblah tribe as a version of how it gained control of its tribal area (Case 163).

> New to southeast Sinai, now inhabited by their tribe for at least two hundred years, the members of the Farārja were fishing the coast, near a spot called Bīr Mālḥa, when they were suddenly visited by members of the ʿAlaygāt confederation, which had preceded them to the area but had long since moved westward. The guests, having come a long way, unsaddled their camels and left them free to graze in the vicinity of the tent of a Farārja elder, where he

had tethered a goat-kid he intended to slaughter for their lunch. One of the camels, nibbling at the buds of an adjacent acacia tree, however, trampled on the kid and killed it. The host, aware of the law and its determination of responsibility in cases of animal damage, demanded of the guests, in mock seriousness, his due, which he termed "the blood-money of the goat-kid" (*diyit al-jidī*), as if a human being had been killed (only human slaughter warrants a payment of blood-money). Playing along with him, the guests asked what he wanted. He replied, "Ownership of your coast." "Granted," they said, and *diyit al-jidī* has since been known as the way in which the Tarabīn in Sinai gained possession of their southeastern lands.[188]

Usually the killing of one animal by another involves camels, in particular a rutting male that attacks a she-camel. It is the Bedouin practice in these cases for the owner of the killer camel to sell it and split the money gained with the owner of the victim camel. In this way, neither loses entirely, and responsibility is assumed by the killer camel's owner, even though his camel, being "a beast that doesn't understand" (*dābba mā bitifham*), is recognized as not entirely under his control. Among the ʿAzāzma Saraḥīn in the central Negev in 1968, for example, a strident Jumʿa al-Khiraynig appropriated an untethered rutting male camel that had just bitten and killed one of his mares (Case 164). Taking up the case of Salmān al-Ghidayfi, the owner of the killer camel, Ḥimayd as-Saddān, the leader of the two contestants' tribal section, asserted that the law awarded Khiraynig only a part of the camel's sale price, to which the latter was constrained to concur.[189] By contrast, the owner of a rutting camel that he has tethered bears no responsibility for injuries caused to another's animal that approaches it.

Damages caused by persons themselves to the animals of others are naturally accountable before the law. Despite the common wisdom that "camels are for everyone" (*al'-bil li-l-jamīʿa*), reflecting the reality that neighbors often utilize each other's freely grazing camels for conveyance or riding (after which they return them), the law stipulates that riding another person's camel without his permission is forbidden and warrants a fine, whether the camel is unharmed, injured, or killed.[190] Likening the gravity of this offense to the heinous crime of dallying with another's woman, Bedouin admonish potential offenders with the saying, "Camels and girls have no companions" (*al'-bil wa-l-banāt mā ilhin ṣaḥbāt*).[191] Under the law too, injured male camels command a higher fine than do she-camels, owing to their greater ("fourfold") ability to convey loads and cover distances in less time. Accordingly, the Bedouin legal maxim stipulates that "A [harmed] male camel is worth four mares" (*in al'-jamal biyjīb arbaʿ niyāg*).[192]

Killing another's dog is also an offense before the law. Although despised for reasons of religion, dogs play a vital role in Bedouin life by "guarding the livestock and scolding approaching men" (*ḥāris al-māl ū-muʿātib ar-rijāl*).[193] Therefore, they cannot be killed with impunity. The traditional fine for the killing of a dog is about one thousand kilograms of grain—that is, the quantity needed to cover an upright stick, the length of which is equal to the space between the deceased dog's head to the end of its tail.[194] Until it is paid, moreover, the law determines that "He who killed the dog must cover all the damage" (*al-kharāb ʿāl kīs illī katal al-kalb*);[195]—that is, whatever harm the livestock subsequently suffers from wolves or whatever property is thereafter stolen must be compensated by the killer of the dog that had been protecting them. Bedouin law also imposes fines for stealing, killing, or injuring donkeys, as it is they who bring drinking water from the source to the encampment. The proverb holds that "The donkey is a tent's water channel" (*al-ḥimār ganāt al-bayt*).[196] Accordingly, in 1979 in the central Negev, the Ameiṭil clan of the ʿAzāzma ʿAṣiyāt were fined the equivalent of $150 for stabbing a donkey belonging to Swaylim Abū Bilayya of the ʿAzāzma Saraḥīn and $900 for bringing about the deaths of seven more (Case 23).[197]

THEFT

Attitudes toward Theft

One might imagine that a society lacking the agencies and infrastructure of law enforcement to protect property would be single-minded in its condemnation of theft. Bedouin society, however, is ambivalent in this regard, giving notable consideration to the motives for theft under various circumstances. For example, aware that living in the desert is impossible without camels and knowing from centuries of experience that camels are most easily and numerously acquired through pillage,[198] Bedouin—until governments finally suppressed camel raiding in the mid-twentieth century—did not view raiding upon the herds of distant tribes as a vice.[199] The perpetrators of camel raids were considered stalwarts and given a hero's welcome on their return home with the plunder.

Theft is also a means employed to deter men from raping women. As mentioned above, when a rape has taken place, the clansmen of the woman are legally entitled to pillage the livestock and kill the men of the offender's clansmen. Pillage is also employed to deter other offenses against women. For example, among the Muzayna confederation in southern Sinai in 1975, when the sons of Munayfī Sālim Jabalī attacked Sālim Jumʿa Abū Ṣabḥā in his tent at night and took hold of his wife, the victim's clansmen went out and pillaged nineteen of the invaders' camels (Case 1).[200] When the attack was finally litigated by the noted judge of honor Sulaymān al-ʿUgbī in 1976, the judge ruled the camels to have been legally taken and not to be restored to Jabalī.[201]

Bedouin law also sanctions two other categories of theft, albeit of a temporary nature, to further the implementation of the hallowed Bedouin values of justice and hospitality. The impoundment of property (*wisāga*), discussed above, is practiced as a measure toward ensuring that relatively weak parties receive justice from stronger and recalcitrant violators.[202] This goal entails stealing their property, normally camels, and depositing them with a third party until they agree to litigate the grievance against them. In regard to hospitality too, as discussed below, Bedouin law allows a person who has received guests to steal a sheep or goat from someone else's flock so as to feed the guests meat in the event that his own flock is absent in distant pastures. This practice, called "aggression" (*ʿadāya*), does not constitute borrowing (despite the legal right of the flock owner to receive compensation), as it is not consensual; it is a forcible act of theft, to which the pillaged person may not agree. In 1799, the conquest of the Negev by tribes of the Tiyāha and Tarabīn confederations from Sinai was a result, albeit indirect, of such *ʿadāya*, when the chief of the dominant Wuḥeidāt confederation took a goat from shepherdesses of the Ramaḍīn confederation who protested the theft (Case 187).[203]

Consideration of the circumstances behind a theft is manifest in other ways as well. Although the punishment for unauthorized theft is usually a fine, called *zuyūd*, which compounds the value of the stolen object, it is not unusual for owners of stolen belongings to concede the fine and be satisfied with the value of the object or the return of the object itself. This tendency is captured in the proverbial sentiment, "The fines for stolen livestock come down to their own withers [that is, the animal itself]" (*zuyūd al-māl ʿal ghawāribha*).[204] In addition to the honor gained through the practice of concession (*fawāt*),[205] an oft-expressed reason for this indulgence is the conviction that people won't steal unless they are hungry or needy, conditions with which all Bedouin are familiar.[206] Accordingly, when in 1946 fellow tribesmen of the future paramount chief of the ʿAzāzma, ʿOwda Abū Muʿammar, appropriated his coffee utensils (dispersed by a flood) and were ultimately fined four times the value of the utensils and ordered to return them, Abū Muʿammar conceded the fine and was content with the return (Case 117).[207] Similarly after Aḥmad Ibn Saʿad of the ʿAzāzma Saraḥīn stole a camel from his fellow tribesman Ḥimayd as-Saddān in 1965, fled with it to his encampment in eastern Sinai, and was fined the price of four camels (the equivalent of $1,000) when the case was tried after the Six Day War of 1967 (which renewed access between the Negev and Sinai), Saddān conceded all, settling for the return of his camel (Case 165).[208] In southern Sinai around the middle of the twentieth century, after people of the Ṭawara tribes of southern Sinai stole a pregnant camel belonging to Ḥusayn al-ʿAlowna of the Tarabīn Ḥasāblah tribe and slaughtered and ate it, they were conceded six of the eight camels they were fined, the owner retaining only two, one each for the butchered mare and the unborn calf it was bearing (Case 166).[209]

Another indication of the relative tolerance for theft in Bedouin society are the laws that relate to accusations against a suspected thief. First, the claimant must prove, primarily by witnesses, that the allegedly stolen object is his. Second, the law posits stringent provisos limiting the testimony of witnesses at trials over theft. One, as noted in chapter 5, specifies that a witness would have had to know a camel before it was stolen as well as when he saw it in the possession of the suspected thief—that is, he must have "see[n] the camel in both couching grounds"—in order for his testimony to be valid. A story from the Negev tells of such a ruling: one Bedouin saw another from the same Tarabīn confederation traveling toward Sinai with a camel bearing the brand of the ʿAzāzma confederation (Case 120). Three years later, hearing of an ʿAzāzma man whose camel had been stolen, he offered him his services—in exchange for the customary informer's fee (*akāl; see below*)—in leading him to the thief and testifying against him. The judge who ruled in the case, however, felt that the probability that the stolen camel was indeed the one seen by the witness was too slight to convict the accused thief.[210] Another story, heard among the Muzayna confederation in southeast Sinai, alludes to the scrutiny exercised by judges toward testimony proffered against a suspected thief of camels no longer in his possession (Case 118).

> Someone once stole three camels from a person and took them to a distant market, such as in Khān Yūnis, where he was seen by an acquaintance while selling them. The thief asked the man to keep their meeting a secret and offered him an Egyptian pound [the price of one camel] for his silence. However, the thief reneged on his payment, whereupon the other went to the owner of the camels and offered to testify against the former before a judge.
>
> The owner then went to the thief and accused him of stealing his camels, and the two agreed upon the judge to hear their case. The thief's condition for litigating, however, was that the witness whom the owner would bring be a person of impeccable character and not his enemy. When the thief saw who the witness was to be and realized that he could neither disqualify him on the basis of his character nor divulge the agreement he had broken with him, he had to change his argument, asserting that he was merely examining, rather than selling, the camels in question. In the presence of the judge, he asked the witness, "Did you see me unbind their fetters" (*shuftnī w-āna fakkayt ʿugūlhin*)? The witness was unable to affirm that he had, so the judge proceeded to dismiss the case, claiming lack of sufficient evidence that the accused had actually stolen the camels.[211]

Punishments for Theft

The above notwithstanding, no Bedouin enjoys being robbed, and the law accordingly seeks to prevent theft. On the most basic level, it holds a thief's entire clan ultimately responsible for rectifying his violation in the event that he absconds. The clansmen of a habitual thief may also be obliged to ensure his desistance from robbery by appointing seven guarantors, to each of whom they must pay a severe *manshad* fine for the violation of their honor if he should prove unrelenting.[212] The law also holds that "The thief has no rights" (*al-ḥarāmī mā lah ḥagg*).[213] Thus, if caught in the act, a thief may be deprived of whatever he has in his possession, including his weapon and mount. He may even be bound (which is otherwise forbidden)[214] and held for ransom, to be paid by his clansmen.[215] Accordingly, in the eighteenth century, a camel thief called Sālim al-ʿĀgir, from the ʿUmrān confederation of the eastern Wādī al-ʿAraba region, was kept bound until he was ultimately released out of mercy by his captor, an Abū Ṭrayfāt of the Ẓullām Janabīb tribe in the central Negev (Case 167).[216] Only if a thief is wounded in the course of his act does the law, always concerned to prevent bloodshed, permit his claim for damages. In the case that he is wounded, his wounds will be assessed before the fine for the camel is set. The law, however, allows the judges for theft to exercise certain discretion in imposing fines so that normally "The fines for property will neutralize the wounds" (*zuyūd al-māl yāklin dammah*) and not incur losses to the owner of the stolen object.[217]

Bedouin consider two categories of theft particularly heinous. The first pertains to stealing things that others have stored. At least as late as the second half of the twentieth century, Bedouin in Sinai and the Negev migrated seasonally,[218] and they were constrained to store utensils, implements, and especially the grain they had cultivated the previous winter in underground "burying pits" (*maṭamīr*; sing. *miṭmāra*), which they dug out for the purpose. The feeling of immunity to theft was so pervasive that the Bedouin left these deposits unguarded. In Sinai, moreover, an entire tent might be folded up and left behind, hanging from the branch of an acacia tree. It was this possibility for Bedouin to leave their cumbersome possessions untended that made migration, and hence life in the desert, practicable. Accordingly, the theft of things stored, called "stealing from the pit" (*sirgit al-miṭmāra*), threatened the very basis of Bedouin life and was considered one of the three most heinous crimes (together with fornicating with a neighbor's wife and betraying the trust of a fellow traveler).[219] In northern Sinai a judge reported imposing a fine consisting of one full-grown camel (*rabāʿ*) for opening someone's pit, two such camels for closing it, ransom for the hand that removed the grain (rather than its amputation), and four times the value of the grain taken.[220] However, the harshest punishment for such a theft is the perpetrator's loss of the right to swear an oath. As an oath taken by someone accused of violating the rights of others is a Bedouin's way of absolving himself of an accusation in the absence of evidence, the loss of that right exposes him to sentence for any accusation directed against him throughout the remainder of his life.

Similarly heavy fines are imposed to ensure the immunity of dates not yet picked from an unguarded tree. Although Bedouin sympathy for hunger allows a passerby to pick a few dates to eat on the spot (and leave the pips in place beside the sign of his camel-brand in the sand) without being considered a thief, the law severely punishes a Bedouin charged with cutting down and stealing a cluster of dates. To highlight the gravity with which such theft is perceived, a Bedouin legal maxim says, "Denuding a palm tree is like unveiling a girl" (*tafrīaʿ nakhla tafrīaʿ bint*).[221]Accordingly, the thief will be tried before a *manshad* judge, whose judgments are feared as the harshest in Bedouin law.

The second category of loathsome theft pertains to stealing things from people to whom the thief enjoys welcome access, such as a host, a neighbor, a clansman, a fellow tribesman or a member of the same confederation, and even the member of another confederation living in peace with the confederation of the thief. Such theft is called "betrayal of the couching-place" (*khōnt al-marāḥ*) and expresses the revulsion Bedouin feel for the betrayal of the trust of someone in the above intimate categories. Accordingly, as most theft naturally transpires among people with whom the thief shares relative social proximity, the most common Bedouin term for a thief is *khāyin*, which in non-Bedouin standard Arabic actually means "traitor" or "betrayer."* By contrast, the standard Arabic words for thief, *ḥarāmī* (lit. "doer of forbidden things") and *sarrāg* (lit. "stealer") are reserved for people who steal from enemies or strangers, such as wayfarers, not people included in the above categories.

Compared to the normal punishments for theft—a fine comprising the value of the stolen object normally compounded by four,[222] payment of the expenses incurred by the original owner in his efforts to obtain justice, and the return of the stolen object or its equivalent value—those for *khōnt al-marāḥ* are more severe in order to highlight its gravity. When, in 1952, a man of the ʿAtayyig clan of the ʿAzāzma Saraḥīn stole goats from the herd of ʿOwda al-Kishkhar of the Ẓullām Janabīb, who had been his host the previous night, the judge, in addition to the fourfold fine for theft, imposed, as separate punishments for the violation of hospitality, the fine of a male and a female camel and 100 Israeli pounds with each camel (Case 88).[223] In northern Sinai the dis-

*By contrast, when a Bedouin refers to an actual traitor or betrayer, he uses the noun *bāyig* (see chapter 5 for more on betrayal).

couragement of the theft of coffee utensils from a host's tent may consist of meticulous fines such as a grown camel for taking a coffee pot (a thoroughbred if the pot was knocked down and thus dishonored); a three-year-old camel for each cup taken (a full-grown camel for each one that is knocked down); two grown camels for extending the hand that would steal, and one such camel for withdrawing the hand that held the object.[224]

The theft of a guest by his host is also viewed with gravity. One past judge, hearing the claim made by the owner of a *ghalyūn* pipe stolen by his host, awarded him a female and a grown male camel, the former to compensate for the guest's longing to inhale and the latter for his lost pleasure of exhaling.[225] The concern for honor and dignity, the retention of which is to be observed even in the stealing of coffee utensils, as cited above, manifests itself too when judges impose severe punishments for the theft of a person's needle, often carried with him or her for immediately mending or fastening an outer garment in the event of a tear or rip.[226]

As in the case of a wounded thief, as noted above, the law empowers judges to stiffen punishments for theft by allowing them to exercise discretion. The most notable practice is to impose a fine for each step—for example, "from the place he [the thief] left to the place he came to" (*min mimshāh ila majāh*), "from its [an animal's] pasture to the place it was hid" (*min maflāha ila makhfāha*), or "from its pasture to where it was couched" (*min maflāḥa ila mankhāha*)[227]—the judge also being free to determine the size of this fine for each step. It can thus come to a sizable total. When, in 1952, as depicted above (Case 88), an al-ʿAtayyig stole goats from his host, ʿOwda al-Kishkhar, he was fined twenty piastres for each step taken "from their pasture to the market" (*min maflāhin ila mabāʿhin*), a distance of 50,000 meters, or steps, worth 10,000 Israeli pounds (approximately $3,000 at the time).[228] If the thief belongs to the same encampment as his victim, the number of steps is determined by someone sitting at the entrance of the tent in question and "throwing a stick" (*garṭ al-ʿaṣa*) with his arms outstretched. The number of steps subsequently needed to cover the distance from the spot where the stick lands (deemed the border of the tent's precinct) to the tent's entrance becomes the basis for the fine, often one full-grown camel for each step.[229] The severity of this punishment was designed to deter theft among neighbors so that Bedouin could migrate and camp with security for their belongings, wherever grazing conditions allowed.

If a case of theft gets to litigation, the person claiming to have been robbed must verify his claim through witnesses, whereas the accused has recourse to an oath to substantiate his innocence. Where camels have been stolen, witnesses may offer their evidence for a fee, called "feeding the witness" (*akāl ash-shāhid* or *ṭiʿmit ash-shāhid*), the amount of which is agreed to by the witness and camel owner. In 1982 in eastern Sinai, when Salīm Warrād al-Lijnān told Ḥimayd Salmān as-Saddān of the ʿAzāzma Saraḥīn that his missing she-camel and foal had been stolen by a fellow tribesman of the Tiyāha, an Ibn Daybis, he was paid a fee of $1,000 (Case 168).[230] If the claimant wins the case, the accused repays him this fee in addition to the other punishments imposed by the judge. If the claimant loses, the witness bears the responsibility for paying the judge's fee; and if the witness reneges on his pledge to testify, he may be tried by the claimant for compensation for the judge's fee and any fines incurred for having dishonored the defendant. In the aforementioned case (Case 168), the reinstitution of the Israeli-Egyptian pre-1967 border in April 1982, denying mutual access to the ʿAzāzma and Tiyāha in question, left the camel theft unresolved.

If someone is found with a camel or other object that has been stolen, he is either asked to swear to his innocence by taking an oath or his clan may be asked to swear in his place, his own oath not being trusted. Such skepticism is reflected in the saying, "As a thief is perfidious, he'll surely swear." An option to the oath is his undergoing the *bishʿa* ordeal, which the Bedouin consider daunting. In 1946 among the ʿAzāzma, when ʿOwda Abū Muʿammar demanded that people who appropriated the coffee utensils he had lost in a flood "lick the fire" to establish their innocence, they directly confessed their crime (Case 117).[231] If, however, a person accused of theft can prove that he unwittingly bought a stolen object, the seller—whether the thief or a merchant in collusion with him—must compensate him and stand trial for theft, while the buyer has no further legal obligation other than to return the object to its original owner.

INHERITANCE

Clansmen Inherit

Property inheres in the Bedouin clan and is viewed as a source of its strength. Hence, inheritance transpires within the male line of a man who dies, always according to blood proximity. If he has living sons, they alone inherit his total wealth. This principle is affirmed in the legal maxim, "There is no heir after the son" (*mā baʿd al-walad warīth*), and is reaffirmed by another maxim: "He who inherits inherits, you can't hold him to account" (*al-wārith wārith—lā tiḥāsbah*).[232] Those who inherit do so on a basis of equality, none of the heirs possessing any rights to the property not possessed by the others; if this rule is violated, the others can legally rectify it. In the 1930s, for example, Jaddūaʿ al-Aʿsam of the Tiyāha Gudayrāt in the northern Negev secretly sold his father's land to a merchant from Gaza (Case 159). When the father died, the trickery was revealed, whereupon Aʿsam's brothers, each of whom was to inherit of their father's land equally, challenged the sale. Through litigation, they forced their wayward brother to effect the return to them of their inherited land.[233] The only exception to this principle pertains to the tent and its appurtenances. In the event that a man leaves one or more minor sons, who will be brought up by their mother in the tent of their father, the youngest will ultimately inherit it, in keeping with the maxim, "The youngest son takes charge of his father's tent" (*aṣ-ṣaghīr wilī ʿala dār abūh*).[234]

Normally, as the Bedouin themselves say, "If there is no son, the brother's son gets the inheritance" (*iza mā fīh walad, ibn akhūh owla bi-l-wirtha*), meaning that the sons of all a man's brothers are next in line to inherit him if he is without male offspring.[235] This dictum, however, ignores one situation, albeit rare, of a man whose sons have died before him but left male children. It is these grandchildren, as the direct descendants of their grandfather, who will inherit him, rather than his brothers' sons. One of the latter may manage the children's legacy until they have reached maturity but will have no share in it except for the expenses incurred on behalf of the wards. Similarly, if the deceased leaves neither sons nor grandsons, and the sons of his brothers, his heirs, are still children, their father will manage their legacy until they have reached maturity. Such a situation pertained in the 1940s with the future chief of the Tiyāha Gudayrāt aṣ-Ṣāniʿ tribe, Ḥasan Ibrahīm aṣ-Ṣāniʿ (Case 169).[236]

The next in line to inherit the total wealth of a deceased man—after his sons, grandsons through deceased sons, and the sons of his brothers or their male children if all are deceased—are the sons of his first paternal cousins. In the absence of these, the heirs must successively be sought one more degree removed from the deceased. The Bedouin saying, "There is no tree without roots" (*mā shajara ila ilha ʿurūg*), indicates the belief that someone with a blood connection through the male line to the deceased will ultimately be found, even if he is no longer in the same clan.[237] Indeed, a legal maxim exists to the effect that "He who inherits from the outside [that is, one who is no longer of the clan] is an heir" (*mitwarrith min barra hū warīth*).[238]

Women Do Not Inherit

According to Bedouin law, daughters, sisters, and wives do not inherit money, livestock, or land from a man or a woman (except that daughters inherit their mother's jewelry and personal belongings). In 1961 a man of the Tiyāha al-Afinish tribe in the northern Negev accused his sister of taking money that their deceased mother had hidden, as she had no right to it (Case 58). The offense seemed to him so grave that he made her swear an oath at the tomb of a holy man to establish her innocence.[239] Similarly, as "land belongs to the men" (*al-arḍ li-z-zlām*), when a man dies, "his land is like a widow that returns to her kin" (*ad-dār armala ū-thannat l-ahal-ha*), an allusion to the general practice of young widows rejoining their paternal family to be remarried.[240] In other words, a man's wife or daughters have no right to his land. Accordingly, in 1949, when Mishrif al-Bagīaʿ of the Tarabīn aṣ-Ṣāniʿ in the northwest Negev died and his wife and daughter began tilling his land, his brothers came and drove them off the land, which they then divided among themselves (Case 170).[241] Also, when Sālim al-ʿUwaywī of the ʿAzāzma ʿAṣiyāt in the central Negev died in the 1950s, his land went to a distant clansman, Ṣubḥī al-ʿUwaywī, rather than to his daughter, Uẓʿeina (Case 171).[242]

The only right a widow has in this regard is to stay in her deceased husband's tent and manage his livestock and land for the welfare of their minor children if these include males. After that, she may stay by leave of the son who adopts his father's tent as his own family's future home. Such was the case of a woman called Faḍiyya, who personally supported her son Sālim and his siblings from the land and flock of her deceased husband, Sulaymān Abū Gardūd of the ʿAzāzma ʿAṣiyāt in the 1980s (Case 172).[243] On the other hand, if the widow's only children still with her are girls—as was the case of the widow of Mishrif al-Bagīaʿ, mentioned above (Case 170)—she has no right to stay on, but she may stay by the de facto leave of her late husband's clansmen. In any case, two legal conditions govern the right of a widow to remain on her late husband's land. One is that "A woman cannot hand over land to anyone else" (*wiliyya mā tiwallī al-arḍ ila wāḥad thānī*);[244] the second is that she must remain unmarried. The fear behind this second restriction is that if a woman remarries, her new husband, from a different clan, might seek rights to the land his wife is tilling. If she marries one of her deceased husband's clansmen, the law understands that the question would be resolved by her moving to her new husband's tent and plot.

In return for their deprivation in inheritance, the daughters of a deceased man are legally entitled to be supported and married off by their brothers or other heirs of their father's estate. In this way, the future wife (as well as cousin) of Ḥasan Ibrahīm aṣ-Ṣāniʿ of the Tiyāha Gudayrāt of the northern Negev was raised by her paternal uncle, Ibrahīm, after her father died without sons and his estate was designated to Ḥasan and his male siblings (Case 169).[245] If denied this support, a bereaved daughter may litigate against her guardian, but only if she manages to obtain the protection of some prominent man to take up her cause.*

*The claim by al-ʿĀrif (*al-Qadāʾ*, p. 125) that proven neglect by the heirs might lead a judge to award the daughters money, livestock, and land from their father's estate was not endorsed by the various Bedouin I consulted. They felt that the judge's rulings against the guardian could be adequately enforced through guaranty, rendering a change in the laws of inheritance unnecessary.

LOANS

Bedouin law establishes that when one Bedouin borrows money from another, it must be paid back on time and in full, in the same way that a fine imposed upon him by a judge or through mediation must be paid. There are two legal maxims in this regard: "A debt is to be paid in full, just as a grave is to be filled" (*mā li-dayn ila wafāh—ū-mā li-gabr ila malāh*), and "Every sum that's fixed must be returned" (*kull maḥdūd mardūd*).[246]

Bedouin law considers loans a personal matter, not requiring the agreement of the borrower's clansmen. The clansmen, however, are responsible to the lender in the event of default. The legal maxim instructs, "What's left unpaid is the responsibility of his clan" (*al-mitibaggī ʿal khamsitah*).[247] Indeed, even reciprocity exists between clans concerning loans. Thus, in 1999 among the ʿAzāzma Saraḥīn in the central Negev and eastern Sinai, Sālim Salāma ar-Rimāg of the Rimāg clan, who owed money to ʿOwda Ibn Saʿad of the Suʿūd clan, demanded that his debt be neutralized on the basis of a debt owned to him by a man called Braym, whom he believed had joined the Suʿūd (Case 34). It was only when a delegation that crossed the border into Sinai clarified that Braym had never joined the Suʿūd that Rimāg's claim of reciprocity was rejected.[248]

As with fines, the best way to ensure repayment of a loan is through a guarantor, owing to the pressure that he himself can, and must, exert on the borrower, lest he, the guarantor, be defamed.[249] Experience has coined the Bedouin proverb, "Money without a bedrock will not arrive" (*māl bidūn magraʿ ma biyījī*).[250] If a loan is not guaranteed, a witness present at the time of its being made will also be useful in subsequent litigation over default. Similarly a witness may be useful to a borrower when he repays the debt, in the event that the repayment is denied or doubted by the lender. An example of the absence of a witness being harmful took place in 1938 among the Ẓullām confederation in the northern Negev, when the claim of Salāma Abū Graynāt that he had paid a debt owed to ʿĪd as-Sareiʿa through the latter's son (Case 12) was rejected.[251] In this case, Sareiʿa's rejection was instructed by the legal principle, conceived to reduce complications over loans, that they be directly repaid to the persons to whom they are owed. The principle is called "the hand and what it handed over" (*al-yad ū-mā sallamat*).[252] In the end, Sarei'a lost the case, but only because he used violence before checking the veracity of Abū Graynāt's claim.

Sanctuary (Ṣiyānit al-Bayt)

THE INVIOLABILITY OF A TENT

In Bedouin law and culture, a tent is more than the mobile shelter of a nomadic family. In an often contentious society, the tent is a sanctuary where strangers, as well as the tent's dwellers, are assured safety from aggression. A Bedouin saying asserts that "Tents save people's lives" (*al-bayt biysallim ar-rigāb*).[253] Such sanctuary is essential to the existence of Bedouin society, ensuring that people have a safe place to meet and gather and to pursue their rights without the threat of harm. Alluding to its inviolability, a Bedouin sentiment proclaims, "The tent is a place of awe" (*al-bayt lah heiba*).[254] Consequently any violation of "the right of a tent" (*ḥagg al-bayt*—that is, its right to sanctuary and nonaggression) is heavily punished. According to experienced judges and other knowledgeable Bedouin, the various fines may range, depending on the gravity of the violation, from two camels each for "entrance and exit" (*khashsh ū-ṭāliʿ*), as in the case of theft;[255] to two camels for each of forty steps from the tent to the outer limits of its legal precincts in four directions, totaling 320 camels;[256] and to fines for each tent pole, rope, and pin that fastens the surrounding curtain to the roof, totaling even greater sums.[257]

Deriving from the role of a tent as sanctuary, much of its owner's honor depends on his maintenance of its reputation for such. The Bedouin thus say, "The tent confers honor—even the tent of a widow" (*al-maʿazza min al-bayt—lō bayt armala*)[258]—that is, even the tent of someone who has no power to protect its reputation for inviolability. Accordingly, Bedouin are zealous to retain their tents' good reputation, even in matters that may seem trivial to a non-Bedouin. In 1979, for example, Sulaymān ʿAliyyān al-Guṣayyir, the paramount chief of the Aḥeiwāt Shawafīn confederation in eastern Sinai, expelled fellow tribesmen of the Nuṣayrāt clan from his tent lest they shame it by conspiring there to secretly sell land to non-clansmen, a scheme that would deny their own clansmen the legal right of preemption (Case 27).[259]

Another example of concern for the good reputation of a tent (in this case a house) took place in November 1999 in the town of El-ʿArīsh (Case 173).

> Ḥamd Muṣliḥ Ibn ʿĀmir of the Tiyāha Ṣugayrāt tribe brought a man, ʿAbd ar-Rahmān Imsallam Abū Nīfa of the Tarabīn Shibaythāt, to trial for entering his house under false pretenses that could dishonor it. Abū Nīfa's aim was to tryst with a woman of the Muzayna Sakhāna, for which he had announced himself as her clansman, though he was from a totally different confederation. Ibn ʿĀmir, having allowed the woman (whose uncle was in the process of buying the house) to stay in it, had become her host and, thereby, also the warden of her sexual propriety and the guardian of her physical welfare on

behalf of her family. Spotting Abū Nīfa sitting beside and dallying with the woman, which was a violation of her family's honor and an act of aggression against the family, Ibn ʿĀmir feared that the good reputation of his house was threatened. At the Bedouin trial over this violation of "the right of the tent," the judge, Sulaymān Nāfiʿ of the Tiyāha Shitayyāt, imposed on Abū Nīfa a fine of forty camels and ordered him to fly a white flag beside Ibn ʿĀmir's house to restore its honor symbolically.[260]

Bedouin concern for the sanctuary of a tent is also manifest in accounts current among them telling of hosts who even desisted from taking revenge on guests who had killed their clansmen, once these guests had entered their tents. One widespread story in the Negev, for example, relates that in the 1870s Dahshān Ṣagr Abū Sitta killed Muḥammad Ḥamdān aṣ-Ṣūfī, a rival leader of the Tarabīn confederation, and took refuge from revenge among the distant Tiyāha ʿAlamāt (Case 109). After some time, however, late one night he and a clansman stealthily returned to Tarabīn territory, where they unknowingly entered the tent of the murdered man's brother, Ḥimayd Ḥamdān aṣ- Ṣūfī. When the fire in the tent was lit for preparing coffee for the guests, in accordance with custom, the adversaries recognized each other. Before Abū Sitta found need to act so as to save his life, Ṣūfī, unwilling to take revenge in his own tent, bolted to the women's section, as if to declare, "Consider me a woman, who does not take revenge." This gave Abū Sitta and his clansman a chance to flee.[261]

Likewise, in the 1950s among the Tiyāha Gudayrāt of the northern Negev, a man was sitting as a guest in a tent of the ʿUthmān (pronounced ʿUsmān) section when news came that one of his clansmen had murdered a man of his host's clan (Case 174). Several lads of that clan, present when the news arrived, immediately leapt forward to kill the guest in instant revenge but were stopped by the host, Muḥammad Sālim al-Aʿsam, who sternly warned them not to perpetrate an act of revenge in his tent. The guest was thereby allowed to leave, deferring the vengeance. To the relief of the host, his honor was maintained, and, to the relief of all, fresh news soon arrived reversing the initial report.[262] Again, among the Ẓullām Janabīb in the central Negev in 1986, a year after someone of the Wujūj clan had killed a man of the Kishkhar clan, a neutral party, in an attempt to gain them reprieve, brought clansmen of the killer, Miẓʿān al-Wajj, to the tent of the elder, Hilayyil al-Kishkhar, saying, "Behold, I have brought you your revenge" (*jibtak as-sadād*) (Case 47). Kishkhar replied, "I don't take revenge in my tent" (*mānī mistadd fī baytī*).[263]

THE TENT-OWNER'S RESPONSIBILITY

Preventing Violence against Persons in a Tent

Beyond the moral and social importance accorded the sanctuary of a tent, Bedouin law, too, endorses it primarily by holding the tent owner (*rāʿī al-bayt*) responsible for the safety of his guest and ward. First, the law orders him to try to prevent harm from befalling that person in the first place. This injunction is reflected in the legal directive, "Defend a guest if he's done good or done bad; keep the violator at bay or pay for his faults" (*aḍ-ḍeif, ḥāmīh bi-khayrah ū-bi-sharrah—yā tilimmah yā tishīl khaṭāh*).[264] Defending a guest or ward may mean keeping assailants away from their intended victim through admonitions, especially if they are still outside the tent. Such was the means chosen, for example, in 1899 by a tent owner about whom the Czech scholar Alois Musil reported from the Syrian desert (Case 177).

> During a bloody attack by men of the Transjordanian Ḥuwayṭāt on a camp of the ʿAneza Sibāʿa, one of the attackers, having killed a lad of the encampment and seeing his retreat blocked, rode his horse close to the tents, leapt into one of them, belonging to a man called Rushayd Ibn Masrab, and asked for protection. As Ibn Masrab at that moment was away fighting off the attackers, his daughter shouted instantly to the pursuers, "Stand still! There is a tent before you. He is our protégé." Then, when her father finally arrived, he too posted himself in front of his tent, liberating the Ḥuwayṭī from the enraged crowd. Even after the grandfather of the slain lad, learning that the killer was in Ibn Masrab's tent, came and offered him twenty camels to turn the protégé over, the latter stood his ground, pleading, "Wouldst thou tarnish my tent, so that I should become an object of contempt?"[265]

Also in the late nineteenth century, but in the Negev, the chief of the Tarabīn Wuḥeidāt tribe, Fāris ʿĪsa al-Wuḥeidī, tried to keep Turkish troops, coming from Beersheba, from remanding an escaped Bedouin prisoner who sought shelter in his tent (Case 78). The Turks demanded that he yield the fugitive, but he refused. The troops then dismounted, intending to enter his tent, whereupon the chief lifted his rifle and shot. When the din and dust settled, everyone was startled to see the beloved filly of the chief lying dead where she'd been tethered near the opening of the tent. The officer asked, "What's the meaning of that?" and was answered by an old man who said, "The chief has just killed what was most dear to him and has nothing more to lose. Look out!" According to the tribal rendition, the troops thereupon left without their man.[266]

In both the above cases, the owner of the tent put his life at risk for the safety of his guests, in keeping with the legal directive, "You will die in front of the one you're protecting" (*inti timūt guddām dakhīlak*).[267] Pursuers in such cases, however, also know that according to the law, if they ignore the tent owner's admonitions and invade his tent, he or his kinsmen have the right to kill them, and to do so without fear of revenge, just as there is no revenge for fornicators or rapists killed in a tent.[268] By the same token, in the event that the invaders raise any claim in court for blood-damages, it will be outweighed by the countervailing claim for their violation of the tent. Furthermore, if pursuers refuse to stop at the entrance to a tent, enter it, and actually murder the tent owner, they become subject to revenge for the murder they have committed in addition to their liability for the violation of the tent.

A tent owner is also legally responsible for protecting a guest or ward from harm by persons who have entered the tent either innocently or by subterfuge. For example, if violence breaks out among guests, the law expects the tent owner or the male members of his family to try to separate the adversaries, even by force if needed. Or if a tent owner observes that a quarrel between guests in his tent may lead to violence, he should try to remove them from his premises by uttering standard admonitions, such as, "The plain is wide" (*al-gāʿa wasīʿa*),[269] as if to say, "There is room for your problems elsewhere; take them outside this tent." The law allows this expulsion of persons from the tent, even overriding the normative injunction against turning guests away, as expressed in the metaphorical saying, "No one snarls at a guest but a dog" (*mā biyhirr aḍ-ḍeif ghayr al-kalb*).[270] The law similarly permits a host to prevent violence by denying a prospective guest entrance to his tent until the latter's adversary, already there when he arrives, has finished eating and drinking and takes his leave. This happened among the ʿAzāzma Saraḥīn in the central Negev in 1974, when ʿAyyāda Sulaymān Abū Bilayya came to greet ʿĪd Swaylim al-Ḥawaṣa in his tent on the occasion of the post-Ramaḍān holiday, ʿĪd al-Fiṭr (Case 43). The host saw Abū Bilayya approach and knew that his clan was in a state of hostility with that of Hilayyil ar-Rimāg, a guest who was already seated with him; thus he rose, exited the tent, and asked Abū Bilayya kindly to wait at some distance until Rimāg had left.[271]

Had Rimāg formally been Ḥawaṣa's protégé (*dakhīl*), Ḥawaṣa would have had to be doubly on the alert. Although the Bedouin ethos, as mentioned above, instructs that anyone coming to a tent is to be automatically welcomed and admitted with no questions asked,[272] a tent owner, once he has taken the responsibility for a ward, must keep him safe by screening other comers, lest one be the ward's enemy. In the case of a ward who is liable to blood-revenge, this scrutiny concerns the entire encampment of the protector. All its residents are legally bound to question any outsiders they meet in its precincts in order to ascertain their objectives. Hence, in 1953, when a murder occurred among the Tarabīn living in the western Negev, the "blood-stained" (*madmiyyīn*) took refuge among the ʿAzāzma Ṣubḥiyyīn, who were encamped only four kilometers to the east (Case 178). The alertness of the protectors and their furtiveness concerning their protégés enabled the latter to live among them undetected by their enemies for eight years.[273]

Again, in the mid-1970s, when murder took place within the Ẓullām confederation in the northern Negev, the killers received the protection of the elder of the ʿAzāzma Saraḥīn, ʿOwda Sulaymān az-Zanūn, with whom they stayed for five years (Case 179). So rigorous were all the members of the protecting encampment, near the Nabatean ruins of Sibayṭa in the central Negev, that the avengers, of the Ṣabāḥ clan, were intimidated from approaching their area. Even years later, local Bedouin recalled their terse warnings, such as, "Get lost or you'll lose your heads! Fly away!" (*baḍiyaʿ ū-baḍāyaʿ rūskū—ṭīr*).[274]

Restoring the Rights of a Violated Guest or Ward

According to Bedouin law, even an inadvertent guest is entitled to the sanctuary of a tent, and a tent owner's responsibility for his safety and property is no less than for those of a ward—that is, someone to whom he has deliberately extended protection (*dakhāla*). They are legally the same. Hence, if either is physically harmed or verbally offended by another stranger to the tent, the law stipulates that "A host gets his own right and demands the right of a guest" (*rāʿī al-bayt yākhidh ḥagg ū-yuṭlub ḥagg*)—that is, he is not only entitled to a legal award for the violated right of his tent, as seen above, but must also act so that his guest-victim, who has been wounded, insulted, or otherwise violated, receives his rights too.[275] Thus, in 1978, when Salāma Ḥusayn az-Zimaylī of the Aḥeiwāt Shawafīn confederation in east-central Sinai learned that the sanctuary of his tent had been violated when, in his absence, his nephew had beaten his wife in it, he brought the young man to justice, achieving for the woman two grown camels (a male and a female) and the appraisal of her wounds as she herself described them, to be fined twofold, having been inflicted in a tent not the couple's own (Case 57).[276] All awards for harm incurred from aggression in a tent are evaluated twofold.

If a tent owner fails to fulfill this legal obligation, the guest or ward can have him heavily fined by a *manshad* court, just as if he were a derelict guarantor, as Bedouin law requires him to guarantee the safety of those in his tent. In 1977, for example, among the Aḥeiwāt confederation of east-central Sinai, Sālim ʿAlī al-Guṣayyir, who had been insulted in the tent of Jumʿa Ibn Kureidim, succeeded in motivating his apathetic host to secure his rights from the man who had violated him only by threatening to initiate legal proceedings against him as an inadequate (*gāṣir*) host (Case 106).[277] Fear of the resultant heavy fines or, alternatively, the legal possibility of having his reputation dishonored by a cairn of blackened stones—such as may be erected by neglected guests to attract attention and queries at a much-frequented well or crossroad—serves to discourage a tent owner from risking being deemed inadequate.

While the rights that a tent owner restores to the violated stranger in his tent are often obtained through litigation, other ways exist as well. For example, a tent owner must see to the replacement of anything stolen from either the guest or the ward, especially if they are of a different tribe from his. Assuming that a tent owner is familiar with all the persons in his own tribe, to which the thief likely belongs, the law stipulates that he either retrieve the stolen item from the latter or replace it himself. If he fails to comply with the law, he will be liable to the accusation of being an inadequate host and suffer the attendant fines and dishonoring. Only by taking an oath that he has no knowledge of the thief or the whereabouts of the object can he gain legal reprieve from his responsibility.

Bedouin law also holds a host responsible for the protection of guests in particular, not only while they are within the legal precincts of his tent (forty paces from the edge of the tent roof in each direction), but also for a subsequent three and a third days after their departure (or, alternatively, until they reach another tent). The responsibility during these additional three and a third days, however, is conditional on a departed person's announcing to an aggressor, such as a thief, that he is under the protection of his erstwhile host. An example of the rigidity of the law in this regard took place in the northern Negev in the late nineteenth century. When a member of the Transjordanian Ḥuwayṭāt Tuwayha, ʿAlī Bin Miṣabbiḥ, was pillaged two days after leaving the tent of Sulaymān al-Asad of the Tiyāha Ḥukūk, he realized that he had forfeited his legal right to engage the latter's help in retrieving his lost herd because he had not managed to declare that he was under Asad's protection (Case 180). However, recalling yet another law of hospitality—namely, that anything left by a guest in the tent of his host is tantamount to his own presence there—he resorted to a subterfuge. He returned to Asad's tent and surreptitiously slipped his rifle under the curtain that separated the women's from the men's section of the tent, where he had been sitting. When Asad himself came to the tent, Bin Miṣabbiḥ proclaimed that he had returned to collect the forgotten firearm he purportedly had left behind and informed his host what had befallen his camels. Aware of his obligation, Asad went to the pillagers and forced them to surrender their plunder.[278]

Other accounts also circulate among the Bedouin of cases in which tent owners, in efforts to preserve their honor, have used force to retrieve the violated right of a ward or guest. In the late nineteenth century, for example,

Ibrahīm Salāma ʿAzzām al-Huzayyil of the Tiyāha Ḥukūk in the northern Negev gave protection to a Bedouin of the Banī Ṣakhr confederation of Transjordan, ʿAlī al-Khureisha, who had fled from enemies in his own tribe (Case 175). Other enemies, of the Ḥuwayṭāt Maṭālga, however, while camel raiding in the Negev, pillaged Khureisha's camels at pasture. Huzayyil thereupon went after them, retook the camels, and even killed their leader, Ḥamd Bin Dhiyāb.[279] Being Huzayyil's ward, Khureisha, his property, and his safety were under Huzayyil's protection, even outside his immediate tent. Apparently, however, although Huzayyil was duty-bound to restore Khureisha's right of property, he did not possess a legal right to kill the head of the raiding party, Bin Dhiyāb. Consequently the Huzayyil felt that revenge against them was legally in order, and it was only averted by a *ḥisnī* agreement they concluded whereby the Ḥuwayṭāt would be considered benefactors of the Huzayyil, and the Huzayyil would henceforth aid them in regaining any camels that the Tiyāha Ḥukūk, the sub-confederation to whom the Huzayyil belonged, later pillaged from them. The agreement prevailed until 1948.[280]

Another example of restoring by force the rights of a guest, occurred in southeast Sinai in the late 1940s. ʿAnayz Sālim al-ʿUrḍī of the Tarabīn Ḥasāblah invited a man of the Aḥeiwāt Ḥammadāt, called aṭ-Ṭawīl, to be his guest at a celebration of a Tarabīn pilgrimage to the grave of one of their ancestors, Ḥimayd, at Nuwaybaʿ, on the coast of the Gulf of ʿAqaba (Case 176). Ṭawīl, who lived at the northern end of the gulf, came to Nuwaybaʿ in the small boat of a man of the Muzayna Sakhāna, the immediate neighbors of the Tarabīn to the south. When the boat arrived, the navigator immediately sent word to fellow tribesmen that Ṭawīl, who had beaten them up a few years earlier when they were fishing the coast in Aḥeiwāt territory, was now nearby. They thereupon hastened to attack him before he reached the festivities, inflicting several knife wounds upon him. Hearing of this attack on his guest, ʿAnayz al-ʿUrḍī immediately mounted a camel and raced after the attackers, whom he shot to kill.[281] Although the attack on Ṭawīl did not take place in ʿUrḍī's tent or its inclusive precincts, the fact that Ṭawīl was a guest from a different tribal confederation made all Tarabīn territory in southeast Sinai his sanctuary from harm.

This story, however, as the previous one, also suggests that wielding force as a first resort to restore a guest's right may not be sanctioned by the law. As told to me, the Tarabīn, fearing that ʿUrḍī had actually killed one or both of the Muzayna attackers, packed up and fled to the nearby mountains to escape revenge. Had ʿUrḍī's resort to force been his legal right, his supposed killing of his guest's assailants (which turned out not to be the case) would have been with impunity, thus obviating the need of the Tarabīn to fear and flee from revenge.

BLOOD-REVENGE IN A TENT: A VIOLATION OF SANCTUARY?

The one issue concerning the rights of a tent that is clouded by legal ambivalence is whether the tent has any right when a *madmī*, or person liable for blood-revenge, is killed in vengeance inside it or its precincts. On the one hand, there are Bedouin who claim that a blood-avenger is subject to no penalty for violating the right of a tent if he manages to get inside and kill the person subject to his revenge. In other words, so long as he has not deliberately ignored the admonitions of the tent owner and entered the tent by force, he will not have violated the right of the tent and will not become subject to fines or even murder on the spot. As depicted by a judge of the ʿAzāzma Masʿūdiyyīn, Salmān Ibn Ḥammād, "An avenger that manages to enter the tent—crouch, for example, by the 'side tent pole' (*ʿāmir al-bayt*)—and shoot his *madmī*, who is having dinner inside, has not violated the tent."[282] Bedouin holding this view argue that blood-revenge is a right in itself and therefore must not be considered aggression. They proffer, in support of this position, the license given by the legal maxim, "The blood-avenger may be bold, whether by day or by night" (*ṣāḥib ad-damm jassār—layl ū-nahār*),[283] even though the maxim does not expressly justify violating a tent. Still, as blood-revenge is so cardinal an element in Bedouin life and law, this attitude cannot be lightly dismissed. Moreover, examples of its application exist. Among the ʿAzāzma confederation in the Negev, for instance, it is recalled that in the 1950s, a man called Musayfir Umm Kharbūsh, from the Abū Shiyyāḥ section of the ʿAzāzma Muḥammadiyyīn, murdered a man from another section of that tribe, thereupon fleeing from revenge and taking refuge among people of the Ẓullām confederation (Case 181). Although the avengers eventually came and shot him in the tent of his protector, the latter made no claim to compensation for violation of the tent.[284]

At least partial additional support of this view that vengeance taken in a tent is not liable to penalty for violation of that tent comes from the Bedouin consensus that a *madmī* ward killed beyond the precincts of his protector's tent entitles the latter to no claim to the violation of his tent. In the 1920s, for example, a leader of the ʿAzāzma Zaraba tribe called Abū Huwayshil gave protection to a man of the ʿAzāzma Ṣubḥiyyīn who had killed a fellow tribesman (Case 182). One day, in a show of bravado, Abū Huwayshil took the man with him to the market in Beersheba. On the way, they passed near to one of the avengers, sitting by the path, eating half a watermelon, his face covered with its juice. The ward said, "There's my enemy!" But Abū Huwayshil ignored his alarm saying, within earshot of the man, "Look at him eating; he's nothing but a fool." On their return, however, the avenger, who meanwhile had fetched a rifle, laid ambush to them near the Turkish bridge in Wadi Beersheba, calling to

Abū Huwayshil to keep away because he was taking revenge on his brother's killer. Abū Huwayshil nonetheless leapt at him in an attempt to protect his ward, but the man managed to shoot the *madmī* dead. Thereupon, Abū Huwayshil, considering the matter closed, simply went home.[285]

Also supportive of the right of an avenger to take blood-revenge with impunity in a tent (albeit of the *madmī* himself) is the depiction of this action as a norm in various accounts of vengeance. One, from the northern Negev in the late nineteenth century, tells of a man of the Abū Hānī family, living among the Bedouin, who took revenge on an Abū ʿUwaylī of the Tarabīn Nabaʿāt, coming to his tent ostensibly to greet him on the occasion of a holiday (Case 46). Abū ʿUwaylī had murdered his brother. As related, this act seems to have closed the conflict without reference to any violation of Abū ʿUwaylī's tent.[286] Another widespread account from the Arabian desert, but circulating in Sinai and the Negev, relates that the elderly father of a lad killed in a raid upon their camp walked a great distance, disguised as a beggar, until he reached the encampment of the raiders and their leader, called Ṣāliḥ (Case 183). One night, he stole into the latter's tent and stabbed him to death in revenge. In the telling of the tale, there is no hint of such revenge being contrary to a legal norm.[287]

By contrast to the foregoing, however, there are Bedouin who insist on the sanctuary of a tent even for a *madmī*. Examples have been presented above showing that blood-revenge within a tent is seen to stain the reputation of its owner, even if he himself is the "possessor of the blood" (*ṣāḥib ad-damm*) and entitled to vengeance. We have also seen the legal obligation of a tent owner to try to stop avengers from entering his tent to fulfill their purpose, as well as his right to kill them with impunity if they disregard his admonitions. These laws and attitudes indicate a Bedouin sentiment that the sanctuary of a tent and the reputation of its owner should prevail over the need and right of another to take blood-revenge.

This sentiment is further endorsed by stories that circulate in Sinai and the Negev. One such story tells of a tent owner in the northern Negev who killed an avenger for having taken revenge on a *madmī* ward in his tent (Case 184).

> He was the son of a chief who had given refuge to a killer from Transjordan twenty years earlier. When that chief and his tribesmen left their encampment on a camel raid, clansmen of the murder victim sought and found the original murderer in the chief's tent and took their revenge on him. The chief was killed during his camel raid, leaving his wife pregnant with child, and this child, a son, grew up unaware of the revenge that had taken place in his father's tent. When he became a young man, however, an old woman apprised him of that event, saying, "Your mother brought you into this world the year your protégé was killed in the tent" (*inti—jabatak ammak sanat mā katalū*

> *dakhīlkū fī-l-bayt*), and he felt he must restore his family's honor. So he made his way to Transjordan and killed the avenger, called Mashʿal, whose revenge in their tent had shamed them.[288]

The story was related with no hint that the tent owner, in avenging the right of his tent, was acting contrary to the law.

Another story highlights the reticence of avengers themselves to take revenge upon a killer in a tent in which the latter has found refuge so as not to dishonor the tent owner. The story, related as having occurred in the northern Negev in 1946, tells of a man who sought to kill the murderer of one of his guests (Case 185). The murderer in question, a poet from the same tribe as the avenger, had killed a more talented bard from a distant tribe out of envy; the bard was a guest in the tent of the avenger. As the murder was perpetrated in the tent owner's absence, he was determined to avenge it so as to restore his honor. When he finally located the murderer, however, the latter had taken refuge with a Bedouin dignitary whose tent the avenger was unwilling to violate, lest he commit the same violation from which he himself had suffered shame. As a result, he exercised patience until his quarry left the tent to water his camel at a nearby well and killed him there. The verdict of a blood-pool judge, as conveyed in this story is of interest to the question of whether a tent owner has the right to avenge the murder in his tent of a *madmi* (or even a guest).[289] Whereas the owner of the tent in which the *madmī* poet had found refuge sought to charge the avenger with plain murder, the judge confirmed the avenger's right to have taken revenge there for the earlier violation of his tent.[290]

ATTACKING ONE WHO DENIES JUSTICE IN HIS TENT

By contrast to the ambivalence regarding the right of a tent in which blood-revenge has taken place, all Bedouin agree that in matters short of murder, the tent of a person who denies another person justice (*ʿāyib* in the Negev; *ʿāṣī* in Sinai) will not serve him as sanctuary. The relevant legal maxim holds that "The tent of him who rejects justice won't protect him" (*bayt al-ʿāyib mā yisallmah*)[291]—that is, after a violated party has taken measures prescribed by the law to bring a violator to justice but has failed, he can resort to using violence against him, even in his tent.[292] In 1955, for example, men of the Kashākhra section of the Ẓullām Janabīb tribe in the central Negev attacked and wounded a man of the Atayyim section of the ʿAzāzma Saraḥīn in the tent of the latter's clansman, after they had despaired of bringing him to justice for striking one of their shepherdesses at a well where she was watering her flock (Case 86). The clansman's tent, legally equivalent to being the perpetrator's own, received no award from a judge for the assault upon it.[293] Similarly in southern Sinai in 1975, the three sons of Munayfī Sālim Jabalī of the Muzayna Jarābʿa attacked Sālim Jumʿa Abū Ṣabḥā of the Muzayna Ghawānma in his tent after failing to persuade him to pay the balance of a fine he had incurred for wounding their father in 1974 (Case 1). When the *manshad* judge, Sulaymān Muḥammad al-ʿUgbī, subsequently fined them for their attack, it was not for the attack itself but for entering the tent without warning the woman inside.[294] The law, as seen above, stipulates in regard to attacking a tent that the attacker first call to his intended victim or, alternatively, to the women possibly present in the tent to come out so that they will neither be hurt nor seen indecently dressed.

AGGRESSION BETWEEN A HOST AND HIS GUEST OR WARD

Perhaps the worst violations of the right of a tent are acts of aggression perpetrated by a tent owner against visitors in his tent or vice versa. If the aggressor is the host, he may suffer the indignity of having a *manshad* judge pronounce his home "unworthy to shelter or shield" (*lā yihjī wala yidhrī*). If he wounds his guest, he will pay fourfold the normal assessment for such a wound.

Within the Ẓullām confederation in the northern Negev in 1938, ʿĪd as-Sareiʿa was fined 100 gold pounds and ordered to whiten, before three tents full of men, the honor of his guest, Salāma Abū Graynāt, at whom he sought to fling the pestle of his coffee mortar in a moment of anger (Case 12). A year earlier, Sareiʿa had loaned Abū Graynāt one gold pound and availed himself of the latter's appearance in his tent to remind him that the maturity date for the loan had passed and to demand repayment. Abū Graynāt maintained that he had already repaid the money to his host's son, in the presence of a witness who could be asked to testify to the rightness of this claim under oath. Doubtful of his guest's story, Sareiʿa, outraged, raised his arm to throw the pestle at Abū Graynāt, only to be restrained by others. The judge not only condemned Sareiʿa for attacking his guest, but also for doing so without first checking his claim.[295]

A tent owner may also be heavily fined for stealing from his guests or wards, for slighting them by offering them no drink or food without explicit apology, for expelling them from the tent without ostensible reason, and for making romantic advances at their womenfolk.

Offenses on the part of a guest or ward toward a tent owner, such as stealing from him or engaging in romantic relations with the women of his household, are also heavily punished. In the central Negev in 1952, after a man called al-ʿAtayyig of the ʿAzāzma Saraḥīn was treated to a freshly butchered meat dinner and spent the night in the tent of ʿOwda al-Kishkhar of the Ẓullām Janabīb, he stole, upon leaving the tent in the morning, some goats of his host's flock, which he then sold in the market in Guṣayma (Case 88). When the theft was discovered and was eventually tried by Ḥammāda Ibn ʿAyyāda of the Ẓullām Gurʿān, a *ziyādī* judge, ʿAtayyig not only had to return the equivalent of the goats stolen, but owing to the gravity of stealing from a host, he also had to give Kishkhar two camels and $200, plus the equivalent of twenty cents for every step he had taken from the host's tent to the market in Guṣayma (approximately fifty kilometers).[296]

In the event of his dallying with a host's womenfolk, a Bedouin may expect to be slain. This is evident in stories and poems that circulate in Sinai and the Negev, as well as in the Arabian deserts. One such account, meant to entertain, tells how the wife of a host seduced a guest one night, subsequently insisting that either he or she relate the happening to her husband the next morning. Aware that death would be his reward, the guest, seated around the morning campfire with the men of the camp, recited a poem relating the night's events —but only as a dream.[297]

THE LEGAL DIFFERENCE BETWEEN SEXUAL AGGRESSION AND THEFT IN A TENT

It is of interest, from a legal point of view, that Bedouin law does not deem theft a violation of the tent so long as it is perpetrated against neither a host nor a guest. In other words, if someone enters a tent or its precincts in order to steal something belonging to the owner and is caught in the act, he will be punished only for the theft itself.

By contrast, when a man violates a woman's honor in a tent, whether consensually or by force, he will be considered to have violated the tent as well. If the woman is of the same clan as the tent owner, the latter will be entitled to two legal awards, one for his violated honor and one for his tent. If, however, she is not a clanswoman of the owner (as in the case of a nonrelated wife) and the violation of her honor was by force, her clansmen will receive an award for her violated honor, while the tent owner will receive an award for his violated tent. Hence, in 1972, when Hilayyil al-Wajj of the Ẓullām Janabīb secretly visited the non-clan wife of Ḥimayd as-Saddān of the ʿAzāzma Saraḥīn in the latter's tent when she was alone one evening, Saddān, for his violated tent received an honor-restoring confession by Wajj in three prominent tents, his own tent to be covered with white cloth, as well as four camels, two for Wajj's entering the tent and two for his exiting it (Case 44).[298] In the Negev, Saddān's award is called "a right that is the brother of an honor award" (*ḥagg akhū manshad*), to designate it as an award for the tent arising from a sexual violation.[299] Accordingly, a *manshad* fine was awarded to the woman's father for the same offense. If Saddān had actually caught Wajj with his wife and killed him, it would have been with impunity, highlighting the law's grave censure of a sexual violation committed in a tent.

In violations of a woman's honor in a tent, Bedouin law makes a distinction depending upon whether the intention is sexual violation or not. In the above example, Wajj's visit to Saddān's wife was interpreted as a violation with sexual intent. No other reason for the visit would be acceptable in court. If, for instance, a man looking for a night's shelter should come upon a tent where a woman was alone, it would be incumbent upon her to send him to the tent nearest to hers, but not have him stay, as if it were daylight. During the day, when her tent is open to sight, by contrast, a woman's receiving a wayfarer and providing him with food and drink is commendable and in accordance with the rules of Bedouin hospitality. In a well-known poem asking God for the ten best things in life, the second is "a wife of good training and breed/Who, when guests come, directly will bring what they need."[300] Over many years, when coming to a tent to look for its owner and finding him away, I have often encountered a woman alone in the tent, and she has invariably invited me to drink tea or coffee. Such an invitation is considered carrying out the tent's obligation toward a guest. Indeed, one explanation for the proverb "She undertook the obligation of her menfolk" (*saddat masadd rijālha*) indicates a woman's obligation to provide the needs of a guest when the men are away.[301]

When the honor of women is violated in a tent that is invaded for reasons other than sexual intent, Bedouin judges impose no fine for the violation of the tent. Within the Muzayna confederation in southeast Sinai in 1975, for example, when the sons of Munayfī Sālim Jabalī, attacking the tent of Sālim Abū Ṣabḥā in retaliation for the latter's refusal to pay their father a fine he owed him, held down Abū Ṣabḥā's wife lest she interfere in the fray, they were subsequently fined for violating the woman's honor but not for violating it in the tent because the initial intention was not sexual (Case 1).[302] Similarly, in 1991 in southwest Sinai, when men of the Tarabīn tribal confederation raided a tent belonging to someone of the ʿAlaygāt confederation, seeking a man to abduct in retaliation for the ʿAlaygāt having kidnapped and bound one of their own men, they legally violated the seclusion, and thus honor, of the women then present in the tent (Case 91). However, as their invasion was to obtain justice and not to violate the women, whom they neither touched nor addressed, they were not fined for violation of the tent.

Afterword

A Major Human Achievement

From outside Bedouin society, Bedouin law has often been seen as a source of chaos, rather than an antidote to it, owing primarily to its allowed use of private violence in the pursuit of justice.[1] Typical of this misunderstanding were the Egyptians, who were wont to say, even during the harshest times of Ottoman rule, that "The oppression of Turks is better than the justice of Bedouin" (*jōr at-turk wala ʿadl al-ʿarab*).[2] Clearly, such an outlook indicates the lack of a comprehensive grasp of the aims, logic, and workings of Bedouin law and of Bedouin culture, from which that law emerged.

However, an ample survey of the Bedouin legal system, as this book has attempted to present, reveals a more positive picture. In the historical absence of any governmental or tribal law-enforcement agencies in the deserts of the Middle East, the Bedouin devised a legal system that constitutes a comprehensive effort to ensure the rights of individuals and to preserve society. One of this system's main instruments for suppressing conflict and ensuring that justice be done is to engage the good offices of neutral persons. For example, to assure weak members of Bedouin society access to justice and to protect them from violations by the stronger, the law endorses the institution of protection, whereby strong members of society, neutral in a given conflict, are legally sanctioned to secure the rights of supplicants unable to do so themselves. Then, through the practice of guaranty, the law enlists powerful neutral persons to commit their honor for ensuring that members of Bedouin society comply with their legal commitments. Similarly the law authorizes persons present at an imminent threat of violence to "throw" their honor, or that of another powerful Bedouin, between the opponents, who will face serious penalties for ignoring it. Also, after a person's rights have actually been violated, neutral parties often seek to mediate between the parties in order to resolve the conflict before it becomes more violent and spreads, the law endowing some of these delegations with specifically legal roles.

Bedouin law also seeks to deter violations by endorsing the principle of mutual liability, according to which every man is accountable for the actions of his clansmen and is subject to punishment for them. Mutual liability thus gives pause to many prospective violators, lest they wreak suffering upon their own clansmen. Bedouin law also tries to reduce the possibility of conflict erupting, through specific injunctions against provocation, insult, collusion to commit a violation, treachery, breaches of trust, and the violation of the helpless.

The mistaken impression often gained by non-Bedouin that Bedouin law is, in fact, lawless mainly stems from the permission given to violated parties to wield private violence to avenge violations. Here, however, the law seeks to mitigate the effect of such license by differentiating between the use of violent revenge as a first resort or a last resort. The former is valid when the ultimate violations of murder or rape have taken place, and the intent of this permission, as with other means employed by the law, is to deter them. At the same time, however, the law sets limits to revenge as a first resort in an attempt to preserve Bedouin society. In particular, revenge cannot be practiced against persons not in the clan of the violator or against women, and it cannot exceed parity—a person for a person. The law also stipulates truces that proscribe revenge until justice is served by peaceful means, the neglect of which is subject to a range of harsh penalties.

Owing to the innate desire of the law to suppress violence, it deems the permission to wield private violence in offenses less than murder or rape as a last resort that, to be legal, must follow previous attempts to resolve the conflict peaceably, especially the dispatch of delegations urging the violator to give justice and resolve the conflict peacefully. At the center of its aim of resolving conflicts without violence, Bedouin law provides a fastidious framework for the litigation of disputes before judges.

Clearly one essential concomitant of the intent of Bedouin law to resolve conflicts peaceably, in the absence of law-enforcement agencies, is the need to enlist a range of fears in order to deter violations. Among these are the fear of violent physical retaliation for offenses, fear of the scope of retaliation that stems from collective responsibility, fear of the might of neutral parties who intercede in a conflict in order to settle it, and fear of heavy fines that may result from litigation.

Whether one condones or condemns the internal logic of Bedouin law, this law must be seen — in the perspective of millennia — as a major human achievement. Few, if any, societies and cultures can claim the great longevity of the Bedouin, and their survival for so long in the deserts of the Middle East without governments to protect them is a feat worthy of our esteem. The fact that Bedouin in modern times still resort, with trust and hope for justice, to the legal system that their earliest ancestors bequeathed them speaks volumes for the soundness of its ways.

Notes

Introduction

1. For example, see Layish and Shmueli, "Custom," pp. 35–41.
2. Bailey, *Proverbs*, p. 101.

Chapter 1. Justice without Government

1. Eph'al, *The Ancient Arabs*, passim.
2. Kister, "al-Ḥīra," passim.
3. See Gibb and Bowen, *Islamic Society*, pp. 219–33; Doughty, *Travels*, vol. 1, pp. 39ff.
4. See Bailey, "Nineteenth Century," pp. 75–76
5. See Musil, *Northern Hegaz*, pp. 1–10.
6. Burckhardt, *Notes*, vol. 2, pp. 131–35.
7. Rosenfeld, "Social Composition," pp. 175–84.
8. For example, Burckhardt, *Notes*, vol. 1, pp. 3, 8; vol. 2, pp. 24, 33, 38.
9. For example, Kister, "Mecca and Tamīm," p. 120.
10. For example, Eph'al, *The Ancient* Arabs, pp. 93–100.
11. Bailey, "Dating," p. 36.
12. For example, Eph'al, *The Ancient Arabs*, pp. 123–252, esp. 206–10.
13. Oral communication, ʿĪd Ibn Darrāj of the Ẓullām Janabīb, June 14, 1975.
14. Al-ʿĀrif, *Ta'rīkh*, p. 107; Bailey, "Nineteenth Century," p. 63, n. 80.
15. Bailey, *Poetry*, pp. 357–60.

16. Eph'al, *The Ancient Arabs*, pp. 94, 98.
17. Hitti, *History of the Arabs*, pp. 78–84.
18. Eph'al, *The Ancient Arabs*, pp. 112–23, 142–47.
19. Hitti, *History of the Arabs*, pp. 140–42.
20. Al-ʿĀrif, *Taʾrīkh*, pp. 190–93; Bailey, "Nineteenth Century," pp. 72–73.
21. Musil, *Northern Hegaz*, p. 7.
22. Musil, *Manners*, p. 132; Burckhardt, *Notes*, vol. 1, pp. 235–37.
23. Burckhardt, *Notes*, vol. 1, p. 7.
24. Ibid. vol. 2, p. 9.
25. Ibid. vol. 1, pp. 3, 5; vol. 2, pp. 24, 33–34, 38; Musil, *Northern Hegaz*, p. 9.
26. Burckhardt, *Notes*, vol. 1, p. 23; vol. 2, p. 35; Bailey, "Nineteenth Century," pp. 53–54, n. 45.
27. Musil, *Northern Hegaz*, p. 9.
28. Ibid., pp. 9–10.
29. Ibid., p. 234.
30. Ibid., p. 2.
31. Burckhardt, *Notes*, vol. 2, p.179.
32. Doughty, *Travels*, vol. 1, p.165.
33. Musil, *Northern Hegaz*, p. 126.
34. Ibid., p. 84.
35. Al-ʿĀrif, *Taʾrīkh*, pp. 242–44; Bailey, "Nineteenth Century," pp. 74–80.
36. Jennings-Bramley, "Bedouin of the Sinaitic Peninsula" (1910), p. 143.
37. Shuqayr, *Taʾrīkh*, p. 287.
38. Cole, "Tribal and Non-Tribal Structures," pp. 124–25.
39. For studies of Bedouin social structure in Sinai and the Negev, see Marx, *Bedouin of the Negev*, ch. 3, and Bailey, *Proverbs*, ch. 4.
40. See chapter 3 for more on the *khamsa*.
41. Bailey, *Proverbs*, p. 190.
42. Musil, *Northern Hegaz*, p. 7.
43. Oral communications from Ḥimayd Salmān as-Saddān of the ʿAzāzma Saraḥīn, May 4, 1973, and Sālim Muḥammad Abū Jilaydān of the ʿAzāzma ʿAṣiyāt, December 3, 1975.
44. Musil, *Northern Hegaz*, p. 24.
45. Oral communication from Ḥimayd's clansman, Swaylim Sulaymān Abū Bilayya, March 23, 1974.
46. Bailey, *Proverbs*, pp. 189–90.
47. Oral communication from Sālim Jumʿa Abū Ṣabḥā of the Muzayna Ghawānma, July 23, 1975.
48. Bailey, *Proverbs*, pp. 424–25.
49. Ibid., p. 147.
50. Blunt, *Bedouin Tribes*, p. 307.
51. Ibid., pp. 322–23.
52. See chapter 6 for more on "closest-cousin marriage."
53. Blunt, *Bedouin Tribes*, p. 324
54. This account is based on my personal witness.

55. Bailey, *Proverbs*, p.147.

56. Oral communication from Jumʿān Huwayshil Maṣābḥa, chief of the Dawāghra Maṣābḥa, April 15, 1981.

57. Musil, *Northern Hegaz*, p. 19.

58. Ibid., p. 20.

59. Ibid.

60. Musil, *Arabia Deserta*, pp. 177–80.

61. See below and Bailey, "ʿ*Adl*," pp. 133–35, for a discussion of the image of being "tilted" or "out of balance" (*māyil*) as injustice.

62. For the preceding two maxims, not found in Bailey, *Proverbs*, see the "Index of Bedouin Legal Maxims."

63. Bailey, *Proverbs*, p. 238.

64. Oral communication from Muḥammad Salmān Abū Jarabīaʿ of the ʿAzāzma Masʿūdiyyīn, May 26, 2001; cf. Nawi, "Law among the Bedouin," pp. 11–12.

65. For the complete poem and the Arabic text, see Bailey, *Poetry*, pp. 30–32.

66. See chapter 5 for more on *fawāt*.

67. Bailey, *Proverbs*, p. 332.

68. Ibid.

69. See chapter 2 on *badwa* delegations.

70. See chapter 4 for more on wounds caused to a violator in an act of retaliation.

71. This account is based on a hearing before several judges concerning this case, tape-recorded by me at Abū Rudays, Sinai, July 23, 1975, and an oral communication from Salmān Muḥammad Abū Ṣabḥā of the Muzayna Ghawānma, January 27, 2007.

72. See chapter 2 for more on guaranty.

73. See chapter 2 for more on denunciation.

74. Oral communication from Rāḍi Swaylim ʿAtayyig of the Muzayna Darārma, June 30, 2005.

75. Oral communication from Salmān Muḥammad Abū Ṣabḥā of the Muzayna Ghawānma, January 27, 2007.

76. Oral communication from Swaylim Sulaymān Abū Bilayya of the ʿAzāzma Saraḥīn, October 5, 1999.

77. See al-ʿĀrif, *al-Qaḍāʾ*, p. 83.

78. Oral communications from Muḥammad Sālim al-Aʿsam of the Tiyāha Gudayrāt, October 16, 1995; ʿĀyid ʿUbayd as-Sareiaʿ of the Tarabīn Shibaythāt, November 10, 1996; and Muḥammad Salmān Abū Ghuraygāna of the Aḥeiwāt Ghuraygāniyyīn, December 3, 1997.

79. Oral communication from Ḥājj Murayshid Rashīd al-Marāshda of the Suwārka Zuyūd, January 30, 1977.

80. From a tape recording that I made of the reconciliation meeting, January 31, 1977.

Chapter 2. Honor and Private Might in the Service of Justice

1. See chapter 3 for more on clans and clan solidarity.

2. See chapter 5 for more on honor fines and *manshad* (honor) judges.

3. See Bailey, "Nineteenth Century," pp. 61–67, and al-ʿĀrif, *Tāʾrīkh*, pp. 175–81.

4. See chapter 4 for more on the camel-truce (*jīra*).

5. Oral communication from Muḥammad Ḥusayn al-ʿAlōwna of the Tarabīn Ḥasāblah, June 17 and 29, 1998; for a verbatim rendition of the account, see Bailey, "Arabah," p. 261.

6. The following is an oral communication from Judge Amīra Salāma Abū Amīra of the Masaʿīd Awāmra, January 18, 2001.

7. See chapter 4 for more on abduction.

8. See chapter 6 for more on exchange marriages.

9. Oral communications from Swaylim Sulaymān Abū Bilayya, February 26, 1978, and ʿOwda Sulaymān al-Hadōbe, June 23, 1998, both of the ʿAzāzma Saraḥīn.

10. See Stewart, *Texts*, vol. 1, pp. 80–81.

11. Bailey, *Proverbs*, p. 284.

12. See Bar-Tsvi, *Jurisdiction*, p. 76, and chapter 4 below for more on violence as a first resort.

13. See Kressel, "Ḥaqq Akhū Manshad," pp. 22–28.

14. Oral communication from Swaylim Sulaymān Abū Bilayya of the ʿAzāzma Saraḥīn, February 15, 1974.

15. See Stewart, *Texts*, vol. 1, p. 152.

16. Oral communications from Swaylim Sulaymān Abū Bilayya, June 30, 1998, and Frayj Ḥimayd as-Saddān, December 30, 2004, both of the ʿAzāzma Saraḥīn.

17. See chapter 6 for more on closest-cousin marriage.

18. Oral communication from Swaylim Sulaymān Abū Bilayya of the ʿAzāzma Saraḥīn, May 20, 1973.

19. See the "Index of Bedouin Legal Maxims" for the proverb.

20. From the testimony of Ḥimayd Salmān as-Saddān before Judge Ḥamdān aṣ-Ṣūfī, tape-recorded by me at Rafaḥ, Gaza Strip, July 14, 1984.

21. See Bar-Tsvi, *Jurisdiction*, pp. 66–67.

22. See Kressel, "Ḥaqq Akhū Manshad," pp. 25–26. Although Kressel calls the emissary "a messenger," he was tantamount to a *jāha*, even though he was but one person. See the "Index of Bedouin Legal Maxims" for the proverb.

23. See chapter 4 for more on truces.

24. See Bar-Tsvi, *Jurisdiction*, p. 97.

25. Ibid. pp. 26–29. For more on this type of protection, called "throwing the face," see below.

26. Oral communications from ʿAnayz Abū Sālim al-ʿUrḍī of the Tarabīn Ḥasāblah (April 10, 1984), a poet who composed a poem on the subject (see Bailey, *Poetry*, pp. 91–97); and Amīra Salāma Abū Amīra of the Masaʿīd Awāmra, the judge who ultimately ruled on the case, January 18, 2000.

27. Oral communication from Ḥimayd Salmān as-Saddān of the ʿAzāzma Saraḥīn, May 15, 1975. Cf. Bailey, "Arabah," p. 253, for more of the story. The Saʿīdiyyīn are residents of Wādī al-ʿAraba, which separates the Negev from southern Jordan.

28. Bailey, *Proverbs*, p. 395, where an alternative meaning is given.

29. Oral communications from Swaylim Sulaymān Abū Bilayya, December 1, 1974, and ʿOwda Sulaymān al-Hadōbe, June 23, 1998, both of the ʿAzāzma Saraḥīn.

30. Oral communication from Salmān Muḥammad Abū Ṣabḥā of the Muzayna Ghawānma, January 27, 2007.

31. See Bar-Tsvi (who was present at the *jāha*), *Jurisdiction*, pp. 46–47.

32. See chapter 4 for more on impoundment.

33. Bailey, *Proverbs*, p. 188.

34. See chapter 5 for more on the concession of fines.

35. Oral communication from Swaylim Sulaymān Abū Bilayya of the ʿAzāzma Sarahīn, September 14, 1977.

36. The following discussion is based on a tape recording of the *jāha* in question, September 16, 1977.

37. Bailey, *Proverbs*, p. 340.

38. See below on concession.

39. Oral communication from Sulaymān Salāma ar-Rimāg (the brother of Jumʿa), December 12, 2004. The following discussion is based on my tape recording of the *jāha* concerned, December 13, 2004.

40. See chapter 5 for more on guaranty.

41. See Bar-Tsvi, *Jurisdiction*, p. 46.

42. See Bar-Tsvi, *Jurisdiction*, pp. 138–39.

43. Bailey, *Proverbs*, p. 333.

44. Figures based on Bar-Tsvi (who tape-recorded the trial), *Jurisdiction*, pp. 138–39.

45. Oral communications from Sulaymān Jumʿa Abū Ṣabḥā, June 29, 1995, and Salmān Muḥammad Abū Ṣabḥā, January 27, 2007, both of the Muzayna Ghawānma and a brother and cousin respectively of Sālim Abū Ṣabḥā.

46. Cf. Bailey, *Proverbs*, p. 249.

47. See Bar-Tsvi, *Jurisdiction*, pp. 97–98.

48. For the population figures, see Bailey and Peled, *Bedouin Tribes in Sinai*, pp. 110, 111.

49. From a recording of the *jāha* session that I made at Rās al-Aḥmar, January 31, 1977.

50. See chapter 4 for more on blood-price.

51. Oral communications from ʿAbdallah Muʿattig al-Wajj, November 10, 1976, and Muḥammad Sulaymān al-Kishkhar, December 14, 1981, both of the Ẓullām Janabīb; cf. Marx, *Bedouin of the Negev*, p. 124.

52. Oral communication from Swaylim Sulaymān Abū Bilayya of the ʿAzāzma Sarahīn, October 5, 1999.

53. Bailey, *Proverbs*, p. 42.

54. Oral communication from Swaylim Sulaymān Abū Bilayya of the ʿAzāzma Sarahīn, February 4, 1974.

55. Bailey, *Proverbs*, p. 393.

56. The foregoing account is based on notes I made at the *jāha*, near Subayṭa, May 30, 1974.

57. Most Bedouin in Sinai and the Negev pronounce this as *sāmil*, conveying the meaning, as in Classical Arabic, of "dregs" or "remainder" (Hava, *Al-Farāʾid Arabic-English Dictionary*, p. 337; Lane, *Lexicon*, p. 1431). Some pronounce it as *ṣāmil* (see Stewart, *Texts*, vol. 2, pp. 265–66).

58. See Bailey, *Poetry*, pp. 317–19.

59. Oral communication from Swaylim Sulaymān Abū Bilayya of the ʿAzāzma Sarahīn, December 13, 1996.

60. See chapter 5 for more on ʿ*ugbī* judges.

61. See Stewart, *Texts*, vol. 1, pp. 124–25, 134.

62. See chapter 5 for more on witnesses.

63. Oral communications from Swaylim Sulaymān Abū Bilayya, December 12, 1984, and Frayj Ḥimayd as-Saddān, February 4, 2006, both of the ʿAzāzma Saraḥīn. Abū Bilayya was one of the appointed guarantors. Saddān was the accused's son.

64. See Stewart, *Texts*, vol. 1, pp. 27–33.

65. See Bar-Tsvi, *Jurisdiction*, pp. 44–45.

66. See Stewart, *Texts*, vol. 1, p. 32.

67. Bailey, *Proverbs*, p. 364.

68. See chapter 3 for more on expulsion from a clan.

69. Oral communication from Salāma ʿĪd Abū Bilayya of the ʿAzāzma Saraḥīn, December 15, 1996.

70. See al-ʿĀrif, *al-Qaḍāʾ*, pp. 93–94. See chapter 5 for more on moral punishments.

71. See Bar-Tsvi, *Jurisdiction*, p. 112.

72. See Abū Ḥassān, *Turāth*, p. 150.

73. Bailey, *Proverbs*, p. 300.

74. Ibid., p. 292.

75. Ibid., pp. 292–93.

76. Ibid., p. 293.

77. Ibid.

78. Ibid.

79. Ibid. p. 297.

80. Ibid. p. 301.

81. Oral statement delivered by Ḥimayd as-Saddān at a trial of this case before Judge Ḥamdān aṣ-Ṣūfī in Rafaḥ, the Gaza Strip, July 14, 1984.

82. The imagery comes from Bailey, *Proverbs*, pp. 23–24: "A man is like a China cup, which, once cracked, is useless" (*ar-rājil zay finjāl ṣīnī—in anthalam khirib*).

83. Ibid., p. 294.

84. Oral communication from Muḥammad Salmān Abū Ghuraygāna of the Aḥeiwāt Ghuraygāniyyīn, December 3, 1997.

85. See Stewart, *Texts*, vol. 1, p. 122.

86. Oral communication from Sālim Salāma ar-Rimāg of the ʿAzāzma Saraḥīn, December 20, 1999; also see chapter 6 for more on loans.

87. See chapter 5 for more on oaths.

88. See Bailey, *Poetry*, pp. 97–101.

89. See Bar-Tsvi, *Jurisdiction*, pp. 28–29.

90. See Stewart, *Texts*, vol. 1, p. 116.

91. See Bar-Tsvi, *Jurisdiction*, p. 26.

92. Oral communication from Swaylim Sulaymān Abū Bilayya of the ʿAzāzma Saraḥīn, May 5, 1973.

93. See Stewart, *Texts*, vol. 1, p. 142.

94. See Bar-Tsvi, *Jurisdiction*, p. 27.

95. See chapter 5 for more on choosing judges.

96. See Bar-Tsvi, *Jurisdiction*, p. 26.

97. See Stewart, *Texts*, vol. 1, p. 161.
98. Musil, *Manners*, pp. 438–40.
99. Bailey, *Proverbs*, p. 281.
100. Bailey, *Poetry*, pp. 134–35, for the poem.
101. Bailey, *Proverbs*, p. 125.
102. Bailey and Peled, *Bedouin Tribes in Sinai*, pp. 111–12.
103. Oral communications from Judge Swaylim al-Gunbayzī of the Tarabīn Ḥasāblah, November 29, 1999, and Muḥammad ʿĪd Ibn ʿĀmir of the Tiyāha Ṣugayrāt, November 30, 1999.
104. See chapter 4 for more on blood-revenge.
105. Oral communications from Ṣabāḥ Ṣāliḥ al-Ghānim of the ʿAgaylī ʿAgūl, November 21, 1996, and Ibrahīm Ḥasan ʿAṭiyya of the Suwārka Manṣūriyyīn, December 1, 1999.
106. Oral communication from Swaylim Sulaymān Abū Bilayya of the ʿAzāzma Sara-ḥīn, November 10, 1974.
107. See Stewart, *Texts*, vol. 1, pp. 66–73.
108. Oral communication from Swaylim Sulaymān Abū Bilayya, December 1, 1974, and ʿOwda Sulaymān al-Hadōbe, June 23, 1998, both of the ʿAzāzma Saraḥīn.
109. Stewart, *Texts, vol. 1*, p. 66, for the recorded statements.
110. Oral communications from Swaylim Sulaymān Abū Bilayya, December 15, 1996, and Frayj Ḥimayd as-Saddān, June 27, 2006, both of the ʿAzāzma Saraḥīn.
111. See chapter 3 for more on the responsibility of a clan for its women.
112. Oral communication from Swaylim Sulaymān Abū Bilayya of the ʿAzāzma Sara-ḥīn, February 13, 1974.
113. See Kressel, "Ḥaqq Akhū Manshad," pp. 22–28.
114. Bailey, *Proverbs*, p. 173.
115. Oral communication from ʿOwda Sulaymān al-Hadōbe of the ʿAzāzma Saraḥīn, June 23, 1998.
116. Bailey, *Proverbs*, p. 177.
117. See Bar-Tsvi, *Jurisdiction*, p. 43.
118. Ibid., p. 112.
119. Bailey, *Proverbs*, p. 174.
120. Ibid., p. 176.
121. Oral communications from Salāma ʿĪd Abū Bilayya, December 18, 1996, and Frayj Ḥimayd as-Saddān, December 10, 2005, both of the ʿAzāzma Saraḥīn.
122. See Bar-Tsvi, *Jurisdiction*, pp. 116–17.
123. Oral communication from ʿOwda Sulaymān al-Hadōbe of the ʿAzāzma Saraḥīn, June 23, 1998.
124. Oral communication from Swaylim Sulaymān Abū Bilayya of the ʿAzāzma Sara-ḥīn, February 26, 1978.
125. See Stewart, *Texts*, vol. 1, pp. 74–87.
126. Bailey, *Proverbs*, p. 175, for the preceding three proverbs.
127. Cited in Stewart, *Texts*, vol 1, p. 74.
128. Ibid., pp. 77, 81.
129. Oral communication from Swaylim Sulaymān Abū Bilayya of the ʿAzāzma Sara-ḥīn, February 26, 1978.

130. Bailey, *Proverbs*, p. 175.

131. Ibid., p. 176.

132. Oral communications from Ṣabāḥ Ṣāliḥ al-Ghānim of the ʿAgaylī ʿAgūl, November 21, 1994, and Ibrahīm Ḥasan ʿAṭiyya of the Suwārka Manṣūriyyīn, December 1, 1999.

133. See Nicholson, *Literary History*, pp. 56–57.

134. See chapter 6 for more on this custom.

135. Oral communication from Shaykh Salāma ʿAwwād Masʿūd of the Suwārka Zuyūd, January 22, 1972.

136. Oral communication from Sālim Muḥammad al-ʿUgbī of the Tiyāha Banī ʿUgba, February 12, 1972; cf. al-ʿĀrif, *Taʾrīkh*, pp. 117–20, and Bailey, *Poetry*, pp. 212–15.

Chapter 3. The Role of Collective Responsibility in Achieving Justice

1. From the *Washington Post*, February 24, 1996.

2. Bailey, *Proverbs*, p. 131.

3. Oral communication from ʿOwda Sulaymān al-Hadōbe of the ʿAzāzma Saraḥīn, June 23, 1998.

4. Oral communication from Judge ʿOwda Ṣāliḥ of the Muzayna Shaẓāẓna, November 22, 1994.

5. Oral communications from Sulaymān Sālim Ibn Jāzī (December 2, 1977) and Jumʿa ʿĪd al-Farārja (December 4, 1977), both of the Tarabīn Ḥasāblah.

6. Oral communication from Judge Amīra Salāma Abū Amīra of the Masaʿīd Awāmra, January 18, 2000.

7. For the proverbs, see Bailey, *Proverbs*, pp. 131, 135, 136.

8. Oral communication from Swaylim Sulaymān Abū Bilayya of the ʿAzāzma Saraḥīn, November 1, 1998.

9. Bailey, *Proverbs*, p. 136.

10. See Stewart, *Texts*, vol. 1, pp. 97–98, for a good discussion by Bedouin of this obligation.

11. Bailey, *Proverbs*, p. 134.

12. Ibid., p. 135.

13. Ibid., p. 137.

14. Oral communication from ʿOwda Sulaymān al-Hadōbe of the ʿAzāzma Saraḥīn, June 23, 1998.

15. Oral communication from Swaylim Sulaymān Abū Bilayya of the ʿAzāzma Saraḥīn, October 10, 1999.

16. See Stewart, *Texts*, vol. 1, pp. 36, 50–51.

17. Ibid., pp. 67–68, 98.

18. Ibid., p. 89.

19. Oral communication from Sālim ʿOwda aṭ-Ṭimṭāwī of the ʿAzāzma ʿAṣiyāt, July 12, 1975.

20. See Stewart, Texts, *vol.* 1, pp. 67–68.

21. Bailey, *Proverbs*, p. 139.

22. See chapter 5 for more on "blood-pool" judges.

23. See Stewart, *Texts*, vol. 1, pp. 89–92, for a clear discussion of these points by Bedouin.
24. Bailey, *Proverbs*, p. 139.
25. See Stewart, *Texts*, vol. 1, p. 84, n. 73.
26. Bailey, *Proverbs*, p. 123
27. Ibid., p. 124.
28. Doughty, *Travels*, vol. 1, p. 319; emphasis in the original.
29. Bailey, *Proverbs*, p. 137.
30. Ibid., p. 414.
31. Ibid., p. 153.
32. Bailey, "Religious Practices," pp. 78–79.
33. Oral communication from Jumʿa ʿĪ d al-farārja of the Tarabīn Ḥasāblah, November 30, 1999.
34. Oral communication from Swaylim Sulaymān Abū Bilayya of the ʿAzāzma Saraḥīn, April 15, 1975. Most other clan issues are decided by majority vote (cf. Stewart, *Texts*, vol. 1, pp. 97–98).
35. Oral communication from Sulaymān Ḥusayn al-Khiraynig of the ʿAzāzma Saraḥīn, November 10, 1996.
36. Oral communication from ʿĀyid ʿUbayd Ibn Sarīaʿ of the Tarabīn Shibaythāt, September 24, 1971.
37. See chapter 5 for other uses of this symbolic act.
38. Oral communication from Judge Muḥammad Ḥusayn al-ʿAlowna of the Tarabīn Ḥasāblah, June 29, 1998. Cf. Stewart, *Texts*, vol. 1, pp. 56–57. See chapters 4 and 6 for more on bondage-marriage.
39. Bailey, *Proverbs*, p. 126.
40. Ibid., p. 128.
41. Ibid., p. 127.
42. From my conversation with ʿAyyāda Sulaymān Abū Bilayya of the ʿAzāzma Saraḥīn, October 15, 1974.
43. Bailey, *Proverbs*, p. 131.
44. Ibid., p. 129.
45. See chapter 4 for more on blood-revenge.
46. Bailey, *Proverbs*, p. 159.
47. See Stewart, *Texts, vol.* 1, p. 92; see chapter 5 below for more on treachery.
48. Tribal number from Raswan, *Black Tents*, p. 4.
49. Musil, *Arabia Deserta*, pp. 238–42.
50. Bailey, "Nineteenth Century," p. 62, and al-ʿArif, *Taʾrīkh*, p. 177.
51. See Bar-Tsvi, *Jurisdiction*, pp. 97–98.
52. See Stewart, *Texts*, vol. 1, pp. 11–25, 83–85.
53. See Bar-Tsvi, *Jurisdiction*, p. 26.
54. Ibid., p. 31.
55. See Stewart, *Texts*, vol. 1, p. 36.
56. Ibid., pp. 68–69.
57. Oral communication from ʿAlī Ḥasan Munaynaʿ of the Suwārka ʿAradāt, June 29, 1998.

58. Oral communication from ʿIshaysh ʿAnayz al-ʿUrḍī of the Tarabīn Ḥasāblah, November 4, 2005.

59. See Bar-Tsvi, *Jurisdiction*, pp. 35–36.

60. Bailey, *Proverbs*, pp. 140–41.

61. Oral communication from Muḥammad Ḥusayn al-ʿAlōwna of the Tarabīn Ḥasāblah, November 20, 1995.

62. Cf. Stewart, "The Woman," pp. 121ff., where the author draws legal comparisons between Bedouin women and domestic animals.

63. Ibid., pp. 104, 107.

64. Bailey, *Proverbs*, p. 258.

65. See chapter 6 for more on inheritance.

66. See chapter 6 for more on striking women and divorce.

67. Cited in Musil, *Arabia Deserta*, p. 7.

68. Bailey, *Proverbs*, p. 138, for the proverbs.

69. Ibid., p. 404.

70. Oral communication from Swaylim Sulaymān Abū Bilayya of the ʿAzāzma Saraḥīn, October 1, 1973.

71. Oral communication from ʿAnayz Sālim al-ʿUrḍī of the Tarabīn Ḥasāblah, December 3, 1997.

72. Oral communication from Frayj Ḍeifallah al-Musāʿida of the Tarabīn Ḥasāblah, January 30, 2001; also see Bailey, *Proverbs*, p. 264.

73. Bailey, *Proverbs*, p. 263.

74. Ibid.

75. Oral communication from ʿAnayz Sālim al-ʿUrḍī of the Tarabīn Ḥasāblah, December 2, 1997.

76. Oral communication from Swaylim Sulaymān Abū Bilayya of the ʿAzāzma Saraḥīn, May 12, 1998.

77. Oral communication from Swaylim Sulaymān Abū Bilayya of the ʿAzāzma Saraḥīn, June 30, 1997; for more details, see *Ḥadashōt* (erstwhile daily newspaper, Tel Aviv), July 19, 1985.

78. For more details, see *Yediōt Aḥaronōt* (daily newspaper, Tel Aviv), April 8, 2006.

79. Bailey, *Proverbs*, p. 267.

80. Ibid., p. 268.

81. Ibid., p. 269.

82. Oral communication from "Saʿīd" of the Tiyāha Abū ʿAbdūn, January 10, 2003.

83. Oral communications from Swaylim Sulaymān Abū Bilayya (February 13, 1974) and Frayj Ḥimayd as-Saddān (June 16, 2005), both of the ʿAzāzma Saraḥīn.

84. See Stewart, *Texts*, vol. 1, pp. 68–71.

85. See Kressel, "Ḥaqq Akhū Manshad," pp. 22–23.

86. Oral communication from Judge Amīra Salāma Abū Amīra of the Masaʿīd Awāmra, January 18, 2000.

87. Oral communications from Salāma ʿĪd Abū Bilayya of the ʿAzāzma Saraḥīn, November 27, 1997, and Judge Muḥammad Ḥusayn al-ʿAlowna (June 30, 1998) and ʿAnayz Sālim al-ʿUrḍī (November 1, 1998), both of the Tarabīn Ḥasāblah.

88. See chapter 4 for more on revenge for sexual violation.

89. See Bar-Tsvi, *Jurisdiction*, p. 54.

90. Oral communication from ʿAlī ʿAwwād Abū-l-Gīʿān of the Tiyāha Abū-l-Gīʿān, March 25, 2006.

91. Bailey, "Weddings," pp. 126–27.

92. Bailey, *Proverbs*, p. 404.

93. Oral communication from Frayj Ḥimayd as-Saddān of the ʿAzāzma Saraḥīn, July 4, 2001.

94. Oral communication from Swaylim Sulaymān Abū Bilayya of the ʿAzāzma Saraḥīn, October 1, 1973.

95. Oral communication from Frayj Ḥimayd as-Saddān of the ʿAzāzma Saraḥīn, July 4, 2001.

96. Oral communication from Muḥammad Ḥusayn al-ʿAlōwna of the Tarabīn Ḥasāblah, June 29, 1998.

97. Bailey, "Dating," p. 41.

98. Oral communication from Shaykh Sulaymān Salīm Ibn Sarīaʿ of the Tarabīn Shibaythāt, September 24, 1971.

99. Oral communication from Sālim al-Ameiṭil of the ʿAzāzma ʿAṣiyāt, May 14, 1975.

100. Bailey, *Proverbs*, p. 159.

101. Oral communication from Jumʿa ʿĪd al-Farārja of the Tarabīn Ḥasāblah, July 10, 2001.

102. Bailey, *Proverbs*, pp. 159–60.

103. Oral communication from the chief of the Ḥasāblah tribe, Sulaymān ʿĪd Ibn Jāzī, January 17, 1980.

104. Oral communication from Swaylim Sulaymān Abū Bilayya of the ʿAzāzma Saraḥīn, May 22, 1973.

105. Oral communication from Swaylim Sulaymān Abū Bilayya, of the ʿAzāzma Saraḥīn, November 10, 1974.

106. Oral communication from Swaylim Sulaymān Abū Bilayya of the ʿAzāzma Saraḥīn, May 12, 1998.

107. Bailey, "Nineteenth Century," pp. 67–72.

108. See Bailey, *Poetry*, pp. 253–55.

109. Ibid., pp. 91–97, for the poem.

110. Oral communication from Ḥimayd Salmān as-Saddān of the ʿAzāzma Saraḥīn at a trial of the case before the Tarabīn judge, Ḥamdān aṣ-Ṣūfī, at Rafaḥ, the Gaza Strip, July 14, 1984.

111. Oral communication from ʿAnayz Sālim al-ʿUrḍī of the Tarabīn Ḥasāblah, June 17, 1998.

112. Ibid.

113. Bailey, *Proverbs*, p. 170.

114. Oral communication from Salāma ʿĪd Abū Bilayya of the ʿAzāzma Saraḥīn, November 27, 1997.

115. Oral communications from Swaylim Sulaymān Abū Bilayya of the ʿAzāzma Saraḥīn, October 15, 1998, and Ṣāliḥ Sālim az-Zalbānī of the Ḥuwayṭāt Zalābya (Jordan), October 29, 1998. Cf. Hilw and Darwish, *Customary Law*, p. 88.

116. Oral communication from ʿAlī Ḥikmat al-Wuḥeidī of the Tarabīn Wuḥeidāt and great-grandson of the chief in question, March 15, 1980. See chapter 6 for an enlarged version of this account and for more on sanctuary.

117. See Shuqayr, *Taʾrīkh*, pp. 410–12, for a list of benefactions that he recorded in Sinai early in the twentieth century.

118. See Bailey, "Arabah," pp. 256–57, for details of the original story.

119. Oral communication from Shaykh Salāma ʿAwwād Masʿūd of the Suwārka Zuyūd, January 22, 1972.

120. Oral communication from Muḥammad Ḥusayn al-ʿAlowna of the Tarabīn Ḥasāblah, October 20, 1999. For the complete story, see Bailey, "Arabah," p. 257.

121. Oral communication from ʿAnayz Sālim al-ʿUrḍī of the Tarabīn Ḥasāblah, July 28, 1999.

Chapter 4. The Role of Private Violence in Achieving Justice

1. Bailey, *Proverbs*, p. 248, and the "Index of Bedouin Legal Maxims" for the three preceding proverbs.

2. See below on the "special arrangements," per "the camel of sleep."

3. Bailey, *Proverbs*, p. 251.

4. Ibid., p. 252.

5. Ibid., p. 250.

6. Ibid., p. 256.

7. Ibid., p. 255.

8. Ibid., p. 330.

9. Thesiger, *Arabian Sands*, p. 107.

10. Musil, *Manners*, p. 496; also oral communications from Muḥammad ʿAlāya of the Liyāthna (Jordan), April 25, 1996, and Muḥammad Ḥusayn al-ʿAlowna of the Tarabīn Ḥasāblah, June 30, 1998.

11. See Bailey, *Poetry*, p. 78.

12. Bailey, *Proverbs*, pp. 257–58.

13. Ibid., p. 118.

14. Oral communication from ʿĀyid ʿUbayd Ibn Sarīaʿ of the Tarabīn Shibaythāt, December 3, 1997.

15. Burckhardt, *Travels*, pp. 513–16.

16. See chapter 6 for more on theft.

17. Thesiger, *Arabian Sands*, p. 107.

18. Oral communication from Salāma ʿĪd Abū Bilayya of the ʿAzāzma Saraḥīn, November 27, 1997.

19. See chapters 3 and 6 for more on murder for fornication.

20. Bailey, *Proverbs*, p. 253.

21. Ibid., p. 254.

22. *New York Times*, January 21, 1981.

23. Oral communications from ʿĀrif Abū Rubayʿa, April 8, 2008, and ʿAṭiyya Slaym Ibn Jāzī, April 25, 2008.

24. Oral communication from Frayj Ḥimayd as-Saddān of the ʿAzāzma Saraḥīn, July 4, 2001.

25. *Ha'aretz* (Tel Aviv), March 26, 2006.
26. Oral communication from Anwar al-Khaṭīb at-Tamīmī, Jerusalem, September 9, 1969; cf. Peake, *History*, pp. 188–89, for a different version of the origin of the name.
27. Oral communication from ʿUmar Al-ʿAyāyda, ʿArāba, February 8, 2000.
28. Bailey, *Proverbs*, p. 254.
29. Ibid., p. 255.
30. Ibid., p. 262.
31. Oral communication from Shaykh Khalīl Farhūd Abū-l-Gīʿān of the Tiyāha Abū-l-Gīʿān, April 7, 2006; cf. Bar-Tsvi, *Jurisdiction*, pp. 54–57, for the background of the case.
32. Oral communication, May 28, 2006, from an anonymous member of the Tiyāha Ramaḍīn who was present on the occasion.
33. Hence, the Bedouin noun for rape (*ghaṣab*) derives from the verb "to force" (*ghaṣab*).
34. Oral communication from Salīm Ḥusayn al-ʿAgaylī of the Masaʿīd Marābda, September 3, 1975.
35. See below for attitudes toward pillage during blood-revenge.
36. Bailey, *Proverbs*, p. 264.
37. Ibid., p. 354.
38. See ibid., p. 355. For additional such sayings, see chapter 6.
39. See chapter 5 for more on oaths and the ordeal.
40. From a recording I made while attending the session; cf. Bar-Tsvi, *Jurisdiction*, pp. 57–58, for the account that the Negev judges approved.
41. Oral communication from Amīra Salāma Abū Amīra of the Masaʿīd Awāmra (the appeals judge in the case), Jalbāna, Egypt, January 18, 2000; cf. Bailey, *Poetry*, pp. 91–97, for a Tarabīn account.
42. Oral communication from Judge Amīra Salāma Abū Amīra of the Masaʿīd Awāmra, January 18, 2000.
43. Bailey, *Proverbs*, p. 403.
44. Oral communication from Judge Amīra Salāma Abū Amīra of the Masaʿīd Awāmra, January 18, 2000; see chapter 6 for a more complete rendition of the story.
45. Oral communication from ʿAnayz Sālim al-ʿUrḍī of the Tarabīn Ḥasāblah, April 5, 1983.
46. Oral communication from ʿIshaysh ʿAnayz al-ʿUrḍī of the Tarabīn Ḥasāblah, November 8, 2005.
47. Oral communication from Jumʿa ʿĪd al-Farārja of the Tarabīn Ḥasāblah, July 8, 2001.
48. See chapter 3 for more on relations with a non-clan wife.
49. Bailey, *Proverbs*, p. 238.
50. Ibid., p. 239.
51. See Bar-Tsvi, *Jurisdiction*, pp. 68–69.
52. As heard from ʿAnayz Sālim al-ʿUrḍī of the Tarabīn Ḥasāblah, April 5, 1983.
53. Bailey, *Proverbs*, p. 284.
54. See Bar-Tsvi, *Jurisdiction*, pp. 54–57.
55. Bailey, *Proverbs*, p. 328.
56. See chapter 2 for more on resolution and power.

57. From my tape recording of a hearing of this case at Abū Rudays, in Sinai, August 20, 1975.

58. Bailey, *Proverbs*, p. 265.

59. Oral communications from Ṣabāḥ Ṣāliḥ al-Ghānim of the ʿAgaylī ʿAgūl, November 21, 1996; ʿĀyid ʿUbayd Ibn Sarīaʿ of the Tarabīn Shibaythāt, December 3, 1996; and ʿAlī Ḥasan Munaynaʿ of the Suwārka ʿAradāt, June 29, 1998; cf. affirmations in the literature (e.g., Musil, *Arabia Petraea*, p. 365, and al-ʿĀrif, *al-Qaḍāʾ*, pp. 79–80).

60. Oral communications from Swaylim Sulaymān Abū Bilayya (February 17, 2000) and Frayj Ḥimayd as-Saddān (March 26, 2006), both of the ʿAzāzma Saraḥīn; also from Jumʿa ʿĪd al-Farārja (December 4, 1997) and Judge Muḥammad Ḥusayn al-ʿAlowna (June 29, 1998), both of the Tarabīn Ḥasāblah, all expressing contempt for pillage during blood-revenge.

61. Bailey, *Proverbs*, p. 286.

62. See Bar-Tsvi, *Jurisdiction*, p. 88; also pp. 45–46, for a further example of effective impoundment.

63. Bailey, *Proverbs*, p. 287.

64. See chapter 2 for more on protection.

65. Oral communication from Swaylim Sulaymān Abū Bilayya of the ʿAzāzma Saraḥīn, May 12, 1998.

66. Bailey, *Proverbs*, p. 286.

67. Ibid.

68. See chapter 6 for more on sanctuary.

69. Oral communication from Muḥammad Ḥusayn al-ʿAlowna of the Tarabīn Ḥasāblah, November 29, 1999.

70. Nicholson, *Literary History*, pp. 84–85.

71. See al-ʿĀrif, *al-Qaḍāʾ*, p. 114.

72. Oral communication from ʿAnayz Sālim al-ʿUrḍī of the Tarabīn Ḥasāblah, October 21, 1999.

73. Bailey, *Proverbs*, p. 240.

74. Oral communications from Lāfī Faraj Sulaymān of the Rumaylāt Busūm, October 15, 1970, and Ibrahīm Ḥasan of the Suwārka Manṣūriyyīn, December 1,1999.

75. Oral communications from Swaylim Sulaymān Abū Bilayya of the ʿAzāzma Saraḥīn, May 12, 1998; Judge Amīra Salāma Abū Amīra of the Masaʿīd Awāmra, January 18, 2000; and ʿAnayz Sālim al-ʿUrḍī of the Tarabīn Ḥasāblah, January 30, 2001; see also Shuqayr, *Taʾrīkh*, pp. 110–11.

76. Oral communication from Judge Amīra Salāma Abū Amīra of the Masaʿīd Awāmra, January 18, 2000.

77. Oral communications from ʿĀyid ʿUbayd Ibn Sarīaʿ of the Tarabīn Shibaythāt, November 10, 1996, and Judge Salmān Ibn Ḥammād of the ʿAzāzma Masʿūdiyyīn, November 8, 1998.

78. Bailey, *Proverbs*, p. 253.

79. See chapter 5 for more on fines for treachery.

80. Oral communications from Ḥājj Swaylim Zāyid al-Gunbayzī of the Tarabīn Ḥasāblah, November 29, 1999, and Muḥammad ʿĪd Ibn ʿĀmir of the Tiyāha Ṣugayrāt, November 30, 1999.

81. Bailey, *Proverbs*, p. 258.

82. Abū Ḥassān, *Turāth*, pp. 180–82.

83. Oral communication from Jumʿa ʿĪd al-Farārja of the Tarabīn Ḥasāblah, December 4, 1997. In table 4.2 the Abū Huwaymil lineage is not shown in its entirety.

84. See the "Index of Bedouin Legal Maxims."

85. Oral communication from Muḥammad Ḥasan an-Nabārī of the Tiyāha Gudayrāt, December 5, 2005.

86. See chapter 3 for more on blood-fine groups.

87. Oral communication from Muḥammad Ḥusayn al-ʿAlowna of the Tarabīn Ḥasāblah, November 28, 1999.

88. Bailey, *Proverbs*, p. 258.

89. See ibid., pp. 254–55, for the preceding three maxims.

90. Ibid., p. 256.

91. Oral communications from Ṣabāḥ Ṣāliḥ al-Ghānim of the ʿAgaylī ʿAgūl, November 21, 1996, and Ḥasan Ibrahīm ʿAṭiyya of the Suwārka Manṣūriyyīn, December 1, 1999.

92. Bailey, *Proverbs*, p. 256.

93. Ibid., p. 257.

94. Oral communication from Swaylim Sulaymān Abū Bilayya of the ʿAzāzma Saraḥīn, October 3, 1973.

95. See Bar-Tsvi, *Jurisdiction*, pp. 99–100.

96. Oral communication from Sālim Salāma ar-Rimāg of the ʿAzāzma Saraḥīn, November 25, 2006.

97. Based on a tape recording of the reconciliation conclave, which I attended at Rās al-Aḥmar, northern Sinai, January 31, 1977.

98. Oral communication from Dodik Shoshani, Kibbutz Lahav, March 29, 2006. Cf. Bar-Tsvi, *Jurisdiction*, p. 100.

99. Bailey, *Proverbs*, p. 259.

100. Ibid., p. 273, for the preceding two maxims.

101. Ibid., p. 275.

102. Ibid., p. 276, for the preceding two maxims.

103. Oral communication from ʿAyyāda Sulaymān Abū Bilayya of the ʿAzāzma Saraḥīn, October 15, 1974.

104. Oral communication from Ḥimayd Salmān as-Saddān of the ʿAzāzma Saraḥīn, October 10, 1981.

105. Bailey, *Proverbs*, p. 275.

106. From my tape recording of the *jāha* in question, September 16, 1977.

107. Ibid., p. 277.

108. Oral communication from Frayj Ḥimayd as-Saddān of the ʿAzāzma Saraḥīn, July 11, 2001; cf. al-ʿĀrif, *al-Qaḍā'*, p. 86.

109. Oral communication from Jumʿa ʿĪd al-Farārja of the Tarabīn Ḥasāblah, June 16, 1998.

110. See Bar-Tsvi, *Jurisdiction*, pp. 69–70.

111. Oral communication from ʿAnayz Sālim al-ʿUrḍī of the Tarabīn Ḥasāblah, October 21, 1999.

112. Bailey, *Proverbs*, p. 274.
113. Ibid.
114. Oral communication from Swaylim Sulaymān Abū Bilayya of the ʿAzāzma Saraḥīn, October 1, 1973.
115. Oral communication from Swaylim Sulaymān Abū Bilayya of the ʿAzāzma Saraḥīn, November 10, 1974.
116. See chapter 2 for more on "throwing the face."
117. Bailey, *Proverbs*, pp. 277–78, for the preceding two maxims.
118. Abū Ḥassān, *Turāth*, pp. 155–56.
119. See Bar-Tsvi, *Jurisdiction*, pp. 97–98.
120. Bailey, *Proverbs*, p. 254.
121. Ibid., p. 274.
122. Oral communication from Muḥammad Sulaymān al-Kishkhar of the Ẓullām Janabīb, December 14, 1981.
123. Based on 1931 figures from al-ʿĀrif, *al-Qaḍāʾ*, for population (pp. 7–15) and number of camels (pp. 223–24).
124. Oral communication from Frayj Ḥimayd as-Saddān of the ʿAzāzma Saraḥīn, July 4, 2001.
125. See chapter 5 for a discussion of these canons.
126. See Bailey, *Proverbs*, p. 279, for the legal maxim.
127. Ibid., p. 278.
128. From my tape recording of a hearing on the case, at Abū Rudays, Sinai, August 20, 1975.
129. Bailey, *Proverbs*, p. 278.
130. Ibid.
131. Oral communication from Judge Amīra Salāma Abū Amīra of the Masaʿīd Awāmra, January 18, 2000.
132. Oral communication from Swaylim Zāyid al-Gunbayzī of the Tarabīn Ḥasāblah, November 29, 1999.
133. Oral communication from Shaykh Salāma ʿAwwād Masʿūd of the Suwārka Zuyūd, January 22, 1972.
134. Oral communication from Muḥammad Sālim Abū Ghuraygāna of the Aḥeiwāt Shawafīn, December 3, 1997.
135. Oral communication from Swaylim Sulaymān Abū Bilayya of the ʿAzāzma Saraḥīn, May 17, 1998.
136. See chapter 5 for more on "burying the pebble."
137. Oral communication from Sulaymān ʿĪd Ibn Jāzī of the Tarabīn Ḥasāblah, April 18, 1996; cf. Stewart, *Texts*, vol. 1, pp. 111–13, and Bailey, *Poetry*, pp. 77–82.
138. Oral communication from ʿĀyid ʿAwwād Jumʿa of the Muzayna Sakhāna, September 15, 1973.
139. Oral communication from Swaylim Sulaymān Abū Bilayya of the ʿAzāzma Saraḥīn, May 28, 1998.
140. Also "covenant and friendship" (*ḥilf ū-wilf*).
141. Shuqayr, *Taʾrīkh*, p. 404.
142. Bailey, *Proverbs*, p. 67.

143. Another term for this position is "accountant" (*ḥasīb*; pl. *ḥasaba*), "he who keeps account."

144. Oral communication from ʿAnayz Sālim al-ʿUrḍī of the Tarabīn Ḥasāblah, October 20, 1999.

145. Shuqayr, *Taʾrīkh*, p. 406.

146. Oral communication from Swaylim Sulaymān Abū Bilayya of the ʿAzāzma Saraḥīn, October 15, 1998.

147. Oral communication from Lāfī Faraj Sulaymān of the Rumaylāt Busūm, October 15, 1970.

148. Oral communication from Judge Murayshid Rashīd al-Marāshda of the Suwārka Zuyūd, February 12, 1977.

149. Oral communication from Ṣabāḥ Ṣāliḥ al-Ghānim of the ʿAgaylī ʿAgūl, November 21, 1996.

150. Oral communication from Salmān Ibn Ḥammād of the ʿAzāzma Masʿūdiyyīn, September 9, 1997; cf. al-ʿĀrif, *al-Qaḍāʾ*, pp. 60–61.

151. Oral communication from Judge Amīra Salāma Abū Amīra of the Masaʿīd Awāmra, January 18, 2000.

152. Oral communication from Muḥammad Ḥusayn al-ʿAlowna of the Tarabīn Ḥasāblah, November 28, 1999.

153. Shuqayr, *Taʾrīkh*, pp. 110; see Bailey, "Dating," pp. 32–33, for determining the date.

154. Bailey, "Nineteenth Century," pp. 55–58.

155. Bailey, *Proverbs*, pp. 156–57.

156. Oral communication from Salīm ʿĪd Ibn Jāzī of the Tarabīn Ḥasāblah, March 29, 1972.

157. Bailey, *Proverbs*, p.189, for the preceding two proverbs.

158. Oral communications from Sālim ʿOwda aṭ-Ṭimṭāwī (February 23, 1974) and ʿAliyyān ʿĪd aṭ-Ṭimṭāwī (February 11, 2001), both of the ʿAzāzma ʿAṣiyāt.

159. Bailey, *Proverbs*, p. 187.

160. See Stewart, *Texts*, vol. 1, pp. 41–51.

161. Bailey, *Proverbs*, p. 198.

162. See chapter 2 for more on *badwa* delegations.

163. See chapter 2 for more on *jāha* delegations.

164. See Bar-Tsvi, *Jurisdiction*, pp. 45–47.

165. See Stewart, *Texts*, vol. 1, pp. 158–61.

166. Oral communication from Salmān Muḥammad Abū Ṣabḥā of the Muzayna Ghawānma, January 27, 2007.

167. Oral communication from ʿAnayz Sālim al-ʿUrḍī of the Tarabīn Ḥasāblah, November 1, 1998.

168. Al-ʿĀrif, *al-Qaḍāʾ*, p. 159.

169. Bailey, *Proverbs*, p. 189.

170. Ibid., p. 328.

171. Oral communication from Judge Muḥammad Ḥusayn al-ʿAlowna of the Tarabīn Ḥasāblah, June 30, 1998.

172. See Stewart, *Texts*, vol. 2, p. 8, for the Arabic text. Stewart translates *ṭīz* as cunt, but it refers here to ass.

173. Ibid., vol. 1, p. 10.

174. Oral communication from Khalīl Farhūd Abū-l-Gīʿān of the Tiyāha Abū-l-Gīʿān, July 7, 2006.

175. Bailey, *Proverbs*, p. 183.

176. Oral communications from ʿĀyid ʿUbayd Ibn Sarīaʿ of the Tarabīn Shibaythāt, November 10, 1996, and Zāyid ʿUbaydallah al-ʿUrḍī of the Tarabīn Ḥasāblah, December 3, 1997.

177. Oral communication from Judge Muḥammad Ḥusayn al-ʿAlowna of the Tarabīn Ḥasāblah, June 30, 1998. See chapter 5 for more on fines for an ejected eye.

178. Oral communications from Swaylim Sulaymān Abū Bilayya (May 30, 1973) and ʿOwda Sālim al-Owraydī (March 15, 1974), both of the ʿAzāzma Saraḥīn.

179. See chapter 2 for more on "blackening."

180. See Bar-Tsvi, *Jurisdiction*, p. 88.

181. Ibid., p. 76.

182. Oral communication from Chief Sulaymān Salīm Ibn Sarīaʿ of the Tarabīn Shibaythāt, September 24, 1971.

183. See Stewart, *Texts*, vol. 1, pp. 74–76.

184. Bailey, *Proverbs*, p. 260.

185. See chapter 5 for more on wounds.

186. Oral communication from ʿĀyid ʿUbayd Ibn Sarīaʿ of the Tarabīn Shibaythāt, November 10, 1996.

187. Bailey, *Proverbs*, p. 260.

188. Ibid., p. 357.

189. Ibid., p. 367.

190. Ibid., p. 396.

191. Oral communications from Judge Murayshid Rashīd al-Marāshda of the Suwārka Zuyūd, February 12, 1977, and Judge Amīra Salāma Abū Amīra of the Masaʿīd Awāmra, January 18, 2000.

192. Oral communication from Judge Muḥammad Ḥusayn al-ʿAlowna of the Tarabīn Ḥasāblah, June 29, 1998.

193. Oral communication from Chief Sālim Salāma Rajawīn of the Dawāghra Naghāmsha, March 13, 1977.

194. From a tape recording I made of the *jāha* session at which the fine was determined, September 16, 1977.

195. Oral communication from ʿĀyid Frayj al-Farārja of the Tarabīn Ḥasāblah, January 31, 2001.

196. See the "Index of Bedouin Legal Maxims."

197. Oral communication from Judge Amīra Salāma Abū Amīra of the Masaʿīd Awāmra, January 18, 2000.

198. Oral communications from Sulaymān ʿĪd Ibn Jāzī (December 2, 1997) and Jumʿa ʿĪd al-Farārja (December 4, 1997), both of the Tarabīn Ḥasāblah.

199. Oral communication from Muḥammad Sālim al-Aʿsam of the Tiyāha Gudayrāt, October 15, 1995; cf. al-ʿĀrif, *al-Qaḍāʾ*, p. 293.

200. Bailey, *Proverbs*, p. 212.

201. Oral communication from ʿAnayz Sālim al-ʿUrḍī of the Tarabīn Ḥasāblah, July 28, 1999.

202. Bailey, *Proverbs*, p. 171.
203. Ibid., p. 170.
204. Musil, *Manners*, p. 496; also oral communications from judges Muḥammad ʿAlāya of the Liyāthna (Jordan), April 25, 1996, and Muḥammad Ḥusayn al-ʿAlowna of the Tarabīn Ḥasāblah, June 30, 1998.
205. Oral communication from Sālim Salāma ar-Rimāg of the ʿAzāzma Saraḥīn, September 30, 1997.
206. Oral communication from Swaylim Sulaymān Abū Bilayya of the ʿAzāzma Saraḥīn, October 5, 1999.
207. See the "Index of Bedouin Legal Maxims" for the preceding two proverbs.
208. Bailey, *Proverbs*, p. 102.
209. Ibid., p. 416.
210. Oral communication from Frayj Ḥimayd as-Saddān of the ʿAzāzma Saraḥīn, December 10, 2005.
211. Oral communication from Muḥammad Ḥusayn al-ʿAlowna of the Tarabīn Ḥasāblah, June 17, 1998.
212. Bailey, *Proverbs*, p. 418, for the preceding two sayings.
213. See Bar-Tsvi, *Jurisdiction*, pp. 116–17.
214. As discussed in ibid., pp. 117–18.
215. Bailey, *Proverbs*, p. 419.
216. Ibid., p. 336.

Chapter 5. The Role of Litigation in Achieving Justice

1. Bailey, *Proverbs*, p. 281.
2. Ibid., p. 282.
3. Ibid., p. 244.
4. See chapter 2 for more on denunciation.
5. See Stewart, *Texts*, vol. 1, pp. 135–38, 150–53.
6. Ibid., p. 29, for a Bedouin discussion of this measure.
7. See below for more on this ordeal; also Ginat, *Bishʿah Justice*, passim.
8. See Stewart, *Texts*, vol. 1, pp. 9–10.
9. Ibid.
10. Al-ʿĀrif, *al-Qaḍāʾ*, pp. 60–61; for a list of the judges as of 1931, see Abu-Rabiʿa, *Bedouin Century*, p. 61. Also see El-Barghuthi, "Judicial Courts," pp. 34–65.
11. See chapter 4 for more on tribal agreements.
12. Oral communication from Judge Salmān Ḥusayn Ibn Ḥammād of the ʿAzāzma Masʿūdiyyīn, September 30, 1997.
13. See Bar-Tsvi, *Jurisdiction*, pp. 27–28.
14. Oral communication from Judge Amīra Salāma Abū Amīra of the Masaʿīd Awāmra, January 18, 2000.
15. Al-ʿĀrif, *al-Qaḍāʾ*, pp. 60–61.
16. For example, see Hilw and Darwish, *Customary Law*, p. 94 and passim; also oral communication from Judge Amīra Salāma Abū Amīra of the Masaʿīd Awāmra, January 18, 2000.

17. Bailey, *Proverbs*, p. 349. In the Arabic, "a ruling" is *ḥagg* (normally "right" or "law"), as it determines what the law is.

18. Oral communication from Shaykh Sālim Ḥusayn ʿAgaylī of the Masaʿīd Marābda, September 3, 1975.

19. Bailey, "Dating," pp. 27–28.

20. Oral communication from Judge Amīra Salāma Abū Amīra of the Masaʿīd Awāmra, January 18, 2000.

21. Oral communication from an anonymous host in the Masaʿīd tent at the annual camel races near El-ʿArīsh, November 21, 1996.

22. See Bar-Tsvi, *Jurisdiction*, pp. 124–25.

23. Bailey, *Proverbs*, pp. 348–49.

24. Shuqayr, *Taʾrīkh*, pp. 117–18; al-ʿĀrif, *Taʾrīkh*, pp. 117–20; Bailey, *Poetry*, pp. 212–15.

25. Bailey and Shmueli, "Settlement," pp. 28–31.

26. See Kennett, *Bedouin Justice*, p. 108.

27. Oral communication from Ḥājj ʿĪd ʿOwda Abū Rīsh of the ʿAyāyda Salāṭna at Jinayfa, Egypt, October 25, 1973.

28. Murray, *Sons of Ishmael*, p. 234.

29. Oral communication from Yosef Ginat of Haifa University, January 2, 2005.

30. Oral communication from Ḥusayn Salīm Ḥasan of the ʿAyāyda Salāṭna, March 8, 1972.

31. Oral communication from Yosef Ginat, January 2, 2005.

32. Bailey, *Proverbs*, p. 305.

33. Ibid., p. 306.

34. See Stewart, *Texts*, vol. 1, p. 160.

35. See the "Index of Bedouin Legal Maxims."

36. Oral communication from ʿAnayz Sālim al-ʿUrḍī of the Tarabīn Ḥasāblah, November 9, 1996.

37. Oral communication from Judge Salmān Ḥusayn Ibn Ḥammād of the ʿAzāzma Masʿūdiyyīn, September 30, 1997.

38. Oral communication from Muḥammad Salmān Abū Jarabīaʿ of the ʿAzāzma Masʿūdiyyīn, May 26, 2001; cf. al-ʿĀrif, *al-Qaḍāʾ*, pp. 196–97, for a similar expression of Bedouin disdain for peasants.

39. Oral communication from Judge Muḥammad Ḥusayn al-ʿAlowna of the Tarabīn Ḥasāblah, November 1, 1998.

40. Bailey, *Proverbs*, p. 290.

41. See Stewart, *Texts*, vol. 1, pp. 4–7.

42. Oral communication from Sālim Jumʿa Abū Ṣabḥā of the Muzayna Ghawānma, November 22, 1994.

43. Oral communication from Swaylim Sulaymān Abū Bilayya of the ʿAzāzma Saraḥīn, October 1, 1973.

44. See Stewart, *Texts*, vol. 1, p. 70.

45. Bailey, *Proverbs*, p. 310.

46. Ibid., p. 309.

47. Ibid., p. 362.

48. See Stewart, *Texts*, vol. 1, pp. 22–25.

49. From my tape recording of this hearing at Abū Rudays, in Sinai, August 20, 1975.

50. Oral communication from Ḥājj Swaylim Zāyid al-Gunbayzī of the Tarabīn Ḥasāblah, November 29, 1999.

51. See chapter 2 for more on guaranty.

52. Bailey, *Proverbs*, p. 295.

53. Ibid., p. 290.

54. See Bar-Tsvi, *Jurisdiction*, p. 88.

55. Bailey, *Proverbs*, p. 307.

56. Ibid., p. 299.

57. Ibid., p. 295.

58. Ibid., p. 291.

59. Ibid., p. 297.

60. Ibid.

61. See al-ʿĀrif, *al-Qaḍāʾ*, pp. 93–94.

62. See Bar-Tsvi, *Jurisdiction*, pp. 112–13.

63. Bailey, *Proverbs*, p. 304.

64. Ibid., p. 308.

65. Ibid., p. 307.

66. Ibid., p. 306.

67. Ibid.

68. See Stewart, *Texts*, vol. 1, pp. 135, 173, for examples.

69. See Bar-Tsvi, *Jurisdiction*, p. 131, for an example from the trial of Sālim Abū Ṣabḥā against the sons of Munayfī Jabalī, all of the Muzayna confederation of southeast Sinai.

70. Bailey, *Proverbs*, p. 313.

71. See below for more on oaths.

72. Oral communication from Judge Muḥammad Sālim al-Āʿsam of the Tiyāha Gudayrāt, December 14, 1995; cf. Bailey, *Proverbs*, p. 314.

73. Bailey, *Proverbs*, p. 312.

74. Ibid., p. 313.

75. Ibid., p. 314.

76. Oral communication from Judge Amīra Salāma Abū Amīra of the Masaʿīd Awāmra, January 18, 2000.

77. Oral communication from Shaykh ʿAwaḍallah Misfir of the Bilī Magābla, August 21, 1975.

78. Oral communication from Shaykh Salāma ʿAwwād Masʿūd of the Suwārka Zuyūd, January 22, 1972.

79. See Stewart, *Texts*, vol. 2, pp. 29–30 (my translation).

80. Oral communication from Sālim Jumʿa Abū Ṣabḥā of the Muzayna Ghawānma, November 22, 1994; cf. Bar-Tsvi, *Jurisdiction*, pp. 131–34, as tape-recorded at the trial (June 24, 1976).

81. For tape-recorded examples, see Bar-Tsvi, *Jurisdiction*, p. 135, and Stewart, *Texts*, vol. 1, pp. 45–48.

82. Oral communication from Swaylim Sulaymān Abū Bilayya of the ʿAzāzma Saraḥīn, June 9, 1974.

83. Bailey, *Proverbs*, p. 315.

84. Based on my tape recording of a hearing of the case at Abu Rudays, Sinai, July 25, 1975.

85. Bailey, *Proverbs*, p. 279.

86. See Bar-Tsvi, *Jurisdiction*, p. 107.

87. Ibid., pp. 27–28.

88. Bailey, *Proverbs*, p. 287.

89. Ibid., p. 316.

90. Ibid., p. 189.

91. Recall the saying mentioned in chapter 3: "When one turns to his cousin, even if he's wrong, he's not" (*illī biyījī l-ibn ʿammah—lō lih shī mā lih shī*). Ibid., p. 127.

92. See Bar-Tsvi, *Jurisdiction*, p. 118.

93. Bailey, *Proverbs*, p. 310.

94. Ibid., p. 316.

95. Ibid., p. 267.

96. See Bar-Tsvi, *Jurisdiction*, pp. 27–28.

97. Oral communication from Frayj Ḥimayd as-Saddān of the ʿAzāzma Saraḥīn, July 4, 2001.

98. Bailey, *Proverbs*, p. 389.

99. Oral communication from Ṣabāḥ Muḥammad Jumʿa of the Muzayna Iḥsaynāt, July 26, 1999.

100. See Bar-Tsvi, *Jurisdiction*, p. 51; Bar-Tsvi had heard the account from Chief ʿAwwāḍ Abū Rugayyig of the Tiyāha confederation.

101. Oral communication from ʿAnayz Sālim al-ʿUrḍī of the Tarabīn Ḥasāblah, December 2, 1997.

102. Oral communication from Amīra Salāma Abū Amīra of the Masaʿīd Awāmra, January 18, 2000.

103. See Bailey, *Proverbs*, pp. 199–201, for more on hospitality judges.

104. Ibid., p. 349.

105. Ibid., p. 351.

106. Ibid., p. 317.

107. See Bar-Tsvi, *Jurisdiction*, pp. 41–42.

108. Oral communication from Ṣabāḥ Muḥammad Jumʿa of the Muzayna Iḥsaynāt, July 26, 1999.

109. Oral communication from Judge Amīra Salāma Abū Amīra of the Masaʿīd Awāmra, January 18, 2000.

110. Oral communication from ʿAliyyān aṭ-Ṭimṭāwī of the ʿAzāzma ʿAṣiyāt, December 12, 2004.

111. Oral communication from Swaylim Sulaymān Abū Bilayya of the ʿAzāzma Saraḥīn, May 22, 1973.

112. See chapter 6 for more on oaths taken over claims to land ownership.

113. Bailey, *Proverbs*, p. 318.

114. Ibid., p. 317.

115. See Bar-Tsvi, *Jurisdiction*, p. 45.

116. I tape-recorded the details of this case at a trial held at the home of the judge, Ḥamdān aṣ-Ṣūfī, at Rafaḥ, in the Gaza Strip, July 14, 1984.

117. Oral communication from Shaykh ʿAlī Salāma Abū Graynāt of the Ẓullām Abū Graynāt, February 23, 1974.

118. See Bar-Tsvi, *Jurisdiction*, pp. 99–100.

119. See ibid., p. 66.

120. Oral communication from ʿAnayz Sālim al-ʿUrḍī of the Tarabīn Ḥasāblah, November 9, 1996.

121. Bailey, *Proverbs*, p. 318, for the preceding two proverbs.

122. Ibid., p. 319.

123. See Bar-Tsvi, *Jurisdiction*, pp. 31–32.

124. See the "Index of Bedouin Legal Maxims" for the preceding two sayings.

125. Bailey, *Proverbs*, p. 317.

126. Ibid., p. 267.

127. Ibid., p. 320.

128. See Bar-Tsvi, *Jurisdiction*, pp. 31–32.

129. Oral communication from ʿAnayz Sālim al-ʿUrḍī of the Tarabīn Ḥasāblah, April 5, 1983.

130. Oral communication from Sulaymān ʿĪd Ibn Jāzī of the Tarabīn Ḥasāblah, December 2, 1997.

131. Bailey, "Weddings," pp. 126–29.

132. Bailey, *Proverbs*, p. 319, for the two preceding proverbs.

133. Ibid., p. 320.

134. See the "Index of Bedouin Legal Maxims" for the preceding two sayings.

135. Oral communication from ʿAnayz Sālim al-ʿUrḍī of the Tarabīn Ḥasāblah, April 5, 1983.

136. Details tape-recorded at the trial, July 14, 1984.

137. Oral communication from Shaykh ʿAlī Salāma Abū Graynāt of the Ẓullām Abū Graynāt, February 23, 1974.

138. See al-ʿĀrif, *al-Qaḍāʾ*, pp. 255–64; Bailey, "Religious Practices," pp. 74–76; Bar-Tsvi et al., *Graves*, passim.

139. Oral communication from Sulaymān Ḥusayn Khiraynig of the ʿAzāzma Saraḥīn, December 4, 2004.

140. Oral communication from Sulaymān ʿĪd Ibn Jāzī of the Tarabīn Ḥasāblah, December 2, 1997.

141. See Bar-Tsvi, *Jurisdiction*, pp. 27–28.

142. Oral communication from Swaylim Sulaymān Abū Bilayya of the ʿAzāzma Saraḥīn, May 25, 1973; cf. Burckhardt, *Notes*, vol. 1, pp. 128–29.

143. Oral communication from Sulaymān Ḥusayn al-Khiraynig of the ʿAzāzma Saraḥīn, July 25, 2005.

144. See Bar-Tsvi, *Jurisdiction*, pp. 65–66.

145. Oral communication from ʿAnayz Sālim al-ʿUrḍī of the Tarabīn Ḥasāblah, April 5, 1983.

146. See chapter 6 for more on abduction.

147. Details tape-recorded at the trial, July 14, 1984.

148. Bailey, *Proverbs*, p. 320.

149. Burckhardt, *Notes*, vol. 1, pp. 290–91.

150. Bailey, *Proverbs*, p. 319.

151. Oral communication from Frayj Ḥimayd as-Saddān of the ʿAzāzma Saraḥīn, March 25, 2006.

152. See the "Index of Bedouin Legal Maxims."

153. See Bar-Tsvi, *Jurisdiction*, pp. 105–6.

154. Ibid., p. 67.

155. See Stewart, *Texts*, vol. 1, p. 129.

156. See Bar-Tsvi, *Jurisdiction*, p. 107.

157. Ibid.

158. Ibid., p. 53.

159. Ibid., p. 105.

160. See the "Index of Bedouin Legal Maxims."

161. See Bar-Tsvi, *Jurisdiction*, p. 67.

162. The following procedures are as demonstrated by the *mubashshaʿ* ʿAyyād ʿAwwād al-Jarabīʿa in a documentary film, *Bishʿa*, produced by Elia Sides, 1998.

163. Oral communication from Judge Amīra Salāma Abū Amīra of the Masaʿīd Awāmra, January 18, 2000.

164. Stewart, *Texts*, vol. 1, pp. 111–13.

165. Ibid., p. 214.

166. Oral communication from Ḥājj ʿĪd ʿOwda Abū Rīsh of the ʿAyāyda Salāṭna, at Jinayfa, Egypt, October 25, 1973.

167. See Bar-Tsvi, *Jurisdiction*, pp. 118–19.

168. Oral communication from Ḥusayn Salīm Abū Rīsh of the ʿAyāyda Salāṭna, March 8, 1972.

169. Oral communication from Shaykh Sālim Naṣṣār Salāma of the ʿAyāyda Salāṭna, March 15, 1974.

170. Bailey, *Proverbs*, p. 322, for the preceding two maxims.

171. Oral communication from ʿAnayz Sālim al-ʿUrḍī of the Tarabīn Ḥasāblah, November 9, 1996.

172. See Bar-Tsvi, *Jurisdiction*, pp. 65–66.

173. Oral communication from Judge Amīra Salāma Abū Amīra of the Masaʿīd Awāmra, January 18, 2000; cf. Bailey, *Poetry*, pp. 91–97.

174. Oral communication from Judge Amīra Salāma Abū Amīra of the Masaʿīd Awāmra, January 18, 2000.

175. Oral communication from ʿAnayz Sālim al-ʿUrḍī of the Tarabīn Ḥasāblah, June 29, 1998.

176. Oral communication from Judge Amīra Salāma Abū Amīra of the Masaʿīd Awāmra, January 18, 2000.

177. Oral communication from ʿAnayz Sālim al-ʿUrḍī of the Tarabīn Ḥasāblah, June 29, 1998.

178. See the "Index of Bedouin Legal Maxims."

179. Oral communication from ʿAnayz Sālim al-ʿUrḍī of the Tarabīn Ḥasāblah, November 9, 1996.

180. See Bar-Tsvi, *Jurisdiction*, p. 78.

181. Ibid., p. 26.

182. Ibid., pp. 41–42.
183. Ibid., p. 68; Bailey, *Proverbs*, p. 285.
184. See Bar-Tsvi, *Jurisdiction*, p. 69.
185. See the "Index of Bedouin Legal Maxims."
186. See Bar-Tsvi, *Jurisdiction*, pp. 52, 57.
187. See the "Index of Bedouin Legal Maxims."
188. Oral communication from ʿAnayz Sālim al-ʿUrḍī of the Tarabīn Ḥasāblah, November 1, 1998.
189. See Bar-Tsvi, *Jurisdiction*, p. 109, for a *ghurra* presented after murder within the same clan.
190. See chapter 6 for examples of the *ghurra* penalty.
191. See Bailey, *Proverbs*, pp. 341–42.
192. Oral communication from Jum'a ʿĪd al-Farārja of the Tarabīn Ḥasāblah, December 4, 1997; see Bar-Tsvi, *Jurisdiction*, pp. 56, 109, for examples of a husband's unfettered brutality to his *ghurra* wife.
193. Oral communication from ʿOwda Ṣāliḥ Imbārak of the Muzayna Shaẓāẓna, November 22, 1994; also see Bar-Tsvi, *Jurisdiction*, pp. 62–64, 137–38, and Hilw and Darwish, *Customary Law*, pp. 68–71.
194. Oral communication from Swaylim Sulaymān Abū Bilayya of the ʿAzāzma Sarahīn, May 20, 1973.
195. Oral communication from Sālim Jumʿa Abū Ṣabḥā of the Muzayna Ghawānma, November 22, 1994; cf. Bar-Tsvi, *Jurisdiction*, pp. 131–34.
196. See Hilw and Darwish, *Customary Law*, pp. 74–75; in a case of rape cited above, the judge ordered the placing of three white flags at various places, such as where the act took place, the tent of the *ḍraybī* judge who issued the verdict and sent the contestants to the *manshad* judge for the sentence, and the tent of the girl's guardian.
197. Oral communications from Swaylim Sulaymān Abū Bilayya (February 13, 1974) and Frayj Ḥimayd as-Saddān (December 13, 2004), both of the ʿAzāzma Sarahīn.
198. See Hilw and Darwish, *Customary Law*, pp. 52–53.
199. Oral communication from Swaylim Sulaymān Abū Bilayya of the ʿAzāzma Sarahīn, October 15, 1998; cf. Judge Ṣāliḥ Sālim az-Zalābya of the Ḥuwayṭāt Zalābya (Jordan), October 29, 1998; Hilw and Darwish, *Customary Law*, p. 88 (for the Bilī version in Sinai, as heard from Judge Ibrahīm ʿOwda Abū Dahathūm, September 1, 1987). By contrast to what is herein stated, al-ʿĀrif (*al-Qaḍā'*, p. 56) quotes the *gaṣṣāṣ*, ʿAwwād Ibn Dallākh, of the Bilī, as awarding twenty, rather than ten, camels for the loss of one eye.
200. Al-ʿĀrif, *al-Qaḍā'*, p. 56.
201. Shuqayr, *Ta'rīkh*, p. 415.
202. Oral communication from Jumʿa ʿĪd al-Farārja of the Tarabīn Ḥasāblah, December 4, 1997. See the "Index of Bedouin Legal Maxims" for the proverb.
203. Bailey, *Proverbs*, p. 327.
204. Oral communication from Salmān Muḥammad Abū Ṣabḥā of the Muzayna Ghawānma, January 27, 2007.
205. Bailey, *Proverbs*, pp. 356–57.
206. Oral communication from Sālim Ḥusayn al-ʿAgaylī of the Masaʿīd Marābda, September 3, 1975.

207. See chapter 6 for more on beating a wife.

208. Oral communication from Sulaymān ʿĪd Ibn Jāzī of the Tarabīn Ḥasāblah, April 18, 1996.

209. See the "Index of Bedouin Legal Maxims."

210. For example, see Musil, *Manners*, p. 398.

211. Oral communication from ʿAnayz Sālim al-ʿUrḍī of the Tarabīn Ḥasāblah, April 5, 1983.

212. Oral communication from Muḥammad Ḥusayn al-ʿAlowna of the Tarabīn Ḥasāblah, June 17, 1998.

213. See chapter 4 for more on the obligations toward a companion.

214. Bailey, *Proverbs*, p. 389.

215. See Bar-Tsvi, *Jurisdiction*, p. 76.

216. Oral communication from ʿAnayz Sālim al-ʿUrḍī of the Tarabīn Ḥasāblah, December 2, 1997.

217. See Bar-Tsvi, *Jurisdiction*, p. 88.

218. See chapter 4 for more on blood-truces.

219. See chapter 4 for more on "the camel of sleep."

220. See chapter 2 for more on the "guarantor of warmth."

221. Shuqayr, *Taʾrīkh*, p. 414.

222. Oral communication from ʿOwda Ṣāliḥ Imbārak of the Muzayna Shaẓāẓna, November 22, 1994.

223. See Bar-Tsvi, *Jurisdiction*, p. 107.

224. Oral communication from Muḥammad Ḥusayn al-ʿAlowna of the Tarabīn Ḥasāblah, June 17, 1998.

225. Based on my tape recording of the *jāha* at which the fines were determined and conceded, September 16, 1977.

226. Oral communication from ʿAlī Abū-l-Gīʿān, Ḥūra village, July 1, 2008.

227. Bailey, *Proverbs*, p. 332.

228. See the "Index of Bedouin Legal Maxims."

229. Bailey, *Proverbs*, pp. 333–35, for the preceding four expressions.

230. Ibid., p. 334.

231. Ibid., for the preceding two proverbs.

232. Oral communication from Swaylim Sulaymān Abū Bilayya of the ʿAzāzma Saraḥīn, May 8, 1998.

233. Bailey, *Proverbs*, p. 335.

234. The following discussion is based on my tape recording of the *jāha* in question, September 16, 1977.

235. Bailey, *Proverbs*, p. 347, for the preceding two maxims.

236. Ibid., p. 338.

237. Ibid., p. 340.

238. Ibid., p. 260.

239. Cf. Bar-Tsvi, *Jurisdiction*, pp. 45–47, 65–66, 97–98, for more instances of kissing a victim at reconciliation.

240. Bailey, *Proverbs*, pp. 344–46, for these and other expressions of reconciliation.

241. Ibid., p. 299.
242. See chapter 2 for more on "blackening" remiss guarantors.

Chapter 6. Laws Pertaining to Women, Property, and Sanctuary

1. See chapter 3 for more on the upbringing of women.
2. See chapter 2 for more on honor and strength.
3. Bailey, *Proverbs*, p. 238.
4. See chapter 5 for more on judges and punishments.
5. See Kressel, "Ḥaqq Akhū Manshad," passim.
6. Oral communication from Amīra Salāma Abū Amīra of the Masaʿīd Awāmra, January 18, 2000.
7. See the "Index of Bedouin Legal Maxims."
8. Bailey, *Proverbs*, p. 279.
9. Ibid.
10. Oral communications from Sulaymān Jumʿa Abū Ṣabḥā of the Muzayna Ghawānma, April 20, 1996.
11. Oral communication from Amīra Salāma Abū Amīra of the Masaʿīd Awāmra, January 18, 2000.
12. Bailey, *Proverbs*, p. 354.
13. Oral communication from Swaylim Sulaymān Abū Bilayya of the ʿAzāzma Saraḥīn, February 13, 1974.
14. See chapter 5 for an example of such a plea.
15. Bailey, *Proverbs*, p. 355.
16. Oral communication from Amīra Salāma Abū Amīra of the Masaʿīd Awāmra, January 18, 2000.
17. See Bar-Tsvi, *Jurisdiction*, pp.62–63.
18. Forty also has holy significance for the Bedouin, adding to the awe of the punishment; see Bailey, "Religious Practices," p. 83.
19. Oral communication from Sālim Ḥusayn al-ʿAgaylī of the Masaʿīd Marābda, September 3, 1975.
20. Bailey, *Proverbs*, p. 352.
21. Ibid., p. 126.
22. Ibid., p. 123.
23. Oral communication from Shaykh Sālim Ḥusayn ʿAgaylī of the Masaʿīd Marābda, September 3, 1975.
24. Bailey, *Proverbs*, p. 352.
25. Ibid.
26. Oral communication from Shaykh Sālim Salāma Rajawīn of the Dawāghra Naghāmsha, March 13, 1977.
27. From the author's tape recording of a hearing of this case at Abū Rudays, in Sinai, August 20, 1975.
28. See chapter 4 for more on the camel-truce; also Bailey, *Proverbs*, pp. 277–79.
29. Recall the dictum noted above: "He whose camel is couched is ready for the honor trial." Bailey, *Proverbs*, p. 279.

30. See chapter 4 for more on violence as a last resort.

31. See the "Index of Bedouin Legal Maxims."

32. See Bar-Tsvi, *Jurisdiction*, pp. 136–38; Bar-Tsvi attended and recorded the trial.

33. Oral communication from Sulaymān Jumʿa Abū Ṣabḥā of the Muzayna Ghawānma, June 29, 2005.

34. I attended and tape-recorded the hearing, August 20, 1975.

35. See Bar-Tsvi, *Jurisdiction*, pp. 121–40, for a tape recording of the proceedings.

36. See below for more on theft; also see Bailey, *Proverbs*, p. 364.

37. Oral communication from the judge's son, Amīra Salāma Abū Amīra of the Masaʿīd Awāmra, January 18, 2000.

38. Oral communication from Swaylim Sulaymān Abū Bilayya of the ʿAzāzma Sarahīn, November 10, 1974.

39. Oral communication from Sālim Jumʿa Abū Ṣabḥā of the Muzayna Ghawānma, November 22, 1994; cf. Bar-Tsvi, *Jurisdiction*, p. 132. See chapter 5 for Abū Ṣabḥā's plea.

40. From my tape recording of a hearing of this case at Abū Rudays, in Sinai, August 20, 1975.

41. Oral communication from Judge ʿOwda Ṣāliḥ Imbārak of the Muzayna Shaẓāẓna, November 22, 1994.

42. Bailey, *Proverbs*, p. 353.

43. Ibid., p. 285.

44. Oral communication from ʿAnayz Sālim al-ʿUrḍī of the Tarabīn Ḥasāblah, November 9, 1996.

45. Oral communication from the judge's son, Amīra Salāma Abū Amīra of the Masaʿīd Awāmra, January 18, 2000.

46. See below for more on invading tents.

47. Oral communication from ʿAnayz Sālim al-ʿUrḍī of the Tarabīn Ḥasāblah, December 2, 1997.

48. Bailey, *Proverbs*, p. 351.

49. Oral communication from Sālim Muḥammad Abū Jilaydān of the ʿAzāzma ʿAṣiyāt, July 5, 1974.

50. Oral communications from Swaylim Sulaymān Abū Bilayya (February 13, 1974) and Frayj Ḥimayd as-Saddān (December 13, 2004), both of the ʿAzāzma Saraḥīn.

51. Oral communication from Amīra Salāma Abū Amīra of the Masaʿīd Awāmra, January 18, 2000.

52. Bailey, *Proverbs*, pp. 350–51, for the previous two sayings.

53. See chapter 3 for more on women in the clan.

54. Bailey, *Poetry*, pp. 139–40.

55. Oral communication from Sālim Salāma ar-Rimāg of the ʿAzāzma Saraḥīn, November 22, 2000.

56. Oral communications from Swaylim Sulaymān Abū Bilayya (May 30, 1973) and ʿOwda Salmān al-Owraydī (January 10, 1974), both of the ʿAzāzma Saraḥīn.

57. Bailey, *Proverbs*, p. 268.

58. Ibid., p. 416.

59. Oral communication from Swaylim Sulaymān Abū Bilayya of the ʿAzāzma Saraḥīn, October 1, 1973.

60. See below for more on divorce.

61. Oral communication from ʿAyyāda Sulaymān Abū Bilayya of the ʿAzāzma Saraḥīn, July 18, 1974.

62. Bailey, *Proverbs*, pp. 404–5.

63. See chapter 4 for more on limiting violence.

64. Bailey, *Proverbs*, pp. 256–57.

65. For example, see Stewart, *Texts*, vol. 1, p. 24.

66. Oral communication from Swaylim Sulaymān Abū Bilayya of the ʿAzāzma Saraḥīn, October 1, 1973.

67. Oral communications from ʿAnayz Sālim al-ʿUrḍī of the Tarabīn Ḥasāblah, November 9, 1996, and December 2, 1997.

68. See Bar-Tsvi, *Jurisdiction*, p. 51.

69. Oral communication from Swaylim Sulaymān Abū Bilayya of the ʿAzāzma Saraḥīn, March 21, 1996.

70. Oral communication from ʿAtayyig Jumʿa al-Farārja of the Tarabīn Ḥasāblah, June 25, 2005.

71. See chapter 3 for more on a clan's responsibility for its women's moral behavior.

72. See Stewart, *Texts*, vol. 1, pp. 14–15.

73. Bailey, "Weddings," p. 130.

74. See Bar-Tsvi, *Jurisdiction*, p. 69.

75. Bailey, *Proverbs*, p. 408.

76. See chapter 5 for more on ʿ*ugbī* judges.

77. Bailey, "Weddings," p. 113.

78. Cf. Hava, *Al-Farāʾid Arabic-English Dictionary*, p. 227.

79. Al-ʿĀrif, *al-Qaḍāʾ*, p. 159.

80. Bailey, *Proverbs*, p. 405; cf. Bar-Tsvi, *Jurisdiction*, p. 69.

81. Oral communication from ʿOwda Sulaymān al-Hadōbe of the ʿAzāzma Saraḥīn, June 23, 1998.

82. See Burckhardt, *Notes*, vol. 1, pp. 107–8; Bailey, "Weddings," pp. 123–25.

83. Oral communication from Muḥammad Marḍī Abū Luhaym of the Jabaliyya Owlād Saʿīd, November 9, 1968. Also see Gardner, *Women*, pp. 202–6, for a vivid example of the powerless disappointment of a girl of the Tarabīn Ḥasāblah tribe in southeast Sinai with the husband chosen for her by her brothers in 1980; cf. Gardner, "Fatma's Story," parts 1 and 2.

84. Bailey, *Proverbs*, p. 147, for the preceding two sayings.

85. Oral communication from ʿAnayz Sālim al-ʿUrḍī of the Tarabīn Ḥasāblah, December 2, 1997.

86. Oral communication from Shaykh Sālim Salāma Rajawīn of the Dawāghra Naghāmsha, March 13, 1977.

87. Bailey, *Proverbs*, p. 146, for the preceding two sayings.

88. Oral communication from ʿOwda Sulaymān al-Hadōbe of the ʿAzāzma Saraḥīn, June 23, 1998.

89. Statement by Ḥimayd Salmān as-Saddān of the ʿAzāzma Saraḥīn, tape-recorded at a trial in the home of Judge Ḥamdān aṣ-Ṣūfī, Rafaḥ, the Gaza Strip, July 14, 1984.

90. Oral communication from Salāma ʿĪd Abū Bilayya of the ʿAzāzma Saraḥīn, July 4, 2001.

91. See chapter 2 for more on protection.

92. Bailey, *Proverbs*, pp. 146–47.

93. Oral communication from Sālim ʿOwda aṭ-Ṭimṭāwī of the ʿAzāzma ʿAṣiyāt, October 22, 1974.

94. Blunt, *Bedouin Tribes*, pp. 222–24.

95. Oral communication from ʿĪd Ibn Darrāj of the Ẓullām Janabīb, December 30, 1997.

96. Oral communication from Frayj Ḥimayd as-Saddān of the ʿAzāzma Saraḥīn, October 9, 1999.

97. See Marx, *Bedouin of the Negev*, pp. 149–50.

98. Oral communication from Sālim ʿOwda aṭ-Ṭimṭāwī of the ʿAzāzma ʿAṣiyāt, December 25, 1972.

99. Oral communication from Swaylim Sulaymān Abū Bilayya of the ʿAzāzma Saraḥīn, May 22, 1973.

100. For more on bride-price, see Bailey, "Weddings," pp. 110–11.

101. See the "Index of Bedouin Legal Maxims."

102. Bailey, *Proverbs*, pp. 149–50.

103. Oral communication from Swaylim Sulaymān Abū Bilayya of the ʿAzāzma Saraḥīn, May 20, 1973.

104. Oral communication from Judge Muḥammad Ḥusayn al-ʿAlowna of the Tarabīn Ḥasāblah, June 29, 1998. See Stewart, *Texts*, vol. 1, p. 69, for a further example from central Sinai.

105. Oral communication from Khalīl Farhūd Abū-l-Gīʿān of the Tiyāha Abū-l-Gīʿān, April 7, 2006.

106. Blunt, *Bedouin Tribes*, p. 224.

107. Oral communication from Zāyid ʿUbaydallah al-ʿUrḍī of the Tarabīn Ḥasāblah, December 2, 1997.

108. Bailey, *Proverbs,* p. 148.

109. See Bailey, "Weddings," pp. 127–29, for more on *dukhla*.

110. Oral communication from Swaylim Sulaymān Abū Bilayya of the ʿAzāzma Saraḥīn, May 20, 1973.

111. Ibid.

112. Ibid.

113. See Bailey, *Proverbs*, pp. 353–54, for the maxim "A companion will save you from an honor trial" (*ar-rafīg yisallmak min al-manshad*), as an unaccompanied abduction leaves room for a violation of the girl's honor.

114. Oral communication from Swaylim Sulaymān Abū Bilayya of the ʿAzāzma Saraḥīn, December 15, 1997.

115. Bailey, *Proverbs*, p. 148; the reference to staff means that the camels belong to the father.

116. Oral communication from ʿĪd Ibn Darrāj al-Wajj of the Ẓullām Janabīb, December 30, 1997.

117. The details of this case were gleaned from the claim that Ḥimayd as-Saddān made at a trial held at the home of the judge, Ḥamdān aṣ-Ṣūfī, at Rafaḥ, in the Gaza Strip, July 14, 1984.

118. Oral communication from Swaylim Sulaymān Abū Bilayya of the ʿAzāzma Sara-ḥīn, May 28, 1998.
119. Oral communication from ʿOwda Sulaymān al-Hadōbe of the ʿAzāzma Saraḥīn, June 23, 1998.
120. Oral communication from ʿAyyāda Sulaymān Abū Bilayya of the ʿAzāzma Sara-ḥīn, February 26, 1978.
121. Oral communication from Swaylim Sulaymān Abū Bilayya of the ʿAzāzma Sara-ḥīn, February 26, 1978.
122. See Bailey, *Poetry*, pp. 91–97, for a depiction of the case and a poem composed in its wake.
123. Bailey, *Proverbs*, p. 153, for both the preceding proverbs.
124. Ibid.
125. Oral communication from ʿAnayz Sālim al-ʿUrḍī of the Tarabīn Ḥasāblah, May 25, 1984.
126. See Liebesney, *The Law*, pp. 133–35.
127. Oral communication from Swaylim Sulaymān Abū Bilayya of the ʿAzāzma Sara-ḥīn, June 13, 1998.
128. For a version of the entire story, see Bailey, *Poetry*, pp. 225–52.
129. Oral communication from Zāyid ʿUbaydallah al-ʿUrḍī of the Tarabīn Ḥasāblah, December 3, 1997.
130. Bailey, *Proverbs*, p. 154.
131. See chapter 3 for more on the legal personality of women.
132. Oral communication from Jumʿa ʿĪd al-Farārja of the Tarabīn Ḥasāblah, November 11, 1996.
133. Oral communication from Swaylim Sulaymān Abū Bilayya of the ʿAzāzma Sara-ḥīn, July 18, 1974.
134. Gardner, *Women*, pp. 211–17; also Gardner, "Fatma's Story," parts 1 and 2.
135. See chapter 5 for more on the *ghurra*.
136. Bailey, *Proverbs*, p. 147.
137. I personally witnessed the events herein related.
138. Bailey, *Proverbs*, p. 150.
139. Shuqayr, *Taʾrīkh*, p. 404.
140. Oral communication from Shaykh ʿAbdallah Darwīsh of the Muzayna Sakh-khāna, September 9, 1972.
141. For details and the complete poem, see Bailey, "Nineteenth Century," pp. 55–58.
142. Oral communication from ʿAnayz Sālim al-ʿUrḍī of the Tarabīn Ḥasāblah, November 9, 1996.
143. Bailey, "Bedouin Budget," pp. 80–81.
144. For rainfall patterns in the Negev, see Evenari et al., *The Negev*, pp. 29–30.
145. See the "Index of Bedouin Legal Maxims."
146. Oral communication from ʿAnayz Sālim al-ʿUrḍī of the Tarabīn Ḥasāblah (who served as a judge in the case), October 31, 1998.
147. Bailey, *Proverbs*, p. 368.
148. Shuqayr, *Taʾrīkh*, p. 419.
149. See chapter 5 for more on oaths.

150. For the background of this case, see Stewart, *Texts*, vol. 1, p. 126.

151. Oral communications from ʿAliyyān aṭ-Ṭimṭāwi of the ʿAzāzma ʿAṣiyāt, December 11, 2004, and Sulaymān Ḥusayn al-Khiraynig of the ʿAzāzma Saraḥīn, July 25, 2005.

152. For more on Swaylim Abū ʿArgūb, a renowned poet, see Musil, *Arabia Petraea*, vol. 3, p. 235; Bailey, *Poetry*, pp. 10, 264, 285.

153. Oral communications from Swaylim Sulaymān Abū Bilayya (December 17, 1974) and Frayj Ḥimayd as-Saddān (June 16, 2005), both of the ʿAzāzma Saraḥīn.

154. See Bar-Tsvi, *Jurisdiction,* p. 26.

155. See Stewart, *Texts*, vol. 1, pp. 123–25.

156. Kressel et al., "Changes," p. 53, n. 45.

157. Ibid.; for the Ẓullām-Yaṭṭa War, see al-ʿĀrif, *Taʾrīkh,* pp. 194–96.

158. Stewart, *Texts*, vol. 1, p. 127.

159. Ibid., p. 139.

160. Oral communication from Dakhlallah ʿĪd Abū Bilayya of the ʿAzāzma Saraḥīn, July 25, 2005.

161. For example, see Stewart, *Texts*, vol. 1, p. 130; Bar-Tsvi, *Jurisdiction*, p. 26.

162. Oral communication from Sulaymān Ḥusayn al-Khiraynig of the ʿAzāzma Saraḥīn, July 25, 2005.

163. Kressel et al., "Changes," pp. 40–41.

164. Kennett, *Bedouin Justice*, pp. 96–97.

165. Ibid., p. 96, in which an additional rule is mentioned—namely, that if more than one clansman or neighbor wishes to buy the plot up for sale, it goes to the highest bidder among them.

166. See Stewart, *Texts*, vol. 1, pp. 123–25; cf. p. 134.

167. Bailey, *Proverbs*, p. 373.

168. Oral communication from ʿAyyāda Sulaymān Abū Bilayya of the ʿAzāzma Saraḥīn, May 19, 1971.

169. Al-ʿĀrif, *al-Qadāʾ*, pp. 150, 234.

170. Ibid., p. 152.

171. Oral communication from Muḥammad Ḥusayn al-ʿAlowna of the Tarabīn Ḥasāblah, October 20, 1999. For a more complete story, see Bailey, "Arabah," p. 257.

172. See chapter 4 for more on dissolution.

173. Bailey, *Proverbs*, p. 418 for the preceding two sayings.

174. Ibid., p. 419.

175. Ibid; also see al-ʿĀrif, *al-Qaḍāʾ*, p. 234.

176. Bailey, *Proverbs*, p. 419.

177. Ibid., p. 63.

178. All the above material on *mathānī* comes from al-ʿĀrif, *al-Qaḍāʾ*, pp. 144–46; as opposed to my understanding of *mathānī* as "returned foals" and *fāyiḍa* as "the copartner's share," al-ʿĀrif presents the meanings as "two foals" and "the swift one" respectively.

179. Bailey, *Proverbs*, p. 425.

180. Ibid., p. 59.

181. Ibid., p. 374.

182. Ibid., p. 373.

183. Bar-Tsvi, *Jurisdiction*, pp. 65–66.
184. Oral communication from ʿIshaysh ʿAnayz al-ʿUrḍī of the Tarabīn Ḥasāblah, November 4, 2005.
185. Oral communication from Frayj Ḥimayd as-Saddān of the ʿAzāzma Saraḥīn, June 3, 2007.
186. Oral communication from Ḥimayd Salmān as-Saddān of the ʿAzāzma Saraḥīn, May 15, 1976.
187. Oral communication from Swaylim Sulaymān Abū Bilayya of the ʿAzāzma Saraḥīn, November 10, 1974.
188. Oral communication from Jumʿa ʿĪd al-Farārja of the Tarabīn Ḥasāblah, June 19, 1972.
189. Oral communication from Frayj Ḥimayd as-Saddān of the ʿAzāzma Saraḥīn, April 26, 2007.
190. Al-ʿĀrif, *al-Qaḍāʾ*, p. 152.
191. Bailey, *Proverbs*, p. 263.
192. See the "Index of Bedouin Legal Maxims."
193. Bailey *Proverbs*, p. 374.
194. Hilw and Darwish, *Customary Law*, p. 86; cf. Burckhardt, *Notes*, vol. 1, pp. 124–25.
195. Bailey, *Proverbs*, p. 374.
196. See the "Index of Bedouin Legal Maxims."
197. I was present when the fines were imposed, September 16, 1977.
198. Bailey, *Proverbs*, p. 67.
199. Sweet, "Camel Raiding," pp. 1132–50.
200. Oral communication from Sulaymān Jumʿa Abū Ṣabḥā of the Muzayna Ghawānma, June, 8, 2005.
201. See Bar-Tsvi, *Jurisdiction*, pp. 136–38.
202. See chapter 4 for more on impoundment.
203. See Bailey, "Nineteenth Century," pp. 39–44, for details of this story.
204. See the "Index of Bedouin Legal Maxims."
205. See chapter 5 for more on concessions.
206. For example, oral communications from Swaylim Sulaymān Abū Bilayya (October 5, 1974) and Frayj Ḥimayd as-Saddān (December 13, 2004), both of the ʿAzāzma Saraḥīn, and Muḥammad Abū Ghuraygāna of the Aḥeiwāt Shawafīn Ghuraygāniyyīn, December 3, 1997.
207. See Bar-Tsvi, *Jurisdiction*, p. 107.
208. Oral communications from Salāma ʿĪd Abū Bilayya (December 15, 1996) and Frayj Ḥimayd as-Saddān (June 16, 2005), both of the ʿAzāzma Saraḥīn.
209. Oral communication from Muḥammad Ḥusayn al-ʿAlowna of the Tarabīn Ḥasāblah, November 29, 1999.
210. See Bar-Tsvi, *Jurisdiction*, pp. 41–42.
211. Oral communications from Ṣabāḥ Muḥammad Jum'a of the Muzayna Ḥusaynāt, July 26, 1999, and Rāḍī Swaylim ʿAtayyig of the Muzayna Darārma, July 8, 2005.
212. Bailey, *Proverbs*, p. 364.
213. See the "Index of Bedouin Legal Maxims."

214. See chapter 5 for more on binding.

215. See Burckhardt, *Notes*, vol. 1, pp. 160–68.

216. See Bailey, "Arabah," pp. 256–57, for details of the original story.

217. Bailey, *Proverbs*, p. 364.

218. Bailey, "Central Negev," pp. 67–69.

219. Bailey, *Proverbs*, p. 389.

220. See Hilw and Darwish, *Customary Law*, p. 87.

221. Bailey, *Proverbs*, p. 365.

222. Sometimes by two or three, according to the circumstances of the case; e.g., see Hilw and Darwish, *Customary Law*, p. 66.

223. Bar-Tsvi, *Jurisdiction*, p. 88.

224. Hilw and Darwish, *Customary Law*, p. 68.

225. Oral communication from ʿAlī al-Kishkhar of the Ẓullam Janabīb, June 11, 1974; cf. Bailey, *Proverbs*, p. 366.

226. Bailey, *Proverbs*, p. 364.

227. Ibid., pp. 364–65.

228. See Bar-Tsvi, *Jurisdiction*, p. 88; oral communication from ʿAlī al-Kishkhar of the Ẓullām Janabīb, June 11, 1974, for details concerning the Kishkhar encampment at the time of the crime.

229. Bailey, *Proverbs*, pp. 362, 364–65.

230. Oral communication from Frayj Ḥimayd as-Saddān of the ʿAzāzma Saraḥīn, June 3, 2007.

231. Bar-Tsvi, *Jurisdiction*, p. 107.

232. Bailey, *Proverbs*, p. 370.

233. Kressel et al., "Changes," pp. 40–41.

234. Bailey, *Proverbs*, p.372.

235. Ibid., p. 370.

236. Bar-Tsvi, *Jurisdiction*, p. 61.

237. Bailey, *Proverbs*, p. 370.

238. Ibid., p. 371.

239. Bar-Tsvi, *Jurisdiction*, p. 31.

240. Bailey, *Proverbs*, p. 371.

241. Bar-Tsvi, *Jurisdiction*, p. 71.

242. Oral communication from Uẓʿeina Sālim al-ʿUwaywī of the ʿAzāzma ʿAṣiyāt, July 25, 2005.

243. Oral communication from Faḍiyya Salmān al-Gurʿānī of the ʿAzāzma ʿAṣiyāt, November 20, 1993.

244. Bailey, *Proverbs*, p. 372.

245. Bar-Tsvi, *Jurisdiction*, p. 61.

246. Bailey, *Proverbs*, p. 372.

247. Ibid., p. 136.

248. Oral communication from Sālim Salāma ar-Rimāg of the ʿAzāzma Saraḥīn, December 20, 1999.

249. See chapter 2 for more on the workings of guaranty; also see Bailey, *Proverbs*, pp. 289–302.

250. Ibid., p. 291.

251. Bar-Tsvi, *Jurisdiction*, p. 76.
252. Bailey, *Proverbs*, p. 372.
253. Bailey, *Proverbs*, p. 362.
254. Ibid., p. 360.
255. Oral communication from Swaylim Sulaymān Abū Bilayya of the ʿAzāzma Sara-ḥīn, December 15, 1997.
256. Oral communication from Sulaymān Salīm Ibn Sarīaʿ of the Tarabīn Shibaythāt, October 19, 1969.
257. For example, see Hilw and Darwish, *Customary Law*, pp. 66–68.
258. Bailey, *Proverbs*, p. 359.
259. Stewart, *Texts*, vol. 1, pp. 131–32.
260. Oral communications (separate) from Muḥammad ʿĪd Ibn ʿĀmir of the Tiyāha Ṣugayrāt, November 30, 1999, and ʿAtayyig Jumʿa al Farārja of the Tarabīn Ḥasāblah, November 30, 1999.
261. Al-ʿĀrif, *al-Qaḍāʾ*, p. 193; for the date, see Bailey, "Nineteenth Century," p. 68.
262. Oral communication from Muḥammad Sālim al-Āʿsam of the Tiyāha Gudayrāt, May 5, 1996.
263. Oral communications from Swaylim Sulaymān Abū Bilayya (December 8, 1991) and Frayj Ḥimayd as-Saddān (December 10, 2005), both of the ʿAzāzma Saraḥīn.
264. Bailey, *Proverbs*, pp. 213–14.
265. Paraphrased from Musil, *Manners*, pp. 447–48.
266. Oral communication from ʿAlī Ḥikmat al-Wuḥeidī of the Tarabīn Wuḥeidāt and great-grandson of the chief in question, March 15, 1980.
267. Bailey, *Proverbs*, p. 175.
268. See chapter 4 for more on the murder of fornicators and rapists.
269. Bailey, *Proverbs*, p. 212
270. Ibid., p. 199.
271. Oral communication from ʿAyyāda Sulaymān Abū Bilayya of the ʿAzāzma Sara-ḥīn, July 24, 1974.
272. See Bailey, *Proverbs*, pp. 197–99, for more on this principle.
273. Oral communication from ʿAliyyān aṭ-Ṭimṭāwī of the ʿAzāzma ʿAṣiyāt, February 11, 2001.
274. Ibid.
275. Bailey, *Proverbs*, p. 213.
276. Stewart, *Texts*, vol. 1, pp. 24–25.
277. Stewart, *Texts*, vol. 1, p. 5; for more details on this case, see ibid., pp. 1–10.
278. Al-ʿĀrif, *al-Qaḍāʾ*, p. 194.
279. Ibid., p. 199, n. 1.
280. Oral communication from ʿAlī Ṣagr al-Huzayyil (director of education in the Bedouin city of Rahaṭ, in the northern Negev), December 27, 2005. See chapter 3 for more on benefaction (*ḥisnī*).
281. Oral communication from Ibrahīm Muḥammad as-Sākhin of the Muzayna Sa-khāna, July 8, 2005.
282. Oral communication from Judge Salmān Ibn Ḥammād of the ʿAzāzma Masʿūdiy-yīn, November 8, 1998.
283. Bailey, *Proverbs*, p. 250; also see chapter 4 for more on blood-revenge.

284. Oral communication from Judge Salmān Ibn Ḥammād of the ʿAzāzma Masʿūdiyyīn, November 8, 1998.

285. Oral communication from Muḥammad Salmān Abū Jarabīaʿ of the ʿAzāzma Masʿūdiyyīn, February 26, 2001; cf. Bailey, *Proverbs*, pp. 241–42.

286. Bar-Tsvi, *Jurisdiction*, p. 112.

287. Bailey, "Narrative Context," pp. 76–81, for the Arabic text of the story.

288. Oral communication from Ibrahīm Abū ʿAyyāda of the Ẓullām Gurʿān, October 7, 2003.

289. See chapter 5 for more on blood-pool judges.

290. Bar-Tsvi, *Jurisdiction*, p. 77.

291. Bailey, *Proverbs*, p. 285.

292. See chapter 2 for bringing violators to trial.

293. Bar-Tsvi, *Jurisdiction*, p. 68.

294. Ibid., pp. 136–38. Bar-Tsvi tape-recorded the trial.

295. Ibid., p. 76.

296. Ibid., p. 88.

297. Bailey, *Poetry*, pp. 198–99; also see pp. 75–76.

298. Oral communications from Swaylim Sulaymān Abū Bilayya (February 13, 1974) and Frayj Ḥimayd as-Saddān (December 13, 2004), both of the ʿAzāzma Saraḥīn.

299. For more on this type of award, see Kressel, "Ḥaqq Akhū Manshad," 17–23.

300. Bailey, *Poetry*, pp. 138–40, for the Arabic text.

301. Bailey, *Proverbs*, p. 118, for a different interpretation.

302. See Bar-Tsvi, *Jurisdiction*, pp. 137–38, for the tape-recorded sentence.

Afterword

1. For example, see Shuqayr, *Taʾrīkh*, pp. 422–24.

2. Burckhardt, *Arab Proverbs*, p. 56.

Glossary of Bedouin Legal Terms

Listed alphabetically according to the Arabic root of the first word

ء = a

a b l	*al'-bil*—camels; 75, 85, 118, 141, 255, 275
a b w	*abū dam'a*—"tearful one": the designation of an as yet uncircumcised boy whose wounds are the subject of litigation; 104, 154
	abū an-niswān—"father of women": the designation of an *'ugbī* judge; 166, 261
a j l	*mawajīl*—legal delays allowed for trials and the obligations of guarantors; 44
a kh w	*akhū manshad*—"brother of an honor trial": cases deriving from the problems of women's honor; 232, 297
	ikhwānah fī lisānah—"he names his brothers with his own tongue": the oft-exercised right of a judge to choose the appeal judges for a current case; 172
a d y	*diya*—blood-price for a homicide; 19, 22, 214, 215 et passim
	ad-diya al-muḥammadiyya—"the Muhammadan blood-price": set at 100 camels; 214–15
a r ḍ	*arḍ ū-'arḍ*—"land and women": putative causes of war between confederations; 92
a k l	*akāl*—"feeding": a fee for helping find stolen camels; 278, 281
a h l	*ahl ad-diyār*—"people of the lands": judges in problems of land; 161, 164, 207, 265

ahl al-ʿarāyish—"people of the palm trees": judges in problems of date palms; 164

ahl ar-rasān—"people of the reins": judges in problems of horses; 164, 273

ب = b

b kh t — *bakht*—"luck": a judge's fate for ruling honestly; 168

b d l — *badl*—exchange marriage; 249, 252, 262–63

b d w — *badwa* (*badwāt*)—"an appearance": a delegation sent to a violator to demand justice; 23, 27–30, 118, 145, 148, 186

b r a — *barī wa-ʿarī*—"absolved and bare": the designation of someone who has undergone the fire ordeal without harm; 205

b r z — *birza*—"the outlying": a bride's tent during her wedding; 84, 253

b r k — *barak* (*yubruk*), *barrak al-jīra*—"to couch the camel": asking for a truce after sexual offense; 134, 136, 233

b r y — *imbarrī*—a companion to an absconding couple; 139, 186, 254

b sh ʿ — *bashaʿ* (*yibshaʿ*)—to administer the fire ordeal; 199

bishʿa—the fire ordeal; 166, 167, 185, 197, 199–205, 209, 267, 282

mubashshaʿ—he who administers the fire ordeal; 159, 166–67, 177, 185, 199, 267

b ṭ n — *ibṭaynī*—one who leads a blood-avenger to his victim; 149

b ʿ r — *baʿīr an-nōm*—"the camel of sleep": payment for exclusion from blood-revenge; 124, 191, 192, 235, 354

b l m — *balam mā yitikallam* (or *mitiballam mā yitikallam*)—"a dumb one that does not speak": designation for a defendant forbidden to speak at his trial; 34, 179

b n y — *ibn ʿamm*—"a paternal uncle's son": a fellow member of a clan; 29, 73–74, 78, 86, 88, 95, 196, 215, 251

bint (*banāt*)—an unmarried, presumably virgin, girl; 82, 248–50

b w q — *bōg*—treachery; 44, 66, 135, 150, 183–84, 193, 222

bōg ar-rafīg—"betraying a traveling companion": one of the offenses that deprive a Bedouin of the privilege of taking oaths to exonerate himself in trials, a thief; 188, 222

bāyig—one who practices treachery; 43, 45, 147, 188, 282 and passim

b y t — *bayt al-ʿimāra*—"the tent of the coexistence agreement"—i.e., where an agreement is signed; 138

b y ḍ — *bayḍā*—"whitening ": the restoration of a woman's, or her family's, honor; 85

bayāḍ—"whitening ": covering a man's tent with white cloth to restore his honor after it has been impugned or violated; 236

b y ʿ — *bayʿ ū-shrī*—"selling and buying": negotiations prior to or during litigation; 193

b y n — *bayn arbāʿha*—"between her four [two thighs and two calves]"—i.e., in flagrante delicto; 195

ت = t

t ḥ t — *taḥt al-frāsh*—"under the carpet": something no longer legally attainable, such as pillaged camels taken to force a rapist to give justice; 238

t r k — *tark al-ʿaṭwa* — "leaving the blood-truce" — i.e., not renewing it when it elapses, an offense subject to a fine; 131

t q y — *tagī nagī* — "God-fearing and clean": depiction of an acceptable witness; 187

t m m — *yitammim ʿala al-mushkila* — resolving a legal problem; 136

ث = th

th a r — *thār* — blood-revenge; 36, 102, 107, 127, 154
astathār — to take blood-revenge; 106
astathār astajār — to request a camel-truce after taking revenge; 136, 229

th l th — *thilāth al-muḥarrimāt* — "three forbidden women [for marriage]": one's mother, one's sister, and one's stepmother (*ʿammtah*), the wife of one's father; 258
thilāthit al-mikhtalfīn — "the three disputants": three judges from each of two confederations who will rule on conflicts between members of their respective groups as either judges of first resort or judges of appeal; 143, 162

th l m — *thilm* — "a crack": a metaphor for the loss of honor by a woman or a guarantor; 243

th n y — *mathānī* — "returned foals": the foals returned to a mare's original owner by her buyer; 41, 272–73

ج = j

j b b — *imjabbab* — a camel with black tent-cloth around its neck, sent to ask for aid against danger; 45

j d d — *al-jidd al-jāmiʿ* — "the gathering forefather" — i.e., the relevant ancestor of a clan; 103

j r r — *jarra* — "the dragging-off fine": (in the Negev) a camel like the one on which a girl was abducted; 26, 140, 255–56

j r d — *jird al-bint* — "uncovering a woman's head": a litigable misdeed; 239
imjarrida — a girl or woman whose head is uncovered; 239

j s r — *jassār* — bold, as an avenger is allowed to be, seeking revenge at all times and places; 103, 293

j l s — *majlis* — a forum of several judges ruling on a legal question together; 96, 173

j l y — *jalāya, majla* — the exile of persons subject to blood-revenge; 102
jalāwiya, majālī — people subject to blood-revenge living in exile; 103, 107

j m l — *al-jamal al-ajrab* — "the mangy camel": one upon which a rapist is forcibly seated so that he pays an indemnity as ransom for the oil-stained parts of his loins; 213, 236
jamal ash-shatt — "a stray camel" — i.e., a child who's father is unknown; 237
jamal ash-sharāda — "camel of abduction": (in Sinai) the fine for abducting a girl; 140, 255
jamal aṭ-ṭulūaʿ — "camel of exit": paid by one wishing to disafilliate from a clan; 67
jamal al-mufaḍḍala — "camel of the worthy one": presented by a man to a moral woman he is divorcing; 258

j n b — *ajnabī* (*ajānib*) — "an outsider": a person not belonging to a specific clan; 62, 73, 79, 187 j h l *jāhil* (*juhāl*) —"ignorant one": designation for a minor child in legal matters; 155

j w r *jōr*—oppression; 53

j y b *jāb bayḍāha*—"he brought them whiteness": said of a nonrelated husband who acted to save the honor of his wife and her family; 114

j y r *astajār*—to request a camel-truce; 136, 229

jīra—a camel-truce, usually sought after a serious violation of a woman's honor; 25–26, 53, 133–37, 184–85, 233, 238, 240

jīra (*jiyār*)—the camel that is sent to request a camel-truce; 132, 134, 233

jīrit iftāsh—"an investigative camel-truce": used to clarify whether an accusation warrants an honor trial; 233

jīrit garḍ ū-farḍ—"a decisive camel-truce": presuming the need of an honor trial; 137, 233

jīrit inshāda—"a camel-truce for searching": used to clarify whether an accusation warrants an honor trial; 137

ح = ḥ

ḥ b s *ḥabasiyya*—"the detainment fine": paid by a proven informer for each day a victim has spent in detainment (*ḥabs*); 150

ḥ t m *iḥtūm al-ʿaṭwa*—"fine for the blood-truce": paid for each day that the recipient of a blood-truce has not renewed an elapsed truce; 131

ḥ j j *yiḥtajj*—to plead before a judge; 236

ḥijja (*ḥajaj*)—a plea before a judge; 179–85

ḥ r b *aḥrab*—"He acts belligerently": to desist from greeting a person, a litigable offense; 145

ḥ r f *miḥtirif*—deviant (talk); 208

ḥ r m *ḥarāmī* (*ḥaramiyya*)—a thief; 279, 280

ḥ s n *ḥisnī* (*ḥisnāt*)—a benefaction toward someone from another confederation; 99–100, 292

ḥisnā (*ḥasānī*)—benefactor; 99

ḥ ṣ w *ḥaṣā*—a pebble buried in the sand to mark something irrevocable, such as a legal claim or an agreement to join a group or an alliance; 170–72

ḥ ṭ ṭ *ḥaṭṭ* (*yiḥuṭṭ*) *al-girsh*—to pay fines with people of another clan; 86

ḥaṭāṭ girsh ū-akāl girsh—"placing the coin and gaining the coin": (in the Negev) a non-clan group that pays and receives fines together with another clan; 86–87

ḥ ẓ ẓ *ḥaẓẓ*—"luck": a judge's fate for ruling honestly; 168

ḥ q q *ḥagg* (*ḥugūg*) a right: the law; 16–17, 19–20 et passim

ḥagg ibn al-ʿamm—"a closest-cousin's right"—i.e., to marry a girl of his clan; 29, 251

ḥagg al-bayt—"the right of the tent": inviolable sanctuary; 83, 165, 286

ḥagg al-jīra—(in Sinai) the right of murderers to receive a camel from avengers after their revenge; 136

ḥagg ash-shayla—a judicial award for the abduction of a man; 146

ḥigg—a camel paid as a fine for abducting a girl without an escort; 256

ḥ k m *ḥakam* (*yiḥkim*) — to force someone to fulfill an obligation; 78, 174

ḥ l l *ḥilliyya* — part of a wedding ceremony; 254

ḥ l f *ḥalaf* (*yiḥlif*) — to swear an oath; 179, 193–94, 198

ḥilf (*aḥlāf*) — "sworn covenant": a nonaggression pact between two confederations; 140–44, 161

ḥālif (*ḥalafa*) — one who takes an oath; 193, 198

muḥallif — one who obliges an enemy to take an oath; 198

ḥ m d *aḥmadī* (*aḥāmda*) — (in Sinai) a judge ruling on the sanctuary of tents; 162–63, 165, 172–73, 182, 219

ḥ m l *ḥammāl seif* — "bearer of a sword": a lad considered an adult before the law; 102, 104

ḥ w ḍ *ḥowḍ ū-rowḍ* — "trough and grassy valley": a statement of a confederation's role of providing its members with water and pasture; 144, 264

ḥ w f *ḥāyif al-maraḥayn* — "see a camel in both couching-grounds": the legal condition in court for accepting the evidence of a person informing on a camel thief; 211

خ = kh

kh r b *kharāb al-bayt* — "destruction of the tent" — i.e., the sexual violation of its women; 108, 113

kh sh sh *khashsh ū-ṭāliʿ* — "entrance and exit": a basis for fining a thief; 286

kh ṭ ṭ *makhṭūṭ* (*makhaṭīṭ*) — a judge named as lines are drawn in the sand; 172

kh m s *khamsa* (*khamsāt*) — clan; 12, 43–44, 60, 67, 102, 126, 139

kull khamsa bi-khamsit-ha — "each clan against its [specific] clan": a rule for limiting the scope of blood-revenge; 139

kh w l *khāl* (*khwāl*) — one's maternal relative, toward whom one normally has no legal responsibility; 78, 82, 93, 242, 260

kh w n *khōnt al-marāḥ* — "betrayal of the couching-place" — i.e., by stealing from friends and neighbors; 280

khāyin (*khawwān*) — thief: one who steals from friends and neighbors; 147, 193, 280

د = d

d b b *dabbit al-jāra* — "fornicating with a neighbor's wife": one of the offenses that deprive a Bedouin of the privilege of taking oaths to exonerate himself in trials; 188

d kh l *dakhāla, dakhal* — protection; 23, 43, 49, 53–54, 250, 255, 288

dakhīl (*dakhāla*) — partaker in protection (protector or protégé); 53, 81, 289, 290, 295

dukhla — the culmination of a marriage through sexual intercourse; 254

d r y *dārī ū-mārī* — "one who knows and ignores" the immoral acts of his womenfolk; 188

d sh b *dishba* — "the flu": from which one's dying in prison commands a fine from the informer; 150

d ʿ q *madʿag ath-thōb* — "burning one's garment": an act performed upon joining a clan to symbolize one's renouncing dependence on his previous clan's cover, or protection; 71

d f n *dafn al-ḥaṣā* — "burying the pebble": as one states one's claims in court or joins a new clan; 71, 139, 170, 172

d q q *dagga* — "biting" — i.e., rape; 109

d l kh *dalīkha* — the denial of a crime; 244

d m y *damm* — "blood": the category of law comprising a violent physical attack on a man or a sexual attack on a woman; 28, 95–96, 101–03, 189

damawiyya — (in Sinai) a group of non-clansmen who pay blood-fines together; 86–87, 126

damawiyyit ʿaṣa — (in Sinai) "a stick blood-group" — i.e., a clan; 87

damawiyyit girsh — (in Sinai) a "coin blood-group": a group of non-clansmen who pay blood-fines together; 86–87

madmī — "blood-stained": a murderer or his clansmen subject to revenge; 289, 293–95

d y n *dīn* — an oath; 190, 194, 198

dīn bāligha — a declarative oath made on behalf of a woman by her clansman; 188

dīn bi-khaṭṭ ū-sikkīn — "an oath by line and knife": standing in a circle and swearing; 196

dīn ū-khamsa mitgaṭṭrīn — "an oath and five more in train": sworn to overcome doubts as to a defendant's veracity; 194

ذ = dh

dh r ʿ *dhrāʿ hāshimī* — "a Hashemite forearm": the length of a stick (one cubit), which is the maximum allowed for beating one's wife; 247

dh n b *dhanb (dhunūb)* — "a wrong": a woman's act of misbehavior that entitles her husband to beat her; 246

midhnib — wrongdoer; 267

dh y kh *dhīkh* — "Dog!": an example of an epithet that is litigable if addressed by one man to another publicly and justifies a beating if addressed by a wife to her husband privately; 246

ر = r

r b ṭ *marbūṭ* — a three-year-old camel paid as a fine for abducting a girl; 256

r b ʿ *rubaʿ (arbāʿ)* — a section of a clan based on lineage, or a sub-tribe; 12, 66, 125

rabāʿ ū-rabaʿiyya — "two mature camels, male and female": an example of fines; 279, 147

r t b *ritba* — "finger-width": a measure of assessing wounds; 220

r d d *radd ash-sharaf* — "restoring station" — i.e., honor killing; 81

radd an-nagā — "removing the purity": a declaration of war; 141

r z q *ruzga (ruzag)* — "sustenance": a judge's fee; 178–79

r ḍ w *raḍwa* — "satisfaction fee": paid to a witness of the original stating of claims to get his evidence when discrepancies occur; 171

riḍāwa — "satisfaction fine": paid to a wife by an abusive husband; 417

marḍawī—"satisfied one": a witness paid for his evidence of what was said under legal circumstances (the stating of claims, the making of an agreement, litigable threats); 41, 87, 172

r ʿ y — *rāʿī al-bayt*—"tent owner": a preliminary judge or the owner of a tent in which legal obligations were contracted; 25, 171, 182, 288, 290

r f ʿ — *irtifāʿ*—"going up": (in Sinai) appealing to a higher judge; 168

r f q — *rafīg* (*rifāg*)—"a companion": an escort-witness at an abduction; 29, 67, 139, 152–53, 186, 198, 222, 254

rafīg al-janb—"a companion alongside": one who helps another who is attacked nearby; 97–98

rafīga—"the companion fine": paid for failing to bring an escort-witness to an abduction; 26, 256

r q b — *ragaba* (*rigāb*)—"a neck": a life taken or owed in revenge; 103, 104

r m y — *ramī al-wijih*—"throwing the face": the intervention of a notable to stop violence or a violation; 25, 58, 103–04

r w ḥ — *rūḥī li-zlāmkī*—"Go to your clansmen!": the divorce statement to a wife who has behaved dishonorably; 258, 260–61

ز = z

z r m — *zaram* (*yizram*) *ʿend*—to aid a non-clansman in conflict; 89

mazramiyya (also *zaram*, *zarma*)—aiding a non-clansman in conflict; 89–92, 97

z l l — *zalla*—"an error": accidental homicide; 191

z l m — *zalama* (*zlām*)—a clansman; 61, 89, 247, 258, 283

z w j — *jīzit ibn al-ʿamm*—"a paternal cousin's marriage": closest-cousin marriage; 251

jīzit ʿadam—"marriage that destroys rights": an absconding couple's marriage; 256

jawāz dass—"concealed marriage": a marriage kept secret (by the bride's father) from one with a closest-cousin's right; 253

z w d — *azyad*—to warrant compound fines; 222

ziyādī (*zuyūd*)—"an increaser (of wealth)": a judge in matters of theft; 161, 164, 181, 219, 297

zuyūd—fines for theft; 119, 141, 186, 211, 277, 279

س = s

s b b — *sabab*—"reason": the person aided by a nearby non-clansman when attacked; 90, 97

masabba—"slander": particularly of a woman's honor; 242

s b q — *sābigt as-saraḥ*—"preceding the grazers": a shepherdess directly reporting a rape; 110

s d d — *sadd* (*yisidd*)—to fulfill an obligation; 105, 298

yistadd—to take blood-revenge; 287

sadād—accomplished blood-revenge; 287

s r q — *sirgit al-miṭmāra*—"stealing what has been stored": one of the offenses that

deprive a Bedouin of the privilege of taking oaths to exonerate himself in trials; 188, 289
sarrāg—a thief; 287

s k r *sakkar ath-thilm*—"closing the crack": restoring honor to a woman or a guarantor; 243

s l m *sālim adh-dhawārib*—"clean of [legal] defects": a condition for receiving protection; 53

s m ʿ *sāmiʿa*—"listener": a witness to the results of the fire ordeal; 201

s m l *sawāmil al-ḥagg*—"the leftover entitlement": what remains of a fine after concessions; 38, 288

s n d *yistinid*—"going up": (in the Negev) to appeal to a higher judge; 168
istinād—the process of appeal; 168

s h y *sāhya lāhya* (also *sāhī lāhī*)—"unmindful": innocent; 180, 234

s w d *siyād al-ḥagg*—"masters of justice": judges; 177
sawād, taswīd—"blackening": denouncing a person for denying justice or reneging on a guarantee; 28, 44

s w q *sāg (yisūg) al-jīra*—"to drive the truce-camel forward": to request a camel-truce; 134
siyāg—bride-price; 251

ش = sh

sh r d *sharad* (*yushrud*)—to flee, abduct; 71, 76, 175
shrād—abduction of a girl; 111, 186, 254
mishrād—flight from revenge; 71, 76

sh r y *tashrīaʿ al-ḥajaj*—"revealing the pleas": a judge's repeating the pleas before issuing a judgment; 185
sharwa—"purchase": paying the blood-price imposed on a person in exchange for his subsequent paying of fines with the benefactor; 70, 198
sharwat al-yamīn—"buying the oath": paying a demanded sum in place of swearing; 198

sh k l *mashākil ʿār*—"problems of womenkind"—i.e., sexual violations; 108
mashākil al-layl—"problems of the night": incompatibility; 166

sh k w *shākī bāki* (also *shākya bākya*)—"complaining and crying": a woman's informing of sexual violation; 110, 233
shakwa—a legal complaint; 79
shākyit aḍ-ḍaḥa—"a mid-morning complainer": a sexually violated woman who virtuously informs her family directly (i.e., not waiting for the evening); 110

sh m s *tashmīs*—"exposing to the sun": expulsion from a clan; 75
mushammas—"one exposed to the sun": a person expelled from his clan; 75

sh h b *ash-hab al-jild ū-gaṭīaʿ al-wild*—"dry-skinned and devoid of offspring": designation of a person unacceptable as a witness; 193

sh h d *shāhid* (*shuhūd*)—a witness; 119, 187, 189, 191, 281

sh w sh *shāsh ibn ghibn*—"the white cloth of Ibn Ghibn": a flag flown to honor someone for a benefaction; 218

sh y kh — *shaykh* (*shuyūkh*)—"old man": a tribal chief; 6, 13, 14, 127, 262

sh y ʿ — *ishāʿat ad-damm*—"the spreading of the news of bloodshed": a three-day period after murder; 118

ص = ṣ

ṣ ḥ b — *ṣāḥib al-ḥagg*—"possessor of the right": a violated party; 225
ṣāḥib ad-damm—"possesser of blood": a person entitled to seek blood-revenge; 103, 126, 293–94

ṣ f f — *ṣaff* (*ṣufūf*)—"a row": a tribal confederation; 92, 139, 161
ṣaff yigūm ʿa ṣaff—"confederation rising against confederation": a designation of war; 92, 95

ṣ l ḥ — *ṣulḥ*—"mending": reconciliation; 228–30

ṣ w n — *ṣiyānit al-bayt*—the sanctuary of a tent; 286
ṣiyānit al-māl—"protecting livestock": laws for the welfare of livestock; 274
ṣāyinit nafs—"moral self-respect": a woman's modest comportment; 259

ṣ y ḥ — *ṣāyiḥa*—"a screamer": a raped woman; 110, 133, 234

ض = ḍ

ḍ r r — *ḍarra*—a fellow-wife; 258

ḍ r b — *yuḍrub bi-s-seif ū-yigrī aḍ-ḍeif*—"to strike with a sword and feed meat to a guest":the designation for a mature male; 244
ḍraybī (*ḍraybiyya*)—(in Sinai) a preliminary judge for cases of honor; 159, 162–63, 172–73, 176, 190, 192, 233
ḍarrāb seif—"one who wields a sword": a designation for a mature lad; 104

ḍ ʿ f — *ḍaʿīf* (*ḍuʿūf*)—"a weak one": a legal definition for a minor; 154

ط = ṭ

ṭ r d — *ṭarad* (*yuṭrud*)—to seek blood-revenge; 22, 68, 71, 76, 102, 106, 184, 195
ṭard, ṭarād, miṭrād—the seeking of blood-revenge; 71, 76, 105, 230
ṭarrād—an avenger for the shedding of blood; 97
maṭrūda—"banished": woman divorced for immoral behavior; 259

ṭ r q — *maṭrag*—a stick thrown from the entrance of a tent to determine the area of its legal domain; 247

ṭ l b — *maṭālib ʿowjī*—"crooked demands": immoral suggestions to a woman; 208

ṭ l ʿ — *ṭulūaʿ al-ḥagg*—"exposing the law": the delivery of a judgment; 17, 185

ṭ l q — *ṭalāg*—"freeing": divorce; 14, 80, 258–59, 262
intī ṭālig—"You are as something unbound": a writ of divorce; 258
muṭallaga—divorced; 258–59
intī imṭallaga—"you are freed:" a writ of divorce; 258

ṭ m ḥ — *ṭāmiḥ*—"unsubmissive": an unloving wife; 260

ṭ m r — *miṭmāra* (*maṭamīr*)—pit for storing grain or belongings; 188, 289

ṭ n b — *ṭanab ʿala* (*yuṭnub*) "to intertwine the tent ropes with": to receive protection; 53
ṭanīb (*ṭanaba*)—"person of the tent rope": a protégé or protected person; 53
ṭanīb ḥagg—"a protégé in the right": someone acceptable for protection; 53

ṭ w s — *ṭāst al-ʿayyādī*—"the roasting pan of the ʿAyāyda man": the implement for the fire ordeal; 166

ṭ y b   *ṭīb* — reconciliation through payment of blood-price; 46
          ṭība — a fine or blood-price; 87

ظ = ẓ
ẓ l m   *ẓulm* — "darkness": injustice; 54
          ẓālim (*ẓullām*) — one who behaves unjustly; 37

ع
ʿb d   *ʿabd ū-khādim* — "male and female black slaves": a symbolic basis for a fine for
          rape; 221
ʿd d   *ʿadd ū-baʿad jidd* — "by count and the distance of a forefather": criteria for the
          right to disaffiliate from a clan; 64
          ʿadd ū-radd — "count the fee and return": a judge's order to consult a paid
          witness as to the original claims stated by parties to a conflict; 171
ʿd f   *ʿadf* — "preference": the process for choosing appeals judges before a trial; 172
          maʿdūf — "the preferred one": a judge of appeal; 172
ʿd l   *ʿadl* — "restored balance": a rectified right, justice; 18, 263, 299
ʿd m   *ʿādam* (*yiʿādim*) — to make someone an outlaw and subject to allowed violence;
          116
          ʿādmah bi-thilāth badwāt — "Outlaw him through three delegations": the con-
          dition for using violence against one who denies justice; 28, 116
          ʿadam, taʿdīm — violence bereft of justice; 116
          ʿadmān — one who flouts lawful procedure; 5, 116
ʿd w   *ʿadāya* — "aggression": a host's stealing a sheep for a guest's dinner; 58, 277
          mitʿaddī — an aggressor; 116, 147
ʿr d   *maʿrad* — an offer to pay a sum to ransom someone else's oath; 199
ʿr ṣ   *muʿarraṣ* — "Pimp!": an example of a wife's curse directed at her husband,
          justifying his beating her; 246
ʿr f   *iʿtirāf* — confession; 185
ʿr y   *ʿār* — "inexcusable": womankind and its inviolability; 36, 81, 108, 110, 113,
          121–22, 127, 132
          ʿār ʿala dār — the violation of a woman's seclusion; 239–40
ʿz b   *ʿazaba* — "a solitary woman": a previously married woman (either widow or
          divorcee); 15, 248–49
ʿz w   *ʿizwa* — "might": the brothers of a woman acting to safeguard her rights; 78
ʿsh r   *ʿashīra* (*ʿashāyir*) — tribe; 12
ʿṣ b   *ʿaṣabiyya* — the sentiment of tribal solidarity; 88–92, 95
ʿṣ y   *ʿāṣī* — "one who flouts": (in Sinai) a person who denies another person justice;
          5, 116, 295
ʿṭ w   *ʿaṭwa* — "a grant": a blood-truce 40, 42, 129–34, 150–51, 174–75, 223
          ʿaṭwa rās — "a direct truce": a truce needing no clarifications; 133
          ʿaṭwa iftāsh — "an investigative truce": a truce during which the question of
          who offers the truce is clarified; 133
          ʿaṭwa gibāl ʿaṭwa — "truce against truce": a situation of both sides needing a
          truce; 132

	ʿaṭwa manaʿ ash-sharr—"a truce for preventing evil": a truce during which the question of who offers the truce is clarified; 133
ʿ q b	*ʿugbī*—a judge in marital problems between a husband and wife; 41, 164, 247, 253, 258–59, 261
	ʿāgibit as-saraḥ—"one who follows the flock home": a suspect shepherdess who doesn't reveal a sexual violation until she returns with the flock in the evening; 110
ʿ q d	*maʿgūd al-ʿamāma*—"your head-cloth is knotted [as a reminder]": said to someone asked to be a witness; 186
ʿ l q	*yiʿallig al-ʿānī*—"to hang up what's required": to bring the truce-camel; 134
ʿ l m	*ʿilm al-ʿarab*—"knowledge of the Bedouin": Bedouin law; 168
ʿ m r	*ʿimāra*—"living together": a coexistence agreement between different confederations; 138–40
	iʿmārat al-bayt—"rebuilding the tent": the bride-price paid by a fornicator for the cuckholded husband's new wife; 113
	muʿammirit aṣ-ṣaff—"those who a confederation": judges who keep the confederation together by resolving conflicts between members of its various constituent tribes; 139, 161
ʿ w q	*ʿowg ū-bōg*—"deceit and treachery": a treacherous and illegal action; 66, 183–84
	muʿawwag—"twisted": a crippled or infirm person whose wounding warrants compound fines; 104
ʿ y b	*ʿeib*—"shameful behavior": the immoral behavior of a woman; 31, 61, 80, 188–89, 225, 260
	ʿāyib—(in the Negev) a person who denies another person justice; 49, 53, 61, 87, 212, 240, 295
	ʿāyiba—a wife who has behaved immorally; 258–59

غ = gh

gh r r	*ghurra*—"marked girl": a woman given in bondage-marriage as part of a blood-payment 25, 55, 73, 155, 215–17, 262
	mughirr—one who misrepresents a previous claim; 172
gh r m	*gharīm* (*gharama*)—a contestant in a conflict; 45
gh z w	*ghazū*—a camel raid; 140–41
gh s l	*ghassal ʿala*—"to wash up for": to undergo the penalty in place of a person who has violated the law on one's behalf; 90, 97
	ghusūl ath-thiyāb—"washing the clothes": a reconciliation after blood-revenge; 136
gh ṣ b	*ghaṣab*—"force": rape; 109
gh ṭ y	*mughaṭṭiya*—"covered": a woman wearing the proper headgear; 239

ف = f

f kh dh	*fakhdh* (*afkhādh*)—sub-confederation; 13
f r sh	*frāsh al-manshad*—"carpet of the honor judge": a designation for the *ḍraybī* preliminary judge in cases of a woman's honor; 163

f r ʿ — *fārʿa*—"orificed": an unveiled woman; 239
tafrīaʿ al-bint—forcefully removing the veil from a girl; 239, 280

f ṣ l — *faṣṣal ū-rassal*—"to detail and send": specifying a mediator's mission; 29

f k k — *fakāk*—the resolution of a legal problem; 172

f l j — *anfalaj*—to be condemned by a court (a contestant); 169
maflūj—"the guilty one": condemned by a court; 174

f l n — *fulān fi-baṭnak*—"so-and-so's in your stomach": an accusation of murder; 105

f w t — *fawāt*—"concession": the relinquishment of a fine; 19, 35, 224, 228, 277

f w r — *fowrit ad-damm*—"the boiling of the blood": the first three days following a murder; 118, 123

f w ḍ — *fāyiḍa* (*fawāyiḍ*)—"the copartner's share": a foal returned to the seller of a mare subsequent to its birth; 272–73

f w l — *fawwal*—to dissolve the legal commitment of a minor or incompetent person; 155
tafwīl—legal dissolution; 155, 272
mufawwil—the dissolver of an illegal transaction; 156, 272

ق = q

q b l — *gabīla* (*gabāyil*)—a tribal confederation; 12, 88

q t l — *katl ʿend al-ʿār*—"murder for a woman": legally murdering a sexual violator; 114
katlit dhīb—"the killing of a wolf"—i.e., a fornicator warrants no revenge; 112

q r ṭ — *garṭ al-ḥaṣā*—"throwing of the pebble": separating claims at a trial; 171
garṭ ar-rzāg—paying the judge's fee; 178
garṭ al-ʿaṣa—"throwing the stick": a method for determining the legal precincts of a tent; 281

q r ʿ — *magrūaʿ*—"bedrock": ground rules for the abduction of women; 139, 285

q ṣ ṣ — *yingaṣṣ wi-yinthinī*—"to be assessed and doubled": rules for assessing wounds caused treacherously; 104, 132, 221
gaṣṣāṣ (*gaṣṣaṣīn*)—"measurers": auxilliary judges who assess wounds; 159, 164, 248

q ṣ r — *gāṣir*—"short": an inadequate host: a weak elder; 104, 290

q ṣ l — *gaṣal* (*yugṣul*)—to betroth one's child; 250
gaṣala—a cut plant presented to a prospective groom's representative by the father of the bride to indicate his agreement with the betrothal; 250, 253

q ḍ y — *gāḍa* (*yigāḍī*)—to challenge one to litigation; 59
gāḍī (*guḍā*)—"decider": a judge; 36, 159, 168, 180–81, 183, 235
al-guḍā al-baʿīdīn—"the distant judges": the main judges of a confederation; 161
gāḍī al-ghalāṭ—"judge of contentions": a judge for questions of hospitality; 189

q ṭ ʿ — *gaṭʿ al-wijih, tagṭīaʿ al-wijih*—"cutting the face": condemning a guarantor for remissness in his obligation; 42, 47
guṭʿaniyya—assessments of animal damage to crops; 274

q ʿ d — *magʿad (magāʿid)*—"sitting place": the venue of a trial; 177, 215, 240, 242
q l l — *galīl dīn*—"irreligious": a litigable insult if voiced in public; 147
q l d — *galīd (galada)*—a person who is responsible for resolving problems with other, particularly friendly, confederations; 141
q w m — *yigawwim*—"to arouse": to call people, especially guarantors, to fulfill their obligations 175, 230
gōm (giymān)—a lineage in a clan; 66, 72

ك = k

k b r — *kabīr (kibār)*—a tribal elder; a spokesman; 13, 62, 139, 178–79, 272
kabīr yōm ū-dōm—"elder for a day and forever": an elder who serves as spokesman for fellow clansmen in trials; 178
k r m — *karam al-arḍ*—"bequest of land": the gift of a piece of land; 268
k s y — *kiswit al-bayt*—"the covering of a tent" to show its owner's honor; 236
k f l — *kafāla, kafal*—"twofold": guaranty; 22–23, 39–46, 54
kafīl (kafala)— guarantor; 20, 40, 174, 176
kafīl bāyig— remiss guarantor; 43, 45, 188
kafīl mathlūm—"cracked guarantor": one who has been dishonored; 45
kafīl dafā—"guarantor of warmth": one who protects previous violators from revenge; 35, 43–44, 175–76, 230
kafīl as-sāmil—"guarantor of the remainder": one who guarantees the sum after the concession of fines; 20, 40
kafīl sawwāg—"driving guarantor": one who spurs a defendant to trial; 40
kafīl ṣaff ū-mathnī—"a guarantor of doubleness": one who ensures repayment after a guarantor's payment of a fine in place of a defaulting defendant; 176
kafīl aṭ-ṭīb—"guarantor of reconciliation": one who ensures payment after the victim agrees to it; 22, 46
kafīl ʿaṭwa—"guarantor of truce": who ensures that the conditions of a truce will be honored; 40, 175
kafīl ū-ʿamīl—"guarantor-executor": a guarantor who guarantees his own actions; 45
kafīl ʿan gheiba ū-heiba—"guarantor against absence or fright": one who ensures that the defendant appears in court; 40, 174
kafīl wafā—"guarantor of completeness": one who ensures that fines be fully paid; 40, 43–44, 175–76
k l b — *kalb ū-māt*—"a dog that's died": a murdered fornicator who warrants no revenge; 112
k l m — *kalām shaṭāra*—"words of adroitness": the formulas used in court pleadings; 160

ل = l

l th m — *mulaththima*—a (properly) veiled girl; 239
l ḥ s — *laḥas (yilḥas) an-nār*—"to lick the fire": a depiction of undergoing the fire ordeal; 200, 203
l s n — *lisān ḥāl*—"a tongue for the occasion": an ad hoc spokesman for a party on trial; 179

l m m *malamm*—"the place of gathering": a preliminary magistrate; 159, 170–72, 233

م = m

m d d *mādd ū-mīʿād*—"designated time and place": a trial, a hearing; 40
madd al-yad—"extending the hand": the sexual violation of touching a woman; 237

m r a *murūwa*—"manliness": the virtue in aiding someone in danger; 88, 97, 225

m w l *māl*—"wealth": livestock; 69, 174, 184, 273–74, 276–77

m y l *māyil*—"tilting, out of balance": state of having had one's rights violated; 16, 18

ن = n

n kh w *nakha* (*yinkhī li* . . .)—to come to the aid of someone; 154
ankha—to call for help in danger; 95, 97

n dh r *mundhirāt al-ʿarab*—"warner of a camp (against raiders)": thoroughbred camels, which must not be impounded in order to attain justice; 120

n sh d *manshad* (*manāshid*)—"place of appeal for help": the honor court, the honor judge; 24, 28–31, 42–43, 45, 183–84, 210–11 et passim
manshad brāt—an absolution *manshad;* 235
manshad rās—an honor trial at which guilt or innocence is determined beforehand; 178, 233

n sh r *nashr ad-damm*—"spreading the blood": calling for others to help in taking revenge; 95

n ẓ f *naẓīfa sharīfa*—"pure and noble": the designation for a girl whose honor has been upheld in court; 261

n f sh *nāfsha*—"one who pastures freely at night": a woman who fornicates away from her tent; 113

n q ʿ *mangaʿ ad-damm*—"blood pool": the judge who rules in matters of physical attack; 55, 66, 161, 164, 167, 187, 196, 219

n q l *nagal* (*yungul*) *ad-dakhal*—"to convey the protection": a protector's taking a protégé to someone more able to protect him; 54

n h b *nihibi*—abducting a girl; 111, 254

n w r *nūra*—"a light": a girl found fornicating but allowed to live in order to enlighten as to the cause of her lover's murder; 114

n w m *nōm*—"sleeping:" reprieve from vengeance; 124–25
nāyim ʿala frāsh-ha—"lying on the bedding of a woman": a man caught in flagrante delicto; 112

ه = h

h t m *hitaymī*—"member of a despised Hitaym tribe": a litigious insult; 147

h j y *lā yihjī wala yidhrī*—"unworthy to shelter or shield": a host who has violated a guest; 296

h m m *hamm* (*humūm*)—"a concern": a nonviolent or nonsexual violation; 28, 71, 73

h m l *ihmāl al-ʿaṭwa*—"leaving the blood-truce": a punishable failure to renew an elapsed truce; 131

h w n *ihāna*—"demeaning treatment" of a husband toward his wife; 247

و = w

w j h	*wijih*—"face": honor, guaranty; 42, 46, 133
	wajīh (*wajaha*)—a notable; 46
	jāha (*jahāt*)—a delegation of notables sent to a victim of violation; 23, 30–39, 136, 145
w r th	*wārith*, *warīth*—an heir; 44, 282–83
w s kh	*wisikh*—"Filthy one!": a wife's curse directed toward her husband, warranting his beating her; 246
w s ṭ	*wisāṭa*—mediation; 23
w s q	*wisāga*—impoundment; 118, 186, 213, 277
w s m	*wasm* (*wusūm*)—a camel brand; 91, 210, 247
w ṣ f	*towṣīf ahalha*—"describing her family's whereabouts": a form of divorce of a dishonorable or unloving wife; 259
w ʿ d	*mowʿid*—a trial for which the time is set; 174
w gh f	*waghīf*, *mowghūf*, *mayghūf*—one whose tongue has been burned in the fire ordeal as a sign of guilt; 202
w l y	*wilī* (*ūliya*)—a guardian; 242, 283
	wiliyya—"a person under a guardian": the designation for a woman; 242, 244, 284

ى = y

y m n	*yamīn* (*aymān*)—oath; 190–91, 194–95, 198–99, 209, 266

Bibliography

Abū Ḥassān, Muḥammad. *Turāth al-Badū al-Qaḍā'ī* (The Bedouin legal heritage). Amman: Department of Culture and Arts, 1974.

Abu-Rabi'a, 'Aref. *A Bedouin Century: Education and Development among the Negev Tribes in the 20th Century*. Oxford: Berghahn Books, 2001. (*Bedouin Century*)

Al-'Abādi, Aḥmad 'Uwaydī. *al-Qaḍā' 'end al-'Ashā'ir al-Urdunniyya* (Law among the Jordanian tribes). Amman, 1988.

Al-'Ārif, 'Ārif. *al-Qaḍā' bayn al-Badū* (Law among the Bedouin). Jerusalem, 1933. (*al-Qaḍā'*)

——. *Ta'rīkh Bi'r al-Sab' wa-Qaba'iliha* (A history of Beersheba and its tribes). Jerusalem, 1934. (*Ta'rīkh*)

Al-Rāwī, 'Abd al-Jabbār. *al-Bādiya* (The desert). Baghdad: Al-Ani Press, 1949.

Bailey, Clinton. "The Bedouin Budget." *Teva Vaaretz* 18, no. 3. Tel Aviv: Israeli Nature Preservation Society, 1976 (in Hebrew). ("Bedouin Budget")

——. "The Bedouin Concept of *'adl* as Justice." *Muslim World* 66, no. 2 (1976). ("*'Adl*")

——. *Bedouin Poetry from Sinai and the Negev: Mirror of a Culture*. Oxford: Oxford University Press, 1991 (*Poetry*)

——. "Bedouin Religious Practices in Sinai and the Negev." *Anthropos* 72, nos. 1–2 (1982). ("Religious Practices")

——. "Bedouin Weddings in Sinai and the Negev." *Folklore Research Center Studies* 4: *Studies in Wedding Customs*, ed. I. Ben-Ami. Jerusalem, 1974. ("Weddings")

——. *A Culture of Desert Survival: Bedouin Proverbs from Sinai and the Negev*. New Haven: Yale University Press, 2004. (*Proverbs*)

——. "Dating the Arrival of the Bedouin Tribes in Sinai and the Negev." *Journal of the Economic and Social History of the Orient* 28, no. 1 (1985). ("Dating")

——. "The Narrative Context of the Bedouin Qasida Poem." *Folklore Research Center Studies* 3, ed. I. Ben-Ami. Jerusalem, 1972. ("Narrative Context")

——. "The Negev in the Nineteenth Century: Reconstructing History from Bedouin Oral Traditions." *Asian and African Studies* 14, no. 1 (1980). ("Nineteenth Century")

——. "Notes on the Bedouin of the Central Negev." *Notes on the Bedouin* 9. Midreshet Sde Boker: Field Studies School, 1978 (in Hebrew). ("Central Negev")

——. "Relations between Bedouin Tribes on Opposite Sides of the Wadi Arabah, 1600–1950." *Levant Supplementary Series* 3: *Crossing the Rift*, ed. Piotr Bienkowski and Katherine Galor. Oxford: Oxbow Books, 2006 ("Arabah")

Bailey, Clinton, and Rafi Peled. *Shivtei ha-Beduim bi-Sinai* (A survey of the Bedouin tribes in Sinai). Tel Aviv: Israel Ministry of Defense, 1975 (internal document).

Bailey, Clinton, and Avshalom Shmueli. "The Settlement of the Sinaitic ʿAyāydah in the Suez Canal Zone." *Palestine Exploration Quarterly* 109, no. 1 (1977).

Bar-Tsvi, Sasson. *Jurisdiction among the Negev Bedouins*. Tel Aviv: Ministry of Defense Press, 1991 (in Hebrew).

Bar-Tsvi, Sasson, Aref Abu Rabiʿa, and Gideon Kressel. *The Charm of Graves*. Tel Aviv: Ministry of Defense Press, 1991 (in Hebrew). (Bar-Tsvi et al., *Graves*)

Blanc, Haim. "The Arabic Dialect of the Negev Bedouins." *Proceedings of the Israel Academy of Sciences and Humanities* 4, no. 7 (1970).

Blunt, Anne. *Bedouin Tribes of the Euphrates*. New York, 1879.

Burckhardt, J. L. *Arab Proverbs*. London, 1830; repr. 1972. (*Arab Proverbs*)

——. *Notes on the Bedouins and Wahabys*, 2 vols. London, 1831; repr. 1967. (*Notes*)

——. *Travels in Syria and the Holy Land*. London, 1822. (*Travels*)

Cole, Donald P. "Tribal and Non-Tribal Structures among the Bedouin of Saudi Arabia." *Al-Abhath* 30 (1982).

Doughty, Charles M. *Travels in Arabia Deserta*, 2 vols. London, 1888; repr. 1937.

El-Barghuthi, Omar. "Judicial Courts among the Bedouin of Palestine." *Journal of the Palestine Oriental Society* 2 (1922).

Ephʾal, Israel. *The Ancient Arabs: Nomads on the Borders of the Fertile Crescent, 9–5th Centuries B.C.* Jerusalem: Magnes Press, 1989.

Evenari, Michael, Leslie Shanon, and Naphtali Tadmor. *The Negev: Challenge of a Desert*. Cambridge, MA: Harvard University Press, 1971.

Gardner, Ann. "Fatma's Story." WIN Magazine.htm. Pt. 1: issue 43, and pt. 2: issue 45, 2001. ("Fatma's Story")

——. *Women and Changing Relations in a South Sinai Bedouin Community*. Ph.D dissertation, Univ. of Texas at Austin. Ann Arbor: University Microfilms International, 1994. (*Women*)

Gibb, H. A. R., and Harold Bowen. *Islamic Society and the West*, vol. 1, pt. 1. Cambridge, MA: Harvard University Press, 1950.

Ginat, Joseph. *Bedouin Bishʿa Justice: Ordeal by Fire*. Brighton: Sussex Academic Press, 2009.

Hava, J. G. *Al-Farāʾid Arabic-English Dictionary*. Beirut, 1970.

Hilw, Kamal Abdallah al-, and Said Mumtaz Darwish. *Customary Law in Northern Sinai*. Cairo, n.d.

Hitti, Philip. *History of the Arabs*. London: Macmillan, 1958.

Jennings-Bramley, W. F. "Bedouin of the Sinaitic Peninsula." *Palestine Exploration Fund Quarterly*, 1905–1914.

Kennet, Austin. *Bedouin Justice: Law and Custom among the Egyptian Bedouin*. London, 1925; repr. London: Frank Cass, 1968.

Kister, Marvin. "al-Ḥīra: Some Notes on Its Relations with Arabia." *Arabica* 15 (1968). ("al-Ḥīra")

——. "Mecca and Tamīm: Aspects of Their Relations." *Journal of the Economic and Social History of the Orient* 8 (1965). ("Mecca and Tamīm")

Kressel, Gideon. "Ḥaqq Akhū Manshad: Major and Minor Wrongs and Specialized Judges among the Negev Bedouin." *International Journal of Middle East Studies* 25 (1993). ("Ḥaqq Akhū Manshad")

Kressel, Gideon, Joseph Ben-David, and Khalil Abu Rabiʿa. "Changes in the Land Usage by the Negev Bedouin since the Mid-19th Century: The Intra-Tribal Perspective." *Nomadic Peoples* 28 (1991). (Kressel et al., "Changes")

Lane, E. W. *Arabic-English Lexicon*. (1863); repr. Cambridge: Islamic Texts Society Trust, 1984.

Layish, Aharon, and Avshalom Shmueli. "Custom and *Sharīʿa* in the Bedouin Family according to Legal Documents from the Judaean Desert." *Bulletin of the School of Asian and African Studies* 42, no. 1 (1979).

Liebesney, Herbert J. *The Law of the Near and Middle East*. Albany: State University of New York Press, 1975.

Marx, Emanuel. *Bedouin of the Negev*. Manchester: Manchester University Press, 1967.

Murray, G. W. *Sons of Ishmael: A Study of the Egyptian Bedouin*. London: Routledge, 1935.

Musil, Alois. *Arabia Deserta*. New York: American Geographical Society, 1927. (*Arabia Deserta*)

——. *Arabia Petraea*. Vol. 3: *Ethnologishe Reisebericht*. Vienna: Kaiserliche Akademie der Wissenschaften, 1908. (*Arabia Petraea*)

——. *The Manners and Customs of the Rwala Bedouins*. New York: American Geographical Society, 1928. (*Manners*)

——. *The Northern Hegaz*. New York: American Geographical Society, 1926. (*Northern Hegaz*)

Nawi, Eliahu. "Law among the Bedouin." *Notes on the Bedouin* 1. Midreshet Sde Boker: Field Studies School, 1970 (in Hebrew).

Nicholson, R. A. *A Literary History of the Arabs*. Cambridge: Cambridge University Press, 1907; repr. 1966.

Oppenheim, Max von. *Die Bedouinen*, 4 vols. Wiesbaden: Otto Harrassowitz, 1949–1968.

Palmer, E. H. *Desert of the Exodus*. London, 1872.

Palva, Heikki. *Artistic Colloquial Arabic: Traditional Narratives and Poems from al-Balqaʾ (Jordan)*. *Studia Orientalia* 69 (1992). Helsinki: Finnish Oriental Society.

Peake, Frederick. *History and Tribes of Jordan*. Miami: University of Miami Press, 1958.

Raswan, Carl R. *Black Tents of Arabia: My Life among the Bedouins*. Boston: Little, Brown, 1935.

Rosenfeld, Henry. "The Social Composition of the Military in the Process of State Formation in the Arabian Desert." *Journal of the Royal Anthropological Institute* 95, no. 2 (1965).

Shuqayr, Naʿūm. *Taʾrīkh Sīnāʾ wa-l-ʿArab* (A history of Sinai and the Arabs). Cairo, 1916.

Smith, W. Robertson. *Kinship and Marriage in Early Arabia*. London, 1903; repr., n.d.

Stewart, Frank Henderson. *Texts in Sinai Bedouin Law*, 2 vols. Wiesbaden: Otto Harrassowitz, 1988. (*Texts*)

——. "The Woman, Her Guardian, and Her Husband in the Law of the Sinai Bedouin." *Arabica* 38 (1991). ("The Woman")

Sweet, Louise. "Camel Raiding of North Arabian Bedouin: A Mechanism of Ecological Adaptation." *American Anthropologist* 67 (1965).

Thesiger, Wilfred. *Arabian Sands*. London: Longmans, Green, 1959; Penguin Books paperback, 1964.

Volney, Constantin François de Chasseboeuf, comte de. *Travels through Syria and Egypt*. Paris, 1787. English edition: New York, 1798.

Index of Cases and Conflicts and Associated Subjects

Listings are given by chapter and page number.

Index of Bedouin Legal Maxims: (Not found in Bailey, Proverbs*)*

Al-ḥagg ʿala gadr sāyigah — A right is got in keeping with the resolve of him who pursues it. 17

Ḥagg gawīy maʿ aḍ-ḍaʿīf — A right gained by a strong one at the expense of someone weak. 17

Mā yibdī ghayr ar-rafīg — No one joins a *badwa* delegation except a friend. 29

Kalām fī kalām mā bitʿayyib — Words exchanged in argument do not shame. 31

Ad-damm mā fīh gōm ū-gaʿada — Revenge does not require judicial consent. 101

An-nōm bi-l-khāṭir — Sleep [reprieve from vengeance] is by leave. 125

Al-bōg bizyid — The punishment for treachery is compounded. 151

ʿEinha baṣīr wa-īd-ha gaṣīr — Her eye is sharp, but her hand is short. 154

Al-himsh yiraḍḍīh wa-l-kaff yibakkīh — A piece of plain bread will make him content, and a slap will make him cry. 154

Yōm taʿṭīnī riyāl aʿṭīk riyāl — When you give me a riyal, I'll give you a riyal. 168

As-sārig ḥalīf — A thief will also swear. 193

Al-khāyin khāyin — ghayr yiḥlif — As a thief is perfidious, he'll surely also swear. 193, 282

Al-yamīn ilha ḍarār li-l-maṭalīaʿ — An oath entails danger to the offspring. 195

Al-yamīn muʿallag fī sabaʿ manadīl ū-yuṭrud jīl warā jīl — God's wrath from a false oath will be visited on seven men ("head-cloths"), one in each of seven generations. 195

Al-yamīn illī mā lih maʿrad bāṭla — An oath that cannot exact an offer is false. 199

Index of Bedouin Tribal Confederations and Persons

General Index